THE WORLD'S RAREST BIRDS

Erik Hirschfeld, Andy Swash & Robert Still

With contributions by Nick Langley, Stuart Butchart, Brian Clews & Gill Swash

and illustrations by Tomasz Cofta

WILDGuides

PRINCETON

press.princeton.edu

Published by Princeton University Press,
41 William Street, Princeton, New Jersey 08540
In the United Kingdom: Princeton University Press, 6 Oxford Street,
Woodstock, Oxfordshire OX20 1TW
nathist.press.princeton.edu

British Library Cataloging-in-Publication Data is available

Library of Congress Control Number 2012945960
ISBN 978-0-691-15596-8

Production and design by **WILD**Guides Ltd., Old Basing, Hampshire UK
Printed in Singapore

10 9 8 7 6 5 4 3 2 1

The World's Rarest...

Images on Title Page (left-to-right, from top line):

Marbled Murrelet *Brachyramphus marmoratus*. Photo: Tom Middleton (reflectingthewild.com).
Balearic Shearwater *Puffinus mauretanicus*. Photo: Tom Brereton.
Spoon-billed Sandpiper *Eurynorhynchus pygmeus*. Photo: Pavel Pinchuk (aqua-wader.blogspot.com).
Chinese Crested Tern *Brachyramphus marmoratus*. Photo: Michelle & Peter Wong.
Palila *Loxioides bailleui*. Photo: Eric VanderWerf (pacificrimconservation.com).
Ivory-billed Woodpecker *Campephilus principalis*. Illustration: Tomasz Cofta.
Red-crowned Crane *Grus japonensis*. Photo: Huajin Sun (birdnet.cn).
Okinawa Rail *Gallirallus okinawae*. Photo: Ambrosini.
Long-whiskered Owlet *Xenoglaux loweryi*. Photo: Dubi Shapiro (pbase.com/dubisha).
Banded Cotinga *Brachyramphus marmoratus*. Photo: Ciro Albano (nebrazilbirding.com).
Amber Mountain Rock-thrush *Monticola erythronotus*. Photo: Dubi Shapiro (pbase.com/dubisha).
Philippine Eagle *Pithecophaga jefferyi*. Photo: Rich Lindie.
Masafuera Rayadito *Aphrastura masafuerae*. Photo: Peter Hodum (oikonos.org).
Black-browed Albatross *Thalassarche melanophrys*. Photo: David Monticelli (pbase.com/david_monticelli).
Kakapo *Strigops habroptila*. Photo: Shane McInnes.
Golden White-eye *Cleptornis marchei*. Photo: Jack Jeffrey (jackjeffreyphoto.com).

Contents

The Regional Directories

Let the birds speak for themselves…

Araripe Manakin
Antilophia bokermanni
Photo: Ciro Albano (nebrazilbirding.com)

Winning photographs from The World's Rarest Birds photo competition:

CRITICALLY ENDANGERED species (*above left top to bottom*)

1st **Kakapo** *Strigops habroptila*: Shane McInnes – *see page 151*.

2nd **Brazilian Merganser** *Mergus octosetaceus*: Sávio Freire Bruno (uff.br/biodiversidade) – *see page 26*.

3rd **Christmas Island Frigatebird** *Fregata andrewsi*: David Boyle – *see page 45*.

ENDANGERED or DATA DEFICIENT species (*above right top to bottom*)

1st **Asian Crested Ibis** *Nipponia nippon*: Quan Min Li (birdnet.cn) – *see page 101*.

2nd **Red-crowned Crane** *Grus japonensis*: Huajin Sun (birdnet.cn) – *see front cover*.

3rd **Marvellous Spatuletail** *Loddigesia mirabilis*: Daniel Rosengren (scutisorex.se) – *see page 265*.

Migratory CRITICALLY ENDANGERED species (*right*)

1st **Orange-bellied Parrot** *Neophema chrysogaster*: David Boyle – *see page 53*.

The World's Rarest initiative

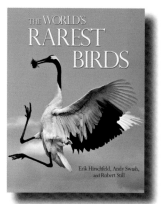

In 2008 and 2009, the *Rare Birds Yearbooks* were published. These were produced in order to put a spotlight on the 190 or so most threatened birds in the world – those that are Critically Endangered – and to present the latest information about them in a form that was readily accessible to everyone. The aim was to increase awareness of the often dire situations faced by many of these species, and to show what each looks like with an accompanying photo or painting. With the rapid development of digital cameras and increased interest in photography among birders, scientists and explorers alike, many fantastic images were becoming available – and so the time seemed right to present these birds with stunning colour pictures. The publication of the *Yearbook* was intended to be annual in order to reflect changes in threat status and to summarize the most recent findings from dedicated researchers across the world.

BirdLife International, the global partnership of conservation organizations that acts as a 'watchdog' over bird species, was supportive of the *Rare Birds Yearbook* concept from the outset. BirdLife's exhaustive compilation of scientific information on each species, augmented with thousands of emails to researchers worldwide for updates, provided the authoritative basis for the Yearbooks. A photo competition was arranged in order to obtain images and the first *Rare Birds Yearbook* was published in 2008. This was followed a year later by the 2009 edition, which was also underpinned by a photo competition. Both photo competitions were mainly sponsored by the quality optics company Minox.

The *Rare Birds Yearbooks* were sold in over 40 countries. They were produced by a small team in Sweden and were successful in generating funds to support BirdLife's Preventing Extinctions Programme. However, the impact of the books outside Europe could have been greater. A fortuitous meeting between Erik Hirschfeld, editor of the *Rare Birds Yearbooks*, and Andy Swash, Managing Director of the British publisher WILD*Guides*, led to a proposal to change the scope of the project to encompass the species that are categorized as Endangered or Data Deficient, in addition to those that are Critically Endangered. WILD*Guides* have recently joined forces with Princeton University Press in the USA and this will help to ensure that the books they produce are available to more people, particularly in the Americas.

Given the increasing number of excellent bird photographs that are being taken, it was decided to produce a large format book featuring as many images of Endangered and Critically Endangered species as possible. This would also provide an opportunity to summarize their current status and the reasons for their being threatened, and to provide some information about their distribution and ecology. In order to make the book as accessible to as many people as possible, regardless of where the reader lives, the decision was made to divide it into eight sections: an introduction to the world's birds and the threats they face; and seven 'regional directories' covering all the species that are found there. A comprehensive review of the threat status of every bird species is undertaken every four years by BirdLife International, as the Red List authority for the International Union for Conservation of Nature (IUCN). The outcome of the most recent review was published in May 2012, and publication of this book has been timed to reflect the new categories. Sadly, 197 species are now categorized as Critically Endangered and 389 as Endangered, and four now only exist in captivity. In addition, 60 species are so poorly known that they are classified as Data Deficient.

The challenge in producing this book was to obtain photographs of as many of these 650 species as possible. To achieve this, an international photo competition was organized and run, with an attractive range of prizes on offer through the generous sponsorship of Minox, the publishers Lynx Edicions, **WILD***Guides* and Princeton University Press, BirdLife International and World Migratory Bird Day. The response was astonishing, with over 3,500 photos submitted by over 300 photographers from around the world. The winning images all appear in this book, together with over 800 others. With these images, and the kind agreement of the photographers to re-use photos submitted for the *Rare Birds Yearbooks*, photos of 515 of the threatened species to be featured (87%) and 21 of the Data Deficient species were obtained and are presented here. For the threatened species that have never been photographed, either because they have rarely been seen or may in fact be extinct, or for which publishable photos could not be obtained (76 species), the highly acclaimed Polish artist Tomasz Cofta kindly agreed to produce an illustration. These amazing works of art are the result of many hours of painstaking attention to detail and provide, for the first time for many species, an indication of how they may appear (or have appeared) in life.

New information about the species covered in this book is coming to light every day. For this reason, readers are encouraged to visit the BirdLife website – **www.birdlife.org** – for the latest information and to subscribe to their newsletters.

Introduction to the world's birds

Diversity and distribution

Over 10,000 species of bird are currently recognized by BirdLife International, which is the IUCN (International Union for Conservation of Nature) Red List authority for all birds. As of May 2012, when BirdLife International's four-yearly update of the status of all the world's birds for The IUCN Red List was released, there were 10,064 birds species (9,934 extant and 130 extinct since 1500), with a number of others awaiting decisions on their

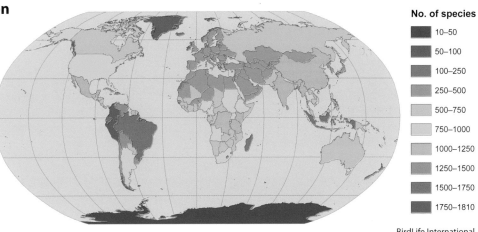

No. of species

| 10–50 |
| 50–100 |
| 100–250 |
| 250–500 |
| 500–750 |
| 750–1000 |
| 1000–1250 |
| 1250–1500 |
| 1500–1750 |
| 1750–1810 |

The number of bird species in each of the world's countries

BirdLife International and NatureServe (2012): bird species distribution maps of the world

validity. These species are not distributed evenly across the world: 3,370 species are concentrated in the American tropics (Neotropics), compared to just 937 in the largest of the world's ecozones, the Palearctic (Europe, Asia north of the Himalayas, North Africa and the Middle East).

The number of species currently known to breed or to occur as regular migrants to each of the world's countries is shown on the map above. Six of the seven countries with the most bird species are in Neotropical South America, led by Colombia with 1,810 species. Indonesia, the only non-Neotropical country among the top seven, comes in fifth place with 1,559 species. The first African country in the league table, the Democratic Republic of the Congo, comes in tenth place, with 1,081 species, behind China with 1,237 and India with 1,166. Yet the Afrotropical realm as a whole holds 21% of the world's bird species.

Birds are found in all major habitat types. Although some species occur in two or more habitats, many are confined to just one. Grasslands, savanna and inland wetlands are all important habitats for birds, each supporting about 20% of species, and shrublands support 39% of birds. Around 45% are found in 'artificial' habitats: those that have been modified by humans, such as agricultural land. But by far the most significant habitat is forest, supporting 75% of all species. Birds occur in all forest types, from subantarctic woodland to equatorial rainforest. The most important types are tropical/subtropical lowland and montane moist forest, which support 50% and 35% of species respectively, with tropical/subtropical dry forest supporting 18%.

Endemic Bird Areas

Most bird species are widespread and have large ranges. However, over 2,500 (about one-quarter of all species) are restricted to an area of less than 50,000 km², within which they are said to be endemic (*i.e.* not found anywhere else). BirdLife International has identified regions of the world that include the entire global distributions of two or more of these restricted-range species, and refers to them as Endemic Bird Areas (EBAs). Worldwide, there are 218 EBAs covering a total area of 7·3 million square kilometres – that is just 4·9% of the Earth's land surface. These are shown on the map opposite. A further 138 areas have been identified as Secondary Areas, which support one or more restricted range species, but do not contain the entire ranges of two or more of them.

EBAs are found around the world, but most (77%) are located in the tropics and subtropics. There are approximately equal numbers of island (105) and mainland EBAs (113). Of the island EBAs, 70% are on oceanic islands and 30% on continental-shelf islands. Of those on the mainland, 42% are largely in montane areas, 35% in lowland areas and 24% span both. The natural habitat in most EBAs (83%) is forest.

The number of restricted-range landbirds occurring in EBAs varies from two to over 50, and they encompass 93% of the world's restricted-range bird species, as well as many other species that are more widespread. Half of all restricted-range species are globally threatened or near threatened and the other half are vulnerable to the loss or degradation of habitat due to the small size of their ranges. EBAs are, therefore, the highest priority for habitat-based conservation.

Important Bird Areas

BirdLife International operates the global Important Bird Area (IBA) Programme, which aims to identify, protect and manage a network of sites that will ensure the survival and long-term viability of bird species for which a site-based approach to conservation is appropriate. IBAs are selected using standard, internationally recognized criteria based on the species and populations of birds they support. Among other criteria, an IBA may be recognized because it regularly holds significant numbers of a globally threatened species, or of a group of species whose ranges define an Endemic Bird Area. To date, over 11,000 IBAs have been identified and these are shown on the map below.

The IBA network may be considered as the minimum suite of sites required to ensure the survival of the bird species across their ranges, should other habitat be lost. BirdLife's IBA Programme aims to guide the implementation of national conservation strategies through the promotion and development of national protected-area programmes. It also aims to inform the conservation activities of international organizations and to promote the implementation of global agreements and regional measures.

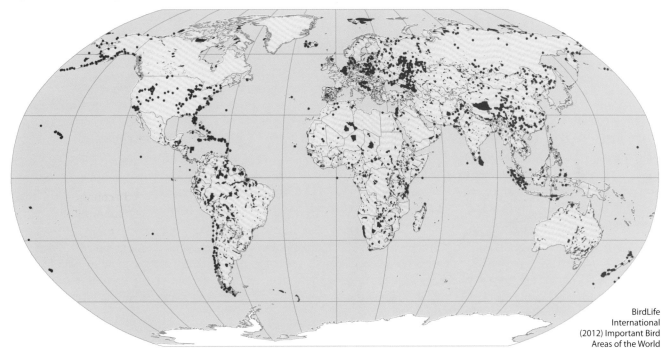

BirdLife International (2012) Important Bird Areas of the World

The global distribution of Important Bird Areas (IBAs)

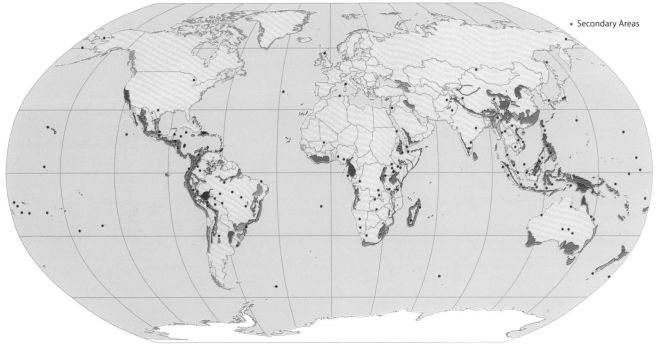

• Secondary Areas

The global distribution of Endemic Bird Areas (EBAs) and Secondary Areas

From: Stattersfield, A.J., Crosby, M.J., Long, A.J. and Wege, D.C. (1998) *Endemic Bird Areas of the World. Priorities for biodiversity conservation.* BirdLife Conservation Series 7. Cambridge: BirdLife International

Birds and humans

Humans have found uses for up to 45% of the world's bird species, from hunting them for food or sport, to keeping them as pets or for their singing or fighting skills, using their feathers for decoration or bedding (eiderdowns and pillows), tanning their skins for leather (ostriches and rheas), or using their melted-down fat to fuel lamps (oilbirds).

The domesticated descendants of the Red Junglefowl *Gallus gallus* now provide a staple of diets across much of the world. This species has been very successfully exploited, and on any one day there are five times as many chickens alive as people. However, when exploitation becomes unsustainable, it can set a species on the path to extinction. The Passenger Pigeon *Ectopistes migratorius,* possibly the most numerous bird species in the world at the beginning of the 19th century, and extinct in the wild by the beginning of the 20th, is the starkest example. But hunting, trapping for the cagebird market and collection of eggs for food are still a significant threat for 194 globally threatened species today.

Birds provide a range of 'services' that often go uncosted, and are therefore overlooked. Members of families such as honeyeaters (Meliphagidae), sunbirds (Nectariniidae) and sugarbirds (Promeropidae) have co-evolved to be the main or exclusive pollinators of some plants and trees. In Hawaii, following the extinction of many honeycreeper species, some endemic trees are unable to set fruit. The loss of the Tui *Prosthemadera novaeseelandiae* and New Zealand Bellbird *Anothornis melanura* from New Zealand's North Island has similarly caused a dramatic fall in fruit-setting by some native plant species.

The role of birds in 'pest control' is better known. An assessment of the impact of birds such as Evening Grosbeak *Coccothraustes vespertinus* on spruce budworm outbreaks in North America estimated that it would cost over US$1,820 per square kilometre per year, over a 100-year rotation, to achieve the same results by spraying. In the Bet-She'an Valley, Israel, Barn Owls *Tyto alba* are estimated to remove at least 80,000 rats and mice from the fields every year.

With the catastrophic decline of vultures across the Indian subcontinent and large parts of Africa, the service they provided in removing animal carcasses and offal and other wastes is being performed by rising numbers of feral dogs and rats, dangerous to humans in their own right, and as vectors of disease. A recent study in India estimates that there has been an increase in the feral dog population of at least 5·5 million, and that this has resulted in more than 47,300 extra human deaths from rabies.

Birds are the source of symbols in our art, and phrases in our languages and music, and models for our dances. In recent decades, they have also become a major focus for our leisure, with one in five people in the USA claiming to spend time watching birds, and one in three in the UK watching or feeding them. Many of these people have been transformed into citizen scientists by events like the Christmas Bird Count in the USA (now spreading to the rest of the Americas and Caribbean) and the Big Garden Birdwatch in the UK. The mass of information these enthusiasts provide has been invaluable in tracking the status of bird populations, and the impacts of climate change.

Ubiquitous, conspicuous and (usually) relatively easily identified, birds are good indicators of environmental states and changes, serving as a proxy for all biodiversity. More is known about the status and distribution of birds than about any other order of animals or plants. This is reflected by the fact that just 60 (0·6%) of the world's bird species are so poorly known that their theat status cannot be determined (see *pages 20* and *322–331*). Sites identified as important for birds (BirdLife's Important Bird Areas), and parts of the world where range-restricted bird species are found (Endemic Bird Areas), have also been found to capture 70–90% of other biodiversity, including mammals, snakes, amphibians and plants.

The lust to possess the Critically Endangered **Bali Starling** *Leucopsar rothschildi* is such that in 1999, when black market prizes soared, an armed raid was launched on the captive breeding centre, snatching most of birds waiting to be introduced to the wild. The free-flying population on Bali remains at fewer than 50 individuals. Photo [captive]: Dolora Batchelor.

The world's rarest birds

This book focuses on the 197 Critically Endangered and 389 Endangered bird species listed by BirdLife International on the 2012 IUCN Red List. 'The World's Rarest' should be taken as shorthand for 'the most threatened', noting that some of these species may still be quite abundant, but declining extremely rapidly, and hence qualifying as Critically Endangered or Endangered under the 'A' criterion of The IUCN Red List (see *page 13*).

Conversely, some rare birds are not globally threatened. The Powerful Owl *Ninox strenua*, with a global population of 2,200–2,800 mature individuals, is naturally sparsely distributed, with huge home ranges of up to 5,000 hectares in eastern and south-eastern Australia. There are fewer than 10,000 Madeira Laurel Pigeons *Columba trocaz* within an area of just 160 km², but they have reoccupied all areas of suitable habitat on the island, following a ban on hunting. Both species are currently considered of Least Concern.

The population of **New Zealand Scaup** *Aythya novaeseelandiae* is estimated to be 5,000–10,000 individuals. Nowhere common, it is spread thinly on clear water lakes and lagoons near the sea on New Zealand's North and South Islands. However, numbers are increasing since hunting was banned, and this 'rare' bird is considered of Least Concern on *The IUCN Red List*. Photo [captive]: Andy & Gill Swash (WorldWildlifeImages.com).

Although still numbered in the hundreds of thousands, **Northern Rockhopper Penguin** *Eudyptes moseleyi* has declined by over 50% in three generations over much of its range in the south Atlantic, and thus qualifies as Endangered. With up to 760,000 individuals, the Marbled Murrelet *Brachyramphus marmoratus* is even more abundant, but this species too has declined by over 50% over 20 years, and is also considered Endangered. Photo: Marie-Hélène Burle.

The IUCN/BirdLife species category assignment process

SPECIES **NOT EVALUATED** ▶ Not Evaluated **NE**

SPECIES **EVALUATED**

Species data **not adequate for assessment** ▶ Data Deficient **DD**

▼

Species data **adequate for assessment** ▶ ASSIGNMENT TO CATEGORIES
using Red List criteria
(*see table opposite for
'threatened' category
assignment thresholds*)

Extinct **EX**

Extinct in the Wild **EW**

T
H
R
E
A
T
E
N
E
D

Critically Endangered **CR**

Endangered **EN**

Vulnerable **VU**

Near Threatened **NT**

Least Concern **LC**

The IUCN Red List categories

As the designated Red List Authority for all birds, BirdLife International is responsible for providing the assessments to IUCN for the Red List. To achieve this, it collates all the relevant data on each species, and applies them to the Red List criteria in order to assign each species to a category of extinction risk. The criteria have quantitative thresholds for each category, and are based on combinations of range and population size, trend and structure (see *table opposite*).

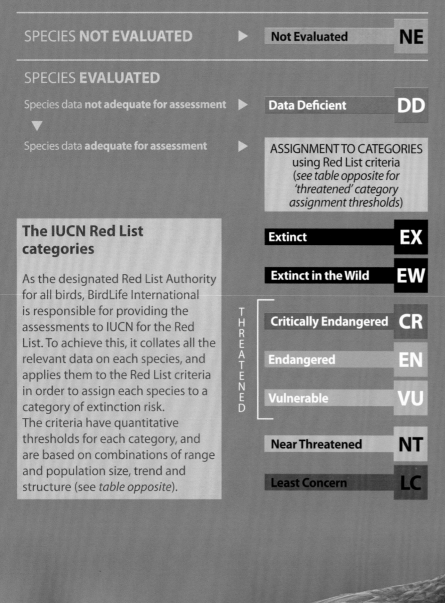

The threat status of the **Hooded Vulture** *Necrosyrtes monachus* jumped from Least Concern to Endangered in 2011. This was based on evidence that it was declining very rapidly because of hunting for bushmeat and traditional medicine, poisoning of carcasses laid out to kill large carnivores, and improvements in rubbish collection and hygiene at abattoirs. Photo: Andy & Gill Swash (WorldWildlifeImages.com).

Simplified overview of thresholds for The IUCN Red List criteria

Criterion		Critically Endangered (CR)	Endangered (EN)	Vulnerable (VU)	Qualifiers and notes
A1:	Reduction in population size	≥ 90%	≥ 70%	≥50%	Over 10 years / 3 generations in the past, where causes are reversible, understood and have ceased.
A2-4:	Reduction in population size	≥ 80%	≥ 50%	≥30%	Over 10 years / 3 generations in past, future or combination.
B1:	Small range (extent of occurrence)	<100 km²	<5,000 km²	<20,000 km²	Plus two of (a) severe fragmentation / few localities (1, ≤5, ≤10), (b) continuing decline, (c) extreme fluctuation.
B2:	Small range (area of occupancy)	<10 km²	<500 km²	<2,000 km²	Plus two of (a) severe fragmentation / few localities (1, ≤5, ≤10), (b) continuing decline, (c) extreme fluctuation.
C:	Small and declining population	<250	<2,500	<10,000	Mature individuals. Continuing decline either (1) over specified rates & time periods or (2) with (a) specified population structure or (b) extreme fluctuation.
D1:	Very small population	<50	<250	<1,000	Mature individuals.
D2:	Very small range	n/a	n/a	<20 km² or ≤5 locations	Capable of becoming CR or EX within a very short time.
E:	Quantitative analysis	≥50% in 10 years / 3 generations	≥20% in 20 years / 5 generations	≥10% in 100 years	Estimated extinction risk using quantitative models *e.g.* population viability analyses.

The IUCN Red List is updated annually, with a comprehensive review undertaken every four years – most recently in 2012. A total of 208 bird species moved between Red List categories in 2011–12 and 559 species between 2008–12. Of the latter, 174 resulted from a genuine change in the status of species (16 improvements versus 158 deteriorations), 206 were a result of improved knowledge of the status of species or the threats impacting them, and 179 resulted from taxonomic revisions.

Ongoing habitat destruction by mining and mining wastes dumped in its high-altitude bog habitats in Peru are amongst the problems faced by the **White-bellied Cinclodes** *Cinclodes palliatus*, which was uplisted from Endangered to Critically Endangered in 2010. Photo: Dubi Shapiro (pbase.com/dubisha).

Flightless Cormorant *Phalacrocorax harrisi.* Photo: Daniel Rosengren (scutisorex.se).

Gouldian Finch *Erythrura gouldiae.* Photo: Don Hadden (donhadden.com).

European Turtle-dove *Streptopelia turtur.* Photo: Greg & Yvonne Dean (WorldWildlifeImages.com).

Populations of the **Flightless Cormorant** *Phalacrocorax harrisi* in Galápagos have repeatedly crashed because of El Niño events. But it recovers quickly, and now appears to be stabilizing at a new population high. Although no longer qualifying as Endangered, this species is listed as Vulnerable because its limited range and flightlessness make it extremely susceptible to catastrophes such as oil spills.

The **Gouldian Finch** *Erythrura gouldiae* is confined to a handful of grassland sites in Northern Australia. Although well below historical levels, the population appears to have stopped declining, and in 2012 it was downlisted from Endangered to Near Threatened. Overgrazing and changes in fire management remain a threat.

Next on the list? In the last 25 years the European population of **European Turtle-dove** *Streptopelia turtur* has fallen by more than 60%. Threats include habitat loss, and unsustainable hunting, especially in blackspots like Malta, where the requirements of the European Birds Directive are regularly ignored during spring migration. Still listed as of Least Concern, this is one of a large number of once common migratory and farmland species that may be plummeting towards threatened status.

The population of the **Red-bellied Grackle** *Hypopyrrhus pyrohypogaster* was previously estimated at less than 2,500 individuals. However, it is being recorded at an increasing number of localities, suggesting that this was an underestimate, and it was downlisted from Endangered to Vulnerable in 2012. Continuing forest clearance within its range in the Colombian Andes remains a significant threat. Photo: Pete Morris (birdquest-tours.com).

Successive surveys have extended the known range of the **Madagascar Red Owl** *Tyto soumagnei*, which is now believed to occupy all suitably large blocks of forest in the east and north of Madagascar. It was downlisted from Endangered to Vulnerable in 2009. Photo: Dubi Shapiro (pbase.com/dubisha).

Recent surveys have revealed that the **Fuerteventura Stonechat** *Saxicola dacotiae* occupies a much larger area of its home island in the Canary Islands than was thought, with a correspondingly larger population, and in 2010 it was downlisted from Endangered to Near Threatened. Photo: Oliver Smart (smartimages.co.uk).

Going or gone?

While this book focuses on Critically Endangered and Endangered species – those believed to be on the brink of extinction – at least 130 species are known already to have gone Extinct since 1500. Four more species are Extinct in the Wild (and another is probably so), and now only exist in captivity. A list of the Extinct species and the date each was last recorded is included in Appendix 1 on *page 336*.

Listing a species as Extinct has significant conservation implications, because conservation funding is, justifiably, not targeted at species that are believed no longer to exist. Conservationists are therefore reluctant to designate a species as Extinct if there is any reasonable possibility that it may still be extant.

For this reason, authorities such as BirdLife International and IUCN take a precautionary approach to classifying extinctions in order to encourage continuing conservation efforts until there is no reasonable doubt that the last individual of a species has died. It also minimizes the danger of 'crying wolf' and reducing confidence in the accuracy of the label Extinct.

However, this approach means that the number of recent extinctions documented on The IUCN Red List is likely to be a significant underestimate. The tags 'Possibly Extinct' and 'Possibly Extinct in the Wild' have therefore been developed to identify those Critically Endangered species that are in all probability already Extinct (or are believed only to exist in captivity), but for which confirmation is required. Fourteen species (see table on *page 18*) are tagged in this way. Although these species are, on the balance of evidence, likely to be Extinct, they can not be formally listed as such until adequate surveys have failed to find them and local or unconfirmed reports have been investigated and discounted.

For example, the last confirmed record of the near-flightless Alaotra Grebe *Tachybaptus rufolavatus*, confined to the Lake Alaotra area of Madagascar, was in 1982. After extensive surveys failed to find it, it was described as Possibly Extinct in 2006, and declared extinct in 2010. On the other hand, the Madagascar Pochard *Aythya innotata*, which had also disappeared from Lake Alaotra, and was also was placed in the new 'Possibly Extinct' category in 2006, was rediscovered later the same year, 300 km north of the lake.

Four species are now Extinct in the Wild but survive as captive populations: **Hawaiian Crow** *Corvus hawaiiensis*, **Guam Rail** *Gallirallus owstoni*, **Alagoas Curassow** *Mitu mitu* and **Socorro Dove** *Zenaida graysoni*. They are described as Critically Endangered (Extinct in the Wild). With the disappearance of the last known wild individual in 2000, a fifth species, **Spix's Macaw** *Cyanopsitta spixii*, is listed as Critically Endangered (Possibly Extinct in the Wild).

Hawaiian Crow *Corvus hawaiiensis*.
Photo: Jack Jeffrey (JackJeffreyphoto.com).

Alagoas Curassow *Mitu mitu*.
Photo [captive]: Luís Fábio Silveira (ib.usp.br/~lfsilveira).

Spix's Macaw *Cyanopsitta spixii*.
Photo [captive]: Al Wabra Wildlife Preservation, Qatar.

Socorro Dove *Zenaida graysoni.* Photo [captive]: Tomasz Doroń.

Guam Rail *Gallirallus owstoni.* Photo: Kurt W. Baumgartner.

One-third of the Possibly Extinct species have not been recorded for more than 50 years, which is in itself strong evidence that they may well be Extinct. For example, **Hooded Seedeater** *Sporophila melanops* is known only from the type specimen collected over 180 years ago. The **Turquoise-throated Puffleg** *Eriocnemis godini* has not been seen since 1850, and the habitat at the type-locality has been almost completely destroyed. However, it cannot yet be presumed to be Extinct because there was an unconfirmed record in 1976. Introduced mammalian predators are the prime candidates for the possible extirpation of the **Jamaican Pauraque** *Siphonorhis americana* and the **Jamaica Petrel** *Pterodroma caribbaea*. Similarly, the **Guadalupe Storm-petrel** *Oceanodroma macrodactyla* has not been recorded since 1912 despite several searches, following a severe decline owing to predation by introduced cats and habitat degradation by goats. Only the difficulty of detecting petrels and storm-petrels at their breeding colonies at night, and the continued survival of other petrels and storm-petrels on these islands, keeps alive the hope that these species still survive. Hunting and logging, and deliberate poisoning by timber companies, drove the **Imperial Woodpecker** *Campephilus imperialis* to possible extinction, but the possibility that some survive in regenerating forest cannot be ruled out. The once-abundant **Eskimo Curlew** *Numenius borealis* declined rapidly more than a century ago because of industrial-scale hunting, followed by destruction of most of its breeding habitat in the Prairies and its wintering grounds in the Pampas. Similarly, **Bachman's Warbler** *Vermivora bachmanii* may have gone extinct as a result of habitat destruction on its breeding and wintering grounds, but not all remaining swamp breeding habitat has yet been searched. In the Hawaiian Islands, the **Olomao** *Myadestes lanaiensis*, **Ou** *Psittirostra psittacea*, **Oahu Alauahio** *Paroreomyza maculata* and **Nukupuu** *Hemignathus lucidus* were seen for what may have been the last times between 1988 and 1996, and the last known **Poo-uli** *Melamprosops phaeosoma* died in captivity in 2004. Not recognised until 2004, the **Ua Pou Monarch** *Pomarea mira* was declared extinct in 2006, but an unconfirmed report in 2010 raised hopes that it may survive.

Bird species that are Possibly Extinct (PE) or Possibly Extinct in the Wild (PEW), and the date they were last recorded

Species	Status	Last recorded
Hooded Seedeater *Sporophila melanops*	PE	1823
Turquoise-throated Puffleg *Eriocnemis godini*	PE	1850
Jamaican Pauraque *Siphonorhis americana*	PE	1860
Jamaica Petrel *Pterodroma caribbaea*	PE	1879
Guadalupe Storm-petrel *Oceanodroma macrodactyla*	PE	1912
Imperial Woodpecker *Campephilus imperialis*	PE	1956
Eskimo Curlew *Numenius borealis*	PE	1963
Ua Pou Monarch *Pomarea mira*	PE	1985
Bachman's Warbler *Vermivora bachmanii*	PE	1988
Olomao *Myadestes lanaiensis*	PE	1988
Ou *Psittirostra psittacea*	PE	1989
Oahu Alauahio *Paroreomyza maculata*	PE	1990
Nukupuu *Hemignathus lucidus*	PE	1996
Spix's Macaw *Cyanopsitta spixii*	PEW	2000
Poo-uli *Melamprosops phaeosoma*	PE	2004

The term 'Romeo Error', meaning to give up hope for a species on the mistaken assumption that it is Extinct, was first applied in the case of **Cebu Flowerpecker** *Dicaeum quadricolor*. This species was rediscovered in 1992 after 86 years without a record. Now listed as Critically Endangered, it may be benefitting from work to protect and regenerate Cebu's remaining forests. Illustration: Tomasz Cofta.

Left to right: Hooded Seedeater *Sporophila melanops*, **Turquoise-throated Puffleg** *Eriocnemis godini*, **Jamaican Pauraque** *Siphonorhis americana* and **Jamaica Petrel** *Pterodroma caribbaea*. Illustrations: Tomasz Cofta

Left to right: Guadalupe Storm-petrel *Oceanodroma macrodactyla*, **Imperial Woodpecker** *Campephilus imperialis*, **Eskimo Curlew** *Numenius borealis* and **Ua Pou Monarch** *Pomarea mira*. Illustrations: Tomasz Cofta

Left to right: Olomao *Myadestes lanaiensis*, **Ou** *Psittirostra psittacea*, **Oahu Alauahio** *Paroreomyza maculata* and **Nukupuu** *Hemignathus lucidus* Illustrations: Tomasz Cofta

Monteiro's Bush-shrike
Malaconotus monteiri.
Photo: A. P. Leventis.

The known unknowns

For 60 bird species, there is insufficient information available to evaluate them against The IUCN Red List criteria, and they are therefore categorized as 'Data Deficient'. Many of these species will probably be found to be Least Concern once further information is available, but some could prove to be to Critically Endangered or Endangered. This suite of birds encompasses a number of different sorts of cases, including:

Mysterious origins: two hummingbirds – Bogotá Sunangel *Heliangelus zusii* and Coppery Thorntail *Discosura letitiae* – are known only from one or two specimens taken 100–150 years ago, labelled as 'Bogotá' and 'Bolivia' respectively, but could quite possibly come from any of the Andean countries. Black-browed Babbler *Malacocincla perspicillata*, known from a single specimen taken in the 1840s, probably in Kalimantan (but possibly from elsewhere in the region), has a similarly mysterious origin.

Taxonomic tangles: in some cases, the lack of information that precludes a Red List assessment may be a consequence of taxonomic uncertainty. For example, Blüntschli's Vanga *Hypositta perdita* was named from two specimens collected in 1931 in south-east Madagascar. The specimens are juveniles, and may refer to juvenile Nuthatch Vanga *H. corallirostris*, which would explain why none have ever been recorded since (although some taxonomists think that the apparently far longer tarsi and shorter toes make this unlikely).

Papuan enigmas: the island of New Guinea (shared by Indonesia and Papua New Guinea) and its satellite islands host the greatest concentration of Data Deficient species – 17 in total. This reflects the paucity of information on the distribution, sensitivity to hunting and habitat loss, and ecology of many of the species of this region, resulting from the limited number of birdwatchers and ornithological researchers visiting the area. Starry Owlet-nightjar *Aegotheles tatei* is a typical example, with the voice of this nocturnal species only recently being described for the first time.

Congo conundrums: the Democratic Republic of Congo, Cameroon and adjacent West African countries host another 12 species that are too poorly known in terms of distribution, ecology and threats to determine their status, including for example, Emerald Starling *Coccycolius iris*. This species is found from Equatorial Guinea to Côte d'Ivoire, but its abundance, sensitivity to habitat degradation and susceptibility to the impact of collection for the cagebird trade are all very poorly known. Somalia, Colombia and the Philippines are additional hotspots for Data Deficient species, with five such species each. The poor security situation in some of these countries in recent decades is part of the explanation for the lack of fieldwork, and hence knowledge of these species.

Emerald Starling *Coccycolius iris*. Photo: David Monticelli (pbase. com/david_monticelli).

Starry Owlet-nightjar *Aegotheles tatei*.
Photo: Tony Sawbridge.

Museum specimens of the **Starry Owlet-nightjar** *Aegotheles tatei* come from close to Papua New Guinea's border with Indonesia, and also from Nunumai in the far south-east. The species has been described as fairly common, but there is no information on its likely distribution extent, population size, trends or threats, and it is classified as Data Deficient.

The few recent records of the Data Deficient **Lesser Masked-owl** *Tyto sororcula* come from the Indonesian islands of Buru in South Maluku, and Yamdena and Larat in the Tanimbar group. One early collector obtained two live birds caught in holes in limestone cliffs on Buru, and this may be the best habitat type to search for the species.

By one estimate, there may be 30,000 **White-vented Storm Petrels** *Oceanites gracilis* in the tropical waters of the eastern Pacific. It is presumed to nest on rocky islets from Chile north to Galápagos, although only one small colony has so far been found. It is listed as Data Deficient, but in the absence of evidence of declines or major threats, the population is thought to be stable.

Problems in differentiating **Monteiro's Bush-shrike** *Malaconotus monteiri* from the very similar Grey-headed Bush-shrike *M. blanchoti* contributed to its previous listing as Data Deficient. Only one of 14 specimens listed as *M. monteiri* in the American Museum of Natural History was found to be correctly identified. Surveys have found it more widely distributed along the escarpment zone of Angola than was thought, but it was classified as Near Threatened in 2012 because of forest loss.

The **Emerald Starling** *Coccycolius iris* is known from Guinea, Sierra Leone and Côte d'Ivoire in West Africa. It is said to be locally common, but because there is uncertainty over how well it copes with altered habitat, it is listed as Data Deficient. Fairly large numbers are caught for the cagebird trade, which gives some cause for concern.

Lesser Masked-owl *Tyto sororcula*. Photo: Denzil Morgan.

White-vented Storm Petrels
Oceanites gracilis.
Photo: Steve N. G. Howell.

The distribution of threatened birds

Nearly all countries and territories worldwide support at least one globally threatened bird. Some regions and countries stand out as having particularly high densities of threatened species: for example, the tropical Andes, Atlantic Forests of Brazil, the eastern Himalayas, eastern Madagascar, and the archipelagos of South-East Asia.

The majority of threatened birds (60%) occur only in one country (and hence are termed single-country endemics), and have small ranges and small populations. Areas of importance for these endemic birds have suffered much more from agricultural expansion than the rest of the world, and 20% of all bird species now occur in a total area of less than two million square kilometres (1% of the world's area), down from 4 million square kilometres in historic times.

Conversely, the ranges of some threatened birds may cross the borders of several countries: the globally Endangered Egyptian Vulture *Neophron percnopterus* tops the list, occurring regularly in 82 countries across Europe, Asia and Africa. In total, 22 threatened species have ranges that encompass 30 or more countries, and 184 are recorded from five or more countries.

On continents, the numbers of threatened birds to some extent reflects the species richness. Of the countries with the most threatened species, four of the top five are also among the top five for the overall number of species: Brazil, Peru, Indonesia and Colombia. But nine of the 'top 20' countries for threatened bird species are in Asia, with Indonesia in third place, China in sixth, and India seventh; all these countries have suffered from the rapid clearance of their lowland forests.

Although just 2% of bird species are found on the islands of the Oceanic realm, compared to 83% from the continental land masses, these islands have a disproportionately high number of threatened species. When continental shelf islands are added to oceanic islands, the total number of threatened bird species reaches 583, compared to 613 for all the continental land masses combined.

For example, Gough Island, one of the world's most important breeding sites for seabirds, has seven threatened species, including a penguin, three albatrosses and a petrel, as well as both its endemic species (a moorhen and a bunting). French Polynesia, the Cook Islands, St Helena and Pitcairn each have fewer than 100 bird species, but 40% are either threatened or already Extinct.

The Endangered **Egyptian Vulture** *Neophron percnopterus* is the most widespread of all Endangered birds, being found across Europe, Asia and Africa. Photo: Clement Francis Martin (clementfrancis.com).

The twenty countries with the highest percentage of globally threatened bird species

	Threat codes: CR = Critically Endangered EN = Endangered VU = Vulnerable	Proportion of bird species that are globally threatened (CR, EN or VU)
1	Cook Islands	42·9%
2	Pitcairn Islands	41·7%
3	French Polynesia	40·7%
4	Heard Island and McDonald Islands	40·7%
5	New Zealand	34·1%
6	St Helena	33·9%
7	Niue	33·3%
8	Norfolk Island	26·8%
9	Wallis and Futuna	25·7%
10	French Southern Territories	25·5%
11	Mauritius	19·6%
12	American Samoa	19·5%
13	Kiribati	15·8%
14	Antarctica	14·7%
15	Madagascar	14·6%
16	Réunion	13·6%
17	Samoa	13·3%
18	Guam	13·2%
19	United States Minor Outlying Islands	12·8%
20	New Caledonia	12·2%

NB Only countries with ten or more species are included in this analysis.

The twenty countries with the largest number of globally threatened bird species

	Threat codes: CR = Critically Endangered EN = Endangered VU = Vulnerable	CR or EN (illustrated in this book)	VU	Total No. of globally threatened species
1	Brazil	63	89	152
2	Peru	42	82	124
3	Indonesia	52	70	122
4	Colombia	44	68	112
5	Ecuador	28	67	95
6	China (mainland)	25	62	87
7	India	29	51	80
8	United States of America (including [Hawaiian Islands])	37 [20]	41 [11]	78 [31]
9	Philippines	27	47	74
10	New Zealand	31	39	70
11	Mexico	26	35	61
12	Bolivia	15	38	53
13	Russian Federation	21	31	52
14	Australia	24	27	51
15	Argentina	16	34	50
16	Thailand	20	27	47
17	Vietnam	22	23	45
	Myanmar	18	27	45
	Malaysia	13	32	45
20	United Republic of Tanzania	19	25	44

NB The figures in these tables include migrant seabirds and are based on an analysis of data held in BirdLife's World Bird Database (2012).

The distribution of globally threatened bird species

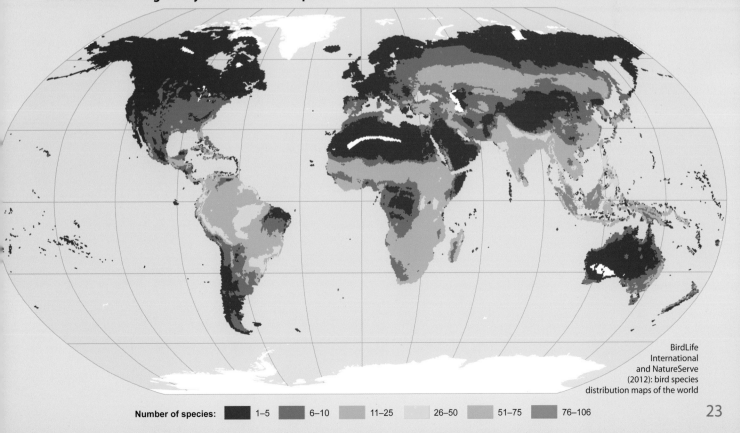

BirdLife International and NatureServe (2012): bird species distribution maps of the world

Number of species: 1–5 6–10 11–25 26–50 51–75 76–106

The Serra do Baturité in north-east Brazil was designated an AZE (Alliance for Zero Extinction) site because it was believed to hold the last population of Critically Endangered **Grey-breasted Parakeet** *Pyrrhura griseipectus*. Photo: Ciro Albano (nebrazilbirding.com).

Three-quarters (76%) of threatened birds are found in forests of different kinds. Marine, inland wetland and grassland habitats each support 16% of threatened bird species. Only 31% of threatened species tolerate human-modified habitats, compared with 50% of all birds. Threatened forest birds are highly dependent upon intact habitat for their survival. Overall, 18% of bird species can be found in degraded forest, but only 3% of threatened birds use such habitat, and for the majority it is of marginal importance.

Seabirds are now more threatened than any other group of birds. Of the 346 seabird species, 97 (28%) are globally threatened, and a further 10% are Near Threatened. Nearly half of all seabird species are known or suspected to be experiencing population declines. Of the main seabird families, which together account for 87% of species, the most threatened are the penguins, and the albatrosses and petrels. Of 22 albatross species, 17 are globally threatened and the rest Near Threatened. The next most threatened group of seabirds are the gadfly petrels of the genera *Pterodroma* and *Pseudobulweria*.

Last chances to save

Of the 586 Endangered and Critically Endangered bird species, exactly 200 are now restricted to single sites. In other words, for each of these species, the entire global population (or, in a few cases, over 95% of it) is restricted to a single Important Bird Area (IBA), National Park or patch of forest. The Alliance for Zero Extinction (AZE), a joint initiative of 76 biodiversity conservation organizations, has identified 588 such sites for 920 highly threatened bird, mammal, amphibian, reptile, conifer or coral species globally.

An AZE site must contain all or the vast majority of the global population of at least one Endangered or Critically Endangered species, either resident, or during part of its life history (breeding or wintering). Protecting AZE sites is an absolute priority for the conservation of these species. Although to survive in the long term, some species will require larger areas than currently covered by AZE sites, it is hoped that preserving such sites will help to at least halt the decline of the species, providing a refuge from which they will be able expand into restored habitat in the future.

The threats birds face

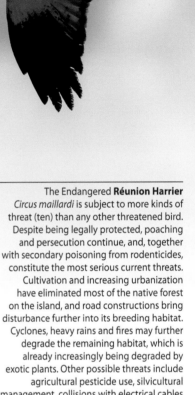

To understand the factors that result in species being threatened with extinction, and to allow comparisons between different species, BirdLife International and other organizations classify these factors using a standard classification scheme. This is hierarchical, with some broad, high-level classes, each of which is divided into more specific categories. For each threat, a score is assigned for its timing (current, future, past, and for the latter a judgement made as to whether it is likely to return in the short or long term), scope (the proportion of the population affected by the threat), and severity (the rate of population decline driven by the threat within the area it affects). These scores are combined to produce a score for threat impact – the magnitude of its effect on the species as a whole.

These data show that a broad range of factors threaten Endangered and Critically Endangered species, with agriculture, logging, invasive species and unsustainable levels of hunting and trapping being most important. A review of each of the main threats is provided on the following pages, with illustrated examples from around the world. The only threat which is not covered in any detail is ecosystem modifications.

The Endangered **Réunion Harrier** *Circus maillardi* is subject to more kinds of threat (ten) than any other threatened bird. Despite being legally protected, poaching and persecution continue, and, together with secondary poisoning from rodenticides, constitute the most serious current threats. Cultivation and increasing urbanization have eliminated most of the native forest on the island, and road constructions bring disturbance further into its breeding habitat. Cyclones, heavy rains and fires may further degrade the remaining habitat, which is already increasingly being degraded by exotic plants. Other possible threats include agricultural pesticide use, silvicultural management, collisions with electrical cables and wind turbines, and human hunting pressure on some if its prey species. Photo: Sarah Caceres & Jean-Noël Jasmin.

The Endangered **Oriental Stork** *Ciconia boyciana* is subject to the second highest number of different threats (nine) of any threatened bird. Deforestation and drainage of wetlands for agricultural development are the main causes of decline in its breeding grounds. Spring fires threaten breeding sites and kill nest trees. Reclamation of wetland has reduced the area of habitat for wintering birds. Over-fishing is a problem at many breeding and wintering sites. In places it is hunted, persecuted as a pest, or collected for zoos. Other threats include pollution, changes in water levels caused by large-scale dams, and collisions with infrastructure such as power-lines. Photo: Huajin Sun (birdnet.cn).

The site of the initial discovery of the Critically Endangered **Forest Owlet** *Heteroglaux blewitti*, in India, has been completely encroached by agriculture. Forest in its range is being lost and degraded by illegal tree cutting, forest fires and irrigation dams, and it suffers increasing predation from native raptors and competition for limited nesting cavities. Local people hunt it for its body parts and eggs. Pesticides and rodenticides may pose additional threats.

The Critically Endangered **Brazilian Merganser** *Mergus octosetaceus* occurs in extremely low numbers at a few highly disjunct localities in south-central Brazil. It is suspected to have declined rapidly over the last ten years due to habitat loss and degradation caused by the expansion of hydroelectric dams, soya cultivation, illegal logging, river pollution and diamond mining. Tourist operations cause disturbance, even in national parks.

Forest Owlet *Heteroglaux blewitti*.
Photo: Dr Jayesh K. Joshi.

Brazilian Merganser *Mergus octosetaceus*.
Photo: Sávio Freire Bruno (uff.br/biodiversidade).

The threats faced by globally threatened birds

This chart shows the total number of Critically Endangered, Endangered and Vulnerable species affected by each of the 15 threat types. It is important to note that many species are affected by more than one threat, and some face many threats. For this reason, the cumulative total is much greater than the actual number of species involved.

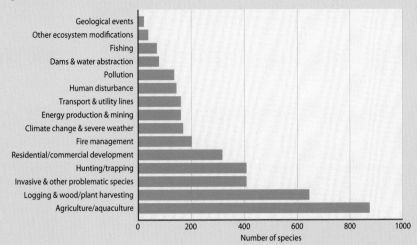

Chart: Number of species
- Geological events
- Other ecosystem modifications
- Fishing
- Dams & water abstraction
- Pollution
- Human disturbance
- Transport & utility lines
- Energy production & mining
- Climate change & severe weather
- Fire management
- Residential/commercial development
- Hunting/trapping
- Invasive & other problematic species
- Logging & wood/plant harvesting
- Agriculture/aquaculture

0   200   400   600   800   1000
Number of species

Few vegetated marshes suitable for the Endangered **Bogotá Rail** *Rallus semiplumbeus* remain in Colombia, because of drainage, agricultural encroachment, pollution and eutrophication caused by untreated sewage and agrochemicals, tourism, hunting, burning, trampling by cattle, harvesting of reeds and increased water demand. Construction of a new road may open up the wetlands to colonization and invasive species such as rats, cats and dogs.

Habitat destruction and hunting for food have caused the decline of the Endangered **Black-capped Petrel** *Pterodroma hasitata*, and remain key threats in Haiti. Birds are also predated by introduced mammals. Urbanization and increases in artificial light (light pollution) may distract birds and lead to collisions with trees, wires and buildings. The proposed development of gas/oil fields off the coast of South Carolina, USA, could devastate an important feeding area.

The Endangered **Masked Finfoot** *Heliopais personatus* is declining very rapidly because of the loss and degradation of wetlands and riverine lowland forest in Asia, driven by agricultural clearance, logging, and dam construction. This species is hunted, its eggs and chicks are collected, and it suffers disturbance from increased traffic on waterways.

Bogotá Rail *Rallus semiplumbeus*. Photo: Murray Cooper.

Black-capped Petrel *Pterodroma hasitata*. Photo: Steve N. G. Howell.

Masked Finfoot *Heliopais personatus*. Photo: Myron Tay (flickr.com/photos/28786551@N04).

AGR Agriculture and aquaculture

The conversion of natural habitats to agricultural land is the most serious threat to globally threatened birds. Across the world, the area of land used for agriculture has increased six-fold during the past 300 years. Much of the usable land that has not yet been developed, but is likely to come under pressure as human populations and levels of consumption grow, is in areas that are important for biodiversity.

In Africa, habitat clearance for agriculture threatens over 50% of Important Bird Areas (IBAs), and almost one third of Europe's IBAs are damaged or at risk from agricultural intensification and expansion.

The growing demand for commodity crops is leading to the rapid and large-scale destruction of tropical forests and grasslands. Brazil alone has over 20,000 km^2 of coffee plantation, most of it replacing primary rainforest. According to the United Nation's Food and Agriculture Organization (FAO), more than 80% of the world's existing oil palm plantations are in Indonesia and Malaysia, where they have replaced lowland forest. World demand for palm oil is predicted to at least double by 2020. Most remaining lowland forest in Myanmar has already been allocated to oil palm concessions, threatening the last stronghold of the Endangered Gurney's Pitta *Pitta gurneyi*, which also faces a bleak future in tiny habitat remnants in Thailand. Studies in Thailand found that bird species richness was 60% lower in oil palm than primary lowland forest, and that following conversion to plantations, 15 out of 16 globally threatened or Near Threatened species disappeared.

The temperate grasslands of southern South America originally covered an area of over one million square kilometres in Argentina, Uruguay, Brazil's Rio Grande do Sul state, and southern Paraguay. Only a tiny percentage remains in a natural state, and even this remnant is threatened by agricultural intensification. Traditional beef producers, whose grazing livestock helped maintain the natural grasslands, have seen their markets captured by intensively-reared 'feedlot' beef, and pasture has instead been turned over to crops such as soya. Endemic grassland-dependent bird species such as Marsh *Sporophila palustris* and Chestnut *S. cinnamomea* Seedeaters, Saffron-cowled Blackbird *Xanthopsar flavus*, Strange-tailed Tyrant *Alectrurus risora* and Ochre-breasted Pipit *Anthus nattereri* have all become globally threatened.

Globalized commodity agriculture also puts indirect pressure on other habitats by displacing small farmers, who may be driven to practice slash-and-burn farming. The rapid expansion of human populations can also lead to incursions into primary habitats, often in protected areas. Species threatened by slash-and-burn agriculture across the world include the Critically Endangered Samoan Moorhen *Gallinula pacifica*. On Mindoro in the Philippines, small-scale cultivation is invading the last remnants of forest used by the Critically Endangered Mindoro Bleeding-heart *Gallicolumba platenae* and Black-hooded Coucal *Centropus steeri,* and the Endangered Mindoro Hornbill *Penelopides mindorensis*. A host of endemic birds on Madagascar are now listed as Vulnerable primarily because of small-scale agricultural encroachment. The fires set while clearing forest can also get out of hand, destroying much larger areas than intended, as happened in Borneo and Sumatra during the late 1990s.

Not all cultivation is legal, and a number of already threatened species in Central and South America are losing habitat to illegal drug production. It is estimated that around 8% of what remains of the habitat of the Critically Endangered Gorgeted Puffleg *Eriocnemis isabellae*, already less than 10 km^2, is damaged every year by illegal coca cultivation. Attempts to stamp out the drug trade by spraying defoliants from the air can do far more damage than the drug-growers, who usually retain some canopy trees to hide their activities. Species affected by such retaliatory herbicide spraying include the Endangered Santa Marta Bush-tyrant *Myiotheretes pernix* and Santa Marta Sabrewing *Campylopterus phainopeplus* in Colombia.

White-headed Duck *Oxyura leucocephala.*
Photo: Andy & Gill Swash (WorldWildlifeImages.com).

Water abstraction for irrigation affects water levels at many sites throughout the range of the Endangered **White-headed Duck** *Oxyura leucocephala*, in Europe, Asia and north Africa. Approximately 50% of its breeding habitat was drained during the 20th century.

The last refuge of the Critically Endangered **Banggai Crow** *Corvus unicolor*, from Indonesia, is at risk from slash-and-burn cultivation made possible by construction of logging roads.

The narrow altitudinal band of dense undergrowth used by the Endangered **Russet-bellied Spinetail** *Synallaxis zimmeri* in the Peruvian Andes is severely threatened by cattle-grazing and clearance for farming.

Expanding pasture and sugarcane production threatens the tiny remnants of upland Atlantic Forest used by the Critically Endangered **Alagoas Foliage-gleaner** *Philydor novaesi* in Brazil. Fires used to clear the plantations can also spread into adjacent forest.

Cultivation of native grassland has virtually extirpated the Endangered **Plains-wanderer** *Pedionomus torquatus* from southern South Australia and Victoria. Even if cultivation ceased, this fragile habitat would take decades to recover.

Banggai Crow
Corvus unicolor.
Photo: Filip Verbelen.

Russet-bellied Spinetail *Synallaxis zimmeri*. Photo: Denzil Morgan.

Alagoas Foliage-gleaner
Philydor novaesi.
Photo: Ciro Albano
(nebrazilbirding.com).

The conversion of mangroves and coastal wetlands for aquaculture – often for short-term enterprises like prawn farming – has destroyed the breeding and wintering habitats of some restricted range species, such as the now Critically Endangered Javan Lapwing *Vanellus macropterus*, and the Endangered Madagascar Teal *Anas bernieri*. Coastal aquaculture also adds to the pressures on migratory shorebirds, particularly those that migrate in short hops and rely on finding frequent stop-over sites where they can rest and refuel along the route, such as the Critically Endangered Spoon-billed Sandpiper *Eurynorhynchus pygmeus*.

Plains-wanderer *Pedionomus torquatus*.
Photo: Andy & Gill Swash (WorldWildlifeImages.com).

Pfrimer's Parakeet
Pyrrhura pfrimeri.
Photo: Ciro Albano
(nebrazilbirding.com).

LOG Logging/plant harvesting

Global demand for timber and paper
pulp is second only to clearance for
agriculture as a driver of deforestation in
the tropics. The two are linked: clear-felling
of forest often preceeds conversion of the land to plantation
crops. In an increasing number of tropical countries, primary
forest is restricted to protected areas surrounded by intensively
cultivated landscapes. In parts of South-East Asia and Indonesia,
secondary forests are being logged for the second or even third
time because there is no unprotected primary forest left.

Communities around forests also take timber for building
materials and wood for fuel. Cumulatively, the impact of these
local activities is huge, and the UN's Food and Agriculture
Organization (FAO) estimates that at the global level, firewood
accounts for about half the wood removed from forests.

Globally, deforestation affected an estimated 13 million
hectares per year between 2000 and 2010, but because
of afforestation and natural expansion, net forest loss
was 5·2 million hectares per year. However, most of the
gains were in temperate and boreal forests, and most of the
losses in tropical forests. The five countries reporting the largest
decrease in primary forest over the last 20 years included two
of the top five for bird species richness (and threatened birds):
Brazil and Indonesia.

Even well-managed selective logging of tropical forest
impoverishes bird communities, with insectivores, particularly
those that feed on the ground, being hardest hit. However, the
proportion of frugivores in the community often increases.

On a more positive note, the FAO found that the amount of
primary forest covered by Protected Areas increased over the
decade 2000–2010.

Streak-breasted Bulbul *Ixos siquijorensis.* Photo: Leif Jonasson.

Regent Honeyeater
Xanthomyza phrygia.
Photo: Chris Tzaros.

Sokoke Scops-owl
Otus ireneae.
Photo: Roy de Haas (agami.nl).

The principal threat to the
Endangered **Pfrimer'**
Parakeet *Pyrrhura pfrimeri* i
selective logging of the smal
area of Brazilian *caatinga* forest i
inhabits. Durable wood to make
fence poles is particularly targeted

The Endangered **Streak-breasted**
Bulbul *Ixos siquijorensis* occurs
on four widely separated island
in the Philippines. But only tiny
patches of degraded forest remain
and logging continues unabated

The remnants of forest used b
the Critically Endangered **Regen**
Honeyeater *Xanthomyza phrygic*
have been heavily cut over
and larger trees are still being
extracted. The resulting habita
changes favour more aggressive
honeyeater species

Many areas of old-growth fores
in the USA and Canada that the
Endangered **Marbled Murrele**
Brachyramphus marmoratus uses
for nesting are slated for logging
Loss of nesting habitat has been
strongly linked to the decline o
this species

Licenced and illegal logging and
woodcutting for subsistence us
are degrading the forest home
of the **Sokoke Pipit** *Anthu*
sokokensis and **Sokoke Scops-ow**
Otus ireneae (both Endangered
in Kenya. The scops-owl nests
in cavities in old *Brachylaene*
huillensis trees, but these tree
are popular with wood-carvers
and few are lef

Invasive and other problematic species

According to BirdLife International, invasive species have been the most important driver of bird extinctions since 1500. Dogs, pigs, mongooses, sheep, rabbits and goats have all been implicated. But predation by introduced rats and cats, and diseases caused by introduced pathogens, have been the most deadly factors.

The threat posed by invasive aliens is especially acute on islands, where long isolation may have led to the evolution of species that lack defences. Of 130 species known to have gone extinct since 1500, 15 are rails from islands, several of which are believed to have been flightless, or weak and reluctant fliers at best.

In total, 625 threatened birds are currently at risk from invasive alien species. The majority are threatened by introduced predators and, once again, rats and cats are far and away the most severe threats, impacting 251 and 174 threatened species respectively. A host of species, including petrels, rails, parrots, pigeons, monarchs and white-eyes, are either confined to small rat- and cat-free islands, or survive only because of rigorous controls on these predators.

On Henderson Island, part of the Pitcairn group, non-native Polynesian (or Pacific) Rats *Rattus exulans* kill and eat 25,000 seabird chicks each year, including those of the Endangered, endemic Henderson Petrel *Pterodroma atrata*. The Ultramarine Lorikeet *Vini ultramarina* was classified as Endangered because it only survived on two or three small islands in the Marquesas, but the tiny populations on two of these may already have been extirpated by recently established Black Rats *Rattus rattus*. Up to 11% of nests of the Critically Endangered Palila *Loxioides bailleui* on Hawai'i (the Big Island) in the Hawaiian Islands are depredated by feral cats each year. On Stewart Island, New Zealand, over 50% of monitored adult Critically Endangered Kakapos *Strigops habroptila* were killed each year by cats, before the last of this population were transferred to cat- and rat-free offshore islands. The Kakapo is thought to be extinct in its natural range.

Common Myna *Acridotheres tristis* is the most significant invasive bird species, impacting 21 species, especially by competing for nest holes with threatened parrots like Endangered Mauritius Parakeet *Psittacula eques* and Rimatara Lorikeet *Vini kuhlii*.

The Brown Tree Snake *Boiga irregularis* was first accidentally introduced to the Pacific island of Guam, where it has been responsible for the extinction of 12 native bird species, and huge population declines in eight more. It has recently become established on several of the nearby Northern Mariana Islands, leading to a number of species being reclassified as Critically Endangered because they are predicted to suffer extremely rapid population declines in the near future. Mariana Crow *Corvus kubaryi* is one such species: the recent introduction of Brown Tree Snakes to Rota is likely to speed up the already rapid decline caused by habitat loss and predation by rats. Rota Bridled White-eye *Zosterops rotensis* and Golden White-eye *Cleptornis marchei* are in similar situations, as is the Nightingale Reed-warbler *Acrocephalus luscinius*.

Endemic birds in the Hawaiian Islands have been severely impacted by avian pox and malaria, transmitted by introduced mosquitoes. The mosquitoes are currently restricted to the lowlands, and cooler high-elevation forests are the last refuges for 18 threatened bird species, mainly Hawaiian honeycreepers. But as temperatures rise because of climate change, the altitudinal zone of malaria risk will also shift upwards.

There are plenty of examples from around the world of successful eradications of invasive species from islands. New Zealand has been a leader in 'de-ratting', while BirdLife partners in the Pacific have a growing track record in successful eradications. In the Indian Ocean, predator removal in Seychelles has helped in the downlisting of three species from Critically Endangered.

Maui Alauahio
Paroreomyza montana.
Photo: János Oláh
(birdquest-tours.com).

The Critically Endangered **Nightingale Reed-warbler** *Acrocephalus luscinius* was probably extirpated from Guam by the Brown Tree Snake *Boiga irregularis*, which is spreading to other islands where the reed-warbler occurs. An invasive gourd is also destroying its habitat.

The most significant threat to the Endangered **Northern Brown Kiwi** *Apteryx mantelli* is predation of adults by introduced dogs and ferrets. Stoats and cats prey on young kiwis.

Introduced dogs, cats, rats and pigs take the eggs, young and even adults of the Critically Endangered **Galápagos Petrel** *Pterodroma phaeopygia*. Nest-site destruction by goats, donkeys, cattle and horses is another major threat.

The proportion of young **Gough Buntings** *Rowettia goughensis* in the population has decreased greatly because of predation of eggs and chicks by House Mice *Mus domesticus*, which also compete with the Critically Endangered birds for food.

Introduced pigs, goats and deer are destroying the habitat of the Endangered **Maui Alauahio** *Paroreomyza montana* on Maui in the Hawaiian Islands. Other introduced mammals, birds and insects predate or compete with it, and disease-carrying mosquitoes are spreading into its range.

Galápagos Petrel
Pterodroma phaeopygia.
Photo: Peter Candido
(aviphile.smugmug.com).

Northern Brown Kiwi *Apteryx mantelli.* Photo: David Boyle.

Gough Bunting *Rowettia goughensis.* Photo: Ross Wanless.

However, the records of other governments in funding the removal of invasive aliens from their overseas island territories has been very poor. Put together, the UK's 16 overseas territories are fifth in the world league table of bird extinctions, with at least ten species lost since 1500, partially or wholly because of the impact of non-native mammals. France's overseas territories hold more than 70 globally threatened species. The USA's record is even worse: for example, the Hawaiian Islands once supported over 100 endemic bird taxa, but more than half of these have been driven to extinction by habitat loss, introduced predators and disease.

Nightingale Reed-warbler *Acrocephalus luscinius.* Photo: Kurt W. Baumgartner.

HUN Hunting and trapping

Some 50 bird species that have become extinct since 1500, or around 40% of the total, have been subject to over-harvesting. In 2012, 507 globally threatened bird species (39%) were affected by overexploitation for human use, primarily through hunting for food, and trapping for the cagebird trade.

Often these are large and conspicuous species, or particularly colourful ones. Some families are severely affected, with more than 10% of their species threatened by exploitation, including 75 species of parrots and 47 species of pigeons and doves. Other families, notably pheasants, guans and curassows, waterfowl, birds of prey and rails, are also heavily hunted or trapped.

Eight out of the ten countries with the highest numbers of birds at risk from exploitation are in Asia, with Indonesia at the top of the list. The well-known plight of the Critically Endangered Bali Starling *Leucopsar rothschildi* has overshadowed that of the Black-winged Starling *Sturnus melanopterus* from Java, also reduced to Critically Endangered status by the cagebird trade, and now almost impossible to find in the wild, even by the most skilled bird-trappers. Soberingly, one of the world's most familiar cagebirds, the once-abundant Java Sparrow *Padda oryzivora*, is now listed as Vulnerable because of excessive trapping.

African countries also play a disproportionately large role in the wild bird trade. Six of the top ten exporters of Convention on International Trade in Endangered Species (CITES)-listed wild birds between 2000 and 2003 were in Africa. Parrots and other species may be 'laundered' through adjacent countries where law enforcement is slack and export paperwork more easily obtained.

Overexploitation is causing rapid declines in both numbers and range for species like the Philippine Cockatoo *Cacatua haematuropygia*, which was once known from 52 islands, but has recently been recorded from just eight, and is now Critically Endangered. The high prices commanded result in chicks being taken from virtually every accessible nest. Trapping is changing the age structure of the remaining population, with fewer and fewer young birds.

Similarly, in Latin America thousands of wild parrots are illegally caught and traded every year despite national laws and international trade agreements. A recent study of markets in Santa Cruz, Bolivia found that over 22,000 individuals of 31 parrot species, the vast majority of which (94%) were wild-caught, were illegally traded every year. The Blue-throated Macaw *Ara glaucogularis* is now Critically Endangered because of illegal trapping.

Hyacinth Macaws
Anodorhynchus hyacinthinus.
Photo: Greg & Yvonne Dean
(WorldWildlifeImages.com).

At least 10,000 Endangered **Hyacinth Macaws** *Anodorhynchus hyacinthinus* were taken for the cagebird trade in the 1980s, in Brazil, and some illegal trapping still continues.

Unsustainable harvesting of eggs combined with human disturbance of nesting grounds has caused the abandonment of many nesting colonies of the Endangered **Maleo** *Macrocephalon maleo* on Sulawesi and Buton Islands.

The main cause of the decline of the Endangered **Yellow Cardinal** *Gubernatrix cristata*, prized for its song, has been constant and chronic trapping in Argentina, Uruguay and southern Brazil.

In Argentina and Paraguay, the meat of the Endangered **Black-fronted Piping-guan** *Pipile jacutinga* is thought superior to other game birds. Its unwary behaviour makes it an easy target.

Interviews with hunters at Madagascar's Lake Alaotra suggest that 450 Endangered **Meller's Ducks** *Anas melleri* are taken each year, constituting 18% of the global population.

Yellow Cardinal *Gubernatrix cristata*
Photo: James C. Lowen (pbase.com/james_lowen).

Widespread hunting for sport (often using falcons) and food has been the main driver of the decline of many of the world's bustard species. The most threatened of all, the Critically Endangered Great Indian Bustard *Ardeotis nigriceps*, is still heavily poached in Pakistan, where 49 birds were hunted out of 63 that were sighted over four years. Some poaching continues in India, including one instance where mine-workers, who lost their livelihoods when mines near Gwalior were closed to make way for the Ghatigaon Bustard Sanctuary, hunted the bustards to undermine the sanctuary's status. (This is a classic case study of how *not* to go about creating a protected area.)

Other Critically Endangered birds that have fallen victim to hunters include the Dwarf Olive Ibis *Bostrychia bocagei* on São Tomé, an event all too likely to be repeated as the forests are opened up by roads serving oil palm plantations. In Myanmar's Gulf of Martaban, the Spoon-billed Sandpiper *Eurynorhynchus pygmeus* is regularly caught in nets that are set to catch other waders for food. Sociable Lapwings *Vanellus gregarius* have been shot in Syria, and one of four known Northern Bald Ibises *Geronticus eremita* from the colony at Palmyra, Syria, was killed by a hunter while migrating through Saudi Arabia.

Black-fronted Piping-guan *Pipile jacutinga*
Photo: Martin V. Sneary (mvsneary.photoshelter.com).

Trapping and shooting on both sides of the Mediterranean are notorious threats to birds migrating between Europe and Africa. Black spots include Cyprus, where songbirds are trapped in huge numbers to provide expensive 'delicacies' (*ambelopoulia*), and Malta and the Straits of Messina in Italy, where raptors and other large migrants are blasted from the sky. But illegal trapping and hunting is a growing problem in eastern Europe and the Balkans too. Songbirds are sourced for the restaurant trade elsewhere in Europe, and larger birds, including threatened species like the Endangered Red-breasted Goose *Branta ruficollis*, are killed by 'hunting tourists'.

Other forms of exploitation include egg-collecting for food, which has become a threat as traditional controls have broken down and human numbers have increased. Two megapodes from the Pacific (Micronesian *Megapodius laperouse* and Polynesian *M. pritchardii*), and the Maleo *Macrocephalon maleo* from Sulawesi and the Buton Islands, are all now considered Endangered because of excessive egg-harvesting.

Maleo
Macrocephalon maleo
Photo: Ch'ien C. Lee
(wildborneo.com.my).

Grenada Dove *Leptotila wellsi.* Photo: Anthony Jeremiah.

DEV   Residential and commercial development

Cities are expanding worldwide, with expectations that more than half of the world's total human population will be living in them by 2030. The associated residential and commercial development, including housing, urban infrastructure, industry, and tourism and recreation, is already having impacts on nearly 30% of all threatened bird species.

Urbanization alone affects 249 species (19% of threatened birds). Urban development is occurring most rapidly in Asia, which holds 31% of the species threatened by residential and commercial development. Urbanization increases biological homogenization, with the extirpation of most native species, especially forest birds, and the establishment of invasive and adaptable birds such as feral Rock Doves *Columba livia* and House Crows *Corvus splendens*.

Demographic pressures – such as high densities or growth rates of human population, and increasing flows of human migrants and refugees – are among the main drivers of the extinction crisis. There is increasing evidence that areas of dense human settlement often coincide with areas of unique and irreplaceable biodiversity. In sub-Saharan Africa, human population density is positively correlated with species richness of terrestrial vertebrates. Similar relationships between the distributions of people and biodiversity have been found in Australia, North America, Europe and, at a smaller scale, in the tropical Andes.

Urban, commercial and industrial development is often concentrated on coastal plains. In many rapidly developing countries along the East Asian–Australasian Flyway, competition for limited land is so great that coastal wetland reclamation can be far cheaper than buying or renting land, especially in urban areas. The pace of coastal land reclamation is fastest around the Yellow Sea, where remote sensing shows losses of up to 60% of intertidal habitats in some key areas for migratory shorebirds.

Spoon-billed Sandpiper *Eurynorhynchus pygmeus.* Photo: Chaiwat Chinuparawat.

Restinga Antwren *Formicivora littoralis*. Photo: Ciro Albano (nebrazilbirding.com).

Araripe Manakin *Antilophia bokermanni*.
Photo: Ciro Albano (nebrazilbirding.com).

All the state-owned land where the Critically Endangered **Grenada Dove** *Leptotila wellsi* occurs is now protected. But the rest is in private hands, in hundreds of expensive tiny parcels earmarked for development.

Tidal flats throughout the migratory and wintering ranges of the Critically Endangered **Spoon-billed Sandpiper** *Eurynorhynchus pygmeus* are being reclaimed for development.

The entire range of the Endangered **Restinga Antwren** *Formicivora littoralis* lies within a holiday development area in south-east Brazil, where surviving fragments of *restinga* beach-scrub are being cleared for real-estate projects.

New homes have encroached on the 28 km² of moist forest used by the Critically Endangered **Araripe Manakin** *Antilophia bokermanni* in north-east Brazil. Protection of the watershed for nearby towns is driving conservation efforts.

Development pressure is resulting in habitat loss at many sites favoured by the Endangered **Belding's Yellowthroat** *Geothlypis beldingi* around the oases in Baja California.

Belding's Yellowthroat *Geothlypis beldingi*.
Photo: Javier Lascurain.

FIRE | Fire and fire management

At least nine Critically Endangered birds are directly threatened by changes in fire regimes. Many others are indirectly threatened, especially when small islands of habitat (as at the Murici Biological Reserve in Brazil's Atlantic Forest, home to 15 globally threatened bird species) are surrounded by plantations of crops such as sugarcane, where fire is used to clear the ground after harvest.

Some major habitats such as *cerrado*, savanna and tropical dry forest rely on fire to maintain the vegetation structure, which in turn is an important determinant of bird community structures. Threats to the integrity of these communities are often the result of changes in the fire regime.

In savannas, regular low-intensity fires burn off old, dry grass, help regenerate new grass, and prevent the invasion of scrub, without doing much harm to savanna trees. When regular fires are prevented or extinguished, the resulting build-up of dry material means that fires, when they come, are uncontrollable, intense and destructive, killing trees and penetrating into the ground where they destroy root systems. Full recovery of these ecosystems can take many years.

Ecuadoran villagers extinguished a large fire that threatened the last patches of habitat only days after the Endangered **Pale-headed Brush-finch** *Atlapetes pallidiceps* was rediscovered. However, the species needs fire to maintain the regenerating scrub in which it lives. Photo: Dusan M. Brinkhuizen (sapayoa.com).

In Australia, the increased threat status of many grassland and scrubland species may be the results of the ending of Aboriginal fire-based management regimes. In south-western Australia, small areas were burned every 5–10 years, resulting in a mosaic of habitats with a high diversity of plant species. Early European colonists burned heathland more often, every 2–3 years. These changes were a major factor in the extinction of at least five bird taxa. Inappropriate fire regimes are recognized as a major threat for almost half of Australia's nationally threatened birds, notably those of heathland and mallee habitats. The Endangered Noisy Scrub-bird *Atrichornis clamosus* avoids areas that are burnt more often than every six years, and reaches its highest densities only after 20–25 years of regrowth. The patches of habitat remaining to the Endangered Mallee Emuwren *Stipiturus mallee* are menaced by increasingly intense wildfires because of drought. Mallee-heath requires 5–10 years of regeneration before it is suitable for the emuwren.

In rainforest, natural fires are extremely rare, and burnt forest may take hundreds or possibly thousands of years to return to its original state. In Indonesia during 1997–1998, fires damaged or destroyed almost 50,000 km² of forest in Borneo and Sumatra. Research at Bukit Barisan Selatan National Park, Sumatra, showed that the density of hornbill species decreased by 28–63% in fire-damaged forest because of the resulting sparse canopy and scarcity of fruit.

Forest fires are responsible for the greatest proportion of habitat loss at Kilum-Ijim, Cameroon, the largest area of montane forest left for the Endangered **Bannerman's Turaco** *Tauraco bannermani*. Photo: Markus Lilje (rockjumperbirding.com).

CLI Climate change and severe weather

More than 400 bird species globally have already undergone range shifts in line with those predicted by climate change modelling. As global temperatures rise, ranges have moved towards the poles and, in the case of mountain species, upwards. For some birds with small ranges at high latitudes and altitudes, there may soon be nowhere left to go.

In North America, over 200 bird species have experienced northward range shifts consistent with climate change. Similar findings have been reported in Europe, where the largest climate change induced range shifts have been recorded. However, the magnitude of these responses may still be insufficient to keep pace with climate change. Effectively, birds are lagging behind climate warming, and the long-term implications of this discrepancy could be profound.

Annual routines like migration and breeding are becoming increasingly mismatched with the life-cycles of other species. The insect prey that provides parent birds and young with high energy, high protein food in turn needs to synchronize its reproduction with trees coming into leaf: too early, and there may be no young leaves for the insect larvae; too late, and the leaves may be too high in tannins.

A preliminary analysis suggests that up to 35% of bird species have characteristics that render them particularly susceptible to climate change. Of these, 72% are not currently considered threatened. But most birds that are already threatened (80%) are also 'climate-change susceptible' and may therefore face an even more uncertain future. Certain groups are particularly sensitive, including seabirds and Neotropical forest-dependent passerines.

The Arctic region has already shown the most pronounced warming of any part of the globe, and this trend is set to continue, with warming of up to 5°C predicted over the rest of this century. Boreal forests are likely to spread northwards into the tundra, and the Endangered Red-breasted Goose *Branta ruficollis* and Critically Endangered Spoon-billed Sandpiper *Eurynorhynchus pygmeus* may lose much or even most of their breeding habitat.

As the climate changes and the oceans become warmer, extreme weather events such as storms, hurricanes and floods are expected to grow in frequency and intensity. In recent years, hurricanes have battered the last populations of a number of Critically Endangered species, including the Grenada Dove *Leptotila wellsi*, the Puerto Rican Amazon *Amazona vittata* and the Tuamotu Kingfisher *Todiramphus gambieri*, and there have been no confirmed sightings of the Cozumel Thrasher *Toxostoma guttatum* since two hurricanes lashed its tiny island home in 2005.

The Critically Endangered **Hooded Grebe** *Podiceps gallardoi* breeds on a few basaltic lakes in Argentina, where until recently it may have been the commonest waterbird. Less snow and rain has fallen in recent years because of climate change, and many former breeding lakes have dried up completely. Photo: Diego Punta Fernández.

A very small rise in temperature could make the tiny range occupied by the Endangered **Ethiopian Bush-crow** *Zavattariornis stresemanni* uninhabitable, making it perhaps the most vulnerable to climate change of all the world's birds. Photo: Paul F. Donald.

Habitat loss following volcanic eruptions, earthquakes and tsunamis is the main danger posed to threatened birds by such geological events. But at vulnerable stages in their life-cycles, they may be impacted more directly.

The Japanese earthquake of March 2011 triggered a tsunami that hit the north-western Hawaiian Islands at night, swamping parts of Midway Atoll and Laysan Island. Around 110,000 of the Near Threatened Laysan *Phoebastria immutabilis* and Vulnerable Black-footed *P. nigripes* Albatross chicks died as a result of this and earlier winter storms. At least a quarter of the adult population of the Critically Endangered Laysan Duck *Anas laysanensis* disappeared, and breeding failed completely that year. The rotting carcasses of the albatross chicks led to a botulism outbreak, and a further 75 Laysan Ducks died as a result.

A number of threatened bird species, such as the Critically Endangered Black-breasted Puffleg *Eriocnemis nigrivestis*, have ranges that are mainly or entirely at risk from volcanic eruption. The Grand Comoro Drongo *Dicrurus fuscipennis*, for example, is classified as Endangered because it has an extremely small population, occupying a very small range at only one location around an active volcano. A single eruption could wipe out the single population of Vulnerable Mount Karthala White-eye *Zosterops mouroniensis*, which is entirely confined to the top of the volcano after which it is named. This white-eye's area of occupancy has already been seriously reduced by heathland fires started by volcanic activity.

The ash falls and acid rain that followed the eruptions on Montserrat not only led to the extirpation of the Montserrat Oriole *Icterus oberi* from much of its former habitat, but also caused rapid declines in the island's population of Forest Thrush *Turdus lherminieri*, which is now listed as Vulnerable.

Volcanic eruptions in the 1990s all but extirpated Montserrat's national bird, the Critically Endangered **Montserrat Oriole** *Icterus oberi*, from its former stronghold in the Soufrière hills. The population has continued to decline, perhaps because of indirect effects such as low insect availability and chronic ill-health from ash falls.

One of only two confirmed locations for the Critically Endangered **Black-breasted Puffleg** *Eriocnemis nigrivestis* is on the ridge-crests of Volcán Pichincha in Ecuador. The volcano has erupted sporadically since 1999, with considerable ash-fall on the tiny area of cloud forest remaining.

Black-breasted Puffleg
Eriocnemis nigrivestis.
Photo: Murray Cooper.

Montserrat Oriole *Icterus oberi*
Photo [captive]: Tomasz Doroń.

MAN Human disturbance

Human disturbance often accompanies or follows other threats to birds, such as logging, hunting, and roadbuilding and other infrastructure development. But disturbance by itself can be a serious threat. The extinction of an endemic hummingbird, Brace's Emerald *Chlorostilbon bracei* from the island of New Providence, Bahamas, is attributed to human disturbance in the late 19th century.

The interior of the island of Tahiti has been opened up with new roads and tracks. This has led to a considerable increase in tourists using four-wheel drive vehicles, which disturb breeding Tahiti Reed-warblers *Acrocephalus caffer,* and the species was *uplisted* to Endangered in 2008. Similarly, increasing use of off-road vehicles in St Helena may be disturbing or destroying the nests of the Critically Endangered St Helena Plover *Charadrius sanctaehelenae.*

Leisure activities – including ecotourism – can cause serious disturbance to breeding birds, and prevent migrating birds from feeding and resting. Popular rock-faces for climbing can be important for breeding raptors. Sport fishing on isolated offshore reefs and islets is a major threat to the Vulnerable Japanese Murrelet *Synthliboramphus wumizusume.* Fish offal discarded by anglers attracts crows and gulls, which then predate eggs and chicks. Similarly, some populations of Critically Endangered Kittlitz's Murrelet *Brachyramphus brevirostris* are repeatedly disturbed by recreational and commercial boat traffic, which causes a 30-fold increase in flight behaviour, driving the murrelets away from the shore until it has passed.

Visits by tourists can cause disturbance to colonies of Critically Endangered Chatham Islands Shags *Phalacrocorax onslowi,* if not supervised carefully. The birds sometimes stampede from their nests when disturbed, breaking their own eggs and exposing them to predation by gulls. Similarly, human disturbance in Namibia and South Africa resulted in the loss of four colonies of Endangered Bank Cormorant *Phalacrocorax neglectus*, and reductions in the populations at six others.

Disturbance is partly blamed for the disappearance of the breeding population of Endangered Black-bellied Terns *Sterna acuticauda* from Chitwan National Park, Nepal, and is thought to be among the causes of the complete loss of the species from Cambodia. Busy river traffic in north-east India, Bhutan and Myanmar has exacerbated the pressures on the Critically Endangered White-bellied Heron *Ardea insignis.*

Although human populations are generally sparse in the Arctic tundra, seasonal activities can cause significant disturbance to nesting birds. For example, in the spring, when domesticated reindeer are being driven on their migration, Siberian Cranes *Leucogeranus leucogeranus* can be forced off their nests, leaving their eggs vulnerable to predation by skuas and gulls.

Ironically, the lack of sensitivity to disturbance played a part in the decline of the Critically Endangered Trinidad Piping-guan, *Pipile pipile*. Hunters reported that shooting one bird did not disturb the flock, allowing others to be picked off.

Ashy Storm-petrel
Oceanodroma homochroa.
Photo: John Sterling
(sterlingbirds.com).

Endangered
Ashy Storm-petrels
Oceanodroma homochroa
may abandon their nests
if disturbed too often, so
are at risk from visits of sea
kayakers to their breeding
islands off California and
Mexico.

Disturbance has led to
the loss of secure feeding,
roosting and nesting areas
for the Critically Endangered
White-shouldered Ibis
Pseudibis davisoni in
South-East Asia. These
birds depend on herbivore-
altered habitats, and with
the extirpation of large wild
ungulates they rely instead
on domestic livestock,
bringing them closer
to human
settlements.

White-shouldered Ibis
Pseudibis davisoni.
Photo: Jonathan C. Eames.

Pollution affects many globally threatened bird species directly, leading to mortality in 6%, and reduced reproductive success in 3%. A total of 170 threatened species is affected by one or more pollutants, of which 97 use marine or freshwater habitats.

Indirect effects include habitat degradation and disruption to the food chain. For example, the decline of the Endangered Guam Swiftlet *Collocalia bartschi* on Guam, and its extirpation from Rota, may have resulted from the scarcity of insect prey because of excessive pesticide use.

The major pollutants are effluents from agriculture, forestry and industry, oil spills, and herbicides and pesticides. Some non-specific herbicides and pesticides can have devastating and immediate effects on whole ecosystems. Like several other Santa Marta endemics, the Critically Endangered Blue-billed Curassow *Crax alberti* has suffered from Colombian government attempts to control illegal marijuana and coca cultivation by spraying its habitat with non-specific herbicides. Large tracts of the primary forest habitat of the Critically Endangered Edwards's Pheasant *Lophura edwardsi* were destroyed by defoliants used during the Vietnam war, and have not recovered.

Highly toxic pesticides, such as carbofurans, are deliberately used to poison large predators, and many vultures, including Endangered White-backed *Gyps africanus* and Hooded *Necrosyrtes monachus* Vultures, are also killed when they feed on poisoned carcasses. Poisoning is the major source of vulture declines in East Africa, and carbofurans continued to be sold in African countries long after they were banned in Europe and the USA. A single poisoned carcass can attract and kill all the vultures from a very wide surrounding area, including those from protected areas, where numbers are also declining fast.

Other pollutants, like heavy metals, and persistent organic pollutants such as PCBs, and DDT and other organochlorine pesticides, accumulate over time, and as they pass up the food chain. The toxic effects of DDT were slow to reveal themselves in declining raptor populations in Europe and the USA, and recoveries after the chemical was phased out were equally slow. DDT and similar chemicals are still sold and used extensively in the developing world. Pesticide accumulation may be reducing the already low reproductive output of the Critically Endangered Philippine Eagle *Pithecophaga jefferyi*.

White-rumped Vulture
Gyps bengalensis.
Photo: Csaba Barkóczi.

Once considered among the world's most abundant large bird of prey, the **White-rumped Vulture** *Gyps bengalensis* has declined by more than 99% since the 1990s. Like two other *Gyps* species in South Asia, the vulture suffers renal failure after eating carcasses of livestock treated with the anti-inflammatory drug diclofenac. All three are now considered Critically Endangered.

Mining activities have polluted Lake Lake Junín, only home of the Critically Endangered flightless **Junín Grebe** *Podiceps taczanowskii*. The north-west part of the lake has been rendered lifeless by iron-oxide sediment, and dead grebes presumed killed by pollutants have been reported.

Historically, pesticides played a role in the decline of the Endangered **Black-faced Spoonbill** *Platalea minor*, and pollution remains a major threat on its wintering grounds in Hong Kong (China).

High levels of heavy metals, especially arsenic and mercury, were reported in Endangered Scaly-sided Mergansers *Mergus squamatus* and their eggs after wintering in the Yangtze catchment, possibly resulting in the low rates of hatching recorded in this population.

Novel chemicals introduced to the environment can do massive damage before their side-effects become known. For example, it took several years before the cause of the catastrophic die-off of vultures in southern Asia was identified as the anti-inflamatory drug diclofenac.

Oil spills in the Gulf of Mexico, off the coasts of New Zealand and Spain, and around Nightingale Island in the Tristan da Cunha group – to mention only some of the most recent – have resulted in the deaths of tens of thousands of seabirds, including many threatened species. Recent large oil spills have impacted populations of Endangered African *Spheniscus demersus* and Northern Rockhopper Penguins *Eudyptes moseleyi*, and pose a significant risk to others, including Galápagos Penguin *Spheniscus mendiculus*. Similarly, moulting and wintering concentrations of seaducks like the Endangered Velvet Scoter *Melanitta fusca* are very susceptible to oil spills and other marine pollutants.

Junín Grebe *Podiceps taczanowski*.
Photo: Denzil Morgan.

Rubbish in the environment is a threat to seabirds and raptors, which can mistake it for food, and pass it on to their chicks. Plastic, nylon, rubber and metal wire have been found in the stomachs of 29% of Black-browed Albatross *Thalassarche melanophrys*. The recovery of the Critically Endangered California Condor *Gymnogyps californianus* in the wild has been seriously set back by nestling mortality caused by swallowing items such as broken glass and plastic cartridge cases. Lead poisoning from shot ingested by adults feeding on carcasses is among the greatest threats to this condor. In total, at least 59 terrestrial bird species are known to have been poisoned by ingesting spent ammunition, nine of which are classified as globally threatened or Near Threatened.

Light pollution from street lamps and other sources is responsible for significant mortality in petrels and shearwaters, which return to their nesting burrows at night. It has been suggested that, among other Endangered petrels, as many as 40–60% of young Endangered Barau's Petrel *Pterodroma baraui* on Réunion are disorientated and suffer light-induced mortality each year. Lights used during night-time construction work at the airstrip on Socorro was believed to have caused the deaths of several Critically Endangered Townsend's Shearwaters *Puffinus auricularis*.

Black-faced Spoonbill *Platalea minor*.
Photo: John & Jemi Holmes
(johnjemi.hk).

TRA Transport and other infrastructure

Poorly planned transport networks can have far-reaching negative impacts on ecosystems, including destruction and fragmentation of habitats, the spread of invasive alien species and pathogens, and direct mortality from collisions. By providing access to previously remote areas, roads can open them up to other kinds of threat including hunting and disturbance, settlement, agriculture and logging.

Damaging road developments currently threaten at least two World Heritage sites of high biodiversity value: Tanzania's Serengeti National Park, and the Yemeni island of Socotra, a hotspot of endemism.

Because of the high price of residential, commercial and agricultural land in affluent countries, road and rail developments can be displaced to land set aside for biodiversity. In the UK in the 1980s, the Government's strategy for roads was memorably described as joining the dots between Sites of Special Scientific Interest. Even in 21st century Europe, which in many ways sets the benchmark for minimizing the environmental impact of infrastructure development, plans to route a bypass through sites of high biodiversity value in Poland were only struck down after work had already begun. In the Caribbean and the Pacific, environmentally disastrous road developments have been provided as bribes by affluent nations seeking votes in institutions as varied as the United Nations and the International Whaling Commission. In continental Asia and Africa, roads and other infrastructure have been built in exchange for access to minerals or land for agriculture, with little or no consideration of environmental and social impacts.

Artificial structures of all kinds, including tall buildings, power-lines, pylons, fences and cell-phone masts, pose a direct threat to many birds, which are killed or injured by collision or electrocution. Large birds such as storks, pelicans, herons and cranes, bustards, swans and geese, and raptors including owls, eagles and vultures, are at particular risk from collisions with power-lines. Among Critically Endangered species that have died in this way are Critically Endangered Galápagos Petrels *Pterodroma phaeopygia*, California Condors *Gymnogyps californianus,* Northern Bald Ibises *Geronticus eremita* in Jordan, and a captive-bred female Spix's Macaw *Cyanopsitta spixii* released to mate with the only male then known to survive in the wild.

Ludwig's Bustard *Neotis ludwigii* was uplisted from Least Concern to Endangered in 2010, on evidence that the population was declining very rapidly because of collisions with power-lines. Collision rates in one part of the South African Karoo alone may exceed one bustard per kilometre per year, with similar rates likely across the Karoo as a whole. Photo: Adam Riley (rockjumperbirding.com).

One of the few fragments of thorn forest left for the Endangered **Honduran Emerald** *Amazilia luciae* is threatened by plans to extend and pave a road. Improved access elsewhere in the bird's range has led to habitat clearance for pineapple plantations. The US government and others have opposed the road, and the World Bank may be putting up cash for an alternative route. Photo: Robert E. Hyman.

The contribution of traditional energy sources ('fossil fuels') to climate change is well and widely known. Climate change is probably the greatest long-term threat to biodiversity and the habitability of our planet, but the processes involved in extracting fossil fuels also cause considerable damage to many already threatened species.

Oil and gas exploration opens remote areas to infrastructure development and settlement, degrades and fragments habitats, and exposes biodiversity to direct threats from spillages and other pollution. Oil and gas production often involves constructing pipelines through previously pristine areas. The Oleoducto de Crudos Pesados Heavy Crude Pipeline, for example, cuts through seven national parks and protected areas in Ecuador, including the Mindo Important Bird Area, which includes the entire global population of Critically Endangered Black-breasted Puffleg *Eriocnemis nigrivestis* and a host of other Chocó endemics. The pipeline's route is prone to earthquakes, with a high risk of pipeline rupture and spillage.

Strip-mining for tar sands, a source of low-grade oil, is damaging forest and wetland habitats in Canada's boreal forest, home to 325 breeding bird species, and the 'nursery' for vast numbers of migratory birds. Over the next 30 to 50 years up to 300,000 hectares of forest and wetland could be directly impacted, while habitat fragmentation by roads and pipelines, pollution and hydrological changes would affect a much larger area. The only wild, migratory population of Endangered Whooping Crane *Grus americana* nests at Wood Buffalo National Park to the north, and migrates over the tar sands region. The techniques used to extract tar sands resemble 'strip mining' for coal: the removal of vegetation, soil and underlying rock over a large area, which can never be fully restored.

The rush to find alternatives to fossil fuels also creates threats for birds. Uranium mining in the Namib Desert risks degrading and fragmenting the habitat of a suite of endemic and threatened birds. Windfarms may be located in areas of strong prevailing winds which are also used as migratory corridors. Biofuels such as palm and jatropha oil, and ethanol from corn and sugarcane, require huge areas of land, which may be taken from existing wilderness areas, or help to destroy them by displacing conventional agriculture. When all factors such as carbon release from land use change, transport and processing are taken into account, biofuels may generate similar or greater quantities of greenhouse gases to the fossil fuels they are intended to replace.

At least a quarter of the breeding area of the endemic and Critically Endangered **Christmas Island Frigatebird** *Fregata andrewsi* has been lost to phosphate mining, and one colony was largely deserted because of continuing dust fallout from phosphate dryers. Future habitat clearance for mining is proposed. Photo: David Boyle.

The forest fragment at Páramo de Frontino, Colombia, one of only two known sites for the Critically Endangered **Dusky Starfrontlet** *Coeligena orina,* is threatened by mining for the rich deposits of gold, zinc and copper that lie beneath it. Photo: Nigel Voaden.

Hydro-electric dams have already altered many of the shingly river beds used for breeding by the Endangered **Black-fronted Tern** *Sterna albostriata* in New Zealand's South Island. Another dam has been approved which would impact the Wairau River, where 12% of the population currently nests.
Photo: Craig McKenzie (flickr.com/photos/craigmckenzie).

WAT Dams and water abstraction

Over 60% of the world's rivers are regulated by dams, which can cause major ecological changes in river basins by flooding forests and other habitats upstream, and depriving downstream wetlands of flows of water and nutrients.

In Africa, the Middle East and Europe, dams pose a threat to over 300 Important Bird Areas, the majority of which contain areas that qualify as wetlands of international importance (Ramsar Sites). In Asia, actual or planned dam projects are likely to have significant impacts on at least ten globally threatened birds, especially waterbirds of lowland floodplains such as the Endangered Masked Finfoot *Heliopais personata*. Large dam projects upstream on the Tigris and Euphrates are preventing the full restoration of Iraq's Mesopotamian Marshes, which were drained by Saddam Hussein's regime. The dams restrict the seasonal pulses of floodwater which maintain the habitat used by Endangered Basra Reed-warbler *Acrocephalus griseldis*, and have reduced the marsh area to less than one-third of its original extent.

The construction of China's Three Gorges Dam has changed the hydrological pattern of the lower Yangtze River, resulting in lower water levels in winter, and more frequent floods and droughts. The bird most at risk of extinction from the resulting degradation of wetland habitat is probably the Critically Endangered Siberian Crane *Leucogeranus leucogeranus*, but a number of other birds currently listed as Vulnerable could be brought within the scope of this book by the impact of the Three Gorges Dam, including Hooded *Grus monacha* and White-naped *G. vipio* Cranes, and Swinhoe's Rail *Coturnicops exquisitus*.

Dams have already destroyed the type locations of two newly-discovered birds: the Critically Endangered Carrizal Seedeater *Amaurospiza carrizalensis* from Isla Carrizal in the Río Caroní, Venezuela, and the Endangered Marsh Tapaculo *Scytalopus iraiensis* from south-eastern Brazil. An impending hydroelectric project would flood what appears to be the global stronghold of the Critically Endangered Cone-billed Tanager *Conothraupis mesoleuca*, in gallery forest along the Alto Rio Juruena, Mato Grosso, Brazil. The Cone-billed Tanager was only rediscovered in 2003 after more than 60 years without a record.

Water abstraction, for irrigation or domestic and commercial consumption, also threatens a range of species, including the Critically Endangered Araripe Manakin *Antilophia bokermanni* from around the springheads on the slopes of the Chapada do Araripe, Brazil, and the Endangered White-winged Flufftail *Sarothrura ayresi*, which is known from a few tiny seasonal marshlands in South Africa, Zimbabwe and Ethiopia. By 2025, it is predicted that water abstractions will increase by 50 percent in developing countries and 18 percent in developed countries, with potentially devastating effects on wetlands and other ecosystems.

The river marshes along the upper Río Lerma, one of only four known areas for the Endangered **Black-polled Yellowthroat** *Geothlypis speciosa*, are becoming increasingly fragmented by water abstraction to supply México City and Toluca. Photo: Manuel Grosselet (tierradeaves.com).

FISH Fishing

Each year longline, trawl, and gillnet fisheries are responsible for the incidental deaths of hundreds of thousands of seabirds. Such 'bycatch' impacts at least 40 threatened seabird species.

Of the world's 22 albatross species, 17 are globally threatened, and fishing bycatch is the main factor driving many of them towards extinction. These and other seabirds are at risk because their foraging grounds include the most productive areas of the world's oceans, which are also targeted by commercial fisheries.

Numbers of the Critically Endangered Amsterdam Albatross *Diomedea amsterdamensis* are now so low that bycatch exceeding six individuals per year would be enough to cause a potentially irreversible population decline. Some of the species worst affected, such as the Critically Endangered Tristan Albatross *Diomedea dabbenena*, are also having to contend with predation of their eggs and chicks by invasive alien mammals. Losses from bycatch, which may amount to 2–5% per year, are unsustainable, as these long-lived birds are slow to reproduce. The median age at first breeding in some species is ten years, and many produce their single young only every two years.

Up to 600 adult and immature Endangered **Indian Yellow-nosed Albatrosses** *Thalassarche carteri* may be killed every year by longline fisheries. Photo: Jean-Florent Mandelbaum.

Shearwaters and petrels also die in large numbers in the world's fisheries. Mass deaths of up to 100 Critically Endangered Balearic Shearwaters *Puffinus mauretanicus* have been recorded in encounters with longline or purse seine fishing boats.

Thanks to the work of BirdLife's Albatross Taskforce, and lobbying of Regional Fisheries Management Organizations by conservationists, bycatch mitigation measures are being introduced in many areas where fishing fleets and seabirds meet. Europe currently lags behind many south Atlantic and Pacific nations in the implementation of bycatch mitigation.

Gillnets (static curtains of netting designed to entangle fish by their gills) are anchored vertically in the water. In coastal waters they are a threat to pursuit-diving species, such as divers (loons), grebes, seaducks, auks and cormorants. Fishing with similar nets from boats on the high seas (driftnets) has now been banned, but driftnets can still be used in coastal fisheries, where they may be responsible for tens of thousands of seabird deaths.

In Europe alone, based on studies in the Baltic and North Seas, gillnets could be responsible for the deaths of at least 90,000 and possibly as many as 200,000 birds per year. Long-tailed Duck *Clangula hyemalis*, the most frequently entangled species, was uplisted from Least Concern to Vulnerable in 2012, and may warrant uplisting to Endangered if declines elsewhere match those in the Baltic. Gillnets have also been responsible for significant mortality in Endangered Marbled Murrelet *Brachyramphus marmoratus* and other threatened auks.

Gillnets are also used in freshwater fisheries, where they have been implicated in the declines of several grebe species, and the Critically Endangered Madagascar Pochard *Aythya innotata*.

The population of **Titicaca Grebe** *Rollandia microptera* on Lake Umayo, Peru, crashed from 1,147 birds in 1986 to just four in 2001. The principal driver of this decline, here and on other freshwater lakes on the Peruvian and Bolivian altiplano, is the use of monofilament gillnets. Photo: Daniel Rosengren (scutisorex.se).

The need for conservation

Conservation can work, provided it is properly resourced, based on sound science, and with sufficient political will behind it. Five of the following case histories describe interventions that may have come just in time. For the sixth, Spix's Macaw, action began too late to prevent probable extinction in the wild. Ironically the breeding stock that may make its reintroduction possible is being provided by the very collectors who caused its decline in the first place.

Phosphate mining on Christmas Island has reduced the breeding habitat of **Abbott's Booby** *Papasula abbotti* by at least a third. But the most serious threat to this and other Christmas Island endemics is the introduced Yellow Crazy Ant *Anoplolepis gracilipes*, which alters island ecology by killing the dominant life-form, the Red Crab *Gecarcoidea natalis*. The ants also 'farm' scale insects for their honeydew, and the resulting increase in scale insects can kill trees and cause the canopy to die back. A control programme eliminated the crazy ant from much of its former extent, and in 2004 the booby was downlisted from Critically Endangered to Endangered. The ants have since recovered, and conservationists are seeking a more effective poison bait which is not toxic to other invertebrates, such as the crabs. The Christmas Island National Park has been extended to cover most Abbott's Booby breeding areas, and an agreement with the phosphate company forbids further clearance of primary rainforest.

Conservation began in time to reverse the fortunes of one of Brazil's large blue macaws. Until 1978, when a wild population was located, **Lear's Macaw** *Anodorhynchus leari* was known only from individuals intercepted in the cagebird trade, which had drastically reduced its numbers. From the mid-1990s, thanks to intensive efforts to protect it, the population began to increase rapidly, and in 2008 it was downlisted from Critically Endangered to Endangered. Trapping continues on a much reduced scale, but infiltration of trading networks and better surveillance at the sandstone breeding cliffs has resulted in arrests of poachers, smugglers and collectors.

The last known Critically Endangered **Spix's Macaw** *Cyanopsitta spixii* in the wild, which paired with a female Near Threatened **Blue-winged Macaw** *Primolius maracana*. Photo: Luiz Cláudio Marigo.

Endangered **Abbott's Booby** *Papasula abbotti*. Photo: David Boyle.

Endangered **Lear's Macaw** *Anodorhynchus leari*. Photo: Ciro Albano (nebrazilbirding.com).

Endangered **Cauca Guan**
Penelope perspicax.
Photo: Juan Manuel Cardona
(pbase.com/caranpaima/nature).

Spix's Macaw *Cyanopsitta spixii* was also known only from traded birds, and one individual shot by Johann Baptist von Spix. In 1985, three macaws were located in north Bahia, Brazil, but all were subsequently trapped. A single male was found at the site in July 1990, and a captive female was released to join it, but disappeared soon afterwards. The male was seen for the last time in 2000. Around the world, there are perhaps 120 Spix's Macaws in captivity, and these form the basis of a reintroduction programme, overseen by Brazil's Chico Mendes Institute. Land around the site where the last birds were seen has been purchased, habitat is being restored, and the first captive-bred birds should be released in 2013.

Land purchases by foundations like the World Land Trust and Ecuador's Fundación Jocotoco have protected the last areas of intact habitat for some of the world's most threatened birds, and lobbying by NGOs like SAVE Brasil and Guyra Paraguay has persuaded governments to create larger protected areas. But without the cooperation of local communities, conservation is doomed to fail. Awareness-raising can lead to the establishment of groups passionately committed to saving 'their' birds, and also persuade government and protected area authorities to take their responsibilities seriously by enforcing regulations.

There are recent records of **Cauca Guan** *Penelope perspicax* from just four areas in the West and Central Andes of Colombia. Killing for food and sport, even in protected areas, has been a factor in its decline, and conservation actions include an educational programme about this species and other guans and curassows, particularly aimed at limiting hunting. Similarly a public awareness campaign has been launched to try to prevent encroachments by settlers, loggers and gold-miners into the protected areas covering some of the five locations where the **Jocotoco Antpitta** *Grallaria ridgelyi* clings on in Ecuador and Peru.

Linking conservation to the interests of local communities, particularly their livelihoods, can be a very successful approach. The Critically Endangered **Colourful Puffleg** *Eriocnemis mirabilis* is known from a few locations in and around the Munchique National Park on the Pacific slope of the West Andes in south-west Colombia. The local economy was formerly based on the fruit crop 'lulo', a relative of the tomato, which was grown under the forest canopy, and hence deterred logging. But a fungal disease destroyed the crop in the 1980s, and logging recommenced.

The replanting of lulo fruits is now being encouraged, with workshops designed to involve local communities in conservation efforts, and to teach integrated pest management practices. In 2004, the Colombian NGO Fundación ProAves established a 1,090 hectare (2,700 acre) reserve to protect the narrow belt of montane cloud forest needed by both the puffleg and the Munchique Wood-wren *Henicorhina negreti*, which is also Critically Endangered.

Critically
Endangered
Colourful Puffleg
Eriocnemis mirabilis.
Photo:
Luís Mazariegos.

Endangered
Jocotoco Antpitta
Grallaria ridgelyi.
Photo:
Glenn Bartley
(glennbartley.com).

Threats without borders

Almost one-fifth of the world's extant bird species migrate, making regular cyclical movements beyond their breeding grounds. Apart from around 80 single-country endemics, they cross one or more national boundaries on their travels.

In 2008, BirdLife analyzed the status of 1,593 of these species, and found that 11% were either threatened or Near Threatened, including 12 that are now categorized as Critically Endangered and 25 as Endangered. Of these, ten are trans-regional migrants, breeding in one of the regions covered in this book and wintering, at least partly, in another. The other 27 species migrate between breeding and non-breeding areas that are entirely within one of these regions.

The main threats to these migratory species are habitat degradation caused by agriculture, and hunting and trapping, although infrastructure such as powerlines and wind turbines are a growing menace. Climate change is expected to exacerbate many of the threats.

Groups that are particularly threatened include large soaring birds, such as cranes and raptors, which migrate along narrow corridors subject to rapid changes in land use and new infrastructure; and waterbirds, which are finding more and more of the coastal wetland stopover sites they need to rest and refuel disappearing because of land reclamation.

After breeding, the Critically Endangered **Sociable Lapwing** *Vanellus gregarius* disperses across much of Central Asia and via the Middle East to winter in Sudan, Eritrea, Israel and India. Its breeding grounds in Kazakhstan are reverting to natural steppe after the end of collective farming. The reasons for its decline are poorly understood, and it may be increasing again.

When Saddam Hussein ordered the draining of Iraq's Mesopotamian Marshes, the Endangered **Basra Reed-warbler** *Acrocephalus griseldis* lost its main breeding area. Restoration of the marshes is hampered by dams higher up the Tigris and Euphrates rivers. This species migrates to eastern Africa, where a key wintering site, Kenya's Tana Delta, is threatened by biofuel plantations.

Mystery surrounds the Critically Endangered **Slender-billed Curlew** *Numenius tenuirostris*. With one known breeding area in Siberia, it formerly migrated through central and eastern Europe to southern Europe and North Africa. The last confirmed sighting was in Hungary in 2001. Breakdown of social behaviour in this highly gregarious bird may have prevented its recovery.

Sociable Lapwing *Vanellus gregarius*. Photo: Soner Bekir.

Basra Reed-warbler *Acrocephalus griseldis*.
Photo: Omar Fadhil Abdulrahman
(natureiraq.org/site/en).

Slender-billed Curlew
Numenius tenuirostris.
Photo: Chris Gomersall.

The Critically Endangered **Eskimo Curlew** *Numenius borealis* bred in north-west Canada and migrated via the Caribbean to South America, wintering on the Pampas and possibly as far south as Patagonia. Already rare by the early 1900s because of industrial hunting and habitat loss, Eskimo Curlew was last seen on the wintering grounds in 1939. The last confirmed individual was 'collected' in Barbados in 1963. Illustration: Tomasz Cofta.

Red-breasted Goose *Branta ruficollis with a few* **Greater White-fronted Goose** *Anser albifrons.* Photo: David Tipling.

The Endangered **Red-breasted Goose** *Branta ruficollis* breeds on remote peninsulas in Siberia, migrating via Kazakhstan to the Black Sea and occasionally the Aegean. Hunting along its entire flyway, and tourist developments and windfarms around the Black Sea coast, are the major threats.

The migration routes of Endangered and Critically Endangered 'land' birds

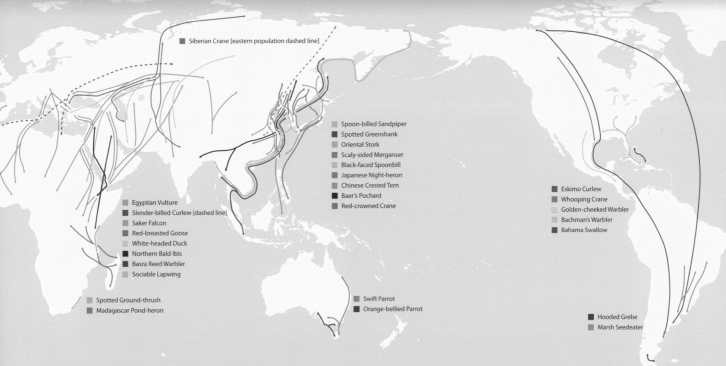

Siberian Crane [eastern population dashed line]

Spoon-billed Sandpiper
Spotted Greenshank
Oriental Stork
Scaly-sided Merganser
Black-faced Spoonbill
Japanese Night-heron
Chinese Crested Tern
Baer's Pochard
Red-crowned Crane

Eskimo Curlew
Whooping Crane
Golden-cheeked Warbler
Bachman's Warbler
Bahama Swallow

Egyptian Vulture
Slender-billed Curlew [dashed line]
Saker Falcon
Red-breasted Goose
White-headed Duck
Northern Bald Ibis
Basra Reed Warbler
Sociable Lapwing

Spotted Ground-thrush
Madagascar Pond-heron

Swift Parrot
Orange-bellied Parrot

Hooded Grebe
Marsh Seedeater

Based on an analysis of data held in BirdLife's World Bird Database (2012)

51

Whooping Crane *Grus americana*.
Photo: Joseph Duff
(operationmigration.org).

The most significant known cause of death to fledgling Endangered **Whooping Cranes** *Grus americana* is collision with powerlines. Thousands of wind turbines are planned for the cranes' migration corridor, which could dramatically increase the number of fatal collisions.

A proposed dam at Poyang Lake in China would flood the foraging grounds used by the vast majority of wintering Critically Endangered **Siberian Cranes** *Leucogeranus leucogeranus*.

The non-migratory population of Endangered **Red-crowned Crane** *Grus japonensis* on Hokkaido, Japan, is stable, although genetic diversity is low and disease a constant threat. On the Asian mainland, the cranes are over-concentrated in a few rapidly shrinking wintering and breeding sites.

The Endangered **Spotted Greenshank** *Tringa guttifer* has declined to a few hundred individuals because of the loss of wetlands along the Asian coast, and overgrazing and hunting on its breeding grounds.

The tidal flats used as stopover sites by the Critically Endangered **Spoon-billed Sandpiper** *Eurynorhynchus pygmeus* are being reclaimed for industry, infrastructure and aquaculture, and are increasingly polluted.

Loss of wintering habitat in south-east Australia is the biggest threat to the Critically Endangered **Orange-bellied Parrot** *Neophema chrysogaster*, although a single sea-storm could wipe out much of the tiny population as it migrates between Tasmania and the mainland.

Siberian Cranes *Leucogeranus leucogeranus*
Photo: Hu Jinglin (birdnet.cn).

Trans-regional terrestrial migrants
Critically Endangered species
Northern Bald Ibis *Geronticus eremita*
Siberian Crane *Grus leucogeranus*
Sociable Lapwing *Vanellus gregarius*
Eskimo Curlew *Numenius borealis*
Slender-billed Curlew *Numenius tenuirostris*

Endangered species
Red-breasted Goose *Branta ruficollis*
Velvet Scoter *Melanitta fusca*
White-headed Duck *Oxyura leucocephala*
Saker Falcon *Falco cherrug*
Egyptian Vulture *Neophron percnopterus*
Basra Reed-warbler *Acrocephalus griseldis*

Intra-regional terrestrial migrants
Critically Endangered species
Crested Shelduck *Tadorna cristata*
Hooded Grebe *Podiceps gallardoi*
Bengal Florican *Houbaropsis bengalensis*
Spoon-billed Sandpiper *Eurynorhynchus pygmeus*
Orange-bellied Parrot *Neophema chrysogaster*
White-eyed River-martin *Eurochelidon sirintarae*
Blue-crowned Laughingthrush *Garrulax courtoisi*
Chinese Crested Tern *Sterna bernsteini*
Bachman's Warbler *Vermivora bachmanii*

Endangered species
Madagascar Teal *Anas bernieri*
Baer's Pochard *Aythya baeri*
Scaly-sided Merganser *Mergus squamatus*
Storm's Stork *Ciconia stormi*
Oriental Stork *Ciconia boyciana*
Greater Adjutant *Leptoptilos dubius*
Black-faced Spoonbill *Platalea minor*
White-eared Night-heron *Gorsachius magnificus*
Japanese Night-heron *Gorsachius goisagi*
Madagascar Pond-heron *Ardeola idae*
Ludwig's Bustard *Neotis ludwigii*
Lesser Florican *Sypheotides indicus*
White-winged Flufftail *Sarothrura ayresi*
Whooping Crane *Grus americana*
Red-crowned Crane *Grus japonensis*
Spotted Greenshank *Tringa guttifer*
Black-billed Gull *Larus bulleri*
Black-fronted Tern *Sterna albostriata*
Swift Parrot *Lathamus discolor*
Hyacinth Macaw *Anodorhynchus hyacinthinus*
Grey-cheeked Parakeet *Brotogeris pyrrhoptera*
Bahama Swallow *Tachycineta cyaneoviridis*
Spotted Ground-thrush *Zoothera guttata*
Golden-cheeked Warbler *Dendroica chrysoparia*
Marsh Seedeater *Sporophila palustris*

Red-crowned Crane *Grus japonensis.*
Photo: Eric VanderWerf
(pacificrimconservation.com).

Spotted Greenshank *Tringa guttifer.*
Photo: Michelle & Peter Wong.

Spoon-billed Sandpiper *Eurynorhynchus pygmeus.*
Photo: Zheng Jianping.

Orange-bellied Parrot *Neophema chrysogaster.* Photo: David Boyle.

The Regional Directories

The following Directory of species is divided into seven sections, as shown on the map on *page 57*. The sections have been arranged in order to provide as logical a flow as possible: starting in Europe and the Middle East (*page 58*); and then covering Africa and Madagascar (*page 68*); Asia (*page 100*); Australasia (including the Australasian oceanic islands) (*page 150*); the other Oceanic Islands (*page 180*); the Caribbean, North and Central America (*page 236*); and ending with South America (*page 264*).

Within each section, the species are arranged in broadly taxonomic order, so that the birds that are closely related appear near to each other. The order of species follows that adopted by BirdLife International, although in a very few cases a species has been moved forward of backwards by no more than one page to enable species within the same genus to appear on the same page.

Lists of birds are maintained by various authorities, and these vary in the way different taxa are treated. Some of these taxa are 'split' and treated as full species by authorities such as the International Ornithologists' Union (IOC), but not by others. However, in preparing this book the taxonomy adopted by BirdLife International has been followed, since this provides the official basis for the species covered in The IUCN Red List.

The distribution of a few species, principally the terrestrial migrants and some seabirds, spans more than one region. For the sake of completeness these species are covered, and illustrated, in all the regional sections in which they occur. The exception is with the seabirds, which are only covered in a regional section if they actually breed there. The Oceanic Islands section only includes islands that are truly oceanic, and excludes continental islands that were once joined to the mainland (*e.g.* the Falkland Islands (Islas Malvinas), which were once part of mainland South America). The consequence is that the species that occur on Oceanic Islands situated close to a continental land mass (*e.g.* São Tomé just off the west coast of Africa) are included in the Oceanic Islands section of this book. Whilst such species are usually included in the list of birds for the nearby continent (including by BirdLife), this different approach has been adopted here in order to highlight the particular threats faced by birds that are restricted to oceanic islands.

Structure of the regional sections

A **map** is included at the beginning of each regional section that delineates the region as covered in this book. The combined distribution of Endangered and Critically Endangered birds within the region, and all the Important Bird Areas (IBAs) are shown on the map.

Within each regional section is a variable number of '**features**' that summarize the conservation issues and illustrate some of the key hotspots for threatened birds. At the start of the **species accounts** is a table summarizing the number of Critically Endangered and Endangered species in each bird family.

The individual **species accounts** are set out as follows:

The 2012 IUCN Red List category

The following coding is used throughout this book:

EW	Extinct in the Wild
CR	Critically Endangered
CR (PE)	Critically Endangered (Possibly Extinct)
CR(PEW)	Critically Endangered (Possibly Extinct in the Wild)
EN	Endangered
DD	Data Deficient

Species name and scientific name

The English and scientific names adopted by BirdLife International are used throughout, although alternative English names used by other recognized authorities are given (apart from Americanized spellings of, for example, 'colour' or 'grey').

Population trend

This is indicated by an icon as follows:

▼	Decreasing
▲	Increasing
=	Stable
?	Unknown
†	Not applicable as the species is Extinct in the Wild

Population size

The 2012 estimate of the global number of mature individuals is shown (IN RED); this is the figure used to determine The IUCN Red List category. In those instances where the number of mature individuals is not known, the total number of individuals is given (IN BLACK). For those species that occur in more than one region, the global population figure is presented throughout; the number has not been subdivided to show the population of birds within each region.

Threat summary

For each species, the main threats it is believed to face are coded from left to right in their order of significance. The codes used for each of the 15 threat types are shown in the 'Threat codes' table to the right.

The impact of these threats is shown using differing typefaces, as follows (using AGR as an example):

AGR	High impact
AGR	Medium impact
AGR	Low impact

Additional notation is used as follows:

AGR?	Indicates threats that may have an impact
(AGR)	Codes are shown in parentheses if the threat had an impact in the past (but could possibly return)

Threat codes

AGR	Agriculture
CLI	Climate change & severe weather
DEV	Residential/commercial development
ECO	Other ecosystem modifications
EGY	Energy production & mining
FIRE	Fire & fire management
FISH	Fisheries
GEO	Geological events
HUN	Hunting/trapping
SPP	Invasive & other problematic species, and diseases
LOG	Logging/plant harvesting
MAN	Human disturbance
PLN	Pollution
TRA	Transportation & utility lines
WAT	Water abstraction & dams

Species text

The text for each species aims to provide a concise summary of its distribution, the particular threats it faces and any conservation action that has been implemented, is planned or may be needed. In some instances, where space permits, information is provided on behaviour or ecology.

For the 19 species that appear in more than one regional section, the text reflects its status in that region, and is cross-referenced in the body text to the relevant page(s) in other regional section(s).

Where a species is illustrated in the introductory chapters or regional features, this is cross-referenced to the right of the scientific name in a box with the relevant page number(s) as follows 50 . All other references to the species, wherever they occur in the book, are included in the Index.

Photograph or illustration

Wherever possible a photograph of each species is shown. For those species that are sexually dimorphic, these photographs in most cases depict males in breeding plumage (where this is not the case the caption indicates otherwise). The name of the photographer appears next to each photo, with other information or details of their association or website where this has been requested. For the 76 species for which no photograph is believed to exist, or for which a publishable image could not be obtained, an illustration by Tomasz Cofta is included.

Distribution map

A map is provided for each species, summarizing its current distribution and key migration routes (where appropriate). A limited number of map templates have been used, the intention being simply to provide an indication of the species' range. For the 19 species that occur in more than one region, the same map is used.

The colour-coding used on the maps is as follows:

	Resident distribution
	Breeding distribution
	Non-breeding distribution
	Migration route
	presumed former distribution (for species that are Possibly Extinct)

QR code

A QR code has been included for every species. This innovation enables quick access to the relevant page containing the species factsheet on BirdLife International's website **www.birdlife.org/datazone/species**. These factsheets are updated annually and provide detailed information about the species, the reason(s) for it being considered threatened, and a summary of the conservation actions underway or proposed. They also contain a high resolution distribution map.

The code can be accessed via a QR Reader which can be downloaded as an app for smart phones or tablet computers. Simply scan the code.

Glossary of terms

Whilst every effort has been made to keep the text in the species accounts as non-technical as possible, some technical terms have inevitably had to be used. Those that are perhaps most likely to require explanation are defined here.

Altiplano — An extensive area of high plateau in the Andes.

Boreal forest — Circumpolar, subarctic forest of high northern latitudes that is dominated by conifers.

Bycatch — An unintentional catch during animal harvesting or collecting; usually related to fisheries.

Caatinga — Dry scrubland and thorn forest, and a region in north-east Brazil characterized by this vegetation.

Camelid — A member of the family Camelidae, the New World representatives of which are the llamas, alpacas, vicuñas and guanacos.

Cash crop — A crop that is grown for sale.

Cerrado — The vast tropical **savanna** covering 21% of Brazil's land area. Four types are described depending on the density and height of trees.

Chapada — A flat-topped mountain in Brazil.

Conspecific — Two or more individual organisms, populations or **taxa** that belong to the same **species**.

Dipterocarp — A member of the tree family Dipterocarpaceae, which has about 500 mainly tropical lowland rainforest species, told by two-winged fruits.

Endemic — Unique to a defined geographic location (*e.g.* an island, country or other defined area).

Epiphyte — A plant that grows upon another plant (such as a tree), non-parasitically.

Extant — A **taxon** that is not **extinct**.

Extinct — A **taxon** that has died out.

Extirpate — The bringing of a **species** to extinction within a part of its range.

Feral — An organism that has changed from being domesticated to being wild or untamed.

Gallery forest — A forest forming a corridor along a river bank or adjacent to a wetland.

Genus (pl. genera) — A unit of **taxonomic** classification comprising a number of **species** that are more closely related to one-another than to other species in other genera.

Lek — A communal display ground where males gather to attract and court females.

Mallee — A 2–3 m tall scrub community in southern Australia dominated by *Eucalyptus* species.

Maquis — Drought-resistant tall scrub vegetation.

Mesic — Receiving a moderate supply of moisture.

Mesquite savanna — Open thorn-woodland dominated by mesquite (*Prosopsis*) and acacia (*Acacia*), where trees are widely separated by sparse ground cover.

Migrant — A species that undertakes periodic movements to or from a given area, usually along well-defined routes at given times of year.

Miombo woodland — Tropical woodlands dominated particularly by Miombo *Brachystegia* spp. trees, that cover a wide area across Africa from Angola to Tanzania.

NGO — Non-Governmental Organization.

Nominate — The **subspecies** that was originally described and which has the same name as the specific name (*e.g. Falco cherrug cherrug*).

Páramo — Montane meadow and scrub vegetation that occurs between the tree line and the snow line in the Andes (South America).

Passerine — A member of the avian order Passeriformes, often referred to as 'songbirds'.

Pluvial — An area of abundant rainfall.

Primary (or old-growth) forest — Forest that has attained great age without significant disturbance and reached a steady state (sometimes termed a climax community).

Restinga — A distinct type of coastal tropical and subtropical moist broadleaf forest found in Brazil.

Riparian — Along river margins and banks.

Savanna — A type of tropical vegetation dominated by grasses, in which any trees are so small or widely spaced that a closed canopy does not form.

Second(ary) growth/ forest — Vegetation that has partially re-grown after a major disturbance such as fire, clearance for agriculture, logging, insect infestation, or windthrow.

Sierra — A long, jagged mountain chain.

Sky island — Mountains isolated by surrounding lowlands and forming a different environment.

Sp. or Spp. — Abbreviation for '**species**' (singular and plural respectively).

Species — The basic unit of **taxonomic** classification that describes a group of species which are capable of interbreeding and producing viable offspring.

Split — Treated as a separate **species**.

Steppe — A Eurasian temperate vegetation type dominated by grasslands.

Storey — A vegetation layer in a forest (also called strata).

Subspecies — A sub-unit of **taxonomic** classification of a **species**; some species have two or more subspecies that are capable of interbreeding and producing fertile offspring but often do not do so due to geographic isolation or other factors.

Sympatric — Existing in the same geographic area and therefore coming into regular contact.

Taxon (pl. taxa) — A group of one or more populations of a biological organism.

Taxonomy — The science of defining groups of biological organisms on the basis of shared characteristics.

Terra-firme — Ground above the flood level; usually used in relation to forest in the Amazon Basin.

Tundra — A treeless plain of the Arctic and Antarctic characterized by short vegetation.

Type — The specimen(s) of an organism to which the scientific name of the species is formally attached.

Vagrant — An individual that wanders outside the species' normal range.

Várzea — Seasonally flooded forest along rivers in the Amazon Basin.

Watershed — The area of land (catchment) from which a watercourse or a groundwater system derives its water.

Xerophytic — Adapted to survive in a dry environment.

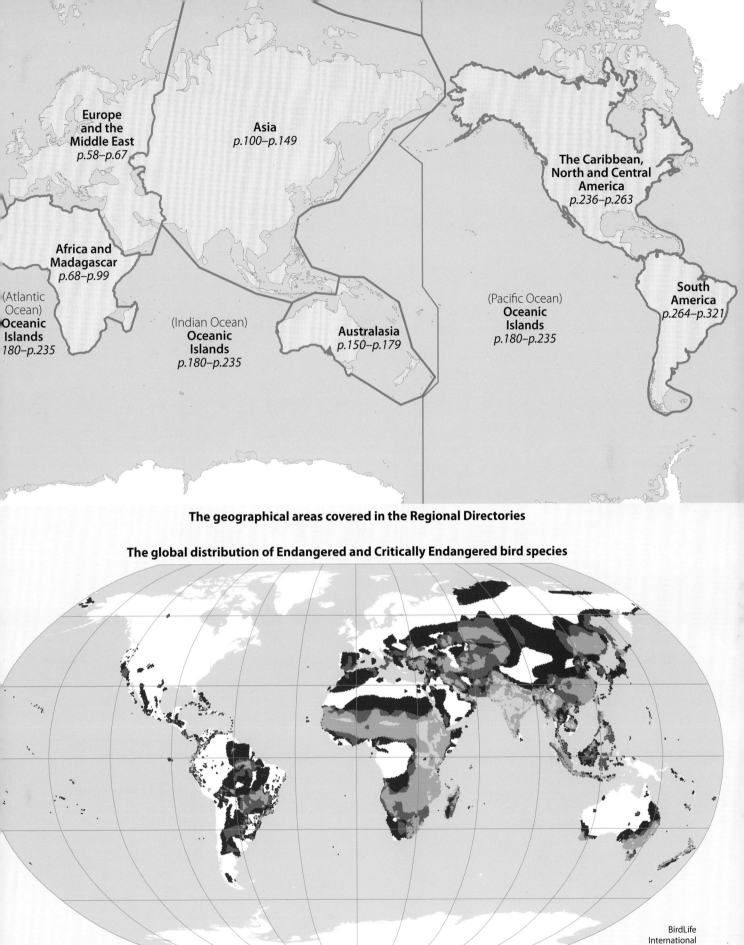

Europe and the Middle East
p.58–p.67

Asia
p.100–p.149

The Caribbean, North and Central America
p.236–p.263

Africa and Madagascar
p.68–p.99

(Atlantic Ocean)
Oceanic Islands
180–p.235

(Indian Ocean)
Oceanic Islands
p.180–p.235

Australasia
p.150–p.179

(Pacific Ocean)
Oceanic Islands
p.180–p.235

South America
p.264–p.321

The geographical areas covered in the Regional Directories

The global distribution of Endangered and Critically Endangered bird species

Number of species: 1 2 3–4 5–6 7–8 9–12

BirdLife International and NatureServe (2012): bird species distribution maps of the world

Europe and the Middle East

Critically Endangered **Balearic Shearwater** *Puffinus mauretanicus*. Photo: Mark Darlaston.

The distribution of Endangered and Critically Endangered species

- 1–4 species
- 5+ species

NORWEGIAN SEA

ICELAND

FAROE ISLANDS

NORWAY
SWEDEN
FINLAND

BALTIC SEA

ESTONIA
LATVIA
LITHUANIA

NORTH SEA
DENMARK

BELARUS

IRELAND
UNITED KINGDOM
THE NETHERLANDS
BELGIUM
LUXEMBOURG
GERMANY
POLAND
CZECH REPUBLIC
UKRAINE
SLOVAKIA

ATLANTIC OCEAN

FRANCE
LIECHTENSTEIN
SWITZERLAND
AUSTRIA
HUNGARY
MOLDOVA
SLOVENIA
ROMANIA
CROATIA
BOSNIA & HERZEGOVINA
SERBIA
Bay of Biscay

ANDORRA
Corsica
FRANCE
ITALY
MONTENEGRO
BULGARIA
BLACK SEA
SPAIN
MACEDONIA
ALBANIA
TURKEY
PORTUGAL
Sardinia
ITALY
GREECE

Balearic Islands
SPAIN

Gibraltar

MALTA

MEDITERRANEAN SEA

CYPRUS
SYRIA
LEBANON

ISRAEL

PALESTINIAN TERRITORIES
JORDAN

EGYPT

TROPIC OF CANCER

BirdLife Partners

Andorra	L'Associació per a la Defensa de la Natura (ADN)	**Bulgaria**	Bulgarian Society for the Protection of Birds (BSPB)
Armenia	Armenian Society for the Protection of Birds (ASPB)	**Cyprus**	BirdLife Cyprus
Austria	BirdLife Austria	**Czech Republic**	Czech Society for Ornithology (CSO)
Azerbaijan	The Azerbaijan Ornithological Society (AOS)	**Denmark**	Dansk Ornitologisk Forening (DOF)
Bahrain	Bahrain Natural History Society (BNHS)	**Estonia**	Estonian Ornithological Society (EOS)
Belarus	BirdLife Belarus (APB)	**Faroe Islands**	The Faroese Ornithological Society (Føroya Fuglafrøðifelag)
Belgium	BirdLife Belgium (Natuurpunt - natagora)	**Finland**	BirdLife FINLAND
		France	Ligue pour la Protection des Oiseaux (LPO)

Europe and the Middle East

In this book, Europe and the Middle are treated as a single region that includes the whole of continental Europe, European Russia and the Middle East, including the island of Socotra. The eastern boundary runs south along the Urals to the Caspian Sea and down its eastern shore to Iran before turning east and south along Iran's eastern borders with Turkmenistan, Afghanistan and Pakistan. The oceanic islands of the Azores, Madeira and the Canary Islands in Macaronesia are not covered in this section, but are included in the Oceanic Islands section (*page 180*). The total land area is approximately 16·6 million square kilometres (6·4 million square miles), or just over 11% of the Earth's land surface. The region encompasses a wide range of habitats, some of which cover large areas, but there are only nine Endemic Bird Areas.

A total of 730 species has been recorded in Europe and the Middle East, including 40 that are globally threatened. Of these, 13 are Endangered or Critically Endangered, of which all bar one are migrants.

RUSSIAN FEDERATION

ZERBAIJAN

CASPIAN SEA

IRAN

KUWAIT

BAHRAIN
QATAR
PERSIAN GULF

UNITED ARAB EMIRATES

UDI ABIA

OMAN

EMEN

ARABIAN SEA

Socotra
YEMEN

BirdLife Partners

Georgia	Georgian Centre for the Conservation of Wildlife (GCCW)	**Palestinian Authority Territories**	Palestine Wildlife Society (PWLS)
Germany	Nature And Biodiversity Conservation Union (Naturschutzbund Deutschland, NABU)	**Poland**	Polish Society for the Protection of Birds (OTOP)
Gibraltar	Gibraltar Ornithological and Natural History Society (GONHS)	**Portugal**	Portuguese Society for the Study of Birds (SPEA)
Greece	Hellenic Ornithological Society (HOS)	**Qatar**	Qatar (Friends of the Environment Centre)
Hungary	Hungarian Ornithological and Nature Conservation Society (MME)	**Romania**	Romanian Ornithological Society (SOR)
Iceland	Fuglavernd – BirdLife Iceland (ISPB)	**Saudi Arabia**	Saudi Wildlife Commission (SWC)
Iraq	Iraq (NI)	**Slovakia**	Slovak Ornithological Society/BirdLife Slovakia (SOS/BirdLife Slovakia)
Ireland	BirdWatch Ireland	**Slovenia**	BirdLife Slovenia (DOPPS)
Israel	Society for the Protection of Nature in Israel (SPNI)	**Spain**	SEO/BirdLife
Italy	Lega Italiana Protezione Uccelli (LIPU)	**Sweden**	Swedish Ornithological Society (SOF)
Jordan	Royal Society for the Conservation of Nature (RSCN)	**Switzerland**	SVS/BirdLife Switzerland
Kuwait	Kuwait Environment Protection Society (KEPS)	**Syria**	Syrian Society for Conservation of Wildlife (SSCW)
Latvia	Latvian Ornithological Society (LOB)	**The Netherlands**	Netherlands Society for the Protection of Birds (Vogelbescherming Nederland, VBN)
Lebanon	Society for the Protection of Nature in Lebanon (SPNL)	**Turkey**	Doga Dernegi (DD)
Liechtenstein	Botanisch-Zoologische Gesellschaft (BZG)	**Ukraine**	Ukrainian Society for the Protection of Birds (USPB)
Lithuania	Lithuanian Ornithological Society (LOD)	**United Kingdom**	The Royal Society for the Protection of Birds (RSPB)
Luxembourg	Lëtzebuerger Natur- a Vulleschutzliga (LNVL)	**Yemen**	Yemen Society for the Protection of Wildlife (YSPW)
Macedonia	Macedonian Ecological Society		
Malta	BirdLife Malta		
Norway	Norwegian Ornithological Society		

Europe and the Middle East – the conservation challenges

Human activities over millennia have reduced the naturally occurring forests and grasslands across much of Europe. Over-abstraction of water, major dam projects and climate change-related drought are causing increasing desertification, which threatens over 2·5 million square kilometres – or one fifth of the total area.

Rapid development in the oil-rich countries of the Gulf is putting pressure on remaining habitats, notably coastal and inland wetlands, which are internationally important for wintering waterfowl. Some of the most important seabird islands in the region are in the Gulf, in the path of busy oil tanker shipping lanes, and collisions and major oil spills are an ever-present threat.

New infrastructure also threatens the large soaring birds, including a number of threatened raptor species and the tiny eastern population of the Critically Endangered Northern Bald Ibis *Geronticus eremita*, which migrate through the Middle East via the Rift Valley and Red Sea Flyways.

Eleven Endangered and Critically Endangered species have been recorded in the Middle East, but a number of endemic Middle Eastern species, including the Yemen Warbler *Sylvia buryi* and Yemen Thrush *Turdus menachensis* in the South West Arabian Mountains, and the Socotra Bunting *Emberiza socotrana*, Socotra Buzzard *Buteo socotraensis* and Socotra Cormorant *Phalacrocorax nigrogularis*, are listed as Vulnerable and are still declining rapidly.

Like the Middle East, Europe has relatively few Endangered and Critically Endangered birds – 11 in total. However, the overall picture is of the rapid decline of large numbers of species still regarded as common. In 2004, 226 of 526 European bird species were assessed as having unfavourable conservation status, compared with 195 species out of 511 assessed in 1994 – a rise from 38% to 43% of species in just ten years.

Species faring particularly badly in Europe include farmland birds, waders and raptors. Many long-distance Afro-Palearctic migrants are also in long-term and accelerating decline, as are some of the continent's most widespread and familiar species, such as House Sparrow *Passer domesticus* and Common Starling *Sturnus vulgaris*. European Union policies for agriculture and fisheries are implicated in many of the declines. Europe lags behind the global South in the implementation of measures to prevent seabird bycatch in fisheries, a serious threat to the Critically Endangered Balearic Shearwater *Puffinus mauretanicus*.

The shocking decline of **Egyptian Vulture** *Neophron percnopterus*, from Least Concern to Endangered in 2007, is attributed to multiple threats, from the disappearance of wild ungulates over large parts of its range, to poisoning of animal carcasses near its breeding grounds, collisions with powerlines, and the growing veterinary use of the anti-inflammatory drug diclofenac in Africa. Photo: Roger & Liz Charlwood (WorldWildlifeImages.com).

The wild Moroccan population of the Critically Endangered **Northern Bald Ibis** *Geronticus eremita* has remained stable since the 1980s. This population is non-migratory. But in Syria, where local people say it was abundant up to 30 years ago, just 1–2 breeding pairs of the migratory population remain. Photo: Adam Riley (rockjumperbirding.com).

The Endangered **Red-breasted Goose** *Branta ruficollis* breeds in Asia but winters mainly on the Black Sea coast. In both Bulgaria and Romania, measures have recently been implemented to encourage goose-friendly farming practices, and many of the other key threats to this species on its European wintering grounds, such as hunting, are also being addressed. Photo: David Tipling.

The Critically Endangered **Sociable Lapwing** *Vanellus gregarius* migrates through Europe and the Middle East *en route* from Asia to its African wintering grounds. Recent conservation initiatives have shown that Turkey and Syria host particularly important stopover sites for this species. An international working group is planning cross-border actions to protect this species across its extensive range. Photo: Maxim Koshkin.

Europe and the Middle East

Native species recorded	730
Extinct in the Wild (EW)	**0**
Critically Endangered (CR)	**6**
Endangered (EN)	**7**
Vulnerable (VU)	**27**
Data Deficient (DD)	**0**

Approximately 730 species have been recorded breeding or wintering on the continental land mass of Europe and the Middle East, or migrate regularly through the region. This figure excludes the many species that have occurred as vagrants from other regions, as well as those that are endemic to the oceanic islands of the Azores, Madeira and the Canary Islands.

Forty of these species – or over 5% – are globally threatened, 13 of which are Endangered or Critically Endangered. Two other Endangered species are often included on the European list – Azores Bullfinch *Pyrrhula murina* and Zino's Petrel *Pterodroma madeira* – but these occur only on the Azores and Madeira respectively, and are therefore included in the Oceanic Islands section (*page 180*). In addition, two Endangered species of albatross – Black-browed *Thalassarche melanophrys* and Atlantic Yellow-nosed *Thalassarche chlororhynchos* – have occurred as vagrants in European waters during their ocean wanderings and these too are covered in the Oceanic Islands and other sections.

Eleven of the 13 Endangered and Critically Endangered species included in this section occur in the Middle East, two of which have not been recorded in Europe: the Endangered Basra Reed-warbler *Acrocephalus griseldis* and, at least in historical times, the Critically Endangered White-rumped Vulture *Gyps bengalensis*. Eleven Endangered and Critically Endangered species also occur in Europe, one of which, the Critically Endangered Balearic Shearwater *Puffinus mauretanicus*, is only found here, although does wander to coastal waters off west Africa. Another, the Endangered Rueppell's Vulture *Gyps rueppellii* has occurred in Europe as a wanderer from Africa and may be establishing a toehold.

With the exception of White-rumped Vulture, all the Endangered and Critically Endangered species that occur in Europe and the Middle East are migrants, although one, the Endangered White-headed Duck *Oxyura leucocephala* has resident populations in Spain and parts of the Middle East and some Saker Falcons *Falco cherrug* are resident in eastern Europe.

The Endangered or Critically Endangered species come from nine bird families. These are summarized in the following table and further contextual information, such as the number of species in each family and the proportion that is globally threatened, can be found in Appendix 2 on *page 339*.

A summary of the most threatened bird families in Europe and the Middle East

Family	CR	EN	Tot.	Family	CR	EN	Tot.
Ducks & geese (Anatidae)	–	3 (1)	**3** (1)	**Cranes** (Gruidae)	1 (1)	–	**1** (1)
Petrels & shearwaters (Procellariidae)	1	–	**1**	**Plovers** (Charadriidae)	1 (1)	–	**1** (1)
Ibises (Threskiornithidae)	1	–	**1**	**Sandpipers & allies** (Scolopacidae)	1 (1)	–	**1** (1)
Falcons (Falconidae)	–	1	**1**	**Old World warblers** (Sylviidae)	–	1	**1**
Vultures & eagles (Accipitridae)	1	2 (1)	**3** (1)				
(n) = number of non-breeding migrants.				**TOTAL (9 FAMILIES)**	**6** (3)	**7** (2)	**13** (5)

EN **Red-breasted Goose** *Branta ruficollis*   `51`

▼ **POPULATION: 37,000** | **THREATS:** EGY, MAN, HUN, CLI, FISH

This attractive migratory goose breeds in Asia (see *page 121*) but winters mainly on the western Black Sea coast (Bulgaria, Romania and Ukraine) and occasionally in Greece and Turkey. Small numbers also winter in Azerbaijan. As it associates with Greater White-fronted Geese *Anser albifrons* during migration and at its wintering sites, which is a legal quarry species for wildfowlers, it is often shot illegally. Frequent disturbance by hunters, fishermen and tourists can hamper its ability to build up fat reserves before migration, and key wintering sites are also being lost due to changes in agricultural practices. A recent major threat is the expansion of windfarms in many wintering areas.

Photo: David Tipling

EN **Velvet Scoter** *Melanitta fusca*

▼ **POPULATION: 250,000** | **THREATS:** FISH, PLN, WAT, EGY, MAN, HUN, SPP, CLI?

The majority of this highly migratory sea-duck breed in northern Europe (on Fennoscandian coasts), and across into Asia (see *page 122*). Although this population winters mainly in the Baltic Sea, it also occurs around other northern and western European coasts. A small population that breeds in Turkey, Armenia, Georgia and Turkmenistan is presumed to be the birds found wintering on the Black and Caspian Seas. This species was uplisted from Least Concern in 2012 due to rapid population declines and the risk of further declines as a consequence of marine pollution and interactions with commercial fisheries. Other threats include loss and degradation of breeding habitat, predation and disturbance.

Photo: Anders Blomdahl

EN **White-headed Duck** *Oxyura leucocephala* `28,29`

▼ **POPULATION: 5,300–8,700** | **THREATS:** AGR, HUN, SPP, PLN, CLI, WAT, FISH, LOG

Although the stronghold of this duck is in Asia (see *page 123*), populations also occur in Africa (see *page 82*), as well as Europe and the Middle East. In this region it has been extirpated as a breeding species from many countries around the Mediterranean, but small populations remain in Iran, Turkey and Spain. Birds also winter in Israel, Syria, Bulgaria and Romania. The main threat to the non-migratory Spanish population was hybridization with Ruddy Duck O. jamaicensis, an introduced species from North America. However, measures to control that species in Europe have succeeded in dramatically increasing the Spanish population. Historically, loss of wetlands due to drainage for agriculture has led to significant habitat loss.

Photo: Robert Tizard (ocellata.com)

CR **Balearic Shearwater** *Puffinus mauretanicus*

▼ **POPULATION: 9,000–13,000** | **THREATS:** FISH, SPP, PLN, EGY, DEV, (HUN)

A medium-sized and long-lived shearwater of coastal seas and small islets, this species breeds between February and June, only in the Balearic Islands in the Mediterranean. Its post-breeding range in the eastern Atlantic has increasingly moved northwards, possibly in response to changes in food availability due to rising water temperatures. It is now seen regularly around the British Isles, with singles observed north to Scandinavia. Before breeding, large numbers gather along the productive continental shelf off north-eastern Spain, foraging for herring, sardines and squid before entering the Mediterranean. The main threats are accidental fisheries bycatch and predation by introduced mammals in the breeding colonies.

Photo: Mark Darlaston

CR **Northern Bald Ibis** *Geronticus eremita* `62`

▼ **POPULATION: 200–249** | **THREATS:** AGR, HUN, SPP, DEV, (WAT), (MAN), (PLN), (ECO)

This ibis is known from two disjunct populations: one in north-west Africa (see *page 83*) and one in Turkey and Syria. The eastern population was believed to be extinct in the wild until a tiny colony was rediscovered in Syria in 2002. Satellite tracking has shown that these birds migrate through the Middle East to winter in Ethiopia. The Turkish population of around 100 birds is not included in population estimates as they are taken into care over the winter to prevent migration. Hunting, particularly on migration, is now the main threat to Syrian birds, but habitat degradation, disturbance and predation are also important factors. Captive breeding schemes exist, or are planned, in several European countries

Photo: Jens & Hanne Eriksen

EN **Saker Falcon** *Falco cherrug*

▼ **POPULATION:** 12,800–30,800 | **THREATS:** AGR, HUN, PLN, WAT?, DEV?

This falcon has a wide range across Asia (see *page 125*), but in this region breeds mainly in eastern Europe and the Middle East, wintering as far west as Italy. It also winters in Africa (see *page 86*). The loss and degradation of steppe and grasslands due to agricultural intensification, or the abandonment of grazing, has been the main cause of population declines. In the Arabian Peninsula, many migrant Sakers are trapped annually for traditional falconry, as they are the favoured species for such purposes. Females are particularly sought after due to their larger size, and are estimated to comprise three quarters of captured birds

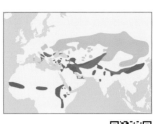

Photo [captive]: Todor Todorov

EN **Egyptian Vulture** *Neophron percnopterus*   22,62

▼ **POPULATION:** 13,000–41,000 | **THREATS:** AGR, EGY, MAN, SPP, PLN, TRA, HUN, (ECO)

A scavenger in lowland and montane regions, this is the most widespread vulture in the world, also occurring in Africa and Asia (see *pages 84 & 126*) and on the Canary and Cape Verde Islands. The population in southern and eastern Europe is migratory, but on the Arabian Peninsula it is mainly resident. Disturbance, poisoning (direct, and indirect from lead shot), electrocution by powerlines, collision with wind turbines, reduced food availability and changes to its habitat are the main reasons for declines in Europe. The establishment of feeding stations in some countries has supplemented its diet, and a release programme of captive-bred birds is underway in Italy.

Photo: Csaba Barkóczi

CR **White-rumped Vulture** *Gyps bengalensis*   42,111

▼ **POPULATION:** 2,500–9,999 | **THREATS:** PLN, HUN, (ECO)

The historical range of this rapidly declining Asian vulture (see *page 126*) formerly extended westwards as far as south-east Iran, east from Hormuz. It is a species of open regions, foothills and farmlands. Although mainly sedentary, it forages over large areas and immatures are often nomadic. It is known in Iran from only a few records prior to 1970, and although its present status is unknown, it is thought to be probably extinct in the region. Elsewhere in its range, a collapse in the populations of large wild ungulates and improved animal hygiene, including the removal of dead livestock from the environment, has resulted in food shortages.

Photo: Roger & Liz Charlwood (WorldWildlifeImages.com)

EN **Rueppell's Vulture** *Gyps rueppellii*

▼ **POPULATION:** 30,000 | **THREATS:** AGR, HUN, PLN, MAN

Although the range of this large vulture is mostly confined to sub-Saharan Africa (see *page 85*), since the 1990s there have been a series of records involving small numbers of individuals in Spain and Portugal. These birds are believed to have crossed the Strait of Gibraltar with migrating Griffon Vultures *G. fulvus*, but it is not known yet whether breeding has taken place. As the African population of this species is declining rapidly, it remains to be seen whether the recent trend of birds moving into southern Europe will be sustained.

Photo: Greg & Yvonne Dean (WorldWildlifeImages.com)

CR Siberian Crane *Leucogeranus leucogeranus*

52

▼ **POPULATION: 3,000–4,000** | **THREATS:** AGR, WAT, DEV, MAN, HUN, PLN

Two breeding populations of this beautiful crane are recognized: one in Arctic Russia and another in Central/West Siberia, which is divided into two flocks (see *page 129*). The westernmost flock migrates to winter in Iran, but only a single bird has arrived there in recent years. Hunting on migration, and on its wintering grounds, is the key threat to this population, with wetland degradation at wintering sites affecting the Arctic Russian population. A programme of captive rearing is underway in an attempt to maintain the central and western Asian flocks.

Photo: Pete Morris (Birdquest-tours.com)

CR Sociable Lapwing *Vanellus gregarius*

50,67

▼ **POPULATION: 11,200** | **THREATS:** HUN, AGR, PLN, CLI?

Flocks of this striking lapwing migrate from their central Asian breeding grounds (see *page 130*) to staging areas in the Middle East, before heading to wintering grounds in Africa (see *page 87*). Several thousands have been counted in Turkey and Syria on migration, and small numbers overwinter in Israel and Arabia. The knowledge of this species' status has been improved in recent years as a result of satellite-tracking of individual birds. This has led to the discovery of the location of important new staging areas. Single birds regularly turn up as vagrants in western Europe in flocks of Northern Lapwings *V. vanellus*. Migratory birds face a particular threat from illegal hunting.

Photo: Jens & Hanne Eriksen

CR Slender-billed Curlew *Numenius tenuirostris*

50

▼ **POPULATION: <50** | **THREATS:** HUN, AGR?, ECO?

Considered as common in the early 19th century, this gregarious species is now one of the rarest wading birds in the world, with the last confirmed record from Hungary in 2001. Its historic migration routes from breeding grounds in Asia (see *page 130*) were through central and eastern Europe (a flock of 19 was recorded in Italy in 1995) to southern Europe and north Africa. It wintered as far west as Morocco (see *page 87*) and Spain, preferring brackish marshes fed by freshwater streams. Drainage of wetlands on its wintering grounds and hunting have probably taken their toll on the population. A second migration route may have led to the Middle East, as there are records of birds wintering in Iraq.

Photo: Richard Porter

EN Basra Reed-warbler *Acrocephalus griseldis*

50

▼ **POPULATION: 1,500–7,000** | **THREATS:** WAT, EGY, DEV, (MAN)

This warbler winters in Africa (see *page 93*) but breeds mainly in the Mesopotamian Marshes of south-east Iraq, and probably in south-west Iran. Two breeding pairs have also recently been found in Israel. Since the 1950s, there has been considerable loss of suitable habitat due to large-scale hydrological projects but this was exacerbated by extensive damage to reedbeds during the Iran-Iraq War (1980-88) and subsequent wetland drainage ordered by Saddam Hussein. From 2003, a large-scale project successfully restored extensive areas of marsh, but drought and continued dam construction is threatening what had been achieved. Improved access to the region has resulted in increased human disturbance and water pollution.

Photo: Mudhafar A. Salim

Africa and Madagascar

Endangered **Loveridge's Sunbird** *Nectarinia loveridgei*. Photo: Werner Suter.

Endangered **Gabela Helmet-shrike** *Prionops gabela*. Photo: Dayne Braine (batisbirdingsafaris.com).

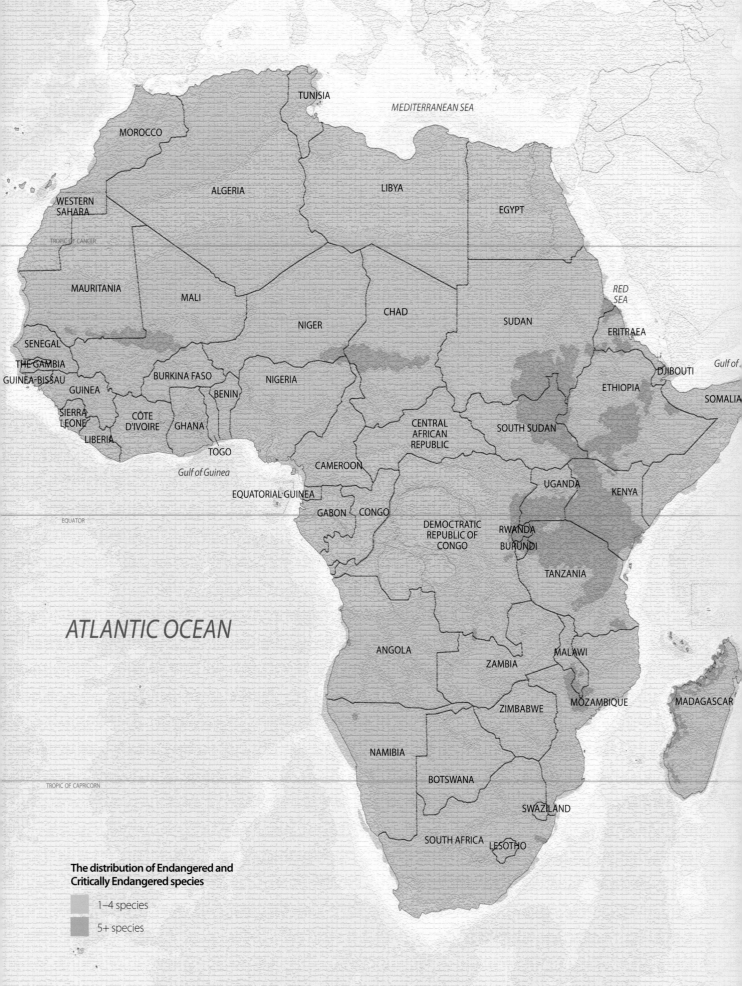

MEDITERRANEAN SEA

TUNISIA

MOROCCO

ALGERIA

LIBYA

EGYPT

WESTERN
SAHARA

TROPIC OF CANCER

RED
SEA

MAURITANIA

MALI

NIGER

CHAD

SUDAN

ERITRAEA

Gulf of

SENEGAL

THE GAMBIA

GUINEA-BISSAU

GUINEA

BURKINA FASO

NIGERIA

BENIN

DJIBOUTI

ETHIOPIA

SOMALIA

SIERRA
LEONE

CÔTE
D'IVOIRE

GHANA

CENTRAL
AFRICAN
REPUBLIC

SOUTH SUDAN

LIBERIA

TOGO

CAMEROON

EQUATORIAL GUINEA

UGANDA

KENYA

GABON

CONGO

EQUATOR

DEMOCRATIC
REPUBLIC OF
CONGO

RWANDA

BURUNDI

ATLANTIC OCEAN

TANZANIA

ANGOLA

ZAMBIA

MALAWI

MOZAMBIQUE

MADAGASCAR

ZIMBABWE

NAMIBIA

BOTSWANA

SWAZILAND

SOUTH AFRICA

LESOTHO

TROPIC OF CAPRICORN

Gulf of Guinea

**The distribution of Endangered and
Critically Endangered species**

1–4 species

5+ species

Africa and Madagascar

Africa and Madagascar form the second largest continent, covering an area of over 30 million square kilometres (11·6 million square miles), or just over 20% of the Earth's land surface. Africa straddles the equator and is about 8,000 km (5,000 miles) from north to south. About 60% of the continent is desert, mostly in the northern half, and the climate ranges from tropical to subarctic on the highest peaks. The diversity of habitats is very wide, ranging from arid scrub through extensive areas of savanna and steppe to dense rainforest. There are 52 Endemic Bird Areas or Secondary Areas in continental Africa and Madagascar, reflecting the great diversity of habitats and the number of restricted-range species that have evolved within isolated areas.

This section covers the species that have been recorded from continental Africa and Madagascar only. Some 92 species that are restricted to oceanic islands are often treated as part of the African avifauna. However, the Endangered and Critically Endangered species that occur on these islands have been included in the Oceanic Islands section (*page 180*). The 2,224 species that occur regularly in continental Africa and Madagascar include many wintering migrants that breed in Europe, the Middle East and Asia, as well as non-breeding seabirds that are regular visitors to coastal waters.

DIAN OCEAN

BirdLife INTERNATIONAL

BirdLife Partners

Botswana	BirdLife Botswana (BLB)		**Malawi**	Wildlife and Environmental Society of Malawi (WESM)
Burkina Faso	NATURAMA (La Fondation NATURAMA)		**Nigeria**	Nigerian Conservation Foundation (NCF)
Burundi	Association Burundaise pour la Protection des Oiseaux (ABO)		**Rwanda**	Association pour la Conservation de la Nature au Rwanda (ACNR)
Cameroon	Cameroon Biodiversity Conservation Society (CBCS)		**Sierra Leone**	Conservation Society of Sierra Leone (CSSL)
Côte d'Ivoire	Côte d'Ivoire (SF)		**South Africa**	BirdLife South Africa (BLSA)
Djibouti	Djibouti Nature (DN)		**Tanzania**	Wildlife Conservation Society of Tanzania (WCST)
Egypt	Nature Conservation Egypt		**Tunisia**	Association 'Les Amis des Oiseaux' (AAO)
Ethiopia	Ethiopian Wildlife and Natural History Society (EWNHS)		**Uganda**	NatureUganda (NU)
Ghana	Ghana Wildlife Society (GWS)		**Zambia**	Zambian Ornithological Society (ZOS)
Kenya	NatureKenya		**Zimbabwe**	BirdLife Zimbabwe (BLZ)
Liberia	The Society for Conservation of Nature in Liberia (SCNL)			
Madagascar	Asity Madagascar			

Africa and Madagascar – the conservation challenges

Of the 2,224 bird species currently recognized in continental Africa and Madagascar, 86 are considered Endangered or Critically Endangered, and a further 109 are globally Vulnerable – a combined total of 195 species (nearly 9% of the total). Remarkably, there have been no known bird extinctions in Africa in the last 500 years, but the Liben Lark *Heteromirafra sidamoensis*, now confined to a tiny area of grassland in Ethiopia, looks set to become the first – unless last-ditch conservation initiatives are successful.

Much of Africa's endemic bird diversity is concentrated in areas such as the forests of West Africa, the coastal forests of Kenya and Tanzania, the Eastern Arc mountains, and the island of Madagascar. Land-use change, particularly deforestation, related to rapidly growing populations, unsustainable development, and the large-scale exploitation of Africa's natural and mineral resources by global industries, are the primary threats. For example, large areas of woodland and wetland habitat in and around the East African coastal forests, including the Dakatcha Woodlands in Kenya, home of the Endangered Clarke's Weaver *Ploceus golandi*, are being targeted by international business interests for biofuel cultivation.

The Endangered **Algerian Nuthatch** *Sitta ledanti*, discovered in 1975, is the only bird species endemic to Algeria. It is confined to four known sites, all within 30 km of each other, although separated by tracts of unsuitable habitat. Fire and overgrazing by livestock have destroyed forest and understorey and prevented regeneration. Photo: David Monticelli (pbase.com/david_monticelli).

The Critically Endangered **Madagascar Fish-eagle** *Haliaeetus vociferoides* survives in low numbers along the west coast of Madagascar, and now numbers only about 120 breeding pairs. Deforestation and the development of wetland areas for rice-paddies is causing loss of nesting and foraging habitat. Direct competition with fishermen reduces food availability. It is persecuted by shooting and nest destruction, and occasionally drowned in nets. Photo: Denzil Morgan.

This is one of very few photographs of the Endangered and little-known **Congo Bay-owl** *Phodilus prigoginei*, last recorded in 1996. It appears to require a mosaic of grassland and montane or bamboo forest, and is threatened by clearance for farmland, which accelerated following a yield-reducing maize blight in the early 1990s. Photo: Thomas M. Butynski & Yvonne A. de Jong.

Africa lacks resources for conservation, including sufficient people with the necessary skills, and political will from governments – whose priorities, understandably, are poverty reduction and the provision of the basic necessities of a decent life, such as clean water, sanitation and education. Although many of Africa's national parks are internationally renowned, there is a huge shortfall in the money needed to manage the continent's protected area system.

Political instability is a persistent threat, and has thwarted conservation efforts in many countries. Although parts of some important countries, such as Sudan and the Democratic Republic of Congo, are still too dangerous for biodiversity surveys and conservation work, the situation in others, including Liberia and Sierra Leone, has improved markedly since the end of their civil wars.

The Endangered **Ibadan Malimbe** *Malimbus ibadanensis* is confined to south-west Nigeria, where surveys found it at only 19 of 52 forest patches, leading to an estimate of just 112 km² of occupied habitat. Its range appears to have contracted by two-thirds since 1970. It has very rarely been photographed. Photo: A. P. Leventis.

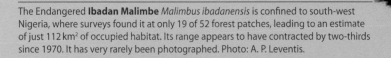

The Endangered **African Penguin** *Spheniscus demersus* has been severely affected by a reduction in suitable breeding burrows due to past mining of guano, but there are indications that the installation of artificial nests might help redress this. Mortality from oil spills is an immediate threat. The world's largest oil-shipping route lies offshore of its entire breeding range, and a single slick could affect tens of thousands of birds. Photo: Adam Riley (rockjumperbirding.com).

Madagascar

Madagascar has been separated from the African mainland for at least 150 million years, and its extraordinary endemic birdlife is the result of a combination of speciation among the isolated founder populations and random colonization from all around the Indian Ocean and beyond.

Taxonomists disagree as to whether there are six bird families endemic to Madagascar and the nearby Comoros Islands (included in this book in the Oceanic Islands section (*page 180*)), or just three. There are 37 endemic bird genera, many of them containing just one species, and 109 endemic species, amounting to more than half the island's total of 209 breeding species. Of these, 13 are currently considered Endangered or Critically Endangered. Two species are now Extinct, including the Alaotra Grebe *Tachybaptus rufolavatus*, whose death sentence was pronounced in 2010. A further 22 are listed as Vulnerable, and 14 are Near Threatened. In addition, the Data Deficient Blüntschli's Vanga *Hypositta perdita* would almost certainly be treated as Critically Endangered if it proved to be a valid species.

Sakalava Rail *Amaurornis olivieri*. Photo: Mikael Bauer.

The Endangered **Sakalava Rail** *Amaurornis olivieri* has probably been affected by the loss of fringing water-lily habitat, following the conversion of wetlands to rice cultivation, and by the impact of introduced fish.

The range of the Endangered **Madagascar (or Bernier's) Teal** *Anas bernieri* encompasses a narrow coastal strip along the whole of Madagascar's west coast. But these coastal wetlands are coming under increasing pressure as more and more people migrate to them from degraded and agriculturally exhausted regions inland. Hunting is a threat; the birds are considered a delicacy, and still appear in local markets.

The Critically Endangered **Madagascar Pochard** *Aythya innotata* was rediscovered in 2006 following the last previous sighting in 1991. Fishing with small-mesh nets undoubtedly contributed to the decline of this medium-sized diving duck, but habitat loss, siltation and the introduction of exotic fish, especially *Tilapia*, had the most devastating impacts. The single remaining wild site is not optimal, and breeding success is low.

Madagascar (or Bernier's) Teal *Anas bernieri*. Photo: Dubi Shapiro (pbase.com/dubisha).

Madagascar Pochard *Aythya innotata*. Photo: Dubi Shapiro (pbase.com/dubisha).

The majority of the threatened species have restricted ranges within Madagascar, which is regarded by BirdLife International as having seven separate Endemic Bird Areas (EBAs). These include two secondary areas holding one species each, one being Ile de Sainte-Marie (Nosy Boraha), former home of the Extinct Snail-eating Coua *Coua delalandei*, which was last seen in the 1830s.

Madagascar has extensive wetlands, which have been divided into two EBAs corresponding to the dry, low-lying western region and the humid, mountainous east. The West Malagasy Wetlands EBA is home to six highly threatened species: one Critically Endangered (Madagascar Fish-eagle *Haliaeetus vociferoides*) and five Endangered (Madagascar Heron *Ardea humbloti*, Madagascar Sacred Ibis *Threskiornis bernieri*, Madagascar Teal *Anas bernieri*, Meller's Duck *Anas melleri* and Sakalava Rail *Amaurornis olivieri*). The East Malagasy Wetlands EBA also has Meller's Duck and the fish-eagle, and contains the entire global range of the Critically Endangered Madagascar Pochard *Aythya innotata* and Endangered Slender-billed Flufftail *Sarothrura watersi*, and formerly the Alaotra Grebe.

These wetlands have long been important to the Malagasy people for fishing, hunting and agriculture. In recent decades resource use has become more intensive and less sustainable. The most serious and widespread threats are conversion of wetland habitats to intensive rice production, or draining for agriculture; bird hunting, often for sale rather than subsistence; over-fishing, using fine-mesh nets which also catch aquatic birds; and invasive alien species, especially plants and fish, which have impoverished the species composition of many wetlands.

The many endemic forest types, from the spiny forests of the south to humid evergreen montane forests, have been much reduced since human colonization around 2,000 years ago. Very little primary lowland forest remains, and large areas of shrubland and savanna have been created where primary forest once stood.

On paper, Madagascar has an extensive and representative protected area system, but lack of resources and political instability have jeopardized the status of many important areas. Key tree species like rosewoods *Dalbergia* spp. are targeted by illegal loggers for overseas trade. But some forests and wetland complexes are gaining a more effective kind of protected status, under a Malagasy law which enables community groups to take control of natural resources. These areas are now being managed in conjunction with local people, with plans in place that incorporate sustainable use and conservation.

The rarest of Madagascar's endemic vangas, the Endangered **Van Dam's Vanga** *Xenopirostris dami* is known from just two sites in the north-west. These are undergoing extensive logging, and burning and conversion for agriculture. However, there is much suitable habitat between the two sites that has not been thoroughly surveyed.

The Endangered **Amber Mountain Rock-thrush** *Monticola erythronotus* is restricted to a single mountain, in northern Madagascar. Its range and population are small, and while not currently at risk, its habitat may come under the same pressures as forests elsewhere on Madagascar.

Van Dam's Vanga *Xenopirostris dami*.
Photo: Dubi Shapiro (pbase.com/dubisha).

Amber Mountain Rock-thrush *Monticola erythronotus*.
Photo: Dubi Shapiro (pbase.com/dubisha).

Angola

Angola is among Africa's ornithologically least-known countries. Bordered by the Democratic Republic of Congo to the north-east, Zambia to the east, and Namibia to the south, it is a meeting point for the biomes which dominate these better-known neighbours, including Guinea-Congo forest, Zambezian Miombo woodland, Kalahari-Highveld and Namib-Karoo. It also includes an important outpost of the Afrotropical Highlands biome. Of 17 restricted-range species, six, all Angolan endemics, are Endangered.

Several vegetation zones meet in western Angola, an Endemic Bird Area (EBA) bounded to the north by the lowland rainforests of the Zaire basin, to the south by the Namib desert, and to the east by a vast area of Zambezian Miombo woodland. At the western edge of Angola's high plateau is a steep escarpment where the cold Benguela ocean current creates almost continuous cloud cover. A band of semi-evergreen forest extends for about 300 km, but becomes very narrow and dry at the southern end. Several endemic species appear to be confined to the semi-evergreen forests of the escarpment zone. The Endangered Gabela Bush-shrike *Laniarius amboimensis*, Gabela Helmet-shrike *Prionops gabela* and Gabela Akalat *Sheppardia gabela* are known only from the escarpment in

Orange-breasted (or Braun's) Bush-shrike *Laniarius brauni*.
Photo: Dayne Braine (batisbirdingsafaris.com).

Gabela Akalat *Sheppardia gabela*.
Photo: Dayne Braine (batisbirdingsafaris.com).

The **Orange-breasted (or Braun's) Bush-shrike** *Laniarius brauni* appears to have a lower population density than other *Laniarius* bush-shrikes, and is considered rare at all known sites. It is found in the undergrowth of secondary and gallery forest, including degraded and disturbed forest.

The **Gabela Akalat** *Sheppardia gabela* survives in a few patches of relict forest and regenerating shade coffee plantations. The replacement of shade-grown coffee with full sun varieties is a threat, and a new road could reopen the area in which it is found to commercial activities.

Pulitzer's Longbill *Macrosphenus pulitzeri* was thought to have a very small, severely fragmented range and a tiny population. However, recent surveys have found the species to be more numerous and widespread, and tolerant of secondary growth, thickets and plantations. If this is confirmed, it may be downlisted from Endangered in the near future.

Pulitzer's Longbill
Macrosphenus pulitzeri.
Photo: A. P. Leventis.

the vicinity of Gabela, and Pulitzer's Longbill *Macrosphenus pulitzeri* is known from here and one locality further south on the escarpment. Orange-breasted Bush-shrike *Laniarius brauni* has been recorded only from the escarpment in Cuanza Norte. Another Angola endemic, Monteiro's Bush-shrike *Malaconotus monteiri* (which was formerly treated as Data Deficient but is now listed as Near Threatened) is also known from this site but also occurs in the vicinity of Gabela. From the 1930s until the 1970s, most of the forest on the escarpment was under shade-grown coffee production, which left the canopy mostly intact. However, coffee-growing has been largely abandoned, and slash-and-burn agriculture is now the main threat.

Another important habitat in Angola is Afromontane forest, of which there are now only a few isolated patches, mainly in deep mountain ravines. Bird populations here are isolated by 2,000 km or more from their congeners. Four of the restricted-range species are associated with Afromontane vegetation, including the Near Threatened Angola Cave-chat *Xenocopsychus ansorgei*, the only representative of this endemic genus. The Endangered Swierstra's Francolin *Francolinus swierstrai* was known only from forest patches on Mount Moco, but is now uncommon there. The Data Deficient endemic Grimwood's Longclaw *Macronyx grimwoodi* is also found at Moco. Several other Afromontane specialists have been found only there or at one or two other sites in Angola, and face a serious threat of extirpation from the country. Prospects for all these species improved with the discovery of sizeable tracts of pristine Afromontane vegetation in the Namba Mountains, tripling the amount of this habitat known to survive in Angola.

Angola's protected areas cover over 6% of the country, but are understaffed and undermanaged, and most saw the virtual extirpation of larger wildlife during years of civil war. Some critical habitats, including Afromontane forest, are not protected at all. The protected area system is being expanded with the assistance of international NGOs, but the years of conflict mean that baseline data on biodiversity is patchy and outdated.

Gabela Bush-shrike *Laniarius amboimensis*. Photo: Fábio Olmos.

In the early 1970s, a protected area of 50 km² was recommended for the **Gabela Bush-shrike** *Laniarius amboimensis* and other escarpment endemics, but was never established.

There were no records of **Swierstra's Francolin** *Francolinus swierstrai* between 1971 and 2005, when seven birds were seen, and another pair or group were heard, at Mount Moco and Mount Soque. A potentially larger population was recently located in the Namba Mountains.

Swierstra's Francolin *Francolinus swierstrai*. Photo: Dayne Braine (batisbirdingsafaris.com).

Liben Lark *Heteromirafra sidamoensis*
Photo: Andy & Gill Swash (WorldWildlifeImages.com).

CONSERVATION CHALLENGE

Grassland management

Across the world, grassland is the habitat type least represented in protected area systems. Most grassland ecosystems have been used sustainably for centuries, creating modified but stable habitats. But within the last generation or two, pressures on grassland in Africa have increased, with changes from grazing to commodity crops and afforestation, the end of nomadic pastoralism and rise of settled agriculture, and cross-border incursions by herders and others who ignore traditional grazing regimes.

Overgrazing and trampling can denude grasslands, but can also encourage coarse and unpalatable plants, with the loss of the short-grass cover that many grassland bird species need in their habitat mosaics. Suppression of fires that were part of grassland management regimes also leads to an increase in old, coarse vegetation and encroachment of scrub.

With the possible exception of some potentially suitable habitat too dangerous to investigate near the border with Somalia, Liben Lark *Heteromirafra sidamoensis* is restricted to a single 30–36 km^2 patch of tall-grass prairie on Ethiopia's Liben plains. Habitat area and numbers are falling fast. Fieldwork in May 2009 recorded a decline of 40% in the number of birds since 2007, and a contraction of 38% in area occupied. A workshop involving herders and other stakeholders led to a committee to manage the restoration of the Liben Plain, an agreement to oppose further agricultural expansion, and a willingness to work with conservation organizations to preserve pastoralism. Young Ethiopians are being trained in conservation,

Recent surveys indicate that there are now fewer than 100 **Liben Lark** *Heteromirafra sidamoensis* territories. But many are likely to be occupied by bachelor males. Females seem much scarcer, perhaps because overgrazing leaves them exposed to predation on the nest.

There is substantial evidence for local decreases and even local extinction of **Botha's Lark** *Spizocorys fringillaris* within its very restricted distribution. Less than 1% of the global population is currently within protected areas.

Liben Lark *Heteromirafra sidamoensis*.
Photo: Andy & Gill Swash (WorldWildlifeImages.com).

Botha's Lark *Spizocorys fringillaris*.
Photo: Adam Riley (rockjumperbirding.com).

scrub will be cleared, and habitat patches protected from grazing by 'exclosures' and the use of hyena dung as a cattle deterrent.

The Endangered Botha's Lark *Spizocorys fringillaris* occurs in northern Orange Free State and south-east Transvaal, South Africa, and much of its range is covered by a proposed Grasslands Biosphere Reserve. Most of the global population of Vulnerable Rudd's Lark *Heteromirafra ruddi* is thought to occur within the reserve, which is also home to Endangered White-winged Flufftail *Sarothrura ayresi*, and Vulnerable Blue *Grus paradisea* and Wattled *G. carunculatus* Cranes, Southern Bald Ibis *Gerontius calvus* and Yellow-breasted Pipit *Anthus chloris*. The reserve will include some 800 private farms and a considerable amount of state-owned land. Establishing state-owned nature reserves would not necessarily enhance the conservation status of Botha's Lark, which favours grassland kept short by frequent fires and grazing.

Kenya's unique highland grasslands are not included in any protected areas, and are rapidly vanishing. The Kinangop plateau grasslands are probably the stronghold of the Endangered, endemic Sharpe's Longclaw *Macronyx sharpei*. This species prefers short-grass fields with tussocks. The Endangered Aberdare Cisticola *Cisticola aberdare* is thought to occur in the higher parts of the plateau. Since the 1960s, large areas have been ploughed for cultivation or to remove the tussock grass, which livestock find unpalatable. The longclaw seems able to coexist with livestock, provided adequate tussock cover remains, but cannot survive in farmed fields. A local conservation action group, Friends of Kinangop Plateau, has active branches in three parts of the plateau. The Leleshwa Nature Reserve, managed by the Friends, will demonstrate land management that favours the species and provides better economic returns from livestock. It is hoped this will encourage the establishment of new reserves by schools and other organizations.

Aberdare Cisticola *Cisticola aberdare*.
Photo: Patrick L'Hoir (bird-picture.eu).

The Endangered **Aberdare Cisticola** *Cisticola aberdare* nests in moist, tussocky grassland above 2,300 m in central Kenya. However, this type of habitat is becoming increasingly degraded due to intensification of livestock production.

The Endangered **Sharpe's Longclaw** *Macronyx sharpei*, a Kenyan Endemic, is threatened by overgrazing of its tussock grassland habitat. But its disappearance from the Aberdare National Park may be the result of undergrazing, leading to scrub encroachment.

Sharpe's Longclaw *Macronyx sharpei*.
Photo: Adam Riley (rockjumperbirding.com).

Africa and Madagascar

A total of 86 Endangered or Critically Endangered species has been recorded from continental Africa and Madagascar, 77 of which are included in this section. The nine that have been excluded are seabirds (two Critically Endangered and seven Endangered) that occur in coastal waters and are covered in other sections (mostly under Oceanic Islands (*page 180*)).

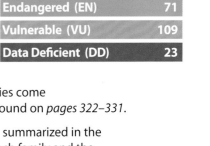

Native species recorded	2,224
Extinct in the Wild (EW)	0
Critically Endangered (CR)	15
Endangered (EN)	71
Vulnerable (VU)	109
Data Deficient (DD)	23

Africa and Madagascar between them have 23 Data Deficient species, the same number as for Asia, but significantly more than for any of the other regions. These species come from 17 different bird families. Further information, and photographs of some, can be found on *pages 322–331*.

The Endangered or Critically Endangered species come from 35 bird families. These are summarized in the following table and further contextual information, such as the number of species in each family and the proportion that is globally threatened, can be found in Appendix 2 on *page 339*.

A summary of the most threatened bird families in Africa and Madagascar

Family	CR	EN	Tot.	Family	CR	EN	Tot.
Francolins & partridges (Phasianidae)	1	4	5	Nightjars (Caprimulgidae)	–	1	1
Ducks & geese (Anatidae)	1	3	4	Wattle-eyes (Platysteiridae)	–	1	1
Penguins (Spheniscidae)	–	2 (1)	2 (1)	Bush-shrikes (Malaconotidae)	1	4	5
Albatrosses (Diomedeidae)	1 (1)	5 (5)	6 (6)	Vangas (Vangidae)	–	1	1
Petrels & shearwaters (Procellariidae)	1 (1)	1 (1)	2 (2)	Crows (Corvidae)	–	1	1
Ibises (Threskiornithidae)	1	1	2	Larks (Alaudidae)	2	2	4
Herons (Ardeidae)	–	2	2	Cisticola & apalises (Cisticolidae)	1	2	3
Cormorants (Phalacrocoracidae)	–	1	1	Bulbuls (Pycnonotidae)	1	1	2
Falcons (Falconidae)	–	1 (1)	1 (1)	Old World warblers (Sylviidae)	1	5 (1)	6 (1)
Vultures & eagles (Accipitridae)	1	5	6	Babblers (Timaliidae)	–	1	1
Bustards (Otididae)	–	1	1	Nuthatches (Sittidae)	–	1	1
Rails (Rallidae)	–	3	3	Thrushes (Turdidae)	1	2	3
Cranes (Gruidae)	–	1	1	Akalats & rock-thrush (Muscicapidae)	–	4	4
Plovers (Charadriidae)	1 (1)	–	1 (1)	Sunbirds (Nectariniidae)	–	2	2
Sandpipers & allies (Scolopacidae)	1 (1)	–	1 (1)	Weavers (Ploceidae)	–	6	6
Turacos (Musophagidae)	–	1	1	Pipits & longclaws (Motacillidae)	–	2	2
Barn Owls (Tytonidae)	–	1	1	Finches (Fringillidae)	–	2	2
Owls (Strigidae)	–	1	1				
(n) = number of non-breeding migrants.				**TOTAL (35 FAMILIES)**	15 (4)	71 (9)	86 (13)

EN Swierstra's Francolin *Francolinus swierstrai* `77`

▼ POPULATION: 1,000–2,499 | THREATS: AGR, HUN, CLI?, (LOG)

Found only in western Angola, this little-known francolin has been recorded from montane forests, tall grass savannas and rocky mountainsides. There were no records between 1971 and 2005, when birds were found at Mount Moco and Mount Soque. It occupies dense undergrowth and breeding is suspected to take place from May to June. The population is suspected to be decreasing as a consequence of habitat loss and hunting pressure, and there may soon be insufficient habitat left to support a viable population. A long-promised protection area on Mount Moco has yet to be established.

Female. Photo: Dayne Braine (Batisbirdingsafaris.com). (See *page 77* for photo of a male.)

EN **Nahan's Francolin** *Francolinus nahani*

▼ **POPULATION: 50,000–99,999** | **THREATS:** AGR, HUN, LOG, MAN, SPP

This forest-dwelling gamebird is found in eastern Democratic Republic of Congo and in central and western Uganda. It is often found in groups in dense primary forest, preferring riverine or swampy areas, searching amongst leaf-litter for invertebrates, shoots, seeds and bulbs. It breeds year-round, nesting on the ground. Its small and severely fragmented range continues to decline in both area and quality, although some populations are found in protected areas. Its distinctive calls may, however, led to new locations being discovered. The effect of hunting has not been thoroughly investigated, but could be a serious threat.

Photo: Pete Morris (Birdquest-tours.com)

CR **Djibouti Francolin** *Francolinus ochropectus*

▼ **POPULATION: 200–500** | **THREATS: AGR**, CLI, MAN, LOG, PLN, HUN

Djibouti's only endemic bird, this francolin occurs in juniper and other woodland above 700 m. Increasing losses of juniper heath, due to grazing, drought and firewood collection, means the descending rattling call of this elusive species is now more likely heard from dense woodland vegetation. It breeds from December to February, but only one nest, situated on an inaccessible mountain ledge, has ever been found. Over 90% of the population has been lost over the last three decades. However, work is underway to gain protected area status for the strongholds of Forêt du Day and Mabla and a juniper restoration project with local involvement has been established.

Photo: Houssein A. Rayaleh

EN **Mount Cameroon Francolin** *Francolinus camerunensis*

▼ **POPULATION: 600–1,700** | **THREATS:** AGR, FIRE, HUN, (GEO)

Restricted solely to the south-east and north-east slopes of Mount Cameroon, this francolin prefers dense undergrowth in primary forest and clearings between 850–2,100 m. One of seven bird species endemic to Cameroon, it has become increasingly scarce since the late 20th century. It feeds on berries, grass seeds and insects and breeds between October and December. Fire occurs naturally on Mount Cameroon, the result of lava flows every couple of decades, but human-induced fires pose an additional threat as they destroy both eggs and young birds. The creation of the Mount Cameroon National Park in 2009 offers some hope for the protection of this species.

Illustration: Tomasz Cofta

EN **Udzungwa Forest-partridge** *Xenoperdix udzungwensis*

= **POPULATION: 2,000–2,700** | **THREATS:** AGR, FIRE, MAN, HUN, SPP

Endemic to Tanzania, this extremely localized partridge inhabits mature montane and submontane evergreen forest above 1,300 m. It occurs on forested ridges, steep rocky slopes with forest cover and flatter ground. Danish biologists on an expedition discovered this species in the early 1990s when they were served a local meal with it as an ingredient. There are two isolated populations, with no apparent gene flow between them. It roosts in trees and forages in small groups of up to a dozen or so birds for invertebrates and seeds in leaf-litter, camouflaged by its barred upperparts, and it has been observed dust-bathing. Its small population is now considered stable but numbers fluctuate between years.

Photo (camera trap): Francesco Rovero (mtsn.tn.it/tropical_biodiversity)

EN **Meller's Duck** *Anas melleri*

`34`

▼ **POPULATION:** 1,300–3,300 | **THREATS: HUN**, AGR, MAN, LOG, SPP, PLN

This duck occurs at inland freshwater habitats on Madagascar, from sea level to 2,000 m. It is often found along small streams but also inhabits lakes, rivers, woodland ponds and marshes, especially in humid, forested areas. It feeds on aquatic seeds, plants, and invertebrates, especially molluscs. Being one of the largest species of wildfowl on Madagascar, it is hunted for food and is now also facing competition from introduced Mallard *Anas platyrhynchos*. Meller's Duck occurs in at least seven protected areas but no regular breeding sites are known. It is highly territorial, defending stretches of water up to 2 km long. An introduced population on Mauritius is believed to be extinct.

Photo: Callan Cohen & Deirdre Vrancken (birdingafrica.com)

EN **Madagascar** (or Bernier's) **Teal** *Anas bernieri*

`74`

▼ **POPULATION:** 1,000–1,700 | **THREATS:** AGR, HUN, LOG, MAN, SPP?

Restricted to western Madagascar, this small duck breeds in seasonally flooded, non-tidal areas dominated by Black Mangrove *Avicennia marina* on the landward side of coastal forest. Pairs mate for life and nest in tree-holes during the wet season (December to March). During its post-breeding moult it becomes flightless and seeks out lakes rich in aquatic vegetation, subsequently moving to coastal wetlands for the remainder of the dry season. It is now severely threatened throughout its range due to extensive habitat loss, hunting and disturbance, and populations are becoming highly fragmented. Competition for nest-holes with other species may now also be a factor in the continuing population decline.

Photo: Adam Riley (Rockjumperbirding.com)

CR **Madagascar Pochard** *Aythya innotata*

`74`

= **POPULATION:** 20–49 | **THREATS:** PLN, (AGR), (WAT), (FISH), (HUN), (SPP)

Endemic to Madagascar, this duck favours shallow freshwater lakes and marshes that combine open water with nearby areas of dense vegetation. It was mainly found in the Lake Alaotra basin until last seen there in 1991. Nine birds were then sensationally rediscovered in 2006 on a volcanic lake 330 km away and, with the site being guarded, numbers rose to 29 adults in 2010. A captive breeding programme has been initiated and is proving to be successful. Being somewhat confiding in behaviour, earlier declines may have been due to hunting pressures. It is believed to feed on invertebrates and aquatic plants and seeds by diving frequently in areas of shallow water.

Photo: Adam Riley (Rockjumperbirding.com)

EN **White-headed Duck** *Oxyura leucocephala*

`28,29`

▼ **POPULATION:** 5,300–8,700 | **THREATS: AGR**, HUN, SPP, PLN, CLI, WAT, FISH, LOG

Most of the population of this species occurs in Asia (see *page 123*), and small numbers are also found in Europe and the Middle East (see *page 65*). In this region, several hundred of these distinctive, primarily nocturnal-feeding diving ducks are resident in Tunisia and Algeria, and birds have increasingly been recorded in Morocco following its recovery in Spain. The preferred habitat is shallow lakes with a water depth of half a metre and extensive fringing emergent vegetation. The courtship display is communal and elaborate. Hunting and changes in water level management are particular threats to this species in Africa.

Photo: Robert Tizard (ocellata.com)

EN **Madagascar Sacred Ibis** *Threskiornis bernieri*

▼ **POPULATION:** 1,500–2,200 | **THREATS:** HUN, LOG, PLN, SPP?

Formerly considered conspecific with Sacred Ibis *Threskiornis aethiopicus*, the Madagascar Sacred Ibis is confined to lowland habitats in saline and brackish coastal zones, occasionally using rice-fields and freshwater lakes. This striking, pale-eyed ibis occurs with two subspecies: the nominate on Madagascar and *abbotti* on Aldabra, Seychelles (see *page 213*). It is a sedentary species and a colonial breeder, nesting either on the ground or in trees. Its confiding nature when breeding makes the eggs, chicks and adults particularly susceptible to hunters. Most of the population resides outside protected areas and work with local communities to protect this species and derive income from eco-tourism are underway.

Photo: Oliver Smart (smartimages.co.uk)

CR **Northern Bald Ibis** *Geronticus eremita* `62`

▼ **POPULATION:** 200–249 | **THREATS:** AGR, HUN, SPP, DEV, (WAT), (MAN), (PLN), (ECO)

This ibis is now restricted to a small sedentary population in Morocco, and a small migratory population in the Middle East that winters in Ethiopia (see *page 65*). Breeding colonies are usually situated in rocky areas in remote arid regions, often near watercourses or on the coast. Birds that migrate to Ethiopia feed on high moors, wet meadows and by fast-flowing mountain streams and lake margins up to 3,500 m. Illegal building and disturbance by humans, as well as changing farm practices and predation, are believed to have been the main causes of a decline in the Moroccan population. A captive-breeding centre has been established in north-east Morocco.

Photo: Todor Todorov

EN **Madagascar Pond-heron** *Ardeola idae*

▼ **POPULATION:** 1,300–4,000 | **THREATS:** WAT, HUN, SPP?

Although the breeding population of this small heron is mostly confined to Madagascar, small numbers also breed on oceanic islands (see *page 213*). It is migratory, ranging across many central and East African countries during the non-breeding season. On Madagascar it principally inhabits freshwater wetlands, particularly shallow water bodies fringed with vegetation and trees. It nests in mixed-species colonies with other herons, often including Squacco Heron *Ardeola ralloides*, with which it sometimes hybridizes. Habitat loss and heavy exploitation of the young and eggs are thought to be the main threats, although introduced fish may compete for food resources.

Photo: Dubi Shapiro (pbase.com/dubisha)

EN **Madagascar Heron** *Ardea humbloti*

▼ **POPULATION:** 1,000 | **THREATS:** AGR, CLI, FISH, HUN, LOG, PLN

Although restricted to western Madagascar and not a migratory bird, this heron is prone to wandering and there have been vagrant records from Réunion and Mayotte, and once from the African mainland. It appears to breed year-round, usually as single pairs in heronries of other species. It feeds on large fish and crustaceans. The degradation of natural wetland habitats is the main reason for its decline, while the felling of nesting trees has been documented at one site. Reduced food availability due to competition with the local fishing industry may also be a factor affecting the population.

Photo: Mark Sheridan Johnson (apertureafrica.com)

EN **African Penguin** *Spheniscus demersus*

`73`

▼ POPULATION: 52,000 | THREATS: CLI, FISH, SPP, (EGY), (MAN), (HUN), (PLN)

This penguin breeds colonially on 25 islands and at four mainland sites in South Africa and Namibia, with seven islands supporting 80% of the global population. Adults are mainly sedentary but movements of generally no more than 400 km can occur in response to prey availability. It prefers to nest in burrows, often excavated in guano, but guano harvesting in the past has led to nesting in the open becoming increasingly common. As a consequence, they are more prone to heat stress, flood events and predation by gulls and feral cats. However, food shortages due to the impact of commercial fisheries, oil spills, and disturbance are also factors contributing to population declines.

Photo: David Monticelli (pbase.com/david_monticelli)

EN **Bank Cormorant** *Phalacrocorax neglectus*

▼ POPULATION: 5,600 | THREATS: MAN, SPP, PLN, FISH, (DEV)

This large cormorant occurs in Namibia and South Africa, its distribution broadly reflecting areas with extensive kelp beds, usually no more than 10 km offshore. There are 45 breeding colonies of up to 100 pairs that nest on sea cliffs and rocky islands, mainly from May to October in the south, and April to November in the north. Adults are usually highly sedentary, whilst juveniles often disperse some distance. Young birds are at risk from predation by seals, large gulls and pelicans. The recent rapid population decline is to due to a combination of human disturbance, displacement by seals, food shortages and, locally, oil spills.

Photo: Eric VanderWerf (pacificrimconservation.com)

CR **Madagascar Fish-eagle** *Haliaeetus vociferoides*

`72`

▼ POPULATION: 240 | THREATS: AGR, FISH, HUN, LOG, MAN, PLN

An endemic species restricted to the west coast of Madagascar, this eagle is found in wooded areas adjacent to water bodies where it feeds on fish, spectacularly snatched from the surface. Of some nine fish species recorded in the eagle's diet, seven are introduced, including two types of easily caught *Tilapia*. Breeding birds hold territories from May to October, nesting in large trees or on cliffs. It suffers low reproduction rates as only one chick is raised due to siblicide, and in one third of breeding attempts eggs are not laid. The main threats are habitat conversion and persecution due to direct human competition for fish stocks, but eagles also become entangled in fishing nets.

Photo: Pete Morris (birdquest-tours.com)

EN **Egyptian Vulture** *Neophron percnopterus*

`22,62`

▼ POPULATION: 13,000–41,000 | THREATS: AGR, EGY, MAN, SPP, PLN, TRA, HUN, (ECO)

The bulk of the resident population of this vulture occurs across sub-Saharan Africa, with a small, isolated, population in Angola and Namibia. North of the Sahara, the breeding populations are migratory. Birds from Europe, the Middle East and Asia (see *pages 66 & 126*) winter in Africa and often outnumber the residents. Loss of wild ungulates and overgrazing led to the initial population declines, but these threats are exacerbated by the use of diclofenac to treat cattle (see *page 110*). In Morocco, at least, the species has been hunted for medicinal purposes. Research is underway to assess the factors impacting on this species in its wintering areas and along its migration routes.

Photo: Ken Logan

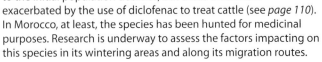

EN **Hooded Vulture** *Necrosyrtes monachus*

▼ **POPULATION: 197,000** | **THREATS:** HUN, PLN, AGR, SPP

This small, sub-Saharan vulture occupies a wide range of habitats and is often associated with human settlements. A widespread and generally sedentary species, occuring in many protected areas, it was uplisted to Endangered in 2011 following rapid population declines. Major threats include accidental poisoning, capture for traditional medicine and bushmeat, and direct persecution. Poachers may carry out intentional poisoning of vultures in some areas in order to prevent attention being drawn to the locations of their kills. Declines have also been attributed to land conversion for development and improvements to abattoir hygiene and rubbish disposal.

Photo: Andy & Gill Swash (WorldWildlifeImages.com)

EN **White-backed Vulture** *Gyps africanus*

▼ **POPULATION: 270,000** | **THREATS:** AGR, HUN, PLN, TRA

Ranging across much of sub-Saharan Africa, this lowland vulture is typically found in open wooded savanna, particularly areas of *Acacia*. It breeds in small, loose, tree-based colonies, generally raising just a single young. It faces a wide variety of environmental pressures, including habitat conversion, non-target poisoning and localized hunting. Although congregations of these distinctive birds can still be seen on thermals over roost sites and carcasses, is has declined rapidly over much of its range, by as much as 90% in some areas, and for this reason it was uplisted to Endangered in 2012. Numbers are apparently stable in Ethiopia, Tanzania and southern Africa.

Photo: Andy & Gill Swash (WorldWildlifeImages.com)

EN **Rueppell's Vulture** *Gyps rueppellii*

▼ **POPULATION: 30,000** | **THREATS:** AGR, HUN, PLN, MAN

Often soaring at great heights, this wide-ranging vulture inhabits the open woodlands, grasslands and arid montane regions across central Africa. However, it has also been recorded in southern Europe (see *page 66*). This magnificent 9kg bird can live for up to 50 years and forms breeding colonies of up to 1,000 pairs. The very rapid population decline is due to habitat loss and degradation as a consequence of changes in agricultural practices, declines in wild ungulate populations, hunting for trade, persecution, collision and poisoning. However, disturbance by recreational climbers and collection of vulture parts for traditional magic practices are particular threats.

Photo: Andy & Gill Swash (WorldWildlifeImages.com)

EN **Madagascar Serpent-eagle** *Eutriorchis astur*

▼ **POPULATION: 250–999** | **THREATS:** AGR, FIRE, MAN, EGY, HUN, LOG

This rare endemic eagle inhabits lowland and mid-altitude rainforest in north-east Madagascar. With no definite records for over 60 years, the first nest was discovered in 1997 after its territorial call became known. It mainly eats lizards (chameleons and geckos make up 83% of its diet) and frogs that it flushes out from leaf-litter and epiphytes. It requires large blocks of pristine, undisturbed forest and is particularly susceptible to slash-and-burn agriculture and commercial logging activities. Other threats include uncontrolled bush fires, mining and human persecution. It has a slow reproduction rate, which adds to its vulnerability.

Photo: Dubi Shapiro (pbase.com/dubisha)

EN **Saker Falcon** *Falco cherrug*

▼ **POPULATION:** 12,800–30,800 | **THREATS:** AGR, HUN, PLN, WAT?, DEV?

This falcon is a winter visitor to north and east Africa from its breeding grounds in Europe and the Middle East (see *page 66*), and from Asia (see *page 125*). It migrates along the Nile to Ethiopia, its southernmost regular wintering site, although birds have also been recorded in western Africa and Kenya. Most of the known threats are on the breeding grounds, where loss and degradation of grasslands and steppe has been the main cause of population declines. Sakers are also much sought after for falconry purposes, especially females as they are larger and perceived to be more powerful, and are regularly trapped on migration.

Photo: Roger & Liz Charlwood (WorldWildlifeImages.com)

EN **Ludwig's Bustard** *Neotis ludwigii*

`44`

▼ **POPULATION:** 56,000–81,000 | **THREATS:** **TRA**, HUN

This long-lived bustard is restricted to the plains, shrubby veld and arid regions of the Namib and Karoo biomes of southern Africa, where flocks of up to 70 have been recorded. There is strong evidence that it undertakes local movements following rains in pursuit of grasshopper and locust hatchlings, but vegetable matter remains an important part of its diet. The breeding season spans August to December and it nests on bare ground. Collisions with powerlines have contributed greatly to recent declines and new wind farms are likely to exacerbate the problem. It is highly susceptible to being caught in mammal snares on farmland and is also threatened by hunting, poisoning and disturbance.

Photo: Adam Riley (rockjumperbirding.com)

EN **White-winged Flufftail** *Sarothrura ayresi*

▼ **POPULATION:** 700 | **THREATS:** AGR, WAT, FIRE, MAN, LOG, PLN

Very little is known about this tiny rail that occurs in seasonal wetlands in the central highlands of Ethiopia and in eastern South Africa. Its movements, in particular, are still a mystery. A single population may migrate between Ethiopia and South Africa, although it seems more likely that each country hosts its own subpopulation. It nests in balls of woven sedges and other plant stems from July to August, rearing up to six chicks. After breeding, it moves to lower altitudes. It eats both plant and animal matter, including small frogs and fish. Habitat loss and degradation (primarily due to drainage and overgrazing) and disturbance are probably the biggest threats to this species.

Photo: Warwick Tarboton (warwicktarboton.co.za)

EN **Slender-billed Flufftail** *Sarothrura watersi*

▼ **POPULATION:** 250–999 | **THREATS:** AGR

An extremely localized, tiny rail, endemic to eastern Madagascar, where this species has been recorded reliably from three well-separated areas. It is found in permanent wetlands dominated by short, dense grasses and clumps of sedges and rushes in montane areas, a habitat that is severely threatened. Difficult to see and presumed to be sedentary, its repetitive clucking call is most frequently heard during the rainy season between October and February. Nothing is known about its breeding behaviour or diet. The conversion of grass-dominated marshes to rice-fields in order to feed the increasing human population is a major constraint to the conservation of this species.

Photo: Pete Morris (birdquest-tours.com)

Photo: Mikael Bauer

EN **Sakalava Rail** *Amaurornis olivieri*

▼ **POPULATION: 250–999** | **THREATS:** AGR, FIRE, HUN, LOG, SPP?

Endemic to western Madagascar, this small rail is usually found in areas of dense, tall, marginal vegetation in streams, lakes and marshes. It prefers areas with patches of open water and floating vegetation, particularly water-lilies. It feeds on invertebrates taken from floating vegetation, and on sub-surface crustaceans. It seems to have an extended breeding season, between July and March, and may be double-brooded. Its wetland habitats are severely threatened by destruction and degradation, such as *Phragmites* clearance and marsh fires, and introduced predatory fish may also be having an impact on the population. As this species is considered taboo in some areas, it is not subjected to egg-collecting and hunting.

EN **Grey Crowned-crane** *Balearica regulorum*

▼ **POPULATION: 50,000–64,000** | **THREATS:** AGR, TRA, WAT, EGY, FIRE, MAN, HUN, LOG, PLN

This attractive crane favours wetlands in eastern and southern Africa, making seasonal movements in response to variations in the availability of water, food and nest sites. Although a solitary nester in waterside grassland, it will roost in groups of up to 200 in water or nearby trees. It breeds in response to localized rainfall, but most often between December and February. It faces a wide range of threats but is particularly susceptible to habitat degradation and disturbance. This crane is also hunted, trapped illegally for the bird trade and sometimes persecuted as a crop pest. These factors have led to a rapid decline in recent decades and it was uplisted to Endangered in 2012.

Photo: Greg & Yvonne Dean (WorldWildlifeImages.com)

CR **Sociable Lapwing** *Vanellus gregarius*

50,63

▼ **POPULATION: 11,200** | **THREATS:** HUN, AGR, PLN, CLI?

Most of the population of this plover, which breeds in Kazakhstan and south-central Russia (see *page 130*), migrates through the Middle East (see *page 67*) to winter in Sudan. The birds arrive in October and inhabit open areas with short vegetation, often adjacent to water. They depart for their breeding grounds in March and April. Illegal hunting may pose a threat and climate change may be leading to changes in habitat, although the impact is currently uncertain. As a result of satellite-tracking, previously unknown populations have recently been found and the species may qualify for downlisting in the future.

Photo: Niranjan Sant

CR **Slender-billed Curlew** *Numenius tenuirostris*

50

▼ **POPULATION: <50** | **THREATS:** HUN, AGR?, ECO?

This small, migrant curlew, which has only been confirmed breeding in Siberia (see *page 130*), may still have a wintering toe-hold in Africa. Historically, it was recorded from Algeria and Tunisia, and from Morocco, where it was last recorded in 1994. Historical records suggest that it may have wintered in large flocks, favouring coastal wetlands. Following the initial population decline, social behaviour patterns may have been disrupted, effectively preventing its recovery. It is also possible that smaller groups or individuals had difficulty in locating suitable stop-over sites on migration through Europe and the Middle East (see *page 67*), instead joining flocks of Eurasian Curlew *N. arquata* that led them to unsuitable wintering habitat.

Photo: Richard Porter

EN **Bannerman's Turaco** *Tauraco bannermani*

38

▼ **POPULATION:** 1,500–7,000 | **THREATS:** **AGR**, **FIRE**, LOG, CLI?, HUN?

This secretive turaco is an arboreal frugivore found in montane forests of western Cameroon. It breeds during the early rainy season from March to June, building a flimsy platform nest; both sexes take turns incubating. The greatest threat is habitat loss, mostly as a result of forest fires. It can survive in degraded secondary forest provided fruiting trees remain. However, as it is reluctant to fly across open habitats the loss of forest fragments is becoming a limiting factor. The crimson flight feathers are used in hats as an ornamental indicator of social status. Efforts have been made to focus conservation action in the Bamenda Highlands but are proving difficult to coordinate.

Photo: Pete Morris (Birdquest-tours.com)

EN **Congo Bay-owl** *Phodilus prigoginei*

73

▼ **POPULATION:** 2,500–9,999 | **THREATS:** AGR, CLI?

The type specimen of this owl was collected in 1951, and although there are possible records from Burundi in 1974 and Rwanda in 1990, the next confirmed record was from the Democratic Republic of Congo in 1996. It is currently known from montane gallery forest at 1,800 m and appears to require a grassland / forest mosaic, and may be able to tolerate human activities nearby. It is threatened by the conversion of forest to small-scale agriculture, primarily as a consequence of a maize blight since the early 1990s reducing yields and forcing farmers to clear new areas. Clearance of forest for livestock farming is also a threat.

Photo: Thomas M. Butynski & Yvonne A. de Jong

EN **Sokoke Scops-owl** *Otus ireneae*

31

▼ **POPULATION:** 2,500–9,999 | **THREATS:** CLI, EGY, LOG, AGR

This tiny owl inhabits forests dominated by *Cynometra* trees in Tanzania and Kenya, occurring at highest densities in undisturbed areas. There are three colour morphs: dark brown, grey-brown and rufous. It feeds on invertebrates, hunting from a perch and dropping down onto its prey. Although rediscovered in 1965, its breeding habits remain little known, but it may nest in cavities in old *Brachylaena* trees. It roosts during the day, usually in pairs. It faces a range of environmental threats, especially (often illegal) extraction of *Brachylaena* trees for timber or firewood. Forest clearance for agriculture and a planned titanium mine could also have a severe impact.

Photo: Jon Hornbuckle

EN **Itombwe** (or Prigogine's) **Nightjar** *Caprimulgus prigoginei*

▼ **POPULATION:** 2,500–9,999 | **THREATS:** AGR

Named after the Itombwe Mountains in the Democratic Republic of Congo, this nightjar is known only from a specimen, a female, taken in February 1955. It resembles Fiery-necked Nightjar *C. pectoralis*, which occurs commonly to the south. Calls believed to be of this species, but yet to be confirmed, have been heard or recorded in northern Congo, Cameroon and Gabon, giving hope that it may be fairly widespread. With just one confirmed record, nothing is known about its ecology, but clearance of forest for grazing and agriculture may be affecting the population. Significant survey work is necessary in order to establish the true status of this mysterious nocturnal bird.

Illustration: Tomasz Cofta

EN **Banded Wattle-eye** *Platysteira laticincta*

▼ **POPULATION: 2,500–9,999** | **THREATS: AGR, FIRE**, LOG, CLI?

Found only in Cameroon, this small flycatcher occupies montane forest fragments dominated by species such as *Podocarpus*, *Schefflera* and *Prunus*. It inhabits thick understorey and seems to favour streams or dry stream courses. Despite its distinctive plumage, this species' call and song are very subdued, making it difficult to locate. The population is centred in the Bamenda Highlands, an area increasingly under pressure from human activity, leading to habitat loss and degradation. Forest fires are probably the greatest threat as this species forages and nests close to the ground, but plans for a large oil palm plantation could also pose a threat.

Photo: Markus Lilje (Rockjumperbirding.com)

EN **Gabela Helmet-shrike** *Prionops gabela*

▼ **POPULATION: 600–1,700** | **THREATS: AGR, LOG, TRA?**

The most recent records for this poorly known species, which is endemic to Angola, have all come from dry forest at around 300 m elevation in a narrow belt below the north-west escarpment. It has also been recorded in gallery and sand forests, dry thickets and cultivations, and occurs in forests underplanted with coffee. After 30 years with no sightings, a group of eight birds was found in 2003 and several other groups were located in 2005. In the early 1970s, 50 km^2 of this species' small and fragmented range was recommended as a protected area but this has yet to be established. Continuing forest clearance for agriculture and charcoal production is the main threat.

Photo: Jon Hornbuckle

EN **Mount Kupe Bush-shrike** *Telophorus kupeensis*

▼ **POPULATION: 50–249** | **THREATS: AGR, LOG, CLI?**

This bush-shrike, endemic to Cameroon, was thought to only occur in extremely small numbers in primary forest regions centred on Mount Kupe. However, birds have recently been found at two sites in the Bakossi Mountains where larger areas of its preferred habitat exist, but where road-building projects might lead to additional pressures on its habitat. It seems to prefer more open understorey at these locations. It occurs in one wildlife sanctuary that affords some protection. The range spans altitudes from 900–1,500 m. Logging concessions, opening up of roads that facilitate access, and clearance of forest for agriculture are the main threats.

Photo: Callan Cohen & Michael Mills (birdingafrica.com)

CR **Uluguru Bush-shrike** *Malaconotus alius*

= **POPULATION: 2,400** | **THREATS: LOG, AGR, CLI?, SPP?**

Endemic to Tanzania, this bush-shrike is found only in the newly formed Uluguru Forest Reserve and adjacent unprotected forest, much of which has recently been lost. It inhabits the canopy of moist submontane and montane forest, seeming to prefer areas with the highest precipitation and least disturbance, but has been found in degraded secondary forest. Whilst nothing is known of its breeding ecology, it probably forages alone or in pairs, feeding on large arthropods with its stout bill. It may join mixed-species flocks. Continuous habitat loss and degradation remains a threat despite the protected status of much of this species' range.

Illustration: Tomasz Cofta

EN Orange-breasted (or Braun's) Bush-shrike *Laniarius brauni*

▼ **POPULATION:** 250–999 | **THREATS:** AGR, LOG. CLI?

76

This little-studied, brightly coloured bush-shrike is endemic to forested escarpments in north-west Angola, where it inhabits undergrowth in highly fragmented pockets of secondary and gallery forest. Although it can be very vocal, it is a shy bird, foraging in dense cover while searching for large invertebrates and small rodents. Not known before first being collected in 1939, it has rarely been recorded since. However, the population may be benefiting from the recent neglect of coffee plantations, as it is also known to occur in degraded and disturbed forest. Increasing slash-and-burn cultivation and timber extraction are the main threats.

Photo: Dayne Braine (batisbirdingsafaris.com)

EN Gabela Bush-shrike *Laniarius amboimensis*

▼ **POPULATION:** 250–999 | **THREATS:** AGR, LOG, TRA, CLI?

77

Restricted to Angola's north-west escarpment, this species is named after the small area in which it was first found. However, surveys in 2005 extended its known range a little further south to the Kumbira Forest. Little known, it appears to favour dry, evergreen forest undergrowth but has also been recorded in degraded habitats. Much of the area that this species inhabits is increasingly being converted to commercial crop production and the removal of understorey vegetation to facilitate the establishment of plantations is a particular threat. In the 1970s, a small part of its range was scheduled for protection but this has yet to be implemented.

Photo: Fábio Olmos

EN Van Dam's Vanga *Xenopirostris damii*

▼ **POPULATION:** 1,500–7,000 | **THREATS:** AGR, FIRE, LOG

75

Endemic to Madagascar, this vanga occurs in, or adjacent to, dense, undisturbed, dry deciduous forest in the north-west of the island. It is considered to be the rarest and most threatened species of vanga. It forages for invertebrates in dead wood, peeling back bark from branches and leaf clumps to reach them, often in the company of other vanga species. The breeding season lasts from October to January and it occurs at a density of four pairs per square kilometre. Although only known from two sites, both of which are under great pressure mainly due to fire, extensive areas of suitable habitat have yet to be surveyed, giving some hope that the population is larger than currently estimated.

Photo: Glen Valentine

EN Ethiopian Bush-crow *Zavattariornis stresemanni*

▼ **POPULATION:** 10,000–19,999 | **THREATS:** **CLI**, **LOG**, AGR, FIRE, SPP, DEV

29

Endemic to southern Ethiopia, this starling-like crow occupies a unique, well-defined, climate pocket that is cooler, drier and more seasonal than the surrounding area. Within this limited range it favours a park-like landscape of open pasturelands interspersed with taller vegetation, especially *Acacia*. It feeds mainly by extracting pupae and larvae from soil and dung, and also by pursuing flying insects. Scrub encroachment due to changes in management practices may be reducing the extent of suitable feeding habitat. There are encouraging signs that recent conservation initiatives will take account of the needs of this species. However, in the long term, the impact of climate change may be the greatest threat.

Photo: Andy & Gill Swash (WorldWildlifeImages.com)

EN **Ash's Lark** *Mirafra ashi*

▼ **POPULATION: 2,500–9,999** | **THREATS:** HUN, DEV, ECO?, (CLI)

A locally common endemic of Somalia, this lark is found in semi-arid, open coastal plains, with scattered bushes. It is only known from one site north of Mogadishu but may occur in other, unexplored, coastal sites and been overlooked due to the presence of several other species of lark. It was described as new to science in 1982, but very little is known about its ecology or threats. If the range of this lark is as limited as thought, coastal development and a reduction in the numbers of livestock and wild ungulates due to drought and over-hunting could have a detrimental impact on habitat extent and quality.

Illustration: Tomasz Cofta

CR **Liben Lark** *Heteromirafra sidamoensis* 78

▼ **POPULATION: 90–256** | **THREATS:** AGR, CLI, FIRE, SPP, (MAN)

This small, short-tailed lark is restricted to just one site, the Liben Plains, in southern Ethiopia. It favours grassland 5–15 cm tall, avoiding areas of very short grass, bare ground or bushes; it has never been recorded from croplands. It was known from just two specimens collected in 1968 and 1974, but since 1994 very small numbers have regularly been recorded in areas subsequently brought into agricultural use or which have become vegetated with bushes due to fire suppression. Aerial display flights have been recorded from January to May. Recent fieldwork revealed a 40% drop in the population between 2007 and 2009 and there is a strong possibility that this species will soon go extinct.

Photo: David Erterius

CR **Archer's Lark** *Heteromirafra archeri*

▼ **POPULATION: 50–249** | **THREATS:** AGR?, CLI?

Found in the border areas of Somalia and Ethiopia, this lark inhabits both open grassland and open, rocky country with sparse bush and limited grass cover. The last confirmed sighting was in 1955 and recent searches in the region have failed to relocate this species. Very little is known about its ecology or behaviour, although it was known to fly only reluctantly and nests have been recorded in June. Refugee settlements in the 20th century resulted in the loss of perennial grassland, and the area has subsequently become intensively farmed and grazed.

Illustration: Tomasz Cofta

EN **Botha's Lark** *Spizocorys fringillaris* 78

▼ **POPULATION: 1,000–3,300** | **THREATS:** **AGR**, FIRE, SPP, CLI, EGY

This lark is restricted to well-grazed natural upland grasslands in eastern South Africa. It is usually found singly or in pairs, dispersing locally in small flocks outside the November to January breeding season, and seems to require ready access to water. The main threat is the loss of grassland to arable cropping and, to some extent, forestry. However, nest predation resulting from inappropriate grassland management practices, particularly burning, is another important factor. It is currently not known to breed in any protected area, although a proposal to designate the Wakkerstroom area as a Biosphere Reserve is being considered. There may be an overlooked population in eastern Free State.

Photo: Adam Riley (rockjumperbirding.com)

EN Aberdare Cisticola *Cisticola aberdare*

▼ **POPULATION:** 50,000–99,999 | **THREATS:** AGR, FIRE, SPP, CLI?

This well-marked cisticola inhabits moist grasslands above 2,300 m on either side of the Rift Valley in central Kenya, one of these areas being the Aberdare Mountains. It is locally common but populations are threatened by continuing habitat fragmentation. Its trilling song is heard mainly in the breeding season between March and June. A flimsy nest of grass, with a side-entrance facing away from prevailing winds, is constructed just above the ground. However, tussocks suitable for nesting are becoming increasingly scarce due to loss of grasslands and intensification of livestock production leading to habitat degradation.

Photo: Patrick L'Hoir (bird-picture.eu)

CR Taita Apalis *Apalis fuscigularis*

▼ **POPULATION:** 210–430 | **THREATS:** AGR, CLI?

Restricted to the Taita Hills, Kenya, this medium-sized, arboreal warbler is only found in a few tiny habitat fragments, totalling 1·5 km². It inhabits the understorey of montane forest, favouring gaps and edges with thick undergrowth but also occurs in disturbed forest and seems to tolerate wood-cutting and other human activity. It is normally seen in pairs or small family parties searching for invertebrates, berries and seeds. Most of the original Taita forest has been cleared for cultivation or re-forested with non-native trees, but the Forest Department is now safeguarding the remaining remnants and there are proposals to restore indigenous forest.

Photos: Daina Samba and Ken Norris [inset]

EN Yellow-throated Apalis *Apalis flavigularis*

▼ **POPULATION:** 1,500–7,000 | **THREATS:** AGR, EGY, LOG, (FIRE)

Endemic to three mountain ranges in south-eastern Malawi, this apalis is found in evergreen and riparian forest between 600–2,400 m. It also inhabits nearby secondary growth and thickets, and moves to lower altitudes outside its September to December breeding season. It forages by gleaning from leaves and twigs and will sometimes hover or hawk insects in flight. An increasing human population, and the consequent forest destruction for agriculture and wood, poses severe pressures on this species' small and extremely fragmented range. The granting of a mining concession in 2011 could also have disastrous consequences.

Photos: Nik Borrow (birdquest-tours.com) and Tiwonge Mzumara [inset]

EN Prigogine's Greenbul *Chlorocichla prigoginei*

▼ **POPULATION:** 2,500–9,999 | **THREATS:** AGR, LOG

This is one of several species named after the Belgian Alexandre Prigogine (1913–1991), a prolific collector and zoologist. It is known from two areas of eastern Democratic Republic of Congo, where it occupies forest patches, thickets and gallery forest along the upper courses of rivers at 1,300–1,800 m. Birds have also been located in slightly degraded, damp, montane forest. It feeds on seeds, fruit and small caterpillars. Forest at one location, the Lendu Plateau, has now been lost and it is thought that very few, if any, birds remain there. The status of the forest at its other locality is largely unknown, but it is suspected that uncontrolled logging and an encroaching human population is having a negative impact.

Illustration: Tomasz Cofta

CR Liberian Greenbul *Phyllastrephus leucolepis*

▼ **POPULATION: 250–999** | **THREATS: AGR, LOG**

Described as recently as 1985, this rare greenbul, endemic to Liberia, occurs in the transitional zone between evergreen and semi-deciduous forest. It was known from only two locations in the Upper Guinea rainforest and, despite targeted survey work at its two known sites in 2010, there are no recent records. Although little known, it has been observed feeding 4–8 m up in branches close to tree-trunks, and appears to join mixed-species flocks. The main threat is habitat fragmentation due to logging and clearance for smallholder farming, which was exacerbated by the civil unrest between 1989 and 2003.

Illustration: Tomasz Cofta

CR Long-billed Tailorbird *Artisornis moreaui*

▼ **POPULATION: 50–249** | **THREATS: LOG, AGR, CLI?, SPP?**

This species occurs in two populations in montane areas over 1,000 km apart: the nominate subspecies in Tanzania and the little-known subspecies *sousae* in Mozambique. It appears to prefer early successional forest habitats such as clearings but avoids areas subject to human disturbance. Despite its secretive nature and dull plumage, its repetitive metallic song often reveals its presence. It can be found in mixed-species flocks and prefers to forage for invertebrates near the ground in tangled vegetation. Pressure on unprotected forest for wood products, and increasing human disturbance, such as clearance of vegetation around powerlines, are believed to be the main threats.

Photo: Nik Borrow (birdquest-tours.com)

EN Grauer's Swamp-warbler *Bradypterus graueri*

▼ **POPULATION: 20,000–49,999** | **THREATS: AGR, CLI, LOG, (EGY)**

Although found in montane marshes in Burundi, eastern Democratic Republic of Congo and south-west Uganda, one site in Rwanda possibly holds two-thirds of the total population of this warbler. It favours marshes dominated by grasses and sedges, probably breeding from February to May, and nesting in dense undergrowth fairly close to the ground. The population is suspected to be declining due to the drainage of marshes for agriculture and the cutting and burning of vegetation. A hydroelectric dam project has afforded some protection to one site, the Rugezi Swamp in Rwanda. This is one of the region's endemics that may be most susceptible to climate change.

Photo: Claudien Nsabagasani

EN Basra Reed-warbler *Acrocephalus griseldis* `50`

▼ **POPULATION: 1,500–7,000** | **THREATS: WAT, EGY, DEV, (MAN)**

Breeding mainly in the Middle East (see *page 67*), this long-distance migrant warbler winters in eastern Africa, from Sudan to Mozambique. At its wintering sites it has been recorded in dense wetland vegetation, coastal *Suaeda monoica* saltbush, and occasionally in herbaceous woodland undergrowth. It occurs mostly singly or in pairs, but during migration has been recorded in loose groups. A key wintering site, a 130,000 ha river delta in Kenya, is threatened by large-scale conversion for agriculture (food and biofuels). However, in 2011 the Tana Delta planning initiative was launched, which it is hoped will result in a long-term strategic land-use plan and sustainable management.

Photo: Omar Fadhil Abdulrahman (natureiraq.org/site/en)

EN Pulitzer's Longbill *Macrosphenus pulitzeri*

▼ POPULATION: 250–999 | THREATS: AGR, FIRE

76

Known only from western Angola, this warbler occurs in dry, evergreen forest at 800–1,030 m. Although its range is small and fragmented, recent studies suggest that it can commonly be found in disturbed areas and abandoned coffee plantations, where it forages near to the ground in dense vegetation. Very little is known about its ecology but vocalizations include repetitive, high-pitched sparrow-like notes. Birds in breeding condition have been encountered in September and December, suggesting this is the breeding season. The conversion of coffee plantations to subsistence agriculture is a major threat to this elusive species.

Photo: A. P. Leventis

EN Usambara Hyliota *Hyliota usambara*

▼ POPULATION: 600–1,700 | THREATS: AGR, LOG

This little-known, flycatcher-like warbler, which was split from Southern Hyliota *H. australis* in 1997, has a small and fragmented range in the foothills of the East Usambara Mountains in Tanzania. It is an uncommon resident of mid-altitude forest, forest edge and coffee plantations, where it spends much of its time feeding on insects inconspicuously and silently high in the canopy. The main threats are habitat loss and degradation due to expanding cultivation for agriculture and the removal of timber. The high human population density in the area, and the demand for land and timber, has hampered forest restoration projects, even in protected areas.

Illustration: Tomasz Cofta

EN Turner's Eremomela *Eremomela turneri*

▼ POPULATION: 6,000–15,000 | THREATS: AGR, LOG

There are two subspecies of this small warbler. The nominate is known from fragmented populations in Kakamega and South Nandi Forests in western Kenya, where it is most often found in the canopy of large trees, showing a strong preference for *Croton megalocarpus*. Subspecies *kalindei* has been recorded in the equatorial forest belt of east-central Democratic Republic of Congo. The population decline is suspected to be due to the effects of forest clearance for cultivation, small-scale and commercial logging activities and intense grazing by livestock. There are plans for this species to become the flagship for a long-term, community-based monitoring scheme for the birds of the South Nandi Forest.

Photo: Adam Riley (rockjumperbirding.com)

EN White-throated Mountain-babbler *Kupeornis gilberti*

▼ POPULATION: 6,000–15,000 | THREATS: AGR, LOG, FIRE

Found in Cameroon and Nigeria, this distinctive babbler occurs in montane primary forest with high rainfall, and mature secondary growth, at 950–2,100 m. It mainly feeds on insects that it finds in bark crevices and epiphytic mosses, and it moves through its territory in small but noisy groups, often in mixed-species flocks. A survey in 1998 at one site, Bakossi Mountains, indicated a population there of several thousand individuals. Although some locations are subject to conservation programmes, there is still much pressure on remaining habitat. Plans for a large oil palm plantation in south-western Cameroon, if approved, may be a significant threat.

Photo: Markus Lilje (rockjumperbirding.com)

EN **Algerian Nuthatch** *Sitta ledanti*

▼ **POPULATION: 250–999** | **THREATS:** AGR, LOG, TRA, MAN?, (FIRE)

Algeria's only endemic bird, this nuthatch was discovered as recently as 1975. It is known from four localities in the Petite Kabylie region in the north-east of the country, where it is restricted to montane forests that contain a diverse mix of deciduous oaks, cedar and fir; a dense understorey, abundant deadwood and many epiphytes are also key habitat features. The habitat extent at one location (Djebel Babor) has been severely reduced and degraded by fire, and the area remains highly threatened. Other threats to this species include ongoing illegal deforestation, overgrazing that inhibits tree regeneration and creates an impoverished understorey, and human disturbance.

Photo: David Monticelli (pbase.com/david_monticelli)

EN **Spotted Ground-thrush** *Zoothera guttata*

▼ **POPULATION: 600–1,700** | **THREATS:** AGR, LOG, EGY, FIRE, MAN, SPP, PLN

This secretive thrush occupies shady forests with deep leaf-litter from sea level to 1,700 m. It has a disjunct distribution across seven African countries, involving five subspecies, two of which are known to be migratory and at least one that is resident. Avoiding all forms of disturbance, it forages at low levels and, as it nests on the ground, broods suffer a high predation rate. Surveying for this well-camouflaged bird is hampered by its tendency to freeze for some minutes when disturbed. Populations at known sites range from a few tens to a few hundred. In 2003, an International Spotted Ground-thrush working Group was set up to coordinate and implement conservation plans.

Photo: Dave Rimmer

CR **Taita Thrush** *Turdus helleri*

▼ **POPULATION: 930** | **THREATS:** AGR, CLI?

Confined to a tiny range of approximately 3·5 km² in the Taita Hills, southern Kenya, this thrush is found in just four cloud forest fragments. It forages amongst leaf-litter on the forest floor, where it keeps itself well hidden in the shady undergrowth, feeding mainly on invertebrates and fruit. In one population there is a highly male-biased sex ratio, which may have a significant impact on its long-term survival. Most of the original Taita forest has been cleared for cultivation or re-afforested with non-native trees, but a tree nursery of indigenous trees for replanting has been established and a translocation project is underway.

Photo: Valérie Lehouck

EN **Thyolo** (or Cholo) **Alethe** *Alethe choloensis*

▼ **POPULATION: 1,500–7,000** | **THREATS:** AGR, LOG, MAN, DEV, TRA, (FIRE)

This small, thrush-like terrestrial bird of submontane evergreen forest, breeds at mid-altitudes (mainly above 1,200 m) in Malawi and Mozambique. Originally known from just 16 areas of forest, additional, significant populations were discovered at new locations in 2005, almost doubling the presumed numbers. Its occurrence is closely linked with ants' nests and it follows army ants to take advantage of the insects they disturb. Its range remains small and there are increasing threats to both the extent and quality of its habitat. However, although populations are declining rapidly in Malawi due to deforestation, new populations may yet be discovered in unsurveyed areas of Mozambique.

Photo: Tiwonge Mzumara

EN **Gabela Akalat** *Sheppardia gabela* 76

▼ **POPULATION:** 10,000–19,999 | **THREATS:** **AGR**, LOG, TRA, CLI?

Known only from a few sites in western Angola, this very shy, drab robin inhabits the dense understorey of fragmented primary and secondary forest at 810–1,280 m. It has also been observed in abandoned shade-grown coffee plantations but probably requires intact forest nearby. Very little is known about its ecology, but it is likely to feed on insects that it gleans from the undergrowth. It is thought to breed in September, coinciding with the rainy season, but juveniles have only been noted once. With peace returning after a lengthy civil war, commercial activity in the region is increasing. Habitat clearance for subsistence agriculture also remains a significant threat.

Photo: Nik Borrow (birdquest-tours.com)

EN **Usambara Akalat** *Sheppardia montana*

▼ **POPULATION:** 28,000 | **THREATS:** AGR, LOG, CLI?

This largely ground-dwelling, little-known forest robin is a Tanzanian endemic that occurs in the West Usambara Mountains. There is probably no more than 140 km² of suitable habitat remaining. It occupies montane forest undergrowth, thickets and degraded woodland at 1,600–2,300 m, replacing Sharpe's Akalat *S. sharpie*, which is found at lower altitudes. It forages on the forest floor, often following ant swarms, as well as on trunks and lianas, and by sallying in mid-air. Its breeding ecology is little known. Although much of its range is in forest reserves, habitat loss and fragmentation remains a serious threat, primarily due to subsistence agriculture.

Photo: Denzil Morgan

EN **Rubeho Akalat** *Sheppardia aurantiithorax*

▼ **POPULATION:** Unknown | **THREATS:** AGR, LOG

Probably the least known of the African akalats, this species is endemic to Tanzania, where it is restricted to the understorey of moist, montane forest at 1,660–2,400 m. It was first discovered in 1989, but only formally described in 2004. It is considered to be fairly common within its small range. It probably feeds on invertebrates, which it takes from the ground or from low branches. Although its range includes one of the largest intact blocks of forest in the Eastern Arc Mountains, and incorporates some protected areas, forest loss and degradation remains a threat. Cannabis cultivation occurs on a fairly large scale in this remote area and can have an impact on the bird's habitat.

Illustration: Tomasz Cofta

EN **Amber Mountain Rock-thrush** *Monticola erythronotus* 75

▼ **POPULATION:** 3,300 | **THREATS:** AGR, LOG

This attractive rock-thrush is found in just a single montane humid evergreen forest block, from 800–1,300 m, on Amber Mountain, Madagascar. Very little is known about its ecology, but it forages inconspicuously for terrestrial prey and nests from October to November in tree hollows or in crevices under overhangs. There are currently few threats in its limited range but habitat destruction due to commercial logging and clearance for subsistence agriculture could become issues in the future. Although this species was recently split from Forest Rock-thrush *M. sharpei*, which also occurs on Madagascar, subsequent studies indicate that such taxonomic treatment may not be valid.

Photo: Pete Morris (birdquest-tours.com)

EN **Amani Sunbird** *Anthreptes pallidigaster*

▼ **POPULATION: 1,500–7,000** | **THREATS:** AGR, LOG

This small, iridescent sunbird is found only in Kenya and Tanzania, occurring in the canopy of mature trees within intact *Brachystegia* forest, or in submontane evergreen forest. Usually found in family groups and often joining mixed-species flocks, it feeds on nectar, insects and arthropods. Egg-laying has been recorded from March to June and from September to December. The nest is built high up in a tree and three eggs are laid. Forest clearance is the main threat, although it seems to survive, at least temporarily, in nearby degraded habitats. The Arabuko-Sokoke Forest in Kenya is now the focus of a project to promote long-term forest conservation, and remains the most reliable site for the species.

Photo: Steve Garvie

EN **Loveridge's Sunbird** *Nectarinia loveridgei*

▼ **POPULATION: 37,000** | **THREATS:** AGR, LOG

Endemic to Tanzania, this spectacular sunbird is confined to the Uluguru Nature Reserve, where it prefers montane forest between 1,200–2,500 m. Intolerant of habitat degradation, and keeping to altitudes above areas of arable conversion, it is often gregarious around flowering plants but also feeds alone, or in pairs, and joins mixed-species flocks. Breeding is believed to take place from August to the following March. Since management agreements with surrounding communities aim to reduce the pressure to expand farmland, and native trees are being replanted, this species may soon be eligible to be downlisted to a lower threat category.

Photo: Werner Suter

EN **Bates's Weaver** *Ploceus batesi*

▼ **POPULATION: 250–999** | **THREATS:** AGR, SPP?, ECO?

Only ever known from nine sites in southern Cameroon, this colourful weaver favours lowland forest but has also been recorded in degraded forest alongside villages. Very little is known about its ecology and detailed study is required. However, it appears to forage on insects, bark-gleaning in the manner of other similar weavers, with which it may compete. It occurs singly or in pairs although there is one record from a mixed-species flock. Despite recent and intensive searches, it was last seen 1996 in the Dja Nature Reserve. The precise reasons for its increasing rarity may relate to the loss of specific habitat features that are not yet understood.

Illustration: Tomasz Cofta

EN **Clarke's Weaver** *Ploceus golandi*

▼ **POPULATION: 2,000–4,000** | **THREATS:** AGR, LOG

Known only from the Arabuko-Sokoke forest in south-east Kenya and nearby lowland *Brachystegia* woodland, Clarke's Weaver occurs in noisy but erratic groups, feeding high in the forest canopy, sometimes with mixed-species flocks. It may not currently breed within its known range as it appears to be absent between April and July before re-appearing with young in August. Since 1998, the Dakatcha Woodlands near Malindi, where the strongest evidence of breeding was last noted, have been regularly surveyed but just a single young bird being fed was found. The main threat to the population is clearance of woodland for agriculture.

Photos [digital merge]: Steve Garvie

EN **Golden-naped Weaver** *Ploceus aureonucha*

▼ **POPULATION:** 250–999 | **THREATS:** AGR

This very rare weaver is found in dense primary forest and secondary forest retaining tall trees in eastern Democratic Republic of Congo. A pair recorded in Uganda in 2006 has extended its known distribution by about 80 km. First discovered in 1920, it was not encountered again until seen several times in 1986, including a flock of 60 on one occasion. It has only been observed a few times subsequently and adults feeding juveniles were last seen in 1993. The greatest threat is deforestation, which is perhaps increasing due to civil unrest in the area. Part of its range lies within the Okapi Faunal Reserve, and more could become protected if the Virunga National Reserve were to be extended.

Illustration: Tomasz Cofta

EN **Usambara Weaver** *Ploceus nicolli*

▼ **POPULATION:** 600–1,700 | **THREATS:** AGR, MAN, LOG, CLI?

Found in low densities in mountains of Tanzania from 900–2,200 m, this weaver inhabits montane evergreen forest, forest edge and disturbed forest. It is also reported from plantations and cultivated areas where mature trees remain. It forages in the upper canopy and can be quite vocal. It usually occurs in mixed-species flocks, often with Dark-backed Weaver *P. bicolor*. Habitat loss and degradation is the greatest threat but in some areas local initiatives aim to increase the area of suitable habitat that is protected or covered by community-based forest management. Two subspecies are described: the nominate from the Usambara Mountains and *anderseni* from the Uluguru and Udzungwa Mountains.

Photo: Nik Borrow (birdquest-tours.com)

EN **Gola Malimbe** *Malimbus ballmanni*

▼ **POPULATION:** 6,000–15,000 | **THREATS:** AGR, LOG

This large weaver survives in just three populations: in Liberia and neighbouring Sierra Leone, Côte d'Ivoire and Guinea. It inhabits primary forest, lightly logged high forest and very old secondary forest below 400 m where it forages for insects in the middle storey, often joining mixed-bird flocks. Although a solitary nester, cooperative nest-building takes place, with females generally working from the inside of the nest and males from the outside. The main breeding period is from September to November, although it also nests from June to August. Severe habitat loss and degradation, in combination with political turmoil, are the main threats.

Photo: David Monticelli (pbase.com/david_monticelli)

EN **Ibadan Malimbe** *Malimbus ibadanensis*

▼ **POPULATION:** 930–2,900 | **THREATS:** AGR, SPP, LOG

Restricted to south-western Nigeria, this weaver lives in forest, secondary woodland and even farmland and gardens. It is usually seen in flocks of up to five, or in groups together with Red-headed Malimbe *M. rubricollis*. Although it occurs in a range of habitats and breeds year-round, but mainly from May to August, its scarcity suggests that it is poorly adapted to degraded habitats. It appears to be particularly sensitive to isolation of forest patches, perhaps due to a low dispersal capability. It feeds in the middle storey, often in mixed-species flocks. Widespread forest clearance for subsistence agriculture since the end of the 20th century is believed to be a major cause of this species' decline.

Photo: A. P. Leventis

EN **Sharpe's Longclaw** *Macronyx sharpei*

▼ **POPULATION:** 6,000–15,000 | **THREATS:** AGR, WAT, EGY, DEV, ECO

Endemic to Kenya, this scarce terrestrial bird is restricted to high-altitude permanent grassland, although rarely above 2,800 m. It undertakes short-distance movements in response to drought. It requires tussocks in which to nest, and feeds mainly on beetles and grasshoppers. The species often forms small groups, sometimes related, which occupy territories of up to 5 ha. It occurs almost exclusively on privately-owned land, where other types of land use, particularly arable cultivation, are rapidly replacing livestock rearing. By early 2012, conservation organizations had secured 58 ha of grassland, leading to the creation of Leleshwa Nature Reserve and it is hoped that similar initiatives will follow.

Photo: Adam Riley (rockjumperbirding.com)

EN **Sokoke Pipit** *Anthus sokokensis*

31

▼ **POPULATION:** 6,000–15,000 | **THREATS:** AGR, LOG, SPP, ECO

This pipit has a highly fragmented distribution along the coast of Kenya and Tanzania. Probably extirpated from many sites, its remaining stronghold is Kenya's Arabuko-Sokoke Forest. The highest population densities are found in dense, undisturbed Miombo *Brachystegia* forest. It is mainly terrestrial, favouring areas of bare ground covered with leaf-litter, and with high densities of ants and termite mounds. Forest loss and degradation due to clearance for agriculture, logging and charcoal production are ongoing threats. However, Arabuko-Sokoke is the focus of a long-term conservation project and, in Tanzania, a large area of suitable habitat is now protected within a National Park and other forest restoration projects are underway.

Photo: Johan Heggen (bird-picture.eu)

EN **Yellow-throated Seedeater** *Serinus flavigula*

▼ **POPULATION:** 250–999 | **THREATS:** AGR, FIRE, (MAN)

Endemic to a small area of eastern Ethiopia, this canary was known from just three 19th century specimens until it was rediscovered in 1989. It occurs in just a few locations, seeming to prefer semi-arid desert scrub, savannah, rocky hillside scrub and tussocky grasslands. It has never been reported from cultivated or degraded land and seems highly susceptible to habitat alteration and disturbance. Very little is known about its ecology, but it forages in grassland and beneath *Acacia*, and is known to favour the seeds of *Lavandula*. The only nest recorded was in a small *Acacia* bush. Further studies are urgently required to better understand this species' status and habitat requirements.

Photo: Andy & Gill Swash (WorldWildlifeImages.com)

EN **Warsangli Linnet** *Carduelis johannis*

▼ **POPULATION:** 250–999 | **THREATS:** LOG, CLI?

Endemic to the northern highlands of Somalia, this finch has been recorded from the areas of Daalo and Mashacaleed, where it is thought to be common but very local. Its ecology is little known but juniper woodland is probably a key habitat component and birds showing signs of breeding have been seen in May and July. It feeds on the seeds of grasses and *Salvia* and has been observed sitting high in elevated dead branches for prolonged periods. Field studies have not been possible for several years due to the unstable political situation in Somalia and it may be some time before the true status of this species can be confirmed.

Photo: Callan Cohen & Michael Mills (birdingafrica.com)

Asia

RUSSIAN FEDERATION

SEA OF OKHOTSK

KAZAKHSTAN

MONGOLIA

UZBEKISTAN

KYRGYZSTAN

SEA OF JAPAN

JAPAN

NORTH KOREA

CASPIAN SEA

TURKMENISTAN

TAJIKISTAN

SOUTH KOREA

AFGHANISTAN

CHINA

EAST CHINA SEA

Izu Islands
JAPAN

PAKISTAN

Ryukyu Islands
JAPAN

NEPAL

BHUTAN

Taiwan
CHINA

BANGLADESH

PHILIPPINE SEA

INDIA

MYANMAR

LAOS

Hainan

Luzon

Bay of Bengal

THAILAND

SOUTH CHINA SEA

PHILIPPINES

Andaman Is.
INDIA

Mindoro

CAMBODIA

VIETNAM

Panay

Cebu

ANDAMAN SEA

Negros

SULU SEA

Mindanao

PALAU

SRI LANKA

Sulu Archipelago

MALAYSIA

BRUNEI

CELEBES SEA

SINGAPORE

Sarawak

Sumatra

Borneo

Halmahera

INDIAN OCEAN

Sulawesi

Sula Is.

I N D O N E S I A

Buru

Seram

Papua

JAVA SEA

BANDA SEA

PAPUA
NEW GUINEA

Java

Flores

Wetar

Bali

Sumba

Timor

The distribution of Endangered and Critically Endangered species

- 1–4 species
- 5+ species

Asia

Asia is the largest continent on Earth, covering almost 38 million square kilometres (about 14·6 million square miles), over one-quarter of the total land area. In the context of this book, the region adopted by BirdLife International is followed, whereby Asia includes the 26 counties on the continental land mass, with the western boundary running south along the Urals to the Caspian Sea and down its eastern shore before heading east and south along Iran's eastern border. The region includes the whole of Indonesia and the eastern boundary therefore runs along the border between Papua and Papua New Guinea (half-way across the island of New Guinea). The volcanic islands of Narcondam in the Bay of Bengal and the Ogasawara-Shoto Islands in western Pacific are encompassed in the Oceanic Islands section (*page 180*).

There are 96 Endemic Bird Areas or Secondary Areas in Asia, by far the largest number of all of the regions, reflecting the size of the continent, diversity of habitats and the degree of isolation of many areas. A total of 3,148 bird species has been recorded in Asia, almost one-third of the 9,934 species currently recognized by BirdLife International. However, 341 of these species – approaching 11% – are globally threatened, with 127 species either Endangered or Critically Endangered.

CIFIC OCEAN

TROPIC OF CANCER

EQUATOR

BirdLife Partners

Hong Kong	Hong Kong Bird Watching Society (HKBWS)	**Nepal**	Bird Conservation Nepal (BCN)
India	Bombay Natural History Society (BNHS)	**Philippines**	Haribon Foundation (HF)
		Singapore	Nature Society (Singapore)
Indonesia	Burung Indonesia	**Sri Lanka**	Field Ornithology Group of Sri Lanka (FOGSL)
Japan	Wild Bird Society of Japan (WBSJ)		
Kazakhstan	The Association for the Conservation of Biodiversity of Kazakhstan (ACBK)	**Taiwan**	Chinese Wild Bird Federation (CWBF)
		Thailand	Bird Conservation Society of Thailand (BCST)
Kyrgyzstan	NABS Public Association in Kyrgyzstan	**Uzbekistan**	Uzbekistan Society for the Protection of Birds (UzSPB)
Malaysia	Malaysian Nature Society (MNS)		
Myanmar	Biodiversity and Nature Conservation Association (BANCA)		

Asia – the conservation challenges

Asia holds more than 3,100 bird species, well over a quarter of all the world's birds. The region's richness in bird species and other biodiversity reflects the great variety of climates and habitats, ranging from Arctic tundra to tropical forest, desert, steppe grassland and boreal forest, as well as the world's highest mountains.

But Asia as a whole has a more rapidly expanding economy and population than any other continent. Throughout the region, forests, grasslands and wetlands are being degraded or lost as a result of human activities, while bird populations are also under great pressure from over-exploitation. Additional threats to Asia's birds and their habitats include invasive species and pollution. As a result, the conservation status of Asia's birds is deteriorating faster than is any other region except Oceania. In all, 342 of the region's bird species are threatened with global extinction. Of these, 72 are Endangered, and 53 Critically Endangered.

The Asia region as defined by BirdLife extends from Pakistan to Indonesia, and northwards to China, Mongolia and eastern Russia. Its great diversity of climates and habitats makes it extremely rich in bird species. Arctic tundra, boreal forest and steppe grassland in the north support huge numbers of breeding birds that disperse in the northern winter. The original vegetation in parts of South Asia and most of South-East Asia was moist tropical forests, the most biodiverse biome on Earth. In between lie the Himalaya and other mountain ranges, deserts, grasslands, temperate forests, inland and coastal wetlands, and the basins of some of the world's greatest rivers.

BirdLife has also identified 2,293 Important Bird Areas (IBAs), covering 7·6% of the Asia region's land area. Sixty-four percent of these include forests, 42% cover wetlands, and 19% are grassland sites.

More than half of Asia's IBAs are wholly unprotected, or only partly protected, including many sites of importance for Endangered and Critically Endangered birds. Those on the Asian mainland include the Inner Gulf of Thailand (Spoon-billed Sandpiper *Eurynorhynchus pygmeus*, Spotted Greenshank *Tringa guttifer* and Black-faced Spoonbill *Platalea minor*), the Bikin river basin in south-east Russia (Scaly-sided Merganser *Mergus squamatus* and Blakiston's Fish-owl *Ketupa blakistoni*), and the Ngawun IBA in Myanmar (Gurney's Pitta *Pitta gurneyi* and Storm's Stork *Ciconia stormi*).

Lack of protection also threatens key sites on the islands of Indonesia and the Philippines. Sangihe island, off northern Sulawesi, holds three Critically Endangered endemic species (Cerulean Paradise-flycatcher *Eutrichomyias rowleyi*, Sangihe Shrike-thrush *Colluricincla sanghirensis* and Sangihe White-eye *Zosterops nehrkorni*), plus one Endangered endemic (Elegant Sunbird *Aethopyga duyvenbodei*). The forest at Mbeliling on the Indonesian island of Flores supports important populations of Flores Hanging-parrot *Loriculus flosculus*, Flores Monarch *Monarcha sacerdotum*, and Flores Crow *Corvus florensis*, all endemic, and all Endangered.

The decline of the Endangered **Scaly-sided Merganser** *Mergus squamatus* coincided with the large-scale conversion of the Russian taiga, and the breeding habitat of the species is further threatened by changes in the law reducing the width of the band of forest required to be left intact on either side of Russia's rivers. Illegal spring hunting is a growing threat in Russia. In the Korean peninsula and China, dams, dredging and canalization of rivers, and industrial pollution are degrading the merganser's habitat. Photo: Martin Hale (martinhalewildlifephoto.com).

The Endangered **Blakiston's Fish-owl** *Ketupa blakistoni* requires dense, undisturbed old-growth forest, with large trees, near lakes and rivers that remain unfrozen in winter. Over-fishing has reduced food availability, and the owl is also drowned in fishing nets, and killed in collisions with power-lines. Photo: David Tipling.

Gurney's Pitta *Pitta gurneyi* was downlisted from Critically Endangered to Endangered in 2005, after a large and previously unknown population was found in southern Tenasserim, Myanmar. But much of the lowland forest there has been assigned to plantation concessions, and could be rapidly destroyed as the relaxation of the country's hard-line military regime makes Myanmar more open to external investment. Photo: Kanit Khanikul.

Tawi-Tawi island in the Philippines has three Critically Endangered species endemic to the Sulu archipelago (Sulu Bleeding-heart *Gallicolumba menagei*, Blue-winged Racquet-tail *Prioniturus verticalis* and Sulu Hornbill *Anthracoceros montani*) and one Endangered species (Tawitawi Brown-dove *Phapitreron cinereiceps*), as well as an important population of the Critically Endangered Philippine Cockatoo *Cacatua haematuropygia*. Mount Siburan on Mindoro holds the largest tract of lowland forest remaining for the Critically Endangered Mindoro Bleeding-heart *Gallicolumba platenae* and Black-hooded Coucal *Centropus steerii*, and the Endangered Mindoro Hornbill *Penelopides mindorensis*.

The population of the large and impressive Endangered **Green Peafowl** *Pavo muticus* has declined catastrophically throughout most of its former South-East Asian range and is now severely fragmented. This decline has been due to hunting for its meat and feathers, its eggs and chicks being collected, and extensive habitat modification. It has now been extirpated from the Thai-Malay Peninsula and much of the rest of Thailand. Photo: Fletcher & Baylis (wildsidephotography.ca).

Philippine Eagle *Pithecophaga jefferyi*.
Photo: Rich Lindie.

Isabela Oriole *Oriolus isabellae*. Photo: Merlijn van Weerd.

The Critically Endangered **Isabela Oriole** *Oriolus isabellae* is endemic to Luzon, where fewer than 250 mature individuals are believed to survive. Extensive habitat loss has resulted in the remaining suitable habitat becoming extremely fragmented. Ongoing deforestation, even in protected areas, means that further declines can be expected unless urgent action is taken.

The Critically Endangered **Philippine Eagle** *Pithecophaga jefferyi* first breeds when it is five (for females) or seven (for males) years old, and the complete breeding cycle lasts two years, with successful pairs raising one offspring. Any recovery will consequently be extremely slow. The eagle's old growth habitat is being rapidly lost, but uncontrolled shooting is perhaps the most significant threat in the short term.

A rapid decline driven by collecting for the cagebird trade has left a population of around 1,000 **Philippine Cockatoos** *Cacatua haematuropygia*. There are 250–700 on Palawan and its satellite islands, and 100–200 on Tawitawi. Apart from these, any remaining populations are likely to be tiny and not viable in the long term. It is known from five protected areas, three of which were specially created for this Critically Endangered species. Conservation efforts on Rasa Island, Palawan, resulted in a recovery from 25 individuals in 1998 to around 280 in 2012. Former poachers have been trained as wardens.

Just 10% of the forest remaining on the islands of Negros and Panay, where the Endangered **Flame-templed Babbler** *Dasycrotapha speciosa* occurs, lies within a suitable elevational range for this species. Highest densities have been recorded in the thick undergrowth of degraded secondary forest, where birds stay in deep cover and are unobtrusive unless singing.

Flame-templed Babbler *Dasycrotapha speciosa*.
Photo: Ivan Sarenas.

The Philippines

The Philippines is remarkable for very high levels of endemism, including many species that are confined to certain islands or island groups, including Cebu, Luzon, Mindanao and the eastern Visayan Islands, Mindoro, Negros and Panay, Palawan, and the Sulu archipelago. The majority of the country falls within seven Endemic Bird Areas, and three Secondary Areas of endemism.

The largest island, Luzon, has around 40 endemic or restricted range species. But here, as elsewhere in the Philippines, the lack of observer coverage is a problem, and three of these are considered Data Deficient (Brown-banded Rail *Lewinia mirifica*, Luzon Buttonquail *Turnix worcesteri* and Whitehead's Swiftlet *Collocalia whiteheadi*). Of the remainder, only one species, the Critically Endangered Isabela Oriole *Oriolus isabellae*, falls within the scope of this book, but nine more are Vulnerable and 12 Near Threatened. In total, 27 species found in the Philippines are Endangered or Critically Endangered.

Philippine Cockatoo
Cacatua haematuropygia.
Photo: David Tipling

The natural habitat throughout most of the Philippines is tropical forest, including lowland rain and peat swamp forest, montane rain and pine forest, and mangrove forest around the coasts. Industrial and subsistence agriculture, logging, and encroachment by human settlements are the main threats.

The Critically Endangered Rufous-headed Hornbill *Aceros waldeni*, for example, is now extinct on Guimaras in the Western Visayas, and survives only in the tiny areas of forest left on Panay and Negros. Hunting for meat, and nest raiding for food and the pet trade, have had severe impacts in the recent past, although two-thirds of the nests in the Central Panay Mountain Range, the main stronghold, are now covered by a nest-guarding scheme, and the species is believed to be increasing. It may warrant downlisting to Endangered if the situation continues to improve.

The Negros *Gallicolumba keayi*, Sulu *G. menagei* and Mindoro *G. platenae* Bleeding-hearts, however, already confined to shrinking patches of closed-canopy forest, continue to be hunted and trapped. All three are listed as Critically Endangered. The Mindoro Bleeding-heart has been recorded from only four sites since 1980, and there have been very few recent sightings of the Negros Bleeding-heart, and none at all of the Sulu Bleeding-heart since unconfirmed local reports in 1995.

Some highly threatened species, like the Critically Endangered Cebu Flowerpecker *Dicaeum quadricolor* and Endangered Black Shama *Copsychus cebuensis*, have been found to tolerate degraded forest, provided there is intact forest nearby. But both are thought to be continuing to decline as remaining forest becomes increasingly fragmented. Both species may benefit from government-backed community management of some forest remnants, and attempts to establish forest corridors between them.

As other parts of the country become more crowded, increasing immigration puts pressure on the remaining forests. In many areas, such as Palawan, the Philippines government, in consultation with local people and NGOs, has concluded that establishing strict protected areas is not viable. Alternatives include networks of Environmentally Critical Areas, which allow a graded system of protection management, ranging from strict control to buffer areas where regulated use is allowed.

The Critically Endangered **Negros Bleeding-heart** *Gallicolumba keayi* occurs on two islands, Panay and Negros, where the population is extremely small and severely fragmented, and probably continuing to decline due to forest loss. It seems to prefer dense forest, the vast majority of which has been destroyed. The wild population is estimated at less than 250 mature individuals, and there are a few birds held in captivity as the nucleus of a breeding programme.

Negros Bleeding-heart *Gallicolumba keayi*.
Photo: Tim Laman (timlaman.com).

Indonesia

Indonesia is divided by the Wallace Line, which separates biodiversity of primarily Asian origin from the species of the transition zone between Asia and Australasia. The line follows the eastern edge of the Sunda Shelf, which lies between Bali and Lombok, and passes between Borneo and Sulawesi. The division is abrupt: for example, the Asian barbets have never colonized eastwards from Borneo to Sulawesi or from Bali to Lombok, sea crossings of only a few tens of kilometres.

The islands either side of the Wallace Line form two of the world's biodiversity hotspots: Sundaland to the west, and Wallacea to the east. BirdLife has further divided these islands into 38 Endemic Bird Area (EBA) and Secondary Areas. Threatened endemic species on the Sundaland side of the line include the Critically Endangered Sumatran Ground-cuckoo *Carpococcyx viridis* (recently rediscovered after an 80 year gap) and Bali Starling *Leucopsar rothschildi*, and the Endangered Bornean Peacock-pheasant *Polyplectron schleiermacheri*, Javan Hawk-eagle *Nisaetus bartelsi* and Javan Trogon *Apalharpactes reinwardtii*.

The **White-tipped Monarch** *Monarcha everetti* occupies an area of less than 200 km² on the island of Tanahjampea in the Flores Sea. The island is unprotected, and logging is an ongoing threat. The monarch appears to be tolerant of some habitat degradation, but because of its small population and tiny range it is listed as Endangered. Photo: Denzil Morgan.

Of the EBAs in Wallacea, Sulawesi alone has 42 restricted-range species, including 12 endemic genera. Seven are globally threatened, including three listed as Endangered. The Lompobatang Flycatcher *Ficedula bonthaina* is only known from the Lompobatang massif at the southern tip of Sulawesi, one of the most densely populated areas of the island, where all forest below 1,000–1,500 m has been cleared. At the northern end of Sulawesi, the Matinan Flycatcher *Cyornis sanfordi* is also losing its lower montane forest habitat, but most forest at higher elevations remains largely untouched. Decreasing connectivity of nesting grounds and forests, hunting and over-harvesting of eggs have caused a rapid decline in the Maleo *Macrocephalon maleo*.

All Wallacea's EBAs hold at least one threatened species. The Timor and Wetar EBA has three Endangered pigeons among its 23 endemic species, and the Banggai and Sula EBA has the Endangered Taliabu Masked-owl *Tyto nigrobrunnea* and Critically Endangered Banggai Crow *Corvus unicolor*. Flores, in the Northern Nusa Tenggara EBA, has four Endangered endemics: Flores Hanging-parrot *Loriculus flosculus*, Flores Scops-owl *Otus alfredi*, Flores Monarch *Monarcha sacerdotum* and Flores Crow *Corvus florensis*.

Formerly common from Bali to Timor, Sulawesi and the Masalembu Islands of the Java Sea, the Critically Endangered **Yellow-crested Cockatoo** *Cacatua sulphurea* is now extinct or close to extinction on many islands because of excessive collecting for the cagebird trade, compounded by habitat loss. The largest population is probably on Sumba, but of the 3,200 birds estimated on the island in the mid-2000s, up to 500 a year are taken by collectors, and the remaining forest is highly fragmented. Photo: Chris Newbold.

The Endangered **Elegant Sunbird** *Aethopyga duyvenbodei* is known only from Sangihe, north of Sulawesi. Still relatively common in the tiny remaining areas of primary forest, it also exists at lower densities in degraded and secondary forest. But human encroachment and agricultural intensification are fast reducing even these modified habitats. Photo: Marc Thibault.

The Critically Endangered **Silvery Wood-pigeon** *Columba argentina* has recently been rediscovered on islets off Siberut, in the Mentawai Islands near the west coast of Sumatra, and may survive on other islands off Sumatra, Kalimantan and Sarawak. There are also plausible reports from the main islands of Sumatra and Siberut. Photo: James Eaton (birdtourasia.com).

The last decade has seen a mixed picture for conservation in Indonesia. Deforestation in Java and Bali has slowed, although much habitat has already been lost. But in Kalimantan (Indonesian Borneo) and Sumatra, very rapid deforestation is taking place to supply the timber, pulp and paper industries, and to provide land for plantation crops such as oil palm. The loss of lowland rainforest has resulted in steep declines in species like the Endangered Storm's Stork *Ciconia stormi* and Bornean Peacock-pheasant *Polyplectron schleiermacheri*. No lowland forest remains in the type localities of the Critically Endangered Rueck's Blue-flycatcher *Cyornis ruckii* in Sumatra, and it has not been recorded since 1918.

The Indonesian government has changed the forest law to allow logging concessions to be managed for conservation. BirdLife's Harapan project in Sumatra will protect over 1,000 km^2 of Sumatra's lowland forest (10% of what remains) for the next hundred years, and by the end of 2011 the government had received another 40 applications for forest restoration concessions, totalling a further 3·9 million hectares. But new regional autonomy laws were enacted in 2000, which empowered regional governments to determine the licensing of forest concessions and exploitation of natural resources. Unfortunately, there has been a significant increase in the rate of logging in protected areas since decentralization, especially in Sulawesi.

Vultures

Asian *Gyps* vultures were once among the world's most abundant large birds of prey. Although they declined throughout much of the twentieth century along with the disappearance of large wild ungulates, they remained common on the Indian subcontinent, feeding on the plentiful carcasses of livestock and domestic animals, offal and other animal waste.

In the 1990s, however, numbers suddenly plummeted. Sick and dying birds displayed a number of symptoms, most strikingly an inability to hold up their heads, which dangled as though their necks were broken. Autopsies found their livers and other organs were covered in crystals of uric acid, a symptom of gout. The 'disease' spread rapidly throughout the subcontinent from Pakistan to Nepal, and it was feared it would spread to Europe and Africa, perhaps via the increasing numbers of Griffon Vultures *Gyps fulvus* wintering in India.

The rates of decline were shocking: Indian Vulture *G. indicus* numbers fell by more than 97% over 10–15 years, and White-rumped Vultures *G. bengalensis* by 99.9%. These, together with Slender-billed Vulture *G. tenuirostris*, were listed as Critically Endangered.

It was not until 2003 that researchers uncovered the cause. Birds which had died from gout had high levels of the anti-inflammatory drug diclofenac in their kidneys. Originally developed for use in human medicine, diclofenac had recently begun to be widely used to treat livestock in India and Pakistan. Diclofenac was found to be fatal to vultures at 10% of the recommended dose for cattle. It is eliminated from the bodies of mammals within a few days of treatment, but because vultures congregate to feed at a carcass, it only takes one animal that dies with the drug still in it to extirpate the birds from a huge area.

There are more than 70 Critically Endangered **Indian Vultures** *Gyps indicus* in captive breeding centres, and in 2010, three chicks were fledged in captivity for the first time. Breeding management guidelines are slowly being established. One key finding is that, since Indian Vultures are colonial species, large group aviaries where birds can meet and form pair-bonds are essential to a successful breeding programme. Photo: Roger & Liz Charlwood (WorldWildlifeImages.com).

The **Slender-billed Vulture** *Gyps tenuirostris* (at rear) was split from Indian Vulture *G. indicus* only in 2001, and was immediately listed as Critically Endangered. In contrast to *G. indicus*, it nests in trees, either in small colonies or alone. In the Indian subcontinent, it often associates with other vultures, such as this **Griffon Vulture** *G. fulvus* (in front). Photo: Andy & Gill Swash (WorldWildlifeImages.com).

Although the impact was most apparent in *Gyps* species, declines are also occurring in other vultures. Egyptian Vulture *Neophron percnopterus* and Red-headed Vulture *Sarcogyps calvus* are now classified as Endangered and Critically Endangered respectively. Although reductions in food availability and poisoning from pesticides may play a role, it is thought diclofenac is once again the main culprit.

In 2006, the governments of India, Pakistan and Nepal introduced a ban on the manufacture of diclofenac, and pharmaceutical firms are now encouraged to promote an alternative drug, meloxicam, which is proven to be safe for vultures. In Nepal, efforts by the government and Bird Conservation Nepal to replace diclofenac have been broadly successful, and rates of decline have slowed. Bird Conservation Nepal has also pioneered the use of vulture 'restaurants', providing uncontaminated carcasses while work continues to eliminate diclofenac from the surrounding area.

Captive breeding centres have been established, and there has been some success in breeding White-rumped and Slender-billed Vultures. But larger vultures do not begin breeding until around five years old, and usually produce no more than one fledged chick every two years. By removing and incubating the first egg artificially, they can be encouraged to lay a second.

It is unlikely that anyone now living will see vultures in the kinds of numbers that were typical until the beginning of the 1990s. With evidence that pharmacies in India are flouting the ban on diclofenac by selling drugs intended for human use for veterinary purposes, it is all too possible that within the next ten years, we will witness the extinction of one or more of these species in the wild.

Although not yet on the same scale, there have been steep declines in Africa's vultures too. The declines have been shockingly rapid: Egyptian Vulture went from Least Concern to Endangered in 2004, Hooded Vulture *Necrosyrtes monachus*, formerly ubiquitous in natural and urban habitats throughout much of sub-Saharan Africa, followed the same path in 2011, and both White-backed *Gyps africanus* and Rueppell's *G. rueppellii* Vultures were uplisted from Near Threatened to Endangered in 2012.

Fortunately diclofenac, the scourge of Asia's vultures, does not seem to be much used as a veterinary drug in Africa. The main threats are different in different regions: habitat loss and the disappearance of wild ungulates in West Africa, and mass poisoning by farmers protecting livestock in East Africa. Traditional medicine (*muti*) is behind trapping and colony-robbing in South Africa: eating vulture brains is believed to make you clever and lucky.

Even before diclofenac started to have such a deadly impact, the Critically Endangered **White-rumped Vulture** *Gyps bengalensis* was probably extinct in southern China and Malaysia, and had disappeared from most of South-East Asia because of the loss of populations of large wild mammals. Only in Cambodia, where diclofenac has never been used, is the population apparently stable, although there are thought to be fewer than 200 birds. Photo: René Pop.

The Critically Endangered **Red-headed Vulture** *Sarcogyps calvus* began its decline later than the three *Gyps* species, possibly because the larger vultures kept it away from diclofenac-contaminated carcasses. However, the Red-headed Vulture has also declined in Myanmar and Cambodia, where diclofenac is not used, indicating that factors such as the disappearance of large herbivores and incidental poisoning (from baits aimed at other birds and mammals, and fish) are also at work. Photo: Johannes Pfleiderer (zootierliste.de).

Bustards

Lesser Florican *Sypheotides indicus* adult displaying.
Photo: Mohanram R. Kemparaju (kemparaju.com).

Bustards and floricans are among the species most challenged by the ways of the modern world. Large, shy birds requiring a lot of undisturbed space, they use habitats that are often regarded as wasteland, such as steppe and arid grasslands. These habitats are rarely seen as conservation priorities, particularly on the scale that bustards require. Governments are far more likely to target these areas with large-scale irrigation projects, which can make them productive for agriculture, at least in the short term, but usually result in the disappearance of the bustards.

Bustards also suffer because they are highly visible, good to eat, and a tempting target for sports hunters and falconers. They are slow breeders, taking several years to reach maturity, and thereafter rarely raising more than one chick in a season. Along with the Critically Endangered Great Indian Bustard *Ardeotis nigriceps* and Bengal Florican *Houbaropsis bengalensis*, and the Endangered Lesser Florican *Sypheotides indicus*, Asia also holds the majority of the global population of the Vulnerable Houbara Bustard *Chlamydotis undulata*.

The Lesser Florican is protected by hunting bans in India and Nepal. Hunting caused its decline, but the main threat is now from overgrazing and conversion of its grassland habitat for agriculture. Its population fluctuates greatly with rainfall patterns, and with numbers so reduced it is feared that a prolonged drought could result in its extinction.

There are two disjunct populations of the Bengal Florican. In the Indian subcontinent it hangs on in small numbers in protected areas in Nepal, with a larger (and it is hoped, stable) population in Uttar Pradesh, Assam and Arunachal Pradesh, India. The South-East Asian population is probably confined to Cambodia, where the seasonally flooded grasslands it depends on are being rapidly converted to dry-season rice, exacerbated by a land-grab by more affluent nations wishing to consolidate their food supplies. The Wildlife Conservation Society, BirdLife International and their government partners are engaged in a programme of conservation activities in the Tonle Sap floodplain of Cambodia. They have so far succeeded in establishing 173 km² of breeding and 138 km² of non-breeding habitat as Bengal Florican Conservation Areas (BFCAs), where local people are paid to grow wildlife-friendly deepwater rice, and to help protect the floricans by patrolling, and reporting nests.

The Great Indian Bustard has been extirpated from at least 90% of its former range in the Indian subcontinent. It is principally confined to Rajasthan (around 175 birds), with populations of fewer than 30 birds in Gujarat, Maharashtra and Andhra Pradesh, Karnataka and Madhya Pradesh. It has been heavily hunted in the past, and some poaching continues, with off-road vehicles making even the remotest parts of its range accessible. It requires a mosaic of habitats, including dense cover for nesting, and short, sparse vegetation on elevated ground for displaying. Government irrigation policies have enabled agriculture to spread over vast areas of arid and semi-arid grasslands, and led to a change from bustard-friendly traditional monsoonal crops, such as sorghum and millet, to unsuitable cash crops like sugarcane and cotton. In the past, these 'waste' lands have also been targeted for large-scale tree plantations.

Studies of the movements of the Endangered **Lesser Florican** *Sypheotides indicus* are urgently needed, both for conservation planning, and to find to what extent observed population fluctuations may be the result of birds finding alternatives to drought-hit areas. There are two existing Lesser Florican sanctuaries in Madhya Pradesh, India, but outside these the florican is still hunted. Involving the community in its conservation is a priority.

Lesser Florican *Sypheotides indicus* chick.
Photo: Devesh Gadhvi.

Great Indian Bustard *Ardeotis nigriceps* chick. Photo: Devesh Gadhvi.

Great Indian Bustard *Ardeotis nigriceps*.
Photo: Csaba Barkóczi.

Bengal Florican *Houbaropsis bengalensis*.
Photos: Jonathan C. Eames (standing) and
Adam Riley (rockjumperbirding.com) (in flight).

Viability analysis predicts a high probability of local extinction within 50 years for Critically Endangered **Great Indian Bustard** *Ardeotis nigriceps* populations numbering fewer than 30 individuals – which means most populations outside Rajasthan. Even the largest population cannot survive current levels of hunting, and without more effective protection the species could be extinct within 20 years.

The population of the Critically Endangered **Bengal Florican** *Houbaropsis bengalensis* in Cambodia was estimated at 600 individuals in 2007, down from 3,000 ten years earlier. Research has found that annual burning is important for maintaining suitable habitat, particularly for displaying males, supporting the idea that community-based grassland management that maintains traditional agricultural practices will benefit the species. Females need unburned grassland or other cover for nesting.

Hornbills

The hornbills (Bucerotidae) are an Old World family, with 23 species in Africa, and 32 in Asia. Each continent has its own hornbill genera, with none shared between them. Of the 13 globally threatened hornbill species, only two (both Vulnerable) are from Africa. (The two African ground-hornbill species have been elevated to their own family, Bucorvidae, and are not included in these figures.)

Hornbill species diversity is greatest in South-East Asia, Indonesia and the Philippines. Ten species are found in Malaysia's Temenggor Forest Complex alone. Thirteen occur in Indonesia – some widespread, some island endemics – and ten in the Philippines.

Four of the five most threatened species (two Endangered, two Critically Endangered) are island endemics from the Philippines. The fifth, the Endangered Narcondam Hornbill *Aceros narcondami*, confined to the tiny volcanic island after which it is named, is included in the section on Oceanic Islands (*page 180*).

Some hornbill species appear to be able to adapt to logged and secondary forest, and to make use of woodlots and scattered fruiting trees in heavily modified habitats, but all seem to be dependent upon nearby larger tracts of closed-canopy forest for nest sites. Deforestation is therefore the greatest threat, although some are also hunted, shot as pests or poached as nestlings.

The Endangered Visayan *Penelopides panini* and Critically Endangered Rufous-headed Hornbill *Aceros waldeni* are both confined to the

Mindoro Hornbill *Penelopides mindorensis*.
Photo: Bram Demeulemeester (birdguidingphilippines.com).

In 1991, it was estimated that the remaining lowland forest on Mindoro would be totally cleared within 10–20 years, although rates of loss may since have slowed. Most recent records of the Endangered **Mindoro Hornbill** *Penelopides mindorensis* come from Mount Siburan, where the forest is effectively part of the Sablayan penal colony. BirdLife Partner the Haribon Foundation has been working with prisoners and the municipality to protect and restore the forest.

The Endangered **Visayan Hornbill** *Penelopides panini* has apparently been extirpated from a number of islands, and remains fairly common only within the proposed Central Panay Mountains National Park, which contains the largest block of forest remaining in the Western Visayas. Trapping of birds for sale is being tackled with alternative livelihoods programmes, but continues. Rehabilitated and captive-bred birds are being released on Panay and Negros.

Visayan Hornbill *Penelopides panini*.
Photos: Female (left) [captive] David Slater;
Male (right) Fletcher & Baylis (wildsidephotography.ca).

Perhaps fewer than 20 pairs of the Critically Endangered **Sulu Hornbill** *Anthracoceros montani* survive in the main mountain range of Tawi-Tawi, and the species is thought to be extinct on Sulu and almost certainly extinct on Sanga-Sanga. The conversion of Tawi-Tawi's remaining forests to oil palm appears to have stalled, but known sites have been cleared for agriculture in recent years, and young birds may still be 'harvested' for food. Photo: Ivan Sarenas.

western Visayan Islands in the central Philippines. Both were formerly much more widespread within these islands, but have been extirpated from some, and are much more local where they survive. A few Visayan Hornbills may survive on Masbate and Pan de Azucar, where tiny fragments of forest remain, but the subspecies *ticaensis*, which was abundant on Ticao in the early 1900s, is extinct. As long ago as 1988, it was estimated that just 4% forest cover remained on Negros and 8% on Panay, and shifting *kaingin* (slash-and burn) cultivation has continued to erode the forests. The Rufous-headed Hornbill survives only on Panay, and on Negros, where it may be functionally extinct, although a captive breeding stock is being established for future reinforcement of the Negros population. Conservation measures include incentives to persuade farmers to abandon *kaingin* and establish permanent agricultural plots. The Central Panay Mountain Range, the site of a proposed National Park, may be the stronghold for both species.

The lowland forest of Mindoro has been largely cleared, and slash-and-burn agriculture, logging and firewood collection are encroaching on the fragments where the Endangered Mindoro Hornbill *Penelopides mindorensi* survives. In the 1970s, it was still thought common and widespread. Similarly, Sulu (Jolo) and Sanga-Sanga have apparently been almost completely deforested, and the Critically Endangered Sulu Hornbill *Anthracoceros montani* is thought to survive only in parts of the mountains of Tawi-Tawi where the terrain is too rugged to have been logged and converted for agriculture, although this remains a threat.

All four highly threatened Philippines Hornbills are killed for food. Being large, noisy and bold, they are very easy targets.

Of the remaining six Philippines species, the Palawan Hornbill *Anthracoceros marchei* is globally Vulnerable, and two are Near Threatened. The three species currently listed as Least Concern are all thought to be in decline because of habitat destruction and hunting. Two have global ranges of around 100,000 km², but one, the Samar Hornbill *Penelopides samarensis* is confined to less than 25,000 km² on a few islands in the east-central Philippines.

Like the Visayan Hornbill *Penelopides panini*, the Critically Endangered **Rufous-headed Hornbill** *Aceros waldeni* is benefiting from a community nest-warden scheme in the Central Panay Mountains. Thanks to this nest protection, nearly 500 broods with up to three young fledged in 2006. The number of active nests has increased, and the scheme is to be extended. The decline of this population may have been halted and even reversed, but there have been no breeding records since 1997 (one pair) in the north-west Panay Peninsula, and recent records of wild breeding on Negros are unconfirmed. Photo: Ivan Sarenas.

115

The world's most threatened flyway

The East Asian-Australasian Flyway extends from Arctic Russia to southernmost Australia and New Zealand. It encompasses large parts of East Asia, all of South-East Asia, and eastern India and the Andaman and Nicobar Islands. Over 50 million migratory waterbirds, including eight million waders, use the route annually.

Fifty species that use the flyway are currently considered at risk of global extinction. These include the Siberian Crane *Leucogeranus leucogeranus*, Spoon-billed Sandpiper *Eurynorhynchus pygmeus* and Chinese Crested Tern *Sterna bernsteini*, all Critically Endangered. Twenty-two migratory species, including the Chinese Crested Tern and Endangered Spotted Greenshank *Tringa guttifer*, have their entire global population within the Flyway.

Waders and other waterbirds moving along the East Asian-Australasian Flyway use a number of traditional stopover sites to rest and refuel. The importance of these sites can be tremendous. For example, almost half the 50 migratory shorebird species in the Flyway strongly depend on the intertidal sand- and mud-flats around the Yellow Sea.

But over 80% of East and South-East Asia's wetlands are classified as threatened, and consequently the East Asian-Australasian Flyway is characterized by more waterbird species listed as Near Threatened or threatened than any of the world's other major migratory flyways. Rates of species decline of up to 8–9% per year are among the highest of any ecological system on the planet.

The countries in the Flyway support more than one-third of the global human population, and most are going through a period of dynamic economic growth. This is causing intense pressure for the conversion of coastal wetlands for urbanization, and industrial, agricultural and aquaculture purposes. Other threats include pollution from industrial effluent, sewage and agrochemicals, and unsustainable hunting and exploitation of fish and shellfish.

Loss of intertidal areas within migratory pathways can have extreme consequences for shorebird populations. For example, until the middle of the last decade, Saemangeum on the west coast of South Korea was one of the most important sites for shorebirds around the Yellow Sea, supporting the largest-known on-passage congregations of Spoon-billed Sandpiper and Spotted Greenshank. The site, which encompasses the estuaries of the Mangyeung and Dongjin Rivers, has now been fully enclosed by a 33 km-long seawall. The abundant molluscs and other invertebrates on which shorebirds fed quickly died off, and numbers of birds using the site plummetted. Bird numbers have risen at the adjacent Geum and Gomso estuaries, although by no means mirroring the losses at Saemangeum. These sites too are threatened by reclamation projects.

Populations of waders which used Saemangeum as a stopover on their way to Australia have declined dramatically. Two species have been particularly hard hit: Far Eastern Curlew *Numenius madagascariensis* and Great Knot *Calidris tenuirostris*, which in 2010 were both 'uplisted' from Least Concern to Vulnerable because of the speed of their decline. Around 90,000 non-breeding Great Knots disappeared from the Saemangeum area. Surveys elsewhere in South Korea confirmed they had not been displaced, and a decline of the same magnitude and timing in Australia suggests that the birds previously using Saemanguem had died. Further analysis of available data may reveal even higher rates of decline in these and other species. Of remaining coastal wetlands of international importance in South Korea, only one is not considered at high risk of development.

Endangered **Spotted Greenshank** *Tringa guttifer*. Photo: Michelle & Peter Wong.

Critically Endangered **Chinese Crested Tern** *Sterna bernsteini*. Photo: Photo: Michelle & Peter Wong.

Critically Endangered **Siberian Crane** *Leucogeranus leucogeranus*. Photo: Hu Jinglin (birdnet.cn).

The East Asian-Australasian Flyway

This map shows the distribution of Endangered and Critically Endangered species that migrate along the East Asian-Australasian Flyway. Other species using the Flyway migrate further south to winter in Australasia.

A Critically Endangered **Spoon-billed Sandpiper** *Eurynorhynchus pygmeus* with a Red-necked Stint *Calidris ruficollis* in the background. Photo: Hu Jinglin (birdnet.cn).

Asia

Native species recorded	3,148
Extinct in the Wild (EW)	**0**
Critically Endangered (CR)	**54**
Endangered (EN)	**73**
Vulnerable (VU)	**216**
Data Deficient (DD)	**23**

All bar three of the 127 Endangered or Critically Endangered species recorded in Asia are included in this section. Those that have been omitted are non-breeding seabirds which are recorded regularly in coastal waters. These species – the Critically Endangered Christmas Island Frigatebird *Fregata andrewsi* and the Endangered Barau's Petrel *Pterodroma baraui* and Abbott's Booby *Papasula abbotti* – are covered in the Oceanic Islands section (*page 180*).

Twenty-five of the 45 Endangered or Critically Endangered migratory 'land' birds in the world occur in Asia. Of all the regions, this is by far the highest number and also the highest proportion (20%) of the species in these threat categories. The species concerned are listed in the table on *page 52*, and the map on *page 51* shows the migration routes for the 16 species where this is known. Many of these birds use the East Asian-Australasian Flyway, which is featured on the previous page.

Along with Africa and Madagascar, Asia has the highest number of Data Deficient species of any of the regions covered in this book. These comprise representatives from 17 different bird families. For further information, and photographs of some, see the section on Data Deficient species on *pages 322–331*.

The Asian species that are Critically Endangered or Endangered comprise representatives from 36 bird families. These are summarized in the following table and further contextual information, such as the total number of species in each family and the proportion that is globally threatened, can be found in the taxonomic list of all the species featured in this book at Appendix 2 on *page 339*.

A summary of the most threatened bird families in Asia

Family	CR	EN	Tot.	Family	CR	EN	Tot.
Megapodes (Megapodiidae)	–	2	2	**Barn Owls** (Tytonidae)	–	1	1
Pheasants & quails (Phasianidae)	2	5	7	**Owls** (Strigidae)	2	4	6
Ducks & geese (Anatidae)	3	5	8	**Trogons** (Trogonidae)	–	1	1
Petrels (Procellariidae)	–	1 (1)	1 (1)	**Kingfishers** (Alcedinidae)	–	1	1
Storks (Ciconiidae)	–	3	3	**Hornbills** (Bucerotidae)	2	2	4
Ibises & spoonbills (Threskiornithidae)	2	2	4	**Woodpeckers** (Picidae)	1	–	1
Herons (Ardeidae)	1	2	3	**Pittas** (Pittidae)	–	1	1
Frigatebirds (Fregatidae)	1 (1)	–	1 (1)	**Old World orioles** (Oriolidae)	1	–	1
Boobies (Sulidae)	–	1 (1)	1 (1)	**Shrike-thrushes** (Colluricinclidae)	1	–	1
Falcons (Falconidae)	–	1	1	**Drongos** (Dicruridae)	–	1	1
Vultures & eagles (Accipitridae)	6	2	8	**Monarchs** (Monarchidae)	2	3	5
Bustards (Otididae)	2	1	3	**Crows & jays** (Corvidae)	2	1	3
Rails (Rallidae)	–	2	2	**Swallows & martins** (Hirundinidae)	1	–	1
Finfoots (Heliornithidae)	–	1	1	**Bulbuls** (Pycnonotidae)	–	1	1
Cranes (Gruidae)	1	1	2	**Babblers** (Timaliidae)	1	6	7
Plovers (Charadriidae)	2	–	2	**White-eyes** (Zosteropidae)	1	1	2
Sandpipers & allies (Scolopacidae)	2	2	4	**Nuthatches** (Sittidae)	–	1	1
Coursers (Glareolidae)	1	–	1	**Starlings** (Sturnidae)	2	–	2
Terns (Laridae)	1	1	2	**Thrushes** (Turdidae)	–	1	1
Auks (Alcidae)	1	–	1	**Chats & Old World flycatchers** (Muscicapidae)	1	6	7
Doves & pigeons (Columbidae)	5	5	10	**Flowerpeckers** (Dicaeidae)	1	–	1
Parrots (Psittacidae)	4	3	7	**Sunbirds** (Nectariniidae)	–	1	1
Cuckoos (Cuculidae)	2	–	2	**Buntings** (Emberizidae)	–	1	1

(n) = number of non-breeding migrants. TOTAL (**36 FAMILIES**) **54** (1) **73** (2) **127** (3)

EN Bruijn's Brush-turkey *Aepypodius bruijnii*

▼ **POPULATION: 980** | **THREATS:** HUN, SPP, LOG, CLI?, (FIRE)

Found only on the small island of Waigeo, West Papua, Indonesia, this species was described from skins collected in the late 19th/early 20th century. Despite several searches, it was not rediscovered until 2002. It breeds during April–June, at only ten known sites, on mountain ridges above 600 m. Like other brush-turkeys, males build mounds of vegetation into which the eggs are laid and then incubated by the heat released from the decomposing material. Only about 350 of the mature adults are mound-building males. A number of factors may impact on this species such as selective logging, hunting and predation by introduced mammals. Living on an island, it is also particularly vulnerable to habitat isolation.

Photo: Fabrice Tortey

EN Maleo *Macrocephalon maleo*

34,35

▼ **POPULATION: 8,000–14,000** | **THREATS:** HUN, AGR, EGY, MAN, LOG, DEV, TRA

An unmistakable casqued megapode, endemic to Sulawesi and the Buton Islands, Indonesia, where it breeds on beaches and in inland forest clearings. It is monogamous and, at communal nesting sites, the pair digs a burrow that they abandon immediately after egg-laying, relying on geothermal or solar heat to incubate the eggs. These hatch after 2–3 months and chicks take up to two days to dig themselves out; they are able to fly as soon as they emerge and are immediately independent. In addition to habitat loss and degradation, unsustainable harvesting of eggs is a major threat. However, a number of conservation initiatives are in place and more are planned.

Photo: David & Nancy Massie

CR Himalayan Quail *Ophrysia superciliosa*

? **POPULATION: <50** | **THREATS:** HUN, EGY, (CLI)

Known from the western Himalaya in north-west India, between 1,600 and 2,500 m, this quail has not been recorded with certainty since 1876. It was then found on steep, south-facing hill slopes in groups of up to a dozen birds. However, there have been a number of possible recent sightings. In the 19th century it was probably relatively common but little is known about its life history other than it was difficult to flush and reluctant to fly. Records at Naini Tal and Mussoorie came from winter months, which could indicate that it bred at higher levels and made altitudinal migrations. Given the remoteness of some parts of the Himalaya, there is hope that populations of this species may still survive.

Illustration: Tomasz Cofta

EN Sichuan Partridge *Arborophila rufipectus*

▼ **POPULATION: 1,000–2,499** | **THREATS:** AGR, WAT, LOG

Endemic to Sichuan Province, China, this partridge prefers undisturbed temperate cloud forest between 1,100 and 2,250 m but can occur in nearby secondary forest. It also seems able to recolonize broadleaf plantations once they are 15 years or so old, provided native species are planted. It forages in leaf-litter in open forest, feeding on fruits and invertebrates. The breeding season lasts from April to October and nests are built in a scrape, often among tree roots. It is a nationally protected species and three reserves have been established which now contain the highest recorded population densities. During the breeding season, it is particularly prone to disturbance by people harvesting bamboo shoots, firewood and medicinal plants.

Photo: James Eaton (birdtourasia.com)

119

CR **Edwards's Pheasant** *Lophura edwardsi*

▼ **POPULATION: 50–249** | **THREATS:** AGR, HUN, LOG, TRA, (MAN)

Endemic to Vietnam, this species was thought to be extinct until its rediscovery in 1996. It occurs in lowland forests, favouring areas with thick undergrowth and liana-covered hillsides. The distribution is fragmented, and deliberate forest destruction during the Vietnam War resulted in extensive habitat degradation. Its ecology is little known, but in captivity males breed when 2 years old. A lack of records since 2000 suggests that the wild population may be extinct, with declines driven by hunting and habitat loss. There are, however, over 1,000 in captivity, and these have been screened to purge hybrids with Vietnamese Pheasant *L. hatinhensis* from the captive stock (however, see text for that species below).

Photo [captive]: Tomasz Doroń

EN **Vietnamese Pheasant** *Lophura hatinhensis*

▼ **POPULATION: 600–1,700** | **THREATS:** AGR, HUN, LOG

This pheasant, which is only found in central Vietnam, was discovered in 1964. It is very similar to Edwards's Pheasant *L. edwardsi*, but males have white rather than blue central tail feathers. However, recent studies indicate that Vietnamese is not in fact a valid species, and probably just an inbred form of Edwards's. Thought to be slightly more numerous than Edwards's, it lives mainly in evergreen lowland forest, being most abundant in areas with a closed-canopy. Habitat destruction, especially for rice cultivation, and hunting are the most serious threats. A captive population of fewer than 200 individuals exists in Hanoi Zoo and in several European collections.

Photo [captive]: Tomasz Doroń

EN **Hainan Peacock-pheasant** *Polyplectron katsumatae*

▼ **POPULATION: 250–999** | **THREATS:** HUN, LOG

Endemic to the island of Hainan, China, this species was originally described as a subspecies of Grey Peacock-pheasant *P. bicalcaratum* in 1906, and did not gain specific status until over 100 years later. It prefers dense evergreen and semi-evergreen forests from 600–1,200 m and can apparently tolerate secondary habitats if they are mature. A dramatic decline since the 1950s has resulted from severe habitat loss, a factor that continues to pose a significant threat to the fragmented populations. It is also subject to hunting, and although it occurs in at least three reserves, their effectiveness in protecting this species is not known.

Photo [captive]: Zhang Zhengwang

EN **Bornean Peacock-pheasant** *Polyplectron schleiermacheri*

▼ **POPULATION: 600–1,700** | **THREATS:** HUN, LOG, FIRE

This rare and elusive species is endemic to Borneo, occurring in both Malaysia (Sabah and Sarawak), and Indonesia (Kalimantan). Little known, even to many native hunters, it is thought to inhabit plains and forests of dipterocarp tree species, on moderately fertile soils, up to 1,000 m. It is presumed to be frugivorous and insectivorous, probably feeding by litter gleaning. In captivity, breeding birds lay a single egg on bare soil. Very little of its range is currently protected and it has been recorded as a victim of the bird trade. Large-scale commercial logging and widespread forest clearance for rubber and oil palm plantations, together with hunting, are likely to lead to further significant population declines.

Photo [captive]: John Corder

EN **Green Peafowl** *Pavo muticus*

▼ POPULATION: 10,000–19,999 | THREATS: AGR, MAN, HUN, LOG, DEV

This peafowl was once common and widespread across South-East Asia, from Myanmar to Indonesia. However, it has been extirpated from many areas and the only sizeable populations are in Cambodia, Myanmar and west-central Vietnam. It is now mostly confined to dry deciduous forests up to 2,100 m, with the highest densities occurring near undisturbed rivers and wetlands. Males can reach 3 metres in length when the train of 200 feathers is fully developed. Threats include habitat loss and degradation, human disturbance, hunting for meat and feathers, and the collection of eggs and chicks. It is, however, known from many protected areas and a reintroduction programme is planned for Peninsular Malaysia.

Photo [captive]: Myles Lamont (Hancock Wildlife Research Center)

EN **Red-breasted Goose** *Branta ruficollis* `51`

▼ POPULATION: 37,000 | THREATS: EGY, MAN, HUN, CLI, FISH

Although this goose breeds on the tundra in Arctic Russia, the majority on the Taymyr peninsula, it is highly migratory and winters mostly in south-east Europe (see *page 64*). Breeding success is highest in good lemming years, presumably as the abundance of small rodents provides easy food for predators and reduces pressure on the geese. The nest is often placed near eyries of birds of prey, which may also afford some protection against predators. The population decline is probably due to a combination of factors including habitat changes, disturbance, and hunting and, in the Arctic, habitat loss due to increasing oil and gas operations

Photo [captive]: Andy & Gill Swash (WorldWildlifeImages.com)

CR **Crested Shelduck** *Tadorna cristata*

▼ POPULATION: <50 | THREATS: DEV?

First collected in 1877, this attractive shelduck was not formally described until 1917. Despite some large-scale publicity campaigns during the 1980s and 1990s, the last reliable report of this bird was of a male and two females in 1964 near Vladivostok, Russia. However, unconfirmed reports up until at least 1985 from under-watched areas bordering Russia, China and North Korea offer a small chance it may still survive. There are also locations in South Korea where it may persist. Japanese aviculturists' 19th century name for this species was Korean Mandarin Duck, which hints at its former distribution. If it still exists, it is likely to have only a tiny population.

Illustration: Tomasz Cofta

EN **White-winged Duck** *Cairina scutulata*

▼ POPULATION: 250–999 | THREATS: WAT, MAN, LOG, AGR, HUN, PLN, DEV

This large, forest duck occurs in fragmented populations throughout South-East Asia from north-eastern India to Indonesia. It prefers slow-moving rivers and pools, within or adjacent to evergreen, deciduous or swamp forests and often feeds nocturnally, occasionally diving for aquatic plants, molluscs and even small fish. During the day it roosts in the dense foliage of large trees. It lays up to 13 eggs in tree-hole nests, but suitable large trees with cavities are becoming scarce. The secretive nature of this duck hinders a comprehensive assessment of its population, but decreases seem to be caused by the destruction, degradation and disturbance of riverine habitats and hunting.

Photo: Robert Tizard (ocellata.com)

CR **Pink-headed Duck** *Rhodonessa caryophyllacea*

? **POPULATION:** <50 | **THREATS:** AGR, SPP?, (HUN)

This distinctive duck was known from the Indian subcontinent and Myanmar, but the last conclusive wild record was in 1949. Specific searches in its old haunts during 2008 failed to find any convincing evidence of its continued presence. However, a possible recent sighting and credible reports in 2006 suggest that it may still persist in remote wetlands in northern Myanmar. Although its behaviour is little known, this shy and secretive, possibly nocturnal, species was usually encountered in small groups. It fed on both plant and animal matter by dabbling or diving and bred from June to September. Hunting, in combination with habitat loss, is believed to have caused its decline.

Photo [museum specimen]: Andrew "Jack" Tordoff

CR **Baer's Pochard** *Aythya baeri*

▼ **POPULATION:** 150–700 | **THREATS:** AGR, CLI, HUN, FIRE

Breeding around lakes with rich aquatic vegetation or in flooded tussocky meadows in north-east Asia, this duck migrates to winter on freshwater lakes and reservoirs in South-East Asia, from India to Japan. Nests are usually located on a tussock, in reeds or under shrubs, occasionally within gull colonies. Eggs may also be laid in the nests of other species of duck. The male guards and feeds the female during incubation, the first chicks staying near the nest until all the eggs have hatched. The reasons for the rapid increase in the rate of this species' decline are unclear, but wetland destruction and hunting are likely to be key factors.

Photo [captive]: Andy & Gill Swash (WorldWildlifeImages.com)

EN **Velvet Scoter** *Melanitta fusca*

▼ **POPULATION:** 250,000 | **THREATS:** FISH, PLN, WAT, EGY, MAN, HUN, SPP, CLI?

The Asian population of this migratory sea-duck breeds mostly on Arctic tundra and taiga, and winter in north-west Europe (see *page 65*). It breeds in solitary pairs or loose groups, sometimes in association with gull and tern colonies, especially favouring boulder-covered or small rocky islands with extensive low vegetation. It feeds primarily on molluscs, but also eats other invertebrates and small fish and, on its breeding grounds, plant material. Threats include human exploitation of its breeding areas for natural resources, as well as disturbance from windfarms, and predation. It is hunted in some areas and is also susceptible to avian influenza.

Photo: Anders Blomdahl

EN **Scaly-sided Merganser** *Mergus squamatus*

▼ **POPULATION:** 2,400–4,500 | **THREATS:** HUN, LOG, TRA, WAT, FISH, MAN, PLN, (DEV)

This distinctive 'sawbill' duck breeds in north-east Asia and migrates to central eastern Asia, where most winter on fresh rather than coastal waters. It feeds on fish and aquatic invertebrates. Breeding territories are established in March/April along rivers below 900 m in mountainous areas with tall, primary forest. It nests in tree holes up to 18 m above the ground and, although generally monogamous, up to 20% of males mate with two females. The continuing rapid population decline is suspected to be due to a combination of habitat loss, illegal hunting and disturbance. However, the provision of artificial nest boxes and engagement with local communities at some breeding sites has shown encouraging results.

Photo: Peiqi Liu (birdnet.cn)

EN **White-headed Duck** *Oxyura leucocephala*

▼ **POPULATION:** 5,300–8,700 | **THREATS: AGR**, HUN, SPP, PLN, CLI, WAT, FISH, LOG

Although this diving duck occurs in Europe and the Middle East (see *page 65*) and northern Africa (see *page 82*), the Asian population is by far the largest. It breeds primarily from Russia and Kazakhstan east to Mongolia and migrates to winter in south Asia, mainly in Pakistan, where it is found on deeper, more saline and alkaline waters with less emergent vegetation than at the breeding sites. Wintering flocks of up to 10,000 have been recorded in the past, although numbers have been declining for some years. Major causes of the decline in Asia are drought, changing water levels (mainly due to abstraction for agriculture), disturbance from fisheries, and pollution. Further threats include illegal hunting and lead poisoning.

Photo: Andy & Gill Swash (WorldWildlifeImages.com)

EN **Storm's Stork** *Ciconia stormi*

▼ **POPULATION:** 260–330 | **THREATS:** LOG, FIRE, HUN, TRA

The main population of this secretive stork is found in Indonesia and Brunei, with smaller numbers in Malaysia and Thailand. It occurs at low densities in large areas of undisturbed lowland forest, particularly swamp-forest. Adults perform dramatic aerial displays during courtship and pairs nest singly in trees. It is thought to feed primarily on fish, but also takes amphibians and invertebrates. The very rapid population decline is primarily due to the destruction of lowland forest through logging, dam construction and conversion to oil palm plantations. Major fires on Sumatra and Borneo in the late 1990s may have also had a major impact on its habitat.

Photo: John & Jemi Holmes (johnjemi.hk)

EN **Oriental Stork** *Ciconia boyciana*   `25`

▼ **POPULATION:** 1,000–2,499 | **THREATS:** AGR, MAN, PLN, WAT, FIRE, FISH, HUN, LOG, TRA

This stork breeds mostly along the border of Russia and mainland China, and winters mainly in the lower Yangtze basin and southern China. It prefers to feed in open, freshwater wetlands taking mainly fish but sometimes amphibians, small mammals, invertebrates and birds. It nests alone in loose colonies in tall trees or sometimes on artificial structures such as electricity pylons. The main threats are deforestation, wetland reclamation for agriculture, over-fishing, and disturbance. Satellite tracking has indicated a high rate of juvenile mortality on migration and on its wintering grounds. A number of captive breeding programmes have been established, with birds reintroduced to Japan and South Korea.

Photo: Huajin Sun (birdnet.cn)

EN **Greater Adjutant** *Leptoptilos dubius*

▼ **POPULATION:** 800–1,200 | **THREATS:** HUN, ECO, PLN, AGR, FISH, LOG, SPP?

This imposing stork was once widespread and common across much of South-East Asia but breeding populations are now restricted to India and Cambodia, and possibly Myanmar. It forages in a range of habitats and often scavenges at carcasses and rubbish dumps. It usually builds its bulky nest, sometimes in mixed species colonies, close to large wetlands and often near human habitations. Threats include deliberate destruction of nesting, feeding and roosting sites, habitat modification and pesticide poisoning. In Cambodia, offering incentive payments to owners of nesting trees to protect the birds has proved to be successful in encouraging the conservation of the species.

Photo: Clement Francis Martin (clementfrancis.com)

CR **White-shouldered Ibis** *Pseudibis davisoni* `41`

▼ **POPULATION: 650** | THREATS: **MAN**, **HUN**, AGR, LOG, DEV, FIRE, CLI?

Possibly the most threatened large waterbird in South-East Asia due to widespread habitat loss and degradation, this previously wide-ranging ibis is now mostly found in Cambodia, with small numbers in southern Laos and on the Mahakam River in East Kalimantan, Borneo, Indonesia. Its preferred habitat of either wetlands, grasslands or deciduous dipterocarp forest changes depending on the season. All these habitats are subject to ongoing loss and degradation. It usually nests singly, in trees, but sometimes congregates in large flocks. As it is increasingly being found near human habitation, hunting is becoming a significant threat. Of the three known sites with the highest number of birds, two are unprotected.

Photo [captive]: Johannes Pfleiderer (zootierliste.de)

CR **Giant Ibis** *Thaumatibis gigantea*

▼ **POPULATION: 230** | THREATS: AGR, MAN, HUN, DEV, WAT, LOG, SPP?

Once widespread in Indochina, this huge ibis, which is highly sensitive to human disturbance, was not seen between the 1960s and 1993, when a population was rediscovered in northern Cambodia and extreme southern Laos; it has also been recently recorded from Vietnam. Its preferred habitat is permanent wetlands in lowland dry forests. Seemingly resident, it may wander widely if disturbed, or in response to changes in water levels. Deforestation is projected to continue at an alarming rate but in Cambodia a number of initiatives are in place that may help stabilize the population. Climate change could also have a negative effect on this species.

Photo: Martin Hale (martinhalewildlifephoto.com)

EN **Asian Crested Ibis** *Nipponia nippon*

▲ **POPULATION: 330** | THREATS: HUN, PLN, ECO, (LOG)

Having become extinct from much of its range, only seven of these spectacular birds were known in the wild by 1981. This population has steadily increased to around 500 birds, all in Shaanxi province in central China, mainly due to conservation efforts by the Chinese Government and local people. However, many rice-paddies, in which it often feeds, have been converted to wheat crops, and winter starvation may be a threat. It is tolerant of human activities and utilizes tall trees for nesting and roosting, pairs becoming territorial in March, when the bushy crest is most noticeable. There is a successful captive breeding programme and a reintroduction is planned for Sado Island, Japan and being considered for South Korea.

Photo: Quan Min Li (birdnet.cn)

EN **Black-faced Spoonbill** *Platalea minor* `42,43`

= **POPULATION: 1,600** | THREATS: AGR, PLN, DEV, MAN, HUN

This spoonbill nests on cliffs on small islets off the coast of north-east Asia and migrates to winter in South-East Asia. It is mainly a crepuscular feeder utilizing intertidal mudflats, where it eats fish, shellfish, crustaceans and other invertebrates, occasionally congregating with Eurasian Spoonbills *P. leucorodia*. In 2002–3, an outbreak of botulism in Hong Kong (China) killed 7% of the world population. As this species overwinters in large flocks, and individuals take up to five years to mature, it is particularly prone to the risks from disease or pollution. Although the population is thought to be stable, recent rapid declines are likely to be due to habitat loss and pollution.

Photo: John & Jemi Holmes (johnjemi.hk)

EN **White-eared Night-heron** *Gorsachius magnificus*

▼ **POPULATION: 250–999** | **THREATS:** AGR, LOG, WAT, MAN, HUN, PLN, TRA

This secretive night-heron has a fragmented distribution in southern China and northern Vietnam. It occurs in subtropical and tropical forest, and is regularly recorded close to streams, rivers, reservoirs and rice-fields. Recent discoveries of new sites indicate a wider distribution within China than previously thought. Very little is known about its ecology but it is presumed to be almost entirely nocturnal, feeding on fish, shrimps and invertebrates. It nests solitarily from March to June, and three to five young are raised. Several of its regular sites are within protected areas or nature reserves but hunting and habitat degradation remain major threats.

Photo: Hung Le Manh

EN **Japanese Night-heron** *Gorsachius goisagi*

▼ **POPULATION: 600–1,700** | **THREATS:** AGR, SPP, LOG, HUN, DEV, (GEO)

This night-heron breeds in hilly, heavily forested areas with watercourses in Japan, with recent records from Taiwan (China) and South Korea. It migrates along the coast of China and winters in the Philippines. It is mainly crepuscular, foraging mostly for earthworms. Deforestation is the main threat throughout its range, whilst changes in agricultural practices have led to an increase in undergrowth in forest and farmland, reducing foraging opportunities. Prior to the 1970s, it was common on Miyake-jima in the Japanese Izu Islands, but after the introduction of Siberian Weasels *Mustela sibirica* it declined rapidly. Today, nest predation by corvids is an increasing threat. It is legally protected in Japan and Hong Kong (China).

Photo: Tim Edelsten

CR **White-bellied Heron** *Ardea insignis*

▼ **POPULATION: 50–249** | **THREATS:** AGR, MAN, LOG, PLN, HUN, DEV

This heron is known from the eastern Himalayan foothills in India and Bhutan, to the hills of Bangladesh and Myanmar, with some birds wintering in the Brahmaputra lowlands. It may also occur in south-east Tibet. It is mostly associated with sandy or gravelly rivers, in or near subtropical broadleaf forest, and nests in Chir Pine *Pinus roxburghii* forest. Although a comprehensive population census has yet to be carried out, the widespread loss, degradation and disturbance of forest and wetlands, through pollution and hydroelectric development, are likely to lead to further declines. Captive breeding and satellite-tagging has been implemented for this species.

Photo: Robert Tizard (ocellata.com)

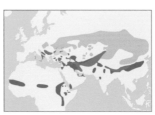

EN **Saker Falcon** *Falco cherrug*

▼ **POPULATION: 12,800–30,800** | **THREATS:** AGR, HUN, PLN, WAT?, DEV?

This wide-ranging species breeds east to China and is either sedentary or migratory depending on prey availability, migrant birds mostly wintering in southern Asia. It also occurs in Europe and the Middle East (see *page 66*) and Africa (see *page 86*). It mainly feeds on rodents by adopting hunting techniques that combine rapid acceleration with high manoeuvrability. It has declined rapidly, mainly due to habitat loss and degradation. Other threats to Asian populations include hybridization with released hybrid falcons, lack of prey due to rodent control, and infrastructure developments. In Mongolia, artificial nests have been erected,

Photo [captive]: Greg & Yvonne Dean (WorldWildlifeImages.com)

EN **Egyptian Vulture** *Neophron percnopterus* `22,62`

▼ **POPULATION: 13,000–41,000** | **THREATS:** AGR, EGY, MAN, SPP, PLN, TRA, HUN, (ECO)

This widespread vulture was once common throughout much of southern Asia. It has undergone a catastrophic decline since the late 1990s, particularly in India where numbers detected on road transects declined by 68% between 2000 and 2003 alone. Northern populations are migratory, wintering in Africa (see *page 84*), while much of the Indian subcontinent population is resident. Poisoning from the veterinary drug diclofenac (see *page 110*) has been the main driver of population declines in South Asia. So-called vulture 'restaurants', where poison-free food is provided, together with ecotourism opportunities have proved beneficial. It also occurs in Europe and the Middle East (see *page 66*).

Photo: Roger & Liz Charlwood (WorldWildlifeImages.com)

CR **White-rumped Vulture** *Gyps bengalensis* `42,111`

▼ **POPULATION: 2,500–9,999** | **THREATS: PLN**, HUN, (ECO)

Described in the 1980s as possibly the most abundant large bird of prey in the world, this vulture occurs widely in South-East Asia. However, there has been a catastrophic population decline of 99% since the mid-1990s, mainly due to the effects of the veterinary drug diclofenac (see *page 110*). Today, the only viable populations, although still declining, are those found in Cambodia and Myanmar. It nests colonially in tall trees, often near human habitation, foraging over large areas in search of carrion. They are voracious feeders, and one group studied cleaned a bullock carcass in 40 minutes. It formerly occurred in Iran in the Middle East (see *page 66*).

Photo: Clement Francis Martin (clementfrancis.com)

CR **Indian Vulture** *Gyps indicus* `110`

▼ **POPULATION: 45,000** | **THREATS: PLN**, ECO

This species, previously considered conspecific with Slender-billed Vulture *G. tenuirostris*, has the most restricted range of all the Asian vultures, being confined to India and a small area in south-east Pakistan. It feeds almost exclusively on carrion and, like the White-rumped Vulture *G. bengalensis* with which it often associates, has suffered a population collapse since the mid-1990s due to diclofenac poisoning (see *page 110*). It nests almost exclusively on cliffs and ruins, rarely in trees, but only half of the nests produce young each year. Captive breeding efforts in India have been ongoing since 2008 and it is currently held in two centres, with birds having recently laid eggs for the first time.

Photo: René Pop

CR **Slender-billed Vulture** *Gyps tenuirostris* `110`

▼ **POPULATION: 1,000–2,499** | **THREATS: PLN**, ECO, HUN, SPP

In India, Nepal and Bangladesh this vulture was common until the mid-1990s, but like other Asian vultures has declined catastrophically due to the impact of diclofenac (see *page 110*). It was common in South-East Asia during the 19th century, but now only small populations remain in Cambodia, Laos and Myanmar. Here, the lack of carrion due to changes in animal husbandry is thought to be the main threat. Its movements are poorly understood, and is is not known whether there is any connectivity between different populations. Such is the concern that in India a collaboration of conservation organizations has established a captive a breeding programme.

Photo: Mridu Paban Phukan

CR **Red-headed Vulture** *Sarcogyps calvus*

▼ POPULATION: 2,500–9,999 | THREATS: **PLN**, AGR, HUN, ECO

This striking vulture occurs throughout much of southern and South-East Asia, from Pakistan to Vietnam, but has become scarce or been extirpated over much of its range. Whilst a suite of factors are probably involved in its catastrophic decline, it feeds on carrion and, in common with other Asian vultures, mortality caused by diclofenac is the most likely cause (see *page 110*). It may, however, be slightly less affected by poisoning due to competitive exclusion at carcasses. Being territorial, it does not occur in large concentrations. In Cambodia this species benefits from vulture 'restaurants' and a captive breeding programme is underway in Thailand.

Photo: H. L. Prakash

CR **Philippine Eagle** *Pithecophaga jefferyi*

106

▼ POPULATION: 180–500 | THREATS: AGR, LOG, PLN, EGY, HUN, SPP

This long-lived, very large but unobtrusive eagle is now known only from Luzon, Samar, Leyte and Mindanao in the Philippines, where it inhabits primary dipterocarp forest, each pair holding a territory of approximately 133 km^2. The birds pair for life, with females maturing at around five years old and males at seven. As just a single chick is raised every two years, and the dispersal and survival rates of immature birds are poor, recruitment into the population is low. These factors, combined with ongoing habitat loss and hunting pressure for food and, formerly, zoos and the bird trade are the greatest threats. A captive breeding programme is underway.

Photo: Ian Merrill

CR **Flores Hawk-eagle** *Nisaetus floris*

▼ POPULATION: 100–200 | THREATS: AGR, HUN

This little-known, small eagle only occurs on a chain of Indonesian islands, where it is mostly found in lowland and sub-montane forests up to 1,600 m. It has been recorded over cultivated areas but always close to forest. Breeding probably takes place during the dry season and displaying birds have been seen on Flores in June and July. Some dispersal, perhaps even between islands, is likely. Habitat loss is the main cause of its decline and the protected areas in which it occurs today are too small to ensure its long-term survival. Population densities are low, perhaps indicative of its inability to adapt to partly cultivated landscapes. It is also persecuted for taking poultry, and trapped for the bird trade.

Photo: James Eaton (birdtourasia.com)

EN **Javan Hawk-eagle** *Nisaetus bartelsi*

▼ POPULATION: 300–500 | THREATS: HUN, LOG, AGR, FIRE, DEV

Endemic to Java, Indonesia, this eagle is widely distributed mainly in primary forest. The home range is typically 400 ha and adults are probably sedentary, immature birds being the main dispersers. Birds mature at three or four years of age and pair for life, breeding biennially, primarily during January–July. Although habitat loss and degradation are probably the greatest threats, its elevation to 'National Bird' of Java seems only to have increased the risk of trapping for the bird trade. A recovery plan is in place, there have been many awareness-raising initiatives, and local communities have successfully assisted with nest protection. A captive breeding programme has been established but so far has had little success.

Photo: Imam Taufiqurrahman (peburungamatir.wordpress.com)

CR **Great Indian Bustard** *Ardeotis nigriceps* 113

▼ **POPULATION:** 50–249 | **THREATS:** AGR, SPP, TRA, EGY, MAN, HUN

Once found throughout the arid and semi-arid grasslands of India and Pakistan, this large bustard has disappeared from 90% of its range. It requires a range of vegetation structures for nesting, displaying, feeding and roosting. An opportunistic feeder, it favours invertebrates, particularly grasshoppers, but also eats seeds. It is thought to make long, nomadic movements. Historically, it was hunted widely for food, sport and recreation, and poaching still occurs in Pakistan. Habitat alteration due to agriculture, industrialization, mining and irrigation projects is now the main threat. Birds have also been killed by discontented miners in response to mine closures in favour of creating a bustard sanctuary.

Photo: Csaba Barkóczi

CR **Bengal Florican** *Houbaropsis bengalensis* 113

▼ **POPULATION:** 250–999 | **THREATS:** AGR, HUN, MAN, LOG

There are two distinct populations of this small bustard: one in the Indian subcontinent and another in Cambodia and possibly southern Vietnam (subspecies *blandini*). It inhabits lowland grasslands that are not intensively managed, performing its elaborate display, including spectacular aerial jumps, from March to May. Most Indian sub-populations are resident, but the South-East Asian birds make local seasonal movements. Across much of its range, grasslands are being converted for agriculture and, as several grassland types are used during the year, all may need conservation action if this species is to thrive. In Cambodia, human disturbance is low and traditional community-based grassland management is proving beneficial.

Photo: Markus Handschuh (accb-cambodia.org)

EN **Lesser Florican** *Sypheotides indicus* 112

▼ **POPULATION:** 1,500 | **THREATS:** AGR, SPP, (CLI), (HUN)

This small bustard breeds in India, where it is mostly found in dry, lowland grasslands. Movements outside the breeding season are poorly understood but some birds are likely to disperse to south-eastern India and it is a rare summer visitor to Nepal. Breeding activities commence in July–September, when males establish territories and perform spectacular displays. Numbers have traditionally fluctuated over many years in response to changes in breeding season rainfall patterns. Two sanctuaries have been established in Madhya Pradesh and it occurs in other protected areas. Working with local communities to ensure favourable grassland management practices is one of the key factors in ensuring this species thrives.

Photo: Mohanram R. Kemparaju (kemparaju.com)

EN **Masked Finfoot** *Heliopais personatus* 27

▼ **POPULATION:** 600–1,700 | **THREATS:** WAT, AGR, MAN, HUN, LOG, PLN, DEV, TRA

Although this secretive species occurs throughout South-East Asia, and is migratory at some sites, its stronghold is Myanmar, which possibly supports the largest remaining population. It is reliant upon undisturbed wetlands, particularly riverine and mangrove habitats, but such areas are being rapidly lost and degraded across its range. As it is especially confiding on the nest, which is built in vegetation overhanging water, it is susceptible to being taken for human consumption, especially as its meat is described as of 'good flavour'. Eggs and chicks are also taken. The planned establishment of a major reserve in Myanmar could safeguard the future of this elusive bird.

Photo: Myron Tay (flickr.com/photos/28786551@N04)

EN **Okinawa Rail** *Gallirallus okinawae*

▼ **POPULATION: 480** | **THREATS:** AGR, WAT, SPP, LOG, DEV, CLI?

This almost flightless rail is endemic to the Japanese island of Okinawa. It forages on the forest floor or in shallow water for invertebrates and lizards, and breeds from May to July, nesting on the ground. As it is mostly ground-dwelling, this species is particularly prone to predation and being killed by vehicles. Although numbers fell dramatically during the 1980s, there are signs that the population may have stabilized, possibly helped by measures to control predatory mammals, in particular the introduced Small Asian Mongoose *Herpestes javanicus*. With the numbers at an all-time low, there are also plans to undertake a captive breeding and reintroduction programme.

Photo: Ambrosini

EN **Talaud Rail** *Gymnocrex talaudensis*

▼ **POPULATION: 600–1,700** | **THREATS:** AGR, HUN, SPP?

This large rail appears to be endemic to Karakelang, in the Talaud Islands, Indonesia. First described in 1998, it is a shy and secretive bird and has only been seen by ornithologists once since, although local reports suggest it is widespread and common. It is little known, but seems to prefer a mosaic of wetland habitat adjacent to forest in the lowlands. What were assumed to be calling birds have been heard from primary riverine forest. The threats have yet to be identified but may include land-use changes, hunting and predation. Although essentially a flightless species, planned searches on other islands in the Talaud group might reveal additional populations.

Photo: Bram Demeulemeester (birdguidingphilippines.com)

CR **Siberian Crane** *Leucogeranus leucogeranus* `52`

▼ **POPULATION: 3,000–4,000** | **THREATS:** AGR, WAT, DEV, MAN, HUN, PLN

Most of the population of this majestic crane breeds in Arctic Russia and winters mainly at Poyang Lake in China. A small remnant population of 10–20 birds from Central/West Siberia that formerly wintered in India and Iran (see *page 67*) appears to be on the brink of extinction. There is concern that the global population will decline extremely rapidly due to dam projects adversely affecting their wintering grounds. A network of wetlands across many central Asian countries is crucial during migration but many of these are also threatened. Captive-raised birds have been released in an effort to maintain the central and western Asian flocks.

Photo: Pete Morris (birdquest-tours.com)

EN **Red-crowned** (or Japanese) **Crane** *Grus japonensis* `52,53`

▼ **POPULATION: 1,650** | **THREATS:** AGR, DEV, HUN, PLN, ECO, MAN?

There are two populations of this attractive crane: one in the border areas of China, Russia and Mongolia; and another in Japan. It breeds in marshes and winters in a range of wetland habitats. Although the Japanese population is resident and stable, the mainland population, which migrates to winter in eastern China and on the Korean Peninsula, is in decline. Degradation of wetlands due to agriculture and industrialization are the main threats. However, deaths of adults in mainland wintering areas have been linked to heavy metal contamination. In Japan, the concentration of birds at feeding stations increases the risk of disease, especially given the population's low genetic diversity.

Photo: Tim Laman (timlaman.com)

CR **Javan Lapwing** *Vanellus macropterus*

? POPULATION: <50 | THREATS: AGR, MAN, HUN

Only ever known for certain from parts of Java, Indonesia, this distinctive lapwing was last seen in 1940. There are also earlier, unsubstantiated, records from Sumatra and Timor. It lived in steppe-like habitat in river deltas, and in damp pastures, agricultural fields and rice paddies, breeding from May to June. It was recorded in isolated pairs, suggesting that densities were always low. Increased human disturbance, together with habitat change through aquaculture and agriculture, are principal factors in its potential demise. Several recent searches have failed to find any birds but not all potential habitat has been surveyed and recent, unconfirmed reports give hope it may still exist.

Illustration: Tomasz Cofta

CR **Sociable Lapwing** *Vanellus gregarius*　50,63

▼ POPULATION: 11,200 | THREATS: HUN, AGR, PLN, CLI?

This migratory lapwing breeds in grassland steppes with bare saline areas near water in Kazakhstan and south-central Russia. Although small numbers winter in the Indian subcontinent and the Middle East (see *page 67*), most winter in Africa (see *page 87*). It underwent a catastrophic decline of some 98% in the 20th century, for reasons that are poorly understood, resulting in concern that just a few hundred remained. However, recent fieldwork in Kazakhstan, supplemented by counts on migration, has shown the population to be substantially larger than previously feared. The greatest threats appear to be on migration and at their wintering areas. Further research may warrant the species being downlisted.

Photo: Paul F. Donald

EN **Moluccan** (or Obi) **Woodcock** *Scolopax rochussenii*

▼ POPULATION: 2,500–9,999 | THREATS: AGR, EGY, LOG, DEV, CLI?, HUN?

This, the largest of all the woodcocks, is confined to dense, moist, montane forests on the small islands of Obi and Bacan, Indonesia, where it has been recorded from just three locations. It is little known but is assumed to be resident and is apparently confiding, only flushing at close range. As local people have an historic name for this species, it may not be particularly rare but verification of the population estimate is needed. Threats include forest clearance for agriculture, illegal gold mining and commercial logging. It probably occurs in the Gunung Sibela Strict Nature Reserve on Bacan and there are proposals for two further protected areas on Obi.

Illustration: Tomasz Cofta

CR **Slender-billed Curlew** *Numenius tenuirostris*　50

▼ POPULATION: <50 | THREATS: HUN, AGR?, ECO?

The last known breeding record of this species was from central Siberia in 1925. It migrates from its breeding grounds in a south-westerly direction to winter in European and African countries bordering the Mediterranean Sea, and on the Arabian Peninsula (see *pages 67 & 87*). It forages on tidal mudflats, steppe grassland and saltpans, presumably feeding on earthworms, larvae, insects and molluscs, although its precise diet is unknown. Any threats to the species in its breeding area are unknown and open to speculation, especially since only two nests have ever been found. It was thought to breed in small colonies.

Photo: Chris Gomersall

EN **Spotted** (or Nordmann's) **Greenshank** *Tringa guttifer* `53,116`

▼ **POPULATION: 330–670** | **THREATS:** AGR, MAN, DEV, HUN, SPP, PLN

This is a long-distance migrant that breeds in north-east Russia and winters across parts of South-East Asia. It is one of the few waders that builds a nest high up in a tree (of larch twigs and lichens), during the very short (May to June) breeding season. Loose colonies of 3–10 pairs use a variety of habitats, up to 10 km inland, including sparse larch forest, wet coastal meadows and the seashore. After hatching the adults lead the young birds to coastal meadows to feed on invertebrates and small fish. The primary threat is development of coastal wetlands and degradation of breeding habitat by grazing reindeer, although wetland pollution is also a concern.

Photo: John & Jemi Holmes (johnjemi.hk)

CR **Spoon-billed Sandpiper** *Eurynorhynchus pygmeus* `36,53,117`

▼ **POPULATION: 240–400** | **THREATS: DEV**, MAN, HUN, SPP, AGR, CLI, PLN

This charismatic small wader is a long-distance migrant, breeding in north-east Siberia and wintering on tidal mudflats in South-East Asia. When breeding it requires a specialized habitat of lagoon spits with crowberry-lichen vegetation or dwarf birch and willow sedges within 5 km of estuaries or mudflats, where it feeds. The population has declined very rapidly due to a combination of factors. Breeding success at some sites has been affected by habitat degradation, human disturbance, predation by dogs, foxes and skuas, and bad weather. However, the main threat is habitat destruction as a result of industrial development and pollution at its migration staging sites. A captive-breeding programme began in 2011.

Photo: Pavel Pinchuk (aqua-wader.blogspot.com)

CR **Jerdon's Courser** *Rhinoptilus bitorquatus*

▼ **POPULATION: 50–249** | **THREATS:** AGR, EGY, MAN, HUN, LOG

Thought to be extinct in 1900, this courser was rediscovered in Andhra Pradesh state, India during 1986. It has since been found at a few other localities in Andra Pradesh and extreme southern Madhya Pradesh, although all known sites are believed to consitute a single population. Its cryptic plumage and nocturnal habits make it difficult to detect in the areas of sparse, scrub forest with bare ground that it inhabits. It eats various invertebrates, especially termites, but little else is known about its biology. Its habitat is becoming scarce and fragmented as this is utilized for firewood collecting, quarrying, livestock grazing and conversion to agriculture. Developments such as road and canal construction are additional threats.

Photo: Navendu Laad

CR **Kittlitz's Murrelet** *Brachyramphus brevirostris*

▼ **POPULATION: 20,000–49,999** | **THREATS:** FISH, MAN, CLI?, (PLN)

The range of this tiny auk is centred on the Bering Sea, with approximately 30% of the population occurring in Russian territory and the remainder in the USA (see *page 252*). One of the rarest breeding seabirds in the North Pacific, it nests in barren, unvegetated scree or on cliff ledges. Birds do not breed until 2–4 years old and may not breed annually. There are strong links between this species' decline and areas of glacial recession, but other threats include increased disturbance by tour-boats, the impacts of pollution, mortality in fishing-nets and changes in the abundance of fish and zooplankton, its preferred food.

Photo: Glen Tepke (pbase.com/gtepke)

CR **Chinese Crested Tern** *Sterna bernsteini*

117

▼ POPULATION: <50 | THREATS: CLI, MAN, HUN, PLN, DEV?

This large, poorly known tern was thought extinct but sensationally rediscovered in 2000 when a family party was noted on an island in the Matsu Archipelago off the east coast of mainland China. It now occurs in three areas off the Chinese coast. Local fishermen often collect tern eggs, for which there is a lucrative market, but this activity is monitored, and fines imposed, by coastguard patrols from Taiwan (China). The indications are that far fewer nests are being plundered as a result. Putative hybrids with Great Crested Tern *S. bergii* have recently been observed and could be a threat. Birds have been found in South-East Asia south to Indonesia, but the overall range is not fully known.

Photo: Michelle & Peter Wong

EN **Black-bellied Tern** *Sterna acuticauda*

▼ POPULATION: 6,700–17,000 | THREATS: SPP, AGR, WAT, FISH, MAN, HUN, LOG

Despite its large range, this small tern is now only locally common in the Indian subcontinent, having declined most rapidly throughout South-East Asia, where it is now almost extinct. It inhabits large, inland rivers in the lowlands, breeding on islands and sand spits, and in marshes. It faces a multitude of threats, including habitat destruction, disturbance, egg collection and predation from mammals and avian predators such as House Crows *Corvus splendens*. Dam construction in rivers can flood nests, and over-fishing also takes its toll. It occurs in some existing protected areas but there is a need to reduce human pressures on riverine ecosystems and for larger stretches of waterways to be protected.

Photo: Greg & Yvonne Dean (WorldWildlifeImages.com)

CR **Silvery Wood-pigeon** *Columba argentina*

109

▼ POPULATION: <50 | THREATS: AGR, EGY, MAN?, HUN?, SPP?, LOG?, DEV?

This rare pigeon occurs on the Mentawai Islands and the island of Simeulue, Indonesia, and possibly other islands in the region. There were no confirmed records from 1931 until 2008, when photographs were obtained. Its similarity to the sympatric and common Pied Imperial-pigeon *Ducula bicolor* (which lacks the red eye-wattles), could explain why it has been overlooked. Little is known about its ecology, but it may prefer mangroves and coastal forests, dispersing to other habitats in response to changes in food supply. A comprehensive assessment has yet to be completed, but habitat destruction for mining and plantations, together with introduced mammalian predators, are likely to be among the main threats.

Photo: James Eaton (birdtourasia.com)

EN **Tawitawi Brown-dove** *Phapitreron cinereiceps*

▼ POPULATION: 250–999 | THREATS: AGR, HUN, LOG, DEV

This shy dove is endemic to the Sulu Archipelago in the Philippines, occupying primary and secondary growth lowland forest, including beach mangroves. It occurs on Tawi-Tawi and Sanga-Sanga, although it is possibly extinct on the latter island as virtually no forest remains. It is little known, but does have a distinctive 'bouncing-ball' call, and is more often heard than seen. There have been decades of forest clearance for cassava plantations but mining developments are an emerging threat. Environmental laws are poorly enforced and hunting and trapping are widespread. Military activity and insurgency also continue to present a serious obstacle to general conservation activity in the archipelago.

Photo: Ivan Sarenas

CR **Mindoro Bleeding-heart** *Gallicolumba platenae*

▼ POPULATION: 50–249 | THREATS: HUN, LOG, AGR, EGY

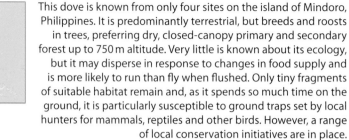

This dove is known from only four sites on the island of Mindoro, Philippines. It is predominantly terrestrial, but breeds and roosts in trees, preferring dry, closed-canopy primary and secondary forest up to 750 m altitude. Very little is known about its ecology, but it may disperse in response to changes in food supply and is more likely to run than fly when flushed. Only tiny fragments of suitable habitat remain and, as it spends so much time on the ground, it is particularly susceptible to ground traps set by local hunters for mammals, reptiles and other birds. However, a range of local conservation initiatives are in place.

Photo: Pete Morris (birdquest-tours.com)

CR **Negros Bleeding-heart** *Gallicolumba keayi* `107`

▼ POPULATION: 50–249 | THREATS: AGR, LOG, HUN, SPP?

Found on the islands of Panay and Negros, Philippines, this dove prefers dense closed-canopy forests at 300–1,200 m, but has also been recorded in degraded forests. Little is known about its habits other than that it feeds on the forest floor, only using trees for roosting or breeding. It tends to run from danger rather than fly. Small populations probably remain in southern Negros and evidence of nesting has come from Panay. However, with so few recent sightings in the wild, a captive breeding programme has been established and there are plans for future reintroductions. There are also proposals to establish more protected areas that will hopefully benefit this species.

Photo: Rob Hutchinson (birdtourasia.com)

CR **Sulu Bleeding-heart** *Gallicolumba menagei*

▼ POPULATION: <50 | THREATS: LOG, AGR, (HUN)

Endemic to the Philippines, this dove has not been recorded with certainty since two specimens were acquired in 1891 from the island of Tawi-Tawi in the Sulu Archipelago. Although the island has since been deforested, in 1995 local reports indicated that this species could still occur on other islets. However, although tiny areas of suitable habitat may remain, no birds have been found, despite repeated surveys. Little is known about the species' ecology, but it is probably a small-island specialist. There are no protected areas in the archipelago and military activity and insurgency continue, presenting a serious obstacle to any conservation activity in the area.

Illustration: Tomasz Cofta

EN **Wetar Ground-dove** *Gallicolumba hoedtii*

▼ POPULATION: 2,500–9,999 | THREATS: AGR, HUN, LOG, FIRE

This small dove inhabits lowland monsoon-forest, and possibly woodland, on West Timor and Wetar in Indonesia, and Timor-Leste. It may be partly nomadic in response to bamboo seeding events, as is the case with several of its congeners. A canopy nester, it probably breeds in the dry season in areas adjacent to permanent water. Although habitat loss is the main threat, this terrestrial bird is also likely to be particularly susceptible to hunting, especially on Timor. In 2004, one of the few remaining birds was rescued from a trapper, suggesting they may be exported for the bird trade. Several protected areas have been proposed on West Timor, and another on Wetar.

Photo: Denzil Morgan

EN **Timor Green-pigeon** *Treron psittaceus*

▼ POPULATION: 600–2,000 | THREATS: AGR, HUN, LOG, DEV, FIRE

Endemic to West Timor and its satellite islands in Indonesia, and to Timor-Leste, this shy pigeon inhabits both wet and dry primary and secondary forests, mostly in the extreme lowlands. It has a very patchy distribution, being absent from many areas of apparently suitable habitat. Possibly nomadic in response to the fruiting cycle of figs, it usually occurs in groups of up to ten birds, but a flock of 140 has been recorded. Although severe habitat loss is the main threat, hunters favour this species of pigeon as it is considered to be particularly good eating. Several protected areas have been proposed, and there is an urgent need to work with local communities to reduce the intense hunting pressure.

Illustration: Tomasz Cofta

CR **Negros Fruit-dove** *Ptilinopus arcanus*

▼ POPULATION: <50 | THREATS: AGR, HUN, LOG, CLI?

This small dove is known only from a single specimen, a female, collected on the island of Negros, Philippines, in 1953. The only subsequent record is an unconfirmed report in 2002. There is no information available on its ecology but a combination of habitat destruction and hunting, which affects all pigeons and doves on Negros, are presumed to be the most likely threats. Only 4% of the island remained forested a few decades ago and remaining forest is under great pressure from human activities. Two species previously only known from Negros, a dove and a jungle-flycatcher, have recently been discovered on the nearby island of Panay, instilling some hope that that Negros Fruit-dove may also occur there.

Illustration: Tomasz Cofta

EN **Mindoro Imperial-pigeon** *Ducula mindorensis*

▼ POPULATION: 600–1,700 | THREATS: AGR, HUN, LOG, CLI?

This little-known pigeon from the central highlands of Mindoro, Philippines, has been recorded at just five sites since 1980, although it is believed previously to have occurred throughout the highlands. It has probably always been uncommon and local, but as it is not easily found unless familiar with its vocalizations, it may be under-recorded. Although once thought to prefer montane forests, it has recently been found at lower altitudes and may be nomadic in response to changes in food supply. Severe habitat loss and subsistence hunting continue to be major threats to this species. In the late 1980s, only 120 km^2 of Mindoro remained forested, and only 25% of this was closed-canopy forest.

Illustration: Tomasz Cofta

EN **Timor Imperial-pigeon** *Ducula cineracea*

▼ POPULATION: 6,000–15,000 | THREATS: AGR, FIRE, HUN, LOG, DEV

Endemic to the islands of Timor and Wetar in Indonesia, with most of the population thought to occur on the latter, this pigeon is most often found in montane forest, monsoon woodland and native *Eucalyptus* forest. Thought to be locally common and possibly sedentary, it has recently been found at several new locations and may undertake altitudinal movements. Hunting is a major issue in Timor and deforestation has greatly reduced the area of monsoon woodland. On Wetar, it occurs commonly down to the lowlands, but is under threat from road development and mining, and agricultural expansion. A large protected area recently established at Gunung Mutis in West Timor may help to safeguard this species.

Photo: James Eaton (birdtourasia.com)

EN Flores (or Wallace's) Hanging-parrot *Loriculus flosculus*

▼ POPULATION: 2,500–9,999 | THREATS: AGR, LOG, DEV, CLI?, FIRE?

The small, arboreal parrot occurs on the island of Flores and its satellite islands, Indonesia. It was thought to only inhabit primary semi-evergreen forest, especially with fruiting figs trees, an important food source, but more recently has also been found in *Eucalyptus* forest and semi-deciduous forest on limestone, and sometimes in degraded habitats. Forest loss and degradation are major threats for this hole-nesting species. Although two areas where this species occurs are proposed as protected areas, there is a need to better understand its ecology and to determine whether it is threatened by the bird trade.

Photos: James Eaton (birdtourasia.com) and Craig Robson [inset]

CR Yellow-crested Cockatoo *Cacatua sulphurea* `108`

▼ POPULATION: 1,500–7,000 | THREATS: HUN, LOG, AGR, SPP, PLN?, (CLI)

This cockatoo is indigenous to Timor-Leste and much of Indonesia, but it is now probably extinct on many islands. A feral population of several hundred occurs in Hong Kong (China). It is found in a wide-range of forest types and requires large cavities in dead or rotting trees for nesting. Its decline is almost wholly attributable to the cagebird trade (*e.g.* 100,000 birds were exported legally during a 12-year period in the late 20th century), but widespread deforestation and the use of pesticides are also threats. It has also been persecuted as it was considered a crop pest. A cooperative recovery plan has been developed and adopted, and moratoria on international trade are in place, although it is likely that a large proportion of the trade is domestic.

Photo: Wong Chi Yin

CR Philippine Cockatoo *Cacatua haematuropygia* `107`

▼ POPULATION: 370–770 | THREATS: HUN, AGR, CLI, LOG, SPP

Endemic to the Philippines, this cockatoo breeds in lowland forests in riverine or coastal areas and frequents agricultural fields at other times. It is partially nomadic, following seasonally fluctuating food resources and using offshore islands for roosting and breeding. Declines are mainly due to widespread habitat destruction but this species' high value results in virtually every chick being taken for the cagebird trade at some sites. It is also persecuted as a crop pest and hunted for food. As the population is so low, it could be particularly hard hit by future weather extremes, such as typhoons. Among several conservation activities, former poachers have been retrained as wildlife wardens, which has proved to be effective.

Photo: Simon Harrap (birdquest-tours.com)

CR Blue-winged Racquet-tail *Prioniturus verticalis*

▼ POPULATION: 50–249 | THREATS: HUN, LOG, AGR, DEV

This little known parrot historically occurred on six islands in the Sulu Archipelago, Philippines but has been in steep decline since 1970 and it is now thought to be extinct on many islands. Despite its name, the distinctive, racquet-shaped central tail feathers can be difficult to see. It inhabits a range of forest types but avoids cultivated areas. Forest clearance is widespread, and the steady erosion of topsoil has disrupted forest regeneration, further exacerbating habitat loss. Hunting pressure is also likely to be a significant threat. There are no protected areas in the archipelago and military activity and insurgency continue, presenting a serious obstacle to any conservation activity in the area.

Photo: Rob Hutchinson (birdtourasia.com)

135

EN **Red-and-blue Lory** *Eos histrio*

▼ POPULATION: 5,500–14,000 | THREATS: HUN, AGR, LOG, SPP?, PLN?

This beautiful parrot is now confined to the Talaud Islands, almost exclusively on Karakelang, Indonesia. The nominate subspecies from from the nearby Sangihe Islands, is probably now extinct. Highest densities occur in primary forest, although it feeds in agricultural areas. It makes short seasonal movements and occasionally roosts on offshore islands. Until recently, 1,000–2,000 birds a year were being exported, most illegally, for the cagebird trade. Stricter export controls are beginning to reduce losses but habitat destruction, the use of pesticides and the transmission of diseases from cage birds remain ongoing threats. Continued community awareness initiatives are a key factor in the protection of this species.

Photo [captive]: Jon Hornbuckle

EN **Purple-naped Lory** *Lorius domicella*

▼ POPULATION: 1,000–2,499 | THREATS: WAT, HUN, EGY, LOG

Endemic to the islands of Seram, Ambon, and perhaps Haruku and Saparua, Indonesia, this parrot, which was uplisted in 2012, has probably always been scarce. It inhabits hill and submontane rainforest within a restricted altitudinal range, most commonly between 600–1,000 m, and appears to be intolerant of habitat degradation. There is a worrying lack of recent records, probably due to ongoing heavy and unsustainable trapping pressure. Habitat loss and degradation due to hydroelectric projects, drilling for oil and commercial logging is an additional threat. A programme of local awareness, focused on conserving the Vulnerable Salmon-crested Cockatoo *Cacatua moluccensis* may also benefit the Purple-naped Lory.

Photo: Rob Hutchinson (birdtourasia.com)

CR **Blue-fronted Lorikeet** *Charmosyna toxopei*

▼ POPULATION: 50–249 | THREATS: AGR, LOG, CLI?

There have been no confirmed records of this parrot, which is endemic to the island of Buru, Indonesia, for many years despite recent searches. However, reports by local people, including of a bird trapped in 1998 and of a *Charmosyna* species seen in plantations in 2006, may relate to this species. Although there has been a significant loss of lowland forest on the island, gardens still contain many indigenous trees, which could potentially support a remnant population. Furthermore, the montane forests are still relatively intact and the island's topography makes these areas inaccessible to loggers. This species is not known from the bird trade. A proposed reserve in the west of the island may help to safeguard this species.

Illustration: Tomasz Cofta

CR **Sumatran Ground-cuckoo** *Carpococcyx viridis*

▼ POPULATION: 50–249 | THREATS: AGR, HUN

This large, little-known cuckoo is endemic to Sumatra, inhabiting primary or undisturbed forest with dense understorey from 300–1,400 m. Unrecorded since 1916, a handful of birds were found in the 1990s, and up to five birds have since been recorded in Bukit Barisan Selatan National Park. Although deforestation is probably the main threat, this terrestrial species is particularly susceptible to being caught in snares set by hunters for other animals. Further surveys, making use of its now-known distinctive, repeated, rising-whistling call are necessary to establish the current population. A number of ecotourism initiatives are underway.

Photo: Nick Brickle

CR **Black-hooded Coucal** *Centropus steerii*

▼ **POPULATION: 50–249** | **THREATS:** AGR, LOG, EGY

Endemic to Mindoro, Philippines, this unobtrusive cuckoo is known from severely fragmented patches of lowland dipterocarp forests up to 760 m, and has only been recorded from three localities since 1980. One of these held five calling birds in 2011. It is restricted to forest interiors, frequenting dense vine-tangles and thick canopy, but the forest is threatened by rattan-collecting, dynamite blasting for marble, selective logging and slash-and-burn cultivation. The species' genetic viability may already be at risk given the small size and fragmented nature of the remaining population. A forest protection scheme aimed at Mindoro Bleeding-heart *Gallicolumba platenae* at one site may also benefit this species.

Photo: Paul Noakes

EN **Taliabu Masked-owl** *Tyto nigrobrunnea*

▼ **POPULATION: 250–999** | **THREATS:** LOG

This poorly known forest owl has only been recorded from the island of Taliabu in the Sula Islands, Indonesia where a bird was collected in 1938. There have been only a handful of recent sightings, including the individual shown here that was photographed in 2009. However, given the difficulty locating this inconspicuous, nocturnal bird, it may also occur on nearby islands. It does appear to be well known to some villagers and recent records suggest it can occupy secondary growth and bamboo thickets in the vicinity of human habitations. Any suitable forest habitat is likely soon to be lost to extensive logging, as most remaining lowland forest on Tailabu is under timber concession.

Photo: Bram Demeulemeester (birdguidingphilippines.com)

EN **Blakiston's Fish-owl** *Ketupa blakistoni* `105`

▼ **POPULATION: 1,000–2,499** | **THREATS:** AGR, LOG, WAT, FISH, MAN, HUN, PLN, DEV, TRA

This huge owl occurs in the coastal mountains of eastern Russia, China and Japan, and probably North Korea. It lives in undisturbed, dense forest using large trees for nesting but, as it hunts for fish by wading through shallow water, also needs to be near water-bodies that do not freeze in winter. Although the widespread loss of riverine forest is a major threat, over-fishing, especially of salmonids, has reduced food availability in Russia and Japan, a factor exacerbated by water pollution. Japanese birds are also subjected to entanglement in nets on fish-farms and collision with powerlines. The Blakiston's Fish-owl Project was initiated in 2005 in Russia, and a range of collaborative projects are either ongoing or planned.

Photo: Roy de Haas (agami.nl)

CR **Forest Owlet** *Heteroglaux blewitti* `26`

▼ **POPULATION: 50–249** | **THREATS:** AGR, FIRE, SPP, LOG, WAT, HUN, DEV, PLN?

Endemic to central India, this small owl was only known from specimens collected in the 19th century until it was rediscovered in 1997. Currently known from fewer than 12 locations, its population is highly fragmented. It is now a sedentary resident of dry deciduous forest but this may be suboptimal habitat as, historically, it was recorded from other forest types. Strongly diurnal, it is easier to detect than many other owl species, and is often seen hunting from bare branches. Threats have yet to be fully assessed but declines are likely to be mainly due to habitat loss and degradation. However, hunting for use of its body parts in traditional customs, and predation by native raptors, are also thought to be contributing factors.

Photo: James Eaton (birdtourasia.com)

137

EN **Serendib Scops-owl** *Otus thilohoffmanni*

▼ **POPULATION: 150–700** | **THREATS:** AGR, LOG, EGY, DEV

Restricted to Sri Lanka, this elusive owl was discovered as recently as 1995 and was formally described in 2004. It is known from just five sites, all of which are within protected areas, although it may also occur in other wet zone forests on the island but remain undetected due to its rather unobtrusive call. It has only been found in disturbed areas with tall, secondary growth in larger blocks (>8·2 km²) of lowland rainforest, suggesting it is particularly sensitive to ongoing habitat loss and fragmentation. It is a nocturnal hunter, foraging in the undergrowth for the first two hours after dark and in higher storeys later in the night. It roosts during the day 1–2·5 m above the ground, sometimes in pairs.

Photo: Adam Riley (rockjumperbirding.com)

EN **Flores Scops-owl** *Otus alfredi*

▼ **POPULATION: 250–2,499** | **THREATS:** AGR, LOG, FIRE, TRA, CLI?

This little-known owl is endemic to the island of Flores, Indonesia, where it is only known from two tiny areas of forest in the western mountains. Originally collected in 1896, it was not recorded again until 1994, and its vocalizations were not described until 2005. It is presumed resident but may make altitudinal movements. Birds have recently been recorded in the newly established Ruteng Nature Recreation Park, where it is hoped active management will benefit this species. Local reports suggest it may also still occur in degraded forest on Gunung Repok, where it was first collected. Continuing habitat loss and degradation is the main threat.

Photo: James Eaton (birdtourasia.com)

CR **Siau Scops-owl** *Otus siaoensis*

? **POPULATION: <50** | **THREATS:** AGR?, LOG?

Endemic to the island of Siau, Indonesia, this owl was formerly considered conspecific with Moluccan Scops-owl *O. magicus*. The type specimen was collected in 1866 but it was not recognised as a species until 1998, and subsequent surveys have failed to confirm whether it is still extant. It is assumed to be a forest owl but very little forest remains on the island and rapid deforestation continues. The size of Siau suggests the population would never have been high. However, local people continue to report observations of this species, giving hope that it might still survive in degraded habitats.

Illustration: Tomasz Cofta

EN **Biak Scops-owl** *Otus beccarii*

▼ **POPULATION: 2,500–9,999** | **THREATS:** AGR, LOG

Found only on the twin islands of Biak-Supiori, Indonesia, this little-known owl is thought to be restricted to tall, lowland forest, including coastal swamp-forest. As it is nocturnal, and there are no recordings of its vocalizations, undertaking surveys is difficult. The current status of this species therefore remains uncertain. Although much of the forest on Biak has been lost or is under severe pressure, recent records suggest this owl may tolerate forest remnants. Much of Supiori is virtually impenetrable forested limestone mountains, potentially affording this species a safe refuge.

Illustration: Tomasz Cofta

EN **Javan Trogon** *Apalharpactes reinwardtii*

▼ **POPULATION: 250–999** | **THREATS:** AGR, DEV

Historically known from just six mountains in West Java, Indonesia, this colourful trogon has recently only been recorded from three of these, with the majority of the population thought to occur in the Gunung Halimun and Gunung Gede-Pangrango National Parks. It favours mid-montane forest from 800–2,600 m, feeding mainly on invertebrates taken by aerial sallying or by perch-gleaning, but sometimes takes fruit. It occasionally joins mixed-species flocks. Habitat loss and fragmentation remain significant threats, primarily due to agricultural encroachment, but tourism and development pressures are increasingly having an impact within this species' limited altitudinal range.

Photo: János Oláh (birdquest-tours.com)

EN **Kofiau Paradise-kingfisher** *Tanysiptera ellioti*

▼ **POPULATION: 250–999** | **THREATS:** AGR, LOG, CLI?

This little-known woodland kingfisher is endemic to the 144 km² island of Kofiau in the West Papuan islands, Indonesia. It is most commonly found in closed-canopy and secondary forests but also occurs in other habitats, including traditional gardens. It perches up to 12 m above the ground, probably feeding by dropping onto insects and other invertebrates, but is not thought to venture into the canopy. In 2009 it was described as abundant in suitable habitat. However, the population is thought to be in decline due to the impact of slash-and-burn agriculture and selective logging. There is no protected area on the island, and a further, comprehensive conservation assessment is needed.

Photos: K. David Bishop and Papua Expeditions/cv.Ekonexion [inset]

CR **Okinawa Woodpecker** *Dendrocopos noguchii*

▼ **POPULATION: 100–390** | **THREATS:** CLI, MAN, SPP, AGR, WAT, LOG, DEV, TRA

Endemic to Okinawa, Japan, where it is confined to one district, this medium-sized woodpecker was thought to be close to extinction in the 1930s. It mainly inhabits subtropical evergreen forest on mountain ridges, requiring large dead and decaying trees for breeding and foraging, but can also be found in coastal forest. It breeds from February to May and females and males have different foraging niches. As its range has become increasingly restricted due to the loss of mature forest to logging and development, it has become more vulnerable to disease and natural chance events such as typhoons; predators are also a significant threat. Many areas in which this species occurs are now protected.

Female. Photo: Ambrosini

EN **Gurney's Pitta** *Pitta gurneyi* `105`

▼ **POPULATION: 10,000–17,200** | **THREATS:** AGR, HUN, LOG, MAN, SPP

Previously restricted to peninsular Thailand, this beautiful pitta was downlisted from Critically Endangered to Endangered following the discovery of a population in southern Myanmar in 2003. It occupies low-lying, secondary, semi-evergreen forest, where it forages for invertebrates in the leaf-litter. Forest clearance for agriculture and commercial plantations is occurring rapidly and, at the current rate, all suitable habitat may soon be lost. In Thailand, trapping for the cagebird trade and predation by snakes are also serious threats. Should the Thai population fall below five pairs, contingency measures are in place that would involve captive breeding and supplementary feeding.

Photo: Kanit Khanikul

CR **Sulu Hornbill** *Anthracoceros montani* `115`

▼ **POPULATION: 27** | **THREATS: LOG**, HUN, AGR?, CLI?, DEV?

Once endemic to three islands in the Sulu Archipelago, Philippines, this hornbill is now thought to exist only on Tawi-Tawi, where it faces imminent extinction. Although probably once widespread and common, it is now only found in dipterocarp forest on rugged mountain slopes where enough large trees survive to provide adequately sized nest holes. The archipelago has been subject to decades of forest clearance for rubber and oil palm plantations. Environmental laws are poorly enforced, and hunting (not just for food but also for target practice) and trapping are widespread. Military activity and insurgency also continue to present a serious obstacle to general conservation activity in the area.

Photo: Rob Hutchinson (birdtourasia.com)

EN **Mindoro Hornbill** *Penelopides mindorensis* `114`

▼ **POPULATION: 250–999** | **THREATS:** HUN, LOG, AGR, EGY, (CLI)

This small hornbill is endemic to the island of Mindoro, Philippines, where it is found in the few remaining, fragmented patches of lowland primary forest, forest edge, secondary growth and isolated woodlots, as well as in fruiting trees in cultivated areas. However, large trees in remnant patches of closed-canopy forest are probably crucial as nest sites. A rapid population decline since the 1970s, primarily due to habitat loss and hunting, was exacerbated by major floods in 1993 that destroyed many nest trees. The species has been recorded from only 17 locations in the last 20 years. However, a range of conservation initiatives are now in place.

Photo: Bram Demeulemeester (birdguidingphilippines.com)

EN **Visayan Hornbill** *Penelopides panini* `114`

▼ **POPULATION: 1,200** | **THREATS:** HUN, AGR, (LOG)

Endemic to the Philippines, two subspecies of this small hornbill are recognised. The nominate occurs in the central mountains of Panay, where it is still fairly common, and on a few offshore islands where it is either rare or extirpated; *ticaensis*, which occurred on Ticao, is extinct. It inhabits primary, evergreen and dipterocarp forest up to 1,100 m sometimes wandering to secondary forest or isolated fruiting trees. Although deforestation and hunting and trapping are still significant threats, a wide range of conservation initiatives are being implemented including captive breeding and reintroduction, the use of artificial nest boxes, and community-based awareness raising.

Photo: Tim Laman (timlaman.com)

CR **Rufous-headed Hornbill** *Aceros waldeni* `115`

▼ **POPULATION: 1,000–2,499** | **THREATS:** HUN, AGR, LOG

Historically, this spectacular hornbill is thought to have occurred only on the islands of Panay, Negros and Guimaras in the Philippines, but only Panay now holds a viable population. It inhabits severely fragmented areas of closed-canopy, low- to mid-altitude forests and occasionally logged areas, and may make local nomadic movements in response to food availability. Large trees are crucial as nest sites. Widescale habitat loss and hunting, either for human consumption or the bird trade, are significant threats. Effective conservation measures on Panay, including a community-based nest-wardening scheme, offer hope that declines can continue to be reversed. Captive breeding is taking place and reintroduction to Negros is planned.

Photo: Tim Laman (timlaman.com)

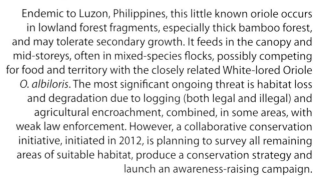

CR **Isabela Oriole** *Oriolus isabellae*

▼ POPULATION: **50–249** | THREATS: LOG, AGR, CLI?

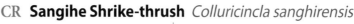

Endemic to Luzon, Philippines, this little known oriole occurs in lowland forest fragments, especially thick bamboo forest, and may tolerate secondary growth. It feeds in the canopy and mid-storeys, often in mixed-species flocks, possibly competing for food and territory with the closely related White-lored Oriole *O. albiloris*. The most significant ongoing threat is habitat loss and degradation due to logging (both legal and illegal) and agricultural encroachment, combined, in some areas, with weak law enforcement. However, a collaborative conservation initiative, initiated in 2012, is planning to survey all remaining areas of suitable habitat, produce a conservation strategy and launch an awareness-raising campaign.

Photo: Wouter Thijs

CR **Sangihe Shrike-thrush** *Colluricincla sanghirensis*

▼ POPULATION: **50–249** | THREATS: AGR, LOG, CLI?

Known from only one locality on the island of Sangihe, Indonesia, this species was rediscovered in 1995, a century after being first documented. A resident of montane forest between 600–750 m on the mountains Gunung Sahendaruman and Gunung Sahengbalira, the tiny population continues to dwindle at an alarming rate due to the loss of forest to agriculture and government initiatives to plant non-native tree species at altitudes of up to 900 m. It may also be susceptible to climate change. Over the years, a number of local initiatives aimed at promoting sympathetic land-use and raising awareness of the threats to this species have been initiated but, so far, these have had limited success.

Photo: Jon Riley

EN **Tablas Drongo** *Dicrurus menagei*

▼ POPULATION: **50–249** | THREATS: AGR, LOG

Only recently split from Hair-crested Drongo *D. hottentottus*, this drongo is only found on the island of Tablas, Philippines. It inhabits severely fragmented remnants of relatively mature closed-canopy forest and forest edge, often near streams. Very little suitable habitat is left, most of the forest having been cleared for agricultural use. It is likely that small-scale logging remains a threat and the population may now be confined to just one forest block that has no formal protection. Conservation action is urgently needed and any further reduction in the area of habitat is likely to qualify this species for uplisting to Critically Endangered.

Photo: Des Allen

CR **Cerulean Paradise-flycatcher** *Eutrichomyias rowleyi*

▼ POPULATION: **13–90** | THREATS: AGR, HUN, LOG, CLI?, (DEV)

Endemic to the island of Sangihe, Indonesia, this unmistakable flycatcher favours steep-sided valley slopes in primary montane forest. Only a fragment of suitable habitat remains and there were no records for over a century until a tiny population was found in 1998. Loss of forest to agriculture and government initiatives to plant non-native tree species are significant threats. Over the years, a number of local initiatives aimed at promoting sympathetic land-use and raising awareness of the threats to forest birds have been initiated but, so far, have had limited success. However, there is now a small bird tourism industry on the island that, it is hoped, will provide economic incentives to residents to conserve the remaining forest.

Photo: Jon Riley

EN **Flores Monarch** *Monarcha sacerdotum*

▼ **POPULATION:** 2,500–9,999 | **THREATS:** AGR, FIRE, TRA, LOG, DEV, CLI?

Found only on the western half of the island of Flores, Nusa Tenggara, Indonesia, this flycatcher appears to be extremely local and largely uncommon. It mostly inhabits primary semi-evergreen rainforest from 350–1,000 m, but also occurs in deciduous monsoon forest and may tolerate some limited habitat degradation. Although mainly feeding at around 20 m in the sub-canopy, it has been noted hunting nearer the forest floor, occasionally in mixed-species flocks. Although recent records suggest a northward range extension, the extent of native forest continues to decline at an alarming rate. One key site is proposed for establishment as a protected area.

Photo: James Eaton (birdtourasia.com)

EN **White-tipped** (or Tanahjampea) **Monarch** *Monarcha everetti*

▼ **POPULATION:** 600–1,700 | **THREATS:** LOG, DEV

108

Endemic to the comparatively well-forested island of Tanahjampea in the Flores Sea, Indonesia, this little-known flycatcher was considered still fairly common during a brief survey in 1993, when between two and four individuals were seen together, and it was regularly observed associating with mixed foraging flocks. The main threat is probably loss of forest to agriculture and logging (for house and boat construction), although it may tolerate some degree of habitat degradation. Both adults and juveniles were seen in rattan shrubbery in 2011 and subsequently photographed (shown here). As far as is known, no conservation actions have been taken.

Photo: Rob Hutchinson (birdtourasia.com)

CR **Black-chinned Monarch** *Monarcha boanensis*

▼ **POPULATION:** 70–130 | **THREATS:** AGR, LOG

Confined to the island of Boana, off north-west Seram, South Maluku, Indonesia, this small flycatcher was believed to be restricted to forests in the higher parts of the island (150–700 m). However, recent observations have come from forests at lower elevations. After its discovery in 1918, it was not recorded again until 1991. The first record since 1994 came in 2011 when about 30 individuals were located and the first photographs taken (shown here). Forest loss has been reported to be decimating the ecology of this small island and ongoing population declines are likely. It is possible that the neighbouring islands of Kelang and Manipa may also support this species.

Photo: James Eaton (birdtourasia.com)

EN **Biak Monarch** *Monarcha brehmii*

▼ **POPULATION:** 2,500–9,999 | **THREATS:** AGR, LOG

This attractive monarch is endemic to the twin-islands of Biak-Supiori in Geelvink Bay, Papua (formerly Irian Jaya), Indonesia. The varying amount of yellow on the head could be related to sex or age. The very few observations have come from lowland forest, but suitable habitat is severely fragmented and declining rapidly due to logging and clearance for agriculture. However, although Biak is subject to rapid development, Supiori is far more impenetrable and may support important populations of this species. There are two protected areas on the islands but no comprehensive survey of the birds has been carried out for some years. However, the opportunities for such studies are increasing as Biak becomes more accessible.

Photo: Mikael Bauer

CR **Javan Green Magpie** *Cissa thalassina*

▼ **POPULATION: 50–249** | **THREATS:** AGR, HUN, LOG, EGY

Only recently split from Bornean Green Magpie *C. jefferyi*, this species is endemic to western Java, Indonesia. There have been very few records this century and it may only be extant in four protected areas. It usually inhabits forests from 500–2,000 m, but sometimes ranges into adjacent cultivated areas. Remaining populations are highly fragmented and recent rapid declines are likely to continue due to ongoing trapping for the cagebird trade and the loss and degradation of suitable habitat, even within protected areas. Research and informed conservation actions are urgently needed to increase the chances of this species' survival.

Illustration: Tomasz Cofta

CR **Banggai Crow** *Corvus unicolor* 29

▼ **POPULATION: 50–249** | **THREATS:** AGR, LOG, EGY?, SPP?, (HUN)

Endemic to the Banggai Archipelago, Sulawesi, Indonesia, this crow was only known from specimens taken in 1884 until it was rediscovered on the largest island, Peleng, early this century. Although little studied, it has been found in mosaics of forest remnants and cultivations, and is thought to maintain group territories and have extensive home ranges. Habitat loss due to logging and the conversion of forest to agriculture remains the greatest threat. More recent concerns include potential mining concessions and competition with Slender-billed Crow *C. enca*. Local initiatives have resulted in an awareness campaign and the promotion of sustainable agriculture. Unknown populations may still occur in remote, montane forests.

Photo: Filip Verbelen

EN **Flores Crow** *Corvus florensis*

▼ **POPULATION: 600–1,700** | **THREATS:** AGR, SPP, LOG

Endemic to the islands of Flores and Rinca, Nusa Tenggara, Indonesia, this small crow is known chiefly from the western half of Flores. It inhabits forests from sea level to 950 m, especially along watercourses. Although it will sometimes feed in degraded habitats, it has not adapted well to forest fragmentation. The pressure of brood parasitism by cuckoos (Asian Koel *Eudynamys scolopaceus* and less frequently Channel-billed Cuckoo *Scythrops novaehollandiae*) and cuckooshrikes may exacerbate the ongoing threat of rapid habitat loss as forests are converted for small-scale agriculture. It occurs in two protected areas but further ecological studies are required.

Photo: James Eaton (birdtourasia.com)

CR **White-eyed River-martin** *Eurochelidon sirintarae*

▼ **POPULATION: <50** | **THREATS:** HUN, AGR?, WAT?, MAN?

One of the most enigmatic species in South-East Asia, White-eyed River-martin was first known from 12 specimens collected in Thailand in 1968 from amongst roosts of wintering hirundines. It has not been recorded with certainty since 1978, despite recent surveys, although there have been two unconfirmed reports up to 1986. Unconfirmed reports have also come from Cambodia and Myanmar, indicating that there may be another refuge for any remaining birds. Virtually nothing is known about its ecology but it could be nocturnal, as suggested by its large eyes, and it may not be associated with rivers. Should any birds remain extant, intensive trapping of hirundines for food and habitat destruction at roost sites would be severe threats.

Photo: H. E. Mclure

EN Streak-breasted Bulbul *Ixos siquijorensis*

`30`

▼ **POPULATION:** 2,500–9,999 | **THREATS: LOG**, AGR, SPP?

This little known but vociferous bulbul occurs in three subspecific populations on four widely separated islands in the Philippines: *monticola* on Cebu, *cinereiceps* on Tablas and Romblom and the nominate on Siquijor. It lives in forest, forest edge and secondary growth and tolerates degraded habitats, although at lower densities, and only when adjacent to forest. Population declines are primarily due to continuing rapid habitat loss through logging and conversion to agriculture throughout the species' range, but competition from other species of bulbul is also likely to be a contributing factor. Although a few populations occur in areas that have some level of protection, habitat deterioration remains an issue.

Photo: Leif Jonasson

EN Negros Striped-babbler *Stachyris nigrorum*

▼ **POPULATION:** 600–1,700 | **THREATS:** AGR, LOG, CLI?

Found only on the island of Negros, Philippines, this small babbler inhabits tiny fragments of montane forest and associated areas of degraded habitat at between 950–1,600 m. It usually forages in small parties in the understorey for small fruits and insects, sometimes associating with mixed-species flocks and giving a high-pitched call. Stricter implementation of existing laws governing forest destruction may help protect this species but, despite recent conservation initiatives, its population is thought to still be in decline and it may soon qualify for uplisting to Critically Endangered. Near one of its key sites, logging now extends to a higher altitude (1,250 m) than anywhere else on Negros.

Photo: Apolinario B. Cariño

EN Flame-templed Babbler *Dasycrotapha speciosa*

`106`

▼ **POPULATION:** 2,500–9,999 | **THREATS:** AGR, LOG

Endemic to the islands of Negros and Panay in the Philippines, this colourful but unobtrusive babbler prefers thick undergrowth in forests from sea level up to 1,000 m, with highest densities recorded from degraded secondary growth. It occurs in mixed-species feeding flocks, foraging for insects at low levels. Breeding has been recorded from December to August. It is estimated that only 10% of the little forest that remains on Negros and Panay lies within the altitude range favoured by this species and unrelenting habitat clearance could lead to its demise in the near future. Although it occurs in two protected areas, their protection is only nominal and effective conservation measures are urgently needed.

Photo: Ivan Sarenas

EN White-throated Wren-babbler *Rimator pasquieri*

▼ **POPULATION:** Unknown | **THREATS:** AGR, WAT, TRA

Restricted to a tiny area in the Hoang Lien Mountains, northern Vietnam, this little-known, rarely seen species has only been found in montane and submontane forests at 1,200–2,500 m, where it seems to favour areas of dense undergrowth dominated by dwarf bamboo of the genus *Arundinaria*. Habitat loss and degradation is largely being driven by a rapid increase in the cultivation of cardamom, which involves the removal of forest undergrowth. The undisturbed habitat this species requires is now almost impossible to find. Major infrastructure projects are also likely to lead to large-scale habitat loss. The species was uplisted from Least Concern to Endangered in 2011.

Photo: Luu Thi Thanh Lan / Vietnam Birding

CR **Blue-crowned Laughingthrush** *Garrulax courtoisi*

▼ **POPULATION: 50–249** | **THREATS:** HUN, TRA, DEV

Breeding at just six localities in Jiangxi province, China, the wintering sites of this migratory laughingthrush are unknown. It forages in vocal groups and nests in May and June in trees adjacent to human habitation and near rivers. Not recorded for almost 50 years, it was only found in the wild in 2000 after birds were discovered in captivity in Europe. Historically, trapping for the bird trade was a major cause of decline but habitat loss due to development pressures is becoming a more significant threat. A conservation action plan is in place, education work is ongoing and some small protected areas have been established. Around 170 individuals are also being maintained in captivity.

Photo: H. E. Shu-hui (52pp.com)

EN **Collared Laughingthrush** *Garrulax yersini*

▼ **POPULATION: 2,500–9,999** | **THREATS:** LOG, AGR, HUN, CLI?

A resident of the Da Lat Plateau, in Vietnam's Western Highlands, this striking laughingthrush inhabits dense montane forest undergrowth at 1,500–2,400 m. It is known from eleven severely fragmented localities but has only been recorded from eight of these recently; however, its true status is poorly known due to a lack of data. It is highly social, regularly occurring in small flocks, but is often only revealed by its characteristically loud song. The already fragmented populations are under increasing pressure due to a government resettlement programme that has resulted in further habitat degradation. This species has also been reported as being available in the illegal domestic bird trade.

Photo: Hung Le Manh

EN **Black-chinned Laughingthrush** *Strophocincla cachinnans*

▼ **POPULATION: 2,500–9,999** | **THREATS:** AGR, WAT, DEV, CLI?, PLN?

Endemic to montane areas in north-west Tamil Nadu, north-east Kerala and south-west Karnataka, southern India this sedentary laughingthrush has two subspecies: the nominate and *jerdoni*. It inhabits areas of severely fragmented, dense forest undergrowth generally above 1,600 m, sometimes visiting gardens, but avoiding commercial plantations. Populations have declined as forests are lost to plantations, agriculture and settlements and the indiscriminate use of inorganic pesticides may also be a threat. Small parts of its range already have some degree of formal protection, but widescale habitat restoration and awareness raising are key to the future of this species.

Photo: Ramki Sreenivasan (wildventures.com) / Conservation India

EN **Grey-crowned Crocias** *Crocias langbianis*

▼ **POPULATION: 1,500–7,000** | **THREATS:** AGR, WAT, FIRE, LOG, TRA, CLI?

Long thought to be restricted to the Da Lat Plateau, Vietnam, this babbler occurs in tropical montane evergreen forest at 900–1,700 m. First found in 1939, there were no further sightings until 1994. Since then it has been located with increasing frequency and, in 2012, two pairs were discovered at a new location 300 km to the north in Kom Tun Province. It is arboreal, feeding mainly on caterpillars, and sometimes accompanying mixed-species flocks. A government resettlement programme on Da Lat puts extra pressure on already fragmented forests, with conversion to agriculture, firewood collection, logging and charcoal production being the main threats at all the known sites.

Photo: Luyen Nguyen

CR Sangihe White-eye *Zosterops nehrkorni*

▼ **POPULATION:** <50 | **THREATS:** AGR, LOG, CLI?, SPP?

Endemic to the island of Sangihe, Indonesia, this white-eye may survive at only one locality. It inhabits the mid-storey to upper canopy of primary broadleaved ridge-top forest at 750–1,000 m, of which just 8 km² remains. Although discovered in the late 19th century it was not seen again until 1996. The last record was in 1999, when only four birds were found during five months of searching. Virtually the whole island has been cleared of forest and converted to agriculture. A number of local initiatives aimed at promoting sympathetic land-use and raising awareness of the threats to this species have been initiated but, so far, have had limited success.

Illustration: Tomasz Cofta

EN Rufous-throated White-eye *Madanga ruficollis*

▼ **POPULATION:** 2,500–9,999 | **THREATS:** AGR, LOG, DEV, CLI?

Endemic to the island of Buru in South Maluku, Indonesia, this montane species is only known from four specimens collected prior to 1920 and a few recent field observations. Little is known about its ecology but it has been observed following mixed-species feeding flocks and foraging along tree trunks in the manner of nuthatches, and it is believed to take invertebrates. Although the area of suitable habitat is thought to remain largely undisturbed, some habitat degradation is likely to be occurring, particularly at lower altitudes. Accurate information on the species' population status is lacking but current evidence suggests that it is either highly elusive, very localized, or occurs at low densities.

Photo: Rob Hutchinson (birdtourasia.com)

EN White-browed Nuthatch *Sitta victoriae*

▼ **POPULATION:** 2,500–9,999 | **THREATS:** AGR, LOG, CLI?

Only known from the southern Chin Hills, Myanmar, this dainty nuthatch favours *Quercus semicarpifolia* and *Rhododendron arboreum* forests at 2,300–3,000 m. It feeds in mixed-species flocks, usually gleaning food from outer branches. It breeds in March/April, making a cavity nest, but does not use mud to modify the entrance hole as do other nuthatches. Although much of its range falls within Natma Taung National Park, it is unclear how effective this protection is likely to become. Extensive habitat loss and degradation has occurred at lower altitudes, and slash-and-burn clearance for agriculture is still a major threat.

Photo: John & Jemi Holmes (johnjemi.hk)

EN Sri Lanka Whistling-thrush *Myophonus blighi*

▼ **POPULATION:** 600–1,700 | **THREATS:** AGR, EGY, MAN, LOG, PLN, CLI?

This secretive, terrestrial bird is confined to a few severely fragmented areas of dense forest above 900 m in the central mountains of Sri Lanka. It is usually found close to streams, especially in gorges and ravines, where it nests on rocky ledges next to waterfalls or rapids, or in the forks of trees. Although this species, and some areas in which it occurs, are legally protected, its habitat continues to be lost and degraded due to conversion to agriculture and plantations, the collection of firewood and water pollution. Food supplies have also been affected as indigenous trees have been replaced with monoculture plantations. Gem mining is also a serious threat.

Male on left; female on right. Photos [digital merge]: Gehan de Silva Wijeyeratne

CR **Bali Starling** *Leucopsar rothschildi*

▼ POPULATION: <50 | THREATS: **HUN**, SPP?, (AGR)

Endemic to the island of Bali, Indonesia, this large starling has become virtually extinct in the wild, primarily due to illegal exploitation for the cagebird trade. This problem is ongoing and is compounded by loss of this species' preferred lowland savanna and forest habitats. The wild population has been maintained only by the release of captive birds in West Bali National Park and on the nearby island of Nusa Penida; both populations are breeding and apparently increasing. A Bali Starling Recovery Plan is in place, although the value of the birds is so high that one of the breeding centres has even been robbed of starlings at gunpoint.

Photo: Gregory Guida (gguida.com)

CR **Black-winged Starling** *Sturnus melanopterus*

▼ POPULATION: 600–1,700 | THREATS: HUN, PLN?

Uplisted to Critically Endangered in 2010, this starling is endemic to the islands of Bali and Java, Indonesia, but has occasionally been found on adjacent islands. It occurs in a variety of habitats but is chiefly found in agricultural and grazed areas in the extreme lowlands. Although nominally legally protected, it has been one of Java's most popular cagebirds. However, its current rarity in the trade suggests that the level of exploitation has been unsustainable. Excessive use of pesticides in its foraging areas and loss of genetic integrity as a result of birds from different subspecies mixing after escaping from captivity, may also be significant issues. Surveys are urgently required to obtain an accurate assessment of the global population.

Photo [captive]: Adam Riley (rockjumperbirding.com)

EN **Nilgiri Blue Robin** *Myiomela major*

▼ POPULATION: Unknown | THREATS: AGR, LOG, WAT, DEV, TRA, CLI?

The range of this chat-like flycatcher is restricted to just a few isolated hills, typically at altitudes of between 900–1,500 m, in the states of Kerala and Karnataka in the Western Ghats, southern India. It is a secretive ground-feeder that forages in the dense undergrowth of sheltered woods. Habitat destruction and degradation, particularly for agriculture, plantations and forest products, and infrastructure projects continue to be major threats. As it also lives close to the maximum altitude within its range, it may be susceptible to the effects of climate change. Some populations occur in protected areas and efforts are being made to restore natural habitats in some parts of its range.

Photo: Clement Francis Martin (clementfrancis.com)

EN **White-bellied Blue Robin** *Myiomela albiventris*

▼ POPULATION: Unknown | THREATS: AGR, LOG, WAT, DEV, TRA, CLI?

This chat-like flycatcher is found only on a few isolated mountain-tops across the states of Kerala and Tamil Nadu in southern India. It occurs between 1,000–2,200 m, favouring wet undergrowth, often along streams, in forested areas, but has also been recorded in gardens and plantations. Although sedentary, it may make some altitudinal movements. Habitat destruction and degradation for agriculture and forestry, and infrastructure development are the major threats. Since it lives close to the maximum altitude within its range, it may also be susceptible to the effects of climate change. Although some populations occur in protected areas, comprehensive population studies are urgently needed.

Photo: Vivek Tiwari (flickr.com/photos/spiderhunters)

EN **Black Shama** *Copsychus cebuensis*

▼ **POPULATION: 670–3,300** | **THREATS:** AGR, EGY, MAN, LOG, DEV

This distinctive chat is endemic to the island of Cebu, Philippines, where it favours primary forest and dense undergrowth in secondary habitats, but has also recently been recorded from urban areas. It is a secretive bird and its ability to mimic the calls of other species makes census work particularly difficult. However, recent surveys have shown it to be more widespread than previously believed and breeding territories are now known to cover 0·2–0·5 km². Very little forest remains on Cebu, and the few remnants are being continually degraded. However, a range of local conservation projects has been initiated, including the development of an action plan, giving hope for the future of this species.

Photo: Raul Benjamin Puentespina

EN **White-throated Jungle-flycatcher** *Rhinomyias albigularis*

▼ **POPULATION: 2,500–9,999** | **THREATS:** AGR, LOG

This secretive flycatcher is endemic to the islands of Negros, Guimaras and Panay, Philippines. It is presumed extinct from Guimaras, where the last record was in 1887, but is probably under-recorded on Panay. It inhabits shady, primary montane forests, mostly at or below 950 m but occasionally up to 1,350 m. It forages for invertebrates in the lower levels of the forest and along forest edges, and has also been recorded in secondary growth. Little suitable habitat remains and ongoing forest loss is a major threat. Encouragingly, this species has recently been discovered at new sites but better protection of existing forest reserves and the formal protection of other key sites is crucial if its future is to be secured.

Photo: Jon Hornbuckle

EN **Lompobatang Flycatcher** *Ficedula bonthaina*

▼ **POPULATION: 2,500–9,999** | **THREATS:** AGR, LOG, DEV, CLI?

This tiny, unobtrusive flycatcher is only known from one population on the Lompobatang massif at the southern tip of Sulawesi. Although apparently common until the 1930s, there have been few subsequent records and it was not photographed until 2010. Recent observations were in dense, heavily shaded understorey in disturbed montane forest, above 1,100 m. Very little is known about its ecology or behaviour, but birds have been seen making very low, short sorties to the ground and amongst vegetation. Habitat loss has been severe within the known range of this species, and forest that remains at higher elevations continues to be threatened by human activities.

Photo: Mikael Bauer

EN **Matinan Flycatcher** *Cyornis sanfordi*

▼ **POPULATION: 6,000–15,000** | **THREATS:** AGR, DEV, LOG, CLI?

Endemic to northern Sulawesi, Indonesia, this drab flycatcher is a presumed resident of primary lower and upper montane rainforest and moss forest above 1,400 m, but may make local altitudinal movements. It is little studied but thought to have similar habits to Blue-fronted Flycatcher *C. hoevelli*, which occurs in southern Sulawesi. Population declines are suspected to be taking place due to rapid habitat loss within the lower altitudes of its range as a result of shifting agriculture and transmigration settlements. An increase in logging concessions is also a potential threat as a consequence of changes to laws in 2000 which gave regional governments the power to determine how resources can be exploited.

Photo: Filip Verbelen

CR **Rueck's Blue-flycatcher** *Cyornis ruckii*

? POPULATION: <50 | THREATS: AGR, LOG

Thought to be endemic to the lowlands of northern Sumatra, this beautiful flycatcher is only known from two specimens collected there in 1917 and 1918. Although no forest remains in the vicinity of where it was collected, it cannot be categorized as Extinct because apparently suitable habitat in Sumatra has been relatively poorly surveyed. The specimens were collected in 'exploited forest', which suggests the species may be tolerant of some degree of habitat degradation. Although recent searches have failed to relocate this species, since the specimens were taken in January and April, there is a small chance that it is a migratory bird that winters on or passes through the island.

Illustration: Tomasz Cofta

CR **Cebu Flowerpecker** *Dicaeum quadricolor* `18`

▼ POPULATION: 60–70 | THREATS: AGR, EGY, LOG, DEV, TRA, SPP?

Endemic to the island of Cebu, Philippines, this flowerpecker was only rediscovered in 1992, having been thought extinct since early in the 20th century. It is now known from just five tiny areas, although no more than four birds have ever been seen together. It was once regarded as a strictly forest species but has been found foraging in adjacent selectively logged areas and secondary forest. Although the little forest that remains is difficult to cultivate, it is still threatened by a range of factors. Competition for habitat with Red-striped Flowerpecker *D. australe* may also be a threat. A range of conservation initiatives are being implemented, including habitat rehabilitation, and research is being undertaken into the species' ecology.

Illustration: Tomasz Cofta

EN **Elegant Sunbird** *Aethopyga duyvenbodei* `109`

▼ POPULATION: 13,000–29,000 | THREATS: AGR, LOG

Known only from the island of Sangihe, Indonesia (and an historical record from nearby Siau), this large sunbird is a resident of primary forest and isolated areas of secondary habitat, up to 1,000 m. Its ecology is little known but it is often found in mixed-species flocks, feeding on insects and nectar. Sangihe's primary forest has been almost completely cleared, and although this species appears to tolerate secondary habitats, these areas are also being lost to agricultural intensification. A number of local initiatives aimed at promoting sympathetic land-use and raising awareness of the threats to this species have been initiated but, so far, have had limited success.

Photo: Marc Thibault

EN **Rufous-backed** (or Jankowski's) **Bunting** *Emberiza jankowskii*

▼ POPULATION: 250–999 | THREATS: AGR, WAT, MAN, SPP?, (FIRE), (DEV)

Now breeding only in south-east China and the extreme north-east of North Korea, having disappeared from Russia, this bunting disperses short distances south and west outside the breeding season. It is declining rapidly, primarily due to conversion of its preferred grassland habitat for agriculture and forestry. Unless additional stable populations are discovered it may soon qualify for uplisting to Critically Endangered. Suitable habitat is likely to remain in Russia, and probably North Korea, but is threatened by the Tumangan Project, which aims to increase regional economic development. Surveys are urgently required to determine the species' status and underpin the promotion of favourable management practices.

Photo: Martin Hale (martinhalewildlifephoto.com)

Australasia

Critically Endangered **Kakapo** *Strigops habroptila*. Photo: Shane McInnes.

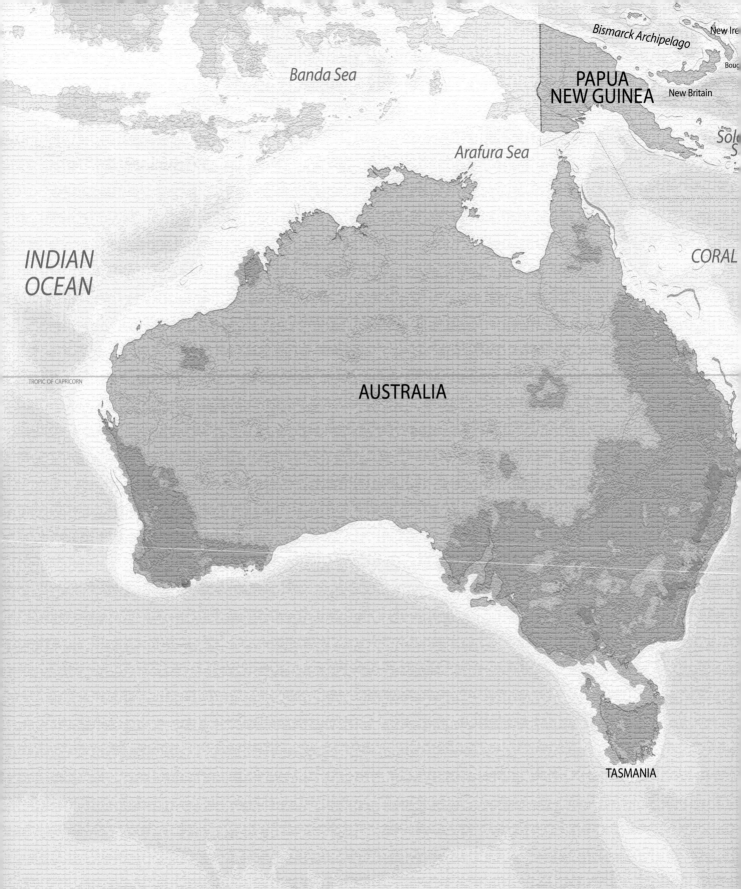

INDIAN
OCEAN

Banda Sea

Arafura Sea

PAPUA
NEW GUINEA

Bismarck Archipelago

New Ire

Boug

New Britain

Sol
S

CORAL

TROPIC OF CAPRICORN

AUSTRALIA

TASMANIA

**The distribution of Endangered and
Critically Endangered species**

1–4 species

5+ species

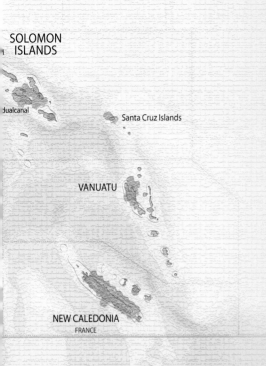

SOLOMON
ISLANDS

Guadalcanal

Santa Cruz Islands

VANUATU

NEW CALEDONIA
FRANCE

Australasia

In the context of this book the Australasian region extends from the tropics to the subantarctic and includes Australia, Tasmania, New Zealand, Papua New Guinea, and neighbouring islands and island groups such as Norfolk Island, Lord Howe Island, New Caledonia, the Bismarck Archipelago (including New Britain and New Ireland) and the Solomon Islands and Vanuatu, as well as the southern oceanic islands as far south as Macquarie Island. The north-western boundary of the region runs down the middle of the island of New Guinea (the western half, Papua, which is part of Indonesia, is covered in the Asia section (*page 100*)). The total land area of Australasia is approximately 8·4 million square kilometres (3·2 million square miles).

For the other continents, birds endemic to their associated oceanic islands are included in the Oceanic Islands section (*page 180*). However, this approach has not been followed with Australasia principally due to the geography of the region. The only the exception is Christmas Island, which is covered in the Oceanic Islands section.

Many individual islands and island groups are Endemic Bird Areas or Secondary Areas. Among the 40 such areas that BirdLife has identified in Australasia are New Zealand's North and South Islands (five and seven endemic species respectively), and Tasmania (15 species). While mainland Australia has five EBAs (plus a number of secondary areas where one endemic species is found), mainland Papua New Guinea has seven.

Of the 1,326 species that have been recorded in Australasia and its oceanic islands, 165 – over 12% – are globally threatened, with 67 species (5% of the total) either Endangered or Critically Endangered.

PACIFIC OCEAN

Norfolk Island
AUSTRALIA

Lord Howe Island
AUSTRALIA

BirdLife INTERNATIONAL	**BirdLife Partners**
Australia	BirdLife Australia
New Caledonia	Société Calédonienne d'Ornithologie (SCO)
New Zealand	Forest & Bird

North Island

NEW ZEALAND

SMAN SEA

South Island

CHATHAM ISLANDS
NEW ZEALAND

Chatham Island   Pitt Island

Stewart Island

Bounty Islands
NEW ZEALAND

Antipodes Islands
NEW ZEALAND

Auckland Islands
NEW ZEALAND

Campbell Island
NEW ZEALAND

Macquarie Island AUSTRALIA

Australasia has a dreadful record of bird extinctions, with 28 known in historical times which of course excludes previous catastrophes like the extermination of at least nine species of moa from New Zealand, and with them their only predator before the arrival of humans, the gigantic Haast's Eagle). Two island species of emu were hunted to extinction by settlers in the early 19th century, and a suite of rails, quails, doves, parrots, gallinules, ducks and thrushes, many of them flightless (including the Stephens Island Wren *Traversia lyalli*), and all of them fearless of humans, were eradicated by settlers and the cats, rats and pigs they brought with them.

Of 1,326 extant Australasian bird species, 95 are Near Threatened and 165 threatened, including 50 Endangered and 17 Critically Endangered. A further 15 are Data Deficient.

Although 37 of Papua New Guinea's 702 recognized species are globally threatened, only two, the Endangered White-eyed Starling *Aplonis brunneicapillus* and Critically Endangered Beck's Petrel *Pseudobulweria becki*, fall within the scope of this book. The French overseas territory of New Caledonia, by contrast, with 125 species, has three Endangered and four Critically Endangered birds (two of which have not been seen for a century), plus one Extinct gallinule. Like other overseas territories, such as those of the UK in the south Atlantic, New Caledonia is not eligible for international biodiversity funds because it is not an independent nation, and conservation has not been a high priority for France or its regional government.

New Zealand has an impressive record of moving remnant populations of very threatened island species to small rodent-free islets, and then reintroducing them after their larger island homes have been 'de-ratted'. Notable successes include the Campbell Islands Teal *Anas nesiotis*, downlisted from Critically Endangered to Endangered in 2011, seven years after the species was reintroduced to Campbell Island from a temporary captive population on Codfish Island.

Continuing intensive conservation management is the key to the survival of many of these species. The Norfolk Island Parakeet *Cyanoramphus cookii* has for more than a decade been regarded as a conservation success, one of the 'extinctions we have prevented'. In 2012, however, it was uplisted once again from Endangered to Critically Endangered, following a reported slackening of conservation effort, which has led to an increase in predation by rats and cats. A proposal to reintroduce burrow-nesting seabirds to the island, and hence in the long term to restore the nutrients on which native plant communities depend, has not been followed through.

The Regent Honeyeater *Xanthomyza phrygia* was also uplisted to Critically Endangered in 2012. Despite a programme of captive breeding and reintroduction, the fragmentation and degradation of its habitat appears to have left it at a competitive disadvantage against more aggressive honeyeaters. Its dramatic decline also coincides with a 12-year period of reduced rainfall in south-eastern Australia. Perhaps this drought is early evidence of the impact of climate change, which could put the final nails into the coffins of many more of the region's endemic species.

Long known only from three specimens collected in the 19th century, and presumed Extinct, the Critically Endangered **New Zealand Storm-petrel** *Oceanites maorianus* was rediscovered in 2003, off the Mercury Islands to the north of New Zealand's North Island. Subsequently, a flock of 10–20 was observed and photographed near Little Barrier Island. Its breeding grounds are yet to be found. It may be at risk from invasive predators, or may already have benefitted from the 'de-ratting' of some of New Zealand's offshore islands. Photo: Marcus Lawson.

Over the last century the Endangered **Golden-shouldered Parrot** *Psephotus chrysopterygius* has vanished from most of its range in Cape York Peninsula, Queensland, Australia. One of three confirmed breeding populations was last reported in the 1920s, one has contracted and continues to decline, and one is depleted but stable. Changes to the fire regime resulting in invasion of grassland by woodland are implicated, along with the loss of termite mounds that are used for nest sites. Photo: Ueli Weber.

Endemic to New Zealand, the Endangered **Kaka** *Nestor meridionalis* is found on and around both South (*N. m. meridionalis*) and North Island (*N. m. septentrionalis*). Three generations ago, over 90% of the population would have been on the main islands, but recent information suggests the species has almost disappeared from the mainland except for a few intensively managed sites, and valleys that remain free of possums. Mortality from introduced predators is highest in nesting females, but relatively large numbers of males can remain highly visible long after a population has become reproductively unviable. Photo: Liz Whitwell

The Endangered **Kagu** *Rhynochetos jubatus* is endemic to New Caledonia. Its main population in Parc Provincial Rivière Bleue is increasing, and elsewhere it is believed to be stable. However, 15% of the Rivière Bleue population died during the 2006 breeding season, probably of disease, highlighting the vulnerability of birds with small populations and tiny ranges to chance extreme events. Dogs and other predators kill the birds, and introduced deer are degrading some areas of forest, which is also being eroded by logging and mining. Photo: Roger & Liz Charlwood (WorldWildlifeImages.com)

Australia

Forty-spotted Pardalote *Pardalotus quadragintus*.
Photo: Don Hadden (donhadden.com).

Australia is ranked fourteenth in the world for the number of globally threatened species. Over the past 200 years, clearance and modification of native vegetation for agriculture and urban expansion has left many of the country's landscapes highly fragmented. Even though broad-scale vegetation clearance has come to an end in most states (with the notable exception of Tasmania), the loss of connectivity of natural habitats remains one of the greatest threats to the survival of Australia's birds.

Changes in fire regimes have impacted a number of Australia's threatened species in different ways. The disappearance of the Endangered Noisy Scrub-bird *Atrichornis clamosus* from most of its former range has been attributed to the end of Aboriginal fire management. In 1976, the single remnant population survived in an area protected from fire by the terrain. A combination of translocation and habitat management has resulted in local increases, but recent fires have caused substantial declines in the largest subpopulation.

The large mallee Important Bird Areas (IBAs) in South Australia and Victoria have been burnt so often in recent years that species such as the Endangered Mallee Emuwren *Stipiturus mallee* are increasingly restricted to precariously small and isolated populations. The Endangered Eastern *Dasyornis brachypterus* and Western *D. longirostris* Bristlebirds require regular fires to prevent their heathland habitat becoming too dense, and long-term suppression or prevention of fires may threaten their populations. But wildfires at intervals of fewer than 5–10 years, which have become increasingly frequent, destroy the low heath or understorey upon which they depend. Conversely, annual fires after the first rains of the wet season are thought to be important in maintaining the open structure of the grassland habitat favoured by the little-known, Endangered Buff-breasted Buttonquail *Turnix olivii*.

Tasmania's most threatened endemic species are all at risk from habitat degradation and fragmentation, particularly the unchecked clearance of old-growth native forest, much of which is done to provide woodchip rather than timber. Even when logging is selective, the old, large trees chosen tend to be those that provided nesting hollows for Endangered Swift Parrots *Lathamus discolor*. Competition for nest holes with introduced Common Starlings *Sturnus vulgaris* puts additional pressure on this species and the Critically Endangered Orange-bellied Parrot *Neophema chrysogaster*.

Several Endangered species including Eastern Bristlebird, Black-eared Miner *Manorina melanotis* and some of those endemic to small islands, like Lord Howe Woodhen *Gallirallus sylvestris*, are found within protected areas. All five populations of the Rufous Scrub-bird *Atrichornis rufescens* are in national parks (but the species continues to decline). Others, like the Plains-wanderer *Pedionomus torquatus*, which changes its range according to the availability of suitable habitat, and the Swift Parrot, which nests in different forests depending on which are flowering, are less well served by the protected area system.

Climate change is likely to impact all Australia's threatened birds in coming decades, with increased drought and wildfires, and temperature increases beyond those tolerated by some species. Species now regarded as Least Concern may become threatened. The Golden Bowerbird *Prionodura newtoniana*, which occurs in montane forests in north-east Australia, for example, is predicted to decline to extinction if temperatures rise by 5°C. Others likely to be significantly affected include species that are relatively poor dispersers, such as scrub-birds and bristlebirds.

Carnaby's Black-Cockatoo
Calyptorhynchus latirostris.
Photo: Don Hadden
(donhadden.com).

The Endangered **Forty-spotted Pardalote** *Pardalotus quadragintus*, endemic to Tasmania, is found exclusively in open white gum woodland. Around 60% of occupied habitat is protected, but timber-clearance, sheep-grazing and settlement threaten the rest, even in areas adjacent to reserves. Drought has caused habitat degradation and may be the greatest long-term threat to this species.

Endemic to south-western Australia, the Endangered **Carnaby's Black-Cockatoo** *Calyptorhynchus latirostris* disappeared from over one third of its range between the 1970s and 1990s, with both local extinctions and reduced density in occupied areas. The number counted at night roosts in the Swan Region, which includes the Perth metropolitan area, has fallen by 40% in two years, from 6,700 in 2010, to 4,000 in 2012. Habitat clearance for housing development is thought to be an important factor, and heatwaves and hailstorms have caused mass cockatoo deaths.

Between 1961, when it was rediscovered, and 1976, the Endangered **Noisy Scrub-bird** *Atrichornis clamosus* was largely confined to the Mount Gardner area of the Two Peoples Bay Nature Reserve on the south coast of Western Australia. As a result of translocations, and natural recolonization from the Mount Gardner population, the range has since increased. However, a series of lightning-induced fires in the Two Peoples Bay-Mount Manypeaks area between 2000 and 2004 severely impacted the largest subpopulation. After a fire, it may take ten years before the habitat is once again suitable.

The Endangered **Mallee Emuwren** *Stipiturus mallee* has a severely fragmented distribution in the Victorian and South Australian mallee regions, south and east of the Murray River. In recent years, wildfires have wiped out many subpopulations, to the point where a single fire could now be catastrophic for the species. Mallee-heath requires 5–10 years of regeneration before it is once again suitable. Birds are unlikely to disperse more than 5 km, meaning that subpopulations are effectively isolated. Much apparently suitable habitat is unoccupied.

After breeding, the Endangered **Swift Parrot** *Lathamus discolor* migrates north from Tasmania to mainland Australia. While in most years a large part of the population winters in central Victoria, during periods of extreme drought the parrots undertake movements of up to 1,000 km to wetter coastal areas of New South Wales. But these drought refuge habitats are being cleared for coastal developments.

Swift Parrot
Lathamus discolor.
Photo: David Stowe
(pbase.com/davidstowe).

New Zealand

Before the arrival of humans around 800 years ago, New Zealand had just two native land mammals, both bats. Beginning with Polynesian Rats *Rattus exulans* brought by the first Polynesian settlers, alien mammal predators including Black Rats *Rattus rattus*, possums, cats, stoats, pigs and hedgehogs devastated the islands' birds, many of which were flightless and ground-nesting. By some accounts, half of New Zealand's vertebrate species were driven to extinction, including around 50 birds. The current list of 220 bird species includes 15, all endemic, that have become Extinct over the last 200 years.

Cats were the main culprits in the decline of the Critically Endangered Kakapo *Strigops habroptila*, killing up to 50% of adults every year, an unsustainable level of predation for any bird species, let alone one that breeds only every two to five years according to the fruiting patterns of its main food plants. Introduced herbivores, such as Red Deer *Cervus elaphus*, have degraded New Zealand's forest and other habitats. Deer compete directly with the Endangered Takahe *Porphyrio hochstetteri* for snow tussock grasses, one of the bird's two staple foods, and were a major factor in its decline.

Over one-third of New Zealand's extant bird species are globally threatened. Of these, all six Critically Endangered species and 21 out the 25 Endangered species are endemic (the exceptions are three albatrosses, and the Australasian Bittern *Botaurus poiciloptilus*).

Extirpation of the southern subspecies of Endangered **New Zealand Dotterel** *Charadrius obscurus* from its last refuge on Stewart Island has been averted by poisoning the cats that preyed on them. The survival of this population depends on continuing intensive management. But the status of the northern subspecies on North Island is uncertain, and populations in some areas have undergone substantial declines because of predation, disturbance, and habitat change caused by dune-stabilising plants. A known breeding site has been bulldozed as part of a storm protection programme. Photo: Tim Rumble (flickr.com/photos/timrumble).

Numbers of the Endangered **Black-billed Gull** *Larus bulleri* have plummeted by as much as 90% over the last 10–20 years, because of nest predation by mammals including hedgehogs, river modification by dams, and increasing disturbance by recreational river users. One of the gull's remaining strongholds in Southland is threatened by opencast mining for lignite, a low quality and dirty form of coal. Photo: Tim Rumble (flickr.com/photos/timrumble).

New Zealand was largely covered in forests, but over two-thirds of the native forest has been cleared for timber, settlement and agriculture. More modern threats include damming of rivers for hydro-electricity. The Endangered Blue Duck *Hymenolaimus malacorhynchos*, confined to mountain areas by habitat clearance, saw its forested river habitats further reduced by dam-induced changes in water flow (although in the last ten years flow rates have been increased to reduce these impacts). Meeting New Zealand's target for hydro-electricity as part of its switch to renewables would require many more of the country's major rivers to be dammed.

Despite this commitment to renewables, opencast coal mining has in recent decades destroyed large areas of habitat, and now threatens the Denniston Plateau, one of the strongholds of the Vulnerable Great Spotted Kiwi *Apteryx haastii*. New Zealand is already ranked fourth in the world for per capita greenhouse gas emissions. Hotter and drier conditions at the Endangered Northern Royal Albatross *Diomedea sanfordi* colony at Taiaroa Head, South Island, are already reducing breeding success, causing eggs to overheat and increasing fly-strike on chicks.

New Zealand and its surrounding islands are sometimes called 'the seabird capital of the world'. At least 86 species breed, including more than half the world's 22 albatross species. The most threatened seabirds include two Endangered endemic penguins, the Erect-crested *Eudyptes sclateri*, now confined to around 20 km² of breeding habitat on a few small islands, and Yellow-eyed Penguin *Megadyptes antipodes*.

New Zealand is probably the world leader in 'de-ratting' small islands, and in recent years has turned its attention to mainland forests, using the biodegradable mammal toxin 1080, which has been found 90% effective in killing possums, and 98% effective on rats. The breeding population of Kokako *Callaeas cinereus* increased tenfold in Mapara Forest in the Waikato after four aerial 1080 operations in eight years, and numbers of Yellowhead *Mohoua ochrocephala* have also begun to bounce back in areas where 1080 has been used to control possums, rats and stoats.

The last confirmed sightings of the South Island subspecies of the Endangered **Kokako** *Callaeas cinereus* were in 1967, and it is now considered extinct. On North Island it survives only where predators are intensively managed. It has been introduced to several rat-free islands, and also by the 'Ark in the Park' project to the Waitakere Ranges, along with the Vulnerable Stitchbird *Notiomystis cincta*.
Photo: Trevor Feltham (surfbirds.com/blog/albums/tf1044).

Numbers of the Endangered **Northern Brown Kiwi** *Apteryx mantelli* have probably shrunk by at least 90% since 1900, and are declining at 2·5% annually in unmanaged mainland populations. Following the splitting of Northern and Southern Brown *A. australis* Kiwis in 1995, a third species, the Okarito Brown Kiwi *A. rowi*, from the west coast of South Island, has been proposed. It is not yet recognized by BirdLife, although is under review. Its global population would be fewer than 300 individuals.
Photo: Simon Fordham (naturepix.co.nz).

THREATENED BIRD HOTSPOT
Australasian Islands

Many islands and island groups belonging to Australia and New Zealand have high levels of bird endemism, although sadly also high levels of endemic species extinction. The most northerly of these have conservation issues that perhaps have more in common with the islands of the tropical Pacific.

Australia's Norfolk Island supports the entire global populations of the Critically Endangered White-chested White-eye *Zosterops albogularis* (arguably Australia's rarest bird, if not already extinct) and Norfolk Island Parakeet *Cyanoramphus cookii*. The Slender-billed White-eye *Z. tenuirostris* and Norfolk Island Gerygone *Gerygone modesta* were both downlisted from globally threatened to Near Threatened in 2012 because their populations were believed to be stable. But the surviving endemic landbirds occupy less than 15% of the island's area, mostly in protected remnant forests in the Norfolk Island National Park. The island has a depressingly long list of extinct birds, and of petrels and other seabirds which no longer nest there.

In common with other Australasian islands, Norfolk Island also has many endemic subspecies which are highly distinct from their mainland counterparts, and which may be slipping away unregarded because of quibbles over their taxonomic status. For example, subspecies of Island Thrush *Turdus poliocephalus* from Norfolk Island, Lord Howe Island and New Caledonia's Maré Island have all gone extinct.

The Chatham Islands lie 800 km east of South Island, New Zealand. Only five endemic landbirds are extant today, including Chatham Oystercatcher *Haematopus chathamensis* and Shore Plover *Thinornis novaeseelandiae*, both Endangered, and the Black Robin *Petroica traversi*, now Endangered, but distinguished by having recovered from the lowest population recorded for any bird species – three males and two females, only one of which proved to be fertile.

The Endangered **Lord Howe Woodhen** *Gallirallus sylvestris* is found only in the island group in the Tasman Sea after which it is named. Now a World Heritage Site, Lord Howe Island is the subject of a $9 million Australian government project to exterminate rodents. But at least nine birds endemic to the Lord Howe group are already extinct, including the White Gallinule *Porphyrio albus*, Lord Howe Gerygone *Gerygone insularis*, Robust White-eye *Zosterops strenuus* and Norfolk Island Starling *Aplonis fusca*. Photo: Dave Watts (davewattsphoto.com).

The Endangered **Shore Plover** *Thinornis novaeseelandiae* is endemic to the Chatham Islands, but now breeds only on two of them (South East Island/Rangatira, and Mangere Island), with vagrants to Pitt Island. Attempts to relocate the species to other islands near the main New Zealand islands have had mixed success, because of predation and disease, but a population of around 100 has been successfully established on an undisclosed private island off North Island. Photo: David Boyle.

Following the establishment of a 'stable and secure' population of **Norfolk Island Parakeet** *Cyanoramphus cookii*, and its downlisting to Endangered in 2000, conservationists appear to have taken their eyes off the species, both literally and figuratively. Monitoring has ceased, but anecdotal reports suggest reduced numbers of sightings and alarming levels of feral cat predation. With some authorities fearing that the population has once again fallen below 50, the parakeet was uplisted to Critically Endangered in 2012. Photo: Rob Morris.

Four predator-free and relatively undisturbed islands in the group support breeding Critically Endangered Chatham Islands Shag *Phalacrocorax onslowi*. The Endangered Pitt Island Shag *P. featherstoni* is also confined to the Chatham group. The Endangered Chatham Petrel *Pterodroma axillaris* is endemic, and the Critically Endangered Magenta Petrel *P. magentae* is known to breed only on Chatham Island, though believed to have once been more widespread.

Among the southernmost of all of Australasia's islands, the subantarctic Antipodes (New Zealand) and Macquarie Island (Australia) support millions of nesting seabirds. Macquarie has colonies of two Endangered albatrosses, and the Antipodes one, plus the Endangered Erect-crested Penguin *Eudyptes sclateri*.

Like 'mainland' Papua New Guinea, its associated island groups have very high levels of endemism, but only one species is Critically Endangered (Beck's Petrel *Pseudobulweria becki*, which is strongly suspected to nest on New Ireland, although this remains to be proved), and one is Endangered (White-eyed Starling *Aplonis brunneicapillus* of the Solomon Islands). However, levels of threat are increasing among the endemic birds of these islands. For example, the total number of restricted-range species classified as globally threatened or Near Threatened on New Britain as a result of forest clearance for oil palm plantations has increased from 12 to 21.

There are no mammalian predators on New Zealand's Bounty or Antipodes Islands where the Endangered **Erect-crested Penguin** *Eudyptes sclateri* breeds. However, both breeding populations have declined rapidly, for reasons not fully understood. In common with other *Eudyptes* species, oceanic warming may be causing changes in the distribution of its prey species (mainly krill and squid). Photo: David Boyle.

The Endangered **Chatham Oystercatcher** *Haematopus chathamensis* is endemic to the Chatham Islands. Thanks to conservation efforts, the population has increased from 44 breeding pairs in 1987/8 and now appears to have to stabilized at about 100 pairs. Breeding success is affected by introduced predators and plants, and trampling by livestock. Photo: David Boyle.

New Caledonia

Uvea Parakeet *Eunymphicus uvaeensis.*
Photo: Tun Pin Ong (flickr.com/photos/tunpin).

The French Overseas Territory (Territoire d'outre-mer or TOM) of New Caledonia includes the island of New Caledonia itself (Grande Terre), the nearby Loyalty Islands of Uvea, Lifou and Mar, and a number of smaller islands including Île des Pins.

New Caledonia ranks high among Pacific islands for endemic bird species. The majority are found on Grande Terre, the most ecologically diverse of the islands, notable exceptions being the Large and Small Lifu White-eyes, *Zosterops inornatus* and *Z. minutus*, and the Endangered Uvea Parakeet *Eunymphicus uvaeensis* (split from the Vulnerable Horned Parakeet *E. cornutus* of Grande Terre in 1998).

Of New Caledonia's four Critically Endangered species, two have not been seen in the last 100 years (New Caledonian Rail *Gallirallus lafresnayanus* and New Caledonian Lorikeet *Charmosyna diadema*). The recent rediscovery of a third, the New Caledonian Owlet-nightjar *Aegotheles savesi*, after a similar lapse of time, is a reminder of the dangers of giving up hope of the survival of a species before all possible locations have been exhaustively surveyed. New Caledonia's remaining montane forests are largely inaccessible, and both 'lost' species may survive there.

The fourth Critically Endangered species, the Crow Honeyeater *Gymnomyza aubryana*, was uplisted from Endangered in 2009, when surveys indicated it had declined from an estimated 1,000–3,000 to 70–400 individuals in ten years. Logging, mining and fires have destroyed much of its forest habitat, but the main factor is almost certain to be nest predation, mainly by introduced Black Rats *Rattus rattus*. Nests are poorly camouflaged, and recently fledged birds tend to move about on the ground where they are vulnerable to cats, dogs and pigs.

New Caledonian Owlet-nightjar
Aegotheles savesi.
Illustration: Tomasz Cofta.

The **Kagu** *Rhynochetos jubatus* can live for 20 years in the wild, and pairs apparently mate for life. It lays one egg per year, in a poorly-concealed nest on the ground. The young of previous years help in defending the parents' territory, and reproductive success is linked to the size of the family group. But this breeding strategy makes the birds especially vulnerable to predation, because they cannot respond to lower densities by lifting their reproductive output. Photo: Adam Riley (rockjumperbirding.com).

Half the area of Grande Terre is now covered by secondary forest, savanna and grassland. Logging is restricted to a few small areas but can still have a significant impact on the severely depleted forests. Fires started in the dry season to regenerate grazing lands or clean overgrown cultivated fields often spread into forest edge and maquis. The island has an estimated 50% of world stocks of nickel, and open-cast mining has overtaken logging as the main threat to native habitats. The resulting erosion is among the worst anywhere in the world.

Increasing fragmentation of habitat is a particular risk for New Caledonia's national bird, the Endangered Kagu *Rhynochetos jubatus*, which require large forest territories to breed. The Kagu is also vulnerable to introduced mammalian predators throughout its life. Its eggs are eaten by pigs, its chicks are killed by dogs, cats and rats, and feral dogs and hunting dogs kill the flightless adults.

Invasive mammals may have wiped out the Endangered White-throated Storm-petrel *Nesofregetta fuliginosa* on New Caledonia, as they have wiped out petrels on many other Australasian Islands. Three or four breeding pairs were found in 1996–7, but repeated surveys ten years later failed to locate any. It is hoped it may still breed on atolls north of Grande Terre.

On Uvea (Ouvéa), most of the population of the Endangered Uvea Parakeet *Eunymphicus uvaeensis* occurs in 20 km² of forest. Their nest holes are cut open and made unsuitable for further use by poachers involved in the illegal cagebird trade. Invasive bees also compete for nest holes.

With the exception of Parc Provincial de la Rivière Bleue (the only site where Kagu numbers are increasing), most protected areas in New Caledonia exist on paper only, because of a lack of funding. Some are too degraded for there to be much value in attempting to conserve them, and others are covered by mining concessions.

New Caledonian Lorikeet *Charmosyna diadema*. Illustration: Tomasz Cofta.

A conservation programme has resulted in the Endangered **Uvea Parakeet** *Eunymphicus uvaeensis* becoming celebrated as the island of Uvea's emblem. Bird guides employed by the Association for the Protection of the Ouvéa Parakeet help protect nests from poachers. The population has steadily increased from an estimated 600 birds in 1993 to 2,090 birds in 2009, and is expected to spread naturally from the 20 km² of forest currently occupied into the 60 km² of suitable habitat elsewhere on the island.

The Critically Endangered **Crow Honeyeater** *Gymnomyza aubryana* occurs in small populations scattered throughout the south of New Caledonia's main island. Recent surveys have found it declining in, or absent from, sites where it was known just ten years earlier. But it is an unobtrusive species, and large areas of potentially suitable habitat have yet not been searched. In 2011 it was relocated on Mount Paine in the north of the island.

The **New Caledonian Rail** *Gallirallus lafresnayanus* has not been reliably recorded since the early 20th century, and the **New Caledonian Lorikeet** *Charmosyna diadema* was last observed in 1913, although reports from local people provide some hope that both species might yet survive in remote montane and cloud forests. A third 'lost' species, the **New Caledonian Owlet-nightjar** *Aegotheles savesi*, was known only from a specimen collected in 1880, until one was sighted by a team from BirdLife in 1998. All three are listed as Critically Endangered.

New Caledonian Rail *Gallirallus lafresnayanus*. Illustration: Tomasz Cofta.

Australasia

Native species recorded		1,326
Extinct in the Wild (EW)		0
Critically Endangered (CR)		17
Endangered (EN)		50
Vulnerable (VU)		98
Data Deficient (DD)		15

Sixty-two of the Endangered or Critically Endangered species from Australasia are included in this section; five non-breeding seabirds recorded in coastal waters are covered in the Oceanic Islands section (see *page 180*). See *pages 322–331* for information on the Data Deficient species that occur in this region.

A summary of the most threatened bird families in Australasia

Family	CR	EN	Tot.	Family	CR	EN	Tot.
Ducks (Anatidae)	–	3	**3**	**Sandpipers & allies** (Scolopacidae)	–	2	**2**
Penguins (Penguins)	–	2	**2**	**Gulls & terns** (Laridae)	–	2	**2**
Albatrosses (Diomedeidae)	–	4 (2)	**4 (2)**	**Parrots** (Psittacidae)	5	8	**13**
Petrels & shearwaters (Procellariidae)	3	2 (1)	**5 (1)**	**Scrub-birds** (Atrichornithidae)	–	2	**2**
Storm-petrels (Hydrobatidae)	1	1	**2**	**Honeyeaters** (Meliphagidae)	2	1	**3**
Shags (Phalacrocoracidae)	1	1	**2**	**Bristlebirds** (Dasyornithidae)	–	2	**2**
Rails (Rallidae)	2	2	**4**	**White-eyes** (Zosteropidae)	–	2	**2**
Other families: All have 1 species (bold names = monotypic families): Kiwis (Apterygidae); Herons & egrets (Ardeidae); Frigatebirds (Fregatidae); Boobies (Sulidae); **Kagu** (Rhynochetidae); Buttonquails (Turnicidae); Oystercatchers (Haematopodidae); Stilts (Recurvirostridae); Painted-snipes (Rostratulidae); **Plains-wanderer** (Pedionomidae); Doves & pigeons (Columbidae); Owlet-nightjars (Aegothelidae); Australasian wrens (Maluridae); Pardalotes (Pardalotidae); Thornbills & gerygones (Acanthizidae); Wattled Crows (Callaeatidae); Monarchs (Monarchidae); Australasian Robins (Petroicidae); Starlings (Sturnidae).	3 (1)	16 (1)	19 (2)				
(n) = number of non-breeding migrants. See Appendix 2 (*page 339*) for more information on these families.				**TOTAL (33 FAMILIES)**	17 (1)	50 (4)	67 (5)

EN **Northern Brown Kiwi** *Apteryx mantelli*

`33,159`

▼ **POPULATION: 35,000** | **THREATS: SPP**, AGR

Once widespread throughout the islands of New Zealand, populations of this kiwi have become fragmented due to predation and habitat loss. It favours dense native forests, but can also be found in a variety of other habitats. Mainly nocturnal, kiwis have poor eyesight, but excellent senses of smell and hearing. Pairs stay together for life, usually 10–15 years, and breed twice a year. Males dig the tunnel nest, up to 2 m long, and incubate the, usually, single egg. Being terrestrial, kiwis are highly susceptible to introduced mammalian predators, and many mainland populations are in serious decline, although rates have been slowed due to intensive predator control. A captive breeding and reintroduction programme has also been established.

Photo: Simon Fordham (naturepix.co.nz)

EN **Blue Duck** *Hymenolaimus malacorhynchos*

▼ **POPULATION: 1,200** | **THREATS: SPP, AGR, MAN, (WAT)**

The only member of its genus, this duck, known locally as Whio Whio after its high-pitched call, occurs along fast-flowing rivers and streams on North and South Islands, New Zealand. It feeds on aquatic invertebrates and has a unique 'lip' on its upper mandible that enables it to scrape caddisfly larvae off rocks without damaging its bill. Once widespread, the range of this species is now severely fragmented, primarily due to the impact of predation by introduced mammals. It is hoped that an ongoing species recovery plan, which includes a captive breeding and reintroduction programme and intensive predator control, will help to secure the survival of this species in the wild.

Photo: Trevor Feltham (surfbirds.com/blog/albums/tf1044)

EN **Brown Teal** *Anas chlorotis*

▲ POPULATION: 1,300 | THREATS: CLI, TRA, AGR, SPP, (HUN)

Once probably the most abundant species of wildfowl on New Zealand, this small duck is now restricted to the Great Barrier Island, the east coast of Northland and the Coromandel Peninsula (where it was reintroduced). Initial population declines due to the loss of wetland habitats and hunting in the early 20th century were exacerbated by predation from introduced mammals and the native Purple Gallinule *Porphyrio porphyrio*. Drought-induced habitat change and road deaths are more recent threats. A species recovery plan is in place, which includes releases of captive bred birds at suitable locations, and intensive predator control is ongoing.

Photo: Liz Whitwell

EN **Campbell Islands Teal** *Anas nesiotis*

▲ POPULATION: 100–200 | THREATS: CLI, SPP

The introduction of rats to remote Campbell Island, New Zealand, led to this flightless duck being considered extinct for around 30 years until a small group was rediscovered on nearby, predator-free, Dent Island in 1975. In 1984, four birds were translocated to New Zealand to start a captive breeding programme and subsequent conservation efforts have proved very successful. In recent years many birds have been reintroduced onto Campbell Island itself, from which rats were eventually eradicated in 2001. Its natural predators are skuas, gulls and giant-petrels. A small wild population is now breeding successfully in a variety of habitats and it was downlisted from Critically Endangered in 2011.

Photo: Ian R. McHenry

EN **Erect-crested Penguin** *Eudyptes sclateri* `161`

▼ POPULATION: 130,000–140,000 | THREATS: **CLI**

Known to breed only on the Bounty and Antipodes Islands, New Zealand, the population of this penguin has declined by over 50% during the three decades up to 2011. It breeds in large, conspicuous colonies on rocky terrain, and feeds on krill, squid and occasionally fish. Its wintering distribution remains largely unknown, with just a few records from the Cook Strait and off the east coast of South Island. The reason for such a rapid population decline over just 3 generations is uncertain, but may be due to changes in oceanographic or climatic conditions, as mammalian predators (except for mice) do not occur on the breeding sites.

Photo: Alan Tate (aabirdpix.com)

EN **Yellow-eyed Penguin** *Megadyptes antipodes* `150`

▼ POPULATION: 3,500–4,200 | THREATS: AGR, CLI, SPP, (FIRE), (LOG), (ECO)

Endemic to New Zealand, this sedentary penguin breeds along the south-east coast of South Island and on nearby offshore islands. It feeds up to 15 km from land along the edge of the continental shelf, diving to 160 m when foraging for fish and squid. It forms life-long pair-bonds and as it nests on the ground in patches of forest and scrub, introduced mammalian predators are the greatest threat. Habitat degradation and human disturbance are also exacerbating population declines. Other threats include periodic food shortages due to changes in sea temperature, drowning in fishing nets and avian diseases. Conservation initiatives including the fencing of colonies, predator control and habitat restoration projects are underway.

Photo: Bill and Jack Moorhead (wildiaries.com/users/73)

EN **Northern Royal Albatross** *Diomedea sanfordi* `202,205`

▼ **POPULATION: 17,000** | **THREATS:** FISH, HUN, SPP, (CLI)

Most of the population (99%) of this huge albatross breeds on the remote Chatham Islands, New Zealand, with the remainder occurring on the south-east tip of South Island and on Enderby Island in the Auckland Island Archipelago. When not breeding, it disperses around the southern oceans. As the majority of the breeding population occurs at just one site, freak events, such as a storm in 1985 that resulted in the loss of most of the vegetation and led to prolonged low annual productivity, are an ongoing threat. However, should the current population remain stable it may qualify for downlisting in the near future.

Photo: Bill and Jack Moorhead (wildiaries.com/users/73)

EN **Black-browed Albatross** *Thalassarche melanophrys* `202,205`

▼ **POPULATION: 1,150,000** | **THREATS: FISH**, SPP, CLI?, (GEO)

Most of the world population of this albatross breeds on islands in sub-polar waters off South America (see *page 284*), but small numbers also breed on the Heard and McDonald Islands and Macquarie Islands (Australia), and on the Campbell, Snares and Antipodes Islands (New Zealand), as well as on other oceanic islands (see *page 209*). Although many populations elsewhere are declining, the around 600 pairs on Heard Island appears to be increasing, despite periodic volcanic eruptions. An explosion in rabbit numbers on Macquarie Island since 1999 has led to extensive habitat destruction and soil erosion at nest sites, but an eradication programme commenced in 2010.

Photo: David Monticelli (pbase.com/david_monticelli)

CR **Magenta Petrel** *Pterodroma magentae*

▲ **POPULATION: 80–100** | **THREATS:** SPP, CLI, LOG?, (AGR), (HUN)

First collected at sea in 1867, there were no further records of this petrel until 1978, when it was found breeding in the south-west corner of Chatham Island, New Zealand. It nests in burrows in dense forest and predation by introduced mammals over many years took its toll. In 2006, only 25 breeding pairs were known but intensive conservation management, particularly predator control, has led to a slow increase in numbers. Some chicks have been successfully moved to predator-free areas prior to fledging in the hope that they will form new colonies, and females have been introduced to burrow clusters that contain unpaired males. Outside the breeding season, birds range across the southern Pacific Ocean.

Photo: Otto Plantema (pbase.com/otto1)

CR **Chatham Petrel** *Pterodroma axillaris*

▲ **POPULATION: 1,100** | **THREATS:** SPP, CLI?, (HUN)

Once one of the most common petrels on islands in the Chatham Islands group, New Zealand, breeding is currently restricted to South East Island, Pitt Island and Chatham Island, having been recently successfully reintroduced to the latter two islands. Most birds breed at around five years of age, but they face fierce competition for nest-burrows from Broad-billed Prions *Pachyptila vittata*. Successful conservation measures, which include the development of artificial burrow entrance flaps that allow petrels to pass but not prions, have led to a population increase since 2000. However, introduced mammalian predators still remain a threat on Pitt and Chatham. Post breeding, it migrates eastwards to spend the rest of the year in the northern Pacific Ocean.

Photo: David Boyle

CR **Beck's Petrel** *Pseudobulweria becki*

▼ **POPULATION: 50–249** | **THREATS:** SPP?, ECO?

Known only from two specimens taken at sea of Papua New Guinea and the Solomon Islands in the early 1900s, there were no further records of this unusual gadfly petrel until 2003, when several birds, thought to be this species, were reported in the Bismarck Archipelago. Although subsequent expeditions have recorded up to 160 birds around the same location, this species remains little known. It may have declined due to predation by introduced mammalian predators on its breeding grounds, but these have yet to be discovered. As petrels are nocturnal at their nesting grounds, they are notoriously difficult to detect.

Photo: Hadoram Shirihai / © The Tubenoses Project

EN **Hutton's Shearwater** *Puffinus huttoni*

= **POPULATION: 300,000–350,000** | **THREATS:** CLI, FISH, SPP

This shearwater breeds in burrows only at 1,200–1,800m in the Kaikoura mountains of South Island, New Zealand. The habitat at most of the colonies known in the 20th century has been destroyed due to soil erosion and trampling, mainly caused by feral pigs, and this remains a potential threat to the two colonies that remain. Historically, introduced mammalian predators may have contributed to declines but reduced food availability due to the impact of over-fishing may now prove to be a more severe threat. Although the population is thought to be stable, work is underway to establish a third colony through the translocation of chicks. In the non-breeding season birds migrate to waters off Australia.

Photo: Tony Palliser

CR **New Zealand Storm-petrel** *Oceanites maorianus* `154`

? **POPULATION: <50** | **THREATS:** SPP?

Presumed extinct since the 1800s, this storm-petrel was spectacularly rediscovered in 2003 off the North Island of New Zealand. Efforts to locate the breeding sites by catching several birds at sea and fitting them with transmitters have, so far, been unsuccessful. This information is, however, critical in determining the size of the population and providing protection. Although the population may be decreasing owing to the impacts of alien, invasive predators, this remains speculation. It is possible that breeding birds have already benefited from rat-eradication programmes on offshore islands. Reports of individuals off south-east Australia and New Caledonia suggest it could be migratory.

Photo: Marcus Lawson

EN **White-throated** (or Polynesian) **Storm-petrel** *Nesofregetta fuliginosa*

▼ **POPULATION: 250–999** | **THREATS:** SPP, AGR, HUN

The majority of the breeding population of this storm-petrel occurs on islands scattered throughout the southern Pacific (see *page 212*), but a few pairs have also bred on New Caledonia and Vanuatu. Introduced mammalian predators are the primary reason for the rapid decline. Repeated visits to New Caledonia in 2007 failed to produce any records and it may now be extinct there. However, it has since been sighted twice off the northern tip of the island and may possibly breed on offshore atolls. Although it is also thought to be extinct on Vanuatu, there is a slim chance that it may persist. A comprehensive survey is urgently needed in order to assess the true population size.

French Polynesia Islands; August 2007. Photo: Hadoram Shirihai / © The Tubenoses Project

EN **Australasian Bittern** *Botaurus poiciloptilus*

▼ **POPULATION: 1,000–2,499** | **THREATS:** AGR, CLI, WAT, HUN, TRA, ECO

Found only in Australia, New Zealand and New Caledonia, this bittern favours shallow swamps with a mixture of short and tall vegetation, particularly when breeding. However, it disperses widely to other wetland habitats, areas that are especially important during times of drought. It feeds mostly at night, typically having a home range of 16–20 ha. The greatest threat is habitat loss due to wetland drainage for agriculture, but high grazing pressure and salinization are also significant issues. In Australia, which has seen the largest decline, a Bittern Project was initiated in 2007, a few sites are now managed specifically for this species, and it was afforded legal protection in 2011.

Photo: Alan Tate (aabirdpix.com)

CR **Chatham Islands Shag** *Phalacrocorax onslowi*

▼ **POPULATION: 720** | **THREATS:** FISH, MAN, HUN, SPP, CLI?

Restricted to the Chatham Islands group, New Zealand, the population of this large cormorant fluctuates between years, possibly reflecting changes in the marine environment that affect the food supply. It nests on high, exposed rocks or cliff-ledges and forages up to 24 km offshore for small fish. Islands free of introduced predators host the largest colonies, but those on Chatham Island itself are often disturbed by humans and other mammals, which result in egg breakages and subsequent predation by gulls. A breeding survey in 2011 indicated that the rate of decline may have slowed, but, as yet, no conservation action has been specifically directed towards the species.

Photo: János Oláh (birdquest-tours.com)

EN **Pitt Island Shag** *Phalacrocorax featherstoni*

▼ **POPULATION: 1,094** | **THREATS:** HUN, SPP, CLI?

Found on many islands within the Chatham Islands group, New Zealand, this cormorant's distinctive double crest is only present during the breeding season. It breeds in small colonies of between five and 20 pairs on rocky areas and forages offshore, primarily for fish. Even though they tend to nest in inaccessible sites, on Chatham Island and Pitt Island colonies may be affected by disturbance or predation by farm stock and other introduced mammals. Recent declines may be a response to changes in the marine environment that are affecting food supplies, but it is also known that 40–80 individuals are caught annually in crayfish traps and birds are sometimes illegally hunted.

Photo: Tony Sawbridge

CR **New Caledonian Rail** *Gallirallus lafresnayanus*

163

? **POPULATION: <50** | **THREATS: SPP**

Despite surveys in 1998, this large, flightless rail is still only known from specimens taken in New Caledonia during the late 1800s. However, reports from local people suggest that it may still have occurred in inaccessible montane forests up to the 1980s. Very little is known about its behaviour, except that it was possibly crepuscular or nocturnal. It is presumed to favour the same evergreen forest as Kagu *Rhynochetos jubatus* and may have declined for similar reasons, which include introduced predators, especially dogs and pigs. If so, it could benefit from the predator control actions being taken to save the Kagu. If it does still exist, the population must be assumed to be tiny.

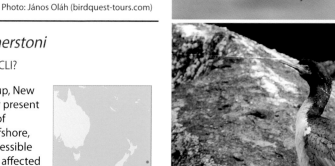

Illustration: Tomasz Cofta

EN **Lord Howe Woodhen** *Gallirallus sylvestris*

160

= **POPULATION: 140** | **THREATS:** CLI, SPP, (HUN)

This confiding, flightless rail is endemic to Lord Howe Island, Australia. Once widespread, by the mid-1800s it was restricted to dense forest on two mountain summits having been eliminated elsewhere due to predation and disturbance by introduced animals, especially feral pigs. By the 1970s fewer than ten breeding pairs remained. In the 1980s, following the eradication of pigs, captive breed birds were successfully reintroduced to the lowlands. The most significant threats today are predation by the introduced Australian Masked-owl *Tyto novaehollandiae* and, especially during the breeding season, perhaps conflict with the Buff-banded Rails *Gallirallus philippensis* that have recolonized the island.

Photo: Dave Watts (davewattsphoto.com)

EN **Takahe** *Porphyrio hochstetteri*

▲ **POPULATION: 227** | **THREATS:** MAN, SPP, AGR?, (CLI), (HUN)

Endemic to New Zealand, the flightless Takahe is the world's largest rail, and can live up to 20 years. It was once widespread on both South and North Islands but habitat modification, harsh winters, and introduced mammalian predators reduced numbers dramatically. It is now restricted to alpine tussock grasslands on the mainland and to a few translocated populations on predator-free offshore islands. A species recovery programme has helped to stabilize populations but some sites are now thought to have reached carrying capacity and inbreeding depression could become a threat. However, if the population continues to increase, the species will warrant downlisting in due course.

Photo: Adam Riley (rockjumperbirding.com)

CR **Makira Moorhen** *Gallinula silvestris*

? **POPULATION: <50** | **THREATS:** HUN, LOG, CLI?, SPP?

Only found on the island of Makira in the Solomon Islands, this moorhen has not been seen for many years, despite intensive recent surveys, although hunters reported it up until 1974. However, there have been a number of credible recent reports, including one of a calling bird in 2004. It is little known, but local hunters report that, being flightless, it climbed vegetation to escape dogs. Introduced mammalian predators are probably responsible for its rapid decline. Most lowland forests have been logged but suitable habitat is thought to remain on remote, steep, inaccessible, rocky slopes, giving some hope that a remnant population survives.

Illustration: Tomasz Cofta

EN **Kagu** *Rhynochetos jubatus*

155,162

= **POPULATION: 250–999** | **THREATS:** FIRE, SPP, AGR, EGY, LOG

This strange, flightless bird, which is the only member of its family, is restricted to a few severely fragmented areas of forest on New Caledonia. Local people know it as 'the ghost of the forest'. Introduced mammals may pose a threat but incidental killing by hunting dogs has probably had the greatest impact on populations. However, there is cause for hope, as recent research shows that the species may be more be widespread than previously thought, and in some areas populations are increasing due to a reduction in hunting, particularly with dogs. There has been a successful captive breeding and reintroduction programme and a species action plan spanning the period 2009–20 is in place.

Photo: Roger & Liz Charlwood (WorldWildlifeImages.com)

EN **Buff-breasted Buttonquail** *Turnix olivii*

▼ **POPULATION: 500** | **THREATS:** AGR, FIRE, SPP?

Restricted to northeast Queensland, Australia, this large buttonquail is one of the country's least-known birds. It is only found sporadically at a few sites within a tiny area, where it seems to favour open grasslands, particularly for breeding. Although fire may be important in maintaining an appropriate vegetation structure, sites may have become unsuitable due to inappropriate burning and grazing regimes that promote the growth of woody weeds. Predation by feral cats may also be a threat. A national recovery plan is in place, and a better understanding of this species is urgently needed in order to identify the most effective conservation strategy.

Illustration: Tomasz Cofta

EN **Chatham Oystercatcher** *Haematopus chathamensis* `161`

▲ **POPULATION: 50–249** | **THREATS:** MAN, SPP, (CLI), (HUN)

Endemic to the remote Chatham Islands, New Zealand, the population of this oystercatcher has been increasing due to intensive conservation efforts but is now mostly stable. However, numbers are known to fluctuate and some islands may have reached carrying capacity. As it nests in shallow scrapes on sandy or rocky beaches, introduced mammalian predators and trampling by farm stock are major threats on some islands. The spread of introduced Marram Grass *Ammophila arenaria* has forced some birds to nest nearer the tideline, making them more vulnerable to flooding by high tides and storms. A range of conservation actions is ongoing, including predator control, dune restoration, and the erection of fencing to prevent disturbance.

Photo: David Boyle

CR **Black Stilt** *Himantopus novaezelandiae*

▲ **POPULATION: 27** | **THREATS:** SPP, MAN, (WAT), (DEV), (ECO)

Once widespread on both South and North Islands, New Zealand, this stilt is now mostly confined to Waitaki Valley, South Island, although small numbers winter on North Island. It breeds on braided riverbeds or in wetlands, feeding mainly on insects, molluscs and small fish. Predation by introduced mammals and native harriers and gulls are the main threats, but habitat loss and disturbance are also important factors. It hybridizes with White-headed Stilt *H. leucocephalus* but this behaviour is becoming less prevalent as the sex ratio evens out. The release of captive-reared birds, in combination with predator control, has almost certainly prevented this species from becoming extinct in the wild.

Photo [adult showing hybrid characters]: Bill and Jack Moorhead (wildiaries.com/users/73)

EN **New Zealand Dotterel** *Charadrius obscurus* `158`

▲ **POPULATION: 1,300** | **THREATS:** SPP, MAN, DEV

This New Zealand endemic, the world's largest species of *Charadrius* plover, has two subspecies. The nominate now breeds only on Stewart Island although it formerly occurred on South Island. It is found inland, often at high altitudes, on bare hilltops and open bog or tussock-grasslands. Numbers are now gradually increasing due to extensive predator control. Subspecies *aquilonius* is more numerous and breeds on beaches and tidal mudflats on North Island. Here, introduced predators remain the greatest threat, although coastal urbanization, habitat changes and disturbance are also important factors. At some sites native avian predators (notably Kelp Gull *Larus dominicanus*) occur at high densities and are a significant threat to eggs and chicks.

Photo: Reg Daves

Photo: David Boyle

EN **Shore Plover** *Thinornis novaeseelandiae*

▲ POPULATION: 156–220 | THREATS: AGR, MAN, SPP, CLI?

After being extirpated from South Island, New Zealand in the late 1800s by introduced predators, this shorebird became confined to the remote Chatham Islands. Most of the population now occurs on South East Island, where it nests on salt meadows, beaches and rocky platforms. A captive breeding programme has led to the translocation of birds to predator-free islands in the Chatham group and to islands off mainland New Zealand, but has had mixed success. Although measures to eradicate introduced predators have been successful, it also faces a range of other threats including fire, habitat loss to expanding New Zealand Fur Seal *Arctocephalus forsteri* colonies, disease, human disturbance and predation by native birds such as skuas and gulls.

EN **Australian Painted-snipe** *Rostratula australis*

▼ POPULATION: 600–1,700 | THREATS: AGR, WAT, SPP

Recently split from Greater Painted-snipe *R. benghalensis*, this species has been recorded in a variety of wetland types throughout Australia but is more common in eastern states. It is thought to be crepuscular, or possibly nocturnal, and although some populations are resident, others may be dispersive or even migratory. Females are more colourful than males. The drainage of wetlands and the diversion of water for agriculture and reservoirs since European settlement have led to extensive habitat loss. However, the impact of invasive plants on wetland vegetation structure and trampling by farm stock may be more recent threats and further studies and conservation initiatives are underway.

Photo: Paul Hackett

EN **Plains-wanderer** *Pedionomus torquatus*

29

▼ POPULATION: 1,000–2,499 | THREATS: AGR, SPP, PLN?

This quail-like bird is endemic to eastern Australia where it is dependent upon lightly grazed, natural grasslands with bare ground. It cannot tolerate intensive agricultural management. Although sedentary, it may make local movements in response to habitat changes. The female is larger and more brightly coloured than the cryptically plumaged male, which is left to tend the eggs and young. Although numbers fluctuate naturally in response to the effects of drought, regular surveys have revealed an ongoing decline. Whilst the loss of suitable habitat is the greatest threat, pesticides used to control locusts may kill birds, directly or indirectly through the food chain, but this activity is now regulated

Female. Photo: Dr Liz Still

EN **Black-billed Gull** *Larus bulleri*

158

▼ POPULATION: 96,000 | THREATS: SPP, MAN, (EGY), (TRA)

Endemic to New Zealand, this gull has undergone a very rapid decline. The majority of the population breeds in Southland, mainly on braided river systems, but it uses farmland for feeding and roosting, sometimes scavenging in urban areas. Birds first breed when they are 2–6 years of age. Introduced mammalian predators are a major threat, often taking hundreds of chicks in a season. The spread of weeds, such as introduced lupins, has significantly reduced suitable nesting habitat on riverbeds but other habitat changes and human disturbance are also important factors. Conservation actions underway include further research, population monitoring and habitat restoration and protection.

Photo: Simon Fordham (naturepix.co.nz)

EN **Black-fronted Tern** *Sterna albostriata*

`46`

▼ POPULATION: 2,500–9,999 | THREATS: **SPP**, WAT, MAN, ECO

Breeding only on inland riverbeds in South Island, New Zealand, this tern returns to the coast for the winter, rarely venturing more than 10 km offshore. Major breeding failures have been a consequence of predation by introduced mammals and Australian Magpies *Gymnorhina tibicen*, and some native birds, but disturbance by grazing livestock is also a factor. Habitat loss and degradation are also significant threats and human recreational activities are increasingly affecting both breeding and wintering sites. Although breeding success has improved at some colonies due to predator control, the very rapid population decline is predicted to continue.

Photo: Tim Rumble (flickr.com/photos/timrumble)

EN **Santa Cruz Ground-dove** *Gallicolumba sanctaecrucis*

▼ POPULATION: 600–1,700 | THREATS: SPP, AGR, HUN?, LOG?

This terrestrial dove is known from uninhabited Tinakula and little-visited Utupua (Solomon Islands), but is now probably extinct on both, and from Espiritu Santo (Vanuatu), where there have been a few unconfirmed recent records. It occurs in rainforest at 300–1,000 m, including isolated patches surrounded by agriculture. Population data are lacking but declines are likely to be ongoing due to habitat loss, predation by introduced mammals and hunting. A recently identified threat is the establishment of the invasive vine *Merremia peltata* in the Vatthe Conservation Area on Espiritu Santo, which causes the death of large numbers of canopy trees.

Illustration: Tomasz Cofta

EN **Kaka** *Nestor meridionalis*

`155`

▼ POPULATION: 2,500–9,999 | THREATS: SPP, LOG, (HUN)

This highly vocal parrot is endemic to New Zealand. The subspecies *septentrionalis* occupies large forests on North Island and the nominate is found on South Island, from where it has almost disappeared, and some offshore islands. Populations have declined rapidly due, historically, to habitat loss and hunting, but introduced mammalian predators are now a severe threat. Although it has a varied diet, introduced wasps *Vespula* spp. compete for honeydew, one of its favoured foods, and this may also be a factor contributing to declines. Intensive predator control is ongoing in some areas but work is underway to determine the most sustainable long-term conservation measures.

Photo: Tony Sawbridge

CR **Kakapo** *Strigops habroptila*

▲ POPULATION: 78 | THREATS: (SPP)

Once found throughout New Zealand, this extraordinary, flightless, nocturnal parrot, weighing up to 4 kg, can live for up to 90 years. Uniquely amongst parrots, males create a scrape in the ground from which they display, using a far-ranging booming sound to attract females. Being extremely tame, numbers declined rapidly following human colonization and it became extinct on North Island in 1927 and South Island in1987. Recent declines have been due to predation by introduced mammals, especially cats. Between 1980–92 birds that remained on Stewart Island were transferred to predator-free offshore islands. In 1999 there were only 62 Kakapos left in the wild, but this had increased to 126 by early 2012, including 78 breeding adults.

Photo: David Boyle

EN **Baudin's Black-cockatoo** *Calyptorhynchus baudinii*

▼ **POPULATION: 1,000–1,500** | **THREATS:** HUN, SPP, LOG, EGY, CLI?, (AGR)

This long-lived cockatoo is endemic to south-west Australia, where it favours *Eucalyptus* forests but also disperses to commercial orchards, where it is considered a pest. Only about 10% of the population breeds each year and suitable nest holes are only found in trees over 130 years old. Declines are primarily due to ongoing habitat loss and competition with feral bees for the few remaining suitable nest sites. However, illegal hunting and increasing competition for nest sites with Australian Wood Ducks *Chenonetta jubata* are also important factors. The use of non-lethal control methods in orchards and the retention of old-growth forest are being promoted, and a feral honey bee control strategy developed.

Photo: Don Hadden (donhadden.com)

EN **Carnaby's Black-cockatoo** *Calyptorhynchus latirostris* `156`

▼ **POPULATION: 40,000** | **THREATS:** AGR, SPP, HUN, TRA, CLI?

Endemic to south-west Australia, this cockatoo favours the wheatbelt and the Swan Coastal Plain, but also occurs in forested areas, where it overlaps with the very similar Baudin's Black-Cockatoo *C. baudinii*. Breeding success is dependent upon the presence of heathland feeding areas within 12 km of its woodland nest sites. Coastal pine plantations, which are important roosting and feeding sites for non-breeding birds, are due to be felled when they reach maturity and a food shortage then may occur. It faces a range of threats, including habitat loss to agriculture, competition for nest sites, the illegal bird trade and extreme weather conditions.

Photo: David Stowe (pbase.com/davidstowe)

CR **New Caledonian Lorikeet** *Charmosyna diadema* `163`

? **POPULATION: <50** | **THREATS:** AGR?, EGY?, SPP?

Only found on New Caledonia, the last record of this lorikeet was in 1913. There are unconfirmed reports from an experienced forester of two birds in the central mountains in 1953/4, and again in 1976, but despite intensive searches in 1998 and from 2002–7, there are no further records. However, since *Charmosyna* lorikeets are notoriously difficult to detect, being unobtrusive and nomadic, ranging from montane to lowland forests, there is a slim chance this species persists. As lowland forests have nearly disappeared from the island, the population may have declined due to habitat loss, but introduced disease (such as avian malaria) and predation (notably by rats) may also be important factors.

Illustration: Tomasz Cofta

EN **Uvea** (or Ouvéa) **Parakeet** *Eunymphicus uvaeensis* `162`

▲ **POPULATION: 2,090** | **THREATS:** HUN, SPP, LOG, AGR?, CLI?

Restricted to the island of Uvea, off New Caledonia, this parakeet is becoming well known and celebrated as the island emblem. When breeding it requires old-growth forest with suitable nest holes, but uses adjacent cultivated areas for feeding. Monitoring has revealed that only half the fledglings survive their first month, mostly due to capture for the illegal bird trade. Predation of juveniles by Brown Goshawks *Accipiter fasciatus* and perhaps other predators, and completion for nest sites with bees are also important threats. Encouragingly, numbers are steadily increasing due to conservation efforts, with the presence of local guides believed to be have been particularly effective at preventing nest poaching.

Photo: Tun Pin Ong (flickr.com/photos/tunpin)

CR **Norfolk Island Parakeet** *Cyanoramphus cookii* `161`

▼ **POPULATION:** 50–249 | **THREATS:** SPP, CLI?, (AGR), (LOG)

Once found throughout Norfolk Island, Australia, this parakeet is now confined to the one area of remaining forest, where it nests in tree-hollows, visiting adjacent orchards to feed on soft fruit. By the mid-1990s only four breeding females and around 30 males remained. The population increased up until about 2008 due to conservation management, but is now declining again. Lack of suitable habitat is an ongoing issue and predation of burrow-nesting seabirds by introduced mammals has led to changes in vegetation, which has an adverse effect on this species. Disease and competition for nest sites with introduced Crimson Rosella *Platycercus elegans* and, to a lesser extent, Common Starling *Sturnus vulgaris* and feral honey bees are also important threats.

Photo: Rob Morris

EN **Chatham** (or Forbes's) **Parakeet** *Cyanoramphus forbesi*

= **POPULATION:** 50–249 | **THREATS:** SPP, CLI?, (AGR), (FIRE)

Restricted to the islands of Little Mangere and Mangere in the Chatham Islands group, New Zealand, this parakeet favours dense, unbroken forest and scrub. It has a varied, omnivorous diet. It nests in natural crevices or tree hollows, as well as abandoned petrel burrows and other holes in the ground. The greatest threat was hybridization with the Chatham Island subspecies of the Vulnerable Red-crowned Parakeet *C. novaezelandiae chathamensis*, with 50% of the population being hybrids at one point. However, this is monitored biennially and appears to be rapidly reducing. It has recently been recorded visiting adjacent islands and a translocation to a predator-free area on Chatham Island is planned for 2017.

Photo: Bill and Jack Moorhead (wildiaries.com/users/73)

CR **Malherbe's Parakeet** *Cyanoramphus malherbi*

▲ **POPULATION:** 50–249 | **THREATS:** SPP, (LOG)

This parakeet is now known from just three forested valleys on South Island, New Zealand, where it requires mature trees, particularly *Nothofagus* beech, for nest cavities and feeding. Breeding success is linked with the irregular seeding of *Nothofagus* and in good beechmast years pairs will often have more than one brood. Introduced mammalian predators are a major threat and, in 2000, the population crashed from perhaps 500–700 birds to around 100–200 after irruptions of rats but appears to have stabilized, albeit in much smaller numbers. Intensive predator control is ongoing and there have been successful translocations to predator-free offshore islands.

Photo [captive]: Jonathan Kearvell

EN **Golden-shouldered Parrot** *Psephotus chrysopterygius* `154`

▼ **POPULATION:** 2,500 | **THREATS:** AGR, FIRE, SPP

Only found on the Cape York Peninsula, Queensland, Australia, this unobtrusive parrot has been lost from most of its historical range. Today the areas around Morehead River and the Staaten River National Park hold the only populations. It nests in large, 30+ year-old termite mounds, relying on open country where there is minimal cover for predators. Afterwards it disperses through open woodland to feed on the super-abundant seeds of fire grass *Schizachyrium* spp. Despite intensive conservation efforts, ongoing population declines are thought to be due to changes in agricultural management, particularly burning regimes, an increase in predators, principally Pied Butcherbird *Cracticus nigrogularis*, and a lack of suitable nest sites.

Photo: Graeme Chapman (graemechapman.com.au)

CR **Orange-bellied Parrot** *Neophema chrysogaster*

▼ **POPULATION:** <50 | **THREATS:** AGR, SPP, ECO, DEV, CLI, EGY

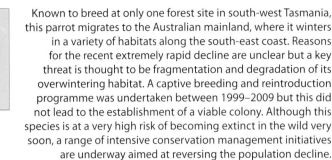

Known to breed at only one forest site in south-west Tasmania, this parrot migrates to the Australian mainland, where it winters in a variety of habitats along the south-east coast. Reasons for the recent extremely rapid decline are unclear but a key threat is thought to be fragmentation and degradation of its overwintering habitat. A captive breeding and reintroduction programme was undertaken between 1999–2009 but this did not lead to the establishment of a viable colony. Although this species is at a very high risk of becoming extinct in the wild very soon, a range of intensive conservation management initiatives are underway aimed at reversing the population decline.

Photo: Tony Sawbridge

EN **Swift Parrot** *Lathamus discolor*   157

▼ **POPULATION:** 1,000–2,499 | **THREATS:** AGR, LOG, DEV, TRA, CLI, MAN, HUN, SPP

Making the longest migration of any parrot, this species can travel up to 5,000 km from its Tasmanian breeding sites to wintering grounds on mainland Australia. It feeds primarily on nectar and is highly dependent upon Tasmanian Blue Gum *Eucalyptus globulus* when breeding. However, as this tree flowers infrequently, breeding may only occur in three years out of ten. The main threat is ongoing habitat loss and degradation, both on the wintering and breeding grounds, but competition for nest sites from introduced Common Starlings *Sturnus vulgaris*, disease, and illegal capture for the bird trade are also important factors. It also suffers high mortality due to collision with windows, vehicles and fences.

Photo [captive]: Dave Watts (davewattsphoto.com)

EN **Night Parrot** *Pezoporus occidentalis*

▼ **POPULATION:** 50–249 | **THREATS:** AGR?, SPP?, ECO?

This nocturnal parrot is endemic to Australia where there are very few confirmed records from the 20th century, despite dedicated searches. The only recent records are of three birds in 2005, a dead juvenile in 2006, and three possible sightings in 2010. It seems likely that this easily overlooked species occurs at low density, as there have been unverified sight records from inland regions of all mainland states. However, there has almost certainly been a decline in abundance since the 1880s, probably due to predation by non-native mammals. Most specimens have come from arid grasslands or scrublands, and the two nests recorded were in tunnels in densely vegetated areas.

Illustration: Tomasz Cofta

CR **New Caledonian Owlet-nightjar** *Aegotheles savesi*   162

▼ **POPULATION:** <50 | **THREATS:** EGY?, FIRE?, SPP?, LOG?

Endemic to New Caledonia, this large owlet-nightjar is known from only two specimens, a sighting in the 1990s, and a handful of other reports. It has not been recorded this century despite intensive fieldwork from 2002–7. If still extant, it either occurs in very low numbers or is restricted to the most remote forest massifs. Like other owlet-nightjars, it probably nests and roosts in holes in trees and predates small animals, foraging from perches or on the ground. It has unusually long legs for an owlet-nightjar, which may indicate a terrestrial behaviour. It is likely to have declined due to predation by introduced rats and possibly cats, or habitat loss through fire, mining and logging.

Illustration: Tomasz Cofta

EN **Rufous Scrub-bird** *Atrichornis rufescens*

▼ **POPULATION: 20,000–49,999** | **THREATS:** CLI, FIRE, ECO, (LOG)

Endemic to Australia, this secretive, terrestrial bird has two severely fragmented populations: subspecies *ferrieri* in New South Wales and the nominate subspecies in south-eastern Queensland. It is usually found in rainforest above 600 m, requiring dense undergrowth associated with gaps in the canopy, a moist microclimate and deep leaf-litter. Most suitable habitat was cleared in the 19th century and the majority of the population now occurs within protected areas. Inappropriate management, particularly logging and burning, continues to reduce habitat quality, and there are concerns that drier conditions caused by climate change may lead to its disappearance from much of its current range.

Photo: David Stowe (pbase.com/davidstowe)

EN **Noisy Scrub-bird** *Atrichornis clamosus* `157`

▼ **POPULATION: 1,000–1,500** | **THREATS:** FIRE, SPP?, (AGR), (CLI), (WAT)

This skulking but noisy bird is only found on the south coast of Western Australia, where it is restricted to just five locations. It nests in areas that contain a mosaic of mature, dense, low vegetation with small, open areas, and feeds on a range of invertebrates in leaf-litter. Several decades of intensive conservation work, involving a combination of translocation and habitat management, resulted in a population increase. However, large lightning-induced fires have since caused significant further declines in population size and habitat quality, from which any recovery is likely to be slow. Other, smaller-scale declines may be due to predation by introduced mammals.

Photo: Graeme Chapman (graemechapman.com.au)

EN **Mallee Emuwren** *Stipiturus mallee* `157`

▼ **POPULATION: 7,500–35,500** | **THREATS:** FIRE, DEV, CLI?, (AGR)

Endemic to southern Australia, this rapidly declining emuwren is only found in areas dominated by mallee vegetation. Suitable habitat is already severely fragmented due to loss to agriculture, and is continuing to be lost due to the combined pressures of drought and wildfires. As birds are unlikely to disperse more than 5 km, remaining populations are becoming increasingly isolated. Anecdotal evidence suggests that rainfall might affect the health of hummock grassland and, in turn, the abundance of insect prey; annual rainfall gradually increases heading eastwards, and may explain why eastern areas of this species' range seem to be a stronghold.

Photo: Tony Crittenden (tcphotos.net)

CR **Crow Honeyeater** *Gymnomyza aubryana* `163`

▼ **POPULATION: 50–249** | **THREATS:** SPP, AGR, EGY, LOG

This unobtrusive honeyeater is endemic to New Caledonia, where its small population is now mainly confined to the south of the island in an area of probably less than 400 km². It is thought to favour a matrix of humid forest and maquis scrub but has recently been recorded from dry forest in the north of the island, in an area where it has not been seen for some years. It is usually found singly or in pairs in the canopy or mid-storey, feeding on invertebrates and nectar. Although habitat loss and degradation is likely to be an ongoing threat, severe predation by introduced rats and cats, and possibly other, native, endemic predators, is probably the major limiting factor.

Photo: Adam Riley (rockjumperbirding.com)

EN **Black-eared Miner** *Manorina melanotis*

▼ POPULATION: 250–999 | THREATS: CLI, FIRE, SPP, (AGR)

Endemic to the Murray Mallee region of southern Australia, this honeyeater's range and numbers declined dramatically during the 1990s. By 1995, just 25 birds were known in the wild. Highest densities occur in mature mallee, but extensive clearance of this habitat for agriculture has created isolated colonies and resulted in high levels of hybridization with Yellow-throated Miner *M. flavigula*. Intensive conservation efforts, including the establishment of a captive breeding colony, have led to a recovery in the population, but loss of habitat due to drought and associated wildfires is a significant ongoing threat. This species may soon qualify for uplisting to Critically Endangered.

Photo: Pete Morris (birdquest-tours.com)

CR **Regent Honeyeater** *Xanthomyza phrygia*   `30,31`

▼ POPULATION: 350–400 | THREATS: AGR, SPP, LOG, DEV, CLI?

Only found in south-east Australia, this honeyeater now has an extremely patchy distribution. Birds concentrate at a small number of sites when breeding, but numbers fluctuate greatly between years and sites, and movements outside the breeding season are poorly understood. It is usually observed within box-ironbark eucalypt associations, seeming to prefer wetter, more fertile lowland sites, but is also found in riparian and wet coastal forests. Recent declines are driven primarily by drought, compounded by habitat loss caused by historic clearance for agriculture, and possibly competition with other native species, particularly Noisy Miner *Manorina melanocephala* and Noisy Friarbird *Philemon corniculatus*. Captive breeding is underway, with the first birds released in 2008.

Photo: Chris Tzaros

EN **Western Bristlebird** *Dasyornis longirostris*

▼ POPULATION: 1,000 | THREATS: CLI?, SPP?, (AGR), (FIRE)

Formerly found along the coast of south-western Australia, this terrestrial, sedentary bird is now confined to a few patches of dense coastal heath in protected areas. Historically, extensive areas of habitat were lost to agriculture, but habitat loss and degradation due to wildfires is now the greatest threat. A series of particularly severe fire events this century has resulted in the population becoming perilously low and action is being taken to prevent further losses. A translocation to a new site appears to have been unsuccessful but further attempts are planned. Other threats include predation by introduced mammals, disturbance by livestock, weed invasion and changes in hydrological regimes.

Photo: Graeme Chapman (graemechapman.com.au)

EN **Eastern Bristlebird** *Dasyornis brachypterus*

▼ POPULATION: 2,550 | THREATS: FIRE, AGR, MAN, SPP

This secretive, terrestrial bird is endemic to Australia. The northern population, subspecies *monoides,* which is critically endangered, inhabits grass tussocks in open forests in south-eastern Queensland and north-eastern New South Wales. The nominate subspecies occurs in eastern New South Wales and eastern Victoria and has a more stable population. It lives in dense, low vegetation, particularly heath, but also in surrounding woodlands. Habitat is degraded by feral pigs and overgrazing but the main threat results from inappropriate burning. Predation by introduced mammals and human disturbance are also important factors. The northern population is the focus of a captive breeding and reintroduction programme.

Photo: Matthew Rodgers

EN **Forty-spotted Pardalote** *Pardalotus quadragintus*

`156`

▼ **POPULATION:** 1,000–1,500 | **THREATS:** AGR, FIRE, SPP, LOG, DEV, CLI?

Restricted to Tasmania, Australia, about 90% of the population of this tiny bird occurs on offshore islands. It is found exclusively in open White Gum *Eucalyptus viminalis* forest. A significant proportion of its habitat continues to be lost to agriculture and urban development, or degraded as a result of overgrazing and extended periods of low rainfall. Although climate change may be the greatest threat in the long-term, wildfires, human disturbance and the impact of potential competitors or predators such as Noisy Miner *Manorina melanocephala* and introduced Laughing Kookaburra *Dacelo novaeguineae* are also of concern. A recovery plan is in place and a key site has been protected.

Photo: Dave Watts (davewattsphoto.com)

EN **Yellowhead** *Mohoua ochrocephala*

▼ **POPULATION:** 1,000–2,499 | **THREATS:** SPP, (AGR)

Endemic to New Zealand, this striking bird is found only on South Island, where the majority of remaining birds occur in the Fiordland and Mount Aspiring National Parks. It formerly occurred on Stewart Island but is now extinct. The preferred habitat is lowland Red Beech *Nothofagus fusca* forest on river terraces, where it often associates with feeding flocks high in the canopy. Recent very rapid population declines and extirpation of some subpopulations has followed irruptions in the numbers of introduced Stoat *Mustela erminea*, which take eggs, chicks and a disproportionate number of adult females. However, a captive breeding and translocation programme has led to the successful establishment of new populations on predator-free offshore islands.

Photo: Simon Fordham (naturepix.co.nz)

EN **Kokako** *Callaeas cinereus*

`159`

▲ **POPULATION:** 1,000 | **THREATS:** SPP, (AGR), (LOG)

The North Island subspecies *wilsoni* of this New Zealand endemic was formerly common throughout the island's forests, but remaining populations are now severely fragmented. The last confirmed sighting of the nominate subspecies from South Island was in 1967 and it is now considered extinct. The species has a reputation for being a beautiful songster and birds are highly territorial. Numbers are increasing in areas where intensive predator management occurs, but declines continue elsewhere, with populations at most unmanaged sites now extinct. The majority of the remaining habitat is protected and populations have been successfully established on offshore islands and new areas on the mainland.

Photo: Simon Fordham (naturepix.co.nz)

EN **Santa Cruz Shrikebill** *Clytorhynchus sanctaecrucis*

▼ **POPULATION:** 1,000–2,499 | **THREATS:** AGR, LOG, SPP?

This little-known bird is endemic to Nendo in the Santa Cruz Islands of the Solomon Islands. It is only known from two specimens taken in 1927 and two pairs seen in 2004, which were found in rainforest near the summit of the island (550 m) and at about 80 m. Local reports suggest that it is uncommon and only found deep in old-growth forest, possibly near to streams, and it is suspected to occur at ten sites. The population may be declining due to small-scale forest clearance for subsistence farming and also possibly as a result of predation by introduced mammals. However, the population estimate is based on few data and poor knowledge of the area of potentially suitable habitat.

Illustration: Tomasz Cofta

EN **Black Robin** *Petroica traversi*

▲ **POPULATION: 224** | **THREATS:** SPP, CLI?

The reversal in the fortunes of the Black Robin is undoubtedly one of the most remarkable successes in species conservation. Endemic to the Chatham Islands group, New Zealand, in the 1980s this species was considered doomed to extinction, with just one breeding female left. In 1976, following forest deterioration on Little Mangere Island, the seven surviving birds had been relocated to Mangere Island, where thousands of trees were planted to provide sufficient habitat. Subsequent intensive conservation management led to a spectacular recovery and it was successfully introduced to South East Island. However, chronic inbreeding and loss of genetic diversity may impact on breeding success in future.

Photo: David Boyle

EN **Splendid White-eye** *Zosterops luteirostris*

▼ **POPULATION: 250–999** | **THREATS:** AGR, LOG, CLI?

This little-known white-eye is endemic to the island of Ghizo in the Solomon Islands. It seems to prefer forest edge, regrowth and mature secondary forest, but also occurs in scrub close to large trees and in plantations, although it is not known whether such habitats support sustainable breeding populations. Remaining tall or old-growth forest is very fragmented and totals less than 1 km². Since the 2007 tsunami, habitat loss and degradation, and human habitation, have increased, particularly in the interior of the island. Comprehensive surveys have not yet been conducted in the interior, but are urgently needed to assess the status of the species.

Photo: Guy Dutson

CR **White-chested White-eye** *Zosterops albogularis*

▼ **POPULATION: <50** | **THREATS:** SPP, CLI?, (LOG)

Endemic to Norfolk Island, Australia, this white-eye may be functionally extinct. Although there have been several reports since 1978, the last in 2006, formal surveys during the last three decades have failed to find any birds. The remaining population, if any exists, is likely to be very small and highly threatened. It appears to have occurred mostly in weed-free indigenous forest, feeding high in shrubs and trees. However, there are also old records of it nesting in orchards and feeding on olive fruits. The decline is believed to be a result of predation by introduced rats, exacerbated by habitat destruction and degradation through invasion of exotic weeds.

Illustration: Tomasz Cofta

EN **White-eyed Starling** *Aplonis brunneicapillus*

▼ **POPULATION: 600–1,700** | **THREATS:** HUN, LOG, AGR

This little-known starling is currently only found on the island of Bougainville, Papua New Guinea and the islands of Choiseul, Rendova and Guadalcanal in the Solomon Islands, but may yet be discovered on other islands. It breeds in colonies of up to 40 nests in lowland swamp and hill forest. Foraging birds have been observed feeding on fruits, occasionally in small flocks that may also contain Metallic Starlings *A. metallica*. Already a scarce species due to deforestation, habitat loss continues and further declines are suspected to have occurred. A further contributing factor may be the harvesting of nest colonies for food, as was recorded historically.

Illustration: Tomasz Cofta

Oceanic Islands

Endangered **Black-browed Albatross** *Thalassarche melanophrys*. Photo: Tim Laman (timlaman.com).

Critically Endangered **Akohekohe** *Palmeria dolei*. Photo: Michael Neal (nealstudios.net).

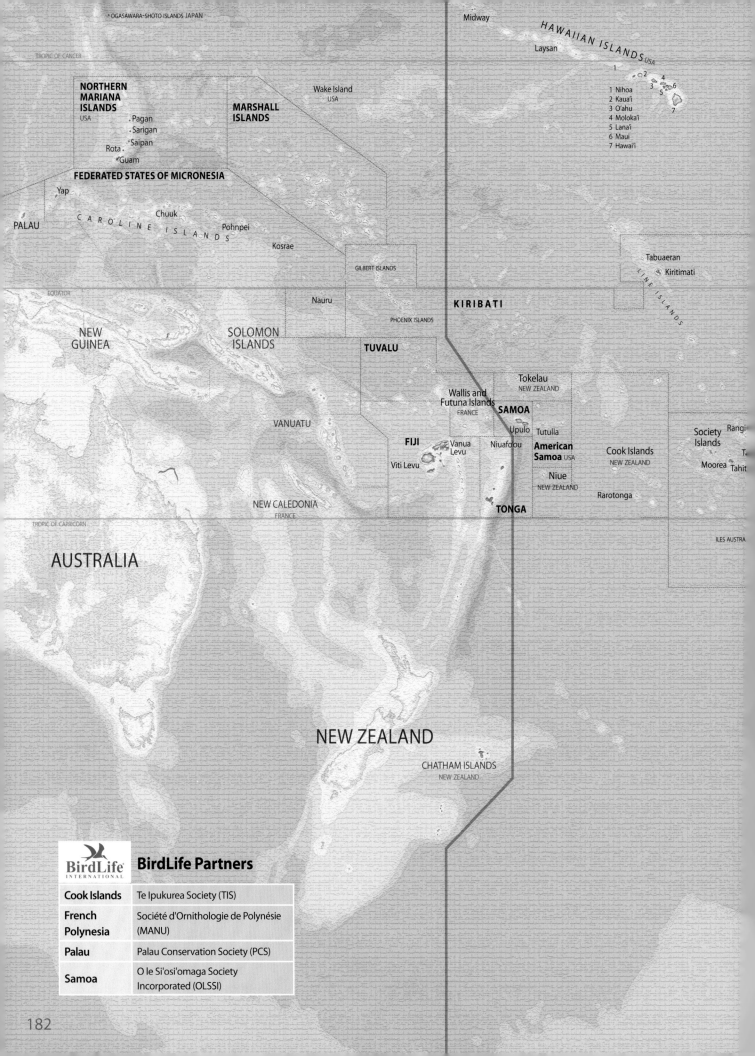

Ogasawara-Shoto Islands JAPAN

Midway

HAWAIIAN ISLANDS USA

Laysan

TROPIC OF CANCER

1

2
3   5
4   6
7

1 Nihoa
2 Kaua'i
3 O'ahu
4 Moloka'i
5 Lana'i
6 Maui
7 Hawai'i

NORTHERN MARIANA ISLANDS
USA

Wake Island
USA

MARSHALL ISLANDS

Pagan
Sarigan
Saipan
Rota
Guam

FEDERATED STATES OF MICRONESIA

Yap

CAROLINE   ISLANDS

Chuuk

Pohnpei

PALAU

Kosrae

Tabuaeran
Kiritimati

GILBERT ISLANDS

LINE ISLANDS

EQUATOR

Nauru

KIRIBATI

PHOENIX ISLANDS

NEW GUINEA

SOLOMON ISLANDS

TUVALU

Tokelau
NEW ZEALAND

Wallis and
Futuna Islands
FRANCE

SAMOA

Society
Islands

Rangi

VANUATU

FIJI

Vanua
Levu

Upulo

Tutulla

Niuafoou

**American
Samoa** USA

Cook Islands
NEW ZEALAND

Moorea

T.

Tahit

Viti Levu

Niue
NEW ZEALAND

Rarotonga

NEW CALEDONIA
FRANCE

TONGA

TROPIC OF CAPRICORN

ILES AUSTRA

AUSTRALIA

NEW ZEALAND

CHATHAM ISLANDS
NEW ZEALAND

BirdLife Partners

Cook Islands	Te Ipukurea Society (TIS)
French Polynesia	Société d'Ornithologie de Polynésie (MANU)
Palau	Palau Conservation Society (PCS)
Samoa	O le Si'osi'omaga Society Incorporated (OLSSI)

Oceanic Islands

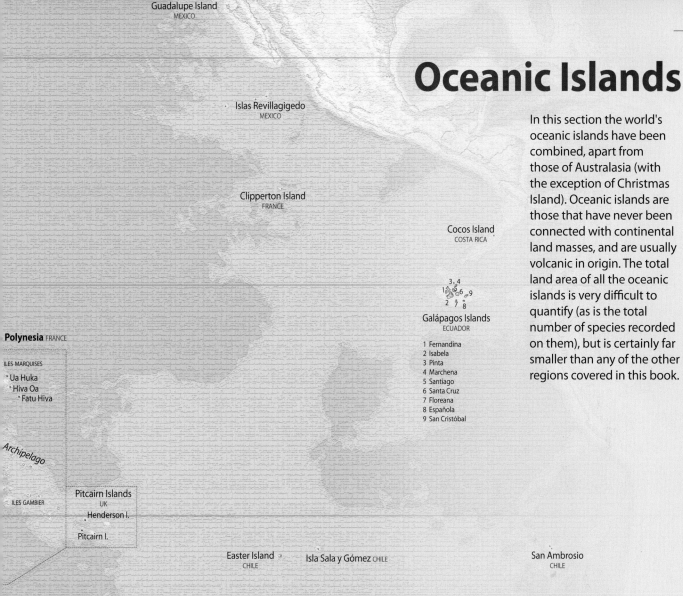

Guadalupe Island
MEXICO

Islas Revillagigedo
MEXICO

Clipperton Island
FRANCE

Cocos Island
COSTA RICA

3 4
1 5 6 9
2 7 8
Galápagos Islands
ECUADOR

1 Fernandina
2 Isabela
3 Pinta
4 Marchena
5 Santiago
6 Santa Cruz
7 Floreana
8 Española
9 San Cristóbal

Polynesia FRANCE

ILES MARQUISES
Ua Huka
Hiva Oa
Fatu Hiva

Archipelago

ILES GAMBIER

Pitcairn Islands
UK
Henderson I.

Pitcairn I.

Easter Island
CHILE

Isla Sala y Gómez CHILE

San Ambrosio
CHILE

Juan Fernández Islands
CHILE

In this section the world's oceanic islands have been combined, apart from those of Australasia (with the exception of Christmas Island). Oceanic islands are those that have never been connected with continental land masses, and are usually volcanic in origin. The total land area of all the oceanic islands is very difficult to quantify (as is the total number of species recorded on them), but is certainly far smaller than any of the other regions covered in this book.

A high element of chance has been involved in the formation of the biodiversity of oceanic islands (for example, the arrival of vagrant birds in breeding condition), which often consists of a relatively small number of often highly distinctive species. Galápagos and Seychelles are the best-known examples. But even the tiny island of Nauru, where only 27 bird species have been recorded, has its own endemic reed-warbler (the Vulnerable Nauru Reed-warbler *Acrocephalus rehsei*). The number of species is usually related both to the island's size, and its distance from the nearest continent.

There are large oceanic island groups, like the archipelagos of the tropical Pacific, the sub-Antarctic South Georgia, South Sandwich, South Orkney and South Shetland islands, and the Aleutian islands between Kamchatka and Alaska. Some oceanic islands are the remotest spots of land on Earth, such as Ascension Island and the St Helena and Tristan da Cunha groups in the south Atlantic, Pitcairn and Easter Island in the Pacific, and Amsterdam, Kerguelen and the Crozet Islands in the southern Indian Ocean.

But not all are remote. The islands of São Tomé and Príncipe lie within the Gulf of Guinea. They are closer to the African mainland than the Falkland Islands (Islas Malvinas) are to the coast of South America. Being part of an ancient volcanic chain, they have always been separate from the mainland, while the Falklands/Malvinas are part of a projection of the Patagonian continental shelf, a fragment of the ancient continent of Gondwanaland.

Globally, there are approximately equal numbers of island Endemic Bird Areas (105) and mainland EBAs (113). Of the island EBAs, 70% are on oceanic islands, and 30% are on continental-shelf islands. The two EBAs of São Tomé and Príncipe, for example, have around 25 endemic species (including some distinctive island subspecies proposed but not yet recognized), with two endemic, monospecific genera.

A disproportionately high number of threatened birds, almost half, occur on islands, particularly oceanic islands. Island species often evolved in the absence of the pressures to which continental species are exposed, and are poorly adapted to deal with new threats, especially introduced predators.

AZORES PORTUGAL
· São Miguel

MADEIRA
PORTUGAL

Bermuda
UK

CANARY ISLANDS SPAIN
1 Tenerife
2 Gran Canaria
3 Fuerteventura

TROPIC OF CANCER

CAPE VERDE
1 São Nicalau
2 Raso
3 Fogo
4 Santiago

AFRICA

ATLANTIC OCEAN

Gulf of Guinea   SÃO TOMÉ &   Bioko
PRÍNCIPE   EQUATORIAL GUINEA
1 São Tomé
2 Príncipe   Annobón
EQUATORIAL GUINEA

EQUATOR

Fernando de Noronha
BRAZIL

Ascension Island
UK

SOUTH
AMERICA

St Helena
UK

Martin Vaz Islands
BRAZIL

TROPIC OF CAPRICORN

Tristan da Cunha UK
Inaccessible Island · Tristan da Cunha
Nightingale Island
Gough UK

Falkland Islands UK
(Islas Malvinas)

South Georgia UK
Shag Rocks   (Georgias del Sur)

South Sandwich Islands UK

South Orkney Islands UK

South Shetland Islands UK

Bay of Bengal

ARABIAN SEA

Narcondam Island
INDIA

SEYCHELLES

OS ISLANDS
more 1 3
2

Aldabra Islands SEYCHELLES

Agalega Islands MAURITIUS

Mayotte
FRANCE

Ile Tromelin FRANCE

Cargados Carajos MAURITIUS

MAURITIUS

ADAGASCAR

Rodrigues
MAURITIUS

Réunion
FRANCE

Christmas Island
AUSTRALIA

Cocos Islands
AUSTRALIA

INDIAN OCEAN

AUSTRALIA

Iles Amsterdam
FRANCE

Iles St Paul
FRANCE

Islands
CA

Iles Crozet
FRANCE

Iles Kergeulen
FRANCE

Heard & MacDonald Islands
AUSTRALIA

BirdLife
INTERNATIONAL

BirdLife Partner

Seychelles   Nature Seychelles

Oceanic islands – the conservation challenges

While only 17% of the world's bird species are restricted to islands, the number of threatened island species is almost equal to those found on continents. Of these, the majority are found on oceanic islands.

For example, out of 115 species, the Northern Mariana Islands have 15 globally threatened species, including five Critically Endangered and four Endangered. Guam, to the south, shares many of the same threatened endemics, plus one that is Extinct, and one Extinct in the Wild.

Three-quarters of all threatened bird species occurring on oceanic islands are at risk from introduced species. Introduced herbivores like goats, cattle and deer degrade habitats, and introduced parasites and microorganisms reduce the fitness of individual birds and the breeding success of entire populations.

The wave of extinctions on islands due to introduced predators may be slowing, but perhaps only because the susceptible species are mostly Extinct. However, the introduction or reintroduction of invasive alien species will always be a threat. Pigs were successfully eradicated from Clipperton Island in the 1950s, and breeding seabird numbers, reduced to hundreds, increased by tens of thousands. But rats came ashore following shipwrecks in 1999 and 2001, and are feeding heavily on eggs and nestlings. When an oil tanker struck Nightingale in the Tristan group in 2011, the prospect of rats escaping onto the previously rodent-free island was considered as serious a threat as the direct impact of spilled oil on the globally important breeding colonies of Endangered Northern Rockhopper Penguins *Eudyptes moseleyi*.

Development, particularly the exploitation of remote islands for their tourism potential, is exacerbating existing threats and bringing new ones. Islands that were once visited by ships only occasionally are now in far more regular contact with the outside world. Socotra, which lies 190 km east of the horn of Africa, has very high levels of endemism, including at least six endemic birds. Formerly cut off during the monsoon season because of rough weather, it now has its own airport. Settlements and resorts are expanding, along with infrastructure including roads. Although much of the island's unique vegetation is heavily degraded, local people have devised sustainable regimes for wood-cutting and grazing. But newcomers often ignore these regimes.

Until 2007, the Endangered **Rimatara Lorikeet** *Vini kuhlii* was confined to Rimatara in French Polynesia, and three islands in the republic of Kiribati. On at least two islands, populations were declining because of nest predation by introduced Black Rats *Rattus rattus*. Historically, the lorikeet had also been found in the Cook Islands, but was driven to extinction by excessive exploitation for its red feathers. Following its reintroduction to Atiu in the Cook Islands, where Black Rats are absent, numbers have steadily increased. Photo: Phil Bender.

The **Narcondam Hornbill** *Aceros narcondami* is endemic to the tiny (6·82 km²) island of Narcondam, east of India's Andaman Islands. Although the population is stable, there are thought to be fewer than 250 mature birds, and so it is listed as Endangered. A few trees are cut every year on the island, and there is some hunting of hornbills for food. Feral goats have mostly been removed from the island, but a substantial population of feral cats may be a threat. Photo: Niranjan Sant.

The Critically Endangered **Laysan Duck** *Anas laysanensis* was once widespread in the Hawaiian Islands, but by the beginning of the 20th century was confined to Laysan. The population increased following the removal of rabbits from the island, but has fluctuated between 100 and 700 because of drought and disease. Up to 25% of adults on Laysan may have died after the tsunami triggered by the 2011 Japanese earthquake swept through part of the breeding area, followed by a botulism outbreak. Breeding failed completely in that year. Further reintroductions to other Hawaiian Islands are planned. Photo: James H. Breeden Jr.

Stalled plans to build an airport on St Helena were revived in 2012, with the aim of opening up the island to development for tourism. The airport will be built in one of the breeding areas of the Critically Endangered St Helena Plover *Charadrius sanctaehelenae*, the only extant member of a suite of nine endemic bird species. Planned infrastructure threatens more sites, and nests are already being destroyed by increasing recreational use of off-road vehicles.

Aircraft can also carry mosquitoes and other vectors of disease which would not survive a long sea crossing.

Many island bird species are exposed to a combination of threats from alien species and modern development. On Guam, predation by the introduced Brown Tree Snake *Boiga irregularis* reduced the Critically Endangered Mariana Crow *Corvus kubaryi* from 350 birds in 1981 to two individuals (both males) by 2008, and none have been seen since 2011. On Rota in the Northern Mariana Islands, the crow declined from 1,318 birds in 1982 to 85 pairs in 2008. Recent typhoons have devastated its habitat on Rota, and forest has been cleared for settlement and resort and golf-course construction.

Conservation interventions such as the eradication of introduced predators can be spectacularly successful at the island scale, when combined with biosecurity regimes agreed with local people to prevent alien species reinvading. Eradication of cats, rats and other predators has led to the recovery of highly threatened species in the Seychelles, in a growing number of Pacific islands, and a few important seabird islands on the edge of Antarctica. Once alien species disappear, native vegetation often begins to regenerate, helped in some cases by replanting projects. As techniques and materials continue to improve, it is likely that many more island restoration projects will become feasible in the coming years. But sea-level rise as the world's oceans grow warmer will be a more intractable problem.

Mohéli Scops-owl *Otus moheliensis*.
Photo: Pete Morris (birdquest-tours.com).

Kiritimati Reed-warbler *Acrocephalus aequinoctialis*.
Photo: Eric VanderWerf (pacificrimconservation.com).

Wilkins's Bunting *Nesospiza wilkinsi*.
Photo: Peter Ryan (fitzpatrick.uct.ac.za).

The Critically Endangered **Mohéli Scops-owl** *Otus moheliensis* has an extremely small range, occurring on only one mountain ridge on Mohéli in the Comoros Islands. It occurs in dense, humid forest, which now only remains on the peak and upper slopes of the central mountain. However, this forest is being felled and degraded primarily due to subsistence agriculture and, as a result, the population and range of this owl are suspected to be in decline.

The Endangered **Kiritimati Reed-warbler** *Acrocephalus aequinoctialis* has been extirpated from one of the three coral atolls in the Northern Line Islands, Kiribati, where it formerly occurred. It is patchily distributed but still locally common on Kiritimati, where surveys since 2007 indicate the population may have stabilized. Should it be found not to be declining overall, it would warrant downlisting.

The Endangered **Wilkins's Bunting** *Nesospiza wilkinsi* is restricted to Nightingale Island in the south Atlantic Ocean, where the population is probably about 100 pairs. Although there are no immediate and serious threats, and numbers are believed to be stable, there is permanent risk from the accidental introduction of mammalian predators which could prey on eggs, chicks and nesting birds.

The stronghold of the Endangered **Phoenix Petrel** *Pterodroma alba* is Kiritimati in the Line Islands (Kiribati), with smaller populations in the Phoenix Islands, the Marquesas (French Polynesia) and Pitcairn Island. It appears only to survive on islands without feral cats, which are the targets of a so far unsuccessful eradication programme on Kiritimati. The recent arrival of Black Rats *Rattus rattus* on Kiritimati is a major worry and is likely to lead to a very rapid population reduction.

The Critically Endangered **Golden White-eye** *Cleptornis marchei* occurs only on Saipan and Aguijan in the Northern Mariana Islands. Its ability to use different habitats has enabled it to survive in high numbers despite typhoon damage and extensive habitat modification. But the Brown Tree Snake *Boiga irregularis* may be establishing itself on Saipan, which following the pattern elsewhere in the Northern Marianas is likely to lead to a catastrophic collapse in populations of this and other endemic species, such as the Critically Endangered Nightingale Reed-warbler *Acrocephalus luscinius*.

Phoenix Petrel *Pterodroma alba*.
Photo: Mike Thorsen (southernphotoguides.com).

Golden White-eye *Cleptornis marchei*. Photo: Chris Collins.

Hawaii

The Hawaiian archipelago (the state of Hawaii, USA) is a chain of volcanic islands in the Pacific, stretching from Nihoa and other uninhabited islands in the north-west (the oldest and smallest in the chain), to the the youngest and largest, Hawai'i (also known as the 'Big Island'), in the south-west.

The Hawaiian Islands once supported over 100 endemic bird taxa, but beginning with the arrival of the Polynesians, more than half of these have been driven to extinction by hunting, habitat loss (especially clearance of lowland forests), introduced predators, herbivores, competitive bird species, aggressive ants and wasps, invasive plants, and disease. The resident human population and numbers of tourists have rapidly expanded, contributing to the pressures which have forced surviving endemic species into refuges of native vegetation of declining size and quality.

The extant endemic species include ducks, geese, petrels, a hawk, thrushes and warblers (millerbirds). Best known are the Hawaiian honeycreepers, sometimes assigned (by default) to their own family, the Drepanididae, (though BirdLife includes them with the Fringillidae, as their ancestor is now almost universally agreed to have been a cardueline finch). Honeycreepers are found throughout the archipelago, reaching their greatest diversity in the central and south-eastern islands.

Of Hawai'i's 16 known endemic species, nine are now extinct. The survivors are found largely above 500 m, although originally they probably occurred in the lowlands too. Forests above 800 m may still hold the Ou *Psittirostra psittacea*, although it has not been seen since 1987 and is now listed as Critically Endangered (Possibly Extinct). The Palila *Loxioides bailleui* is found in Māmane *Sophora chrysophylla* forests above 2,000 m. But drought on top of habitat loss and degradation, and predation by introduced species, caused the population to fall from 5,337 to 1,200 birds between 2005 and 2010, and the Palila was uplisted to Critically Endangered in 2008.

Palila *Loxioides bailleui*. Photo: Eric VanderWerf (pacificrimconservation.com).

Akohekohe *Palmeria dolei*. Photo: Jack Jeffrey (JackJeffreyphoto.com).

Akikiki *Oreomystis bairdi*. Photo: Jack Jeffrey (JackJeffreyphoto.com).

Most of the population of the Critically Endangered **Palila** *Loxioides bailleui* is confined to 30 km² of forest on Hawai'i.

The Critically Endangered **Akohekohe** *Palmeria dolei* is now confined to a tiny area on Maui.

Once widespread on Kaua`i, the Critically Endangered **Akikiki** *Oreomystis bairdi* has retreated to a few dozen km² of high-elevation forest.

All known populations of the Endangered **Hawaii Creeper** *Oreomystis mana* are declining, and one has disappeared since the 1980s.

The Endangered **Maui Alauahio** *Paroreomyza montana* once also occurred on Lana'i but is now restricted to Maui.

Hawaii Creeper *Oreomystis mana*. Photo: Peter LaTourrette (birdphotography.com).

Maui Alauahio *Paroreomyza montana*.
Photo: Michael Neal (nealstudios.net).

191

Of all the Pacific Endemic Bird Areas, the Central Hawaiian Islands have the highest number of threatened restricted-range species in total, and of Critically Endangered endemics in particular. Among those not seen in recent decades are the Olomao *Myadestes lanaiensis*, Nukupuu *Hemignathus lucidus*, Oahu Alauahio *Paroreomyza maculata* and Poo-uli *Melamprosops phaeosoma*, all of which are now listed as Critically Endangered (Possibly Extinct). Three more species have been declared Extinct since 2000. The bird taxonomy of these islands is still in a state of flux; the elepaio (*Chasiempis*), an endemic genus of monarch flycatcher, was in 2010 split into three species, all being immediately listed as threatened, with the Oahu Elepaio *Chasiempis ibidis* categorized as Endangered.

The pressures on the Hawaiian Islands' surviving bird species are being exacerbated by the effects of climate change, including increases in the frequency of cyclones and droughts. Rising temperatures are enabling disease-bearing mosquitos to increase their altitudinal range, bringing them closer to the high-elevation forests that provide the last refuges for 18 threatened bird species, mainly honeycreepers.

The Critically Endangered **Maui Parrotbill** *Pseudonestor xanthophrys* is now restricted to montane mesic and wet forest, which is probably marginal habitat. Photo: Eric VanderWerf (pacificrimconservation.com).

The Endangered **Akiapolaau** *Hemignathus munroi*, endemic to Hawai'i. Photo: Eric VanderWerf (pacificrimconservation.com).

The Critically Endangered **Nihoa Finch** *Telespiza ultima*, found only on one 2 km² island. Photos: Mark Alexander MacDonald (male) and Robby Kohley (female).

The Endangered **Hawaiian Duck** *Anas wyvilliana*. On O'ahu, Maui and Hawai'i there are very few pure birds remaining, because of hybridization with Mallard *A. platyrhynchos*. Photo: Michael Neal (nealstudios.net).

Polynesia & Micronesia

A mixture of high volcanic islands and low coral atolls, the islands of Polynesia and Micronesia are mostly small, with correspondingly low species diversity, but high levels of endemism. Polynesia includes both independent states and overseas dependencies, including Samoa, Tonga, the Cook Islands, Tuvalu, Tokelau, Niue, Wallis and Futuna, Pitcairn, Easter Island, and French Polynesia. Similarly, Micronesia comprises territories of the USA like the Mariana Islands and Wake Island, as well as the independent states of Kiribati, Palau, the Marshall Islands and the Federated States of Micronesia. While strictly part of Melanesia, Fiji is included in this biodiversity hotspot.

Species extinction rates in Polynesia and Micronesia approach the highest in the world, especially for birds. By one estimate, 2,000 bird species have been lost since the prehistoric beginning of human colonization.

Marquesan Imperial-pigeon *Ducula galeata.* Photo: Tim Laman (timlaman.com).

A range of invasive aliens, including rats, cats, dogs, mongooses, snakes, ants, plants and pathogens, continue to pose serious threats to the survival of native species. Some small Pacific islands are close to losing both their last forest areas and their endemic landbirds. Some are already coconut plantation monocultures. The avifauna of many islands has been reduced to a suite of less specialized, disturbance-tolerant species, many of them widespread in the region, or exotic.

For example, the Marquesas Islands in French Polynesia have been devastated by overgrazing and fire, and much of the original dry forest has been reduced to grassland. Most of the native plants survive only in relict forest patches, and on some small islands little vegetation of any kind remains.

The *Pomarea* monarchs, a genus endemic to the Marquesas, Cook and Society islands in Eastern Polynesia, are emblematic of the region's unique birdlife, and its fate. Of nine known species, all are, or were, confined to small islands, with ranges no larger than 100 km² and often much smaller. Three are Extinct, one Critically Endangered (Possibly Extinct), two Critically Endangered, one Endangered and two Vulnerable. The Critically Endangered Fatuhiva Monarch *P. whitneyi* was still common (though considered Vulnerable because of its small range) on the well-forested island of Fatu Hiva, until the first Black Rats *Rattus rattus* appeared around the turn of this century.

There are some brighter notes from the region, including new initiatives to deal with alien invasives and prevent inappropriate development activities, and action to preserve forests (as on Palau) to protect island watersheds.

Micronesian Megapode *Megapodius laperouse.* Photo: Mandy Etpison (necomarine.com).

The Endangered **Marquesan Imperial-pigeon** *Ducula galeata* was downlisted from Critically Endangered in 2008, on evidence that the population was slowly increasing. Until 2000, it survived only in inaccessible valleys on the rat-free island of Nuku Hiva. Illegal hunting, the main threat, has been reduced following a publicity campaign. A translocation programme has established a second breeding population on Ua Huka, and further reintroductions are planned.

The Endangered **Micronesian Megapode** *Megapodius laperouse* occurs in Palau and the Northern Mariana Islands. It is extinct on Guam. Illegal egg-collecting is a threat in Palau, and disturbance by tourists is increasing. Predation by rats, cats, dogs, pigs and monitor lizards is a threat on all islands. On Kayangel Atoll, where Palau's biggest population is found, rats have been eradicated with the enthusiastic participation of local people, because of the dramatic improvement in crop yields that has followed.

The improving status of the **Rarotonga Monarch** *Pomarea dimidiata* shows how changing attitudes and intensive conservation work can bring even the most depleted species back from the brink. Thought to be extinct by the early 1900s, it was rediscovered in the 1980s, and the population has grown from as few as 20 birds to almost 400. In 2000 it was downlisted from Critically Endangered to Endangered, and in 2012 to Vulnerable. But its entire global range is just 2 km^2, it is vulnerable to cyclones and other extreme events, and it survives only because of the intensive trapping of rats.

The decline of the Endangered **Ultramarine Lorikeet** *Vini ultramarina* followed the establishment of Black Rats *Rattus rattus* in its small range in the Marquesas Islands, French Polynesia. It has vanished from Ua Pou and Nuku Hiva since the 1990s, and birds introduced to Fatu Hiva disappeared in the decade after rats were seen there. A single captive pair was introduced to Ua Huka in the 1940s, and the population has since grown to around 2,000. Local people are participating in the work to keep rats out of Ua Huka, and rat-proof nestboxes are being installed.

The Endangered **Tuamotu Sandpiper** *Prosobonia cancellata* has steadily disappeared from islands in the Tuamotu Archipelago, French Polynesia, as Black Rats *Rattus rattus* and cats have spread. Although conversion of islands to coconut plantations is not necessarily a threat, it increases the number of boat visits, and the risk of rodent introductions. Visiting birdwatchers could also bring rats with them. The greatest long-term threat could be sea-level rise due to climate change. The population of birds on Tahanea crashed by 55% in less than a month in 2011 due to starvation after a strong swell contaminated the water table with seawater. Photos: Eric VanderWerf (pacificrimconservation.com) (perched) and Marie-Hélène Burle (feeding on flower).

Mangrove Finch *Camarhynchus heliobates*.
Photo: Roger Ahlman (pbase.com/ahlman).

Medium Tree-finch *Camarhynchus pauper*.
Photo: David Peters (dpphotoimages.com).

Galápagos

The volcanic islands of Galápagos straddle the equator west of mainland Ecuador, to which they belong politically. The entire Galápagos archipelago is protected as a National Park, Biosphere Reserve and World Heritage Site, but its popularity with tourists and scientists means an ever-present risk of the introduction of rats and new diseases.

Of 21 endemic landbird species (plus the Galápagos Heron, now considered the subspecies *sundevalli* of Striated Heron *Butorides striata*), 13 are the famous 'Darwin's finches'. There are also four endemic mockingbirds, the birds whose differences actually triggered Darwin's thinking about natural selection and the stability of species.

Three of the four mockingbirds are threatened. Confined to the island after which it is named, and a small satellite island, the Española Mockingbird *Mimus macdonaldi* still appears common, but is listed as Vulnerable because of the risk of extreme weather events and the accidental introduction of rats (which are currently not present). The Endangered San Cristóbal Mockingbird *M. melanotis* is declining because of predation, habitat destruction and disturbance, but is possibly more threatened by diseases and parasites introduced by the expanding chicken-farming industry on the island. More severe weather, and a warming and more humid climate, are likely to make the mockingbird more susceptible. Extreme weather events also cause numbers of the Floreana Mockingbird *M. trifasciatus* to fluctuate. In 2008, the population fell below the Critically Endangered threshold and it was uplisted from Endangered.

Two Darwin's finches are Critically Endangered. The Mangrove Finch *Camarhynchus heliobates* and Medium Tree-finch *C. pauper* have both suffered heavy predation from introduced species, but the greatest threat is probably from the nest-parasite *Philornis downsi*. Unknown in Galápagos until they began to be found in the nests of Darwin's finches in the late 1990s, the larvae of this fly emerge at night to feed on the blood and flesh of developing nestlings. It is spreading through the islands, has been found in the nests of the Floreana Mockingbird, and is already present on San Cristóbal.

Among seabirds which breed only or mainly on Galápagos, the Critically Endangered Galápagos Petrel *Pterodroma phaeopygia* is heavily predated by cats, dogs, pigs and rats, and its nests burrows are destroyed through trampling by cattle. Numbers of the Flightless Cormorant *Phalacrocorax harrisi* decline and then recover after El Niño events, but it is listed as Vulnerable because of its tiny range on Fernandina and Isabela.

Black Rats *Rattus rattus* are are believed to have been the major reason for the high nesting failure (70% in 2007) of the Critically Endangered **Mangrove Finch** *Camarhynchus heliobates* on Isabela. The first case of nesting mortality due to parasitization by the blood-sucking fly *Philornis downsi* was recorded in 2007, and this threat is becoming relatively more prominent as rats are reduced around the nest areas. A trial reintroduction to a rat-controlled site elsewhere on Isabela seems to have been successful, and others are planned. There have been recent reports of sightings on Fernandina, where the species was thought extinct.

The Critically Endangered **Medium Tree-finch** *Camarhynchus pauper* occurs only in an area of 23 km² in the highlands of Floreana. The population was found to have declined by 39% between 2004 and 2008, to a density of about 60 birds per square kilometre, and it was uplisted to Critically Endangered in 2009. Although the Galápagos National Park incorporates most of Floreana, it does not include the agricultural zone of the island that is the prime habitat for this species.

The Endangered **Galápagos Penguin** *Spheniscus mendiculus* is the most northerly breeding penguin. Its distribution is linked to the cool, nutrient-rich oceanic waters of the western Galápagos, which provide a high density of prey year-round. El Niño events cause the water to warm, and the penguin population crashes (by 77% in 1982–3, and 65% in 1997–8). Climate change is likely to increase the frequency of El Niño events, reducing the penguin's chances of regaining numbers between them.

Galápagos Penguin *Spheniscus mendiculus*.
Photo: Tim Laman (timlaman.com).

Waved Albatross *Phoebastria irrorata*. Photo: Mick Dryden.

Galápagos Petrel *Pterodroma phaeopygia*. Photo: Mick Dryden.

Similarly, the small range of the Lava Gull *Larus fuliginosus* has led to its listing as Vulnerable, although numbers appear stable. The Data Deficient White-vented Storm-petrel *Oceanites gracilis* is suspected to breed around Galápagos, but a nest has yet to be found in the archipelago.

Virtually the entire global population of the Critically Endangered **Waved Albatross** *Phoebastria irrorata* breeds on the island of Española. Birds first breed when four to six years of age and nest annually from March to December, immatures and non-breeding adults wandering to the coastal waters off the Pacific coast of South America. Although the main threat is probably incidental bycatch by longline fisheries, intentional but illegal harvesting to supply food and feather markets also appears to be a key factor in its ongoing decline.

The Critically Endangered **Floreana Mockingbird** *Mimus trifasciatus* became extinct on Floreana in the late 19th century, and has since been confined to Champion (0·1 km²) and Gardner-by-Floreana (0·8 km²). The Charles Darwin Foundation and Galápagos National Park Service have launched the Floreana Project, a long-term programme to restore the island's ecosystem, and reintroduce endemics including the mockingbird, using individuals from both islet populations to maximize genetic diversity. Photo: Luís Ortiz-Catedral.

The Critically Endangered **Galápagos Petrel** *Pterodroma phaeopygia*, which breeds in the highlands of five of the islands in the archipelago, has undergone an extremely rapid population decline over the past three generations (60 years). The principal threat is predation by introduced mammals, particularly rats, although a long-standing intensive rat control programme is being carried out around known colonies on four islands and is beginning to show some success.

The Endangered **San Cristóbal Mockingbird** *Mimus melanotis* is endemic to San Cristóbal. It occupies about one-quarter of the island's area, where the population density is about 60 birds per square kilometre. It was uplisted to Endangered in 2006 on evidence that the population was declining, particularly due to the impact of introduced species, parasites and diseases, the prevalence of which may become greater due to the increased humidity associated with more frequent and intense El Niño events. Photo: Eric VanderWerf (pacificrimconservation.com).

Barau's Petrel *Pterodroma baraui*. Photo: YaBaLeX (faune-reunion.com).

Pink Pigeon *Nesoenas mayeri*. Photo: Photo: Gary Jenkins.

Indian Ocean Islands

Like Madagascar, the islands that surround it in the Indian Ocean – Seychelles and Aldabra, the Mascarene Islands of Mauritius, Réunion and Rodrigues, and the Comoros – have high numbers of endemic species.

The best-known of Mauritius's endemic birds, the Dodo *Raphus cucullatus*, is one of ten endemic species known only from sub-fossils. Most of the island's forests have been converted to plantations, and what remains is severely degraded by introduced animals and plants. The surviving endemic birds are threatened by habitat loss, and nest-predation by introduced rats, monkeys and birds. But Mauritius can boast three outstanding conservation successes. The Vulnerable Mauritius Kestrel *Falco punctatus* was brought back from four wild birds in the 1970s to around 400 now; however, numbers have fallen since the late 1990s, and one subpopulation is thought to be extinct, probably because exotic plants have reduced the availability of natural nesting sites and invaded the more open areas the birds need for hunting. Similarly, the Endangered Pink Pigeon *Nesoenas mayeri* and Mauritius Parakeet *Psittacula eques* have both been brought back from near extinction. All three species depend upon ongoing conservation management. The Critically Endangered Mauritius Olive White-eye *Zosterops chloronothus* is similarly intensively managed, and also benefitting from translocation to predator-free islands, as is the Endangered Mauritius Fody *Foudia rubra*, which may soon warrant downlisting to Vulnerable.

Réunion has one threatened landbird, the Critically Endangered Réunion Cuckooshrike *Coracina newtoni*, but may also be the only breeding area for the Critically Endangered Mascarene Petrel *Pseudobulweria aterrima* and Endangered Barau's Petrel *Pterodroma baraui*. Rodrigues, home of an extinct relative of the Dodo and an extinct, endemic starling, has an endemic warbler *Acrocephalus rodericanus* which is increasing thanks to habitat restoration and may soon be downlisted from Endangered. Restoration to protect watersheds has also led to an increase in the Vulnerable Rodrigues Fody *Foudia flavicans*, which was reduced to 5–6 pairs in the late 1960s.

Equidistant from continental Africa and Madagascar, the Comoros islands are politically divided between the republic of the Comoros

The Endangered **Barau's Petrel** *Pterodroma baraui* nests in upland forest on Réunion and Rodrigues, dispersing as far east as Australia when not breeding. Illegal shooting in the 1990s may have been responsible for a rapid population decline, although numbers have apparently recovered. However, both the small population and very restricted breeding range are believed to be declining again, primarily due to predation by introduced cats and rats.

Although once common, the Endangered **Pink Pigeon** *Nesoenas mayeri* survives only in the Black River Gorges of south-west Mauritius and on Ile aux Aigrettes off the eastern coast. Severe loss of habitat has been compounded by continued predation of nests and adults by introduced Crab-eating Macaques *Macaca fascicularis*, Small Asian Mongoose *Herpestes javanicus*, rats, and feral cats. The pigeons are managed to maximise genetic diversity, with birds moved between subpopulations. Photo: Gary Jenkins.

The Critically Endangered **Anjouan Scops-owl** *Otus capnodes* rediscovered in the 1990s after over a century, survives in remaining fragments of native upland forest, but has been found in human-affected forest areas where large trees remain. Although it may be threatened by introduced Black Rats *Rattus rattus* and Common Mynas *Acridotheres tristis*, its apparent ability to adapt to suboptimal habitat gives hope that a larger population than is currently estimated may exist. Photo: Charlie Marsh.

The population of the Endangered **Seychelles Paradise-flycatcher** *Terpsiphone corvina* appears to have increased substantially in the last 20 years, at least partly owing to a variety of habitat management measures. Numbers on its last refuge on La Digue doubled between 1988 and 1997, but appear to have stabilized at 150–200 individuals. A population translocated to Denis Island in 2008 began breeding the following year.

The Critically Endangered **Réunion Cuckooshrike** *Coracina newtoni* is now only found in two small forested areas in the north-west of Réunion, although 95% of the current range is within the 38 km² reserve of Roche Ecrite. Two-thirds of the approximately 75 remaining individuals are males, possibly due to the effect of predation on incubating females by introduced rats and cats.

(Grand Comoro, Mohéli and Anjouan) and Mayotte, a French overseas department. Each island has its own endemic birds (five on Grand Comoro, one on Mohéli, three on Anjouan, and three on Mayotte), mostly dependent upon evergreen forest, which has been largely cleared from the lowlands. The Critically Endangered Grand Comoro Scops-owl *Otus pauliani* and Endangered Grand Comoro Drongo *Dicrurus fuscipennis* and Grand Comoro Flycatcher *Humblotia flavirostris* are found only on Mount Karthala, an unprotected site which is steadily losing its forest to logging and agriculture.

Beginning with the purchase of Cousin Island by BirdLife's predecessor, the International Council for Bird Preservation (ICBP), to save the last population of the then Critically Endangered Seychelles Warbler *Acrocephalus sechellensis*, a programme of habitat restoration and alien species control on a succession of islands has seen a suite of bird species moved to lower threat categories. The Cousin Island population of the warbler has now reached carrying capacity, and populations on Cousine, Denis, Aride and most recently Frégate appear secure. Now listed as Vulnerable, the warbler may soon be removed from the threatened species list altogether. Four of these islands also hold thriving populations of Endangered Seychelles Magpie-robin *Copsychus sechellarum*, once reduced to 12–15 individuals on Frégate. Steady improvements in habitat quality and extent have enabled the Seychelles White-eye *Zosterops modestus* to recover. Recategorized as Endangered in 2005, it may already be eligible for further downlisting. The Endangered Seychelles Scops-owl *Otus insularis* is thought to be stable in 31 km² of secure habitat on the island of Mahé. Only the Seychelles Paradise-flycatcher *Terpsiphone corvina* remains Critically Endangered, but has been increasing because of habitat management, and may be downlisted within the next few years if the population reintroduced to Denis becomes self-sustaining.

But south-west of the Seychelles, Aldabra's endemic warbler *Nesillas aldabrana* is extinct, and its endemic drongo, Aldabra Drongo *Dicrurus aldabranus*, Near Threatened. The status of several other taxa, currently classed as subspecies, is unclear; among them, the endemic subspecies of White-throated Rail *Dryolimnas cuvieri aldabranus* has the grim distinction of being the only extant flightless bird in the western Indian Ocean.

Seychelles Paradise-flycatcher
Terpsiphone corvina.
Photo: Jon Hornbuckle.

Réunion Cuckooshrike *Coracina newtoni*. Photo: Maxime Loubon.

THREATENED BIRD HOTSPOT

Atlantic Ocean Islands

The Atlantic islands include the four Macaronesian groups (the Azores, Madeira, Canary and Cape Verde Islands); the remote, mid-ocean Ascension, St Helena and the Tristan Group; the islands of São Tomé and Príncipe, nestling close to the coast of West Africa; and South Georgia and the South Sandwich Islands, which lie south-east of southernmost South America.

The Portuguese archipelagos of the Azores and Madeira have a Mediterranean climate, and share with the Canaries a unique laurel-dominated cloud forest. The Cape Verde Islands, off the coast of Mauritania and Senegal, are much more arid. São Tomé and Príncipe are equatorial, and the South Sandwich Islands are subantarctic.

The subantarctic islands are important for seabirds, and there are no resident landbirds on the South Sandwich Islands. Ascension Island has 11 breeding seabirds (many confined to surrounding stacks, although expected to return to the main island once feral cats have been eradicated), including the Vulnerable endemic Ascension Frigatebird *Fregata aquila*, which currently breeds only on the 1 km² cat-free Boatswainbird Island.

Gough Island, south of the Tristan da Cunha group, has been described as 'a strong contender for the title of most important seabird colony in the world', although is being ravaged by House Mice *Mus domesticus* which kill and eat up to 60% of the chicks of Critically Endangered Tristan Albatross *Diomedea dabbenena* and Endangered Atlantic Petrel *Pterodroma incerta*. Gough also has two endemic landbirds, the Vulnerable Gough Moorhen *Gallinula nesiotis* and Critically Endangered Gough Bunting *Rowettia goughensis*, which is undergoing contraction of its already tiny range because of predation and competition from House Mice.

São Tomé and Príncipe are two in a chain of four volcanic islands, along with Bioko and Annobón, which are all recognized as Endemic

The Critically Endangered **São Tomé Fiscal** *Lanius newtoni* was rediscovered in 1990 near the source of the Rio Xufexufe, in the south-west of the island. There have since been regular records from the Xufexufe catchment, and sightings of other birds in the centre and south-east of the island. The population may be greater than previously thought, but the area of suitable habitat (primary lowland and mid-altitude forest with little or no undergrowth) is limited.

Split from the African Olive Ibis *Bostrychia olivacea* on the basis of its much smaller size, colour differences in bare parts and plumage, and distinct vocalizations, the Critically Endangered **Dwarf Olive Ibis** *B. bocagei* was known only from historical records and anecdotal evidence from hunters, until a confirmed sighting in 1990. Unfortunately the hunters' anecdotes were often of birds killed, including 16 during six months in 1997. The ibis is apparently relatively widely, if thinly, distributed in the south of São Tomé.

The Critically Endangered **São Tomé Grosbeak** *Neospiza concolor* occupies a very small area of unprotected primary forest. The area is relatively remote and used only by hunters who do not represent a threat to the species. But plans to develop coffee plantations and restore and extend abandoned oil palm plantations are likely to result in the loss of suitable habitat. There are probably fewer than 50 individuals, and numbers are likely to be declining.

A massive forest fire in August 2010 at the only known breeding colony of the Endangered **Zino's Petrel** *Pterodroma madeira* killed several breeding adults, and only one chick survived to fledge. Before the next breeding season, 100 natural nests were restored, 60 artificial nests were installed to replace those that had collapsed, and coconut matting was laid to prevent further soil erosion. In 2011, 45 nests were found to be occupied and 16 chicks fledged. Ongoing surveys may yet reveal more breeding sites.
Photo: off Madeira; May 2010; Hadoram Shirihai / © The Tubenoses Project.

Bird Areas. São Tomé's distinctive avifauna includes two endemic monospecific genera, the Vulnerable São Tomé Short-tail *Amaurocichla bocagei* and the Critically Endangered São Tomé Grosbeak *Neospiza concolor*, two 'giants', the Vulnerable Giant Sunbird *Nectarinia thomensis* and Giant Weaver *Ploceus grandis*, and a 'dwarf', the Critically Endangered Dwarf Olive Ibis *Bostrychia bocagei*. Príncipe too has a unique monospecific genus, the Príncipe Thrush-babbler *Horizorhinus dohrni*, something of a taxonomic puzzle. All endemic species on both islands are threatened by forest loss and fragmentation, exacerbated by conversion to oil palm plantations, which is already affecting key areas of forest on São Tomé.

Madeira and the Canary Islands are home to three endemic laurel pigeons, none of which are now thought globally threatened following habitat restoration and hunting control. The recently split Vulnerable Monteiro's Storm-petrel *Oceanodroma monteiroi* breeds on two islets in the Azores, and the Endangered Zino's Petrel *Pterodroma madeira* only on a few mountain ledges in the central massif of Madeira. Among other Canary Islands endemics, the Fuerteventura Stonechat *Saxicola dacotiae* was downlisted from Endangered to Near Threatened in 2011 when its range and population were found to be larger than previously thought. The Azores Bullfinch *Pyrrhula murina* also proved more widespread and numerous than had been feared, although restoration of natural vegetation also played a part in its recovery from Critically Endangered to Endangered.

The impacts of high human populations and agriculture are the main threats to the birds of the Cape Verde Islands. Both the Endangered Cape Verde Warbler *Acrocephalus brevipennis* and the Critically Endangered Raso Lark *Alauda razae* have suffered range contractions because of habitat loss, although new populations of the warbler are being discovered, and it may be eligible for downlisting.

The Endangered **Azores Bullfinch** *Pyrrhula murina* appears entirely dependent upon native vegetation for food during many months of the year, and its historical decline and extremely small range are probably the result of native forest being replaced with plantations and agriculture. It is confined to the east of the island of São Miguel, where it was formerly believed to occupy just 6 km² on the slopes around Pico da Vara. In 2008, a simultaneous survey of all suitable habitat found its range to be much larger. Conservation measures include replanting native species, and establishing orchards to give local farmers an economic incentive to conserve the species and its habitat.
Photo: Carlos Ribeiro (flickr.com/photos/cazeribeiro1).

Suitable breeding habitat covers barely half the 7 km² island of Raso in the Cape Verde Islands, sole home of the Critically Endangered **Raso Lark** *Alauda razae*. Dramatic fluctuations in its numbers are thought to be linked to rain and drought. Censuses of the island in 1998 and 2003 found 92 and 98 birds respectively, but following rain in 2004 the population rapidly increased to 130 individuals in 2005, 190 in 2009, and 1,490 by November 2011. When the population is low, only a third of birds are female. Long-term desertification in the Cape Verdes is clearly a major threat.
Photo: Adam Riley (rockjumperbirding.com).

The albatross conundrum

Of the 22 species of albatross, 17 are globally threatened, and the remaining five Near Threatened. Albatrosses are naturally long-lived birds, which take many years to reach breeding maturity, and tend to mate for life. The larger species breed only every two years, producing one young, and even among the smaller 'annually' breeding species, a proportion of each population may not actually breed every year. The loss of any breeding birds, let alone many, can therefore have a significant impact on the long-term viability of populations, especially of the less numerous species. These impacts may not become visible until declines are well advanced, and any recovery in numbers following reductions in bycatch will also be slow.

Albatrosses forage in nutrient-rich parts of the oceans, over sea-mounts or the upwellings of currents, where fish biomass is highest. These are also the areas targeted by fishermen. Remote tracking has found extensive overlap between albatross foraging grounds and some of the world's major fisheries.

By one estimate, an albatross dies every five minutes, on the hooks of longline fishing vessels, drowned in the nets of trawlers, or fatally injured by collisions with the cables that secure the nets. Longlining is a fast-growing industry. At least three billion baited hooks are set every year, and an estimated 100,000 albatrosses are killed annually.

The threat status of the world's albatross species		
Amsterdam Albatross	*Diomedea amsterdamensis*	CR
Antipodean Albatross	*Diomedea antipodensis*	VU
Atlantic Yellow-nosed Albatross	*Thalassarche chlororhynchos*	EN
Black-browed Albatross	*Thalassarche melanophrys*	EN
Black-footed Albatross	*Phoebastria nigripes*	VU
Buller's Albatross	*Thalassarche bulleri*	NT
Campbell Albatross	*Thalassarche impavida*	VU
Chatham Albatross	*Thalassarche eremita*	VU
Grey-headed Albatross	*Thalassarche chrysostoma*	VU
Indian Yellow-nosed Albatross	*Thalassarche carteri*	EN
Laysan Albatross	*Phoebastria immutabilis*	NT
Light-mantled Albatross	*Phoebetria palpebrata*	NT
Northern Royal Albatross	*Diomedea sanfordi*	EN
Salvin's Albatross	*Thalassarche salvini*	VU
Short-tailed Albatross	*Phoebastria albatrus*	VU
Shy Albatross	*Thalassarche cauta*	NT
Sooty Albatross	*Phoebetria fusca*	EN
Southern Royal Albatross	*Diomedea epomophora*	VU
Tristan Albatross	*Diomedea dabbenena*	CR
Wandering Albatross	*Diomedea exulans*	VU
Waved Albatross	*Phoebastria irrorata*	CR
White-capped Albatross	*Thalassarche steadi*	NT

Simple, inexpensive mitigation measures, such as weighting the hooks so that they sink faster, attaching pennants to lines, dyeing bait blue, or setting hooks only at night, can reduce seabird bycatch dramatically, especially when used in combination. South of Chile, bycatch was reduced from over 1,500 birds in one year to zero through the adoption of modified fishing gear. Every hooked albatross represents the loss of a piece of bait, and potentially a fish, so these mitigation measures make good economic sense. A study of a three-vessel fishing fleet in Argentina demonstrated that 'bird-scaring lines' could lead to savings of between $1–2 million over ten years. Most regional fisheries management organizations in the southern oceans have made bycatch mitigation measures mandatory.

Albatrosses also suffer loss of eggs and nestlings to alien rodents and other predators. Predation of Critically Endangered Tristan Albatross *Diomedea dabbenena* chicks by mice on Gough Island has reduced fledging success to half that at other *Diomedea* colonies.

The most threatened of all albatrosses, the Critically Endangered Amsterdam Albatross *Diomedea amsterdamensis*, has a global population of around 170 birds, including 80 mature adults, of which 26 pairs breed each year. The only breeding colony, on Amsterdam Island in the southern Indian Ocean, has been reduced in area and quality by introduced cattle. Predators, particularly feral cats, are also a major threat. The foraging range overlaps with longline tuna fisheries, and a recent analysis indicates that bycatch exceeding six individuals per year would be enough to cause a potentially irreversible population decline. But the the Amsterdam Albatross is threatened primarily by diseases, including avian cholera, that already affect breeding Indian Yellow-nosed Albatrosses *Thalassarche carteri* just 3 km away from the colony. Increased chick mortality in recent years suggests the population is already affected.

In 1985, a cyclone hit the breeding sites of the Endangered Northern Royal Albatross *Diomedea sanfordi* on the Chatham Islands, reducing soil cover and destroying most of the vegetation. Breeding success plummeted to 8–18% due to egg breakage and high temperatures. By 2007, vegetation cover had recovered to about 70%, and breeding productivity has continued to improve, but is still below that of the 1970s. Too much vegetation cover can also limit breeding success, preventing adults from nesting, or trapping fledglings. Two Critically Endangered Waved Albatross *Phoebastria irrorata* colonies in Galápagos were abandoned after goats were removed, allowing vegetation to invade the nesting grounds.

In a rare piece of good news for albatrosses, breeding Black-browed Albatross *Thalassarche melanophrys* numbers on the Falkland Islands (Islas Malvinas) have been increasing by at least 4% annually since 2005. The reasons are not entirely clear, but efforts to reduce seabird bycatch and beneficial feeding conditions are likely to have contributed. If the increase is sustained, the species will be considered for downlisting from Endangered.

The **Black-footed Albatross** *Phoebastria nigripes*, downlisted from Endangered to Vulnerable in 2012, is one of only four species of albatross that are increasing in numbers. An 80 km (50 mile) Protected Species Zone bans longline fishing around the Northwestern Hawaiian Islands where it breeds, and fishing vessels in Hawaiian waters are required to use a range of measures to reduce seabird bycatch. Photo: Roger & Liz Charlwood (WorldWildlifeImages.com).

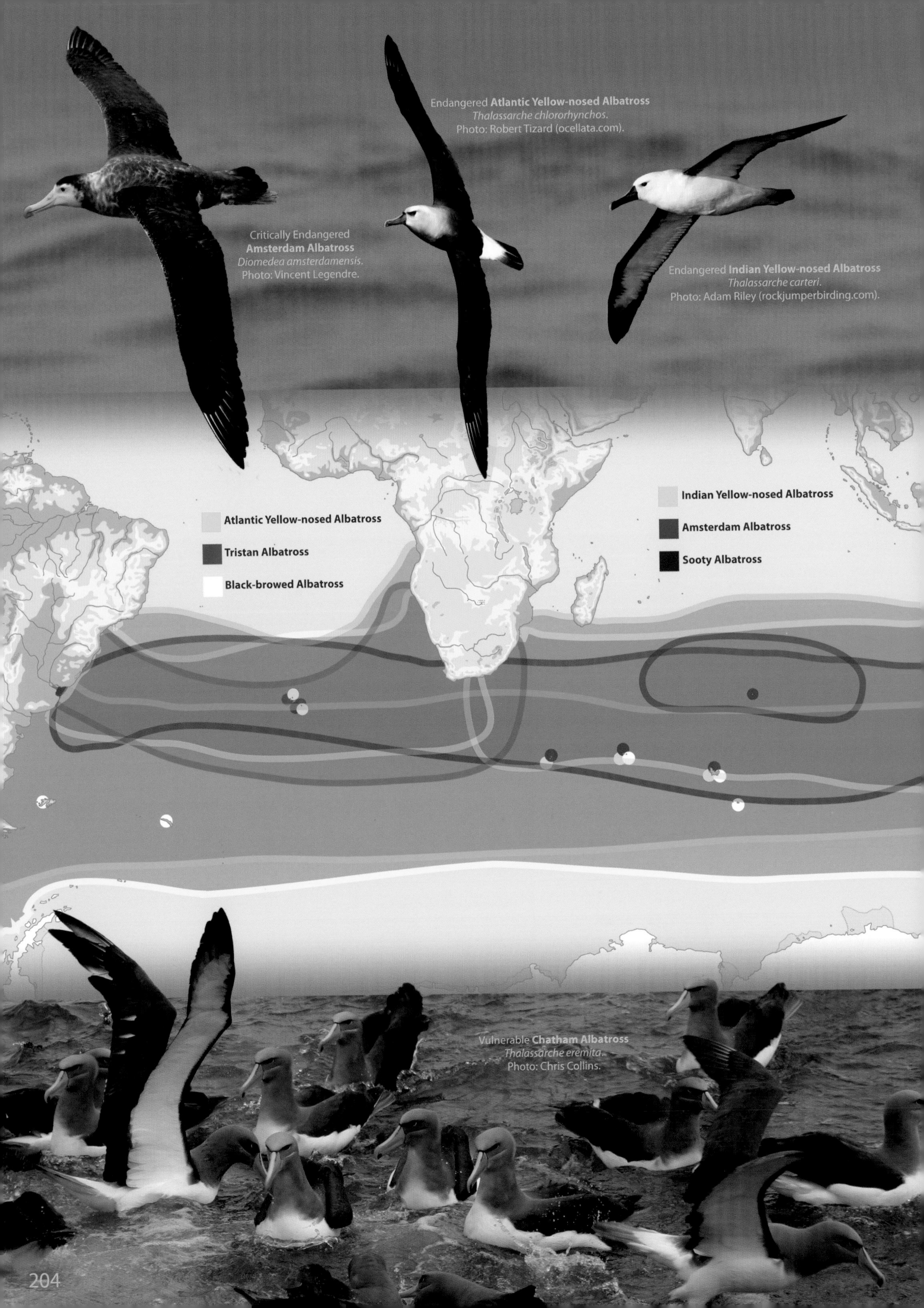

Critically Endangered
Amsterdam Albatross
Diomedea amsterdamensis.
Photo: Vincent Legendre.

Endangered **Atlantic Yellow-nosed Albatross**
Thalassarche chlororhynchos.
Photo: Robert Tizard (ocellata.com).

Endangered **Indian Yellow-nosed Albatross**
Thalassarche carteri.
Photo: Adam Riley (rockjumperbirding.com).

- Atlantic Yellow-nosed Albatross
- Tristan Albatross
- Black-browed Albatross

- Indian Yellow-nosed Albatross
- Amsterdam Albatross
- Sooty Albatross

Vulnerable **Chatham Albatross**
Thalassarche eremita.
Photo: Chris Collins.

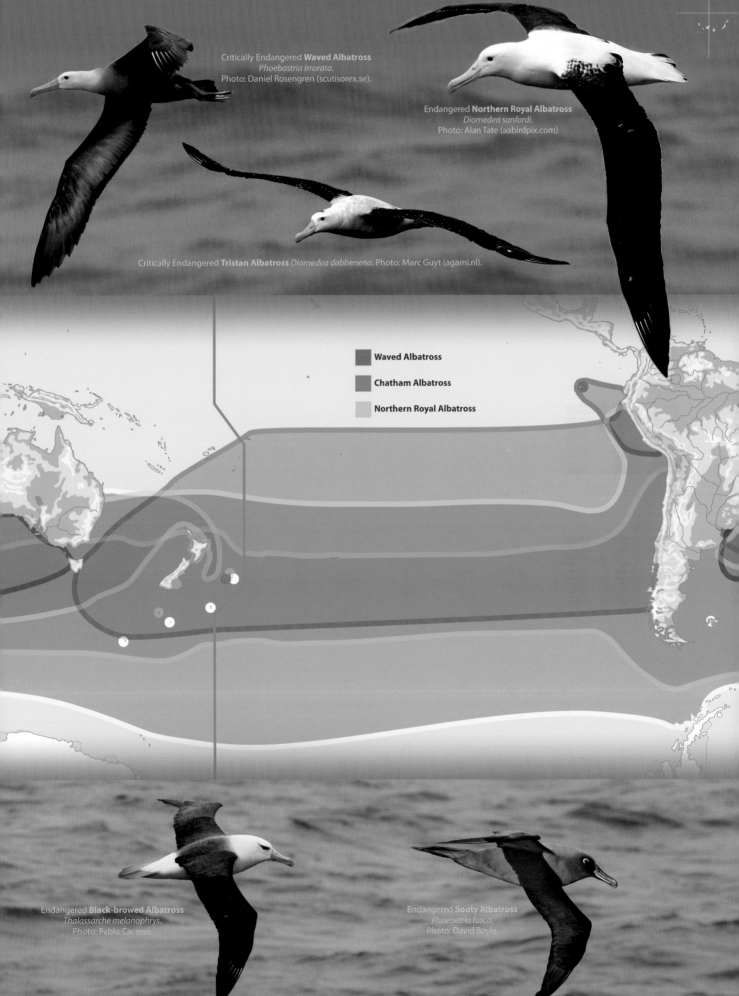

Critically Endangered **Waved Albatross**
Phoebastria irrorata.
Photo: Daniel Rosengren (scutisorex.se).

Endangered **Northern Royal Albatross**
Diomedea sanfordi.
Photo: Alan Tate (aabirdpix.com)

Critically Endangered **Tristan Albatross** *Diomedea dabbenena*. Photo: Marc Guyt (agami.nl).

■ Waved Albatross

■ Chatham Albatross

□ Northern Royal Albatross

Endangered **Black-browed Albatross**
Thalassarche melanophrys.
Photo: Pablo Caceres.

Endangered **Sooty Albatross**
Phoebetria fusca.
Photo: David Boyle.

Oceanic Islands

This section covers 115 of the 130 Endangered or Critically Endangered species that breed on oceanic islands across the world, plus three that are Extinct in the Wild. Those excluded are Egyptian Vulture *Neophron percnopterus*, which breeds on some Macaronesian islands but is covered in three of the other regional sections and the 14 species restricted to Australasian oceanic islands (included in the Australasia section (*page 150*)).

Extinct in the Wild (EW)	**3**
Critically Endangered (CR)	**55**
Endangered (EN)	**61**
Vulnerable (VU)	**87**
Data Deficient (DD)	**1**

A summary of the most threatened bird families on Oceanic Islands (excluding species from Australasian islands)

Family	CR	EN	Tot.	Family	CR	EN	Tot.
Albatrosses (Diomedeidae)	3	4	7	**Old World warblers** (Sylviidae)	2	6	8
Petrels & shearwaters (Procellariidae)	4	7	11	**White-eyes** (Zosteropidae)	3	3	6
Pigeons (Columbidae)	1	6	7	**Mockingbirds** (Mimidae)	2	1	3
Parrots (Psittacidae)	1	4	5	**Thrushes** (Turdidae)	3	–	3
Owls (Strigidae)	3	1	4	**Finches & Hawaiian honeycreepers** (Fringillidae)	11	5	16
Monarchs (Monarchidae)	4	3	7	**Buntings & allies** (Emberizidae)	3	1	4

Other families: The number of species in each family is shown in square brackets: Megapodes (Megapodiidae) [2]; Ducks (Anatidae) [2]; Penguins (Spheniscidae) [2]; Storm-petrels (Hydrobatidae) [2]; Ibises (Threskiornithidae) [2]; Herons (Ardeidae) [1]; Frigatebirds (Fregatidae) [1]; Boobies (Sulidae) [1]; Harrier & vulture (Accipitridae) [2]; Rails (Rallidae) [2]; Plovers (Charadriidae) [1]; Sandpipers & allies (Scolopacidae) [1]; Swifts (Apodidae) [1]; Hummingbirds (Trochilidae) [1]; Kingfishers (Alcedinidae) [2]; Hornbills (Bucerotidae) [1]; Ovenbirds (Furnariidae) [1]; Honeyeaters (Meliphagidae) [1]; Cuckooshrikes (Campephagidae) [1]; Shrikes (Laniidae) [1]; Drongos (Dicruridae) [1]; Crows (Corvidae) [2]; Martins (Hirundinidae) [1]; Larks (Alaudidae) [1]; Starlings (Sturnidae) [1]; Chats & Old World flycatchers (Muscicapidae) [2]; Weavers & allies (Ploceidae) [1].   15   20   35

See Appendix 2 (*page 339*) for more information on these families. **TOTAL (39 FAMILIES)** | **55** | **61** | **116**

EN **Micronesian Megapode** *Megapodius laperouse*   194

▼ **POPULATION: 1,300–1,700** | **THREATS:** MAN, SPP, HUN, (CLI), (GEO)

Having been extirpated from Guam, this megapode is now only found on the island of Palau and on the Northern Mariana Islands. It breeds in forests on limestone or volcanic soils but also occurs in secondary habitat and coconut plantations. The diet is varied and consists of crabs, insects and plant matter. The Palau subspecies *senex* makes mound-nests from leaf-litter, or burrows into sand, but on the Marianas Islands the nominate subspecies uses chambers that are heated geothermally or by the sun, dug into cinder soil. It is subject to many threats, including disturbance, predation and volcanic activity, and, in the recent past at least, eggs have been collected and birds hunted.

Photo: Mandy Etpison (necomarine.com)

EN **Polynesian Megapode** *Megapodius pritchardii*

▼ **POPULATION: 450–650** | **THREATS:** HUN, SPP, AGR, CLI?, (GEO)

Endemic to Tonga, where the fossil record indicates it was once widespread, this megapode now has only a remnant population on the island of Niuafo'ou and a reintroduced population on Fonualei. As it uses hot volcanic ash to incubate its eggs, nesting sites are confined to areas of loose soil close to vents, either in forest or in open ash, or on the beaches of crater lakes. The population on Niuafo'ou is still declining, possibly due to egg collecting, hunting birds and predation, although natural shifts in geothermal activity may also be a factor. However, the newly established population on uninhabited Fonualei provides new hope for the future of this rare bird.

Photo: Dieter Rinke / BirdLife

EN **Hawaiian Duck** *Anas wyvilliana* `193`

▼ **POPULATION: 1,500** | **THREATS: SPP**, MAN, (AGR), (CLI), (HUN), (DEV), (ECO)

Once found on most of the Hawaiian Islands, this duck is now restricted to Kauaʻi and Niʻihau, and also Oʻahu, Hawaiʻi and Maui where it has been reintroduced. Historically, loss of wetlands and predation by introduced mammals such as mongooses, cats and dogs led to large population declines, but hybridization with feral Mallard *A. platyrhynchos*, brought in for ornamental and hunting purposes, is now the greatest threat to the species' recovery as this increases the danger of genetic introgression. Habitat degradation due to the impact of alien plants and feral animals, and the effects of drought and human disturbance are also important factors. Wetland restoration and captive breeding programmes are underway.

Photo: Eric VanderWerf (pacificrimconservation.com)

CR **Laysan Duck** *Anas laysanensis* `186`

▲ **POPULATION: 500–680** | **THREATS:** CLI, SPP, (HUN)

Endemic to the Hawaiian Islands, where sub-fossil remains indicate it was once widespread, this small duck was confined to Laysan, but in 2004/5 a small population was successfully translocated to Midway Atoll. Brine flies are a particularly important food source during the breeding season. Although close to extinction at the beginning of the 20th century, the population has increased to over 500 birds following the eradication of introduced rabbits. It is subject to extreme population fluctuations, avian botulism killing 160 birds in 2008. However, numbers are currently increasing and Laysan has reached its carrying capacity. This species may warrant downlisting if populations continue to be self-sustaining and stabilize.

Photo: Joe Fuhrman

EN **Northern Rockhopper Penguin** *Eudyptes moseleyi* `11`

▼ **POPULATION: 100,000–499,999** | **THREATS:** FISH, HUN, SPP, ECO, MAN, CLI?

The majority of the population of this penguin occurs on Gough Island and islands in the Tristan da Cunha Archipelago in the South Atlantic, with the remainder found on Amsterdam Island and St Paul Island, in the Indian Ocean. It breeds in huge colonies in a variety of habitats ranging from open, boulder-strewn beaches to among stands of tussock grass, often near freshwater springs or pools. Although, historically, egg collecting and predation may have led to a population decline, the causes of the current ongoing decline are unclear. However, the impact of climate change and commercial fisheries on food supplies may be an important factor.

Photo: Marie-Hélène Burle

EN **Galápagos Penguin** *Spheniscus mendiculus* `196`

▼ **POPULATION: 1,200** | **THREATS:** CLI, FISH, MAN, HUN, SPP, PLN

The most northerly breeding penguin, this species is endemic to Galápagos, where 96% of the population breeds on the western islands of Isabela and Fernandina. It nests at sea level, breeding throughout the year in response to food availability, and forages close to shore at relatively shallow depths. Although the population is subject to severe fluctuations, overall there has been a very rapid decline over the last three decades. The very small breeding range and population make it particularly prone to the effect of marine perturbations on fish stocks, events that may be becoming more extreme. However, predation, disease and human disturbance are also important factors.

Photo: Roy de Haas (agami.nl)

CR **Waved Albatross** *Phoebastria irrorata*

`202,205`

▼ POPULATION: 34,700 | THREATS: CLI, FISH, HUN, SPP, (PLN)

The breeding population of this albatross is now essentially confined to Española, Galápagos, although adults have been seen recently on Genovesa and on the Isla de la Plata off the Ecuadorian coast. In the non-breeding season birds move mainly east and south-east into waters off the Ecuadorian and Peruvian continental shelf. The greatest threat is probably incidental bycatch by longline fisheries, a factor that has been exacerbated by the transition from traditional to more modern fishing techniques in inshore waters around Galápagos. Galápagos Giant Tortoise *Chelonoidis nigra*, the only native herbivore, may play a key role in vegetation control and maintaining suitable habitat for breeding.

Photo: Nigel Voaden

CR **Amsterdam Albatross** *Diomedea amsterdamensis*

`202,205`

▼ POPULATION: 100 | THREATS: SPP, MAN, CLI?, (FISH)

The breeding population of this large albatross is confined to a tiny area on Amsterdam Island in the southern Indian Ocean. In non-breeding years, adults range from the coast of eastern South Africa to the south of Western Australia and possibly New Zealand. Historical declines are due to degradation of breeding habitat by introduced cattle and human disturbance. Today, the population is threatened primarily by the potential spread of bacterial diseases that affect the nearby Indian Yellow-nosed Albatross *Thalassarche carteri* colony. Infection risks are very high and increased chick mortality over recent years suggests the population is already affected. Introduced predators and accidental bycatch by longline fisheries also remain ongoing threats.

Photo: Vincent Legendre

CR **Tristan Albatross** *Diomedea dabbenena*

`202,205`

▼ POPULATION: 4,700 | THREATS: **FISH**, **SPP**, (CLI), (HUN)

This huge albatross is restricted to Gough Island although, in some years, a single pair breeds on Inaccessible Island in the Tristan da Cunha Archipelago. It nests primarily in wet heath where the vegetation is open enough to permit take-off and landings. Outside the breeding season, the species disperses to south Atlantic and South African waters and possibly the Indian Ocean. The main threat comes from interactions with longline fisheries, with a high proportion of *Diomedea* albatross bycatch in southern Brazilian waters being of this species. However, predation of chicks by the introduced House Mouse *Mus domesticus* causes very low breeding success and, alone, has been sufficient to drive a population decline of over 50% over three generations.

Photo: Robert Tizard (ocellata.com)

EN **Sooty Albatross** *Phoebetria fusca*

`202,205`

▼ POPULATION: 28,000 | THREATS: FISH, HUN, SPP

This medium-sized albatross breeds in loose colonies of up to 50–60 nests on several islands in the south Atlantic and Indian Oceans. Non-breeding birds range mainly throughout the southern Indian and Atlantic Oceans, with adults moving north in winter from subantarctic to subtropical seas, whereas immature birds tend to remain in subtropical waters year-round. The very rapid population decline is probably due to interactions with fisheries, although introduced predators and avian disease may also be factors on some islands. However, there is high variability in population counts between years and further data are required to confirm the species' conservation status.

Photo: Robert Tizard (ocellata.com)

EN **Black-browed Albatross** *Thalassarche melanophrys* `202,205`

▼ **POPULATION:** 1,150,000 | **THREATS: FISH**, SPP, CLI?, (GEO)

Foraging widely across the southern oceans, the majority of the population of this medium-sized albatross breeds on islands in the sub-polar waters off South America (see *page 284*). However, small numbers also occur on the Crozet and Kerguelen Islands as well as on Australasian islands (see *page 166*). It first breeds when 8–13 years of age and may not breed every year. During the breeding season, adults range as far as 500 km from the nest to feed. On the Kerguelen Islands, predation by cats is thought to impact upon the breeding colonies at Jeanne d'Arc Peninsula.

Photo: Pablo Caceres (flickr.com/photos/pablocaceres)

EN **Atlantic Yellow-nosed Albatross** *Thalassarche chlororhynchos*

▼ **POPULATION:** 21,000–32,000 | **THREATS:** FISH, (HUN), (SPP) `202,205`

This small albatross breeds on Gough Island and islands in the Tristan da Cunha Archipelago, dispersing throughout the south Atlantic Ocean during the non-breeding season. It is one of the commonest species of albatross attending longline fishing vessels, and large numbers are caught as incidental bycatch. On the Tristan da Cunha islands, the number of breeding pairs dropped from 20,000–30,000 in 1974 to an estimated 3,250 in 2001, a decline that is projected to continue unless current initiatives to address incidental mortality are successful. Although House Mouse *Mus domesticus* and Black Rat *Rattus rattus* occur on some breeding islands, they have no known effects on breeding success.

Photo: Robert Tizard

EN **Indian Yellow-nosed Albatross** *Thalassarche carteri* `202,205`

▼ **POPULATION:** 83,160 | **THREATS: FISH, SPP**

Previosuly considered conspecific with Atlantic Yellow-nosed Albatross *T. chlororhynchos*, most of the population breeds on Amsterdam Island, although there are colonies on other islands in the subantarctic Indian Ocean. Non-breeding birds disperse throughout the southern Indian Ocean, and are frequently observed off southern Africa and south-western Australia, and east to north-eastern New Zealand. The rapid population decline is the result of adult mortality and poor recruitment due to disease and interactions with fisheries. The Amsterdam Island colony lost many chicks to bacterial diseases in the 1980s, and such deaths still occur.

Photo: Jean-Florent Mandelbaum

EN **Henderson Petrel** *Pterodroma atrata*

▼ **POPULATION:** 50,000–99,999 | **THREATS:** SPP, CLI?

Although this gadfly petrel is only known to breed on uninhabited Henderson Island, it is also likely to occur on other islands in the region. The non-breeding range is not well known but the species has been sighted at Easter Island. It nests only in dense forest on the plateau, usually near the coast. Breeding success is low, at less than 20%, primarily due to the predation of chicks by Polynesian Rats *Rattus exulans*, although predation by crabs *Coenobita* spp. is also a possibility. In 2011, a rat eradication operation was carried out. As this species has a very restricted geographical distribution the impacts of climate change could be a particular threat.

Off Henderson Island, August 2007. Photo: Hadoram Shirihai / © The Tubenoses Project

EN **Barau's Petrel** *Pterodroma baraui*

198

▼ **POPULATION: 6,000–8,000** | **THREATS:** SPP, PLN, CLI?, MAN?, (HUN)

Breeding at probably just ten colonies in fewer than five locations, this gadfly petrel is known only from Réunion and Rodrigues, where it nests in burrows in volcanic ash soils on cliff ledges in upland elfin forest. Recent tracking data indicates that they can disperse up to 5,000 km across the central and eastern Indian Ocean during the non-breeding season, where it favours warm waters with low productivity. A long-term decline is suspected to be due to increased juvenile mortality caused by disorientation resulting from light pollution. However, predation by introduced mammals is also a significant ongoing threat. Recent measures to reduce light pollution have had some success.

Photo: Dubi Shapiro (pbase.com/dubisha)

CR **Galápagos Petrel** *Pterodroma phaeopygia*

33,197

▼ **POPULATION: 6,000–15,000** | **THREATS: SPP**, AGR, CLI, FISH?, DEV?

This large, long-winged gadfly petrel is known to breed on five islands in the Galápagos Archipelago, but may occur on others. It nest in burrows or natural cavities in the humid highlands at between 300–900 m. In the non-breeding season it disperses to the Pacific coasts of South and Central America. Its diet consists primarily of squid, fish and crustaceans. Major threats include predation by introduced mammals, agriculture (including consequential nest destruction by livestock), habitat degradation by alien plants and collision with man-made structures. An increase in longline fisheries in inshore waters is likely to affect foraging birds.

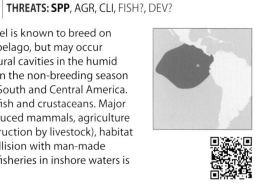

Photo: Daniel Bengtsson

EN **Bermuda Petrel** (or Cahow) *Pterodroma cahow*

▲ **POPULATION: 196** | **THREATS:** CLI, SPP, (PLN), (DEV)

Endemic to Bermuda, this gadfly petrel was thought extinct until specimens were obtained in the early 20th century. In 1951, 18 breeding pairs were discovered on rocky islets, and subsequent conservation management, including the translocation of chicks to form a new colony, has brought this species back from the brink of extinction; 98 pairs nested in 2011. The population recovery was hampered by nest site competition with White-tailed Tropicbirds *Phaethon lepturus* but the petrels have successfully been encouraged to use artificial burrows. In the non-breeding season, birds probably move north into the Atlantic, following the warm waters on the western edges of the Gulf Stream.

Bermuda Island; November 2011. Photo: Hadoram Shirihai / © The Tubenoses Project

EN **Zino's Petrel** *Pterodroma madeira*

201

= **POPULATION: 90–110** | **THREATS:** CLI?, FIRE?, MAN?, (HUN), (SPP)

This gadfly petrel, Europe's most endangered seabird, breeds only on the island of Madeira in burrows on inaccessible mountain ledges at 1,600 m. Its range outside the breeding season is little known. A massive forest fire at the sole known breeding site in 2010 killed 25 young and 3 adults, with only one of 13 surviving birds fledging successfully. It also exacerbated soil erosion and made chicks more vulnerable to predation. However, as birds live for around 15 years, the long-term effects on the overall population will not be known for some time. Before the fire, the population was slowly recovering, primarily due to a successful programme to control Black Rats *Rattus rattus* and feral cats.

Off Madeira; May 2010. Photo: Hadoram Shirihai / © The Tubenoses Project

EN **Phoenix Petrel** *Pterodroma alba* `189`

▼ **POPULATION: 30,000** | **THREATS:** SPP, DEV, (HUN)

Repeated surveys for this petrel have shown population declines and local extinctions and it now probably occurs at fewer than ten locations on islands across Polynesia. However, populations may occur in areas that have yet to be surveyed. During the non-breeding season it disperses over much of the tropical Pacific as far north as Hawaii and as far south as the Kermadec Islands. Birds only survive on islands free of cats and rats, but Black Rat *Rattus rattus* has recently colonized Kiritimati where the majority of birds breed and a very rapid population decline is predicted. There are, however, plans to tape-lure birds to breed on cat-free Jarvis Island.

Photo: Eric VanderWerf (pacificrimconservation.com)

EN **Atlantic Petrel** *Pterodroma incerta*

▼ **POPULATION: 5,000,000** | **THREATS:** SPP, DEV, TRA, (HUN)

Although currently only known to breed on Gough Island, there is a slim chance that this gadfly petrel may still occur on other islands in the Tristan da Cunha group. At sea it feeds across the south Atlantic and, very occasionally, moves into the Indian Ocean. It nests in burrows and fledging success is believed to be very low, at 20% or less. Predation by introduced mice is believed to be the most serious threat but native Southern Skuas *Catharacta antarctica*, of which there is a large population on the island, are also likely to take birds. In the past this species was an important winter food source for Tristan Islanders. Other potential threats include mortality due to hurricanes and grounding of birds due to light pollution.

Photo: Robert Tizard (ocellata.com)

CR **Fiji Petrel** *Pseudobulweria macgillivrayi*

▼ **POPULATION: <50** | **THREATS:** SPP, CLI?, FISH?

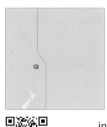

Previously known only from a specimen collected in 1855 on the island of Gau, Fiji, this petrel was rediscovered in 1983. Since then, several immature birds have been reported stranded on local roofs and, in 2009, up to three birds, including the individual photographed here, were documented at sea for the first time: in waters off Gau during the Fiji Petrel Expedition. Its ecology is little known, but it is suspected to breed amongst colonies of Collared Petrel *Pterodroma brevipes* in the rugged interior. The greatest threat is assumed to be introduced mammalian predators but it may also be at risk from longline fisheries. Specially trained 'sniffer' dogs may be able to locate nest burrows in future.

Off Gau Island; May 2009. Photo: Hadoram Shirihai; / © The Tubenoses Project

CR **Mascarene Petrel** *Pseudobulweria aterrima*

▼ **POPULATION: 100–200** | **THREATS:** SPP, DEV, (HUN)

Now known to breed only on the island of Réunion, there are historical records of this gadfly petrel from Rodrigues and more recently from Mauritius, where a roadkill was found in 2002. Five breeding sites are known, all on cliffs, some at 1,000 m altitude. However, recent estimates indicate that perhaps just a few dozen pairs remain. It is, however, possible that they still nest in montane area on Mauritius. The main threats are introduced mammalian predators and light-induced disorientation, particularly in urban areas. A public awareness campaign has led to the successful rescue of many birds involved in light-induced collisions but further conservation measures are urgently needed.

Photo: Nicolas Gaidet & Thomas Gerdil

CR Townsend's Shearwater *Puffinus auricularis*

▼ **POPULATION: 250–999** | **THREATS: SPP**, CLI?, (GEO)

This medium-sized shearwater now breeds only on Socorro in the Revillagigedo Archipelago, Mexico, having been extirpated from nearby Isla Clarión by introduced pigs and rabbits and from San Benedicto by a volcano eruption in the 1950s. It spends the non-breeding season over the adjacent continental shelf. The species nests in rocky burrows within dense bushy areas at the forest edge, usually at around 700 m, in areas that have been heavily degraded by overgrazing and soil compaction caused by sheep. Predation by introduced feral cats is severe and potential infrastructure developments, including a prison, could increase the risk of shearwater deaths due to light pollution.

Photo: Danielle Chelewiak

EN Newell's Shearwater *Puffinus newelli*

▼ **POPULATION: 33,000–38,600** | **THREATS: SPP**, PLN, DEV, TRA, EGY, FISH?, (CLI)

This medium-sized shearwater was previously considered conspecific with Townsend's Shearwater *P. auricularis*. Around 90% of the population nests in montane forests on Kaua`i in Hawaii, with smaller colonies on several other islands in the archipelago. It spends the rest of the year feeding at ocean fronts along the Equatorial Counter Current. Breeding habitat is prone to devastation by hurricanes and modification by alien plants. It is also subject to numerous other threats including predation by introduced mammals, collision with tall, man-made structures, and being grounded by artificial lighting. A range of conservation measures is in place and significant success has been achieved in reducing light attraction and collisions.

Photo: Robby Kohley

EN White-throated (or Polynesian) Storm-petrel *Nesofregetta fuliginosa*

▼ **POPULATION: 250–999** | **THREATS:** SPP, AGR, HUN

This storm-petrel breeds on many islands throughout the south Pacific but numbers have declined rapidly, mainly due to the impact of introduced mammalian predators. It is now thought to be extinct at some sites, although small numbers may still occur in Australasia (see *page 167*). On uninhabited Jarvis Island, a colonization programme has been successful, and a mammal eradication programme that commenced in 2008 on eight of the Phoenix Islands should also benefit this species. However, an attempt to eradicate feral cats on Kirimati has failed to limit predation, and the combined effects of light-attraction and cyclones may impact on the long-term survival of the species in French Polynesia.

Photo: Eric VanderWerf (pacificrimconservation.com)

CR (PE) Guadalupe Storm-petrel *Oceanodroma macrodactyla*

? **POPULATION: <50** | **THREATS:** SPP?

Once abundant on the island of Guadalupe, Mexico, this storm-petrel has not been recorded since 1912, despite several searches. It has probably been driven to extinction by feral cats, compounded by the destruction of nesting burrows by goats. However, this species is difficult to detect and there have been relatively recent records of unidentified storm-petrels calling at night. This, and the fact that breeding Leach's Storm-petrel *O. leucorhoa* still occur on Guadalupe, provides some hope that the species may still breed in rock crevices in areas inaccessible to cats. Goats have now been eradicated and the removal of other introduced species is underway.

Illustration: Tomasz Cofta

19

EN **Madagascar Sacred Ibis** *Threskiornis bernieri*

▼ **POPULATION:** 1,500–2,200 | **THREATS:** HUN, LOG, PLN, SPP?

Although the majority of the population of this ibis is found on Madagascar (see *page 83*), the subspecies *abbotti* occurs on the large coral atoll of Aldabra, where there is a sedentary population of several hundred birds. It feeds on invertebrates and organic material, occasionally taking small vertebrates such as frogs, reptiles and small birds. It differs from the nominate subspecies on Madgasacar in having a blue rather than a white iris. As Aldabra is a Special Reserve of the Republic of Seychelles, it is afforded the strongest level of wildlife protection, and the only permitted human activities are nature conservation and restricted ecotourism.

Photo: Mikael Bauer

CR **Dwarf Olive Ibis** *Bostrychia bocagei* `200`

▼ **POPULATION:** 50–249 | **THREATS:** HUN, AGR, TRA, SPP?

This small, forest ibis is endemic to São Tomé, where it is confined to forested, lowland rivers in the south-west and centre of the island. Previously known only from historical and anecdotal records, the first confirmed sighting was in 1990. Hunting pressure is the most significant threat, with birds still being killed for food. Other ongoing threats include loss of habitat due to agricultural encroachment and predation by introduced mammals, particularly Mona Monkeys *Cercopithecus mona*. It is hoped that a recently initiated programme of advocacy, awareness raising and research will prevent the extinction of this species.

Photo: Nik Borrow (birdquest-tours.com)

EN **Madagascar Pond-heron** *Ardeola idae*

▼ **POPULATION:** 1,300–4,000 | **THREATS:** WAT, HUN, SPP?

The majority of the population of this heron breeds on Madagascar (see *page 83*), but small numbers also nest on Aldabra (Seychelles), Mayotte (Comoros Islands) and Europa (Réunion). It has only recently been discovered breeding on Mayotte, where the population seems to be increasing. On Aldabra it mainly frequents inland pools, lagoon shores and mangroves, where it sometimes builds its bulky nest, but it is occasionally found in areas away from water. It feeds on invertebrates and small vertebrates such as lizards and frogs. As Squacco Herons *A. ralloides* do not occur on these islands, except as vagrants, hybridization has not become an issue, unlike on Madagascar.

Photo: Callan Cohen & Deirdre Vrancken (birdingafrica.com)

CR **Christmas Island Frigatebird** *Fregata andrewsi* `45`

▼ **POPULATION:** 2,400–4,800 | **THREATS:** EGY, FISH, AGR, CLI, HUN, PLN, SPP?

This frigatebird breeds only on Christmas Island and disperses widely in the Indo-Malay Archipelago, and south to northern Australia. It breeds in large forest trees and raises just one fledgling every two years, resulting in a slow reproduction rate. The rapid population decline is probably due to a combination of habitat loss, dust fallout from phosphate mining, marine pollution, over-fishing and bycatch in fishing gear. The introduced Yellow Crazy Ant *Anoplolepis gracilipes*, which has devastated the island's unique ecosystem, has not yet been shown to adversely affect frigatebirds but undoubtedly represents a serious future threat. As two thirds of current nests are in one colony, it is also particularly vulnerable to weather events such as cyclones.

Photo: David Boyle

EN **Abbott's Booby** *Papasula abbotti*

`48`

▼ **POPULATION: 6,000** | **THREATS:** SPP, FISH?, HUN?, PLN?, DEV?, (CLI), (EGY), (TRA)

Having disappeared from most of it breeding range across the Indian and Pacific Oceans, this booby is now thought to nest only on Christmas Island. However, recent records from the Banda Sea, Indonesia, may indicate unknown breeding colonies. Outside the breeding season it disperses throughout the Indian Ocean. Unusually amongst boobies, it nests in tall trees but some areas of suitable habitat are subject to dieback. Ongoing threats include habitat loss, the effect of dust fallout from phosphate mining, marine pollution, over-fishing and cyclones. The introduced Yellow Crazy Ant *Anoplolepis gracilipes* may be a contributory factor in habitat degradation and represents a serious threat.

Photo: Tony Palliser

EN **Réunion Harrier** *Circus maillardi*

`25`

▼ **POPULATION: 200–560** | **THREATS:** PLN, AGR, CLI, EGY, FIRE, HUN, SPP, LOG, DEV, TRA

This harrier is endemic to the island of Réunion, where it mostly occupies forested habitats at 300–700 m, but also forages in open grasslands and cultivated areas. It is believed to be a predator of domestic chickens and is still persecuted, despite legal protection. It is also prone to secondary poisoning from rodenticides and these two factors constitute the most serious current threats. Its tiny range also makes it susceptible to urbanization, infrastructure development and extreme weather events. Public awareness campaigns have met with some success and many birds taken into care have been successfully released into the wild. A species action plan was published in 2011.

Female. Photo: Sarah Caceres & Jean-Noël Jasmin. (See *page 25* for photo of a male.)

EW **Guam Rail** *Gallirallus owstoni*

`17`

† **POPULATION:** Not applicable | **THREATS:** SPP

This flightless rail is endemic to Guam. It was once widespread and found in most habitats, but became extinct in the wild in 1987 due to predation by introduced Brown Tree Snakes *Boiga irregularis*. A captive population survives on Guam in a snake-proof enclosure, and it breeds well in several American zoos. From 1989–2007, 853 captive birds were released on the nearby island of Rota, although this has experienced mixed success, with some populations rapidly declining to extinction, possibly due to predation by feral cats. In 2011, 16 birds were released on Cocos Island off the southern tip of Guam after rats were eradicated, and evidence of breeding has been observed.

Photo [captive]: Greg Neise (inplainsight.net)

CR **Samoan Moorhen** *Gallinula pacifica*

? **POPULATION:** <50 | **THREATS:** AGR, CLI?, SPP?, (HUN)

Endemic to the island of Savai`i, Samoa, where it was restricted to montane forest, this rail was last reliably recorded in 1873. Being flightless, it was easy prey for local hunters and introduced mammals, such as dogs and cats, and these factors, together with habitat destruction caused by pigs and cattle, are likely to have led to its rapid decline. However, unconfirmed reports in 1987 and 2003 suggest that it could still be extant. A 15-day search in 2005 failed to detect any birds but extensive areas of suitable habitat remain and, as it may be nocturnal, this species could be particularly difficult to detect. Habitat loss and degradation in its historical range looks set to continue.

Illustration: Tomasz Cofta

CR St Helena Plover *Charadrius sanctaehelenae*

▲ **POPULATION: 50–249** | **THREATS: ECO**, DEV, MAN, SPP

Only found on the island of St Helena, this plover is known locally as the Wirebird, because of its long, thin legs. Most populations are found in short, dry grasslands but some inhabit areas of semi-desert. An extended rainy season can result in excessive vegetation growth, which can delay or prevent breeding. This factor has been exacerbated by a decline in livestock grazing due to economic constraints. Introduced mammals, and to a lesser extent, introduced Common Mynas *Acridotheres tristis* are probably significant predators, and increased urbanization and plans to build an airport on the island are also potential threats. However, a species action plan is in place and the population is closely monitored.

Photo: David Boyle

EN Tuamotu Sandpiper *Prosobonia cancellata*   195

▼ **POPULATION: 870** | **THREATS: SPP**, AGR, MAN, (CLI)

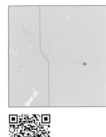

This sandpiper is endemic to the Tuamotu Archipelago, French Polynesia, and probably now only occurs on five islands. It favours the upper reaches of beaches amongst shrubs and open forest where it feeds mainly on invertebrates. However, unusually for a wader, it will also climb into vegetation to glean nectar and other plant material. Predation by introduced rats and cats has eliminated this species from all but the most infrequently visited islands. The area of suitable habitat has also been reduced by the spread of coconut plantations. In 2011, rat eradication programmes were carried out on some islands and, if successful, the translocation of birds will be considered.

Photo: Eric VanderWerf (pacificrimconservation.com)

EN Maroon Pigeon *Columba thomensis*

▼ **POPULATION: 250–999** | **THREATS:** HUN, AGR, LOG, TRA, CLI?

Endemic to São Tomé, this large pigeon is most commonly found in primary forest above 1,000 m but also occurs in other forest types, abandoned coffee plantations and cultivated areas. It mainly feeds on fruit and makes seasonal movements in response to its availability. It seems to occur at low densities and, being rather confiding in nature, is suffering from intense hunting pressure, which may have halved its population in recent years. Although road developments are increasing access to previously remote areas of forest, recent legislation should lead to the creation of a national park. The protection of primary forest as a *zona ecologica* has also been proposed.

Photo: Nik Borrow (birdquest-tours.com)

EN Pink Pigeon *Nesoenas mayeri*   198

▼ **POPULATION: 240–260** | **THREATS:** SPP, (AGR), (CLI), (LOG)

Restricted to mainland Mauritius and offshore Ile aux Aigrettes, the population of this pigeon plummeted due to a severe loss of habitat, compounded by predation by introduced mammals. Invasive plants and extreme weather events have also reduced habitat quality. Only ten birds remained in the wild in 1990 but intensive conservation management, including a successful captive-breeding programme, has resulted in a spectacular population increase. However, the disease *Trichomonosis* was brought to Mauritius by alien pigeons (which now act as a reservoir for the disease) and this, together with inbreeding depression is thought to be limiting population growth.

Photo: Gary Jenkins

EW **Socorro Dove** *Zenaida graysoni*

† **POPULATION:** Not applicable | **THREATS:** SPP, (HUN)

Endemic to Socorro in the Revillagigedo Archipelago, Mexico, this dove was common in the 1950s but had become extinct in the wild by 1972. It is highly terrestrial and is thought to have preferred forests above 500 m with a dense understorey. It is unclear why it became extinct, but a combination of hunting, predation by feral cats and habitat degradation due to overgrazing by sheep are likely factors. Fortunately, a few birds were taken into captivity in the 1920s and populations have been maintained in the USA and Europe. Projects are now underway to eradicate cats and sheep from the island, restore native vegetation and re-establish a breeding population.

Photo [captive]: Tomasz Doroń

CR **Polynesian Ground-dove** *Gallicolumba erythroptera*

▼ **POPULATION:** 70–130 | **THREATS:** AGR, SPP, CLI, (HUN)

This small dove is found on tiny wooded islets throughout the Tuamotu Archipelago in French Polynesia, where it favours primary forest. The nominate subspecies is known from Tahiti and Moorea in the Society Islands (now extinct) and from the Acteon Group in the southern Tuamotus. The subspecies *pectoralis* is known from the central and northern Tuamotus (but is possibly extinct). The main threats are predation by rats and feral cats, habitat loss and deterioration, mainly due to the spread of coconut plantations, and extreme weather events. However, a species action plan is in place and the translocation of captive birds to predator-free islands is being considered.

Photo: Pete Morris (birdquest-tours.com)

EN **Tooth-billed Pigeon** *Didunculus strigirostris*

▼ **POPULATION:** 600–1,700 | **THREATS:** SPP, AGR, HUN, (CLI)

Endemic to Samoa, this unusual, secretive pigeon is a flagship species for conservation awareness, but intensive surveys in 2006 recorded it at only ten locations. It is an arboreal species of primary forest, forest edge and clearings up to 1,600 m, where it specializes in feeding on the seeds of *Dysoxylum* trees (mahoganies), using its unique bill to saw through the tough outer layer of the fruits. Population declines are continuing due to hunting and habitat loss and degradation (partly driven by cyclones) resulting in the establishment of agressive non-native trees. The lack of recent records suggests that subpopulations are now so small that the species may warrant uplisting to Critically Endangered in the near future.

Illustration: Tomasz Cofta

EN **Mariana Fruit-dove** *Ptilinopus roseicapilla*

▼ **POPULATION:** 1,500–7,000 | **THREATS:** AGR, SPP, HUN, CLI?

Found only on the islands of Saipan, Tinian, Rota and Aguijan in the Northern Mariana Island group, this dove primarily inhabits mature limestone forest but also occurs in disturbed mixed woodlands and secondary growth. It has become extirpated from Guam due to predation by introduced Brown Tree Snakes *Boiga irregularis*. Ongoing habitat loss is likely to remain a major threat but it is also at great risk from the recent introduction of Brown Tree Snake to Saipan and probably Tinian. However, a conservation campaign on Rota has resulted in legislation fully protecting the species from hunting and trapping and a wider island conservation programme is in place.

Photo [captive]: Johannes Pfleiderer (zootierliste.de)

EN **Polynesian Imperial-pigeon** *Ducula aurorae*

▲ **POPULATION:** 100–500 | **THREATS:** SPP, DEV, (EGY), (HUN)

This large pigeon is known from Tahiti in French Polynesia, where it may already be extinct, and Makatea in the Tuamotu Archipelago. Formerly found only in dense forests, it has adapted to habitat loss and is increasingly found in secondary habitats and even gardens. A recent survey on Makatea has shown that the population may be slowly increasing, probably due to a cessation of phosphate mining and a reduction in hunting. However, it remains at risk due to plans for infrastructure development. It is also possible that Swamp Harrier *Circus approximans*, which may have contributed to the extinction of this species elsewhere, could colonize the island.

Makatea Island, French Polynesia; August 2008. Photo: Hadoram Shirihai; contributed from the forthcoming *Photographic Handbook of the Birds of the World*, Jornvall & Shirihai © Bloomsbury Publishing Plc.

EN **Marquesan Imperial-pigeon** *Ducula galeata* `194`

▲ **POPULATION:** 200 | **THREATS:** HUN, SPP, CLI?

This pigeon was formerly only known from the Marquesan island of Nuku Hiva but a translocation to the nearby island of Ua Huka, which began in 2000, appears to have been successful. There is also an 18th century record from Tahiti. It is an arboreal species favouring remote, wooded valleys from 250–1,300 m, but also occurs in secondary forest and at the edges of orange and banana plantations. This bird is revered in local culture and although hunting is forbidden, it still continues. However, an awareness-raising campaign focusing initially on local school children has met with success, and has now been expanded to the general public. As a result, hunting pressure appears to have been reduced.

Photo: Tim Laman (timlaman.com)

EN **Mauritius** (or Echo) **Parakeet** *Psittacula eques*

▲ **POPULATION:** 300–350 | **THREATS:** SPP, CLI, (AGR), (LOG)

Following extinction on Réunion, this parakeet is now confined to remnants of native upland forest and scrub in south-west Mauritius, having been lost from most of the island due to severe habitat loss and degradation. In the 1980s, only around ten birds were known to survive, but intensive conservation management, including a captive-breeding and reintroduction programme, has led to a steady increase in the wild population. However, the very little suitable habitat that remains continues to be highly degraded by cyclones, the influences of past forestry practices, the spread of introduced plants and the effect of introduced feral mammals. Predation, nest-site competiton, and nest parasites are also important threats.

Photo: Vikash Tatayah

EN **Socorro Parakeet** *Aratinga brevipes*

▼ **POPULATION:** 300 | **THREATS:** AGR, SPP, CLI?

This small parakeet is endemic to Socorro in the Revillagigedo Archipelago, Mexico, where it inhabits forests between 350–850 m. It nests exclusively in cavities in *Bumelia socorroensis* trees, and fruits of this species comprise over 50% of its diet. Further population declines are expected due to ongoing habitat degradation caused by overgrazing and the defoliation of indigenous forest by swarms of the resident locust *Schistocerca piceifrons*. There is also a high risk of rats being accidentally introduced to the island. However, a captive breeding progamme has been instigated, measures to eradicate sheep from the island are being implemented, and artificial nest boxes are being provided.

Photo: Alejandro Boneta (aboneta.com)

EN **Rimatara Lorikeet** *Vini kuhlii*

▼ **POPULATION:** 1,300 | **THREATS:** SPP, CLI?, (HUN)

Until recently, this beautiful, nectar-feeding parrot was restricted to Rimatara in the Tubuai Islands (French Polynesia), and to Teraina, Tabuaeran and Kiritimati (Kiribati). Historically, it occurred on at least five of the Southern Cook Islands, but is thought to have become extinct there due to exploitation of its red feathers. In 2007, birds were reintroduced to Atiu in the Southern Cook Islands and a few have already spread to the neighbouring island of Mitiaro. On Rimitara, it favours mixed horticultural woodlands, but on other islands is confined to coconut plantations. Nest predation by rats remains the most significant threat, but predation by cats on Kiritimati and Common Mynas *Acridotheres tristis* on Atiu are also ongoing concerns.

Photo: Phil Bender

EN **Ultramarine Lorikeet** *Vini ultramarina*

▼ **POPULATION:** 1,000–2,499 | **THREATS:** AGR, FIRE, SPP

Although populations of this attractive parrot may still occur on a few tiny islands in the Marquesas group, French Polynesia, recent surveys indicate that it is now only likely to remain extant on Ua Huka. It feeds on the nectar and pollen of a wide variety of flowering trees and nests in tree cavities. Although, historically, population declines are likely to have been due to extensive loss of native forest due to the impact of grazing and fire, the arrival of Black Rats *Rattus rattus* on many islands in the group are likely to have led to extinctions. The species may qualify for uplisting unless mitigation measures are taken to prevent accidental introduction of rats to Ua Huka.

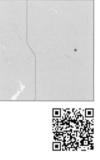

Photo: Pete Morris (birdquest-tours.com)

CR **Red-throated Lorikeet** *Charmosyna amabilis*

▼ **POPULATION:** <50 | **THREATS:** SPP, AGR, LOG, CLI?

Although this parrot was known to have occurred on several islands in Fiji, there have been very few confirmed sightings in recent years, despite considerable survey effort. It has been recorded in mangroves but probably favours mature forests and may still persist in very remote areas at high altitudes. It is usually found in small flocks high in the canopy feeding on nectar and pollen from flowering trees, and probably roams seasonally in search of food. Its breeding ecology is unknown. Major threats include further habitat loss due to ongoing logging and road construction, and predation by introduced mammals, particularly Black Rat *Rattus rattus*.

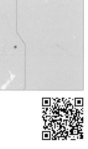

Photo: Bill Beckon

EN **Seychelles Scops-owl** *Otus insularis*

= **POPULATION:** 249–284 | **THREATS:** AGR, CLI, SPP, LOG, DEV, ECO, MAN?

Endemic to the island of Mahé in Seychelles, this small owl favours undisturbed sheltered valleys and slopes above 400 m in areas of high rainfall. It inhabits mixed forest with a high, often mist-shrouded, canopy, where it forages from low in the understorey up to the lower canopy. Although much of its range lies within protected areas, small-scale habitat loss, mainly due to infrastructure projects, is likely to continue, and introduced predators remain a constant threat. In recent years, many nesting trees have been lost to a fungal disease and an increase in extreme weather events due to climate change, which may destroy areas of forest, is also a major concern.

Photo: Bill Coster (billcoster.com)

CR **Anjouan Scops-owl** *Otus capnodes* `199`

▼ **POPULATION: 50–249** | **THREATS:** AGR, CLI, HUN, SPP, LOG

This small owl was only rediscovered on the island of Anjouan in the Comoros Islands in 1992, after going unrecorded for 106 years. It favours native forest but also occurs in degraded forest and plantations. Habitat loss, degradation and fragmentation due to clearance for agriculture, logging and charcoal manufacture has been severe, introduced Black Rats *Rattus rattus* are abundant and may predate nests, and introduced Common Mynas *Acridotheres tristis* may compete for nest holes. Cyclones are a regular threat to remaining forest fragments. However, this species may be able to adapt to suboptimal habitat provided large trees remain, and the population may be larger than previously feared.

Photo: Charlie Marsh

CR **Mohéli Scops-owl** *Otus moheliensis* `188`

▼ **POPULATION: 260** | **THREATS:** AGR, LOG, HUN, SPP, CLI?

Endemic to the island of Mohéli in the Comoros Islands, where it occurs on just one mountain ridge, this small owl was described to science as recently as 1998. It is thought to be relatively abundant in dense, humid forest but is also found at lower densities in degraded forest that has been underplanted for agriculture. Very little intact forest remains on the island, primarily due to conversion for subsistence agriculture, and native forest is also being degraded by invasive exotic plant species. Hunting and predation by introduced mammals are also likely to affect this species. Since its distribution is close to the maximum altitude available within its range, this species is potentially also susceptible to climate change.

Photo: Pete Morris (birdquest-tours.com)

CR **Grand Comoro Scops-owl** *Otus pauliani*

▼ **POPULATION: 1,300** | **THREATS:** AGR, SPP, LOG, TRA, CLI?

Found only on Mount Karthala, an active volcano on Grand Comoro in the Comoros Islands, this small owl favours areas with old, hollow trees along the edges of primary, montane, evergreen forest. Its feeding and breeding ecology are unknown. Although the volcano is active, clearance of forest for agriculture, logging and road construction by the island's large and increasing human population is causing a continuing decline in the area of suitable habitat. Grazing pressure is increasing, even at high altitudes, and could prohibit forest regeneration. Other threats include predation by introduced rats and competition for nest sites with introduced Common Mynas *Acridotheres tristis*.

Photo: Pete Morris (birdquest-tours.com)

EN **Guam Swiftlet** *Collocalia bartschi*

▼ **POPULATION: 2,100–2,300** | **THREATS:** SPP, MAN, PLN?

This swiftlet is endemic to Guam and the Northern Mariana Islands, where colonies remain on Saipan and Aguijan, having disappeared from Rota and Tinian in the 1970s. It was introduced to Oahu (Hawaii) in the 1960s and a single breeding colony still persists. It feeds over forests and grasslands and breeds and roosts in caves. Historically, loss of insect prey through pesticide-use may have caused declines but predation by Brown Tree Snakes *Boiga irregularis* is now a major threat. On Guam, the nests of introduced mud dauber wasps *Vespula* spp. add to the weight of swiftlet nests causing them to fall from cave walls. On Saipan, threats include disturbance by humans and feral mammals, and on Oahu, ongoing rat control is needed to protect the colony.

Photo: Robby Kohley

CR **Juan Fernández Firecrown** *Sephanoides fernandensis*

▼ **POPULATION: 1,700–2,000** | **THREATS:** SPP, (AGR)

This hummingbird is confined to Isla Robinson Crusoe in the Juan Fernández Archipelago. It inhabits native forest, on which it is dependent for breeding, but also feeds on exotic introduced plants. Habitat loss and degradation, and the introduction of herbivorous mammals, such as rabbits, has restricted the availability, quantity and quality of food resources. A recent tsunami also destroyed natural vegetation. As this species is quite tame and approachable, it is particularly prone to predation. There is some competition with Green-backed Firecrown *S. sephaniodes*, which arrived on the island by natural means. A range of conservation measures are being implemented.

Photo: Peter Hodum (oikonos.org)

CR **Marquesan Kingfisher** *Todiramphus godeffroyi*

▼ **POPULATION: 260–320** | **THREATS:** SPP, LOG

Now found only on Tahuata in the Marquesas Islands, French Polynesia, this kingfisher favours dense, humid forest along mountain streams, but also occurs in other habitats including coconut plantations. It was last seen on the nearby island of Hiva Oa in 1997 and recent surveys suggest that it is now extinct there due to predation, principally by introduced Great Horned Owls *Bubo virginianus*. Other alien predators such as Common Myna *Acridotheres tristis* and rats are likely to have contributed to declines on both islands, and ongoing damage to upland forest by feral animals is also a major threat. A public awareness-raising campaign has been implemented with positive results.

Photo: Gouni A/Thétys Editions/SOP Manu

CR **Tuamotu Kingfisher** *Todiramphus gambieri*

▼ **POPULATION: 90** | **THREATS:** SPP, CLI?

The nominate subspecies of this kingfisher became extinct from Mangareva in the Gambier Islands in the early 20th century, and the subspecies *niauensis* is now confined to the island of Niau in the Tuamotu Archipelago. As this species nests in cavities in coconut palms, any change in land management could prove catastrophic. However, a cooperative programme to protect nesting habitat has been initiated with farmers, and management recommendations have been provided. A rat control programme has also been implemented. An experimental translocation on Niau in 2010 proved successful, and translocations to the atoll complex of Anaa in the Gambier Islands may be undertaken in future.

Photo: Pete Morris (birdquest-tours.com)

EN **Narcondam Hornbill** *Aceros narcondami* `187`

= **POPULATION: 50–249** | **THREATS:** AGR, HUN, SPP, LOG, DEV, (CLI)

Restricted to the tiny island of Narcondam, 114 km east of the Andaman Islands (India), this distinctive hornbill inhabits open forest but requires large trees in undisturbed, mature forest for nesting and roosting. Habitat has been lost to buildings and plantations, and degraded by domestic animals, but attempts are being made to remove the large population of feral goats. The proposed installation of communication structures could lead to further habitat loss and cause disturbance. The establishment of a second population on another island in the Andamans is being considered, as is the provision of nest boxes and the planting of fig trees to encourage forest regeneration.

Photo: Niranjan Sant

CR **Masafuera Rayadito** *Aphrastura masafuerae*

= **POPULATION:** 50–249 | **THREATS:** SPP, CLI?

Endemic to the island of Alejandro Selkirk (Más Afuera) in the Juan Fernández Islands, 768 km off the coast of Chile, this ovenbird occurs primarily near streams at 800–1,300 m in lush *Dicksonia externa* fern forest. It nests in man-made or natural holes from December to January. It rarely leaves the safety of dense vegetation and hangs upside-down to forage. Habitat loss and degradation due to trampling by goats, fire and timber-cutting, and predation by introduced mammals,has had a significant impact on the population. Habitat restoration and the eradication of rats, feral cats and goats is a high conservation priority, and nest boxes have been installed to increase the availability of nesting sites.

Photo: Peter Hodum (oikonos.org)

EN **Mao** *Gymnomyza samoensis*

▼ **POPULATION:** 250–999 | **THREATS:** AGR, SPP, (CLI)

This large honeyeater is found only on the Samoan islands of Savai`i and `Upolu, but may occur on Tutuila, where a specimen was collected in the 1920s. Surveys in 2005–6 indicate that although it is widespread in undisturbed native forest at high altitudes, it is now largely absent from the lowlands. It feeds mostly on nectar but insects are also an important part of the diet, particularly in the dry season. The major threats are ongoing habitat degradation, mainly due to slash-and-burn agriculture and invasive plant species, and predation by introduced mammals. Research is being carried out (2010–13) to investigate reproductive success and the effect of habitat modification on nest predation.

Photo: Rebecca Stirnemann (samoanbirds.com)

CR **Réunion Cuckooshrike** *Coracina newtoni* `199`

▼ **POPULATION:** 50 | **THREATS:** HUN, SPP, FIRE, MAN, (AGR), (CLI), (LOG)

This quiet, inconspicuous, closed-canopy specialist is endemic to Réunion, where it is now only found in two small areas of subtropical forest in the north-west of the island. It is mainly insectivorous but will also feed on the fruit of native trees. Although over 95% of its known range falls within a protected area, rats and feral cats predate nests. This may be the primary reason for poor reproductive success and may also explain the skewed sex ratio: almost half of the males are without mates, and only 30% of females produce young. Although there are indications that predator control is proving successful, a wide range of threats remains, including poaching for trade and food.

Photo: YaBaLeX (faune-reunion.com)

CR **São Tomé Fiscal** *Lanius newtoni* `200`

▼ **POPULATION:** <50 | **THREATS:** AGR, LOG, TRA, SPP?

Endemic to São Tomé, this shrike was rediscovered in 1990 in the south-west of the island, having been previously known only from records in 1888 and 1928. There have been several recent sightings, all from near watercourses in primary lowland and mid-altitude forest up to 1,400 m with little or no undergrowth, but with bare ground and rocks. The area of suitable habitat is extremely limited and the population is suspected to be declining due to ongoing habitat degradation and, possibly, the impacts of introduced predators. Recent conservation initiatives include an awareness-raising campaign and the training of local people in the implementation of site-based conservation.

Photo: Martim Melo

EN **Grand Comoro Drongo** *Dicrurus fuscipennis*

= **POPULATION:** 70 | **THREATS:** SPP, AGR, LOG, TRA, CLI?

Only found on Grand Comoro, Comoros Islands, most of the population of this drongo occurs on the south-west slopes of Mount Karthala, an active volcano. It is found primarily within an altitudinal zone of 100–1,150 m and appears to show a preference for forest clearings, forest edge and adjacent areas with a well-developed shrub layer but few high trees. The reasons for this species' rarity are unknown, but the fact that it now occupies mainly degraded areas with exotics plants suggests that its optimal native habitat may have already disappeared at lower altitudes. Introduced mammalian predators may also have an impact on the population.

Photo: Pete Morris (birdquest-tours.com)

CR **Seychelles Paradise-flycatcher** *Terpsiphone corvina* `199`

▲ **POPULATION:** 140–190 | **THREATS:** SPP, DEV

Endemic to Seychelles, the only viable population of this monarch remains on the island of La Digue. It requires mature stands of native high canopy plateau forest but housing developments have led to severe habitat loss. However, it appears to be able to adapt to open woodland close to housing, and an increasing number of tree species are being used for nesting. The establishment of a nature reserve in 1991, and subsequent conservation management has led to an increase in the population but nest-predators remain an ongoing threat. A translocated colony is being established on Denis Island and, if successful, translocation to other suitable islands will be considered.

Female. Photo: Jean-Florent Mandelbaum. (See *page 199* for photo of a male.)

CR **Tahiti Monarch** *Pomarea nigra*

▲ **POPULATION:** <50 | **THREATS:** CLI, SPP

Endemic to Tahiti in the Society Islands, French Polynesia, this monarch is found only in four lowland valleys. Important habitat features are probably watercourses (most nests have been found nearby) and the presence of Mara trees *Neonauclea forsteri*. Predation by introduced rats is the main threat but predation by cats and other birds is also significant. Habitat degradation due to the impact of invasive alien plants and goat grazing is widespread. However, intensive conservation management is reversing the declines and translocation of some birds to the nearby predator-free island of Rimatara is proposed. A recovery group covering this species and Fatuhiva Monarch *P. whitneyi* has been established to formulate a conservation strategy.

Photo: Pete Morris (birdquest-tours.com)

EN **Marquesan Monarch** *Pomarea mendozae*

= **POPULATION:** 160–250 | **THREATS:** CLI, FIRE, SPP

Once widespread in the central Marquesas Islands, French Polynesia, the nominate subspecies of this monarch is now considered extinct from Hiva Oa and Tahuata. The subspecies *motanensis* survives only on Mohotani. Adults are sexually dimorphic: males are entirely black; females are dark with pale wings and tail (the photo shown here is of a juvenile). The species favours native forests, especially areas containing the tree *Pisonia grandis*. On Mohotani, the devastation of native vegetation by feral sheep has been exacerbated by a ban on hunting, and introduced mammalian predators, particularly feral cats and rats, remain a threat.

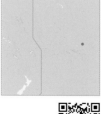

Juvenile. Photo: Eric Olivier & Catherine Chavaillon (atacreation@mail.pf)

CR (PE) Ua Pou Monarch *Pomarea mira*

? POPULATION: <50 | **THREATS:** (FIRE), (SPP)

19

Known only from Ua Pou in the Marquesas Islands group, French Polynesia, this monarch was last recorded in 1985. It was not found during subsequent intensive surveys and was considered extinct. However, a bird matching the description of this species was observed by a walker on the island in 2010 and follow-up surveys are planned. Historically, this mainly insectivorous bird was found in forested valleys at high elevations but probably also occurred throughout lowland forests, which have now been destroyed. Intense grazing pressure, fire and predation, particularly by introduced Black Rats *Rattus rattus*, are the main factors that are likely to have led to the demise of this species.

Illustration: Tomasz Cofta

CR Fatuhiva Monarch *Pomarea whitneyi*

▼ POPULATION: 33 | **THREATS: SPP**, AGR, FIRE

Found only on the tiny island of Fatu Hiva in the Marquesas Islands, French Polynesia, this monarch favours dense, native forest. In 1975, several hundred pairs were known but by 2011 over half of the few birds that remained were restricted to an area of just 2 km². This forest is relatively well preserved but Black Rats *Rattus rattus* were first observed on the island in 2000 and their presence has been strongly correlated with the extinction of monarch populations elsewhere. Predation by feral cats, bush fires, forest clearance and new, unregulated, agricultural tracks in the species' habitat are also increasing threats. A species action plan is in place and rat control has been ongoing since 2008.

Photo: Gouni A/Thétys Editions/SOP Manu

EN Chuuk (or Truk) Monarch *Metabolus rugensis*

▼ POPULATION: 600–1,700 | **THREATS:** AGR, TRA

This sexually dimorphic monarch (females are sooty-black) is widely distributed on nearly all the high lagoon islands and some of the outer reef islets of Chuuk in Micronesia. Although it has probably never been common, it seems to have either disappeared or become very rare at many locations. It favours areas with a thick, leafy understorey, particularly in upland native forest, where it is found in small family groups gleaning prey from the foliage and appears to be strongly territorial. Dramatic declines since the 1940s are likely to be due to extensive agricultural development, a factor that is being exacerbated by a rapidly expanding human population. It may also be subject to direct persecution.

Photo: Jon Hornbuckle

EN Oahu Elepaio *Chasiempis ibidis*

▼ POPULATION: 1,500–2,000 | **THREATS:** AGR, SPP, DEV, FIRE

This small monarch is endemic to O`ahu in the Hawaiian Islands, the name elepaio derives from its shrill call. It is most abundant in moist valleys, preferring mixed-species, tall canopy forest with a well-developed understorey at 200–800 m. The population is still in decline due to the effects of disease, introduced species and ongoing habitat loss and degradation due to agricultural or urban development. Over 80% of birds have been recorded to have malaria and a quarter show signs of avian pox. Nest predation by Black Rats *Rattus rattus* is the most serious current problem, particularly as it leads to a male-biased sex ratio.

Photo: Eric VanderWerf (pacificrimconservation.com)

EW **Hawaiian Crow** *Corvus hawaiiensis*

16

† **POPULATION:** Not applicable | **THREATS:** SPP, (AGR), (MAN), (HUN), (LOG)

Historically, this crow was probably once widespread in a variety of forest types across the Hawaiian Islands, but the last two wild birds were seen in the high mountains of Hawai'i in 2002. Habitat loss and degradation have been severe and the impact of shooting has probably been substantial, even in recent decades. Other significant threats include predation and disease, and it is particularly prone to disturbance when nesting. A captive-breeding programme is in place and in 2011 the population stood at 94 birds. Some areas of its former range are now fenced and free of feral ungulates, and a reintroduction plan is being developed.

Photo: Jack Jeffrey (JackJeffreyphoto.com)

CR **Mariana Crow** *Corvus kubaryi*

▼ **POPULATION:** 50–249 | **THREATS: SPP**, AGR, HUN, DEV, (CLI)

This crow is now confined to the island of Rota in the Northern Mariana Islands. It is probably extinct on Guam, despite the dwindling population having been supplemented by birds translocated from Rota. It inhabits a range of forest types and coastal vegetation but probably only nests in native forest. On Guam, it declined due to predation by introduced Brown Tree Snakes *Boiga irregularis*, despite the protection of nest sites by electrical barriers. On Rota, major threats include habitat loss due to typhoons, housing and infrastructure development, and predation by introduced mammals. Direct persecution has also been an issue.

Photo: Jack Jeffrey (JackJeffreyphoto.com)

EN **Galápagos Martin** *Progne modesta*

▼ **POPULATION:** 250–999 | **THREATS:** SPP?, ECO?

This martin has been recorded on all central and southern islands of Galápagos and is not believed to be migratory. It nests in holes and crevices, and pairs or small groups are found mainly around the highest peaks, and only occasionally in the lowlands (at sites with special characteristics, such as sheer sea cliffs). Little is known about the threats to this species but past declines may be due to introduced diseases and parasites, especially the nest parasite *Philornis downsi* that occurs on all known breeding islands, and introduced nest predators such as rats. It was uplisted from Vulnerable in 2012 and further surveys are needed urgently to obtain accurate population estimates.

Female. Illustration: Tomasz Cofta

CR **Raso Lark** *Alauda razae*

201

= **POPULATION:** 250–999 | **THREATS:** CLI, SPP

Now restricted to the uninhabited island of Raso in the Cape Verde Islands, this lark occurred on other nearby islands until human settlement in the 15th century led to its extinction. It nests on the ground on level plains with volcanic soil and, in some years, predation by the near-endemic gecko *Tarentola gigas* is high. Suitable breeding habitat covers less than half the island and changes in rainfall patterns result in population fluctuations; in wet years there is a rapid increase. Climate change may increase the frequency of drought in the Cape Verdes and, as a ground-nester, the species is also highly at risk from the accidental introduction of mammalian predators.

Photo: Edwin Winkel

EN **Long-legged Thicketbird** (or Warbler) *Trichocichla rufa*

= **POPULATION: 50–249** | **THREATS:** SPP, LOG, CLI?

Endemic to Fiji, this secretive warbler was known from just a few specimens and unconfirmed sightings on the island of Viti Levu, and one specimen in 1974 from Vanua Levu. However, during surveys in 2002–5 and 2012, the nominate subspecies was reported from several sites on Viti Levu, where it was locally common in old-growth forest close to watercourses between 200–800 m, but mostly absent elsewhere. Although the subspecies *clunei* was not found on Vanua Levu, local villagers described its call. This species remains little known and it is easily overlooked unless singing. As a ground dweller, it may be at risk from predation by introduced mammals.

Photo: Patrick Pikacha

CR **Nightingale Reed-warbler** *Acrocephalus luscinius*   `33`

▼ **POPULATION: 2,000–2,499** | **THREATS: SPP**, AGR, FIRE, DEV, (GEO)

Historically, this warbler, which has three subspecies, was known from Guam, the Northern Mariana Islands, and from Yap in Micronesia, but probably remains extant only on Saipan (its stronghold) and Alamagan. It is a secretive bird of dense, often wet, thickets and is more often heard than seen. It sometimes sings at night, hence its name. Habitat loss and degradation due to urbanization, agriculture and invasive plants is an ongoing threat. Predation by the introduced Brown Tree Snake *Boiga irregularis* is likely to have caused its extinction on Guam and this snake may now be established on Saipan. Introduced mammals and, possibly, monitor lizards may be a significant factor in the high proportion of nest failures.

Photo: Jon Hornbuckle

CR **Millerbird** *Acrocephalus familiaris*

= **POPULATION: 250–999** | **THREATS:** CLI, SPP, (FIRE)

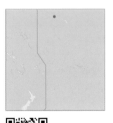

Now only found on uninhabited Nihoa in the Northwestern Hawaiian Islands, this warbler became extinct on Laysan in the early 20th century, probably due to habitat loss through overgrazing. It inhabits dense cover near the ground where it feeds on a variety of prey. The population fluctuates greatly in response to climatic events that affect prey abundance, and this has had a significant impact on genetic diversity. It is now extremely vulnerable to extinction due to factors such as the accidental introduction of mammalian predators, non-native plants or insect species, as well as disease and hurricanes. In 2011, birds were translocated to Laysan and bred successfully during their first breeding season.

Photo: Robby Kohley

EN **Kiritimati Reed-warbler** *Acrocephalus aequinoctialis*   `188`

▼ **POPULATION: 2,500–9,999** | **THREATS:** SPP, AGR, FIRE, HUN, DEV, CLI?

This warbler is confined to just Kiritimati and Teraina in the Northern Line Islands, Kiribati, having been extirpated from Tabuaeran in the 1970s. Surveys on Kiritimati in 2007–11 indicate that the species is widespread and locally common on the mainland, and individuals occasionally visit small islets in the lagoons. It forages near the ground in dense vegetation and Tree Heliotrope *Tournefortia argentea* appears to provide important nesting habitat. Although predation by introduced rats and cats remains a major threat, measures to control rats have had some success. Recent increased immigration to Kiritimati has, however, led to widespread habitat degradation.

Photo: Eric VanderWerf (pacificrimconservation.com)

EN **Tahiti Reed-warbler** *Acrocephalus caffer*

▼ **POPULATION: 250–999** | **THREATS: LOG**, SPP, AGR, MAN, TRA

Endemic to Tahiti in the Society Islands, French Polynesia, this warbler probably formerly occurred on all high islands in the group. Unusually for a warbler, it has dark and pale colour morphs. It is a secretive bird, most easily located by its voice, inhabiting bamboo thickets and second growth forest up to 1,700 m. Infrastructure development has opened up the interior of Tahiti and increased access has led to disturbance and the unregulated collection of bamboo, which is believed to be this species' only nesting habitat. The introduction of feral cats, rats and many alien bird species, including the aggressive Common Myna *Acridotheres tristis*, may also contribute to its rarity.

Photo: Tun Pin Ong (flickr.com/photos/tunpin)

EN **Pitcairn Reed-warbler** *Acrocephalus vaughani*

▼ **POPULATION: 250–999** | **THREATS: SPP**, LOG, CLI?

Only found on the tiny island of Pitcairn in the southern Pacific Ocean, this warbler appears to favour patches of tall forest but also occurs around dwellings and in scrubland. Vegetation on the island has been greatly modified by humans and only remnants of forest now remain. Invasive alien plant species and browsing by goats also threatens native vegetation. It is likely to be predated by Polynesian Rat *Rattus exulans* and feral cats but, after two unsuccessful eradication attempts, there may be little public support for a third attempt. It was uplisted to Endangered in 2008 following the re-establishment of cats on the island.

Photo: Melanie Tankard

EN **Cape Verde Warbler** *Acrocephalus brevipennis*

▼ **POPULATION: 1,500–2,000** | **THREATS: CLI, DEV, SPP**

Until recently this warbler was thought to be confined to Santiago in the Cape Verde Islands. However, it was discovered on São Nicolau in 1998 and on Fogo in 2004. Historically, it was found in scrub on mountain slopes and in valley reedbeds but appears to have adapted to gardens and agricultural habitats with dense undergrowth. The proximity of running water appears to be an important factor. Habitat loss due to the combined effects of successive droughts and an increasing human population may be responsible for the population decline and the species' restricted distribution. Disease and environmental catastrophes are also potential threats to the small, isolated populations.

Photo: Stefan Cherrug (cherrug.se)

EN **Rodrigues Warbler** *Acrocephalus rodericanus*

= **POPULATION: 100** | **THREATS: SPP, MAN?, (AGR), (CLI), (LOG)**

This unobtrusive warbler was once very common on the island of Rodrigues, Mauritius but by 1979 only nine birds remained. Since then, a spectacular population increase has been reported, with an estimated at 3,000–4,000 individuals in 2012. If the population increase is confirmed, this species is likely to be downlisted. Restored native forests, spurred by the need for watershed protection, have been found to support the highest population densities but this insectivorous species has also adapted to dense thickets in remaining, largely exotic, vegetation. Ongoing threats include predation and/ or competition from introduced animals, periods of drought, cyclones, and human disturbance.

Photo: Jon Hornbuckle

CR **Mauritius Olive White-eye** *Zosterops chloronothus*

▼ **POPULATION: 190–296** | **THREATS:** SPP, CLI?, (AGR), (LOG)

Endemic to Mauritius, the population of this white-eye has contracted to a tiny area of less than 25 km² in the south-west of the island due to habitat loss elsewhere. It is restricted to the wettest upland native forests where it feeds on nectar, a particularly important food source, and insects. Habitat degradation due to the impact of invasive alien plants is ongoing and predation by introduced mammals and other birds, notably bulbuls, is a major threat. Intensive conservation management for this species is underway. In 2006/7, birds were translocated to the predator-free offshore Ile aux Aigrettes . These have bred successfully and 26 individuals were present in 2012.

Photo: Michael Buckham

EN **Seychelles White-eye** *Zosterops modestus*

▲ **POPULATION: 50–249** | **THREATS:** FIRE, SPP, CLI?, (AGR), (LOG)

Only found on Seychelles, by 1996 this white-eye was only known from a tiny population on the island of Mahé. However, in 1997 a population was discovered on the island of Conception. The ecology of the two populations differs. On Conception, territories are held in dense mixed woodland with an abundance of native fruiting trees, whereas on Mahé birds seem to prefer exotic plants and are predominantly found in agricultural and residential areas. Conservation management on nearby islands has increased the quantity and quality of habitat, and birds have been successfully translocated to Frégate, North Island and Cousine. Nest predation by rats and birds remains the greatest threat on Mahé.

Photo: David & Nancy Massie

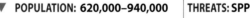

EN **Bridled White-eye** *Zosterops conspicillatus*

▼ **POPULATION: 620,000–940,000** | **THREATS:** SPP

Endemic to the Northern Mariana Islands, this white-eye occurs on the islands of Saipan (which supports about half the population), Tinian (where it is abundant), and Aguijan. It is found in a variety of habitats from native limestone forest, where it forages in large flocks in the upper canopy, to urban areas. The greatest threat on Saipan comes from the introduced Brown Tree Snake *Boiga irregularis*. If this snake becomes established the population of Bridled White-eyes is likely to decline rapidly. In 2008/9, birds were translocated to the island of Sarigan and although the population has increased, it is not yet thought to be self-sustaining.

Photo: Jon Hornbuckle

CR **Rota Bridled White-eye** *Zosterops rotensis*

▼ **POPULATION: 730** | **THREATS:** AGR, CLI, SPP, PLN, DEV

This quiet, inconspicuous white-eye is endemic to Rota in the Northern Mariana Islands, where it is now confined to a tiny area of native, mature, wet limestone forest. It feeds on invertebrates and breeds from December to August. Historical declines are due to habitat loss and degradation as a consequence of agriculture and infrastructure development. However, the recent introduction of Brown Tree Snake *Boiga irregularis* to nearby Saipan is a serious concern. Should it become established on Rota, further rapid population declines are likely. Other threats include predation by introduced rats and birds, including some native species such as the Critically Endangered Mariana Crow *Corvus kubaryi* (*page 224*). A species recovery plan has been published.

Photo: Lainie Zarones

227

EN **Faichuk White-eye** *Rukia ruki*

▼ POPULATION: 350 | THREATS: SPP, LOG, (CLI)

Found only on four tiny islands in the Chuuk Lagoon, Micronesia, this white-eye has a range of only 4 km², but was recently downlisted. It is found in remote native forest, particularly on the summit of Tol South, but ranges into nearby disturbed areas. The only recorded nest was in an endemic Poison Tree *Semecarpus kraemeri*, a species that may be a critical habitat component. Deforestation is widespread across the archipelago but the plateau forests of Tol South are relatively undisturbed due to access difficulties. In addition, superstitious beliefs apparently inhibit islanders from trying to visit the plateau. Potential threats include the introduction of predators and a rise in sea level.

Photo: Chris Collins

CR **Golden White-eye** *Cleptornis marchei*

189

▼ POPULATION: 73,000 | THREATS: SPP, AGR?, DEV?, (CLI)

This white-eye is endemic to the Northern Mariana Islands, with populations on Saipan, its stronghold, and Aguijan. It occurs in a range of wooded habitats, including urban areas, but is more abundant in undisturbed forests. Its ability to utilize different habitats may have enabled this species to persist despite habitat degradation resulting from regular typhoons and human activities. A major threat on Saipan is the recent introduction of Brown Tree Snake *Boiga irregularis*. Should this species become established, a rapid decline in the white-eye population is predicted. In 2011/12, birds were translocated to the island of Sarigan and a captive breeding programme is underway.

Photo: Jack Jeffrey (JackJeffreyphoto.com)

CR **Floreana Mockingbird** *Mimus trifasciatus*

197

= POPULATION: <50 | THREATS: CLI, SPP

This mockingbird is only found on the tiny islets of Champion and Gardner-by-Floreana in Galápagos, having become extinct on nearby Floreana in the late 1800s due to predation by introduced mammals. Significant population fluctuations occur, with numbers only recovering following wet weather conditions. Threats include a significant loss of genetic diversity in the populations, predation by Smooth-billed Ani *Crotophaga ani*, avian pox, and the nest parasite fly *Philornis downsi*. The accidental introduction of rats is also an ongoing threat. Active measures to safeguard existing populations are in place, including the eradication of predators from Floreana and plans for a reintroduction programme.

Photo: Luís Ortiz-Catedral

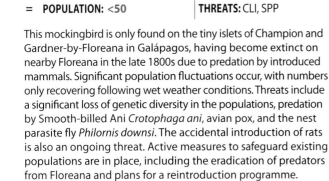

EN **San Cristóbal Mockingbird** *Mimus melanotis*

197

▼ POPULATION: 5,300 | THREATS: SPP, DEV, CLI?

Endemic to the island of San Cristóbal, this was the first mockingbird that Charles Darwin encountered on the Galápagos Islands when he visited in 1835. It inhabits a wide range of habitats from sea level up to the island summit at 715 m. Several factors may be contributing to a population decline, including introduced species (diseases, parasites and predators), habitat degradation, and human disturbance. However, the relative importance and impact of each threat has yet to be determined. Disease vectors include the mosquito *Culex quinquefasciatus* (a vector of avian malaria) and the black fly *Simulium bipunctatus*. The growing number of chicken farms has also led to the introduction of new diseases.

Photo: Andy & Gill Swash (WorldWildlifeImages.com)

CR **Socorro Mockingbird** *Mimus graysoni*

= POPULATION: 190–280 | **THREATS:** SPP

Endemic to Socorro in the Revillagigedo Archipelago, Mexico, this mockingbird was considered a common bird until the mid 20th century, but by 1978 was believed to be on the verge of extinction. It occurs primarily in moist dwarf forest and ravines with a mix of shrubs and trees above 600 m. Overgrazing by sheep has left no suitable nesting or foraging habitat in many areas and, since 1994, forest has been lost due to the impact of a now permanent swarm of the locust *Schistocerca piceifrons* that irrupts twice a year. Predation by feral cats may also occur. Projects are now underway to eradicate cats and sheep from the island and restore native vegetation.

Photo: Eduardo Lugo Cabrera (wildlifeconnection.com)

CR **Pohnpei Starling** *Aplonis pelzelni*

▼ POPULATION: <50 | **THREATS:** AGR?, CLI?, HUN?, SPP?

Endemic to the island of Pohnpei, Micronesia, this small starling has only been recorded with certainty once in recent years (in 1995). It has declined drastically since the 1930s, possibly due to habitat loss, hunting (which is commonly undertaken by local people) and predation by introduced rats. Its ecology is little known but it is believed to favour damp, dark montane forests, although it may once have been widespread in the lowlands. A major source of income for Pohnpei residents is sakau *Piper methysticum*, a cash-crop that has quickly replaced native vegetation and encouraged the spread of invasive species in isolated areas throughout the forest.

Illustration: Tomasz Cofta

CR (PE) **Olomao** *Myadestes lanaiensis* `19`

? POPULATION: <50 | **THREATS:** SPP, CLI?

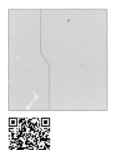

This small thrush is endemic to Hawaii. The nominate subspecies, from the island of Lana'i, was last seen in 1933. The subspecies *rutha* became extinct on Maui in the mid-19th century and the last confirmed record from Moloka'i was in 1980. However, remote plateau areas have not been surveyed recently and could harbour a tiny population. Declines are probably due to the introduction of disease-carrying mosquitoes that, until recently, were restricted to the lowlands but have followed feral pigs as they have penetrated into remote rainforests. Unfortunately, the uplands of Moloka'i are probably too small to provide disease-free refugia. Pigs also degrade native forests as they spread invasive alien plants and destroy the shrub layer.

Illustration: Tomasz Cofta

CR **Puaiohi** *Myadestes palmeri*

▲ POPULATION: 130–330 | **THREATS:** SPP, (CLI)

Endemic to the island of Kaua´i in the Hawaiian Islands, this small thrush obtained its name from the male's mating call, uttered every ten seconds at dusk. It disappeared from many lowland areas at the end of the 19th century and is now restricted to the Alaka´i Wilderness Preserve, where it favours densely vegetated ravines. Destruction of understorey vegetation by pigs has been implicated in its decline but disease, predation by Short-eared Owls *Asio flammeus* and introduced mammals such as rats, and habitat alteration by invasive plants have probably also had an impact. A captive population is maintained and individuals have been successfully reintroduced into the wild, resulting in numbers more than doubling over three generations.

Photo: Eric VanderWerf (pacificrimconservation.com)

CR **Príncipe Thrush** *Turdus xanthorhynchus*

▼ **POPULATION: 50–249** | **THREATS:** SPP, AGR, LOG, HUN?

This confiding forest thrush, which was split from São Tomé Thrush *T. olivaceofuscus* in 2010, is endemic to the island of Príncipe. Having not been recorded since the 1920s, it was only rediscovered in 1997. A dramatic population decline is probably due to deforestation since human colonization in the 1500s. Although habitat loss is still a threat, it is much reduced by the recent protection of the majority of primary forest on the island. Other potential threats include the introduction of alien predators and hunting. It has recently been chosen by the government as one of a suite of indicator species that will be monitored regularly to assess the effectiveness of protected areas for biodiversity conservation.

Photo: Josef C. Uyeda

EN **Seychelles Magpie-robin** *Copsychus sechellarum*

▲ **POPULATION: 120** | **THREATS:** CLI, SPP, (AGR), (HUN), (PLN)

Endemic to Seychelles, this distinctive bird once occurred on eight (possibly 13) islands but, by 1965, only 12–15 individuals remained, on Frégate. Introduced mammalian and bird predators probably precipitated a major population decline, but this was exacerbated by native predators, such as skinks and snakes, and habitat loss and degradation due to an increase in commercial crop production. However, an intensive conservation management progamme, including the successful translocation of birds to Aride, Cousin, Cousine and Denis, has led to a significant population increase. It originally occupied coastal forest but is now found in mature woodland on central plateaux, vegetable gardens and plantations.

Photo: Oliver Smart (smartimages.co.uk)

EN **Grand Comoro** (or Humblot's) **Flycatcher** *Humblotia flavirostris*

▼ **POPULATION: 6,000–15,000** | **THREATS:** AGR, FIRE, SPP, LOG, TRA, CLI?

This flycatcher only occurs in forests on the slopes of Mount Karthala, an active volcano on the island of Grand Comoro, where it occupies a wide altitudinal range. It forages from the lowest branches of small trees or bushes, often feeding in small parties, but has never been observed in mixed-species flocks. The rapidly increasing human population on the island presents a major threat to this species due to the clearance of forest for agriculture. Introduced rats and Common Mynas *Acridotheres tristis* also pose a threat by predating nests. If plans to build a road to Mount Karthala's crater materialize, exploitation and fragmentation of the forest, and the spread of exotic species, could be accelerated.

Photo: Pete Morris (birdquest-tours.com)

EN **Mauritius Fody** *Foudia rubra*

= **POPULATION: 140–170** | **THREATS:** SPP, CLI?, (AGR), (LOG)

Once widespread on Mauritius, this striking weaver is now confined to a tiny area in the south-west of the island. Although clearance of native upland forest in the 1970s, particularly for plantations, led to a catastrophic decline, introduced predators are now the greatest threat: Black Rats *Rattus rattus* and Crab-eating Macaques *Macaca fascicularis* having caused almost total breeding failure in most areas. A captive-breeding programme has, however, resulted in a successful translocation to predator-free offshore Ile aux Aigrettes. A translocation of 32 birds to Round Island in 2010/11 failed, all the individuals having died by early 2012 due, mainly, to predation by the endemic boa *Casarea dussumieri*.

Photo: Dubi Shapiro (pbase.com/dubisha)

CR **São Tomé Grosbeak** *Neospiza concolor*

`200`

▼ **POPULATION:** <50 | **THREATS:** AGR, TRA, SPP?

Endemic to São Tomé, this grosbeak was known from just one 19th century specimen until it was rediscovered in 1991 in lowland, closed-canopy primary forest in the south-west of the island. A lack of recent records may be because it is mostly silent and forages in the canopy. Extensive areas of its lowland forest habitat have been cleared for cocoa plantations, and introduced mammals are potential predators. Although primary forest is now protected, there is little enforcement and human disturbance is an increasing threat. However, plans to develop further commercial plantations may include measures to protect native forest and a conservation-awareness initiative has been implemented.

Photo: August Thomasson

EN **Azores Bullfinch** *Pyrrhula murina*

`201`

= **POPULATION:** 860–870 | **THREATS:** SPP, (AGR), (HUN)

Endemic to the island of São Miguel in the Azores, this finch feeds on buds, seeds and fruit and appears to be entirely dependent upon native forest for food during many months of the year. However, the exotic tree *Clethra arborea* may provide a critical food supply from December to January. Widespread clearance of native forest for forestry plantations and agriculture, and hunting (it was considered to be a pest of fruit orchards) caused its historic decline. Current threats include invasive plants that suppress natural fruit, seed and bud supply, and predation by introduced mammals. A range of conservation initiatives have been successfully implemented and it was downgraded from Critically Endangered in 2010.

Photo: Jérôme Scuiller

CR **Nihoa Finch** *Telespiza ultima*

`193`

= **POPULATION:** 1,400–2,400 | **THREATS:** CLI, SPP, (AGR), (FIRE)

Endemic to Hawaii, this finch is now restricted to the tiny uninhabited island of Nihoa, but may once have occurred on other islands in the group. It inhabits low shrubs and grasses and nests in rocky cavities. The introduced grasshopper *Schistocerca nitens* may be a significant threat as its periodic irruptions can lead to the almost total defoliation of the island. Other potential threats include the accidental introduction of mammalian predators, non-native pest plants, insects, avian diseases and chance events such as hurricanes or fire. A process to evaluate and prioritize potential translocation sites throughout the archipelago is currently underway.

Photo: Jack Jeffrey (JackJeffreyphoto.com)

CR **Maui Parrotbill** *Pseudonestor xanthophrys*

`192`

? **POPULATION:** 250–540 | **THREATS:** SPP, CLI

Endemic to Maui in the Hawaiian Islands, this species is now restricted to wet and mesic montane forests in the north-east of the island. However, this habitat may be suboptimal as heavy rainfall leads to drastic losses during the breeding season. It uses its large, hooked bill to feed on the larvae and pupae of wood- and fruit-boring invertebrates. The habitat within its extremely small range has been heavily degraded by introduced feral ungulates but much of the area is now fenced and may be adequately protected. However, it remains at high risk from extreme environmental events, such as hurricanes, as well as the effects of invasive species, particularly the spread of disease-carrying mosquitoes. A small population exists in captivity.

Photo: Michael Neal (nealstudios.net)

CR (PE) **Ou** *Psittirostra psittacea*

? **POPULATION: <50** | **THREATS:** SPP, (AGR), (CLI), (GEO), (HUN), (LOG)

19

This large finch, which was once widespread in the Hawaiian Archipelago, has not been recorded with certainty since 1987 on Hawai'i and since 1989 on Kaua'i. Its hooked bill is specially adapted for feeding on the fruits of the native 'ie'ie vine *Freycinetia arborea* and, although restricted to wet and mesic forests from 800–1,900 m, it is nomadic in response to seasonal changes in food abundance. It may have been driven to extinction by habitat loss, introduced rats and, in particular, by malaria from introduced mosquitoes. However, as not all suitable habitat has been surveyed, and there have been some recent unconfirmed reports, it is possible that a tiny population may remain.

Illustration: Tomasz Cofta

CR **Palila** *Loxioides bailleui*

▼ **POPULATION: 250–999** | **THREATS: CLI**, SPP, MAN?, (AGR), (FIRE)

190

Prior to human settlement, this large finch occurred across the Hawaiian Archipelago but by the early 20th century it was restricted to Hawai'i, where it is was locally abundant. It is confined to dry, subalpine forest at 2,000–3,000 m, where it feeds primarily on the seeds of the endemic Māmane tree *Sophora chrysophylla*, the availability of which affects productivity and adult survival. Although subject to population fluctuations, since 2005 numbers have declined by 75%, primarily due to a prolonged drought that has reduced Māmane pod production. The main cause of its initial decline is habitat loss and degradation, and predation by introduced cats and rats. A captive breeding programme is underway.

Photo: Robby Kohley

CR (PE) **Nukupuu** *Hemignathus lucidus*

? **POPULATION: <50** | **THREATS:** SPP, (AGR), (CLI)

19

Found only on the Hawaiian Islands, the nominate subspecies of this finch, from O'ahu, went extinct in the mid- to late 1800s. There have been controversial records of the subspecies *hanapepe* on Kaua'i and the subspecies *affinis* on Maui up until the late 1990s. However, there have been no recent sightings despite extensive survey effort and it is almost certainly extinct across its range. If a population remains, it is likely to be tiny. It was last known from high-altitude wet and mesic forests, where it used its peculiar bill to feed on wood-boring invertebrates. Forest at lower elevations has been eliminated by cattle ranching and at higher elevations has been degraded by introduced ungulates.

Illustration: Tomasz Cofta

EN **Akiapolaau** *Hemignathus munroi*

▼ **POPULATION: 800** | **THREATS:** AGR, SPP, LOG

192

Formerly widespread in woodlands on Hawai'i, this species is now restricted to a few tiny fragments of high-altitude wet and mesic forests. The highest population densities are found in secondary growth Koa *Acacia koa*, where it uses its oddly shaped bill to feed primarily on invertebrate larvae prised from under the bark. Like some woodpeckers (Picidae), it also regularly feeds on sap from `ohi`a trees *Metrosideros polymorpha*, which it acquires by drilling holes into the bark. It has favoured trees, which its defends, and which are probably used by successive generations. Habitat degradation, predation and avian diseases are constant threats, but a range of actions, such as replanting Koa trees and removing introduced ungulates are underway.

Photo: Eric VanderWerf (pacificrimconservation.com)

CR Akikiki *Oreomystis bairdi* `191`

▼ **POPULATION: 520–1,200** | **THREATS:** SPP, (AGR), (CLI), (LOG)

Once common on the Hawaiian island of Kauaʻi, this inconspicuous species is now confined to one small area of high altitude forest. It forages slowly along trunks and branches, feeding mainly on invertebrates. The population has declined dramatically since the 1960s primarily due to habitat loss for agriculture, but predation and competition with introduced species are also important factors. Feral pigs are now a major threat, as they disperse alien plants and facilitate the spread of introduced mosquitoes that transmit avian diseases. A programme is being developed for captive rearing and release before the population falls to a critical level.

Photo: Robby Kohley

EN Hawaii Creeper *Oreomystis mana* `191`

▼ **POPULATION: 2,500–9,999** | **THREATS:** SPP, (AGR), (LOG)

Formerly widespread on Hawaiʻi in the Hawaiian Islands, this inconspicuous bird is now restricted to three disjunct populations. Although it favours wet and mesic forests from 1,000–2,300 m, where it sometimes joins mixed-species flocks, it is occasionally found in drier Māmane *Sophora chrysophylla* forest. Habitat loss and degradation due to the impact of feral ungulates, particularly pigs, is ongoing and other threats include predation by introduced rodents and diseases carried by introduced mosquitoes. It has recently disappeared from one area and is declining elsewhere. Measures to protect and restore native forest are in place and the release of captive-bred birds is planned.

Photo: Peter LaTourrette (birdphotography.com)

EN Maui Alauahio *Paroreomyza montana* `32,191`

▼ **POPULATION: 10,000–19,999** | **THREATS:** SPP, (AGR), (FIRE), (LOG)

Endemic to the Hawaiian Islands, this warbler-like finch was historically found on Lanaʻi but now only occurs on Maui, where it mostly inhabits a narrow belt of dense, wet forest on the slopes of Mount Haleakala. It feeds on invertebrates and nectar and is often seen in family groups, or amongst mixed-species flocks. Loss of lowland forest probably led to a significant range contraction, but feral ungulates, especially pigs, and recently goats, have caused extensive habitat degradation and facilitated the spread of disease-carrying mosquitoes. A range of introduced mammals, birds and insects are also potential predators and competitors. However, the strongholds of this species fall within protected areas and habitat restoration is an ongoing priority.

Photo: Michael Neal (nealstudios.net)

CR (PE) Oahu Alauahio *Paroreomyza maculata* `19`

? **POPULATION: 1–7** | **THREATS:** SPP, CLI?, (AGR), (DEV), (TRA)

Only found on Oʻahu in the Hawaiian Islands, where it was once common, the last well-documented observation of this species was in 1985 and it may now be extinct. A number of inconclusive sightings in the 1990s have come from between 300 and 650 m in remnant native lowland wet and mesic forests. It is thought to have fed on wood-boring beetles, typically found in the dead branches of Koa *Acacia koa* trees. As suitable habitat remains, the cause of its decline is thought to have been disease spread by introduced mosquitoes. Although not all the remaining areas of suitable habitat have been thoroughly searched, should a population remain, it is likely to be tiny.

Illustration: Tomasz Cofta

CR **Akekee** *Loxops caeruleirostris*

▼ **POPULATION:** 1,700–3,000 | **THREATS:** CLI, SPP, DEV, (LOG)

This finch-like bird is endemic to Kaua`i in the Hawaiian Islands, where it inhabits wet and mesic high-elevation forests. It feeds almost exclusively in the terminal leaf clusters of `ohi`a trees *Metrosideros polymorpha*, using its unusual, slightly cross-tipped bill, to extract invertebrates. It was considered common until the mid-1990s but the population is now declining extremely rapidly. Habitat loss and degradation has occurred due to development pressures and the spread of alien plants and feral ungulates. However, as much of this species' current range falls within a protected area, disease spread by introduced mosquitos may now be the most significant threat.

Photo: Jim Denny

EN **Akepa** *Loxops coccineus*

▼ **POPULATION:** 9,300 | **THREATS:** SPP, AGR, LOG

Endemic to the Hawaiian Islands, only the nominate subspecies, from Hawai'i, is extant (*wolstenholmei* from O'ahu and *ochraceus* from Maui, last recorded in 1930 and 1988 respectively, are presumed extinct). It inhabits high-altitude wet and mesic forests, where it feeds mainly on invertebrates that it extracts from the terminal leaf clusters of trees using its slightly crossed bill. Habitat loss and degradation, and the impact of predation, competition and the spread of disease by introduced mammals, birds and insects may have all contributed to ongoing declines. A large proportion of the population now occurs within protected forest reserves, where the provision of artificial nest sites has been successful.

Photo: Jack Jeffrey (JackJeffreyphoto.com)

CR **Akohekohe** *Palmeria dolei* `191`

▼ **POPULATION:** 2,500 | **THREATS:** SPP, CLI?, (AGR), (LOG)

This distinctive bird is now confined to a tiny area on Maui in the Hawaiian Islands, having been last seen on Moloka`i in 1907. It occurs in wet and mesic forests from 1,100–2,300 m, where it feeds primarily on the nectar of `ohi`a trees *Metrosideros polymorpha*, which it also seems to favour for nesting. Introduced predators and habitat loss and degradation, particularly due to the spread of feral pigs, have contributed to past declines. This species may now be particularly vulnerable to diseases spread by introduced mosquitoes, as it migrates to lower altitudes in response to food availability. It occurs in protected forests where habitat restoration is underway and a captive-breeding programme has been initiated.

Photo: Eric VanderWerf (pacificrimconservation.com)

CR (PE) **Poo-uli** *Melamprosops phaeosoma* `19`

▼ **POPULATION:** <50 | **THREATS:** SPP, CLI?, MAN?, (LOG)

Restricted to a tiny area of remote `ohi`a *Metrosideros polymorpha* forest on Mount Haleakala on Maui in the Hawaiian Islands, this species was only discovered in 1973, when the population was estimated at 200. By 1998, only three birds were known. However, one died in captivity in 2004 and the remaining two individuals have not been seen since 2003/4. The precise reason for the population decline is unknown but habitat degradation due to the impact of feral pigs, predation and disease may all by factors. Rats and the introduced Garlic Snail *Oxychilus alliarius* are believed to be responsible for the decline of native land snails, an important food source for this species.

Photo: Jack Jeffrey (JackJeffreyphoto.com)

CR **Gough Bunting** (or Gough Finch) *Rowettia goughensis* `33`

▼ **POPULATION: 670** | **THREATS: SPP**

Only found on remote Gough Island in the south Atlantic, this large bunting feeds primarily on invertebrates but also eats fruit and grass seeds, and scavenges dead birds and broken eggs. It nests on the ground amongst or under tussocky vegetation, favouring steep slopes or cliffs. The introduced House Mouse *Mus domesticus* is now abundant in the lowlands and poses the greatest threat through predation and competition, forcing the bunting out of coastal areas into suboptimal upland habitat. The accidental introduction of rats is also a potential threat. A draft operational plan for eradicating mice from Gough was prepared in 2010.

Female. Photo: Marie-Hélène Burle. (See *page 33* for photo of a male.)

EN **Wilkins's Bunting** (or Wilkins's Finch) *Nesospiza wilkinsi* `188`

= **POPULATION: 50–249** | **THREATS: SPP, CLI**

This bunting occurs only on Nightingale Island, part of the Tristan da Cunha Archipelago, where it is largely restricted to areas that support Island Cape Myrtle *Phylica arborea*, a large shrub. It breeds from December to February, nesting near the ground in clumps of vegetation. Although the island is uninhabited, this species is permanently at risk from the accidental introduction of mammalian predators from visiting vessels. Other potential threats are an alien scale insect and a black fungus-like growth, both of which have led to a decline in *Phylica* fruit production elsewhere. Catastrophic weather events could also lead to habitat loss (large swathes of *Phylica* were blown down during gales in 2001).

Photo: Peter Ryan (fitzpatrick.uct.ac.za)

CR **Medium Tree-finch** *Camarhynchus pauper* `196`

▼ **POPULATION: 600–1,700** | **THREATS: SPP, (AGR), (CLI)**

Endemic to the island of Floreana in the Galápagos Islands, this finch is mostly found in humid forests and scrub in the highlands, particularly where its preferred nesting tree *Scalesia pedunculata* is dominant. The most significant threat is the introduced parasitic fly *Philornis downsi*, which is responsible for the majority of nestling mortality. Other major threats include habitat loss and degradation, predation by introduced mammals and human disturbance. Although the agricultural zone of Floreana, which was prime habitat for this species, was not included in the area gazetted as the Galápagos National Park, measures to control introduced mammals elsewhere on the island should benefit this species.

Photo: David Peters (dpphotoimages.com)

CR **Mangrove Finch** *Camarhynchus heliobates* `196`

= **POPULATION: 30–200** | **THREATS: CLI?, SPP?**

This finch, which is renowned for using cactus spines or twigs as a tool to extract grubs from wood, is now restricted to two tiny areas of mangrove on Isabela in the Galápagos Islands, although there have been recent records from nearby Fernandina. It favours mangrove with tall trees, a relatively low canopy cover and abundant leaf-litter and dead wood – a very restricted habitat on Galápagos. Predation by introduced Black Rats *Ratus rattus* is probably the greatest threat, but the impact of other predators and the nest parasite *Philornis downsi* may also be significant. The translocation of birds to former sites, and methods for controlling *P. downsi*, are currently being trialled.

Photo: Michael Dvorak

The Caribbean, North and Central America

Critically Endangered **Ivory-billed Woodpecker** *Campephilus principalis.*Illustration by Tomasz Cofta.

CANADA

USA

Guadalupe Island
MEXICO

Gulf of Mexico

TROPIC OF CANCER

MEXICO

Cozumel Island
MEXICO

CAYMAN ISLAND

Islas Revillagigedo
MEXICO

BELIZE

GUATEMALA

HONDURAS

PACIFIC OCEAN

EL SALVADOR

NICARAGUA

Clipperton Island
FRANCE

COSTA RICA

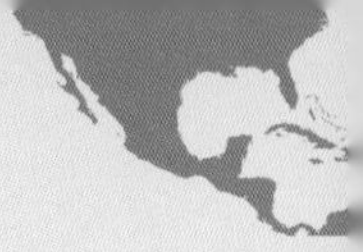

The Caribbean, North and Central America

The region covered in this section extends from the islands and tundras of the arctic north, via the boreal forests of Canada, the grasslands of the great plains and the deserts of south-western United States of America and northern Mexico, to the tropical forests of southern Mexico and the seven countries of Central America (from west to east: Guatemala, El Salvador, Belize, Honduras, Nicaragua, Costa Rica and Panama). The Caribbean islands extend eastwards in an arc which begins in the Gulf of Mexico between Florida and the Yucatán Peninsula, and ends with Trinidad and Tobago just off the north coast of Venezuela in South America. The total land area of the region is 22·5 million square kilometres, of which North America (Canada, the USA and Mexico) accounts for almost 22 million, or 97%. The combined area of the Central American countries is 524,000 km² and the land area of the over 7,000 Caribbean islands is 240,000 km².

There are 44 Endemic Bird Areas or Secondary Areas in the region: ten in the Caribbean, 23 in North America and 11 in Central America. A total of 1,912 bird species has been recorded, 141 (over 7%) of which are globally threatened and 65 (3·4% of the regional total) are Endangered or Critically Endangered.

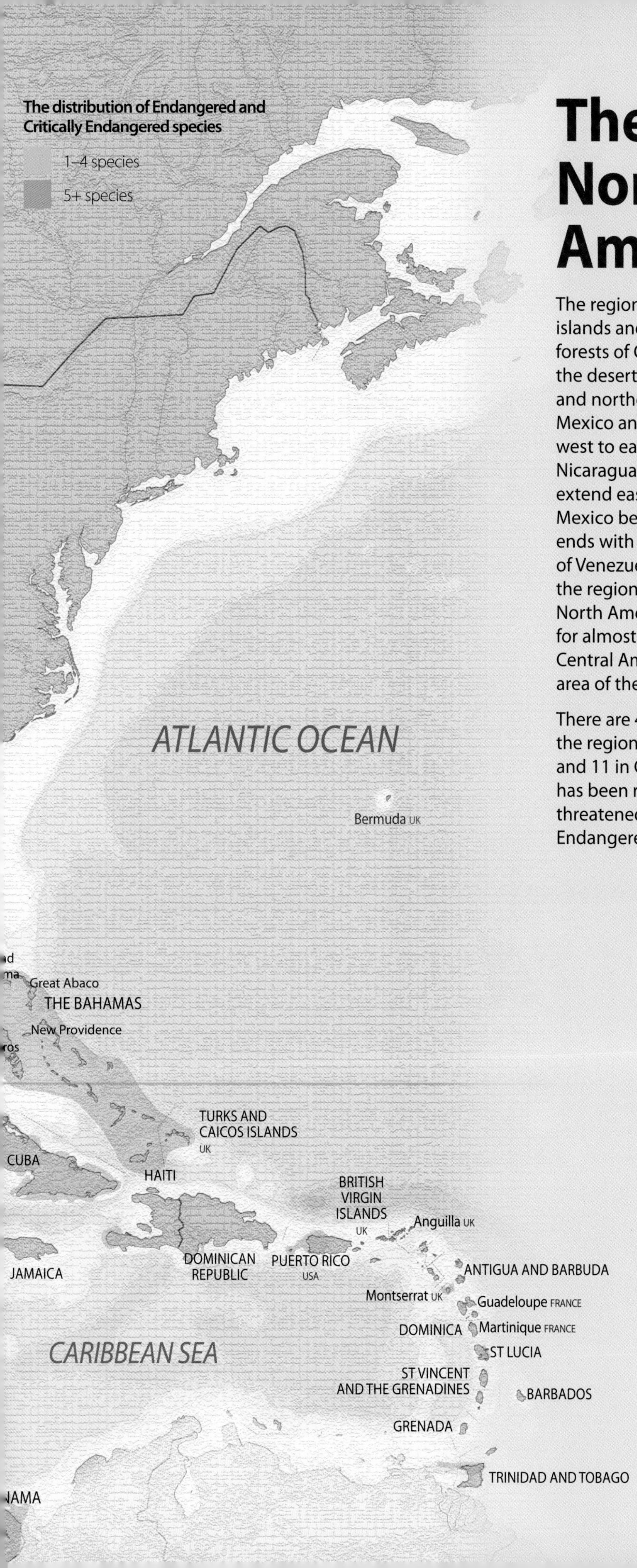

ATLANTIC OCEAN

Bermuda UK

Great Abaco
THE BAHAMAS
New Providence

TURKS AND CAICOS ISLANDS UK

CUBA
HAITI
BRITISH VIRGIN ISLANDS UK
Anguilla UK
DOMINICAN REPUBLIC
PUERTO RICO USA
ANTIGUA AND BARBUDA
JAMAICA
Montserrat UK
Guadeloupe FRANCE
DOMINICA
Martinique FRANCE
CARIBBEAN SEA
ST LUCIA
ST VINCENT AND THE GRENADINES
BARBADOS
GRENADA
NAMA
TRINIDAD AND TOBAGO

BirdLife Partners

Bahamas	Bahamas National Trust (BNT)
Belize	Belize Audubon Society (BAS)
Canada	Nature Canada and Bird Studies Canada (BSC)
Cuba	Centro Nacional de Áreas Protegidas (CNAP)
Dominican Republic	Grupo Jaragua (GJI)
El Salvador	SalvaNATURA (SN)
Mexico	Pronatura
Panama	Panama Audubon Society (PAS)
Puerto Rico	Sociedad Ornitológica Puertorriqueña, Inc. (SOPI)
USA	Audubon

The threatened birds – an overview

Despite its huge land area, Canada has no endemic birds and relatively low bird species diversity, at 460 species, most of which have large ranges, and the majority of which are migrants. The continental USA (not including Hawaii), with a much more varied range of habitats, has over 900 recorded bird species. Among the threatened species shared with Canada are the Endangered Marbled Murrelet *Brachyramphus marmoratus*, and the Endangered Whooping Crane *Grus americana*. The only self-sustaining population of the crane breeds in Canada and winters in Texas.

Species richness begins to increase near the Mexican border. With only one-tenth the land area of its two northern neighbours, Mexico has 1,064 species, 30% more than the USA and Canada combined, of which around 100 are endemic. (Mexico also hosts the largest number of migratory species in North America, since more than 80% of the species classed as Neotropical migrants pass through or winter there.) Mexico also has many more seriously threatened species (once Hawaii is deducted from the USA total). Two bird species have gone extinct in Mexico in historic times, but three more are presumed extinct, including the Imperial Woodpecker *Campephilus imperialis* and Guadalupe Storm-petrel *Oceanodroma macrodactyla*, and the Eskimo Curlew *Numenius borealis*, a transcontinental migrant. Few ornithologists expect to see the Critically Endangered Cozumel Thrasher *Toxostoma guttatum* again either, following a succession of hurricanes that struck its tiny island home in the 1990s and 2000s, although it is not yet listed as Possibly Extinct.

The relatively tiny area covered by the seven Central American countries, clustered together at the end of the isthmus joining North to South America, includes eight Endemic Bird Areas. Costa Rica, with a total area of a little over 50,000 km², has 853 recorded species, of which seven are country endemics. Even tiny Belize, occupying less than 23,000 km², has 549 recorded species. The southernmost of these countries, Panama, has 876 species, including nine endemics (but then its southern neighbour is Colombia, with the world's richest avifauna). These countries are of high importance for neotropical migrants, which either spend the entire winter or stop off on their way further south.

The islands of the Caribbean represent 17 nations and are exceptionally important for global biodiversity conservation. Of 770 bird species, almost one-fifth are endemic to one or more islands. More than 120 species which breed in North America winter in the Caribbean, and the entire populations of species like the Near Threatened Kirtland's Warbler *Dendroica kirtlandii* and Vulnerable Bicknell's Thrush *Catharus bicknelli* spend the winter in small areas of habitat on

The Endangered **Horned Guan** *Oreophasis derbianus* occurs in cloud forest in the Sierra Madre de Chiapas, Mexico, and west-central Guatemala. Subsistence hunting, and habitat loss and fragmentation because of logging, firewood gathering and agriculture are the main threats, and remaining populations are increasingly isolated from one another. The guan is legally protected, and occurs in (more or less) protected areas in both countries. Conservation measures include reforestation, the encouragement of shade-grown coffee cultivation under the shelter of native forest trees, and captive breeding. Photo: Roberto Pedraza Ruiz (sierragorda.net/galeria/Beto).

just a few of the islands. The Critically Endangered Bachman's Warbler *Vermivora bachmanii*, now listed as Possibly Extinct, wintered in Cuba except for a few records from Florida.

This vast and varied region has a corresponding huge range of conservation challenges, from the impact of climate change on tundra-breeding species in the north, to the loss of forests critical for wintering Neotropical migrants in Central America. New, more intensive forms of agriculture and more extensive kinds of resource extraction (such as mountain-top removal and the extraction of tar-sands oil in the boreal forest) are destroying the fragile compromises that enabled grassland and other specialists to cling on after the historic conversion of their habitats. Rubbish and toxic pollutants are finding their way to the remotest places. However, the region is leading the way in trans-boundary conservation initiatives, especially for migratory birds, and centrally-managed protected area systems are being augmented by others, run by (and for the benefit of) traditional communities and indigenous peoples.

Habitat conversion to banana plantations, and forest damage by hurricanes, combined with capture for the cagebird trade, were the principal reasons for the decline of the Endangered **Imperial Amazon** *Amazona imperialis*, which is endemic to the island of Dominica. The trade has been almost eliminated, and protected areas including Morne Diablotin National Park established to protect its habitat. Photo: Dr Paul R. Reillo (rarespecies.org).

The Caribbean

Though covering a land area of just 239,681 km² (about the same size as the state of Arizona in the USA), the Caribbean islands are home to endemic plants and vertebrates amounting to at least 2% of the world's total species complement. Of around 770 bird species, 148 are endemic, with 105 confined to single islands.

Only around 10% of the region's original habitats remains. Forests are being lost to clear-felling and conversion to agriculture (especially bananas, cacao, coffee, and tobacco), and degraded by timber extraction, livestock grazing and shifting cultivation. Bauxite (aluminium ore) mining threatens three-quarters of the largest remaining area of Jamaica's unique karst limestone forest, home to 95% of the global population of the Vulnerable Black-billed Amazon *Amazona agilis*. Charcoal production for fuel has helped destroy all but 2% of Haiti's forests, and is continuing to encroach on the rest. Throughout the region, sand, gravel and limestone is being quarried to support housing and infrastructure construction. Wetlands on all islands are being degraded, drained and developed, or used as dumps. Runaway tourism development is altering whole landscapes with golf courses, non-native vegetation, roads, hotel complexes and holiday villages. Predatory alien species such as pigs, rats, cats and Small Asian Mongoose *Herpestes javanicus* are well established on many islands.

Currently there are 14 Critically Endangered species in the Caribbean, several of which could be rendered extinct through the destruction of relatively small patches of habitat. For example, the Puerto Rican Amazon *Amazona vittata* is confined to just 0·2% of its former distribution because of habitat loss, the cagebird trade, pesticides and alien predators. In 1989, Hurricane Hugo halved the wild population from 47 to about 23. Ridgway's Hawk *Buteo ridgwayi* has lost almost all its primary forest habitat in the Dominican Republic, even in national parks, and secondary forest is fast disappearing too.

The clashes between conservation and development in the Caribbean are well illustrated by the Critically Endangered Grenada Dove *Leptotila wellsi*. All the state land on which the dove occurs is now protected, but its future cannot be assured without protecting habitat on private land. However, this land is divided into hundreds of parcels which, because of their development potential, are far too expensive to be purchased and added to the protected area system.

St Lucia Black Finch *Melanospiza richardsoni*.
Photo: Adams Toussaint.

The Endangered **St Lucia Black Finch** *Melanospiza richardsoni* tolerates a range of natural, modified and degraded habitats, but prefers the dense undergrowth naturally found in ravines within moist montane forest. The clearing of undergrowth, particularly in timber plantations, renders areas completely unsuitable and is probably the major threat. Much apparently suitable habitat on St Lucia is unoccupied.

The Endangered **Blue-headed Quail-dove** *Starnoenas cyanocephala* was once common and widespread across Cuba, but now survives in good numbers only in the lowlands around Zapata, with two smaller but still significant subpopulations elsewhere on the island, and is thought to persist in a number of other areas. It has always been regarded as excellent eating, and is still trapped illegally using drop-traps baited with orange seeds. Hurricanes may significantly affect this species by felling large areas of forest, as happened in the Zapata Swamp in 1996.

Blue-headed Quail-dove *Starnoenas cyanocephala*.
Photo: Rich Andrews (cvlbirding.co.uk).

Hispaniolan Crossbill *Loxia megaplaga*. Photo: Rafy Rodriguez.

Montserrat Oriole *Icterus oberi*. Photo: Gregory Guida (gguida.com).

Out of the Caribbean's 12 Critically Endangered species, four are listed as Possibly Extinct, including the Jamaica Petrel *Pterodroma caribbaea* and Jamaican Pauraque *Siphonorhis americana*, neither of which has been recorded since the 19th century. A fifth, the Ivory-billed Woodpecker *Campephilus principalis*, is very likely to be extinct too.

The 19 Endangered species have declined as a result of habitat destruction, predation by alien species, and in some cases (like the Blue-headed Quail-dove *Starnoenas cyanocephala*) from excessive hunting. As habitat becomes more fragmented, many of the Caribbean's threatened species fall victim to nest-parasitism by Shiny Cowbirds *Molothrus bonariensis*, which are spreading throughout the islands from the mainland, or to competition or nest-predation from more aggressive native species like the Pearly-eyed Thrasher *Margarops fuscatus*.

Puerto Rican Nightjar *Caprimulgus noctitherus*
Photo: Michael J. Morel.

The Endangered **Hispaniolan Crossbill** *Loxia megaplaga* feeds exclusively on pine-seeds. Peak seed crop years in some pinewoods coincide with scant years in others, and the crossbills are highly nomadic, breeding where their food is most abundant. Pinewood logging has been reduced since the 1960s, but clearance for small-scale agriculture continues, especially on the Haitian side of the island. Fires – a necessary part of the pines' regeneration cycle – may burn more of the remaining pine habitat than can be replaced.

Until the 1990s, The Critically Endangered **Montserrat Oriole** *Icterus oberi* occurred throughout the three main forested hill ranges on the island of Montserrat. Volcanic eruptions in 1995–97 destroyed two-thirds of this habitat, and between 2000 and 2006 further eruptions caused heavy ash falls on its remaining stronghold in the Centre Hills. Following an unexplained decline in the years between the two periods of volcanic activity, the population is now thought to be increasing. Further eruptions, habitat destruction by pigs, nest predation by rats and Pearly-eyed Thrashers *Margarops fuscatus*, and the impact of climate change on its montane forest habitat, are among current and potential future threats.

In 2011, the Endangered **Puerto Rican Nightjar** *Caprimulgus noctitherus* was downlisted from Critically Endangered when surveys showed its range and population were larger than had been feared. But it is continuing to lose habitat to residential, industrial and leisure developments, and is further threatened by proposed infrastructure projects including a windfarm and a gas pipeline. The introduction of the Small Asian Mongoose *Herpestes javanicus* in the 1870s may have contributed to its drastic initial decline. Young and eggs may be predated by Pearly-eyed Thrasher *Margarops fuscatus*, fire-ants and feral cats.

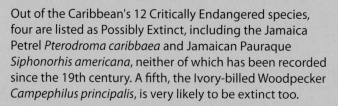

North America

The tri-national Commission for Environmental Cooperation, set up by the governments of the USA, Canada and Mexico, divides the North American continent into 15 eco-regions. Some, like the Hudson Plains, Mediterranean California, and Tropical Dry Forests, lie entirely within one of the countries. Others, like the Marine West Coast Forests and Southern Semi-arid Highlands, cross the boundaries of two countries, and a few, including the Great Plains and North American Deserts, run from north to south through parts of all three countries. Many conservation challenges – especially those affecting migratory species – are now being tackled by regional initiatives, with the sharing and transfer of funds and expertise between countries.

Of the prairie grassland that once covered 3·5 million square kilometres from Canada to southern Texas and Mexico, little remains in a natural state, and the more sustainable kinds of grazing and agriculture are rapidly being replaced by large-scale agribusiness, exacerbated by the switch to crop-based biofuels. Many grassland specialists are becoming more threatened: the Greater *Tympanuchus cupido* and Lesser *T. pallidicinctus* Prairie-chickens and Sprague's Pipit *Anthus spraguei* have all been uplisted from Least Concern to Vulnerable within the last 20 years.

Mining and other extractive industries pose a direct threat to many species. The removal of entire mountain-tops to extract coal in the Appalachians is contributing to the rapid decline of the Vulnerable Cerulean Warbler *Dendroica cerulea*. The dumping of mining waste, seepage from abandoned mining works into rivers, and other kinds of pollution involving highly toxic mining by-products has much wider impacts. The Exxon Valdez oil-spill killed up to 15% of the largest remaining population of Critically Endangered Kittlitz's Murrelet *Brachyramphus brevirostris*, and new oil drilling licences off the coast of Alaska raise the prospect of future spills, which would be catastrophic for this species. Globally 'common' birds regarded as of conservation concern in the USA and Canada suffered the loss of feeding and breeding grounds and stopover sites following the BP oil disaster in the Gulf of Mexico.

Marbled Murrelet *Brachyramphus marmoratus*.
Photo: Glenn Bartley (glennbartley.com).

The Endangered **Marbled Murrelet** *Brachyramphus marmoratus* is found along the west coast of the USA and Canada, with the main population in Alaska. Its rapid decline is thought to be partly due to fragmentation of old-growth forest nesting habitat, accompanied by increased disturbance and predation by crows. Over-fishing has drastically lowered prey availability. In California, following the collapse of the sardine fishery, the murrelets have switched from fish to lower trophic-level prey such as krill, and fewer birds reach breeding condition. Oil-spills and bycatch in gill-nets also cause substantial mortality.

The Endangered **Gunnison Sage-grouse** *Centrocercus minimus* is endemic to the south-western United States, where the largest population is found in the Gunnison Basin, Colorado. It is restricted to sagebrush country where, each spring, males perform elaborate courtship rituals, puffing-up their distinctive plumage to attract females. Despite occurring in a country where the avifauna is well-known, it was overlooked until the 1990s due to its similarity to the Near Threatened Greater Sage-grouse *C. urophasianus*, and only described as a new species in 2000 – making it the first new species of bird to be described from the USA since the 19th century.

The Endangered **Gunnison Sage-grouse** *Centrocercus minimus*. Photo: Mike Danzenbaker (avesphoto.com).

Golden-cheeked Warbler *Dendroica chrysoparia*. Photo: Greg Lasley (greglasley.net).

Tricoloured Blackbird
Agelaius tricolor.
Photo: Glen Tepke
(pbase.com/gtepke).

The extraction of low-grade oil from tar-sands in Canada's boreal forest threatens vast areas of the nursery-grounds of almost 300 songbird and waterbird species, including the already globally Vulnerable Rusty Blackbird *Euphagus carolinus* and Sprague's Pipit. Endangered Whooping Cranes *Grus americana* migrate over the tar-sands regions.

In the arid regions of the southern USA and Mexico, threats to biodiversity come from large-scale urban and tourist development, and the spread of irrigated agriculture, leading to over-abstraction of rivers, disruption to the water table, and water pollution. Three species of *Geothlypis* yellowthroat endemic to Mexico are considered globally threatened: the Endangered Belding's Yellowthroat *G. beldingi* because of tourist and housing development and marsh drainage on the coast of Baja California; the Endangered Black-polled Yellowthroat *G. speciosa* because of water abstraction to supply Mexico City; and the Vulnerable Altamira Yellowthroat *G. flavovelata* because of the conversion of marshes for cattle grazing and, increasingly, industrial development.

Mexico is developing fast economically and industrially, and has a fast expanding population. Ranching and agriculture were responsible for the loss of 50 percent of its forests by 2002; those that remain are threatened both by further exploitation and development, and by illegal drug cultivation and the breakdown of law enforcement that goes with it.

A 2007 analysis which combined the results of the National Audubon Society's Christmas Bird Count (CBC) and Breeding Bird Survey found that many 'common' birds had lost over half their populations in the North American continent since the 1960s. These included tundra-breeding species like Snow Bunting *Plectrophenax nivalis* and Greater Scaup *Aythya marila*, which have declined by 64% and 75% respectively since 1967, partly due to the progressively earlier thawing of the permafrost because of the warming climate. Climate modeling also suggests that species in the south of the continent, including the already Endangered Worthen's Sparrow *Spizella wortheni*, also stand to lose the majority of remaining suitable habitat because of climate change.

Near-endemic to California, the Endangered **Tricoloured Blackbird** *Agelaius tricolor* forms breeding colonies larger than those of any other extant North American landbird. Its rapid decline appears mainly due to low reproductive success in native wetlands and other natural habitats. In silage fields, which hold a significant proportion of the breeding population, harvesting can destroy entire colonies of tens of thousands of nests. Herbicide spraying and contaminated water are suspected to have caused complete breeding failure in several colonies. Reproductive success is significantly higher in non-native upland vegetation, primarily Himalayan Blackberry *Rubus armeniacus*.

The Endangered **Golden-cheeked Warbler** *Dendroica chrysoparia* breeds in juniper-oak woodlands in a small area of Texas, and winters in southern Mexico, Guatemala, El Salvador, Nicaragua and Honduras. Its breeding habitat is being cleared for development and agriculture, resulting in reduced gene-flow between increasingly fragmented populations. But the main factor in its decline is the reduction of its pine-oak wintering habitats, as the area that remains is only sufficient to sustain 15% of the population that could be supported by the available breeding habitat.

Worthen's Sparrow *Spizella wortheni* has suffered a major range contraction and currently only breeds at sites in Coahuila and Nuevo León, Mexico. Its shrub-grassland habitats have been greatly reduced by grazing and agriculture, primarily potato production. Reproductive success is very low, probably because of disturbance by livestock. The known population is thought to be 100–120 individuals, but it qualifies as Endangered rather than Critically Endangered because it breeds at three sites, with at least one subpopulation larger than 50 individuals. Suitable habitat remains elsewhere within its wider historic range, and it is hoped that more thorough surveys will find additional populations.

Worthen's Sparrow *Spizella wortheni*. Photo: René Valdés (birdpicsandmore.com).

Central America

Despite the immense species richness packed into the relatively tiny area of the seven countries of Central America, only 11 species are regarded as Endangered, and just one, the Galápagos Petrel *Pterodroma phaeopygia*, which visits the Pacific coast outside the breeding season, is Critically Endangered.

Several of these Endangered species have tiny ranges. The Yellow-billed Cotinga *Carpodectes antoniae*, which occurs on the Pacific coast of Costa Rica and westernmost Panama, has suffered from the rapid destruction of mangroves, and less than 1,700 km² of suitable habitat remains, with very little of it under effective protection. The Costa Rican endemic Mangrove Hummingbird *Amazilia boucardi* is down to 1,000 km² of habitat, much of it under heavy development pressure. Within the 400 km² distribution of another endemic hummingbird, the Honduran Emerald *Amazilia luciae*, most suitable habitat probably exists as fragments of less than 100 ha in size, with the majority on private land, where relatively sustainable cattle grazing is being replaced by plantation crops. The Black-cheeked Ant-tanager *Habia atrimaxillaris* has a highly restricted distribution on the Osa Peninsula and around the Golfo Dulce in south-west Costa Rica.

There is a surprising amount of forest left in the region. In 2002, Panama was estimated to retain 44% of its original forest cover. In El Salvador, which is the smallest Central American country, and has the highest population density, around 20% of the land is covered by natural vegetation, although some of this is secondary forest growing on abandoned agricultural land. Highland forests tend

Azure-rumped Tanager *Tangara cabanisi*. Photo: Knut Eisermann (cayaya-birding.com).

Yellow-headed Amazon *Amazona oratrix*. Photo: Eduardo Lugo Cabrera (wildlifeconnection.com).

The altitudinal range of the Endangered **Azure-rumped Tanager** *Tangara cabanisi* coincides with the optimal land for coffee cultivation. The tanager has been recorded in degraded and edge habitats, including coffee plantations adjacent to primary forest, but appears to be absent from the interior of intensive coffee plantations. It mostly forages in the upper forest strata and canopy, and has been found nesting in tall trees in shade-grown coffee plantations. Conservation measures proposed include certification schemes to encourage low-intensity shade-grown coffee farming, and birding tourism to provide additional financial incentives for growers.

The site used by the only known breeding population of the Endangered **Yellow-headed Amazon** *Amazona oratrix* in Guatemala was declared a wildlife refuge in 2005, but effective protection is difficult due to organised crime in the area. It is reported that local military authorities are complicit in the illegal trade in the species. In Belize, it is persecuted for damaging crops, and captured for the illicit pet trade by cutting down its nesting trees. It has also suffered extensive loss of pine and palm savanna and coastal scrub habitat.

The current range of the Endangered **Black-cheeked Ant-tanager** *Habia atrimaxillaris* is approximately half what it was in the 1960s. As recently as 1989, it was still common in unprotected forest on Costa Rica's Osa Peninsula. But as logging, roadbuilding and other infrastructure associated with the rapidly growing human population have reduced the extent and continuity of the forest, it has become increasingly scarce outside the Corcovado National Park and Golfito Faunal Refuge. Within these protected areas, populations appear stable.

Black-cheeked Ant-tanager *Habia atrimaxillaris*. Photo: Jonas Langbråten (langbraten.com).

The **Bare-necked Umbrellabird** *Cephalopterus glabricollis* was uplisted from Vulnerable to Endangered in 2008. It breeds very locally on the Caribbean slopes of Costa Rica and Panama, and when not breeding descends to the lowlands and foothills of these countries and adjacent southern Nicaragua. The core of its likely range lies in the Panamanian side of the trans-boundary La Amistad International Park, where its breeding areas are mostly inaccessible. It is suspected to be in rapid decline owing to on-going forest clearance and degradation. Its lowland non-breeding habitat is particularly threatened, and habitat corridors linking the species' breeding and non-breeding areas have been lost.

The Endangered **Mangrove Hummingbird** *Amazilia boucardi* is patchily distributed even within the four or five large mangrove forests in its small range on the Pacific coast of Costa Rica, and is absent from many areas of apparently suitable habitat. The entire Pacific coast of Costa Rica is under heavy development pressure, and although cutting mangroves is illegal in Costa Rica, the law is widely ignored.

Bare-necked Umbrellabird *Cephalopterus glabricollis*. Photo: Michael & Patricia Fogden (fogdenphotos.com).

Mangrove Hummingbird *Amazilia boucardi*. Photo: Glenn Bartley (glennbartley.com).

to be the most intact, and lowland forest (as in Panama's Darién Lowlands EBA) under most pressure from logging, settlement and road construction.

Many Central American countries have very extensive protected area systems, at least on paper. Approximately 36% of the land area of Belize is protected at some level. For Panama, the figure is 34%, and for Costa Rica, 29% (of which around 14% is strictly protected). But in some countries, and particularly in remoter areas, there may be insufficient staff to enforce regulations. Problems within and just outside protected areas include increasing demand for land, timber and mineral resources, and the construction of an extensive network of roads and highways which slice across formerly intact forests and make them more accessible to would-be settlers and developers. In Panama, the remaining lowland and foothill forests on the Caribbean slope, where the Endangered Bare-necked Umbrellabird *Cephalopterus glabricollis* is found, are threatened by clearance for agriculture, even in legally protected areas.

Several of the region's Endangered species have much of their ranges outside the protected area network. About 45% of remaining habitat suitable for the Azure-rumped Tanager *Tangara cabanisi* in Guatemala is unprotected. In Belize, much of the habitat used by the Yellow-headed Amazon *Amazona oratrix* lies outside the national protected area system, and is under heavy development pressure.

The Caribbean, North and Central America

A total of 1,912 species has been recorded from continental North America, Central America and the Caribbean, according to BirdLife International. This number includes about 40 seabirds that do not breed in the region but have been recorded in coastal waters. The land birds that are endemic to the oceanic islands of North and Central America are covered in the Oceanic Islands section (*page 180*). The species concerned are those endemic to the Hawaiian Islands, the Revillagigedo Archipelago (including Socorro), and Cocos Island (which jointly support 33 globally threatened species and two others that are Extinct in the Wild).

Native species recorded	1,912
Extinct in the Wild (EW)	0
Critically Endangered (CR)	22
Endangered (EN)	43
Vulnerable (VU)	85
Data Deficient (DD)	4

Sixty of the 65 Endangered and Critically Endangered species recorded in the region are illustrated in this section. Four of the five that have been omitted are seabirds that are included in the Oceanic Islands section. The fifth species that is not covered here is Red Siskin *Carduelis cucullata* (see *page 316*), which is only present in the region (on Puerto Rico) as an introduced (and declining) population derived from escaped cagebirds.

Five of the Critically Endangered species included in this section are Possibly Extinct: Imperial Woodpecker *Campephilus imperialis*, Jamaican Pauraque *Siphonorhis americana*, Eskimo Curlew *Numenius borealis*, Jamaica Petrel *Pterodroma caribbaea* and Bachman's Warbler *Vermivora bachmanii*.

The globally threatened species in the three sub-regions

Sub-region	Species	CR	EN	VU	TOTAL	% of species	DD
The Caribbean	785	14	19	24	57	7·3%	0
North America	1,252	11 (3)	21 (1)	52	84	6·7%	1
Central America	1,164	1 (1)	11	25	37	3·2%	3

(n) = number of regularly occurring non-breeding visitors.

Five of the 45 Endangered or Critically Endangered migratory 'land' birds in the world breed in this region. They include two of the Possibly Extinct species (Eskimo Curlew and Bachman's Warbler). The other three species are Endangered: Whooping Crane *Grus americana*, Golden-cheeked Warbler *Dendroica chrysoparia* and Bahama Swallow *Tachycineta cyaneoviridis*. The migration routes for all these species are shown on the map on *page 51*.

The Endangered and Critically Endangered species in the region come from 28 bird families. These are summarized in the following table and additional information on these families, such as the total number of species and the proportion that is globally threatened is included in the taxonomic list of all the species featured in this book at Appendix 2 on *page 339*.

A summary of the most threatened bird families in the Caribbean, North and Central America

Family	CR	EN	Tot.	Family	CR	EN	Tot.
Guans (Cracidae)	1	1	2	Hummingbirds (Trochilidae)	1	3	4
Grouse (Phasianidae)	–	1	1	Woodpeckers (Picidae)	2	–	2
Petrels & shearwaters (Procellariidae)	3 (2)	2 (1)	5 (3)	Cotingas (Cotingidae)	–	2	2
Storm-petrels (Hydrobatidae)	1 (1)	1	2 (1)	Tyrant-flycatchers (Tyrannidae)	–	1	1
New World vultures (Cathartidae)	1	–	1	Swallows & martins (Hirundinidae)	–	1	1
Hawks & kites (Accipitridae)	2	1	3	Wrens (Troglodytidae)	–	1	1
Rails (Rallidae)	1	–	1	Thashers & Mockingbirds (Mimidae)	1	1	2
Cranes (Gruidae)	–	1	1	Thrushes (Turdidae)	–	1	1
Sandpipers & allies (Scolopacidae)	1	–	1	Finches (Fringillidae)	–	2 [1]	2 [1]
Auks (Alcidae)	1	1	2	New World warblers (Parulidae)	2	4	6
Doves & pigeons (Columbidae)	1	2	3	New World blackbirds ()Icteridae)	2	3	5
Parrots (Psittacidae)	1	6	7	American Sparrows & allies (Emberizidae)	–	4	4
Cuckoos (Cuculidae)	–	1	1	Tanagers (Thraupidae)	–	1	1
Nightjars (Caprimulgidae)	1	1	2	Grosbeaks, saltators & allies (Cardinalidae)	–	1	1
(n) = number of non-breeding migrants. [1] = introduced to the region.				TOTAL (28 FAMILIES)	22 (3)	43 (1)	65 (4)

CR Trinidad Piping-guan *Pipile pipile*

▼ POPULATION: 50–249 | THREATS: AGR, HUN, LOG, CLI?

Once widespread on Trinidad, this guan is now probably confined to just a small area in the north-west of the island where the only suitable habitat remains. It feeds in the canopy of tall rainforest trees, preferring steep, hilly areas with numerous streams, and seems to tolerate nearby areas of small-scale agriculture provided canopy trees are available and it is not hunted. Although the guan and much of its current habitat is legally protected, enforcement is poor. Ecotourism has helped raise awareness of wildlife conservation with local people but hunting behaviour has remained unchanged and continues to be a serious issue.

Photo: Peter Coe

EN Horned Guan *Oreophasis derbianus* `240`

▼ POPULATION: 600–1,700 | THREATS: AGR, HUN, LOG, SPP, TRA, CLI?

This unmistakable guan occurs at several disjunct locations in south-west Mexico and west-central Guatemala. It is found mostly in cloud forest from 1,400–3,500 m and may make altitudinal movements. Habitat loss and degradation due to logging and clearance for agriculture, especially coffee plantations, is an ongong major threat. Subsistence hunting may still occur but trapping for the bird trade is thought to have ceased. The Mexican federal government has prepared a conservation action plan for this species and, in Guatemala, it has become a 'flagship species' for the development of local tourism. At the end of 2010, the captive population numbered 88 individuals, held by 11 institutions in six countries.

Photo: Roberto Pedraza Ruiz (sierragorda.net/galeria/Beto)

EN Gunnison Sage-grouse *Centrocercus minimus* `244`

▼ POPULATION: 1,700 | THREATS: CLI, AGR, EGY, MAN, SPP, DEV, TRA, (WAT), (HUN)

Confined to the intermontane Gunnison Basin in Colorado and Utah, USA, this grouse is reliant upon areas dominated by sagebrush *Artemisia* spp. The dramatic display of lekking males occurs from March to May in sparse vegetation, but surrounding taller sagebrush is required for nesting. Broods are then reared in nearby riparian areas and mesic uplands. In winter, it moves to snow-free areas near watercourses. Habitat loss and degradation is ongoing, with increasing urbanization a primary factor. Populations are now severely fragmented and inbreeding is occurring. However, since the early 21st century, local conservation initiatives aimed at reversing the population decline have led to significant improvements in habitat management.

Photo: Ian Merrill

EN Ashy Storm-petrel *Oceanodroma homochroa* `41`

▼ POPULATION: 3,500–6,700 | THREATS: FISH, MAN, SPP, PLN, CLI

This storm-petrel breeds colonially in rocky crevices and burrows on a few small islands and offshore rocks off the coast of California, USA, and northern Mexico. Unlike most of its congeners, it remains near its breeding areas year-round. Declines are thought to be due to predation by rats and increasing populations of Western Gull *Larus occidentalis*, Burrowing Owl *Athene cunicularia* and Barn Owl *Tyto alba*. Foraging areas are threatened by organochlorine and oil pollution, and the species is also particularly prone to human disturbance, readily abandoning nests, and to the effects of light pollution. Most of the Californian population nests on protected islands where efforts are being made to eradicate predators.

Photo: John Sterling (sterlingbirds.com)

EN **Black-capped Petrel** *Pterodroma hasitata*

27

▼ POPULATION: 5,000 | THREATS: AGR, HUN, SPP, LOG, PLN, CLI, EGY, DEV, (GEO)

This gadfly petrel breeds on the island of Hispaniola (Haiti and Dominican Republic) and possibly Dominica and Cuba. Historically, it bred on Guadeloupe and perhaps Martinique. At sea, it disperses to north-east USA and north-east Brazil, as well as across the Caribbean. It nests colonially in cliff burrows, often in montane forest, and is primarily nocturnal. When feeding it favours prey associated with *Sargassum* seaweed reefs, but also scavenges behind fishing trawlers. Habitat destruction and hunting for food remain major threats in Haiti. Introduced mammals also predate birds, and urbanization has led to birds becoming disorientated by artificial lighting and colliding with man-made structures and trees.

Photo: Glen Tepke (pbase.com/gtepke)

CR (PE) **Jamaica Petrel** *Pterodroma caribbaea*

19

? POPULATION: <50 | THREATS: CLI?, SPP?, (HUN)

The last confirmed record of this gadfly petrel was in 1879, when 22 birds were collected. The only proven nesting was in the Blue and John Crow Mountains on Jamaica, where islanders knew it as the 'Blue Mountain Duck'. Although its dramatic decline during the 19th century is presumed to have been due to predation by introduced mammals, habitat degradation by introduced pigs, and hunting may also have been important factors. It was searched for without success during the 1990s but cannot yet be presumed to be extinct since nocturnal petrels are notoriously difficult to find and it could potentially occur on Dominica or Guadeloupe.

Illustration: Tomasz Cofta

CR **California Condor** *Gymnogyps californianus*

241

▲ POPULATION: 44 | THREATS: HUN, SPP, (TRA)

Once widespread along the west coast of North America from British Columbia to Baja California, the population of this huge and unmistakable raptor declined drastically during the 20th century until the numbers were so low that the last remaining individuals were taken into captivity in 1987. The decline is principally attributed to persecution and the accidental ingestion of lead from gunshot in carcasses. An intensive conservation programme involving captive breeding and reintroduction has been successful and led to the establishment of a tiny but increasing wild population in California and Arizona/Utah. Birds have also been released in Baja, Mexico, where they have also bred successfully.

Photo: Marcus Lawson

CR **Cuban Kite** *Chondrohierax wilsonii*

▼ POPULATION: 50–249 | THREATS: AGR, HUN, LOG, CLI?

Formerly fairly widespread on Cuba, this striking raptor is now confined to a tiny area of forest in the east of the island. It may be on the verge of extinction, as there have only been a handful of sightings since the 1960s. The decline is mostly due to habitat loss and degradation as a consequence of logging and conversion to agriculture. However, although it feeds chiefly on tree snails *Polymita* spp. and slugs in the understorey, it has also been persecuted by farmers as they believe, mistakenly, that it preys on poultry. A range of conservation measures is being considered, including the reintroduction of tree snails to areas where their population is depleted having been harvested for their beautiful shells.

Illustration: Tomasz Cofta
Photo: Ernesto Reyes [inset]

EN **Gundlach's Hawk** *Accipiter gundlachi*

▼ **POPULATION: 270** | **THREATS:** AGR, HUN, LOG

This hawk was once widespread across Cuba, although never common, and populations have now become severely fragmented. Small numbers of the nominate subspecies breed at three locations in the west and centre of the island, although one population may be extinct. The more numerous subspecies, *wileyi*, occurs in two areas in the east of the island. It is found in a variety of wooded habitats, where it feeds mostly on birds. The chief causes of its decline are habitat loss and disturbance as a result of logging and agricultural conversion. However, as it regularly preys on poultry, it is also subject to human persecution. Some populations occur within National Parks.

Photo: Paul Jones

CR **Ridgway's Hawk** *Buteo ridgwayi*

▼ **POPULATION: 110–160** | **THREATS: AGR**, HUN, LOG, MAN, SPP

Historically widespread on Hispaniola and offshore islands, this hawk is now extinct from Haiti and probably only persists in Los Haitises National Park in north-east Dominican Republic. It inhabits a variety of undisturbed forest types, favouring Hispaniolan Royal Palms *Roystonea hispaniolana* for nesting. Habitat loss due to conversion to agriculture has been severe and it is persecuted because it predates poultry. The National Park currently has no infrastructure in place to prevent ongoing slash-and-burn agriculture. As a consequence, a few birds have been translocated to a private protected area. It seems likely that a captive breeding and reintroduction programme will be key to preventing the extinction of this species.

Photo: Darío Fernández (rovingbiologist.blogspot.com)

CR **Zapata Rail** *Cyanolimnas cerverai*

▼ **POPULATION: 50–249** | **THREATS:** FIRE, SPP, (LOG)

This large rail occurs only in the Zapata Swamp, a tiny area in south-west Cuba. Although it was easily found in the early 1930s, this species was not recorded again until the 1970s. There have been very few recent sightings, suggesting a significant further decline since the beginning of the 21st century. It favours permanently inundated Sawgrass *Cladium jamaicensis* swamp but may disperse to drier areas during wet-season floods. Introduced mammals are probably important predators, but exotic catfish *Clarias* sp. were introduced in 1999 and may predate juveniles. Deliberate dry-season burning is also potentially devastating. Two of the known sites for this species are well protected and managed.

Illustration: Tomasz Cofta

EN **Whooping Crane** *Grus americana*　　52

▲ **POPULATION: 50–249** | **THREATS:** TRA, CLI, MAN, HUN, SPP, PLN, (AGR)

This elegant North American crane declined catastrophically following European settlement due to habitat loss, disturbance and hunting – threats that remain but to a lesser degree. The only remaining natural wild population breeds in prairie wetlands in Canada and migrates to winter in coastal wetlands in Texas, USA. Currently, the most significant threat is death or injury due to collision with powerlines or wind turbines situated along their migration corridor. The species is also threatened by nest predation, increasing urbanization at its wintering grounds, and drought. A reintroduction programme has been successful, with a migratory flock now breeding in Wisconsin and wintering in Florida, and resident populations in Florida and Louisiana.

Photo: Alexander Viduetsky

CR (PE) **Eskimo Curlew** *Numenius borealis*

? **POPULATION:** <50 | **THREATS:** AGR?, CLI?, EGY?, (HUN)

19,50

This long-distance migrant bred on treeless arctic tundra in Canada, and possibly Alaska, and wintered in South America (see *page 288*). However, it has not been reliably reported since a specimen was collected on migration in Barbados in 1963. It was formerly abundant but declined rapidly in the late 19th century primarily due to large-scale hunting for food and sport during the spring in North America. The species was also affected by the loss to agriculture of native North American prairie vegetation, a favoured habitat on migration. Although not all potential breeding areas have been surveyed and there are occasional unconfirmed reports, it is becoming increasingly likely that the Eskimo Curlew is now extinct.

Illustration: Tomasz Cofta

EN **Marbled Murrelet** *Brachyramphus marmoratus*

▼ **POPULATION:** 350,000–420,000 | **THREATS:** **LOG**, FISH, SPP, PLN

31,244

This small auk occurs along the north-west coast of USA and Canada, with Alaska being its stronghold. It travels up to 60 km inland to nest in old-growth trees, favouring forests with multiple canopy layers and, in the southern parts of its range, high mistletoe abundance. The population has declined very rapidly due to a variety of factors including predation, declining fish stocks, oil spills and bycatch in fishing nets. However, habitat loss due to logging is probably the greatest threat. Although some breeding sites fall within protected areas, and some conservation measures are underway, species recovery plans have not yet been fully implemented.

Photo: Roy W. Lowe

CR **Kittlitz's Murrelet** *Brachyramphus brevirostris*

▼ **POPULATION:** 20,000–49,999 | **THREATS:** FISH, MAN, CLI?, (PLN)

Found mostly in the Bering Sea, approximately 70% of the population of this auk occurs in Alaska, USA. The remainder of the population is in Russian territory (see also *page 131*). The current population in Alaska is probably only about 10% of what it was just 15 years ago. Once regarded as a mountain-top breeder in glacial regions, 12 nests found on Agattu, western Aleutians, indicate that it can nest in good densities in areas far from glaciers. Radio-tracking devices fitted on 126 birds are helping to understand their movements. Guidelines have been developed to help minimize disturbance to nesting birds but fisheries related mortality remains a significant threat.

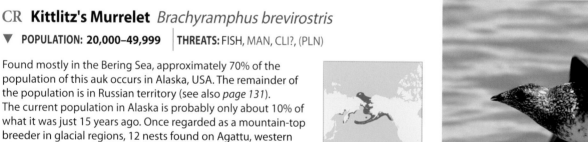

Photo: Edwin Winkel

CR **Grenada Dove** *Leptotila wellsi*

▼ **POPULATION:** 87 | **THREATS:** **AGR**, **DEV**, MAN, SPP

36

Endemic to Grenada in the Lesser Antilles, this dove was once widespread in coastal regions but is now confined to two tiny areas in the south and west of the island, mainly as a result of habitat loss and degradation caused by hurricanes and fire. It seems to favour sparse vegetation in woodland and scrub where frequent natural disturbances (particularly hurricanes) have kept the vegetation in a sub-climax condition. The key threats are overgrazing, increasing urbanization and infrastructure developments, and predation by invasive species. A 10-year species recovery plan drafted in 2010 aims to prevent further declines and to increase the wild population to four self-sustaining subpopulations.

Photo: Anthony Jeremiah

EN **Tuxtla Quail-dove** *Geotrygon carrikeri*

▼ POPULATION: 250–999 | THREATS: AGR, LOG

This terrestrial dove is endemic to the Tuxtla mountain range in the Mexican state of Veracruz, where it inhabits the understorey of humid, evergreen forest from 350–1,500 m. Extensive deforestation for timber and agriculture has led to populations becoming severely fragmented and it now only occurs in three small areas. Although habitat loss may have now abated, and the species occurs in two protected areas (the Santa Marta Biosphere Reserve and Los Tuxtlas Biological Reserve), further work is required in order accurately to determine its current status in the wild. A small captive population is held in a zoo in Pueblo City, Mexico.

Illustration: Tomasz Cofta
Photo: Nick Athanas (tropicalbirding.com) [inset]

EN **Blue-headed Quail-dove** *Starnoenas cyanocephala* 242

▼ POPULATION: 600–1,700 | THREATS: HUN, LOG, CLI?

Endemic to Cuba, this beautiful but shy, terrestrial dove particularly favours areas with abundant leaf-litter in the undergrowth of lowland forest, including inundated areas such as the Zapata Swamp, where it feeds on seeds, berries and snails. However, significant populations also occur in the mountains at La Güira in Pinar del Río province and on the Guanahacabibes Peninsula. The species is also believed to occur elsewhere on the island. It was once common and widespread but excessive hunting and habitat loss due to agriculture, exacerbated by hurricanes, has resulted in a large-scale decline. Although it is legally protected, enforcement is poor and hunting continues.

Photo: Rich Andrews (cvlbirding.co.uk)

EN **Thick-billed Parrot** *Rhynchopsitta pachyrhyncha*

▼ POPULATION: 2,000–2,800 | THREATS: **LOG**, AGR, HUN, (FIRE)

This macaw-like parrot once occurred throughout the Sierra Madre Occidental in western Mexico, and south-west USA, but had disappeared from the USA by the early 1990s. Its favoured habitat is mature pine-oak and coniferous forests above 1,200 m, where it nests in tree cavities. Outside the breeding season it is nomadic in response to food availability. Logging has been intensive throughout its range and as a result it now breeds in just two areas where old-growth forest remains. Fire and the illegal bird trade are also ongoing threats. Initiatives are underway to protect key breeding sites. Attempts to reintroduce this species to the wild in the USA have so far been unsuccessful.

Photo: Roberto Pedraza Ruiz (sierragorda.net/galeria/Beto)

EN **Maroon-fronted Parrot** *Rhynchopsitta terrisi*

▼ POPULATION: 1,000–2,499 | THREATS: AGR, CLI, FIRE, HUN, LOG

The one remaining population of this large parrot is restricted to a small area in the Sierra Madre Oriental in north-east Mexico. It inhabits mature pine, pine-oak and mixed conifer forest from 1,300–3,700 m and feeds almost exclusively on Mexican Pinyon *Pinus cembroides*. It requires daily access to free-flowing water and congregates at clay licks. It is a colonial breeder, nesting in holes in limestone cliffs, and undertakes seasonal and nomadic movements between the northern and southern limits of its range. Major threats include habitat loss due to intensive grazing, conversion to agriculture and regular wildfires, but lack of water and illegal hunting and trapping may also be important factors.

Photo: René Valdés (birdpicsandmore.com)

CR **Puerto Rican Amazon** *Amazona vittata*

= POPULATION: 33–47 | THREATS: CLI, SPP, (AGR), (HUN)

Endemic to Puerto Rico, this parrot once occurred throughout the forests on the island but it is now restricted to a tiny remaining fragment. An endemic subspecies *gracilipes* from nearby Isla Culebra became extinct in 1912. The almost total loss of habitat, hunting for food and pest control, and trapping for the cagebird trade resulted in the historical declines. The principal threats now are predation, competition for nest sites, loss of young to parasitic botflies, and natural disasters such as hurricanes. By 1975, only 13 birds were known to exist, but intensive conservation management, including captive breeding, has led to a slow recovery, and attempts to establish a second wild population appear to have been successful.

Photo [captive]: Jonathan M. Morel

EN **Red-crowned Amazon** *Amazona viridigenalis*

▼ POPULATION: 2,000–4,300 | THREATS: **HUN**, AGR

Natural populations of this parrot are restricted to the Atlantic slope of north-east Mexico, but it formerly occurred south to Veracruz. It inhabits lush areas in arid lowlands and foothills, feeding mainly on fruit, and usually nests in tree cavities. Large, nomadic flocks form in winter. Historically, large areas of suitable habitat have been cleared for agriculture and ranching. However, the cagebird trade has had a major impact on this species, particularly during the late 20th century when thousands of birds were legally imported into the USA. A population has recently become established in Texas, USA, possibly involving wild birds, and introduced populations occur elsewhere in mainland USA, Puerto Rico, Hawaii and Mexico.

Photo [captive]: Dr Paul R. Reillo (rarespecies.org)

EN **Yellow-headed Amazon** *Amazona oratrix*   `246`

▼ POPULATION: 4,700 | THREATS: AGR, HUN, DEV

The highly fragmented populations of this distinctive parrot are found in Mexico (on both the Pacific and Atlantic slopes and the offshore Islas Marías), Belize, extreme eastern Guatemala and extreme north-west Honduras. A number of subspecies have been described. It inhabits a variety of wooded habitats, occasionally up to 500 m. Populations have been severely depleted due to extensive habitat loss and illegal trapping for the cagebird trade. In Guatemala, it is also hunted for food and in Belize it is persecuted for damaging crops. Although it occurs in many reserves, effective protection is difficult due to organized crime in the region. It is bred in captivity, but reintroduction is not currently a feasible option.

Photo [captive]: Manfred Meiners (manfredmeiners.com)

EN **Imperial Amazon** *Amazona imperialis*   `241`

▲ POPULATION: 160–240 | THREATS: AGR, (CLI), (HUN)

This spectacular parrot is endemic to Dominica, where it inhabits forests from 600–1,300 m, foraging at lower altitudes in times of food shortage. It is highly sensitive to habitat modification, readily abandoning traditional foraging and nesting territories. Nests are situated in cavities in tall forest trees but despite intensive study its ecology remains poorly known. Habitat loss (mainly to plantations and hurricane damage), hunting for food, and trapping for the cagebird trade have been major threats in the past. Competition for nest sites with the more numerous Vulnerable Red-necked Amazon *A. arausiaca* is likely to become a significant issue as lowland forest is lost and the two species come increasingly into contact.

Photo [captive]: Dr Paul R. Reillo (rarespecies.org)

EN **Great Green Macaw** *Ara ambiguus*

▼ **POPULATION: 1,000–2,499** | **THREATS:** AGR, HUN, LOG, DEV, CLI?

This large macaw has two subspecies (see also *page 290*). Only the nominate occurs in this region, and is mostly rare, breeding in a few scattered areas of humid lowland and foothill forests from Honduras to Panama. However, the lowlands of southern Nicaragua/northern Costa Rica, which include some protected areas, are thought to hold the second largest global subpopulation (1,530 individuals in 2009). In the non-breeding season it forms flocks that disperse over large distances to visit favoured fruiting trees. High annual deforestation rates combined with illegal capture for the cagebird trade and subsistence hunting has resulted in very rapid and continuing population declines.

Photo: Greg & Yvonne Dean (WorldWildlifeImages.com)

EN **Bay-breasted Cuckoo** *Coccyzus rufigularis*

▼ **POPULATION: 1,500–7,000** | **THREATS:** AGR, HUN, PLN?

Endemic to Hispaniola, this cuckoo's preferred habitat is thought to be the transition zone between dry lowland forest and moist broadleaf forest. It has only been recorded recently from two small areas in the Dominican Republic, may be extinct in Haiti, and has already been extirpated from the offshore island of Gonâve. Major threats include deforestation for agriculture, habitat degradation through overgrazing and hunting for food. The use of agrochemicals may impact on its invertebrate prey, notably cicadas, which are by far the most abundant food item fed to nestlings. Conservation action is urgently required, including the effective protection of known locations and a community education and awareness programme.

Photo: Rafael V. Arvelo C. (rafaelarvelo.com)

CR (PE) **Jamaican Pauraque** *Siphonorhis americana* `19`

? **POPULATION: <50** | **THREATS:** AGR, EGY, SPP?

Endemic to Jamaica, this nightjar has not been recorded with certainty since 1860 and may be extinct. Habitat destruction and predation by introduced mammals are the most likely causes of its demise. However, as it is nocturnal and its voice is unknown, it could easily be overlooked. Specimens were taken from three localities in the lowlands on the southern side of the island, and there is anecdotal evidence that the species could often be found in (what is now assumed to be) the Hellshire Hills. As there have been some recent reports of caprimulgids from this area, and Milk River, that do not appear to be one of the other known species on the island, there is a slim chance it may still survive.

Illustration: Tomasz Cofta

EN **Puerto Rican Nightjar** *Caprimulgus noctitherus* `243`

▼ **POPULATION: 930–1,300** | **THREATS:** EGY, MAN, SPP, DEV

Endemic to Puerto Rico, this nightjar has recently been downlisted as new locations have been found in the south-east of the island, away from its former stronghold in the south-west. It was probably once widespread, but is now most often found in closed-canopy dry forest with abundant leaf-litter, an open understorey and little or no ground vegetation. Predation may be contributing to declines, but habitat loss and degradation due to urbanization and infrastructure projects is the greatest threat. The remaining populations are severely fragmented but it occurs in some protected areas. A revised species action plan will be implemented through a newly established Puerto Rican Nightjar Conservation Network.

Photo: Michael J. Morel

CR **Short-crested Coquette** *Lophornis brachylophus*

▼ POPULATION: 250–999 | THREATS: AGR

Probably confined to the Sierra Madre del Sur in the state of Guerrero, Mexico, this tiny hummingbird is only known from a 25 km stretch of road in the Sierra de Atoyac (north-west of Acapulco). It inhabits semi-humid evergreen and semi-deciduous forests, forest edge and shade-coffee plantations from 900–1,800 m. It has also been reported at lower elevations, which may indicate that it is an altitudinal migrant. In the early 1990s, forests near the road was being rapidly cleared for the cultivation of maize, fruit and coffee. Much of the remaining forest provides cover for the growing of illegal drugs, making an evaluation of habitat quality difficult.

Male; Sierra de Atoyac, Guerrero, Mexico; March 2007. Photo: Hadoram Shirihai; contributed from the forthcoming *Photographic Handbook of the Birds of the World*, Jornvall & Shirihai © Bloomsbury Publishing Plc.

EN **Blue-capped** (or Oaxaca) **Hummingbird** *Eupherusa cyanophrys*

▼ POPULATION: 600–1,700 | THREATS: AGR, (CLI)

Endemic to the Sierra Miahuatlán, an isolated mountain range in southernmost Oaxaca, Mexico, this hummingbird was not described until 1964. It is primarily restricted to cloud forest and the upper reaches of semi-deciduous forest from 1,300–2,500 m, but is occasionally found at lower elevations and may be a seasonal, altitudinal migrant. The cloud forests in this sierra were essentially unspoilt by human activity until the mid-1960s, when huge areas were cut and burnt to plant maize. Lower montane forest is still being cleared, largely for the cultivation of citrus fruits. A hurricane in 1997 destroyed large portions of suitable habitat but the full impact of this event on this species is unknown.

Photo: Manuel Grosselet (tierradeaves.com)

EN **Honduran Emerald** *Amazilia luciae* `44`

▼ POPULATION: 250–999 | THREATS: AGR, TRA

The only species endemic to Honduras, this hummingbird was not recorded between 1950 and 1988, when it was rediscovered in the north-east of the country. Since then, a few other tiny populations have been discovered, most notably in 2008 when birds were seen in western Honduras for the first time since 1935. It inhabits different woodland types in different parts of its range and may tolerate some degree of habitat degradation, undertaking seasonal movements to track food resources. Very little suitable habitat remains, mainly due to the clearance of forest for agriculture. Conservation measures include the creation of a thorn-forest reserve and the promotion of this species as a flagship for local and national conservation.

Photo: Ronald Orenstein

EN **Mangrove Hummingbird** *Amazilia boucardi* `247`

▼ POPULATION: 1,500–7,000 | THREATS: AGR, LOG, CLI, PLN, TRA, DEV?

Only found along the Pacific coast of Costa Rica, this hummingbird is patchily distributed within the few remaining large mangrove forests within its range, probably reflecting the presence of its preferred food-plant, the Pacific Mangrove *Pelliciera rhizophorae*. Its habitat is being destroyed by the construction of salt and shrimp ponds, and selective logging for charcoal production. Other threats include the illegal cutting of mangrove, dyke and road construction (which have affected the hydrology in a number of places), and pollution, particularly around the Golfo de Nicoya port of Puntarenas. The entire Pacific coast of Costa Rica is under heavy development pressure and this species could be affected by a rise in sea level caused by climate change.

Photo: Glenn Bartley (glennbartley.com)

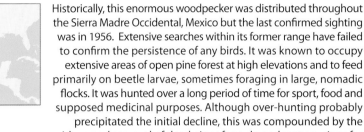

CR (PE) **Imperial Woodpecker** *Campephilus imperialis* `19`

? **POPULATION: <50** | **THREATS:** LOG, CLI?, (HUN)

Historically, this enormous woodpecker was distributed throughout the Sierra Madre Occidental, Mexico but the last confirmed sighting was in 1956. Extensive searches within its former range have failed to confirm the persistence of any birds. It was known to occupy extensive areas of open pine forest at high elevations and to feed primarily on beetle larvae, sometimes foraging in large, nomadic flocks. It was hunted over a long period of time for sport, food and supposed medicinal purposes. Although over-hunting probably precipitated the initial decline, this was compounded by the widespread removal of dead pines for pulp and mature pines for timber. By 1996, only 22 km² of suitable breeding habitat remained.

Illustration: Tomasz Cofta

CR **Ivory-billed Woodpecker** *Campephilus principalis*

▼ **POPULATION: <50** | **THREATS:** AGR?, CLI?, LOG?

This huge woodpecker has two subspecies: the nominate in south-east USA and *bairdii* in Cuba. Historic accounts indicate that it had a very large home range and that extensive, contiguous tracts of mature woodland were required to support a viable population – a habitat that has suffered dramatic losses. Whilst persistent claims have been made that it has occurred in Arkansas and Florida in recent years, the last non-controversial record from the USA was in 1944. The species may still remain extant in Cuba, although searches have been unsuccessful; the most recent records being in the late 1980s. The best hope lies in the Alejandro de Humboldt National Park, where some areas have not been fullly searched.

Illustration: Tomasz Cofta

EN **Yellow-billed Cotinga** *Carpodectes antoniae*

▼ **POPULATION: 150–700** | **THREATS:** AGR, LOG, DEV

This striking cotinga is restricted to a few fragmented areas along the Pacific coast of Panama and Costa Rica. It primarily occurs in extensive mangroves, but is also found in adjacent lowland forest or scrub and occasionally isolated trees in nearby clearings or pastures. Mangroves are being destroyed, primarily for conversion to shrimp/salt ponds, rice cultivation and ranching, and tourism infrastructure developments. Dyke and road construction has also affected the hydrology at several sites. Nearby lowland forests have largely been removed. A population stronghold in Costa Rica is threatened by tentative plans to build an international airport at the headwaters of the Río Sierpe and other nearby development pressures.

Photo: Kevin Easley (costaricagateway.com) and Vivek Tiwari (flickr.com/photos/spiderhunters) [inset]

EN **Bare-necked Umbrellabird** *Cephalopterus glabricollis* `247`

▼ **POPULATION: 1,000–2,499** | **THREATS:** AGR, LOG, TRA, CLI?

This strange cotinga breeds locally in subtropical forests high on the Caribbean slope of mountains in Costa Rica and Panama, where males defend courtship arenas and inflate their bare, red skin during display. After the breeding season birds move to lowland forests as far north as southern Nicaragua. The population is declining rapidly due to habitat loss and degradation, especially in its lowland range, due to conversion to agriculture, the expansion of cattle-ranches and logging. Important habitat corridors linking breeding and non-breeding areas are being lost. In Costa Rica, there is an ongoing initiative to create a biological corridor linking two important protected areas.

Photo: Michael & Patricia Fogden (fogdenphotos.com)

EN **Giant Kingbird** *Tyrannus cubensis*

▼ **POPULATION: 250–999** | **THREATS:** AGR, LOG

Now found only on Cuba, this kingbird has probably always been scarce but is becoming increasingly rare, for largely unknown reasons. It is presumed extinct from the south Bahamas and the Turks and Caicos Islands. It favours transitional habitats such as between forested/open areas and grassland/swamps, as well as riparian forest and open forest with tall trees in montane areas. It uses its massive bill to feed on large insects, lizards (especially *Anolis* spp.), other birds' fledglings and, during the dry season, significant quantities of fruit. Habitat loss, especially the loss of large trees suitable for nesting, due to logging and agricultural conversion, may be factors contributing to its decline.

Photo: Rich Andrews (cvlbirding.co.uk)

EN **Bahama Swallow** *Tachycineta cyaneoviridis*

▼ **POPULATION: 1,000–2,499** | **THREATS: S**PP, DEV, CLI?, FIRE?, (LOG)

This swallow breeds on Grand Bahama, Great Abaco and Andros in the northern Bahamas, and possibly New Providence. Its movements are poorly known but in winter there are records from the southern Bahamas and eastern Cuba, and small numbers appear to be resident on the breeding islands. Vagrants sometimes occur in Florida, USA. It nests in tree cavities in pine woodlands and occasionally around human habitations, and tends to feed in open areas and along coastlines. Loss of habitat to logging, urbanization and hurricanes has probably been exacerbated by competition for nest sites from introduced species such as House Sparrow *Passer domesticus* and Common Starling *Sturnus vulgaris*.

Photo: Craig Nash

EN **Zapata Wren** *Ferminia cerverai*

▼ **POPULATION: 600–1,700** | **THREATS:** AGR, FIRE, SPP?

Endemic to Cuba, this wren is known only from the northern and central parts of the Zapata Swamp. It was reported as common at the time of its discovery in 1926, but anecdotal evidence suggests that it has subsequently declined. It inhabits seasonally flooded freshwater marshes that are dominated by Sawgrass *Cladium jamaicensis* with patches of shrubs, nesting in Sawgrass tussocks. It feeds on invertebrates, small snails, lizards and berries. Deliberate dry-season burning, wetland drainage and agricultural expansion have led to habitat loss and degradation, and it is possibly predated by introduced mongooses and rats. Areas of the Zapata Swamp have protected status, but regulations are poorly enforced.

Photo: Andy & Gill Swash (WorldWildlifeImages.com)

CR **Cozumel Thrasher** *Toxostoma guttatum*

▼ **POPULATION: <50** | **THREATS: CLI**, SPP, DEV

This species, the most threatened in Mexico, is endemic to Cozumel Island, where it was formerly fairly common but became rare immediately after a hurricane in 1988. After further devastating hurricanes in 1995 and 2005, the number of records fell dramatically. The only recent records are four observations of probably the same individual and of another bird elsewhere during extensive surveys in 2004, and a possible sighting in 2006. However, as this species must have evolved with a relatively high hurricane frequency, there may be other reasons behind its decline that are poorly understood. The leading hypothesized threat is predation by *Boa constrictor* snakes (which were introduced to the island in 1971) and feral cats.

Photo: Jon Hornbuckle

EN **White-breasted Thrasher** *Ramphocinclus brachyurus*

▼ **POPULATION: 1,300** | **THREATS:** AGR, SPP, DEV, LOG, PLN, TRA

There are two subspecies of this thrasher: the nominate is restricted to Martinique, and *santaeluciae* to St Lucia. It typically forages on the ground in dry or riparian forests and scrub with abundant leaf-litter. Although it tolerates some habitat degradation, the main threat is ongoing habitat loss, primarily due to agriculture, charcoal production and urbanization, perhaps compounded by predation. On Martinique, the remaining tiny population is restricted to a very small area, most of which is effectively protected. On St Lucia, it is threatened by new tourism developments. Although this species has long coexisted with introduced mammalian predators, they may place an additional burden on an already small population.

Photo: Adams Toussaint

EN **La Selle Thrush** *Turdus swalesi*

▼ **POPULATION: 1,500–7,000** | **THREATS:** AGR, LOG, CLI?

Found only on the island of Hispaniola (Haiti and Dominican Republic), where there are two subspecies (the nominate and *dodae*), this large thrush is now mostly restricted to isolated patches of habitat. It occurs primarily above 1,300 m in moist, montane broadleaf forest, and occasionally pine forest, but only where there is a dense understorey. It mainly forages on the ground for earthworms, insects and fruit. There has been massive habitat loss in Hispaniola, and remaining areas are severely threatened by ongoing deforestation for agriculture and timber. As a consequence, it is likely to have been extirpated (or be on the brink of extirpation) from significant areas of its disjunct range.

Photo: Rafy Rodriguez

EN **Hispaniolan Crossbill** *Loxia megaplaga* `243`

▼ **POPULATION: 400–2,300** | **THREATS:** AGR, FIRE, LOG, SPP, CLI?

Although now found only on the island of Hispaniola (Haiti and the Dominican Republic), there are records of this crossbill from Jamaica in the early 1970s. It is restricted to pine forest, mostly at high elevations, and feeds exclusively on pine seeds, being rather nomadic in response to food availability. Habitat loss due to logging and clearance for agriculture has been extensive. The greatest current threat may be fires that burn more of the remaining forests than can be replaced through regeneration. The vast majority of the population now occurs in the Sierra de Bahoruco National Park (Dominican Republic), but there is no active protection and ongoing loss to agriculture is widespread.

Photo: Rafy Rodriguez

CR (PE) **Bachman's Warbler** *Vermivora bachmanii* `19`

? **POPULATION: <50** | **THREATS:** AGR?, WAT?

This warbler, which bred in several states in south-eastern USA, and wintered in Cuba, and occasionally Florida, has not been reported since 1988, and was last confirmed breeding in 1937. It favoured seasonally flooded swamp-forest, apparently showing a strong association with canebrakes of the bamboo *Arundinaria gigantea*. Wintering habitats appear to have been much more varied. The drainage of swamps, and the near-total clearance of canebrakes in the USA, combined with the conversion of much of Cuba to sugarcane plantation, is the most likely reason for this species' apparent demise. However, there have been recent (unconfirmed) sightings and as small areas of suitable habitat remain, the species may still survive.

Photo: Jerry A. Payne / USDA Agricultural Research Service

EN **Golden-cheeked Warbler** *Dendroica chrysoparia* `245`

▼ POPULATION: 21,000 | THREATS: AGR, EGY, LOG SPP, DEV

This warbler has a fragmented breeding range in central Texas, USA and winters from southern Mexico to Panama. The main cause of decline may be a reduction in pine-oak woodlands in its winter quarters due to logging and agricultural conversion for cattle rearing. However, its breeding habitat (mature juniper-oak woodland) is also being cleared for land development, ranching and agriculture. Predation by rat snakes (*Elaphe* spp.) has a significant effect on adult mortality, accounting for the death of perhaps 15% of breeding females. In the USA, measures are being implemented to protect breeding populations and the ecology of the species on its wintering grounds is being studied.

Photo: Greg Lasley (greglasley.net)

EN **Whistling Warbler** *Catharopeza bishopi*

▼ POPULATION: 2,000–3,300 | THREATS: AGR, GEO, LOG, CLI?

Endemic to the island of St Vincent in the Lesser Antilles, this warbler is mostly found in dense undergrowth and vine-tangles in primary rainforest and palm brake habitat. Shifting agriculture, selective logging for charcoal production and the illegal cultivation of cannabis has led to a reduction in these habitats. However, much of the central part of St Vincent was designated as a wildlife reserve in 1987, and an extensive environmental education programme developed. The population of this species was last surveyed in 1973 and 1986 and, although there are no recent data it is suspected to still be declining at a slow rate due to ongoing habitat degradation.

Photo: John C. Mittermeier (flickr.com/photos/jmittermeier)

EN **Belding's Yellowthroat** *Geothlypis beldingi* `37`

▼ POPULATION: 1,000–2,499 | THREATS: AGR, DEV, CLI?

This warbler is restricted to a few fragmented populations on the Baja California peninsula, Mexico. The nominate subspecies is known from at least 15 sites and *goldmani* from at least 12 sites. It occupies oases of tall vegetation fringing a variety of wetland habitats, and birds usually occur within 15 m of the waters' edge. Baja California's oases are under intense human pressure, especially in the south, and accidental and induced fires, reed-cutting for tourism facilities and house construction, and drainage for agriculture and cattle ranching have all contributed to habitat loss and degradation. However, a range of conservation measures are in place and an action plan was published in 2011.

Photo: Bruno Granados

EN **Black-polled Yellowthroat** *Geothlypis speciosa* `46`

▼ POPULATION: 1,500–7,000 | THREATS: **AGR**, **WAT**, DEV

Currently known from only four areas in central Mexico, this warbler is restricted to lakeshores and river marshes. It appears to require extensive reedbeds and is not found in degraded habitats like many other *Geothlypis* species. The marshes within its range have been greatly reduced in size, mostly as a consequence of being drained for agriculture. Some have become fragmented as a result of water extraction to supply major cities, and in other areas water levels are falling due to a natural build-up of organic material. The population of this species has not been censused since the 1980s, but habitat loss and degradation is likely to be contributing to an ongoing population decline.

Photo: Bjorn Anderson

CR Semper's Warbler *Leucopeza semperi*

? POPULATION: <50 | THREATS: SPP, AGR?, CLI?, LOG?

Endemic to St Lucia, this species has not been recorded with certainty since 1961; sightings in 1965, 1989, 1995 and 2003 have not been confirmed. It is known from the undergrowth of montane and elfin forest and is believed to be largely terrestrial, possibly even nesting on the ground. The introduction of mongooses in 1884 may have contributed to the disappearance of this species, as they probably predated adults, nestlings and eggs. The decline may have been compounded by habitat loss, but suitable forest still remains on the island. As some suitable habitat remains and searches have not been adequately extensive, it possibly still exists.

Illustration: Tomasz Cofta

CR Bahama Oriole *Icterus northropi*

▼ POPULATION: 93–180 | THREATS: SPP, AGR, CLI, FIRE, LOG, TRA

Split from Hispaniolan Oriole *I. dominicensis* in 2009, this species is endemic to the Andros group of islands and cays in The Bahamas. It inhabits open woodlands and, as it relies heavily on palms (including for nesting), the planting of coconut palms in residential areas has allowed it to spread into human settlements. The most significant threats are thought to be brood parasitism by the Shiny Cowbird *Molothrus bonariensis*, which arrived in the 1990s, and lethal yellowing, a disease that has destroyed entire groves of coconut palm on some islands. Additional potential threats include introduced predators (particularly rats and feral cats), and the potential effects of climate change on sea levels.

Photo: Gavin Bieber (wings.com)

CR Montserrat Oriole *Icterus oberi* `40,243`

▼ POPULATION: 920–1,180 | THREATS: **SPP**, CLI, (GEO)

Endemic to the island of Montserrat in the Lesser Antilles, this oriole occurs in most forest types but is absent from very dry locations. Volcanic activity during 1995–7 led to its extirpation from all but two disjunct areas and further ash deposition in the early 21st century has seriously damaged the habitat of the remaining population. It also suffers from high rates of nest predation by rats and native Pearly-eyed Thrashers *Margarops fuscatus*. In 2001 and 2003, drought appeared to reduce laying frequency and clutch size, and this may be an increasing problem now that the species is confined to lower, drier areas. A feral pig population is spreading fast and could cause serious habitat damage if not eradicated.

Male on left; female on right. Photo: Chris Bowden / RSPB

EN Jamaican Blackbird *Nesopsar nigerrimus*

▼ POPULATION: 1,500–7,000 | THREATS: AGR, EGY, SPP, LOG, DEV, CLI?

Endemic to Jamaica, this species is found locally in Cockpit Country, the central hills and the Blue and John Crow Mountains. Pairs occupy large territories in mature, wet montane forests, and forest edge, with heavy epiphytic growth. The most significant current threat is bauxite mining in its stronghold in Cockpit Country. Ongoing habitat loss due to afforestation, coffee plantations, charcoal production, deliberate fires, small-scale farming and development is also a major threat. Habitat degradation has led to an increase in parasitism by Shiny Cowbird *Molothrus bonariensis*, and it may have suffered particularly from the removal of mature trees, since they support the large bromeliads in which it forages.

Photo: Greg & Yvonne Dean (WorldWildlifeImages.com)

261

EN **Tricoloured Blackbird** *Agelaius tricolor* 245

▼ **POPULATION: 250,000** | **THREATS:** AGR, SPP, PLN (HUN)

This blackbird is virtually confined to California, USA, with occasional records from other states and extreme north-west Baja California (Mexico). It nests in massive colonies in freshwater marshes, where reproductive rates are very low, and in non-native vegetation in the uplands, where breeding success is significantly higher. Large numbers often nest in silage fields, increasing the threat of the loss of entire colonies during harvest. It forages in agricultural areas and part of the population migrates to the central Californian coast in winter. Loss of foraging and upland nesting habitats, destruction of breeding colonies, and predation by Cattle Egrets *Bubulcus ibis* are ongoing threats.

Photo: Glen Tepke (pbase.com/gtepke)

EN **Yellow-shouldered Blackbird** *Agelaius xanthomus*

▼ **POPULATION: 1,300** | **THREATS:** SPP, AGR

Formerly widespread on Puerto Rico, this blackbird has two subspecies: the nominate now restricted to the south-west coast of the mainland, and *monensis* on the offshore islands of Mona and Monito. It favours coastal habitats, but brood-parasitism by Shiny Cowbirds *Molothrus bonariensis* has greatly reduced numbers and resulted in most birds now breeding on offshore cays. It gathers at communal feeding sites and large flocks form during the non-breeding season. Competition for nesting areas by Caribbean Martin *Progne dominicensis*, habitat loss to agriculture, nest-predation by Pearly-eyed Thrasher *Margarops fuscatus* and predation by introduced mammals are additional threats. A conservation programme including the installation of artificial nests and predator control is ongoing.

Photo: Michael J. Morel

EN **Sierra Madre Sparrow** *Xenospiza baileyi*

▼ **POPULATION: 2,500–9,999** | **THREATS: AGR**, SPP, LOG, PLN, DEV

This sparrow is found in two disjunct populations in north-western/central Mexico. Only one site remains in the north of its range, which holds three breeding pairs. The species' stronghold is now fragmented upland grasslands in the Valle de México that are subject to agriculture and cattle grazing. Habitat modification due to widespread burning, mostly to promote new growth for livestock, and conversion of grasslands to crops is likely to be the most significant factor in population declines. However, afforestation is also a threat and there is a high level of nest failure due to predation. A community-based conservation project has focused on preserving and restoring habitat with the involvement of landowners and managers.

Photo: Miguel Ángel Sicilia Manzo

EN **Worthen's Sparrow** *Spizella wortheni* 245

▼ **POPULATION: 70–80** | **THREATS:** AGR, SPP?

First described in 1884 in New Mexico, USA, this sparrow has only been recorded in Mexico since that date, where it is now only known from three locations. It is found at 1,200–2,450 m, where it requires a combination of arid, open grasslands grazed at low intensities for foraging, and areas of low, dense shrubs for cover and nesting. Habitat loss due to overgrazing and conversion of grasslands to crops, primarily potato production, are most likely to have led to the population decline. Disturbance and predation by snakes and Coyotes *Canis latrans* may also be important contributing factors. An appropriate management regime is been implemented at one location and fencing has protected an important winter foraging locality.

Photo: René Valdés (birdpicsandmore.com)

EN **Cuban** (or Zapata) **Sparrow** *Torreornis inexpectata*

▼ **POPULATION: 600–1,700** | **THREATS:** FIRE, WAT, MAN, SPP?

Endemic to Cuba, this sparrow has three disjunct populations. The nominate subspecies of the Zapata Swamp inhabits scrub-grassland, xerophytic coastal vegetation and mangroves, and is threatened by drainage and deliberate dry-season burning. Subspecies *varonai* on Cayo Coco off the north coast occurs in semi-deciduous forest, coastal xerophytic thorn-scrub and mangrove. Here, habitat is being lost due to the development of tourism infrastructure. Subspecies *sigmani* on the Guantánamo coast inhabits dry scrub that is being burnt and converted to grassland for sheep rearing. Although each subspecies has been recorded in a protected area, these do not receive effective protection.

Photo: Oliver Smart (smartimages.co.uk)

EN **St Lucia Black Finch** *Melanospiza richardsoni* `242`

▼ **POPULATION: 250–999** | **THREATS:** AGR, SPP?

This finch is found only on the island of St Lucia in the Lesser Antilles. It is mainly terrestrial, and shows a preference for foraging in leaf-litter in dense undergrowth, where it can be found bobbing its tail up and down. It is particularly numerous within moist, montane forests but also occurs in a wide range of other habitats. The clearing of undergrowth, particularly in timber plantations, has resulted in a loss of its preferred habitat in many areas and is probably the most significant threat. Introduced mongooses and rats are also likely to predate eggs, nestlings and adults. The species occurs in a number of forest reserves, such as La Sorcière and Edmond.

Female. Photo: Adams Toussaint. (See *page 242* for photo of a male.)

EN **Azure-rumped Tanager** *Tangara cabanisi* `246`

▼ **POPULATION: 1,500–7,000** | **THREATS:** AGR, DEV

This tanager occurs only in the Sierra Madre de Chiapas of southern Mexico, now at just one locality (El Triunfo), and south-western Guatemala. It inhabits high-altitude, humid, broadleaf evergreen forest but has occasionally bred in adjacent degraded/edge habitats. The altitudinal range of this species coincides with the optimal land for coffee cultivation, and further expansions and intensification of production are the greatest threat, even within some protected areas. The development of ecotourism, particularly in Guatemala, with spin-off economic benefits for local communities, may help safeguard this species, and certification schemes to encourage low-intensity shade-grown coffee farming are also being considered.

Photo: Knut Eisermann (cayaya-birding.com)

EN **Black-cheeked Ant-tanager** *Habia atrimaxillaris* `246`

▼ **POPULATION: 6,000–15,000** | **THREATS:** AGR, LOG

Restricted to the Osa Peninsula and around Golfo Dulce in south-west Costa Rica, the range of this ant-tanager has approximately halved and become increasingly fragmented since 1960. It favours the understorey of dense lowland forest but also occurs in a range of other forest and coastal habitats. Pairs or small groups sometimes join mixed-species flocks. It feeds primarily on invertebrates, but also on the berries of *Melastoma*, a genus of introduced tropical shrubs. The protected areas of the Corcovado National Park and Golfito Faunal Refuge hold significant populations but the vast majority of the forest to the north and east of the Golfo Dulce has been logged and habitat loss is continuing.

Photo: Jonas Langbråten (langbraten.com)

South America

EQUATOR

Galápagos Islands
ECUADOR

VENEZUELA

GUYANA

FRENCH GUIANA

COLOMBIA

SURINAME

ECUADOR

PERU

BRAZIL

BOLIVIA

PARAGUAY

PACIFIC OCEAN

URUGUAY

TROPIC OF CAPRICORN

ATLANTIC OCEAN

ARGENTINA

CHILE

The distribution of Endangered and
Critically Endangered species

1–4 species

5+ species

Falkland Islands UK
(Islas Malvinas)

South Georgia UK
(Georgias del Sur)

South America

South America covers approximately 17·8 million square kilometres (6·8 million square miles), representing almost 12% of the world's land area. The majority of the continent lies within the tropics, and only one of the 12 independent countries – Uruguay – is entirely outside them. The physical geography of South America is deceptively simple: the Andes run the length of the western edge, and the Amazon Basin occupies the centre of the continent, bordered to the north by the Guiana Highlands and the llanos grasslands of Venezuela and Colombia, to the east by the Brazilian Highlands, and to the south by the Pampas. At the southern tail of the continent are the glaciated mountains and steppe-like deserts of Patagonia, surrounded by a rugged fiordal coast that ends in the bleak archipelago of Tierra del Fuego. South America also includes the overseas territory of French Guiana (France). Although, strictly speaking, Trinidad and Tobago are also on the South American continental plate, they are considered geopolitically to be part of the Caribbean and are included in the previous section.

The six Endangered or Critically Endangered species that are endemic to either Galápagos or Juan Fernández Islands are covered in the Oceanic Islands section (*page 180*).

There are 66 Endemic Bird Areas or Secondary Areas in continental South America, second only in number to Asia, and reflecting the wide diversity of habitats and the degree of isolation of many areas. A total of 3,250 bird species has been recorded in South America, almost one-third of the 9,934 species currently recognized by BirdLife International. This figure includes many wintering migrants that breed in North or Central America or the Caribbean, as well as non-breeding seabirds that are regular visitors to coastal waters. However, 384 species are globally threatened – almost 12% of the species – and 168 are ether Endangered or Critically Endangered (over 5% of all South American species).

BirdLife Partners

Country	Partner	Country	Partner
Argentina	Aves Argentinas (AOP)	**Paraguay**	Guyra Paraguay: Conservacion de Aves
Bolivia	Asociacion Armonía	**Suriname**	Foundation for Nature Conservation in Suriname (STINASU)
Brazil	SAVE Brasil		
Chile	Comité Nacional Pro Defensa de la Flora y Fauna (CODEFF)	**Uruguay**	Aves Uruguay (GUPECA)
Ecuador	Aves & Conservación (Corporación Ornitológica del Ecuador)		
Falklands Islands (Islas Malvinas)	Falklands Conservation		

South America – the bird continent

Home to almost one-third of the world's bird species (3,250 recognized in 2012 if Oceanic Islands are excluded), South America includes five of the world's top 20 mega-biodiverse countries, four of which (Colombia, Peru, Brazil, and Ecuador) are also the top four countries for the diversity of their birds.

The many natural barriers presented by the region's geography have led to high levels of endemism. BirdLife International identifies 66 Endemic Bird Areas in mainland South America, including the 'lost worlds' of the Venezuelan Tepuis, Colombia's isolated Santa Marta Mountains, the Andean ridge-top forests and the puna grasslands and páramo of the high Andes, the Amazon flooded forests, the Atlantic Forest, the Mesopotamian grasslands, and Southern Patagonia, home of the recently discovered, rapidly declining and Critically Endangered Hooded Grebe *Podiceps gallardoi*.

The vast ecosystems of the South American continent have correspondingly large conservation problems. The temperate grasslands of southern South America originally encompassed an area of over one million square kilometres, but only a tiny percentage remains in a natural state. The upwellings of the Humboldt Current have made the Pacific coast of South America one of the most productive marine areas in the world, supporting huge congregations of seabirds. But large areas have been over-fished primarily for fertilizer (and foods for farmed fish), and seabird populations have collapsed. Most recently, a BirdLife analysis of projected deforestation in the Amazon Basin, using figures that suggest that up to 40% of the forest may be lost by the middle of the century, resulted in the threat status of 100 bird species being increased. Some that were previously regarded as relatively secure face the loss of all their remaining habitat within a decade or two.

The Endangered **Scissor-tailed Hummingbird** *Hylonympha macrocerca* remains locally common and even abundant on Venezuela's Paría Peninsula. But its range is tiny, and coffee and cacao are encroaching on its understorey habitat. Photo: David J. Southall (tropicalbirdphotos.com).

The Critically Endangered **Munchique Wood-wren** *Henicorhina negreti* has a tiny range in the Andes of south-west Colombia. However, much of its remaining cloud forest habitat is now within a private reserve. Photo: Julio C. Gallardo.

The Critically Endangered **Purple-winged Ground-dove** *Claravis geoffroyi* once occurred in flocks of 100 or more in Brazil, Argentina and Paraguay. The few recent sightings are of five birds at most. Photo: Luiz Cláudio Marigo.

The Endangered **Long-whiskered Owlet** *Xenoglaux loweryi* is one of a suite of species recently discovered in isolated ridge-top forests in Peru. Almost all are threatened. Photo: Dubi Shapiro (pbase.com/dubisha).

Thanks to intensive action, **Lear's Macaw** *Anodorhynchus leari*, restricted to north-east Bahia in Brazil has been downlisted from Critically Endangered to Endangered. But most of the continent's large parrot species are in trouble. Photo: Andy & Gill Swash (WorldWildlifeImages.com).

The Endangered **El Oro Parakeet** *Pyrrhura orcesi* is restricted to the Andean foothills of south-west Ecuador. The wood of its favoured nesting tree is highly sought after for furniture-making. This parakeet tolerates some habitat degradation, but its communal breeding system may make it more vulnerable to a reduction in nesting sites. Photo: Greg & Yvonne Dean (WorldWildlifeImages.com).

Chocó Vireo *Vireo masteri.*
Photo: Dušan M. Brinkhuizen (sapayoa.com).

Baudó Guan *Penelope ortoni.*
Photo: Dušan M. Brinkhuizen (sapayoa.com).

Chocó (Colombia and Ecuador)

Running the length of the Pacific slopes of the Andes in western Colombia and Ecuador, and separated from the Amazon Basin by the mountains, the Chocó supports the largest number of restricted-range birds of any Endemic Bird Area in the Americas, with over 50 endemic species. The original vegetation is primary humid forest, and the Chocó includes some of the wettest land areas on Earth. Between 8,000 and 16,000 mm of rain falls every year on the narrow band of super-wet pluvial forest between the lowland and foothill forest, which possibly has the highest levels of endemism of all.

Many bird species are confined to the tropical lowland and lower subtropical foothill forests, with the remainder primarily found in the subtropical forest on the mid-altitude slopes, and a few in the high-altitude temperate areas. Many have naturally small ranges, and some, particularly hummingbirds such as the Critically Endangered Colourful Puffleg *Eriocnemis mirabilis*, are very localized indeed. Most are suffering rapid contractions of their ranges because of habitat loss, and species with already small and disjunct ranges, like the Vulnerable Turquoise Dacnis *Dacnis hartlaubi*, are approaching the thresholds for higher threat status. The habitat at the type-locality (and only known locality) of the Turquoise-throated Puffleg *Eriocnemis godini* has been almost completely destroyed; there have been no confirmed sightings since the 19th century, and the species is listed as Critically Endangered (Possibly Extinct).

The Chocó has long been a major source of timber for the two countries, and much of the more accessible forest, particularly in the lowlands, has been logged. Forest clearance has been accelerating in recent decades, and deforestation rates in some areas are running at over 3% per year. A growing network of roads has made the forests more accessible to loggers, colonists and small-scale agriculturalists, cattle ranchers, gold miners and illegal coca growers. With new settlements comes subsistence hunting. The Endangered Baudó Guan *Penelope ortoni*, for example, is soon extirpated within a 2–5 km radius around human settlements, and is increasingly restricted to steeper slopes and mountain ridges.

But the major threat to the remaining lowland and foothill forests is conversion to oil palm plantations, to meet the global demand for biofuels. Legislation intended to transfer land rights to indigenous communities has been exploited by large companies to acquire land cheaply, and in places indigenous people are planting oil palms on their own accord.

Infrastructure plans for the Chocó region also include oil pipelines: Mindo in Ecuador, the first Important Bird Area recognized in the Americas, is now crossed by the Heavy Crude Pipeline, fragmenting habitat, adding a new barrier to species movement, and introducing a real risk of catastrophic pollution in this geologically unstable area.

Protected area coverage is limited in the region, especially in lowland and foothill forest, and some of the most important protected areas, such as Colombia's Munchique National Park, are being encroached upon by indigenous communities, settlers and coca-growers. The World Land Trust and the Critical Ecosystems Partnership Fund are among the organizations working to improve the extent and effectiveness of protected areas in the Chocó.

The Critically Endangered **Colourful Puffleg** *Eriocnemis mirabilis* has a known range of just 31 km², and although it has been found at new locations in recent years, its habitat is threatened by forest clearance and coca-growing. Photo: Juan Pablo López Ordóñez.

A proposed new highway threatens the stronghold of the largest subpopulation of the Endangered **Gold-ringed Tanager** *Bangsia aureocincta*. Photo: Nigel Voaden.

The **Turquoise-throated Puffleg** *Eriocnemis godini* cannot yet be presumed extinct, because of one unconfirmed sighting in the 1970s, and the slim chance that it may survive in unsurveyed habitat remnants. It is listed as Critically Endangered (Possibly Extinct). Illustration: Tomasz Cofta.

The Endangered **Baudó Guan** *Penelope ortoni* is very sensitive to habitat modification, yet shows little fear in the presence of humans, and is easily hunted.

Much of the primary cloud forest habitat of the Endangered **Chocó Vireo** *Vireo masteri* is unprotected, and the national parks and reserves in which it is found are threatened by encroachment and disputes over land ownership.

The roadrunner-like **Banded Ground-cuckoo** *Neomorphus radiolosus* seems naturally to occur at low densities, but its populations are becoming increasingly isolated by habitat destruction, and it is hunted for food. Despite the recent discovery of new sites in Ecuador and Colombia, it was uplisted to Endangered in 2009.

The **Chestnut-bellied Flowerpiercer** *Diglossa gloriosissima* went unreported for 40 years until seen at a new site in Antioquia, Colombia, in 2003. It was subsequently rediscovered at the type-locality. It is suspected to be more widespread and tolerant of habitat degradation than feared, and may qualify for downlisting from Endangered.

The combined ranges of Endangered and Critically Endangered birds endemic to the Chocó of Colombia and Ecuador

Chestnut-bellied Flowerpiercer *Diglossa gloriosissima*. Photo: Ciro Albano (nebrazilbirding.com).

Banded Ground-cuckoo *Neomorphus radiolosus*. Dušan M. Brinkhuizen (sapayoa.com).

271

Peru

Peru shares borders with Ecuador and Colombia to the north, Bolivia and Brazil to the east, and Chile to the south. To the west of the Andes is the Pacific Ocean, and the cold Humboldt current; to the east lies the Amazon Basin.

With 1,781 recognized bird species, Peru has the world's second highest avian diversity after Colombia, and the highest number of restricted-range species in the Neotropics. All or part of 19 of South America's 66 Endemic Bird Areas (EBAs) are in Peru. Peru has more members of the families Tyrannidae (240 species), Furnariidae (120 species) and Emberizidae (85 species) than any other country, and a unique genus, the five *Incaspiza* Inca-finches, of which one, Grey-winged Inca-finch *Incaspiza ortizi*, is globally Vulnerable.

Three Inca-finches are found in the Marañón Valley EBA, where following long settlement and cultivation, much of the original riparian and dry forest habitat has been lost. Two endemic hummingbirds, the Purple-backed Sunbeam *Aglaeactis aliciae* and Grey-bellied Comet *Taphrolesbia griseiventris*, have lost much of their range, which was not extensive to begin with, and are now considered Endangered.

Some endemic species have very restricted ranges indeed. Of the seven species unique to the Andean ridge-top forests, six are threatened and one Near Threatened. The Endangered Long-whiskered Owlet *Xenoglaux loweryi* is confined to a few patches of elfin forest totalling just 177 km², while most observations of the Endangered Ash-throated Antwren *Herpsilochmus parkeri* come from 15 km² of habitat on a single isolated mountain ridge.

Similarly, most recent records of the Critically Endangered White-bellied Cinclodes *Cinclodes palliatus* come from just six sites, confined within an area of 24 km diameter in the province of Junín in the High Andes. Like the Critically Endangered Junín Grebe *Podiceps taczanowskii* and Endangered Junín Rail *Laterallus tuerosi*, its habitat is threatened by mining effluent and waste, and peat is increasingly being taken from the mineral-rich bogs it inhabits for mushroom growing, and for gardens and parks in Lima.

The elfin forests on which the Endangered **Golden-backed Mountain-tanager** *Buthraupis aureodorsalis* depends are vulnerable to grazing and fires spreading out of the páramo grasslands above them, and the tree line is receding. Photo: Gunnar Engblom (Kolibri Expeditions).

Fire may actually benefit the Endangered **Royal Sunangel** *Heliangelus regalis*, which is found in stunted forest adjacent to regularly burned areas. Although it is now confined to forest remnants, the poor sandy soil does not support agriculture or cattle ranching. Some of its habitat is protected. Photo: Dubi Shapiro (pbase.com/dubisha).

Fire and grazing are reducing the *Polylepis* woodland the **Royal Cinclodes** *Cinclodes aricomae* needs, but a *Polylepis* conservation programme involving local people may be turning the tide at known sites for this Critically Endangered species. Photo: Matthias Dehling.

Peruvian Plantcutter *Phytotoma raimondii*.
Photo: Murray Cooper (murraycooperphoto.com).

Lulu's Tody-flycatcher *Poecilotriccus luluae*. Photo: Pete Morris (birdquest-tours.com).

The national and private protected area systems cover around 14% of Peru's land area, and ecotourism – bird tourism in particular – is recognized as an increasingly important contributor to the country's economy. Historically, for over a century, birds provided Peru's greatest single source of income, in the form of guano from the seabird colonies that thrived in the productive waters of the Humboldt current. Once the guano was exhausted, the fish themselves – especially the vast shoals of anchoveta – were taken instead to be processed directly into fertilizer. The fishery collapsed in the 1970s, and has never really recovered, and nor have birds like the Endangered Peruvian Tern *Sterna lorata* and Endangered Peruvian Diving-petrel *Pelecanoides garnotii*.

Marañón Spinetail *Synallaxis maranonica*. Illustration: Tomasz Cofta.

Lulu's Tody-flycatcher *Poecilotriccus luluae*, one of Peru's many endemic tyrant-flycatchers, was uplisted to Endangered in 2012 because of projected Amazonian deforestation, but may benefit from attempts to protect the watershed forest at the Abra Patricia-Alto Mayo IBA.

Most of the habitat used by the Endangered **Peruvian Plantcutter** *Phytotoma raimondii* has been converted to plantation agriculture. Firewood collecting, and charcoal-making to supply grilled chicken restaurants in Lima, threaten what is left. The species is being used as an emblem for conservation awareness-raising, and a proposed national protected area on the Illescas Peninsula will cover some of its remaining range.

In 2012, along with a host of other Amazonian species, the **Marañón Spinetail** *Synallaxis maranonica* was uplisted because of projected clearance of forest for commodity crops and cattle in the Amazon Basin. Already confined to just 1,200 km², it is likely to lose 85% of its habitat over the next ten years, and is now considered Critically Endangered.

The Endangered **Junín Rail** *Laterallus tuerosi*, along with the Critically Endangered Junín Grebe *Podiceps taczanowskii*, is endemic to Lake Junín in the high Andes. Its wetland habitat is threatened by pollution and degraded by fluctuating water levels caused by a hydroelectric plant.

Junín Rail *Laterallus tuerosi*. Illustration: Tomasz Cofta.

273

Várzea Piculet
Picumnus varzeae.
Photo: Anselmo d'Affonseca.

Selva Cacique *Cacicus koepckeae.* Illustration: Tomasz Cofta.

The Amazon Basin

The area drained by the River Amazon and its tributaries covers around 40% of South America's land area, including parts of Brazil, Peru, Colombia, Ecuador, Venezuela, Bolivia, Guyana and Suriname. The basin is filled with tropical rainforest of different kinds, including swamp forest, seasonally inundated (várzea) forest and (on higher ground) terra firme forest, which historically covered more than 6·2 million square kilometres.

The Amazon is currently experiencing the highest absolute rate of forest loss in the world. To date around 18% of the region's tropical forest has been cleared, with average annual losses in the last decade of 1·8 million hectares. Projections based on planned roads, which will open up the forest for logging and conversion to agriculture, suggest that up to 40% of forest cover will be lost by 2050 if 'business as usual' continues (including up to 42% of the Brazilian Amazon by 2020). Two-thirds of the forest cover of six major watersheds and 12 eco-regions would go.

Even under the best-case scenario, where the Protected Area Network is expanded and properly enforced, watersheds are protected, and cattle and soya producers yield to pressures to comply with environmental legislation and manage their land soundly, a study calculates that 800,000 km² of forest will be lost by 2050 in the Brazilian Amazon alone.

Yet the overall proportion of Amazonian species in different taxonomic groups assessed as threatened on The IUCN Red List is below the global average, because the Red List assessments have not yet taken account of these projected regional patterns of future deforestation. In 2011, a team from BirdLife International published a reassessment of the status of 814 forest-dependent birds for which Amazonia contains the majority of remaining habitat. They used computer models of predicted deforestation to calculate the extent of suitable habitat likely to be left for each species after three generations.

The Endangered **Várzea Piculet** *Picumnus varzeae* is known from the area between the lower Río Madeira in east Amazonas, and Obidos in extreme north-west Pará, Brazil, although it may have a slightly wider distribution than this. No population estimates are available for this poorly known species, but over 60% of the seasonally flooded forest ('várzea') in its range is projected to be cleared or drowned by hydroelectric projects.

All records of the Endangered **Selva Cacique** *Cacicus koepckeae* come from river margin habitats in Peru. It seems to be extremely local, and to occur at low densities. It has been heard calling from mosaics of forest and cultivated land around a village, suggesting that it can tolerate small-scale settlement and agriculture, but up to 70% of its habitat could be converted to pasture for cattle or cultivated for soya in the next 14 years. It occurs in a number of protected areas including Manu National Park.

Just over 700 km² of suitable dense riverside thicket and river island habitat is currently available to the Critically Endangered **Rio Branco Antbird** *Cercomacra carbonaria*, and it is currently fairly common within this range. But all of it is predicted to be lost over the next 20 years because of accelerating deforestation in extreme north Brazil, and adjacent Guyana. It has been found in dense secondary growth, mainly in overgrown manioc plantations.

Rio Branco Antbird *Cercomacra carbonaria.* Photo: Mikael Bauer.

Amazonian species uplisted to Endangered or Critically Endangered in 2012		2011	2012
Dark-winged Trumpeter	*Psophia viridis*	LC	EN
Várzea Piculet	*Picumnus varzeae*	LC	EN
Rio Branco Antbird	*Cercomacra carbonaria*	EN	CR
Scaled Spinetail	*Cranioleuca muelleri*	LC	EN
Selva Cacique	*Cacicus koepckeae*	VU	EN

Under the 'business as usual' scenario, they predicted that the area of habitat available to Amazonian forest-dependent birds would decrease over the next three generations by 17·9%, with 92 species qualifying as threatened, compared with just 24 species considered threatened on the 2010 IUCN Red List. Even under the best case ('governance') scenario, available habitat would decrease by 15·7%, and 64 species would qualify as threatened.

As a result of BirdLife's reassessment, almost 100 species (including those that moved from Least Concern to Near Threatened) were uplisted in the 2012 Red List update. Among those expected to be worst affected, the Rio Branco Antbird *Cercomacra carbonaria* would lose 100% of its habitat if 'business as usual' continues, and was moved from Near Threatened to Critically Endangered. This, like the Hoary-throated Spinetail *Synallaxis kollari* (Endangered to Critically Endangered) and Várzea Piculet *Picumnus varzeae* (Least Concern to Endangered) is at grave and imminent risk because of recent proposed changes to Brazil's Forest Law, which among other relaxations in the amount of forest required to be maintained on private land, reduces the width of forest buffers that landlords must retain along rivers and streams.

The **Scaled Spinetail** *Cranioleuca muelleri* is found in the undergrowth of 'várzea' (seasonally flooded forest) around the east Amazon in Brazil. Half this habitat could be lost in the next ten years. Photo: Kurazo Okada.

Dependent upon dense lowland rainforest, and hunted for its meat, the **Dark-winged Trumpeter** *Psophia viridis* is only found away from human settlement. This species may lose between one-third and half its habitat over the next 31 years (three generations). Photo: Thiago Orsi Laranjeiras.

Deforestation in the Amazon Basin

■ Extent of the Amazon Basin
■ Deforested and degraded areas

The Atlantic Forest

The Atlantic Forest, or Mata Atlântica, historically extended from the north-eastern tip of Brazil along the coast to its southern states, and inland to extreme north-east Argentina and eastern Paraguay. It encompassed many forest types, from dry restinga on the coast to moist, montane forests up to 2,800 m further inland. It once covered over one million square kilometres but today only around 7% remains intact and it is one of the world's most vulnerable forests.

In south-east Brazil, the lowland Atlantic Forest spans more than 2,500 km of slopes and coastline from central Bahia state south to Rio Grande do Sul, and inland into Minas Gerais. Over 200 birds have been listed as endemic to the lowland Atlantic Forest, including ten endemic bird genera. New species described recently include the Critically Endangered Rio de Janeiro Antwren *Myrmotherula fluminensis* and Endangered Restinga Antwren *Formicivora littoralis*, and the Critically Endangered Bahia Tapaculo *Eleoscytalopus psychopompus*.

There have been no reliable records of the Critically Endangered **Kinglet Calyptura** *Calyptura cristata* since 1996, when two birds were observed in the Serra dos Órgãos north of Rio de Janeiro. Illustration: Tomasz Cofta.

In north-east Brazil, the Atlantic Forest runs along the narrow coastal slope and low-lying mountain ridges in the states of Pernambuco, Alagoas and Paraíba. The Critically Endangered White-collared Kite *Leptodon forbesi* is confined entirely to this area, and a suite of species including the Critically Endangered Alagoas Foliage-gleaner *Philydor novaesi* and Alagoas Antwren *Myrmotherula snowi*, and the Endangered Orange-bellied Antwren *Terenura sicki* and Alagoas Tyrannulet *Phylloscartes ceciliae*, is only found in the tropical evergreen forest on the slopes of Alagoas and Pernambuco. But in 1992 it was estimated that only 2% of the original forest cover remains in Alagoas and Pernambuco states and just 6% in Paraíba. Sugarcane plantations have replaced virtually all the lower-altitude forest, and in higher and steeper areas selective logging, firewood removal and small-scale cultivation are steadily removing the forest.

Before the 2012 IUCN Red List update, which raised the threat status of many Amazonian species, the overwhelming majority of Brazil's threatened birds came from the 12 states that contain substantial remnants of Atlantic Forest. Even after the 2012 update, two-thirds (approximately 100 out of the country's 152 Vulnerable, Endangered and Critically Endangered species) are found in the Atlantic Forest states, with a similar proportion of Near Threatened species. At least one species, the Alagoas Curassow *Mitu mitu*, is Extinct in the Wild, and there are similar fears for the Glaucous Macaw *Anodorhynchus glaucus*.

All Brazil's Atlantic Forest is included within three Endemic Bird Areas. In the state of Bahia alone, at least 33 restricted-range species are found in the few areas of forest that remain. Such figures may be underestimates: since 1994, 15 endemic species new to science have been described from the Atlantic Forest.

The Endangered **Banded Cotinga** *Cotinga maculata* is now known only from a few protected areas in south-east Bahia, north Espírito Santo, and north-east Minas Gerais; it has not been recorded in Rio de Janeiro state since the 19th century. Photo: Ciro Albano (nebrazilbirding.com).

The Critically Endangered **White-collared Kite** *Leptodon forbesi* is now found only in a few remaining Atlantic Forest fragments in the coastal states of north-east Brazil. Many of these areas are protected but are still at risk from fire spreading from adjacent sugarcane plantations. Photo: Andy & Gill Swash (WorldWildlifeImages.com).

The Atlantic Forest – its former & current extent

One of the world's most vulnerable forests, supporting over 100 globally threatened species.

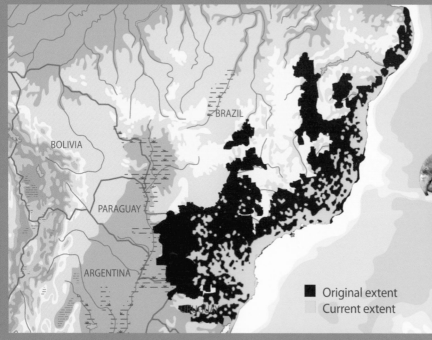

Original extent
Current extent

Atlantic Forest is Brazil's most reduced habitat. It was the location of the earliest European settlement in the country, and in the 400 years since has been cleared for timber, plantations, mining, and towns and cities. Continuing urbanization, agricultural expansion, industrialization, colonization and associated road-building threaten the fragments that remain. When BirdLife's Brazilian Partner, SAVE Brasil, identified 161 Important Areas in the Atlantic Forest states in 2006, it found that over 70% had some form of protection, either within the state protected area networks or as private reserves, but that many still suffered from habitat degradation and severe hunting, and had lost and were losing bird species.

The remnants of lowland forest that the Endangered **Brown-backed Parrotlet** *Touit melanonotus* needs are threatened by urbanization and roads, and adjoining lower montane slope forests are above its altitudinal range. Photo: Ciro Albano (nebrazilbirding.com).

The remaining tracts of forest with dense undergrowth favoured by the Endangered **Fringe-backed Fire-eye** *Pyriglena atra* are becoming ever smaller and more isolated. It has been found in patches of second growth habitat of less than 50 ha, but these tiny populations may not be viable. Photo: Andy & Gill Swash (WorldWildlifeImages.com).

There are recent records of the Endangered **Hook-billed Hermit** *Glaucis dohrnii* from two reserves, but these are under pressure from settlers, fire and road construction, and lack the stream-side habitat the bird favours. Photo: Ciro Albano (nebrazilbirding.com).

CONSERVATION CHALLENGE

Hunting and trapping

Throughout the world, birds in the Order Galliformes tend to be those most exploited by subsistence hunters for their meat, and sometimes their eggs. As 'game' birds, they are also often the primary targets of sport hunters. Two of the five Galliform families, the cracids (guans, curassows and chachalacas) and the New World quails, are confined to the Americas, with most species in Central and especially South America. The cracids have long been an important source of protein for indigenous people, and in recent centuries for landless peasants and farmers. In studies of hunting in Neotropical forests, they usually comprise the largest avian biomass. But recent unsustainable hunting in the wake of habitat conversion, road-building and new settlements, has rendered the cracids the most threatened group of birds in the Americas. The loss of these species leads to long-term habitat impoverishment, since as large avian frugivores, they are important distributors of the seeds of many fruiting trees.

There are current or proposed captive breeding schemes for several threatened cracids, including Horned Guan *Oreophasis derbianus* and Trinidad Piping-guan *Pipile pipile* (both included in the previous section), and **White-winged Guan** *Penelope albipennis*, Black-fronted *Pipile jacutinga*, and Red-billed *Crax blumenbachii* and Helmeted *Pauxi pauxi* Curassows. The Alagoas Curassow *Mitu mitu* survives only as a captive population. The **Red-billed Curassow** has been successfully reintroduced in various states in eastern Brazil, but still hovers at the threshold of Critically Endangered because of continuing losses elsewhere. Various livelihoods initiatives, including an ecotourism project for the Wattled Curassow *Crax globulosa* in Bolivia, and payment of local guards, have been set up to give communities an incentive to leave the birds unharmed. Threatened cracids are found in many protected areas, but are still hunted because of poor enforcement. In Colombia, dedicated reserves have been set up by Fundación ProAves for the Blue-billed Curassow *Crax alberti* (El Paujil Bird Reserve) and the Helmeted Curassow (Pauxi pauxi Bird Reserve), which provide the only adequate protection for these species.

Unsustainable hunting is also a primary factor in the decline of the 12 *Odontophorus* wood-quail species, four of which are threatened, and another four Near Threatened. Many occur in protected areas and on national lists of protected birds, but none appears to be directly targeted by conservation action.

Tens of thousands of wild-caught parrots are still traded every year in South American countries, often in contravention of the Convention on International Trade in Endangered Species (CITES) and national laws. High levels of exploitation are causing local population declines and sometimes national extirpation of the most sought-after species. By a perverse logic, the most threatened parrots can become the most sought-after, their price in illegal international markets rising according to their rarity value.

The Endangered **Gorgeted Wood-quail** *Odontophorus strophium*. Photo: Fundación ProAves (proaves.org).

The Ctitically Endangered **White-winged Guan** *Penelope albipennis*.
Photo: Roger Ahlman (pbase.com/ahlman).

From July 2004 to December 2007, an anonymous wild animal trader from Los Pozos market, Santa Cruz, Bolivia, with a good knowledge of parrots, took daily notes of the species and quantity of individuals that were offered. He recorded over 27,500 individuals from 36 species, of which 64% were adults captured in the wild. Among the threatened species he recorded were two Lear's Macaws *Anodorhynchus leari* (then Critically Endangered, now Endangered), two Critically Endangered **Blue-throated Macaws** *Ara glaucogularis* (a now very local Bolivian endemic), ten Endangered Hyacinth Macaws *Anodorhynchus hyacinthus*, and 47 Endangered Red-fronted Macaws *Ara rubrogenys*. These figures probably represent no more than a quarter of the birds captured. As many as 75% of parrots taken from the wild die from stress, disease, rough handling, asphyxiation or dehydration during capture and transport.

Most parrots were sold locally or in other destinations within Bolivia, but the larger and more expensive species were often taken outside the country. Lear's, Red-fronted and Hyacinth Macaws were sometimes transported across Bolivia from Brazil to be sold in Peru, where authorized wildlife trading routes for a limited number of species appeared to be used to 'launder' threatened species into international markets. Trade in these highly valued species was likely to be under-represented in the street market, since most would be sold directly to middlemen or end-buyers known to be interested in them.

Los Pozos is only one of the four sales points for wild birds in Santa Cruz, and other Bolivian cities also have wild animal markets. Local police refused to be involved, claiming animal traffic was not a priority. Most of the Scarlet Macaws *Ara macao* on sale had been brought from the lowland forest around the borders of Noel Kempff Mercado National Park, indicating that enforcing wildlife laws was a low priority around protected areas too.

Similar findings came from a 2007–8 study of 20 wildlife markets in eight cities in Peru, where four threatened species were traded, including Endangered Grey-cheeked Parakeet *Brotogeris pyrrhoptera*, out of a total of 34 parrot species. Even for the seven species which can be legally traded in Peru, the number of individuals being traded greatly exceeded official quotas.

Of course, parrots are not the only species captured for the cagebird trade. Surveys of eight street markets in Recife, northeastern Brazil, found high levels of trade in songbirds, especially males. The most commonly traded species was the Yellow-bellied Seedeater *Sporophila nigricollis*, which is listed as Least Concern. But as shown by the declining status of other members of this genus, like the Vulnerable Buffy-fronted Seedeater *S. frontalis* (with 'lots' of 100–200 birds offered for sale at certain times in Rio de Janeiro), the Vulnerable Chestnut Seedeater *S. cinnamomea* (heavily trapped for trade) and Endangered Marsh Seedeater *S. palustris* (extirpated from parts of Argentina by trapping and under similar pressure in Uruguay), unsustainable levels of trapping can combine with habitat loss to push previously abundant species towards extinction.

The Endangered
Red-billed Curassow
Crax blumenbachii.
Photos: Ciro Albano
(nebrazilbirding.com).

South America

According to BirdLife International, a total of 3,250 species has been recorded from South America. This figure includes the species found on the Falkland Islands (Islas Malvinas), since these are continental shelf rather than oceanic islands. However, the species restricted to Galápagos, the Juan Fernández Islands and Fernando de Noronha, which are often included on the list of South American species, have been excluded and are covered in the Oceanic Islands section (*page 180*). However, the many seabird species that do not breed in South America or on its continental shelf islands that have been recorded in coastal waters, are included in the totals for each threat category in the tables shown here.

In all, 161 species are included in this section, just over 27% of the total number of species covered by the seven regional 'directory' sections of this book, The eight species recorded from this region that appear elsewhere in the book are all seabirds: the Critically Endangered Tristan *Diomedea dabbenena* and Waved *Phoebastria irrorata* Albatrosses and Galápagos Petrel *Pterodroma phaeopygia*; and the Endangered Northern Royal *Diomedea sanfordi*, Sooty *Phoebetria fusca* and Atlantic Yellow-nosed *Thalassarche chlororhynchos* Albatrosses, Atlantic Petrel *Pterodroma incerta* and White-throated Storm-petrel *Nesofregetta fuliginosa*.

The South American species that are Endangered or Critically Endangered, or are Extinct in the Wild, comprise representatives from 37 bird families. These are summarized in the following table, and additional contextual information, such as the total number of species in each family and the proportion that is globally threatened, is included in the taxonomic list of all the species featured in this book at Appendix 2 on *page 339*.

A summary of the most threatened bird families in South America

Type of bird	EW	CR	CR (PE)	EN	Tot.	Type of bird	EW	CR	CR (PE)	EN	Tot.
Guans & curassows (Cracidae)	1	2	–	7	**10**	**Toucans** (Ramphastidae)	–	–	–	1	**1**
New World quails (Odontophoridae)	–	–	–	1	**1**	**Woodpeckers** (Picidae)	–	–	–	3	**3**
Ducks (Anatidae)	–	1	–	–	**1**	**Manakins** (Pipridae)	–	1	–	–	**1**
Albatrosses (Diomedeidae)	–	2 (2)	–	4 (3)	**6 (5)**	**Cotingas** (Cotingidae)	–	1	–	6	**7**
Petrels Procellariidae	–	1 (1)	–	1 (1)	**2 (2)**	**Tyrant-flycatchers** (Tyrannidae)	–	–	–	10	**10**
Diving-petrels (Pelecanoididae)	–	–	–	1	**1**	**Antbirds** (Thamnophilidae)	–	3	–	10	**13**
Storm-petrels (Hydrobatidae)	–	–	–	1 (1)	**1 (1)**	**Tapaculos** (Rhinocryptidae)	–	2	–	4	**6**
Grebes (Podicipedidae)	–	2	–	1	**3**	**Antpittas** (Formicariidae)	–	2	–	3	**5**
Eagles, hawks & kites (Accipitridae)	–	1	–	2	**3**	**Ovenbirds** (Furnariidae)	–	5	–	7	**12**
Rails & crakes (Rallidae)	–	–	–	4	**4**	**Vireos** (Vireonidae)	–	–	–	1	**1**
Trumpeters (Psophiidae)	–	–	–	1	**1**	**Wrens** (Troglodytidae)	–	3	–	1	**4**
Sandpipers & allies (Scolopacidae)	–	–	1 (1)	–	**1 (1)**	**Gnatcatchers** (Polioptilidae)	–	1	–	–	**1**
Terns (Laridae)	–	–	–	1	**1**	**Finches** (Fringillidae)	–	–	–	1	**1**
Doves & pigeons (Columbidae)	–	2	–	1	**3**	**New World warblers** (Parulidae)	–	–	–	2	**2**
Parrots (Psittacidae)	–	5	–	14	**19**	**New World blackbirds** (Icteridae)	–	–	–	4	**4**
Cuckoos (Cuculidae)	–	–	–	1	**1**	**American sparrows & allies** (Emberizidae)	–	2	–	7	**9**
Owls (Strigidae)	–	1	–	1	**2**	**Tanagers & allies** (Thraupidae)	–	2	–	5	**7**
Nightjars (Caprimulgidae)	–	–	–	1	**1**	**Grosbeaks & allies** (Cardinalidae)	–	1	–	–	**1**
Hummingbirds (Trochilidae)	–	6	–	14	**20**						
(n) = number of regularly occurring seabirds or other migrants that do not breed in the region.						**ALL SPECIES (37 FAMILIES)**	**1**	**46 (3)**	**1 (1)**	**121 (5)**	**169 (9)**

The data in the table opposite shows that very similar numbers of non-passerine and passerine species (85 and 84 respectively) in South America are Endangered or Critically Endangered. Some families have a particularly large number of threatened species and those with ten or more are, in descending order: hummingbirds – 20 (8% of all South American species); parrots – 19 (15%); antbirds – 13 (6%); ovenbirds – 12 (5%); guans and curassows – 10 (23%); and tyrant-flycatchers – 10 (3%).

Four of the 45 Endangered or Critically Endangered migratory 'land' birds in the world breed in this region. A fifth species, Eskimo Curlew *Numenius borealis* is Possibly Extinct but once wintered in the south of the continent. The four breeding migrants are the Critically Endangered Hooded Grebe *Podiceps gallardoi*, and the Endangered Hyacinth Macaw *Anodorhynchus hyacinthinus*, Grey-cheeked Parakeet *Brotogeris pyrrhoptera* and Marsh Seedeater *Sporophila palustris*. The migration routes for all these species are shown on the map on *page 51*.

The eight Data Deficient species recorded in the region are: White-vented Storm-petrel *Oceanites gracilis*; Markham's Storm-petrel *Oceanodroma markhami*; Ringed Storm-petrel *Oceanodroma hornbyi*; Colombian Crake *Neocrex colombiana*; Cayenne Nightjar *Caprimulgus maculosus*; Spot-fronted Swift *Cypseloides cherriei*; Coppery Thorntail *Discosura letitiae*; and Bogotá Sunangel *Heliangelus zusii*. For further information on these species see *pages 322–331*.

South America supports the highest number of bird species of all the continents. It also has the highest number of globally threatened birds, and six of its 14 countries or territories are among the top seven in the world for the number of species recorded. The table below provides a summary of the number of globally threatened species in each of The IUCN Red List categories for all the South American countries.

A summary of the bird species totals for the South American countries (figures exclude oceanic islands)

	Country / territory	Species recorded	EW	CR	CR (PE)	CR (PEW)	EN	VU	GLOBALLY THREATENED	% of species	DD
1	Colombia	1,811	–	13	–	–	31	68	112	6·2%	5
2	Peru	1,781	–	8	–	–	34	82	124	7·0%	3
3	Brazil	1,719	1	22	(2)	(1)	41	88	151	8·8%	–
4	Ecuador	1,558	–	5	(1)	–	17	62	84	5·4%	3
5	Bolivia	1,419	–	2	–	–	13	38	53	3·7%	1
6	Venezuela	1,351	–	2	–	–	13	25	40	3·0%	1
7	Argentina	993	–	6	(2)	–	10	34	50	5·0%	–
8	Guyana	788	–	2	–	–	2	9	13	1·6%	–
9	French Guiana	704	–	–	–	–	–	6	6	0·9%	1
10	Suriname	695	–	–	–	–	–	7	7	1·0%	–
11	Paraguay	688	–	4	(1)	–	6	18	28	4·1%	–
12	Chile	433	–	3	(1)	–	6	22	31	7·2%	3
13	Uruguay	405	–	3	(1)	–	7	14	24	5·9%	–
14	Falkland Islands (Islas Malvinas)	125	–	–	–	–	3	7	10	8·0%	

Photo: Jon Hornbuckle

EN **Baudó Guan** *Penelope ortoni* `270`

▼ **POPULATION:** 7,000–21,000 | **THREATS:** AGR, HUN, LOG, DEV, TRA, EGY

Occurring locally in the Chocó region along the west Andean foothills of Colombia and Ecuador, this guan inhabits early to late successional humid and wet forest, usually below 1,500 m. As it is unafraid of humans, it is easily hunted for food. It is also extremely sensitive to habitat modification, but deforestation has affected large parts of its range, and this is continuing as plans progress for colonization and economic development in more remote regions, aided by the rapid expansion of the road network. Some key protected areas have already been degraded. It is very rare in captivity and little is known about its biology except that it is sedentary and frugivorous.

EN **Cauca Guan** *Penelope perspicax*

`49`

▼ **POPULATION: 250–999** | **THREATS:** HUN, AGR, WAT, LOG, DEV

Found only on the slopes of the West and Central Andes, Colombia, this guan now occupies just 5% of its former range. At higher altitudes (1,600–2,150 m), it is mostly found in humid, primary forest fragments but also occurs in a range of habitats down to 900 m. Its diet consists of a wide variety of fruits, as well as insects, foliage and flowers, sometimes including the young leaves of the exotic Chinese Ash *Fraxinus chinensis*. Habitat loss due to human colonization and deforestation has been severe across its range and ongoing habitat fragmentation is likely to be a major threat. It is also hunted for food, even in some protected areas, a further significant factor contributing to its population decline.

Photo: Murray Cooper (murraycooperphoto.com)

CR **White-winged Guan** *Penelope albipennis*

`279`

▼ **POPULATION: 100–170** | **THREATS:** AGR, HUN, LOG, SPP, EGY

Historically, this guan was probably widely distributed across dry forests in the Tumbesian region, but it is now only known from 22 localities along a 200 km-long band in north-west Peru. It favours areas with permanent water, dense cover and little human disturbance. Habitat loss, primarily due to conversion to agriculture and logging, remains a major threat, and mining concessions in the northern part of its range could potentially lead to further habitat destruction. Hunting has also been a significant factor in declines. However, a reserve has been established specifically for this species, a captive breeding and reintroduction progamme are ongoing, and local people are engaged in ecotourism initiatives.

Photo: Daniel Rosengren (scutisorex.se)

EN **Black-fronted Piping-guan** *Pipile jacutinga*

▼ **POPULATION: 1,500–7,000** | **THREATS:** AGR, WAT, HUN, LOG

Having declined very dramatically, virtually to extinction in the north and south of its range, this distinctive guan is found in humid/riverine forests in north-east Argentina and eastern Paraguay, and in a few localities in the Atlantic Forest of south-east Brazil. Although habitat loss and degradation has been widespread, and is still taking place, illegal hunting is the most immediate threat. The meat of this species is the most prized among the gamebirds in the region and the impact of poaching is severe. Although it does breed in captivity, effective anti-poaching patrols are urgently needed if wild populations are to be maintained.

Photo: Emilio White

EW **Alagoas Curassow** *Mitu mitu*

`16`

† **POPULATION:** Not applicable | **THREATS:** (AGR), (HUN)

Following its discovery in Pernambuco, north-east Brazil, in the mid-17th century, this curassow was not reported again until 1951, when it was rediscovered in Alagoas. By the 1960s, there were probably as few as 20 wild birds remaining. Since the early 1970s, there have only been records from four Atlantic Forest fragments, the most recent being of hunted birds in 1984, and perhaps 1987/8. It is now almost certainly extirpated from the wild due to the ceaseless clearance of lowland forests, chiefly for sugarcane, and poaching. Fortunately, a private captive population was established in 1977, and by 2008 there were 130 birds at two centres (although around 35% were hybrids with Razor-billed Curassow *M. tuberosum*).

Photo [captive]: Luís Fábio Silveira (ib.usp.br/~lfsilveira)

EN **Helmeted Curassow** *Pauxi pauxi*

▼ **POPULATION: 1,000–2,499** | **THREATS:** HUN, AGR, EGY, LOG

The nominate subspecies of this curassow occurs on the north-eastern slopes of the East Andes in Colombia and Venezuela, and in three mountain ranges in Falcón, northern Venezuela. The subspecies *gilliardi* is known from the Sierra de Perijá on the Colombian-Venezuelan border. It is restricted to montane cloud forest at 500–2,200 m. Extensive habitat loss precipitated population declines, but hunting (for food, traditional jewellery and use as an aphrodisiac) is now the most significant threat. In Venezuela, it is legally protected and an education programme is in place. In Colombia, the appropriately named Pauxi pauxi Bird Reserve has recently been established.

Photo [captive]: Myles Lamont / Hancock Wildlife Research Center

EN **Horned Curassow** *Pauxi unicornis*

▼ **POPULATION: 1,000–4,999** | **THREATS:** AGR, HUN, TRA, EGY, LOG

This curassow is known from two disjunct populations. The once-widespread nominate subspecies is now restricted to central Bolivia. Subspecies *koepckeae* of central Peru is possibly a separate species, but probably numbers fewer than 400 individuals; it went unrecorded following its description in 1969 until records from local people were confirmed in 2005. Although both populations occur in dense montane forests in a narrow altitudinal range, the Bolivian population is also found in lowland forests down to 450 m. Historically, the population in both countries has been significantly affected by habitat loss due to colonization and agriculture, but hunting for its meat is now likely to be the greatest threat.

Photo [captive]: Asociación Civil Armonía

CR **Blue-billed Curassow** *Crax alberti*

▼ **POPULATION: 150–700** | **THREATS:** AGR, EGY, HUN, DEV, LOG, TRA, (PLN)

Once a widespread species in the sierras of northern Colombia, only one of the few remaining large areas of lowland tropical forest in its range holds a significant population: Serranía de las Quinchas. Habitat loss and degradation since colonization in the 17th century has been severe and remains a major threat. Hunting and egg collecting for food have contributed to past declines and these activities are likely to continue. New infrastructure development, such as roads, is also creating a barrier between some populations. The El Paujíl Bird Reserve, now the stronghold of the species, was established in 2004, and although numbers here are increasing, declines continue elsewhere, even in protected areas.

Photo: Fundación ProAves (proaves.org)

EN **Wattled Curassow** *Crax globulosa*

▼ **POPULATION: 250–999** | **THREATS:** HUN, AGR, LOG, DEV

Although this curassow is widely distributed across upper Amazonia (Brazil, Colombia, Ecuador, Peru and Bolivia), most locations are remote and little studied. Only Brazil is thought to hold a significant population, perhaps as many as 1,000 birds. In the wet season it possibly migrates from várzea to terra firme forest to feast on canopy fruit and seeds. During the dry season it is known to concentrate around water-bodies. Although ongoing habitat loss is a significant factor in population declines, hunting is the main threat. This species is particularly vulnerable as it is restricted to water-edge habitats that are easily reached by people using rivers for transport.

Photo: Whaldener Endo

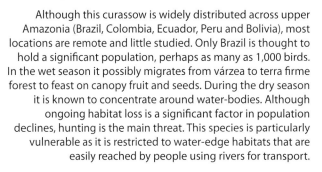

EN **Red-billed Curassow** *Crax blumenbachii*

`279`

▼ **POPULATION: 130–170** | **THREATS:** AGR, HUN, DEV

Formerly widespread from Bahia to Rio de Janeiro states in eastern Brazil, very few, tiny, fragmented wild populations of this curassow are now known, largely restricted to reserves. It occurs in lowland humid forests, but there are recent records from montane forest above 500 m, and disturbed and agricultural habitats, including old, regenerating secondary forest. Habitat loss has been severe, with virtually all lowland forest lost since colonization. Although it is now legally protected, hunting and capture for the bird trade remains a significant threat, even in protected areas. A large population (around 600 birds) is maintained in captivity and reintroduction programmes have been successful.

Photo: Ciro Albano (nebrazilbirding.com)

EN **Gorgeted Wood-quail** *Odontophorus strophium*

`279`

▼ **POPULATION: 1,300–2,900** | **THREATS:** HUN, LOG, AGR, DEV, TRA

This rarely reported forest partridge only occurs on the west slope of the East Andes of Colombia, where it now appears to be largely restricted to the larger oak-laurel forest remnants in the eastern Cordillera. Although probably dependent upon primary forest for at least part of its life-cycle, it has been recorded in degraded habitats and secondary forest. Extensive habitat loss since colonization is likely to have led to significant population declines. Although this species formerly occurred in two protected areas, the recent declaration of the Yariguíes National Park (which comprises a substantial 200,000 ha primary forest fragment) should provide further protection. It was down-listed to Endangered in 2008.

Photo: Alonso Quevedo / Fundación ProAves (proaves.org)

CR **Brazilian Merganser** *Mergus octosetaceus*

`36`

▼ **POPULATION: 50–249** | **THREATS:** AGR, WAT, EGY, MAN, LOG, HUN, PLN

Most recent records of this resident duck are from a few highly disjunct localities in Brazil, its stronghold being the Serra da Canastra area. However, it is also known from Argentina and Paraguay. It inhabits shallow, fast-flowing rivers, particularly in forest, in the upper tributaries of watersheds, ranging into small rivers. Habitat loss and degradation, dam construction and water pollution resulting from deforestation, agricultural expansion and diamond mining have had a significant impact on this species, and there is little suitable habitat left for dispersing birds. Disturbance due to increased tourism is also a threat. Conservation initiatives including the installation of nest boxes are underway, and a captive breeding programme was initiated in 2011.

Photo: Roy de Haas (agami.nl)

EN **Black-browed Albatross** *Thalassarche melanophrys*

`202,205`

▼ **POPULATION: 1,150,000** | **THREATS: FISH**, SPP, CLI?, (GEO)

Although the majority of the population of this albatross breeds in the Falkland Islands (Islas Malvinas), significant colonies also occur on the Islas Diego Ramirez, Ildefonso, Diego de Almagro, Isla Evangelistas and islets in Tierra del Fuego and in the Mallaganes region (Chile), and on South Georgia (Georgias del Sur). It also breeds in small numbers on Oceanic and Australasian islands (see *pages 166 & 209*). Foraging at sea up to 3,000 km from its breeding sites, it is often found in areas where there has been a marked increase in the number of longline fisheries and is one of the albatrosses most frequently killed on hooks (see *pages 202–205*).

Photo: Nigel Voaden

EN **Peruvian Diving-petrel** *Pelecanoides garnotii*

▼ POPULATION: **25,000–28,000** | THREATS: CLI, EGY, FISH, HUN, SPP, DEV

Most of the breeding population of this small seabird is now confined to the Peruvian offshore islands of San Gallán and La Vieja, with further, small colonies on islands off Chile. It remains in coastal waters throughout the year, diving to feed. It excavates nest burrows in thick guano, the harvesting of which continues today and is probably responsible for the massive historical declines. It is also hunted for food and predated by introduced mammals, a factor that probably prevents recolonization of other islands. Commercial fishing reduces food availability and causes mortality through incidental bycatch. The islands on which all known colonies are found are reserves but are poorly protected.

Photo: Ignacio Azocar (chileaves.com)

EN **Titicaca Grebe** *Rollandia microptera*   `47`

▼ POPULATION: **1,600** | THREATS: **FISH**, PLN, HUN, SPP, LOG, WAT?, MAN?

This flightless grebe is endemic to open, freshwater lakes on the altiplano of Peru and Bolivia, where the breeding population is now mostly confined to Lake Titicaca. It feeds by diving for fish and nests in marshes that allow ready access to open water, or amongst floating waterweeds. It faces numerous threats, including accidental bycatch in fishing nets, natural fluctuations in water levels, and changes in lake ecosystems due to introduced exotic fish, chemical contamination from mining and, in Lake Titicaca, the dumping of large quantities of city waste. The harvesting and burning of marsh vegetation has increased, as has disturbance by tourist boats.

Photo: Daniel Rosengren (scutisorex.se)

CR **Junín Grebe** *Podiceps taczanowskii*   `42,43`

▼ POPULATION: **50–249** | THREATS: **WAT**, **PLN**, CLI

Endemic to the shallow, reed-fringed Lake Junín in the Andean highlands of west-central Peru, this flightless grebe was abundant in the 1930s. It feeds in open water near the shore during the (wet) breeding season and in the centre of the lake during the dry austral winter. It feeds mainly on small fish, but these become scarce when water levels drop. A deterioration in water quality due to nearby mining activities, and extreme water-level fluctuations caused by a hydroelectric plant, have adversely affected the lake's ecosystem and led to significant declines. Legal measures to improve water quality and restrict water abstraction have been in place since 2002, but have yet to prove effective.

Photo: Denzil Morgan

CR **Hooded Grebe** *Podiceps gallardoi*   `39`

▼ POPULATION: **660–800** | THREATS: **CLI**, **SPP**, AGR, EGY, GEO

Breeding only on a few basaltic lakes between 500 m and 1,200 m in extreme south-west Argentina, this grebe migrates to winter on the Argentine coast. Aquatic vegetation on its breeding lakes is essential material for its floating nest, and as habitat for several aquatic invertebrates that form its basic diet. The precise reasons for this species' decline are not fully understood, but the key threats are probably climate change (some lakes are now completely dry or have low water levels), and changes in the ecology of some lakes due to the introduction of salmon and trout. In 2010/11, feral American Mink *Neovison vison*, killed more than half the adults in a breeding colony of 24 nests.

Photo: James C. Lowen (pbase.com/james_lowen)

285

CR **White-collared Kite** *Leptodon forbesi*

`277`

▼ POPULATION: 50–249 | THREATS: **AGR, LOG**

This little-known raptor was split from the similar but more widely distributed Grey-headed Kite *Leptodon cayanensis* as recently as the early 1990s. It is restricted to a few remaining fragments of humid Atlantic Forest, up to 600 m, in the coastal states of north-east Brazil. It may once have been much more widespread, but extensive logging for timber and conversion to agriculture has reduced the area of forest in the region to less than 1% of its former extent. The remnant patches of forest that remain are still threatened by logging and uncontrolled fires spreading from adjacent sugarcane plantations. Most of the species' known strongholds are now on private reserves.

Photo: Andy & Gill Swash (WorldWildlifeImages.com)

EN **Grey-backed Hawk** *Leucopternis occidentalis*

▼ POPULATION: 250–999 | THREATS: **AGR**, LOG, DEV

Confined to west Ecuador and north-west Peru, viable populations of this hawk are only likely to survive at a very few sites due to habitat fragmentation. It mostly occurs at elevations of 100–1,400 m, where it inhabits dry deciduous and humid evergreen forests, but is sometimes found feeding in degraded habitats and at forest edges. Nests are built in the upper canopy of tall trees. Habitat destruction has been severe, and building and infrastructure development is ongoing, the expansion of road networks increasing the threat of logging, cattle-ranching, oil palm planting and hunting. Reforestation is underway in several private reserves but many other protected areas remain under considerable threat.

Photo: Roger Ahlman (pbase.com/ahlman)

EN **Crowned Eagle** *Harpyhaliaetus coronatus*

▼ POPULATION: 250–999 | THREATS: **AGR**, HUN, SPP, DEV

This powerful eagle has a very large range east of the Andes, from Argentina, to central Brazil. It is usually found in seasonally dry, semi-open, lowland habitats, including, occasionally, extensively managed cattle ranches. Its movements are poorly understood, and it may be partially crepuscular. Habitat loss and degradation is widespread and ongoing due to the intensification of agricultural practices and, in Brazil, afforestation. In many areas it is persecuted (hunted, poisoned and deliberately disturbed), but other causes of mortality include collision with powerlines and drowning in water-tanks. Measures that would help to safeguard this species include educational campaigns and the establishment of habitat corridors.

Photo: Darío Fernández (rovingbiologist.blogspot.com)

EN **Rusty-flanked Crake** *Laterallus levraudi*

▼ POPULATION: 250–999 | THREATS: **PLN**, AGR, DEV

Endemic to north-west Venezuela, this small rail inhabits dense, aquatic vegetation fringing wetlands, and occasionally dry grasslands, on the lower Caribbean slope. There were very few records between 1946 and 1995, when seven new localities were identified, and it is now known from at least 32 locations. It is probable that deforestation along the eastern flank of the Andes, together with the construction of drainage ditches and pools to water cattle, has led to this species extending its range southwards. However, many factors are currently contributing to wetland degradation, including industrial waste, pesticides, the lowering of water levels and tourist developments.

Yacambu National Park, Lara, Venezuela; December 2011. Photo: Hadoram Shirihai; contributed from the forthcoming *Photographic Handbook of the Birds of the World*, Jornvall & Shirihai © Bloomsbury Publishing Plc.

EN **Junín Rail** *Laterallus tuerosi*

▼ POPULATION: 600–1,700 | THREATS: AGR, CLI, WAT, PLN, SPP?

Endemic to the shores of Lake Junín in the high Andes of central Peru, this tiny, secretive rail is known only from two localities on the south-west shore, but probably occurs elsewhere in the 150 km² of surrounding marshes. The lake and its adjacent wetland habitats have been severely degraded by pollution from nearby mining activities and extreme water-level fluctuations caused by a hydroelectric plant. Predation by Pampas Cats *Leopardus pajeros* may also be a significant threat, particularly during drought when access is easier. Although legal measures to improve water quality and restrict water abstraction have been in place since 2002, they have yet to prove effective.

Illustration: Tomasz Cofta

EN **Plain-flanked Rail** *Rallus wetmorei*

▼ POPULATION: 50–200 | THREATS: PLN, DEV, EGY, HUN, TRA

Found along a short stretch of the north Venezuelan coast, in recent years this little-known rail has only been recorded regularly on the Morrocoy Peninsula. It appears to be sedentary in coastal mangroves and shallow saltwater or brackish lagoons and marshes with emergent and halophytic vegetation. The most significant threat is habitat loss and degradation due to housing, tourism and industrial infrastructure, pollution from domestic sewage and agricultural run-off, sedimentation and the restriction of water flow by road building. Illegal hunting may also be a factor. Surveys are urgently required to help inform the development of appropriate conservation measures.

Photo: David J. Southall (tropicalbirdphotos.com)

EN **Bogotá Rail** *Rallus semiplumbeus* `27`

▼ POPULATION: 1,000–2,499 | THREATS: AGR, HUN, PLN, WAT, LOG, DEV, TRA, SPP?

This vocal rail has two subspecies: *peruvianus* of Peru has probably been extinct since the late 19th century, but the nominate is known from two localities on the Ubaté-Bogotá plateau at 2,500-4,000 m in the East Andes of Colombia. It inhabits savanna and páramo wetlands, favouring marshes fringed by dense, tall reeds and bulrushes, and vegetation-rich shallows. However, major savanna wetlands are seriously threatened, mainly by drainage schemes, but also by a wide range of other factors related to an increasing human population and agricultural intensification. Road construction and illegal settlement have increased the risk of predation by invasive species such as rats and domestic cats and dogs.

Photo: Alonso Quevedo / Fundación ProAves (proaves.org)

EN **Dark-winged Trumpeter** *Psophia viridis* `275`

? POPULATION: Unknown | THREATS: AGR, HUN

Endemic to Brazil, the three subspecies of this large, terrestrial bird (the nominate, *dextralis* and *obscura*) have a contiguous distribution across a wide swathe of the Amazon Basin. It requires large expanses of undisturbed, dense lowland forest in order to thrive. The primary threat to this species is accelerating deforestation as land is cleared for cattle ranching and soya production, facilitated by expansion of the road network. It is also declining as a result of hunting pressure. The subspecies *obscura* that occurs in the north-east of the country may be critically endangered. Currently, no specific conservation actions to benefit this species are known.

Photo: Thiago Orsi Laranjeiras

287

CR (PE) **Eskimo Curlew** *Numenius borealis*

? **POPULATION:** <50 | **THREATS:** AGR?, CLI?, EGY?, (HUN)

Breeding in arctic tundra in Canada, and possibly Alaska (see *page 252*), there have been no records of this long-distance migrant at its wintering grounds in South America since 1939. It formerly migrated down the east coast of the Americas to Argentina and possibly Uruguay, Paraguay, southernmost Brazil and Chile south to Patagonia. It particularly favoured wet pampas grasslands but also occurred on intertidal coastal habitats and semi-desert areas. The return migration is thought to have been along the Pacific coast as far as Central America, and then across the Gulf of Mexico to the Texas coast and northwards through the prairies.

Illustration: Tomasz Cofta

EN **Peruvian Tern** *Sterna lorata*

▼ **POPULATION:** 600–1,700 | **THREATS:** FISH, MAN, SPP, DEV, AGR, WAT, EGY, PLN?

This small tern forages mostly in shallow, inshore waters along the Pacific coast from Ecuador to Chile. Only four breeding sites are known in Peru, and nine in Chile, and it nests either on broad, sandy beaches and dunes, or on desert plains near the coast. The population has not recovered from the collapse of anchovy *Engraulis* spp. stocks (one of its favoured prey) in 1972. The principal threat now is the impact of coastal development and disturbance by human activities such as the use of off-road vehicles. Measures to protect known colonies from habitat destruction, disturbance and pollution are urgently needed to secure its future.

Photo: Denzil Morgan

CR **Blue-eyed Ground-dove** *Columbina cyanopis*

▼ **POPULATION:** 50–249 | **THREATS:** AGR, SPP

This small, terrestrial dove has probably always been scarce throughout the interior of Brazil, but the very few recent records are from just three locations scattered over a wide area; the only viable population is probably in the Serra das Araras. It inhabits cerrado grasslands and, until recently, large areas of potentially suitable habitat remained. However, its population is likely to have declined rapidly since the 1950s due to ongoing habitat loss and degradation, primarily due to conversion to agriculture (including soya production) and afforestation to *Eucalyptus* plantations. It occurs in some National Parks that contain areas of suitable habitat, and at an ecological station in the Serra das Araras.

Illustration: Tomasz Cofta

CR **Purple-winged Ground-dove** *Claravis geoffroyi*

▼ **POPULATION:** 50–249 | **THREATS:** AGR, DEV, HUN

In the early 20th century, this terrestrial dove occurred throughout the Atlantic Forest from Bahia, Brazil to northern Argentina and eastern Paraguay. However, since the early 1990s there have only been a few undocumented, but credible, reports. It appears to prefer forest edge habitats and undertake irregular nomadic movements following the flowering of bamboos, the seeds of which are its favoured food. Suitable habitat is now severely fragmented due to the impact of colonization and agriculture, and the remaining areas are probably not large enough to support a viable population. A small captive population was held by a few Brazilian aviculturists but is believed to have died out.

Photo: Luiz Cláudio Marigo

EN **Tolima Dove** *Leptotila conoveri*

▼ **POPULATION: 600–1,700** | **THREATS:** AGR

Known from only a few valleys on the east slope of the Central Andes, Colombia, this terrestrial dove is now only regularly recorded at one locality (Tolima). It occurs in highly fragmented areas of humid forest and forest borders, mainly in the subtropical zone from 1,600–2,225 m. Its habits are little known but it forages on the forest floor probably feeding on seeds and insects. Since the 1950s in particular, habitat loss and degradation has been extensive within its range due to clearance for agriculture. It has not been recorded from any protected areas but an integrated conservation programme for some areas of forest is underway.

Photo: Alonso Quevedo / Fundación ProAves (proaves.org)

EN **Hyacinth Macaw** *Anodorhynchus hyacinthinus* `34`

▼ **POPULATION: 4,300** | **THREATS:** **HUN**, AGR, DEV

This huge macaw has three isolated populations in Brazil (where its stronghold is the Pantanal), with occasional records from east Bolivia and Paraguay. It occurs in várzea, palm-savannas, cerrado and caatinga, where it feeds mostly on the hard fruit of a few regionally endemic palm species and nests in large tree cavities. Habitat loss and degradation, and local hunting for food and feathers have reduced populations, but the main threat has been the massive illegal trade of this species for the pet market. Although this trade is now much reduced, it still continues. Conservation initiatives are underway, including the provision of artificial nests, and many ranch owners no longer permit trappers on their land.

Photo: Philippe Bourgeat (flickr.com/photos/avidaelinda)

EN **Lear's Macaw** *Anodorhynchus leari* `48,269`

? **POPULATION: 250–999** | **THREATS:** **AGR**, **HUN**, FIRE, CLI?, ECO?

Endemic to north-east Brazil, this macaw was known to science for 150 years before a wild population was found in 1978. It inhabits arid caatinga and nests and roosts colonially on sandstone cliffs. It requires large stands of licurí *Syagrus* palms, the nuts of which are its favoured food. Major threats include habitat loss due to the impact of livestock grazing and illegal trapping. The few areas of suitable habitat that do remain are now particularly vulnerable to fire. Birds are occasionally persecuted for foraging on maize crops and may sometimes be hunted. Conservation initiatives have been successful, leading to a population increase, and the species was downlisted in 2009.

Photo: Ciro Albano (nebrazilbirding.com)

CR **Glaucous Macaw** *Anodorhynchus glaucus*

? **POPULATION: <50** | **THREATS:** AGR?, DEV?, (HUN)

Although last recorded in Brazil in the 1960s, this large macaw may remain extant as large areas of its former range (which included northern Argentina, southern Paraguay, north-east Uruguay) have not been adequately surveyed, and there have been persistent and convincing local reports. Historical records were mostly from along major rivers, although this may reflect human use of rivers for transport rather than the species' true habitat requirements. Its bill appears to be adapted to consuming palm-nuts. It is likely to have declined severely as a result of habitat loss and degradation exacerbated by hunting and trapping. Ongoing genetic studies may indicate that Glaucous and Lear's Macaws *A. leari* are conspecific.

Illustration: Tomasz Cofta

289

CR (PEW) **Spix's Macaw** *Cyanopsitta spixii*

`16,48,49`

? POPULATION: <50 | THREATS: **HUN**, AGR, SPP, ECO?, (EGY)

This small macaw was not known in the wild until three individuals were discovered in north Bahia, Brazil in 1985/6; these were subsequently captured for trade in 1987/8. A male found in 1990 had disappeared by 2000. It probably now only exists in captivity, where there were around 120 birds in 2010. However, not all areas of suitable habitat (gallery woodland) have been surveyed and there is a slim chance it remains extant. The population decline is probably due to the illegal bird trade and habitat loss. Habitat restoration is underway in Brazil and a reintroduction programme planned once conditions are suitable.

Photo [captive]: Al Wabra Wildlife Preservation, Qatar

CR **Blue-throated Macaw** *Ara glaucogularis*

`278`

= POPULATION: 73–87 | THREATS: **HUN**, FIRE?, SPP?, LOG?

Historically trapped in large numbers for the cagebird trade, the wild population of this large macaw was only discovered in 1992 on the Llanos de Mojos in north Bolivia. It has two isolated subpopulations that inhabit fragmented areas of forest in savannas where Motacú Palms *Attalea phalerata* are favoured for feeding and nesting. The threat of illegal trapping has been reduced, but habitat degradation, nest site competition and disturbance remain significant threats. Intensive conservation measures are now in place involving landowners and nest boxes have proved successful. The captive population (some of which is in breeding facilities) is many times larger than the wild population and a reintroduction programme is planned.

Photo: Joe Tobias

EN **Great Green Macaw** *Ara ambiguus*

▼ POPULATION: 1,000–2,499 | THREATS: AGR, HUN, LOG, DEV, CLI?

The nominate subspecies of this large macaw occurs in Central America (see *page 255*) and north-west Colombia. Subspecies *guayaquilensis* is confined to two widely separated populations in western Ecuador, although it has been largely extirpated. It mostly inhabits wet lowland and foothill forests but, in south-west Ecuador, occurs in dry forest. The Darién region of north-west Colombia (and adjacent Panama) holds the largest subpopulation of around 1,700 mature individuals. In Ecuador, the population was estimated at 30-40 individuals in 2012. Annual deforestation rates are very high throughout its range, even in remote areas, due to agriculture, conversion to plantations, urbanization and infrastructure projects.

Photo: David Tipling

EN **Red-fronted Macaw** *Ara rubrogenys*

▼ POPULATION: 670–2,700 | THREATS: AGR, HUN, LOG

Endemic to a few east Andean valleys in south-central Bolivia, this macaw favours dry forests, mostly at 1,100-2,700 m. Its native habitat has been heavily degraded by agriculture and other human activities and it is now mostly found in xerophytic thorny scrub. It usually nests on undisturbed cliffs and its diet includes seeds and fruit. As natural food sources have become increasingly scarce, large flocks sometimes feed extensively on crops and, as a consequence, persecution is now the main threat. Illegal nest poaching and trapping for the local pet trade, and possibly contamination by pesticides applied to crops, are also significant factors. Conservation initiatives involving local communities are proving successful.

Photo [captive]: Greg & Yvonne Dean (WorldWildlifeImages.com)

EN **Golden Parakeet** *Guaruba guarouba*

▼ **POPULATION:** 600–1,700 | **THREATS:** LOG, DEV, TRA, (HUN)

Endemic to Brazil, most records of this striking, semi-nomadic parakeet are from lowland humid forests in the Amazon Basin of Pará, although it has been extirpated from areas nearer to the Atlantic coast. Habitat loss and fragmentation due to increasing colonization and illegal logging is an ongoing threat, and has already been particularly severe in the east of its range. Once extensively trapped, this is no longer a key threat as trade is now usually within the substantial captive population. Although it is known to inhabit protected areas, its protection on intervening land during nomadic movements is also important.

Photo [captive]: Tomasz Doroń

EN **Sun Parakeet** *Aratinga solstitialis*

▼ **POPULATION:** 1,000–2,499 | **THREATS:** HUN, AGR?

This beautiful parakeet is mostly restricted to dry, semi-deciduous forests in northern Roraima state in Brazil, and central Guyana. It may formerly have occurred in Suriname. Due to high demand in the pet trade, this once-common species has declined dramatically since the 1990s and it is now virtually extinct in Guyana; trappers now travel to Brazil to buy birds for export. It is very common in captivity but it is not known what proportion of the birds are hybrids between this taxon and Sulphur-breasted Parakeet *A. (s.) maculata*, which is treated as a species by some taxonomists. Effective conservation measures are urgently needed if the few remaining wild populations of this species are to survive.

Photo [captive]: Greg & Yvonne Dean (WorldWildlifeImages.com)

CR **Grey-breasted Parakeet** *Pyrrhura griseipectus* `24`

▼ **POPULATION:** 30–200 | **THREATS:** HUN, AGR

Once known from four locations in north-east Brazil, this parakeet is now found at just two (Serra do Baturité and Quixadá in Ceará), from where it continues to be extirpated from some localities. It occurs in 'sky islands' of humid forests above 500 m surrounded by semi-arid lowlands. Very little suitable habitat remains due to extensive deforestation and conversion to coffee plantations. However, the principal threat is believed to be ongoing illegal trapping for the bird trade. Conservation initiatives are underway, including a public awareness campaign, the promotion of ecotourism, and the successful use of nest boxes on private reserves. A captive population is maintained and birds could be reintroduced.

Photo: Ciro Albano (nebrazilbirding.com)

EN **Pfrimer's Parakeet** *Pyrrhura pfrimeri* `30,31`

▼ **POPULATION:** 20,000–49,000 | **THREATS:** AGR, FIRE, LOG, HUN, EGY?

This parakeet is restricted to a narrow belt of caatinga forest on limestone outcrops surrounded by cerrado in Goiás and Tocantins states, Brazil. It appears to have a strong reliance on the forest, rarely wandering far from its edge. Deforestation in the area is continuing at a rapid rate, driven by selective logging, fires and conversion to pasture; cement companies are also beginning to target the limestone outcrops. As its range lies close to Brazil's capital, Brasilia, pressures on this species and its habitat are likely to increase. A captive breeding programme was initiated in 2001 but had failed after six years. Although it is rare in captivity, trade remains a potential threat.

Photo: Ciro Albano (nebrazilbirding.com)

EN **Yellow-eared Parrot** *Ognorhynchus icterotis*

▲ **POPULATION: 212** | **THREATS:** AGR, (HUN), (LOG), (DEV)

Once common in Ecuador, this macaw-like parrot has now possibly been extirpated due to hunting for food. However, a population of 81 birds was rediscovered in the Andes of Colombia in 1999. It favours areas dominated by Wax Palms *Ceroxylon quindiuense*, in which it feeds, nests and roosts. Habitat fragmentation due to agriculture and afforestation is ongoing, but the most significant threat currently is the poor recruitment of Wax Palms due to overgrazing, disease and unsustainable exploitation. However, an integrated conservation programme, including land purchase and community projects, has helped reverse the decline of this and other threatened species (*e.g.* Tolima Dove *Leptotila conoveri* (*page 289*)).

Photo: Murray Cooper (murraycooperphoto.com)

EN **Santa Marta Parakeet** *Pyrrhura viridicata*

▼ **POPULATION: 3,300–6,700** | **THREATS:** AGR, SPP, LOG, DEV, HUN?, (PLN)

This little known parakeet is restricted to the Sierra Nevada de Santa Marta, Colombia where it occurs at 1,800–2,800 m in humid montane forests, borders and clearings on the northern slope of the massif. Deforestation in the region has been severe, particularly since the 1950s, primarily due to human immigration and conversion of the forest to narcotic plantations. The spraying of the mountain slopes with herbicides by the Colombian authorities as an anti-drug measure has compounded habitat loss. Other threats include agricultural expansion, logging, burning and afforestation with exotic trees. It is hunted at some localities but has not been found in the local bird trade. Some conservation measures are in place, including the provision of nest boxes.

Photo: Ciro Albano (nebrazilbirding.com)

EN **El Oro Parakeet** *Pyrrhura orcesi*

269

▼ **POPULATION: 250–999** | **THREATS:** AGR, LOG, EGY, SPP?

Only a few highly fragmented populations of this parakeet are now known from cloud forest in the Andean foothills of south-west Ecuador. Its stronghold is the Buenaventura area in El Oro province, the location where this species was first discovered in 1980. It generally occurs in small flocks and breeds communally in tree cavities, and may make seasonal movements to lower altitudes. Deforestation, mainly for timber and agriculture, throughout much of its range has been severe, and mining is also now a threat. A significant proportion of the population occurs in a protected area where a nest box scheme has improved breeding success.

Photo: Greg & Yvonne Dean (WorldWildlifeImages.com)

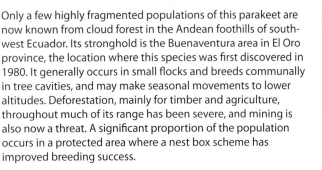

EN **Grey-cheeked Parakeet** *Brotogeris pyrrhoptera*

▼ **POPULATION: 15,000** | **THREATS:** HUN, AGR, LOG

This large parakeet occurs in the Tumbesian region of south-west Ecuador and extreme north-west Peru. It is most numerous in deciduous forests dominated by ceiba trees *Ceiba trichistandra*, but can be found in other forest types, arid scrub and on agricultural land. It feeds on flowers, seeds, fruit and catkins, and will sometimes forage in crops such as bananas and maize. Habitat loss due to agricultural conversion, logging and grazing by goats and cattle, and the illegal bird trade are the principal threats. Persecution as a crop pest may also be a significant issue. Although a few particularly important breeding areas occur in protected areas, these populations are still prone to illegal poaching.

Photo: Glenn Bartley (glennbartley.com)

EN **Brown-backed Parrotlet** *Touit melanonotus*

▼ **POPULATION: 250–999** | **THREATS:** DEV, AGR, TRA?, (EGY)

Known only from a few highly fragmented populations along the south-east coast of Brazil from Bahia to Paraná, this small, secretive parrot inhabits lowland montane Atlantic Forest from near sea level to 1,400 m. New locations have been discovered since the late 20th century following knowledge of its call. Historically, extensive areas of habitat have been lost to agriculture, exotic plantations and mining developments. Current key threats include agricultural expansion, increasing colonization and urbanization, and associated road building. It is legally protected and occurs in many protected areas in the south of its range, but further work is needed to determine its wider distribution and status.

Photo: Ciro Albano (nebrazilbirding.com)

CR **Indigo-winged** (or Fuertes's) **Parrot** *Hapalopsittaca fuertesi*

▼ **POPULATION: 50–249** | **THREATS:** AGR, LOG, SPP?

Until rediscovered in 2002 on the west slope of the Central Andes in Colombia, this parrot was only known from a specimen collected in 1911. It is restricted to cloud forest (mostly at 3,300–3,550 m), where there is abundant mistletoe, the berries of which are a key food source. Habitat loss in the region has been extensive and this species remains highly threatened by loss of forest to cattle pasture and logging. Most mature trees with natural cavities have already been selectively logged, creating a shortage of natural nesting sites. In the Central Cordillera, the species' stronghold, coordinated conservation efforts, including land purchase and the provision of nest boxes, have helped stabilize the population.

Photo: Fundación ProAves (proaves.org)

EN **Red-browed Amazon** *Amazona rhodocorytha*

▼ **POPULATION: 600–1,700** | **THREATS:** AGR, HUN, LOG, DEV

Formerly abundant in the Atlantic Forest of Brazil, the few remaining populations of this large parrot are now highly fragmented due to severe, and ongoing, habitat loss, primarily to plantations and agriculture. Its stronghold is the state of Espírito Santo, where some large forest blocks remain. Capture for the illegal cagebird trade remains a major threat, and it is also persecuted as it sometimes feeds on cash crops such as mangos and bananas. It occurs in protected areas but most provide minimal habitat protection and none are effective against poaching. A range of organizations has collaborated successfully to develop an *ex-situ* captive breeding programme.

Photo: Ciro Albano (nebrazilbirding.com)

EN **Vinaceous-breasted Amazon** *Amazona vinacea*

▼ **POPULATION: 600–1,700** | **THREATS:** AGR, HUN, DEV, (EGY)

Once widespread in the Atlantic Forest of Paraguay, Argentina and Brazil, populations of this parrot are now highly fragmented and close to extinction in many areas; southern Brazil is now probably its stronghold. It mostly occurs in forests up to 2,000 m but is also found at the transition between forest and grasslands and cerrado in some parts of its range. Further rapid population declines are likely, primarily due to ongoing illegal trade and habitat destruction (logging, colonization and plantation agriculture being the main causes). Other threats include a lack of suitable nest cavities and competition with other animals for the few cavities that do remain. It may also still be persecuted as a crop pest.

Photo [captive]: Tomasz Doroń

EN **Banded Ground-cuckoo** *Neomorphus radiolosus* 271

▼ **POPULATION:** 600–1,700 | **THREATS:** AGR, HUN, LOG, DEV, EGY, TRA

Found only in the Chocó region on the Pacific slope of the West Andes in Colombia and Ecuador, this ground-cuckoo has a very small and highly fragmented population. It appears to require continuous expanses of wet foothill forests, and sometimes associates with peccaries and mixed-species bird flocks attending army ant swarms, feeding on disturbed prey. Habitat loss and hunting pressure are increasing rapidly due to advancing colonization, deforestation, and agricultural and infrastructure developments, factors that sometimes also affect protected areas. As remaining subpopulations are predicted to become increasingly small and fragmented, this species was uplisted in 2009.

Photo: Roger Ahlman (pbase.com/ahlman)

CR **Pernambuco Pygmy-owl** *Glaucidium mooreorum*

▼ **POPULATION:** <50 | **THREATS:** FIRE, HUN, LOG

Although this owl was only formerly described in 2002, it was first located by tape recordings in 1990. It was thought to be confined to just one 4·8 km² reserve that protects a fragment of Atlantic Forest in Pernambuco, north-east Brazil but was found at another forest patch in 2001. Its ecology is little known but it has been seen in the canopy of old secondary forest and an unconfirmed report suggests that it is vocal during the rainy months of April/May. Forest loss since colonization has been severe and, despite legal restrictions, losses to fire and illegal logging continues. Searches of other potentially suitable forest fragments have yet to find any birds.

Illustration: Tomasz Cofta

EN **Long-whiskered Owlet** *Xenoglaux loweryi* 269

▼ **POPULATION:** 250–999 | **THREATS:** AGR, LOG, TRA, EGY, CLI?

Only discovered in 1976, this tiny owl is restricted to just a few isolated ridges in the East Andes of northern Peru. It is rarely reported but appears to favour the understorey and mid-storeys of very wet elfin forest and tall forest with abundant epiphytes, bamboo thickets and scattered palms and tree ferns at 1,890–2,400 m (but if local reports are confirmed, down to below 1,200 m). Although this species is legally protected, human immigration in its range is increasing and habitat loss is ongoing. The few areas of suitable habitat that remain are threatened by logging, agriculture, road construction and mining. It does, however, occur in two private conservation areas.

Photo: Dubi Shapiro (pbase.com/dubisha)

EN **White-winged Nightjar** *Eleothreptus candicans*

▼ **POPULATION:** 600–1,700 | **THREATS:** AGR, FIRE?, SPP?

This distinctive nightjar is now known from just a few highly fragmented localities in Brazil, Paraguay, and Bolivia, but is likely to have once been more widespread. It inhabits open, wooded grasslands and cerrado and, although the known populations are believed to be sedentary, may make local movements in response to fires. Habitat loss and degradation has been severe within its range, particularly since the 1950s, due to the conversion of cerrado to agriculture, and afforestation. The remaining populations are relatively well protected in reserves and national parks but wildfires, particularly during the breeding season, are a potential threat.

Photo: Jonathan Newman

EN Hook-billed Hermit *Glaucis dohrnii*

▼ POPULATION: 250–999 | THREATS: AGR, DEV, TRA, FIRE, LOG

Endemic to Brazil, this hummingbird was probably once widespread in humid Atlantic Forest but only a few tiny, fragmented subpopulations are now known. It is generally seen deep in the forest interior, particularly along streambeds with flowering *Heliconia*, but also visits ornamental flowers in areas nearby. The principal cause of this species' decline is the destruction of extensive areas of lowland forest since colonization. Recent records all appear to be from reserves but these are subject to various pressures and generally provide inadequate protection. Perhaps most importantly, few watercourses, and therefore little suitable habitat, are protected by these reserves.

Photo: Ciro Albano (nebrazilbirding.com)

EN Santa Marta Sabrewing *Campylopterus phainopeplus*

▼ POPULATION: 1,500–7,000 | THREATS: AGR, LOG, (PLN)

Restricted to the Sierra Nevada de Santa Marta in north-east Colombia, this large hummingbird is known from only a few locations. It is an altitudinal migrant that occurs in humid forest borders and shade-grown coffee plantations from 1,200–1,800 m during the dry, non-breeding, season (February to May), and open páramo up to 4,800 m in the wet, breeding, season (June to October). Deforestation in the region has been severe, particularly since the 1950s, primarily due to human immigration and conversion of the forest to narcotic plantations. The spraying of the mountain slopes with herbicides by the Colombian authorities has compounded habitat loss. Other threats include agricultural expansion, logging, burning and afforestation with exotic trees.

Illustration: Tomasz Cofta

CR Sapphire-bellied Hummingbird *Lepidopyga lilliae*

▼ POPULATION: 50–249 | THREATS: LOG, PLN, DEV, (TRA)

Endemic to Colombia, this hummingbird is restricted to a small area of the Caribbean coast (Atlántico, Magdalena and Guajira). It appears to be either rare or sporadic at its few known localities and may move locally according to the season. It usually inhabits mangroves but shows a preference for forests of Purple Coral Trees *Erythrina fusca* when they are in flower. Very little is known about its breeding biology. Infrastructure developments in the mid-1970s caused extensive mangrove die-back, and may have precipitated a population decline. Current key threats include pollution, urbanization, the cutting of mangrove and forests, and potentially the building of a large port.

Photo: Pete Morris (birdquest-tours.com)

EN Chestnut-bellied Hummingbird *Amazilia castaneiventris*

▼ POPULATION: 600–1,700 | THREATS: AGR, EGY, LOG, HUN, DEV, TRA

Formerly known from the east slope of the East Andes in Colombia, this hummingbird now appears to be restricted to valleys on the west slope at 340–2,200 m, where it is found in a variety of habitats. Natural habitats continue to be severely fragmented and degraded due to conversion to crops and the introduction of livestock. Other ongoing threats include pollution caused by mining and illegal drug production, immigration into formerly inaccessible areas, and dam construction. It also apparently suffers from subsistence hunting for food. A conservation initiative involving the local community has been implemented in one of the species' strongholds but a large part of its range remains politically unstable.

Photo: Erling Jirle

EN Scissor-tailed Hummingbird *Hylonympha macrocerca* `268`

▼ **POPULATION: 6,000–15,000** | **THREATS:** AGR, EGY

This hummingbird, males of which have a 10cm-long tail, is endemic to the Paría Peninsula, north-east Venezuela. It inhabits the understorey of montane humid forests from 530–1,200m and may make seasonal movements. In primary forest it feeds mainly at bromeliad flowers, and on their insect inhabitants, but in secondary forest it feeds on *Heliconia* and *Costus*. It also hawks insects from exposed perches. Increases in cash crop agriculture since the 1980s have resulted in uncontrolled burning and forest degradation, including the removal of understorey vegetation for coffee and cacao cultivation. Although this species' entire range falls within a National Park, enforcement measures are weak and habitat degradation continues.

Photo: David J. Southall (tropicalbirdphotos.com)

EN Purple-backed Sunbeam *Aglaeactis aliciae*

▼ **POPULATION: 1,000–2,499** | **THREATS:** LOG, AGR?, CLI?

Only known with certainty from a tiny area in the upper Marañón drainage of La Libertad, west Peru, this hummingbird inhabits the understorey of alder *Alnus* woodlands in the temperate zone (2,900–3,500m) but has also recently been reported to feed and roost in introduced *Eucalyptus* trees. However, the species' degree of tolerance of plantations (especially as breeding habitat) is not known. The most significant threat remains the replacement of alder woodlands with *Eucalyptus* plantations in order to provide better timber for the mining industry. Other threats include cutting for firewood and small-scale burning to improve pasture for livestock. A public awareness campaign was carried out in 2009/10.

Photo: Roger Ahlman (pbase.com/ahlman)

CR Dusky Starfrontlet *Coeligena orina* `45`

▼ **POPULATION: 250–999** | **THREATS:** LOG, EGY, DEV

Endemic to the West Andes of Colombia, this hummingbird is known from just two tiny forest fragments at Páramo de Frontino and Farallones del Citará in Antioquia, where the combined area of remaining potentially suitable habitat is probably less than 25km². Its ecology is little known, but it appears to be restricted to elfin forest and timberline-páramo, and adjacent tall, humid forest, and it has been seen at 3,500m feeding on insects. Habitat loss due to mining (gold, zinc and copper) is a serious potential threat but political instability in the region has, so far, prevented exploitation. Colonization and deforestation also remain significant threats. In 2005, a private reserve was established specifically for this species.

Photo: Bjorn Anderson

EN Royal Sunangel *Heliangelus regalis* `272`

▼ **POPULATION: 2,500–9,999** | **THREATS:** AGR, EGY

This hummingbird occupies a highly fragmented and small range in northern Peru and south-east Ecuador. The nominate subspecies occurs in the Cordillera del Cóndor and north-east of Jirillo, San Martín, and the more striking, recently described subspecies *johnsoni* is as yet only known from the Cordillera Azul. It is typically found in very dry, stunted forest habitats growing on sandy soils on ridges from 1,450–2,200m. It feeds mainly on the flowers of a variety of terrestrial and epiphytic plants, but is also partially insectivorous. Although deforestation has been severe in the region, the nutrient-poor soils in the areas favoured by this species do not support agriculture or cattle ranching. Mining operations and road building are the main potential threats.

Photo: Nick Athanas (tropicalbirding.com)

CR **Black-breasted Puffleg** *Eriocnemis nigrivestis*

▼ POPULATION: 140–180 | THREATS: **LOG**, AGR, CLI, EGY, (GEO), (DEV)

Although probably once more widespread and common, the only known site for this hummingbird was Volcán Pichincha in northern Ecuador. However, in 2006, a population was rediscovered in the nearby Cordillera de Toisán. It has been recorded in humid and wet cloud forest from 1,700–3,500 m, and perhaps higher, but its movements remain poorly understood and it may be an altitudinal migrant. Deforestation since colonization has been severe in the region, and remains a major ongoing threat. Human induced fires, mining and infrastructure developments are also serious threats. A few private reserves now protect a key area for this species.

Photo: Murray Cooper (murraycooperphoto.com)

CR (PE) **Turquoise-throated Puffleg** *Eriocnemis godini* 19,271

? POPULATION: <50 | THREATS: AGR?

Thought to be endemic to the Tumbesian region of coastal Peru and Ecuador, this hummingbird has not been recorded since the 19th century. Only the type specimen taken in 1850 from ravines of the Río Guaillabamba south of Perucho, Pichincha, northern Ecuador, had any locality information. It was recorded between 2,100–2,300 m in what was presumed to be an arid area. Searches specifically for this species in 1980 failed to find any birds, as native habitats had been almost completely destroyed. However, it cannot yet be presumed extinct as there was an unconfirmed record in 1976, and further searches of what is thought to be suitable remnant habitat are still required.

Illustration: Tomasz Cofta

CR **Colourful Puffleg** *Eriocnemis mirabilis* 49,271

▼ POPULATION: 250–999 | THREATS: LOG, AGR, FIRE

Endemic to the Tumbesian region, this spectacular but little-known hummingbird, first collected in 1967, is restricted to a tiny area on the slopes of the Andes in Cauca, south-west Colombia. It occurs at low densities in montane forest fragments, and at between 2,800–3,000 m at a recently discovered location. Habitat fragmentation is severe due to deforestation since colonization, and although parts of its range fall within protected areas, small-scale logging, slash-and-burn agriculture, habitat clearance for illegal coca cultivation, and the spread of human-induced fires from lower elevations are ongoing threats. Community-based conservation initiatives are being implemented, and a private reserve has recently been established.

Photo: Juan Pablo López Ordóñez

CR **Gorgeted Puffleg** *Eriocnemis isabellae*

▼ POPULATION: Unknown | THREATS: AGR,TRA

Described as a new species as recently as 2007, this hummingbird is only known from a tiny area of the Serranía del Pinche, Cauca, south-west Colombia. It inhabits the cloud and temperate forest zone, where it appears to be associated with elfin forest on steep slopes along mountain ridges, typically at around 2,600–2,900 m. The remaining area of suitable habitat, which is thought to be less than 10 km², is principally threatened by conversion to agriculture. However, illegal coca cultivation and the potential completion of a new road through the region are also serious threats. A conservation plan that involves local communities, government authorities and conservation organizations is being implemented.

Photo: Alexander Cortes

EN **Black-backed Thornbill** *Ramphomicron dorsale*

▼ **POPULATION:** Unknown | **THREATS:** AGR, FIRE, CLI, LOG

Endemic to the Sierra Nevada de Santa Marta, north-east Colombia, this hummingbird is now known from only one of three historical sites. It inhabits the edges of humid montane forest, elfin forest and páramo, from 2,000–4,600 m. It is thought to breed at the transition between timberline and páramo habitats and appears to forage in all strata, feeding on nectar and taking arthropods. Deforestation for agriculture in the region has now reached this species' altitudinal range, and extensive and regular burning and heavy livestock grazing are causing severe habitat damage. Since 2006, a programme to eradicate exotic pines and replace them with native trees has been implemented.

Photo: Fundación ProAves (proaves.org)

EN **Violet-throated Metaltail** *Metallura baroni*

▼ **POPULATION:** 600–1,700 | **THREATS:** AGR, FIRE, LOG, TRA, CLI?

This hummingbird has a small range in the Western Cordillera of the Andes in southern Ecuador. It is confined to *Polylepis* woodland, shrubby páramo and the upper edge of montane forest at 3,100–4,000 m, where it forages low down for nectar and arthropods. The widespread and regular burning of páramo grassland adjacent to forests to improve grazing for livestock has lowered the tree line by several hundred metres, and led to extensive habitat loss and fragmentation. Other threats include firewood-gathering, road construction and potato cultivation. Conservation measures implemented within one key area (Río Mazán Reserve) appear to have stabilized the population at that location.

Photo: Glenn Bartley (glennbartley.com)

EN **Perijá Metaltail** *Metallura iracunda*

▼ **POPULATION:** 20,000–49,999 | **THREATS:** AGR, EGY, DEV

Restricted to the Sierra de Perijá on the border of Colombia and Venezuela, this hummingbird is only known from old specimens taken from open páramo vegetation at elevations of between 1,850 m and 3,200 m. Native habitats on the lower slopes of the sierra are severely threatened by narcotics cultivation, uncontrolled colonization, cattle-ranching and mineral exploitation, factors that are exacerbated by the many roads approaching the sierra from the Colombian side. Suitable habitat for this species is now probably restricted to just the steepest and least accessible slopes, but security issues in the region make accurate assessments of the current situation difficult.

Illustration: Tomasz Cofta

EN **Grey-bellied Comet** *Taphrolesbia griseiventris*

▼ **POPULATION:** 250–999 | **THREATS:** AGR

Endemic to the Peruvian Andes, this hummingbird is known from only a few, highly fragmented locations on the Pacific slope in Cajamarca, and in the Río Marañón drainage in Cajamarca and Huánuco. It was probably once widespread but there have been very few records since 1950. It inhabits semi-arid country, rocky areas and deep canyons, mainly at elevations of 2,750–3,850 m. It has been observed in cultivated areas but it is not known whether it can complete its life-cycle or occur at normal densities in such areas. Threats include habitat loss and degradation due to deforestation, burning (especially shrubby areas to stimulate regeneration of pastures), agriculture and dam construction.

Photo: Pete Morris (birdquest-tours.com)

EN **Venezuelan Sylph** *Aglaiocercus berlepschi*

▼ **POPULATION:** 1,500–7,000 | **THREATS:** AGR, DEV, TRA

Restricted to the Turimiquire Massif in north-east Venezuela, the adult males of this hummingbird have remarkably long tails (14–15 cm). It inhabits humid montane forest, borders and secondary growth from 1,450–1,800 m, and appears to be less susceptible to the removal of undergrowth to grow shade-grown coffee than other hummingbirds. Ongoing habitat loss and degradation due to widespread forest clearance for agriculture has led to populations becoming increasingly fragmented. However, extensive areas of forest remain, and if new evidence reveals that the species has a larger range than currently thought, or that habitat fragmentation is not a serious concern, it may warrant downlisting.

Photo: Phil Gunson

EN **Marvellous Spatuletail** *Loddigesia mirabilis*

▼ **POPULATION:** 250–999 | **THREATS:** AGR, HUN?

Endemic to Peru, this spectacular hummingbird is only known from two tiny areas: the eastern slopes of the Río Utcubamba valley and the Cordillera del Coláns in Amazonas, and further east in San Martín. It is usually found at 2,100–2,900 m, where it favours impenetrable *Rubus* thickets mixed with alder *Alnus* trees, but also occurs in other forest edge and scrub habitats. Adult males form leks and display their tail 'spoons' to attract females. Deforestation in its range has been widespread but the species' apparent habitat preference may reduce its vulnerability to habitat loss and degradation. A protected area for this species was established in Amazonas in 2006.

Photo: Dubi Shapiro (pbase.com/dubisha)

EN **Chilean Woodstar** *Eulidia yarrellii*

▼ **POPULATION:** 800 | **THREATS:** AGR

This hummingbird is now known to breed regularly only in the Azapa and Vitor desert river valleys near Arica, northern Chile; there are no records from the nearby Lluta Valley since 2003. It occurs mostly below 750 m, but has been reported much higher and may migrate altitudinally, requiring continuous vegetation along rivers to undertake such movements. Although it feeds on ornamental plants and crops, it is comparatively rare in cultivated areas, and probably favours native flowers. Due to intensive agriculture in the irrigated valley bottoms, native habitat is confined to just small remnant patches. Conservation measures have been in place since 2004, including a habitat restoration programme.

Photo: Pablo Caceres (flickr.com/photos/pablocaceres)

EN **Esmeraldas Woodstar** *Chaetocercus berlepschi*

▼ **POPULATION:** 250–999 | **THREATS:** AGR, LOG, DEV, FIRE

Endemic to the Tumbesian region, west Ecuador, this tiny hummingbird is only found in a few severely fragmented localities in Esmeraldas, Manabí, Santa Elena and Guayas. It occurs in humid forests close to the coast from sea level to 750 m, appearing to breed at lower elevations in the south of its range between October and April before moving north-west for the rest of the year. Habitat loss has been severe in the region due to logging and clearance for agriculture, and further rapid rates of loss and degradation are expected to continue. Uncontrolled forest fires are also a major threat. However, a project at one location aims to create a biological corridor linking some areas of remnant forest.

Photo: Murray Cooper (murraycooperphoto.com)

EN **Yellow-browed Toucanet** *Aulacorhynchus huallagae*

▼ **POPULATION:** 600–1,500 | **THREATS:** AGR

Only known from the East Andes in northern Peru, with records from La Libertad, Río Abiseo National Park (San Martín) and Leymebambe, this distinctive toucan is restricted to humid montane forests from 2,000–2,600 m where it inhabits epiphyte-laden tree canopies. It may be more widespread, but little of the forest in its potential range is accessible for survey. Although deforestation has been widespread in the region, it has mainly occurred below this species' altitudinal range. However, coca-growers took over one known locality in the early 1990s. Further fieldwork is needed to improve knowledge of this species' status, distribution and ecology.

Illustration: Tomasz Cofta

EN **Speckle-chested Piculet** *Picumnus steindachneri*

▼ **POPULATION:** 6,000–15,000 | **THREATS:** AGR, LOG

This tiny woodpecker is confined to just a very few locations in two East Andean valleys in northern Peru, where it is likely to have been recently extirpated from one location. It inhabits humid montane forests with many epiphytes, and tall secondary growth, at elevations from 1,100 m to at least 2,200 m, and often moves through the canopy with mixed-species flocks. Deforestation has been ongoing since colonization and large areas have been converted to agriculture (especially coffee plantations) and pastures. With the continuing human population growth in the region, this trend is likely to continue and measures are urgently needed to control habitat loss.

Female. Photo: Dušan M. Brinkhuizen (sapayoa.com)

EN **Várzea Piculet** *Picumnus varzeae*

= **POPULATION:** Unknown | **THREATS:** AGR, WAT

274

Endemic to Brazil, this poorly known, tiny woodpecker is restricted to a small area in the Amazonian region east of Manaus. It inhabits seasonally flooded lowland forest (várzea) preferring sections with dense undergrowth, and may tolerate some degree of disturbance. More than half of its habitat is predicted to be lost in the near future due to accelerating deforestation. Its preferred habitat is also threatened with further degradation by the building of hydroelectric plants. The introduction of measures to safeguard riverine forest corridors and encourage habitat restoration is key to the survival of this species.

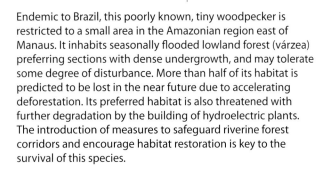

Photo: Anselmo d'Affonseca

EN **Kaempfer's Woodpecker** *Celeus obrieni*

▼ **POPULATION:** 250–2,499 | **THREATS:** AGR, LOG, TRA, FIRE?, (WAT)

Having gone unrecorded for 80 years, this woodpecker was only rediscovered in 2006. It has subsequently been found at several sites across a large range in central Brazil and, as a consequence, was downlisted in 2010. Its ecology remains largely unknown but it has been recorded from cerrado woodlands and shows a strong association with patches of the bamboo *Gadua paniculata*, where it appears to specialize in feeding on ants. The main threat is habitat loss, degradation and fragmentation due to fires, infrastructure development and conversion to crops such as soya, sugarcane and *Eucalyptus*. A potential new threat is the construction of dams for hydroelectricity.

Photo: Ciro Albano (nebrazilbirding.com)

CR **Araripe Manakin** *Antilophia bokermanni*

▼ **POPULATION: 150–700** | **THREATS: DEV**, AGR, WAT, FIRE

Restricted to a tiny area in south Ceará, north-east Brazil, this striking manakin, only described in 1998, is known from just the north-eastern slope and plateau of the Chapada do Araripe. It usually occurs in the lower storeys of gallery forest, particularly near springs and streams. Lowland habitats in the region have largely been lost to agriculture, urbanization and the development of recreational facilities, and forest fires are now a particular threat. Water-flows have also reduced significantly, possibly due to deforestation on the plateau and diversion for human use. A wide range of conservation measures have been implemented and work is underway to establish a fully protected area.

Photo: Andy & Gill Swash (WorldWildlifeImages.com)

EN **Slaty Becard** *Pachyramphus spodiurus*

▼ **POPULATION: 600–1,700** | **THREATS:** AGR, DEV, LOG

This becard is restricted to the Tumbesian region of north-west Peru and the western lowlands of Ecuador. However, there have been very few recent records, particularly from Peru and the north of its Ecuadorian range. It inhabits humid forests and shrubby clearings with scattered trees, mostly below 750 m, but sometimes up to 1,100 m, and is often seen closer to the ground than other becards. Very little suitable habitat remains in either country due to extensive deforestation, and the remaining areas of lowland forest are under severe threat. Apart from the Tumbes Reserved Zone in Peru, it has not been recorded from any other protected area that is large enough to support a viable population.

Photo: Murray Cooper (murraycooperphoto.com)

EN **Palkachupa Cotinga** *Phibalura boliviana*

▼ **POPULATION: 450–530** | **THREATS:** AGR, FIRE, SPP, LOG, CLI

Endemic to the Andes of western Bolivia, this distinctive cotinga went unrecorded for 98 years until rediscovered in 2000. In 2011, it was split from the closely related Swallow-tailed Cotinga *P. flavirostris* of Brazil, Argentina and Paraguay. It occurs along the edge of moist forest fragments on a heavily degraded, intermontane plateau at 1,400–2,000 m. Extensive areas of its favoured native savanna habitats have been lost to agriculture, and continue to be lost at a rapid rate. Breeding success is low, primarily due to predation by jays and extreme weather. Its stronghold is thought to lie around the village of Atén, where a reserve has been established and a community-based conservation project has been underway since 2008.

Photo: Juan Carlos Atienza

EN **Peruvian Plantcutter** *Phytotoma raimondii*

273

▼ **POPULATION: 670–1,600** | **THREATS:** AGR, LOG

Once widespread along the coast of northern Peru, this distinctive and very vocal bird is now known from just four highly fragmented localities. It occurs in desert scrub, riparian thicket and woodlands (usually dominated by *Prosopis* trees with some *Acacia*), up to 550 m. It feeds on fruit and the leaves of *Prosopis* and shrubs, and an understorey layer seems to be a required habitat feature. Very little suitable habitat remains, primarily due to conversion to agriculture, especially large-scale sugar and rice plantations. Illegal subsistence logging for firewood and charcoal are also significant threats. A range of conservation initiatives are underway, including a 'save the Algarrobo' (*Prosopis*) campaign that includes regeneration of grazed areas and replanting.

Photo: Roger Ahlman (pbase.com/ahlman)

EN **Banded Cotinga** *Cotinga maculata*

▼ **POPULATION:** 250–999 | **THREATS:** AGR, LOG, DEV, (HUN)

Once widespread, although probably never common, in the Atlantic Forest of Brazil, this beautiful cotinga is now thought to be restricted to south-east Bahia and north Espírito Santo, where it is confined to just four protected areas. However, there were records from north-east Minas Gerais in 2004/5. It inhabits the canopy of primary, humid, lowland forests, and is often observed along the edge of clearings. However, extensive (and continuing) deforestation within its range has led to populations becoming increasingly isolated. Historically, birds were collected for feather-flower craftwork, and capture for the cagebird trade has also been a threat.

Photo: Ciro Albano (nebrazilbirding.com)

EN **Chestnut-capped Piha** *Lipaugus weberi*

▼ **POPULATION:** 600–1,700 | **THREATS:** AGR?, EGY?

Endemic to Colombia, this dull cotinga is probably confined to just two small populations on the northern slope of the Central Andes, but was once much more widespread. Its distinctive, loud, piercing call is most often heard in the mid- and upper-storeys of primary, wet montane forests from 1,500–1,820 m, and it is sometimes found in mixed-species flocks. Habitat loss and degradation, driven by agriculture and mining, has been severe within its range, and is ongoing. Afforestation with exotic species is an increasing problem. The tiny areas of remaining suitable habitat are becoming increasingly isolated, but two private reserves have recently been established in the region.

Photo: Alonso Quevedo / Fundación ProAves (proaves.org)

EN **White-winged Cotinga** *Xipholena atropurpurea*

▼ **POPULATION:** 3,400–13,000 | **THREATS:** AGR, FIRE, LOG, DEV, HUN

This striking cotinga is endemic to the Atlantic Forest of Brazil. However, its range, from Paraíba in the north to Rio de Janeiro in the south, is now extremely fragmented and it is virtually confined to just 13 protected areas. It occurs in primary lowland and adjacent foothill forests (up to 900 m), mostly near the coast. In the northern part of its range it is sometimes seen in selectively logged forests and fragmented woodlots. It is mostly solitary, gathering only to feed at fruiting trees. Very little suitable habitat remains due to extensive (and continuing) deforestation. Many of the protected areas in which this species occurs are still under threat and inadequately protected.

Photo: Ciro Albano (nebrazilbirding.com)

CR **Kinglet Calyptura** *Calyptura cristata*

▼ **POPULATION:** <50 | **THREATS:** AGR, LOG

Endemic to Brazil, this tiny cotinga, which resembles a kinglet (*Regulus* spp.) in size and shape, was redisovered in Serra dos Órgãos (just north of Rio de Janeiro city) in 1996 after over 100 years without a confirmed record. Although two birds were seen on several days, there have been no further confirmed reports. Historically, it was probably restricted to primary forest in the Atlantic Forest foothills and, although seen in secondary growth in 1996, this habitat is probably suboptimal. Seasonal altitudinal movements are suspected, which might explain the lack of post-1996 records. Although fragments of (presumed) suitable habitat remain, severe deforestation may have led to this species becoming extinct.

Illustration: Tomasz Cofta

EN **Urich's Tyrannulet** *Phyllomyias urichi*

▼ POPULATION: 600–1,700 | THREATS: AGR, DEV, CLI?

This tyrant-flycatcher is endemic to north-east Venezuela, where it is known from the Turimiquire Massif (specimens from four localities but few other records). There is also an unconfirmed report from the extreme west of the París Peninsula. It appears to inhabit montane, humid forest from 800–1,100 m. Habitat loss and degradation has been widespread due to conversion to pasture and, particularly since the 1980s, increases in cash-crop agriculture, including the removal of understorey vegetation for coffee and cacao cultivation. An additional threat is uncontrolled burning. The species probably occurs in two National Parks, although enforcement measures are weak and habitat degradation continues.

Illustration: Tomasz Cofta

EN **Ash-breasted Tit-tyrant** *Anairetes alpinus*

▼ POPULATION: 150–700 | THREATS: AGR, FIRE, LOG

The highly fragmented populations of this small tyrant-flycatcher occur as two subspecies in the high Andes: the nominate in the Cordillera Central and Cordillera Occidental in Peru; and *bolivianus* in the Cordillera Oriental in Peru, and the Cordillera Real in Bolivia. It inhabits *Polylepis-Gynoxys* woodlands at 3,700–4,500 m, and does not appear to persist in fragments smaller than 1 ha. The main threat is habitat loss and degradation due to agriculture, overgrazing, uncontrolled fires, logging, firewood collection and charcoal production, and afforestation. These factors prevent forest regeneration and exacerbate soil erosion. This species is, however, found in some protected areas.

Photo: Fabrice Schmitt (albatross-birding.com)

EN **Antioquia Bristle-tyrant** *Phylloscartes lanyoni*

▼ POPULATION: 600–1,700 | THREATS: AGR, EGY, LOG, DEV, TRA?

This small tyrant-flycatcher has a severely fragmented range in Colombia. It occurs locally on the east and north slopes of the Central Andes in Caldas and Antioquia, and on the west slope of the East Andes in Cundinamarca, Boyacá and Santander. It inhabits lower growth and borders in humid forests from 450–900 m, but is also found in mosaics of remnant forest and agricultural land (perhaps reflecting the lack of optimal habitat). Deforestation in the region has been extensive since colonization, with logging, agriculture, infrastructure development, oil extraction and mining all contributing factors. Habitat loss is ongoing but, in some areas, forest regeneration has begun following land abandonment.

Photo: Alonso Quevedo / Fundación ProAves (proaves.org)

EN **Minas Gerais Tyrannulet** *Phylloscartes roquettei*

▼ POPULATION: 1,500–7,000 | THREATS: **AGR**, **LOG**, EGY, CLI?

Historically, this small tyrant-flycatcher was thought to be endemic to Minas Gerais, east-central Brazil, but in 2009 it was discovered breeding in Bahia. The known extent of its range had already increased significantly this century when it was found at several new localities along the São Francisco river valley and from the Jequitinhonha river basin. It occurs in a variety of cerrado forest types, and appears to prefer the canopy of tall trees. However, only tiny fragments of cerrado remain, most having been cleared for cattle ranching and agricultural development. The São Francisco basin is threatened by quarrying, and a large-scale irrigation project has already resulted in extensive areas of forest being lost.

Photo: Ciro Albano (nebrazilbirding.com)

EN **Alagoas Tyrannulet** *Phylloscartes ceciliae*

▼ **POPULATION: 250–999** | **THREATS:** AGR, FIRE, LOG, DEV, CLI?

First discovered in 1983 in Alagoas, north-east Brazil, this small tyrant-flycatcher has since been found in ten tiny fragments of humid Atlantic Forest, including in Pernambuco. It occurs at elevations of 400–550 m, often joining mixed-species flocks in the mid-storey and subcanopy, where it forages for small arthropods. There has been extensive clearance of Atlantic Forest in the region, largely as a result of logging and conversion to sugarcane plantations and pastureland. The loss of forest continues, despite local conservation initiatives, and remaining areas, some of which are protected, are severely threatened by fires spreading from adjacent plantations.

Photo: Ciro Albano (nebrazilbirding.com)

EN **Bahia Tyrannulet** *Phylloscartes beckeri*

▼ **POPULATION: 2,500–9,999** | **THREATS:** AGR, LOG, CLI?

Only discovered in 1992, this small tyrant-flycatcher is now only known from seven severely fragmented localities in Bahia and two in north-east Minas Gerais in eastern Brazil. It is only reasonably common at two of the sites in Bahia. It occurs at 800–1,200 m in the canopy and borders of montane Atlantic Forest remnants, where pairs or small family groups can be found foraging for arthropods. Very little suitable habitat remains due to logging and conversion to pasture and sugarcane plantations. Although one of the key locations for this species is a National Park, this does not provide effective protection. However, its other stronghold is a well-protected private reserve.

Photo: Ciro Albano (nebrazilbirding.com)

EN **Kaempfer's Tody-tyrant** *Hemitriccus kaempferi*

▼ **POPULATION: 6,000–12,000** | **THREATS: AGR**, DEV, TRA, CLI, (LOG)

Now only known from south-east Brazil (north-east Santa Catarina and south-east Paraná), this tyrant-flycatcher inhabits the lower growth and edges of humid lowland Atlantic Forest, appearing to favour alluvial forests along rivers from sea level to 50 m. Deforestation has been extensive, and is ongoing in the vicinity of all known sites, primarily due to conversion to agriculture and timber plantations, and urbanization of the coastal plain. The potential construction of a new road system would lead to further habitat fragmentation, and sea-level rise is a longer-term threat. This species is known from two reserves, and as recent records have extended its known range, it was downlisted in 2009.

Photo: Sandro Cardoso da Luz (ecophoto.com.br)

EN **Lulu's Tody-flycatcher** *Poecilotriccus luluae*

▼ **POPULATION: 1,500–7,000** | **THREATS:** AGR, MAN, LOG, TRA

This small, distinctive tyrant-flycatcher is known from just six localities on the east slope of the Andes in northern Peru, where it occurs in montane forest from 1,800–2,900 m. It usually favours bamboo thickets but also inhabits shrubby second growth. Deforestation in the region has been extensive due to clearance for timber and agriculture, and to secure land ownership, and at some locations all remaining forest might soon be lost. However, this species may benefit from the creation of areas of secondary growth and from abandonment of pasture in some parts of its range. A local initiative has led to the protection of one large area of forest as a watershed.

Photo: Pete Morris (birdquest-tours.com)

EN **Santa Marta Bush-tyrant** *Myiotheretes pernix*

▼ **POPULATION: 600–1,700** | **THREATS:** AGR, LOG, DEV, (PLN)

Only known from one locality on the north slope of the Sierra Nevada de Santa Marta, north-west Colombia, this large tyrant-flycatcher is found from 2,100–2,900 m in the borders of shrubby forest and secondary growth, and on overgrown hillsides. Habitat loss and degradation in the region has been severe, particularly since the 1950s, primarily due to human immigration, the conversion of forests to narcotic plantations, and the spraying of mountain slopes with herbicides by the Colombian authorities as an anti-drug measure. Although the sierra is nominally legally protected, agricultural expansion, logging, burning and afforestation with exotic trees continue.

Photo: Pete Morris (birdquest-tours.com)

EN **Rufous Flycatcher** *Myiarchus semirufus*

▼ **POPULATION: 1,500–7,000** | **THREATS:** AGR, HUN, SPP, LOG

Once widespread in the Tumbesian lowlands of western Peru, this tyrant-flycatcher is now restricted to habitat fragments in the north of its former range. It favours thorny desert, xerophytic steppes and mesquite savannas, but will tolerate degraded habitats. Habitat loss and degradation is widespread due to an increasing human population, expansion of plantations (particularly sugarcane) and overgrazing by goats. As it nests in cavities and recesses, often in standing dead wood, the widespread collection of firewood is likely to reduce breeding sites. It is also believed to predate bees around hives and is therefore persecuted. It occurs in two protected areas and uses artificial nest boxes provided for swallows at one locality.

Photo: Denzil Morgan

EN **Recurve-billed Bushbird** *Clytoctantes alixii*

▼ **POPULATION: 150–700** | **THREATS:** AGR, EGY, LOG, DEV, WAT

After an absence of 40 years, this large but inconspicuous antbird, with its bizarre bill, was only rediscovered in extreme north-west Venezuela and north Colombia in 2004/5. The lack of records may, however, be due to political instability in the region precluding surveys. It inhabits lowland and foothill forests from 185–1,750 m and is often found in dense undergrowth and edge habitats. Deforestation has been severe since colonization due to logging, conversion to agriculture and, since 1996, gold mining and narcotics cultivation. At one location, the proposed construction of a hydroelectric dam is a major threat. It occurs in two private reserves, one of which was established specifically to safeguard this species.

Photos: Luis Eduardo Urueña and Johana Andrea Borras [female - inset]

CR **Rio de Janeiro Antwren** *Myrmotherula fluminensis*

▼ **POPULATION: 50–249** | **THREATS:** **AGR**, **DEV**, LOG

Discovered in 1982 near Santo Aleixo, Majé, in central Rio de Janeiro state, Brazil, this antwren has not been seen there subsequently. However, since 1994 there have been unconfirmed reports from a private reserve, where birds have typically been seen in secondary forest adjacent to old clearings from 35–200 m, usually in mixed-species flocks and typically foraging low down in dense vine-tangles. The taxonomic status of this species remains uncertain: it may possibly be a local variation of the eastern Brazil subspecies of White-flanked Antwren *M. axillaris luctuosa*, with which it is sympatric, or a hybrid between that species and the Near Threatened Unicoloured Antwren *M. unicolor*.

Illustration: Tomasz Cofta

305

CR **Alagoas Antwren** *Myrmotherula snowi*

▼ **POPULATION: 30–200** | **THREATS: AGR, LOG**, FIRE, DEV, CLI?

First discovered in an Atlantic Forest remnant in Alagoas, Brazil in 1979, this antwren was subsequently found in three isolated forest fragments in Pernambuco earlier this century. It forages in the mid-storeys of semi-humid forest at 400–550 m. Habitat loss and degradation has been severe in the region due to logging and clearance for sugarcane and pastures, and all remaining areas of forest are at high risk of fire spreading from adjacent plantations. It is known to occur in protected areas, some of which are private reserves, but lack of effective protection is likely to result in further population declines.

Photo: Ciro Albano (nebrazilbirding.com)

EN **Ash-throated Antwren** *Herpsilochmus parkeri*

▼ **POPULATION: 250–999** | **THREATS:** AGR, LOG, DEV, TRA

Known from just two sites on the east slope of the Andes in San Martín, northern Peru, this antwren was only discovered in 1983. It appears to favour the mid- and upper storeys of humid montane forests from 1,250–1,450 m, in areas with a relatively closed canopy and many epiphytes, but has also been seen regularly at the transition between humid forests and drier savanna-forests. Major threats include habitat loss and degradation due to widespread and ongoing deforestation, principally for coca and coffee cultivation. This has been exacerbated by recent road improvements and immigration. Further survey work is needed to improve knowledge of this species' distribution.

Photo: Aidan G. Kelly

EN **Restinga Antwren** *Formicivora littoralis*

37

▼ **POPULATION: 1,000–2,499** | **THREATS: DEV**, EGY

The highly restricted range of this antwren falls within a major tourist area centred around Cabo Frio in Rio de Janeiro state, Brazil, where it occupies restinga scrub on sand dunes and other scrub vegetation on coastal hillsides. Ongoing threats include habitat loss due to real estate projects (especially holiday resorts) and the increasing presence of illegal settlers. One locality is severely threatened by the salt industry. However, in 2010 a species action plan was published, and in 2011 local authorities created the Costa do Sol State Park, which encompasses most of the species' range. It was downlisted in 2012 as it had recently been found to occupy a larger range than previously thought.

Female. Photo: Ciro Albano (nebrazilbirding.com). (See *page 37* for photo of a male.)

EN **Black-hooded Antwren** *Formicivora erythronotos*

▼ **POPULATION: 600–1,700** | **THREATS:** AGR, DEV

Endemic to Brazil, this antwren was only rediscovered in 1987, having gone unrecorded for over 100 years. It is known from just seven localities on a narrow coastal plain around the Baía da Ilha Grande in southern Rio de Janeiro state. It occurs in restinga, overgrown clearings and plantations, and woodland undergrowth. Habitat loss and degradation has been severe within its range, primarily due to the development of tourism infrastructure and beachside housing. There has also widespread clearance of native palms *Euterpe* spp., a typical tree of restinga forests, for pasture and plantations. The species is protected under Brazilian law and occurs in the buffer zone of the Serra da Bocaína National Park.

Photo: Ciro Albano (nebrazilbirding.com)

EN **Paraná Antwren** *Stymphalornis acutirostris*

▼ **POPULATION: 6,000–15,000** | **THREATS:** AGR, EGY, FIRE, SPP, DEV, CLI, MAN

Known from just a small area in coastal Paraná, Santa Catarina and São Paulo, southern Brazil, this antwren was only discovered in 1995. It is restricted to marshes dominated by Giant Bulrush *Schoeneoplectus californicus* where it forages in low, dense vegetation, occasionally visiting adjacent habitats. Habitat loss and degradation is ongoing due to constant human pressures, including fires, allotments and landfills. Other threats include land acquisition, disturbance from boat traffic, erosion, sand extraction, invasive vegetation and cattle grazing. The taxonomic position of birds in São Paulo requires clarification, as these may represent an undescribed species.

Photo: Ciro Albano (nebrazilbirding.com)

EN **Orange-bellied Antwren** *Terenura sicki*

▼ **POPULATION: 250–999** | **THREATS:** AGR, FIRE, LOG, DEV, CLI?

This antwren is restricted to severely fragmented remnants of Atlantic Forest in Alagoas and Pernambuco, north-east Brazil, where it inhabits the upper strata of humid forests at 400–700 m (although there is a recent record from 76 m). Only females show orange plumage; males are grey and black. Very little suitable habitat remains in the region as a result of logging and conversion to sugarcane plantations and pasture. Remaining forest fragments remain at risk of clearance, and are threatened by uncontrolled fires spreading from adjacent land. It occurs in some protected areas, where it is known to have declined and to have nearly been extirpated from one location.

Female. Photo: Ciro Albano (nebrazilbirding.com)

EN **Yellow-rumped Antwren** *Terenura sharpei*

▼ **POPULATION: 1,500–7,000** | **THREATS:** AGR, DEV

Restricted to the Yungas (humid to wet forests) on the east slope of the Andes from south Peru (Cuzco) to west Bolivia (Cochabamba), this unmistakable antwren is rarely seen, even in what appears to be prime habitat, and may be naturally rare. It has been recorded from 1,000–1,850 m, foraging high in the dense outer edges of canopy trees. Any areas of suitable habitat accessible to humans are being cleared for cultivation of coffee, citrus trees and, at lower altitudes, coca and tea, factors exacerbated by recent immigration at some locations. Although it probably occurs in some protected areas, this does not necessarily ensure effective habitat conservation.

Illustration: Tomasz Cofta

CR **Rio Branco Antbird** *Cercomacra carbonaria*   274

▼ **POPULATION: 6,000–15,000** | **THREATS: AGR**, FIRE

Found only along the Rio Branco and some of it tributaries in extreme northern Brazil (Roraima) and adjacent Guyana, this antbird inhabits the dense undergrowth of riparian woodland and humid forests below 200 m. Historically, some habitat has been lost due to conversion to agriculture, and selective logging and widespread fires have also had an impact. However, the primary threat is now accelerating deforestation in the Amazon Basin as land is cleared for cattle ranching and soya production, facilitated by expansion of the road network. Although this species is currently fairly common within its limited range, as its habitat is predicted soon to be lost, it was uplisted in 2012.

Female. Photo: Anselmo d'Affonseca. (See *page 274* for photo of a male.)

307

EN **Fringe-backed Fire-eye** *Pyriglena atra*

`277`

▼ **POPULATION: 600–1,700** | **THREATS: AGR, LOG, DEV**

Endemic to north-east Brazil, this antbird is restricted to just a few fragments of lowland Atlantic Forest below 250 m in north-east Bahia and Sergipe. Although it is reported most frequently from larger forest fragments, this species tolerates degraded forest and secondary growth provided a dense understorey remains. Habitat loss within its range has been severe due to widespread urbanization and conversion to agriculture and plantations, and is likely to continue. Although it was discovered at several new locations earlier this century, all remaining tracts of suitable habitat are predicted to become smaller and increasingly isolated.

Female. Photo: Ciro Albano (nebrazilbirding.com). (See *page 277* for photo of a male.)

EN **Slender Antbird** *Rhopornis ardesiacus*

▼ **POPULATION: 600–1,700** | **THREATS: AGR, LOG, CLI?**

Found only in a small area of eastern Brazil (the interior of southern Bahia and north-east Minas Gerais) this antbird is restricted to dry, deciduous forest between 100–900 m, where it requires a fairly open understorey with an abundance of lianas and patches of huge terrestrial bromeliads. Habitat loss and degradation, primarily due to clearance for cattle pasture and firewood has been rapid and is continuing. The few remaining remnant forests are often trampled by livestock, suppressing forest regeneration, and at some localities bromeliads are harvested for sale. Since 2004, a local conservation project has been underway at one location and, in 2010, a 10,000 ha National Park and a 17,000 ha wildlife refuge were established.

Photo: Ciro Albano (nebrazilbirding.com)

EN **Scalloped Antbird** *Myrmeciza ruficauda*

▼ **POPULATION: 600–1,700** | **THREATS: AGR, FIRE, LOG**

Endemic to the Atlantic Forest of Brazil, this antbird has two subspecies: the nominate occurs from south-east Bahia to Espírito Santo; and *soror* is found further north from Alagoas to Paraíba. It is usually seen on or near the ground in dense undergrowth within dry to humid forests below 500 m. In the north-east of its range, logging and clearance for sugarcane and pastures has reduced the remaining forest to isolated and fragmented patches that are now at high risk of fire spreading from adjacent plantations. Further south, little forest remains as a consequence of conversion to plantation agriculture. Although it occurs in some protected areas, this does not necessarily ensure effective habitat conservation.

Photo: Ciro Albano (nebrazilbirding.com)

CR **Stresemann's Bristlefront** *Merulaxis stresemanni*

▼ **POPULATION: <50** | **THREATS: AGR**

This unusual tapaculo remained unrecorded for 50 years until it was rediscovered in 1995 in south-east Bahia, Brazil. Despite searches, there were no subsequent records but, in 2004, a small population was found at one location in the extreme north-east of Minas Gerais. It is confined to a strip of steep, humid valley-floor forest at 700–800 m, where it inhabits dense undergrowth and forages on or near the ground. Much of this area has recently been cleared for conversion to agriculture and pasture. Although a private reserve has now been established in a small part of this species' known range, all other remaining forest in the vicinity remains virtually unprotected.

Female. Photo: Ciro Albano (nebrazilbirding.com)

EN **Marsh Tapaculo** *Scytalopus iraiensis*

▼ POPULATION: 250–999 | THREATS: WAT, SPP, DEV, AGR, EGY, FIRE, TRA

Only discovered in 1997, this tapaculo is now known from 20 localities in Minas Gerais, Paraná, and Rio Grande do Sul in south-east Brazil. It inhabits dense, tussocky, seasonally inundated grasslands adjacent to gallery forest, usually from 750–950 m. On the coastal plain it is also present in peat swamps. Habitat loss due to the construction of dams is a major threat, and has already led to the extirpation of this species from one site. Drainage schemes, sand extraction, urbanization, industrial development and road building are also significant threats. This species does, however, occur in two National Parks and one private reserve.

Photo: Lílian Mariana Costa

EN **Upper Magdalena Tapaculo** *Scytalopus rodriguezi*

▼ POPULATION: 1,500–7,000 | THREATS: AGR, LOG

Described as recently as 2005, this tapaculo is endemic to the Central Andes of Colombia, where it has a small and severely fragmented range. It is currently known from just two localities in the Huila region of the upper Rio Magdalena valley, but may also occur on the East Andes side of the valley. It is little known, but appears to favour the dense understorey of primary humid forests from 2,000–2,300 m. Habitat loss and degradation has been widespread and is continuing, even within the one protected area in the region. Forest clearance to create pasture, the trampling of vegetation by free-roaming livestock and the selective logging of hardwoods are the most significant contributory factors.

Juvenile. Photo: Nigel Voaden

EN **Ecuadorian** (or El Oro) **Tapaculo** *Scytalopus robbinsi*

▼ POPULATION: 2,500–9,999 | THREATS: **AGR**

Endemic to south-west Ecuador, this tapaculo has a very small and severely fragmented range at elevations of 700–1,250 m on the slopes of the Andes, where it is now known from Azuay and El Oro. It inhabits the undergrowth of wet forest, appearing to favour the most humid areas and to be intolerant of any significant habitat modification. Deforestation, mainly for timber and agriculture, throughout much of its range has been extensive. The species' stronghold in Azuay has been particularly severely affected by the loss of primary forest, and it has become harder to find in Buenaventura (a protected area in El Oro) where it was reportedly common in the late 20th century.

Illustration: Tomasz Cofta

EN **Paramillo Tapaculo** *Scytalopus canus*

▼ POPULATION: 250–999 | THREATS: AGR, FIRE, CLI

This tapaculo is currently only known from Páramo de Paramillo and Páramo de Frontino in the West Andes of Colombia, but may occur elsewhere in the Cordillera Occidental. It was first described in 1915 but was treated as a subspecies of Magellanic Tapaculo *S. magellanicus* until 1997. Recent taxonomic studies of this complex genus have, however, resulted in a number of species now being recognized. It is restricted to a narrow band of dense, low-growing tree-line vegetation at the transition between montane forest and páramo grasslands. Major threats include ongoing deforestation and accidental fire. Páramo de Paramillo is a National Park but poorly protected. However, a small area of suitable habitat is effectively protected as a private reserve.

Illustration: Tomasz Cofta

CR **Bahia Tapaculo** *Eleoscytalopus psychopompus*

▼ POPULATION: 50–249 | THREATS: AGR

Endemic to south-east Bahia, Brazil, this tapaculo was rarely recorded in the 20th century, but recent surveys have significantly increased the number of known localities. It occurs in the undergrowth of lowland Atlantic Forest up to 200 m, appearing to favour swampy areas close to watercourses where it forages in dense vegetation. Habitat loss since colonization has been extensive in the region and remaining habitat is highly fragmented. However, it occurs in two protected areas and at one locality conservation measures have been successful. As this species has recently been found to have a larger range than previously thought, it may qualify for downlisting pending further investigation.

Photo: Ciro Albano (nebrazilbirding.com)

CR **Táchira Antpitta** *Grallaria chthonia*

▼ POPULATION: <50 | THREATS: AGR

This antpitta is only known from four specimens taken at the same locality (within what is now El Tamá National Park) in 1955/6 in the Andes of Venezuela (south-west Táchira). The specimens were collected in dense cloud forest at 1,800–2,100 m from an area that has since been deforested. Searches in nearby areas of similar habitat in the late 20th century failed to find any birds. However, although this part of the Andes is one of the most seriously threatened by ongoing deforestation for agriculture, fragments of suitable habitat are likely to remain that have yet to be surveyed. Some taxonomists have suggested that Táchira Antpitta may be conspecific with Scaled Antpitta *G. guatimalensis*.

Illustration: Tomasz Cofta

EN **Cundinamarca Antpitta** *Grallaria kaestneri*

▼ POPULATION: 300–800 | THREATS: AGR, LOG

Restricted to the east slope of the East Andes in Colombia (east Cundinamarca), this antpitta inhabits very wet primary and secondary cloud forest from 1,800–2,300 m. It is known from just three locations, where it appears to favour areas with a dense understorey below gaps in the canopy. Large areas of primary forest remain at some localities, but habitat loss due to timber extraction is widespread and ongoing. Although clear-felling is undoubtedly a major threat to this species, selective logging may actually create the gaps that it seems to favour. Forest clearance for agriculture and grazing by goats are also key threats in some areas.

Monterredondo Road, Colombia; Jan. 2010. The first ever photograph of the species in the wild: Hadoram Shirihai; contributed from the forthcoming *Photographic Handbook of the Birds of the World*, Jornvall & Shirihai © Bloomsbury Publishing Plc.

EN **Jocotoco Antpitta** *Grallaria ridgelyi* `49`

▼ POPULATION: 150–700 | THREATS: AGR, EGY LOG, DEV, TRA

This large and distinctive antpitta, which was only discovered in 1997, was thought to be restricted to the east slope of the Andes in Zamora-Chinchipe, southern Ecuador, but has recently been found in Peru. It occurs at 2,300–2,680 m in wet, montane evergreen forest, with bryophyte-clad, generally low trees, and extensive bamboo. It particularly favours steep terrain and appears to spend most of its time close to streams. Much of this species' range is subject to immigration, logging and gold mining, and habitat loss and degradation is a major ongoing threat. One of its strongholds is a private reserve that was affected by a road-widening project in 2009/10.

Photo: Dušan M. Brinkhuizen (sapayoa.com)

CR **Antioquia** (or Urrao) **Antpitta** *Grallaria fenwickorum/urraoensis*

▼ **POPULATION: 50–249** | **THREATS:** AGR, HUN, LOG, EGY

Formally described in 2010, this antpitta is currently known from just one small area in the Páramo de Frontino massif, Antioquia, in the West Andes of Colombia. It appears to be restricted to the understorey of primary and secondary oak-dominated montane forest at 2,500–3,300 m in east-facing or sheltered valleys. Territories are largely restricted to *Chusquea* bamboo thickets. Deforestation in the region has been extensive since colonization and losses to logging, pasture and cultivation are ongoing. Mineral extraction and hunting are also potential threats. However, most of the species' current known range falls within a well-protected private reserve.

Photo: Jon Hornbuckle

EN **Ochre-fronted Antpitta** *Grallaricula ochraceifrons*

▼ **POPULATION: 150–700** | **THREATS:** AGR, LOG, DEV, EGY, TRA, CLI?

Discovered in the northern Andes of Peru in 1976, this antpitta is restricted to a small range in Amazonas and San Martín south of the Río Marañón. It is known from just three locations (Garcia, Cordillera de Colán and Yambrasbamba) where it inhabits the dense undergrowth of epiphyte-laden cloud forest from 1,900–2,500 m. It has only recently been observed in the wild. Habitat loss and degradation in the region has been extensive, particularly at lower altitudes, and this threat is likely to increase due to recent road improvements and immigration and, around Yambrasbamba, mining. This species does, however, occur in a recently established private conservation area in Garcia.

Photos: Dušan M. Brinkhuizen (sapayoa.com) and Jon Hornbuckle [inset]

CR **Royal Cinclodes** *Cinclodes aricomae* `272`

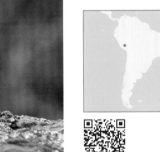

▼ **POPULATION: 50–249** | **THREATS:** AGR, FIRE, LOG

The highly fragmented populations of this cinclodes are found in the high Andes of southern Peru (Apurimac to Puno) and west Bolivia (La Paz), typically from 3,500–4,800 m. It was, however, recorded in Junín in 2008, a significant northwesterly range extension. Although generally confined to humid patches of *Polylepis* woodland and montane scrub, it was recorded in *Gynoxis* woodland in Junín. The main threat is habitat degradation due to fire and overgrazing, which destroy the forest understorey and suppress *Polylepis* regeneration. Cutting for timber, firewood and charcoal are also threats in some areas. Conservation initiatives include *Polylepis* reforestation and the creation of private reserves.

Photo: Matthias Dehling

CR **White-bellied Cinclodes** *Cinclodes palliatus* `13`

▼ **POPULATION: 50–249** | **THREATS:** AGR, EGY, CLI?

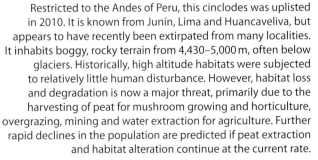

Restricted to the Andes of Peru, this cinclodes was uplisted in 2010. It is known from Junín, Lima and Huancaveliva, but appears to have recently been extirpated from many localities. It inhabits boggy, rocky terrain from 4,430–5,000 m, often below glaciers. Historically, high altitude habitats were subjected to relatively little human disturbance. However, habitat loss and degradation is now a major threat, primarily due to the harvesting of peat for mushroom growing and horticulture, overgrazing, mining and water extraction for agriculture. Further rapid declines in the population are predicted if peat extraction and habitat alteration continue at the current rate.

Photo: Pete Morris (birdquest-tours.com)

EN **White-browed Tit-spinetail** *Leptasthenura xenothorax*

▼ POPULATION: 250–999 | THREATS: AGR, FIRE, LOG

This poorly known species is restricted to a few, severely fragmented populations in the Andes of southern Peru (Apurímac and Cuzco), where it occurs in patches of humid *Polylepis* woodland at 3,700–4,550 m. The principal threat is habitat loss and degradation due to overgrazing, particularly since a shift from using domesticated camelids to sheep and cattle farming, and uncontrolled fires. These factors prevent *Polylepis* regeneration and, in some areas, are exacerbated by cutting of trees for timber, firewood and charcoal. Afforestation with exotic rather than native tree species is also a threat. A conservation project is underway to help protect native forests.

Photo: Fabrice Schmitt (albatross-birding.com)

EN **Perijá Thistletail** *Asthenes perijana*

▼ POPULATION: 150–700 | THREATS: AGR, EGY, DEV

Known only from specimens taken in 1942 and 1974, this thistletail appears to have a very small range in the Sierra de Perijá (particularly Cerro Pintado) on the Colombia-Venezuela border. It inhabits sub-páramo and shrubby vegetation at 3,000–3,400 m, perhaps favouring bamboo. Until recently, habitats at high-elevations where not prone to human pressures but recent immigration and the illegal cultivation of narcotics has left only tiny patches of montane forests on the steepest slopes. Burning, cultivation and mining are also contributing to forest loss. Since its voice is not known and the region it inhabits is politically unstable, obtaining an accurate assessment of this species' status and distribution is difficult.

Illustration: Tomasz Cofta

EN **Pinto's Spinetail** *Synallaxis infuscata*

▼ POPULATION: 250–999 | THREATS: AGR, LOG, DEV, FIRE

Endemic to north-east Brazil, this spinetail is restricted to a few highly fragmented locations in Alagoas and Pernambuco. It inhabits Atlantic Forest remnants from sea level to 500 m, and seems to favour edge habitats, where it forages near the ground in dense thickets. It seems able to tolerate disturbed areas such as coffee plantations, provided forest is nearby. Habitat loss and degradation has been severe in the region, primarily due to logging and clearance for sugarcane and pasture, and all remaining areas of forest are at high risk of fire spreading from adjacent plantations. Although some populations occur in protected areas, these do not necessarily provide a safeguard against habitat degradation.

Photo: Ciro Albano (nebrazilbirding.com)

EN **Blackish-headed Spinetail** *Synallaxis tithys*

▼ POPULATION: 2,500–9,999 | THREATS: AGR, LOG

This spinetail is restricted to a narrow altitudinal range (below 1,100 m) in the Tumbesian region from south-west Ecuador (Manabí) to extreme north-west Peru (Tumbes). It favours the dense undergrowth of dry forests and, during the dry season, has been recorded from degraded secondary forest and hedgerows within cultivated areas. It sometimes joins mixed-species flocks and appears to undertake seasonal movements. Deforestation in the region due to clearance for agriculture is ongoing, and has been particularly severe in the lowlands. Overgrazing, which prevents forest regeneration, is also a serious threat. Populations of this species are becoming increasingly fragmented but some are known to occur in protected areas.

Photo: Gary Rosenberg

CR **Marañón Spinetail** *Synallaxis maranonica*

▼ POPULATION: 6,000–15,000 | THREATS: **AGR**, LOG, EGY

This spinetail is found only in the drier areas of the Río Marañón drainage of extreme southern Ecuador (Zamora-Chinchipe) and extreme north-west Peru (north Cajamarca), at 450–1,800 m. It usually forages near the ground in forest undergrowth, and sometimes in regenerating secondary scrub and riparian thickets. Habitat loss and degradation is widespread and ongoing throughout its range due to conversion for agriculture, oil palm plantations, cattle-ranching and logging. All these factors have been exacerbated by recent improvements to the road network. The lack of recent records from the south of this species' range may be due to local extinctions.

Illustration: Tomasz Cofta

EN **Russet-bellied Spinetail** *Synallaxis zimmeri*

▼ POPULATION: 600–1,700 | THREATS: **AGR**

Endemic to Peru, this distinctive spinetail has a small range in La Libertad and Ancash on the west-central slope of the Andes. It occurs from 1,800–2,900 m, where it inhabits arid montane scrub with occasional short trees, but is sometimes found in adjacent forest and riparian thickets. It is usually encountered in pairs, foraging low down in dense vegetation and vine-tangles for arthropods and seeds. Suitable habitat for this species is being heavily degraded in many areas by livestock grazing, which removes the undergrowth and exacerbates soil erosion; scrub is also being cleared for agricultural expansion. It is not known to occur in any protected area.

Photo: Christian Nunes

CR **Hoary-throated Spinetail** *Synallaxis kollari*

▼ POPULATION: 1,500–7,000 | THREATS: **AGR**, FIRE, PLN, LOG

This little-known spinetail is restricted to extreme northern Brazil (Roraima) and adjacent Guyana. It is extremely rare and local in a narrow corridor of gallery forest along rivers below 200 m, where it inhabits dense, vine-rich, undergrowth and thickets. Although forests within this species' range were formerly remote, they are now being rapidly converted to rice plantations. The plantations receive heavy applications of fertilizers, pesticides and herbicides, and bird and fish die-offs have been reported nearby. Deliberate burning of vegetation may also be a major threat. It is predicted that further forest loss in the region will be extremely rapid.

Photo: Mikael Bauer

EN **Bolivian Spinetail** *Cranioleuca henricae*

▼ POPULATION: 1,000–2,499 | THREATS: AGR, FIRE, GEO, SPP, LOG, TRA

This spinetail occurs in intermontane valleys at 1,800–3,300 m on the east slope of the Andes in western Bolivia (Cochabamba and La Paz), only a few of which now support viable populations. It favours the understorey of dry forest and requires the epiphytic bromeliad *Tillandsia usneoides* (Spanish Moss) for nesting sites, but very little suitable habitat remains. Plantations of *Eucalyptus*, combined with the destruction of native vegetation and high grazing pressure, have led to massive soil erosion and severe landslides, and one of this species' strongholds may soon be lost altogether. Other major threats include firewood collecting and selective logging, and overgrazing and burning that result in poor forest regeneration.

Photo: Victor Garcia / Asociación Civil Armonía

EN **Scaled Spinetail** *Cranioleuca muelleri* `275`

▼ **POPULATION:** Unknown | **THREATS: AGR**

This poorly known spinetail is endemic to Brazil. It ranges from extreme east Amazonas, east to south Amapá and Mexiana Island. It appears to be restricted to the undergrowth of várzea below 200 m, but is uncommon. It often forages in pairs, feeding on arthropods, and is sometimes found in mixed-species flocks. The primary threat is habitat loss due to accelerating deforestation in the Amazon Basin as forest is cleared for cattle ranching and soya production, facilitated by expansion of the road network. This species seems to be particularly susceptible to habitat fragmentation and the narrowing of forest corridors along perennial watercourses.

Photo: Kurazo Okada

CR **Alagoas Foliage-gleaner** *Philydor novaesi* `29`

▼ **POPULATION: 50–249** | **THREATS: AGR, LOG**, FIRE, DEV, CLI?

First discovered at one locality in Alagoas, Brazil in 1979, this foliage-gleaner was subsequently found at another location in the Serra do Urubu, Pernambuco in 2003. It is confined to fragments of Atlantic Forest at 400–550 m, where it inhabits the edges of clearings, often joining mixed-species flocks. Habitat loss and degradation has been severe in the region, primarily due to logging and clearance for sugarcane and pasture, and all remaining areas of forest are at high risk of fire spreading from adjacent plantations. Although both known localities are protected, habitat degradation continues, with illegal charcoal exploitation known to be a particular threat in Pernambuco.

Photo: Ciro Albano (nebrazilbirding.com)

EN **Chocó Vireo** *Vireo masteri* `270,271`

▼ **POPULATION: 13,000–17,000** | **THREATS:** AGR, EGY, LOG, DEV

Restricted to the Chocó region in the West Andes of Colombia and extreme north-west Ecuador, this vireo is found in the canopy and borders of montane cloud forests from 800–1,600 m. It forages primarily in the canopy and often accompanies mixed-species flocks. Much of the region has been subject to ongoing deforestation but logging, small-scale agriculture and gold mining has intensified since the mid-1970s due to immigration as a consequence of a rapidly expanding road network. The cultivation of coca is an increasing threat at lower altitudes. Although this species occurs in some protected areas, these sites remain under threat from logging and local land ownership disputes.

Photo: Dušan M. Brinkhuizen (sapayoa.com)

EN **Apolinar's Wren** *Cistothorus apolinari*

▼ **POPULATION: 600–1,700** | **THREATS:** AGR, WAT, MAN, SPP, LOG, PLN, DEV, TRA

The few severely fragmented populations of this wren occur from 1,800–3,600 m in the East Andes of north-east Colombia, where it inhabits marshes with dense, tall vegetation; on the páramo it is limited to riparian habitats. It has been extirpated or is rapidly declining at many localities, and the current strongholds are Laguna de Tota (Boyacá) and Laguna de Fúquene (Cundinamarca). Habitat loss and degradation is primarily due to the drainage and burning of wetlands for agriculture. Other major threats include changes in wetland vegetation caused by siltation and pollution, and insecticide use, which is likely to reduce food availability or directly poison birds. Nest parasitism by Shiny Cowbird *Molothrus bonariensis* is also an increasing threat.

Photo: Pete Morris (birdquest-tours.com)

CR **Niceforo's Wren** *Thryothorus nicefori*

▼ POPULATION: 30–200 | THREATS: FIRE, LOG, AGR?

Found from 800–2,100 m on the west slope of the East Andes in north-east, Colombia, this wren went unrecorded between the late 1940s and 1989, since when a few birds have been found at several new localities. Its distribution is limited to areas of premontane dry forest dominated by *Trichanthera gigantea* and *Pithecellobium dulce* trees, where a dense understorey with abundant leaf-litter appears to be a key habitat feature. The principal threat is habitat loss and degradation due to livestock grazing, burning, landslides and firewood cutting. In 2008, a new site was discovered in the department of Santander and is now protected by a private reserve.

Photo: Fundación ProAves (proaves.org)

CR **Santa Marta Wren** *Troglodytes monticola*

▼ POPULATION: 50–249 | THREATS: AGR, FIRE, LOG

Endemic to the Sierra Nevada de Santa Marta, Colombia, this wren is known only from specimens taken in 1922, and a record early this century of a pair observed in a small forest fragment at 3,600 m surrounded by heavily degraded páramo. Subsequent searches have proved unsuccessful and as there are currently no known viable populations, it was uplisted in 2011. It is likely to favour low, shrubby vegetation at the transition between páramo and montane forest. However, deforestation, which has affected much of the region, has now reached this species' altitudinal range and it is likely that burning, overgrazing and firewood cutting will lead to further severe degradation and fragmentation of native vegetation.

Illustration: Tomasz Cofta

CR **Munchique Wood-wren** *Henicorhina negreti*   `268`

▼ POPULATION: 250–999 | THREATS: AGR, FIRE, LOG, SPP, CLI?

This wren, which was only formally described in 2003, has a tiny range, and is restricted to the highest peaks of the Western Cordillera in the Andes of south-west Colombia. It inhabits wet, stunted cloud forest from 2,250–2,640 m, and favours successional habitats on steep slopes with a dense understorey. The increasing severity of the dry seasons and general drying of the habitat due to climate change has facilitated an increase in human-induced fires. Human pressure in the region is escalating and deforestation within Munchique National Park, until recently essentially pristine, is now a major issue. However, in 2004 a private reserve that encompasses the majority of the species' range was established.

Photo: Nigel Voaden

CR **Iquitos Gnatcatcher** *Polioptila clementsi*

▼ POPULATION: 50–249 | THREATS: **LOG**, AGR

Only described in 2006, the entire population of this gnatcatcher occurs in the Reserva Nacional Allpahuayo-Mishana, west of Iquitos in the Amazon Basin, Peru. It inhabits humid, tall white-sand forest, but despite significant survey effort, only 15 pairs have been located, and it is becoming increasingly difficult to find. Deforestation in the region has been extensive since colonization, and is likely to have caused historical population declines. However, increased awareness of this bird in the villages surrounding its known range has led to its adoption as the official bird of Iquitos. In 2010, 29 privately owned properties (totaling 480ha) within the eastern section of the reserve were donated to the government agency that administers national protected areas.

Photo: Jose Alvarez Alonso

EN **Red Siskin** *Carduelis cucullata*

▼ POPULATION: 1,500–7,000 | THREATS: **HUN**, AGR

This attractive finch once occurred throughout northern Venezuela and north-east Colombia. It was common in the early 20th century but has become extremely rare and its range severely fragmented. In 2000, a new population was discovered in south-west Guyana. It occurs from 100–1,500 m and makes semi-nomadic and altitudinal movements (seasonally and daily). A massive population decline is due to long-term (and since the 1940s, illegal) trapping for the cagebird trade, primarily because of its capacity to hybridize with canaries. Intensive agriculture continues to reduce the extent of available habitat. Captive-breeding programmes are being hampered by disease and hybrid stock.

Male; Dadanawa Ranch, Guyana; September 2009. Photo: Hadoram Shirihai, contributed from the forthcoming *Photographic Handbook of the Birds of the World*, Jornvall & Shirihai © Bloomsbury Publishing Plc.

EN **Paría Redstart** *Myioborus pariae*

▼ POPULATION: 1,500–7,000 | THREATS: AGR, HUN, DEV, TRA, CLI?

Restricted to the Paría Peninsula in north-east Venezuela, this attractive New World warbler is found from 400–1,150 m in humid montane forest, shade-grown coffee and secondary growth, especially favouring forest borders. Habitat loss and degradation in the region has been widespread due to conversion to pasture and, particularly since the 1980s, increases in cash crop agriculture and uncontrolled burning. This threat has been exacerbated by the construction of a new paved road, which has increased access. Despite the fact that it occurs in a National Park, where the Cerro Humo area appears to be its stronghold, enforcement measures are weak and habitat degradation continues.

Photo: Joe Tobias

EN **Grey-headed Warbler** *Basileuterus griseiceps*

▼ POPULATION: 1,500–7,000 | THREATS: AGR

Endemic to north-east Venezuela, this warbler is restricted to the Turimiquire Massif on the borders of Sucre, Anzoategui and Monagas. It mostly occurs from 1,400–2,400 m, where it favours the interior or edges of undisturbed subtropical forest and natural clearings, but will tolerate disturbed forest provided it has a dense understorey. Ongoing habitat loss and degradation due to widespread clearance of forests for agriculture, particularly shade-grown coffee plantations, has led to populations becoming increasingly fragmented. However, extensive areas of forest remain, and should further evidence indicate that habitat fragmentation is not a serious concern, it may soon qualify for downlisting.

Photo: Phil Gunson

EN **Baudó Oropendola** *Psarocolius cassini*

▼ POPULATION: 600–1,700 | THREATS: AGR, HUN, LOG, DEV, TRA

This poorly known oropendola occurs only in north-west Colombia (Chocó and north-west Antioquia). Although specimens were taken up to 1945, it was not recorded again until 1991. This century, groups of birds have been seen at just two localities (the Siviru and Tipicay river basins). It inhabits humid forest and forest borders from 100–365 m, and appears to favour forests along rivers and sandy coastal plains. Its preferred lowland habitat would have been the first to be deforested as a consequence of human colonization, and conversion to oil palm plantations is now a major threat. This species is also known to be trapped for food and for the cagebird trade.

Photo: Alonso Quevedo / Fundación ProAves (proaves.org)

EN **Selva Cacique** *Cacicus koepckeae*

▼ **POPULATION:** 2,500–9,999 | **THREATS:** AGR

Known only from the Amazon Basin in Peru , this cacique was long known only from its type locality (Balta, in Loreto) until discovered in new areas in the late 1990s. It inhabits humid forested lowlands and foothills at 300–575 m, where it appears to favour habitats along the margins of narrow rivers and forages in small groups in the canopy of tall trees. As it is probably restricted to riverine habitats, it may be particularly susceptible to increasing human colonization and agricultural development. A longer-term threat is accelerating deforestation in the Amazon Basin, exacerbated by an expanding road network.

Illustration: Tomasz Cofta

EN **Mountain Grackle** *Macroagelaius subalaris*

▼ **POPULATION:** 600–1,700 | **THREATS:** AGR, LOG, ECO, DEV

Restricted to the west slope of the East Andes, north-east Colombia (from Norte de Santander to Cundinamarca), this grackle probably once also occurred on the east slope. It inhabits humid forests from 2,100–2,900 m, and shows a strong preference for areas dominated by the oak *Quercus humboltii*; the interface between wetlands and forest also seems to be a key habitat feature. Deforestation in the region has been severe, particularly since the 1960s, due to conversion to agriculture, and further losses are predicted. Mining and landslides are more recent factors contributing to habitat loss. Although some populations of this species occur in protected areas, they are becoming increasingly isolated.

Photo: Nick Athanas (tropicalbirding.com)

EN **Forbes's Blackbird** *Curaeus forbesi*

▼ **POPULATION:** 600–1,700 | **THREATS:** **SPP**, AGR, HUN

Endemic to Brazil, this blackbird is known from a few, widely scattered sites in Alagoas, Pernambuco and Minas Gerais, where it inhabits forest edge and adjacent marshy areas and sugarcane plantations. When breeding, it is highly susceptible to brood-parasitism by Shiny Cowbirds *Molothrus bonariensis*, which may now be the most significant threat. Although habitat destruction has been widespread in the region, this species appears tolerant, to some degree, of the conversion of forests to sugarcane plantations. It has been observed in the bird trade, perhaps due to confusion with the valued Chopi Blackbird *Gnorimopsar chopi*. It known from a few protected areas, but most of its range is unprotected.

Photo: Ciro Albano (nebrazilbirding.com)

EN **Yellow Cardinal** *Gubernatrix cristata*

34,35

▼ **POPULATION:** 1,000–2,000 | **THREATS:** **HUN**, AGR, SPP, LOG

This large, attractive finch was formerly widespread and common throughout much of north/central Argentina and Uruguay, with a few records from southern Brazil (Rio Grande do Sul), where it may now be extinct. It inhabits open thorny woodland (including *Prosopis* woodland), savanna, scrub and shrubby steppe, from sea level to around 700 m. Populations have declined extremely rapidly, and although they are likely to have been affected by habitat loss and degradation (due to the collection of firewood, logging, conversion to cattle pasture and, especially, rapid afforestation with *Eucalyptus* plantations), constant exploitation as a songbird for the cagebird trade remains the greatest threat. Captive-breeding programmes have been established in Uruguay and Brazil.

Photo: Roberto Güller

EN **Plain-tailed Warbling-finch** *Poospiza alticola*

▼ **POPULATION:** 600–1,700 | **THREATS:** AGR, FIRE, LOG, PLN, TRA

Restricted to the high Andes of north-west Peru (Cajamarca to Ancash), this species inhabits shrubby forest and mixed *Polylepis-Gynoxys* woodland at 2,900–4,600 m. It seems to favour ravines, but it is scarce even in optimum habitat. High-altitude woodlands are now highly fragmented and further habitat loss and degradation is predicted. The main causes are cutting for firewood and a lack of regeneration due to burning and overgrazing. Other threats include the change from camelid to sheep and cattle farming, erosion and soil degradation caused by agricultural intensification, road construction and afforestation with exotic tree species. Although it occurs in Huascarán National Park (Ancash), habitat degradation continues.

Photo: Nick Athanas (tropicalbirding.com)

EN **Rufous-breasted Warbling-finch** *Poospiza rubecula*

▼ **POPULATION:** 150–700 | **THREATS:** AGR, LOG

Little-known and secretive, this species occurs at low densities in a few scattered localities in the Andes of west Peru (Cajamarca to Ica). It occurs from 2,350–3,800 m in montane scrub and dry scrub-forest adjacent to *Polylepis* woodland and may undertake seasonal altitudinal movements. Habitat loss and degradation is an increasing threat due to agricultural intensification, a change from camelid to sheep and cattle farming and afforestation with exotic tree species. A particular concern is the rising number of goats in the species' range, and heavy grazing has severely limited tree regeneration at one location (the Zárate forest), a problem that is compounded by cutting for timber.

Photo: Juan Chalco

CR (PE) **Hooded Seedeater** *Sporophila melanops* 18,19

? **POPULATION:** <50 | **THREATS:** Unknown

This seedeater is known only from extreme west-central Goiás, Brazil, where an adult male was collected in 1823 at a lake 15 km north of Registro do Araguaia, on the east bank of the Rio Araguaia. Searches along the floodplain of the Araguaia river, most recently from December 2008–January 2009 and in July 2010, failed to produced any sightings. Although it has not been recorded for almost 190 years, as the region in which type specimen was taken has not been throughly surveyed, and habitat destruction has not been severe, it cannot yet be presumed to be extinct. Studies of the type specimen are also required to confirm the validity of this species.

Illustration: Tomasz Cofta

EN **Marsh Seedeater** *Sporophila palustris*

▼ **POPULATION:** 600–1,700 | **THREATS:** AGR, HUN, SPP, PLN

Breeding in marshes and seasonally flooded grasslands in north-east Argentina, Uruguay and extreme south-east Brazil (and possibly southern Paraguay), this distinctive seedeater migrates to winter in the cerrado of southern-central Brazil. Illegal trapping for the cagebird trade has extirpated the species from parts of its breeding range, and ongoing habitat loss and degradation, not only where it breeds but also along its migration route and at its wintering grounds, is also a major threat. Contributing factors include overgrazing, burning, afforestation, drainage, pollution and the conversion of grasslands to crops. Its year-round range does, however, include a few protected areas in each country.

Photo: James C. Lowen (pbase.com/james_lowen)

EN **Yellow-headed Brush-finch** *Atlapetes flaviceps*

▼ **POPULATION: 250–999** | **THREATS:** AGR

Restricted to the east slope of the Central Andes in Colombia, this brush-finch is still locally common in the Toche valley, Tolima, and has been recorded once in the La Plata Vieja valley, Huila (in 1967). It occurs at 1,300–2,500 m, where it appears to have adapted well to degraded forest, thick secondary vegetation (especially where vines and remnant forest trees are present) and overgrown bean-fields. Deforestation has been ongoing since colonization, but has increased significantly since the 1950s, primarily due to clearance for agriculture. An integrated conservation programme for some areas of forest within its range may benefit this species.

Photo: Alonso Quevedo / Fundación ProAves (proaves.org)

EN **Pale-headed Brush-finch** *Atlapetes pallidiceps* 38

▲ **POPULATION: 226** | **THREATS:** SPP, (AGR), (FIRE), (DEV)

This brush-finch went unrecorded from 1969 until it was rediscovered in 1998. It occupies an extremely small range and is now restricted to one location in Azuay, southern Ecuador. It inhabits scrubby areas in inter-montane Andean valleys from 1,650–1,950 m, typically favouring regenerating landslides and fallow fields. Habitat loss due to clearance for agriculture probably precipitated historical declines, but brood-parasitism by Shiny Cowbird *Molothrus bonariensis* is now the most significant threat. The species' stronghold was established as a private reserve in 1999, and the population has increased due to intensive conservation management. It was downlisted in 2011 as a consequence, but ongoing management is vital.

Photo: Dušan M. Brinkhuizen (sapayoa.com)

EN **Black-spectacled Brush-finch** *Atlapetes melanopsis*

▼ **POPULATION: 1,500–7,000** | **THREATS:** AGR, FIRE

Endemic to the central Andes of Peru (Huancavelica and south Junín), this brush-finch is restricted to just five localities. It is found at 2,480-3,400 m, and favours dry, scrubby areas in zones that have a fairly high seasonal rainfall, but sometimes occurs in adjacent transitional habitats such as forest edge. The main threat to this species is habitat loss and degradation caused by the widespread burning of regenerating natural vegetation in order to maintain available pasture and increase its extent; only steep, rocky areas and ravines are likely to remain unaffected. It is not known to occur in any protected area.

Photos: Denzil Morgan and Fabrice Schmitt (albatross-birding.com) [inset]

CR **Antioquia Brush-finch** *Atlapetes blancae*

? **POPULATION: <50** | **THREATS:** AGR?

This brush-finch was described in 2007 from three specimens collected at the same location in Antioquia in the Central Andes of Colombia. Two of the specimens are undated, but the third was collected in 1971 on the Llano de Ovejas, a small plateau at 2,400–2,800 m. On the assumption that it has similar habitat preferences to other *Atlapetes* brush-finches, it probably occurred in forest borders, and presumed ongoing threats are the conversion of forest to cattle ranching and commercial flower growing. Field surveys in 2007 and 2008 failed to detect the species. However, although there are no known extant populations, there is hope that it may persist.

Illustration: Tomasz Cofta

319

CR **Cone-billed Tanager** *Conothraupis mesoleuca*

▼ **POPULATION: 50–249** | **THREATS:** AGR, WAT?

This tanager went unrecorded after 1938, when a specimen was collected in Mato Grosso, central-west Brazil, until its rediscovery in 2003. It is now known from two localities (one a National Park), where it appears to require permanently or seasonally flooded riverside forests and grasslands. It may be nomadic like the closely related Black-and-white Tanager *C. speculigera*. The factors affecting its status remain largely unknown and populations may be naturally fragmented. However, the ongoing loss and degradation of natural habitats in the region due to conversion to agriculture (particularly soya) may be a threat, and an impending major hydroelectric project is likely to affect the largest population.

Photo: Edson Endrigo (avesfoto.com.br)

CR **Cherry-throated Tanager** *Nemosia rourei*

▼ **POPULATION: 30–200** | **THREATS:** AGR, DEV, CLI?

Endemic to Brazil, this striking tanager is currently only known from Espírito Santo, where it was rediscovered in 1998 having gone unrecorded since 1941. It is now known from just three Atlantic Forest fragments but remains extremely rarely recorded. It occurs primarily in the canopy and borders of humid montane forests from 850–1,250 m, but deforestation in this species' range has been extensive and is ongoing due to conversion to coffee plantations, mining activities and subsistence usage. However, a long-term conservation action plan is now in place and, in 2010, the local government recognised the need for conservation action by identifying ten ecological 'corridors' to reconnect remnant forest patches.

Photo: Ciro Albano (nebrazilbirding.com)

EN **Gold-ringed Tanager** *Bangsia aureocincta*

271

▼ **POPULATION: 600–1,700** | **THREATS:** AGR, EGY, LOG, DEV

This tanager is restricted to the Chocó region on the west slope of the West Andes in Colombia, where it inhabits wet, mossy montane cloud forests, especially along ridges, from 1,600–2,200 m. It is currently known from just five locations and field surveys undertaken in 2008 and 2009 concluded that there may be only 500 birds remaining. Deforestation has been widespread throughout this species' presumed former range, and all known sites remain threatened by human settlement, logging, small-scale agriculture and mining. A recently established private reserve near the city of Medellín now protects a significant proportion of the population.

Photo: Alonso Quevedo / Fundación ProAves (proaves.org)

EN **Golden-backed Mountain-tanager** *Buthraupis aureodorsalis*

272

▼ **POPULATION: 250–2,500** | **THREATS:** FIRE, AGR

Restricted to the east slope of the Andes in north-central Peru (San Martín, east La Libertad and Huánuco), this large, striking tanager is known from five localities in the Cordillera Central, but may also occur in unexplored intervening regions. It is most regularly seen at Bosque Unchog (Huánuco). It inhabits elfin forest at the tree line from 3,000–3,500 m, particularly favouring large islands of forest surrounded by páramo grassland, especially along cloud-covered ridges, and occasionally joins mixed-species flocks. The ongoing destruction of tree-line vegetation due to overgrazing and the spread of fires from adjacent grassland is a major threat, even in remote protected areas.

Photo: Gunnar Engblom (Kolibri Expeditions) (Kolibri Expeditions)

EN **Venezuelan Flowerpiercer** *Diglossa venezuelensis*

▼ **POPULATION:** 1,500–7,000 | **THREATS:** AGR, DEV, TRA

Endemic to north-east Venezuela, this rarely recorded flowerpiercer is restricted to the Turimiquire Massif on the borders of Anzoátegui, Monagas and Sucre, and the westernmost Paría Peninsula. It inhabits montane forest edge, secondary forest and second growth scrub from 900–2,400 m and may undertake seasonal movements. Habitat loss and degradation has been widespread due to clearance for agriculture, particularly shade-grown coffee, cash crops and pasture. Other threats include a proposed gas pipeline and new roads. However, some extensive forest areas remain on the Turimiquire Massif and research into this species' ecology and conservation needs is being undertaken.

Female. Illustration: Tomasz Cofta

EN **Chestnut-bellied Flowerpiercer** *Diglossa gloriosissima* 271

▼ **POPULATION:** 1,000–2,499 | **THREATS:** AGR, EGY, MAN, FIRE?

Restricted to the West Andes of Colombia (Antioquia and Cauca), this flowerpiercer was only rediscovered in 2003, having gone unrecorded since 1965, and has subsequently been found at several locations. It occurs near the timberline from 3,000–3,800 m in semi-humid/humid montane scrub and elfin forest edge, and particularly favours areas with *Polylepis* trees. The key threat to this species is habitat loss and degradation caused by livestock-grazing and frequent fires set by farmers to encourage a fresh growth for stock or caused inadvertently by tourists. However, most of the sites where this species has recently been found are relatively inaccessible and occur in protected areas.

Photo: Murray Cooper (murraycooperphoto.com)

EN **Cochabamba Mountain-finch** *Compsospiza garleppi*

▼ **POPULATION:** 270–2,700 | **THREATS:** AGR, LOG, PLN, HUN, DEV

This mountain-finch is restricted to the central Andes of west Bolivia (Cochabamba and north Potosí) from 2,700–3,900 m. It favours fairly open habitats with scattered low trees and dense, thorny bushes. Although it appears able to tolerate small-scale habitat loss and degradation, patches of native vegetation remain a key habitat feature. All natural habitats in the region have been severely affected by human settlement and agricultural conversion, and ongoing loss and fragmentation is a major threat. This species is also particularly susceptible to disturbance and inadvertent pesticide poisoning. Recent education and awareness-raising initiatives have resulted in two local communities beginning to protect this species.

Photo: German Pugnali

CR **Carrizal Seedeater** *Amaurospiza carrizalensis*

▼ **POPULATION:** <50 | **THREATS:** (WAT)

Endemic to Venezuela, this seedeater was only described in 2003 from a specimen collected on Isla Carrizal in the Río Caroní, Venezuela. This site was destroyed by a dam development but the species has now been found at other localities in the lower Caroní basin. It appears to favour spiny bamboo forest and little is known about its ecology, or the extent of suitable habitat as this cannot accurately be determined by aerial survey as much of it lies beneath the forest canopy. Although this species' range and population may be larger than is currently known, it is maintained as Critically Endangered until further evidence becomes available.

Photo: Miguel Lentino

321

Data Deficient Species

Sixty species are so poorly known that it is not possible to assess their threat status. These birds are categorized as Data Deficient until such time as more information becomes available. All these species are included in this section, with summary information on their presumed population trend, the population size (in the few instances this has been estimated), apparent distribution, and notes on status and, where known, habitat preferences and ecology. It has not proved possible to obtain images of all the Data Deficient species, although photographs are included here for 21 of them.

Data Deficient **Sombre Chat** *Cercomela dubia*. Photo: Andy & Gill Swash (WorldWildlifeImages.com).

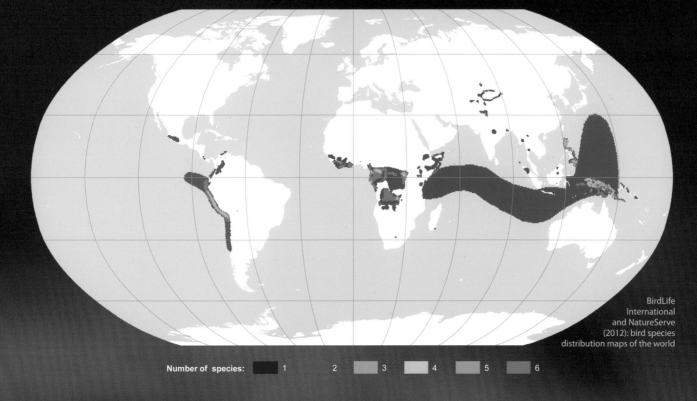

The global distribution of Data Deficient bird species

BirdLife International and NatureServe (2012): bird species distribution maps of the world

Number of species: 1 2 3 4 5 6

DD White-vented Storm-petrel *Oceanites gracilis*

= **POPULATION: 30,000** | **THREATS:** Unknown

Distribution: Tropical waters of the E Pacific; breeds Isla Chungungo, Chile; suspected Galápagos, Ecuador (Oceanic Islands).
Notes: Although numerous, only one small breeding colony has ever been found.

Photo: Pablo Caceres (flickr.com/photos/pablocaceres)

DD Markham's Storm-petrel *Oceanodroma markhami*

? **POPULATION: 50,000+** | **THREATS:** Unknown

Distribution: Tropical waters of the E Pacific; breeds Paracas Peninsula, Peru and probably elsewhere in coastal deserts of Peru and Chile (South America).
Notes: Birds on Paracas Peninsula breed in small colonies close to the sea; young fledge in November. In Chile, grounded fledglings have been found near Iquique in March/April, but the breeding sites remain unknown.

Photos: Jon Hornbuckle

DD Matsudaira's Storm-petrel *Oceanodroma matsudairae*

= **POPULATION: 30,000** | **THREATS:** Unknown

Distribution: Breeds Volcano Islands off southern Japan, and probably elsewhere, ranging as far west as the coast of East Africa (Oceanic Islands).
Notes: Known breeding sites have been little visited, but it is thought to have been extirpated from one island, perhaps due to predation by rats.

Photo: Alan Tate (aabirdpix.com)

DD Ringed Storm-petrel *Oceanodroma hornbyi*

= **POPULATION: 30,000** | **THREATS:** Unknown

Distribution: Coastal Peru and Chile; breeding grounds unknown (South America).
Notes: Thousands have been reported at sea. It may breed on offshore islands or mainland cliffs but the Atacama Desert is the most likely location.

Photo: Dušan M. Brinkhuizen (sapayoa.com)

DD Chestnut-shouldered Goshawk *Erythrotriorchis buergersi*

= **POPULATION:** Unknown | **THREATS:** Unknown

Distribution: New Guinea (Asia and Australasia).
Notes: Rare and little known; recorded from forest at 450–1,580 m.

DD Mayr's Forest-rail *Rallina mayri*

= **POPULATION:** Unknown | **THREATS:** Unknown

Distribution: N New Guinea (Asia and Australasia).
Notes: Known from only a few specimens and although not recorded since the 1960s is probably locally common in montane forest at 1,100–2,000 m in isolated mountain ranges.

White-vented Storm-petrel *Oceanites gracilis.*

Markham's Storm-petrel *Oceanodroma markhami*

Matsudaira's Storm-petrel *Oceanodroma matsudairae.*

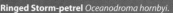
Ringed Storm-petrel *Oceanodroma hornbyi.*

Brown-banded Rail *Lewinia mirifica.*

Luzon Buttonquail *Turnix worcesteri.*

Somali Pigeon *Columba oliviae.*

Lesser Masked-owl *Tyto sororcula.*

DD **Brown-banded Rail** *Lewinia mirifica*

? **POPULATION:** Unknown | **THREATS:** HUN

Distribution: Luzon and Samar, Philippines (Asia).
Notes: Rare, little known and may be endemic but never proven to breed. It may be migratory. The only known threat is hunting.

Photo: Des Allen

DD **Colombian Crake** *Neocrex colombiana*

? **POPULATION:** Unknown | **THREATS:** Unknown

Distribution: N & NW Colombia; W Ecuador; Panama (Central and South America). **Notes:** Two subspecies are described: the nominate is rare across N Colombia and Ecuador; and *ripleyi* is known only from specimens taken in Panama and NW Colombia. It occurs in wetlands and overgrown forest edge up to 2,100 m and is possibly overlooked.

DD **Luzon Buttonquail** *Turnix worcesteri*

? **POPULATION:** Unknown | **THREATS:** HUN?

Distribution: Luzon and Philippines (Asia).
Notes: Virtually all records have derived from bird-catchers and are assumed to be intra-island migrants.

Photo: Arnel B. Telesforo

DD **Somali Pigeon** *Columba oliviae*

= **POPULATION:** Unknown | **THREATS:** INV?

Distribution: N & NE Somalia (Africa).
Notes: May still be locally common in rocky coastal areas but there are a lack of recent survey data.

Photo: Nik Borrow (birdquest-tours.com)

DD **Lesser Masked-owl** *Tyto sororcula* `21`

? **POPULATION:** Unknown | **THREATS:** AGR?, LOG?, IND?

Distribution: North and north-east Somalia (Africa).
Notes: May still be locally common in rocky coastal areas but there are a lack of recent survey data.

Photo: Denzil Morgan

DD **Nicobar Scops-owl** *Otus alius*

= **POPULATION:** Unknown | **THREATS:** Unknown

Region: Asia.
Distribution: Nicobar Islands, India.
Notes: Known from two specimens and a bird trapped in 2003. Possibly inhabits coastal forest.

DD **Maned Owl** *Jubula lettii*

= | **POPULATION:** Unknown | **THREATS:** Unknown

Distribution: Liberia, Côte d'Ivoire; Ghana (old record); Cameroon; Equatorial Guinea; Gabon; Congo; Democratic Republic of Congo (Africa). **Notes:** Poorly known; recorded from 14 sites, all with tall, closed-canopy rainforest.

DD **Papuan Hawk-owl** *Uroglaux dimorpha*

= | **POPULATION:** Unknown | **THREATS:** Unknown

Distribution: New Guinea (Asia and Australasia). **Notes:** Recorded from nine sites in the 1980s and 1990s; occurs mainly in lowland forest, occasionally to 1,500 m.

DD **Cayenne Nightjar** *Caprimulgus maculosus*

? | **POPULATION:** Unknown | **THREATS:** Unknown

Distribution: Rivière Cockioco, French Guiana (South America). **Notes:** Known from just one specimen collected in 1917.

DD **Vaurie's Nightjar** *Caprimulgus centralasicus*

? | **POPULATION:** Unknown | **THREATS:** Unknown

Distribution: Xinjiang, W China (Asia). **Notes:** Known from just one specimen collected in 1929.

DD **Starry Owlet-nightjar** *Aegotheles tatei*

`21`

= | **POPULATION:** Unknown | **THREATS:** LOG?

Distribution: W Papua New Guinea (Australasia). **Notes:** Known from four specimens and a few field reports (the first in 1962, but more often this century) from lowland riverine rainforest close to hills. Although large areas of forest have been logged or cleared, extensive areas still remain intact.

DD **Wallace's Owlet-nightjar** *Aegotheles wallacii*

? | **POPULATION:** Unknown | **THREATS:** Unknown

Distribution: New Guinea (Asia and Australasia). **Notes:** Known from a few specimens and recent observations; recorded from hill-forest below 1,540 m.

DD **Spot-fronted Swift** *Cypseloides cherriei*

? | **POPULATION:** Unknown | **THREATS:** Unknown

Distribution: C & SE Costa Rica; Ecuador; N Venezuela; Colombia (Central and South America). **Notes:** Known only from a few specimens and sight records in montane regions, but likely under-recorded; breeding only proven at four locations. Suitable habitat is probably still relatively intact.

DD **White-fronted Swift** *Cypseloides storeri*

? | **POPULATION:** Unknown | **THREATS:** Unknown

Distribution: SW Mexico (North America). **Notes:** Known only from six specimens and a few sight records from montane forest with waterfalls and ravines at 1,500–2,500 m.

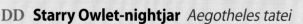

Spot-fronted Swift *Cypseloides cherriei*.
Photo: Nigel Voaden.

Starry Owlet-nightjar *Aegotheles tatei*.
Photo: Jon Hornbuckle.

DD Whitehead's Swiftlet *Collocalia whiteheadi*

▼ POPULATION: Unknown | THREATS: AGR?, LOG?

Distribution: Luzon and Mindanao, Philippines (Asia).
Notes: Two subspecies described: the nominate from Luzon, where not recorded since 1895, and *origenis* from Mindanao. Occurs over forested mountains and may nest on cliffs or in hollow trees. May be migratory.

DD Mayr's Swiftlet *Collocalia orientalis*

? POPULATION: Unknown | THREATS: Unknown

Distribution: Guadalcanal, Solomon Islands; New Ireland and Bougainville, Papua New Guinea (Australasia).
Notes: Known from three specimens, collected in 1927, 1963 & 1979.

DD Papuan Swiftlet *Collocalia papuensis*

= POPULATION: Unknown | THREATS: Unknown

Distribution: New Guinea (Asia and Australasia).
Notes: Known from only a few specimens.

DD Fernando Pó Swift *Apus sladeniae*

? POPULATION: Unknown | THREATS: Unknown

Distribution: W Cameroon; SE Nigeria; Equatorial Guinea; Angola? (Africa).
Notes: Known from a few records; most likely a mountain species.

DD Coppery Thorntail *Discosura letitiae*

? POPULATION: Unknown | THREATS: Unknown

Distribution: Bolivia? (South America).
Notes: Known from two specimens, simply labelled as from 'Bolivia', collected prior to 1852.

DD Bogotá Sunangel *Heliangelus zusii*

? POPULATION: Unknown | THREATS: Unknown

Distribution: E or C Andes of Colombia? (South America).
Notes: Known from a single trade-skin purchased in Bogotá in 1909.

DD Little Paradise-kingfisher *Tanysiptera hydrocharis*

? POPULATION: Unknown | THREATS: LOG?

Distribution: Aru Islands and the Trans-Fly region of S New Guinea (Asia and Australasia). **Notes:** Recent records are only from New Guinea, where it favours undisturbed seasonally flooded alluvial lowland forest that may be threatened by logging.

DD Blue-black Kingfisher *Todiramphus nigrocyaneus*

▼ POPULATION: Unknown | THREATS: LOG?, WAT?

Distribution: New Guinea (Asia and Australasia).
Notes: A rare and little-known species with very few recent records; associated with streams, swamps and ponds in forest to 600 m.

Whitehead's Swiftlet *Collocalia whiteheadi*.
Photo: Jon Hornbuckle.

Little Paradise-kingfisher *Tanysiptera hydrocharis*.
Photo: Pete Morris (birdquest-tours.com).

DD White-chested Tinkerbird *Pogoniulus makawai*

? POPULATION: Unknown | THREATS: Unknown

Distribution: NW Zambia (Africa).
Notes: Known from just one specimen collected in 1964.

DD Yellow-footed Honeyguide *Melignomon eisentrauti*

▼ POPULATION: Unknown | THREATS: Unknown

Distribution: Liberia; Sierra Leone; Côte d'Ivoire; Ghana; Nigeria; Cameroon (two records) (Africa).
Notes: Rare and very poorly known; occurs in mid-strata and forest canopy, mainly in lowland forest, occasionally to 1,500 m.

DD Tagula Honeyeater *Caprimulgus maculosus*

? POPULATION: Unknown | THREATS: Unknown

Distribution: Tagula, Louisiade Archipelago, Papua New Guinea (Australasia).
Notes: Poorly known; probably inhabits forests and forest edge in the lowlands, to 800 m.

DD White-chinned Myzomela *Myzomela albigula*

? POPULATION: Unknown | THREATS: Unknown

Distribution: Louisiade Archipelago, Papua New Guinea (Australasia).
Notes: A little-known species that occurs on a number of small islands that have not been visited by ornithologists in recent years.

Obscure Berrypecker *Melanocharis arfakiana*.
Photo: Nik Borrow (birdquest-tours.com).

DD Obscure Berrypecker *Melanocharis arfakiana*

= POPULATION: Unknown | THREATS: INV?

Distribution: New Guinea (Asia and Australasia).
Notes: A montane species, occurring from 640–1,000 m; appears to tolerate secondary habitats. It is inconspicuous and easily over-looked but has recently been discovered in widely scattered sites.

DD Papuan Whipbird *Androphobus viridis*

= POPULATION: Unknown | THREATS: Unknown

Distribution: New Guinea, mostly Papua (Asia and Australasia).
Notes: Known from five sites in montane forest at 1,400–2,700 m.

DD Blüntschli's Vanga *Hypositta perdita*

? POPULATION: Unknown | THREATS: Unknown

Distribution: SE Madagascar (Africa).
Notes: Known only from two specimens collected in primary forest and grassland in 1931.

DD Tagula Butcherbird *Cracticus louisiadensis*

= POPULATION: Unknown | THREATS: Unknown

Distribution: Tagula Island, Louisiade Archipelago, Papua New Guinea (Australasia).
Notes: Poorly known; probably occurs in forest edge habitats.

Williams's Lark *Mirafra williamsi*.
Photo: Adam Riley (rockjumperbirding.com).

DD **Eastern Wattled Cuckooshrike** *Campephaga oriolina*

▼ POPULATION: Unknown | THREATS: AGR?, LOG?

Distribution: S Cameroon; Gabon, Congo; SW Central African Republic; E & NE Democratic Republic of Congo; SE Nigeria (Africa).
Notes: Uncommon to rare in forest canopy at low altitudes.

DD **Snow Mountain Robin** *Petroica archboldi*

▼ POPULATION: Unknown | THREATS: Unknown

Distribution: Papua, Indonesia (Asia).
Notes: Confined to rocky habitats above the tree line, 3,850–4,150 m, on the Snow Mountains; poorly known, although apparently not uncommon.

DD **African River-martin** *Pseudochelidon eurystomina*

= POPULATION: Unknown | THREATS: Unknown

Distribution: Democratic Republic of Congo; Congo (Africa).
Notes: Although recorded regularly, its distribution and movements remain very poorly known; nests in holes dug into sandbars.

DD **Red Sea Swallow** *Hirundo perdita*

= POPULATION: Unknown | THREATS: Unknown

Distribution: E Sudan (Africa).
Notes: Known only from one specimen: a bird found dead in 1984.

DD **Williams's Lark** *Mirafra williamsi*

= POPULATION: Unknown | THREATS: Unknown

Distribution: N Kenya (Africa). **Notes:** Found in two disjunct populations, one in the Didi Galgalla Desert (north of Marsabit) and the second between Isiolo and Garba Tula. It inhabits rocky desert with low-growing shrubs but is otherwise little known.

DD **Friedmann's Lark** *Mirafra pulpa*

▼ POPULATION: Unknown | THREATS: Unknown

Distribution: Kenya; Ethiopia (once); Tanzania (Africa).
Notes: Poorly known and rarely seen. It appears to prefer fairly dense grassland with bushes, possibly avoiding drier areas, and may be migratory.

DD **Obbia Lark** *Spizocorys obbiensis*

▼ POPULATION: Unknown | THREATS: Unknown

Distribution: SE Somalia (Africa).
Notes: Restricted to a narrow strip of vegetated coastal dunes along about 570 km of coast.

DD **Long-tailed Pipit** *Anthus longicaudatus*

= POPULATION: Unknown | THREATS: Unknown

Distribution: Zambia; Botswana; South Africa (migrant?) and possibly Zimbabwe (Africa). **Notes:** Very poorly known. In the non-breeding season, found in short dry grassland including urban parks and playing fields. Breeding habitat unknown but may be floodplains in Zimbabwe.

Friedmann's Lark *Mirafra pulpa*.
Photo: Nik Borrow (birdquest-tours.com).

Long-tailed Pipit *Anthus longicaudatus*.
hoto: Adam Riley (rockjumperbirding.com).

DD **Tana River Cisticola** *Cisticola restrictus*

? POPULATION: Unknown | THREATS: Unknown

Distribution: W Kenya (Africa).
Notes: Not recorded since 1972, despite surveys; occurred in sandy *Acacia* bushland below 500 m.

DD **Slender-tailed Cisticola** *Cisticola melanurus*

= POPULATION: Unknown | THREATS: Unknown

Distribution: NE Angola; SE Democratic Republic of Congo (Africa).
Notes: Poorly known; from graasy areas in climax Miombo woodland.

DD **Blue-wattled Bulbul** *Pycnonotus nieuwenhuisii*

= POPULATION: Unknown | THREATS: Unknown

Distribution: NE Kalimantan and Sumatra, Indonesia; Brunei (Asia).
Notes: Known from two specimens, and five sight records in 1992; recorded from secondary scrub and lowland tropical rainforest.

DD **Large-billed Reed-warbler** *Acrocephalus orinus*

? POPULATION: Unknown | THREATS: Unknown

Distribution: Probably breeds NE Afghanistan and Badakshan, Tajikistan (Asia); wintering area unknown. **Notes:** Likely breeding sites only found in 2008/9; possibly a long-distance migrant. Very similar to other *Acrocephalus* spp. and possibly overlooked (taxonomic status only recently confirmed).

DD **Short-billed Crombec** *Sylvietta philippae*

= POPULATION: Unknown | THREATS: Unknown

Distribution: NW & W Somalia and adjacent SE Ethiopia (Africa).
Notes: Found in semi-desert from 300–900 m and although fairly common is poorly known.

DD **Black-browed Babbler** *Malacocincla perspicillata*

▼ POPULATION: Unknown | THREATS: INV?

Distribution: South Kalimantan, Indonesia? (Asia).
Notes: Known from a single specimen of uncertain provenance probably collected in the 1840s.

DD **Visayan Miniature-babbler** *Micromacronus leytensis*

? POPULATION: Unknown | THREATS: Unknown

Distribution: Samar, Biliran and Leyte in the Eastern Visayas, Philippines (Asia). **Notes:** Recently split and very poorly known; inhabits undergrowth and canopy of montane broadleaf evergreen forest and forest edge at around 500 m.

DD **Mindanao Miniature-babbler** *Micromacronus sordidus*

▼ POPULATION: Unknown | THREATS: Unknown

Distribution: Mindanao, Philippines (Asia). **Notes:** Recently split from *M. leytensis*; poorly known with few recent records; inhabits undergrowth and canopy of broadleaf evergreen forest and forest edge at 600–1,670 m.

Emerald Starling *Coccycolius iris*.
Photo: David Monticelli (pbase.com/david_monticelli).

Large-billed Reed-warbler *Acrocephalus orinus*.
Photo: Raffael Ayé.

Tessmann's Flycatcher *Muscicapa tessmanni*.
Photo: Nik Borrow (birdquest-tours.com).

Sombre Chat *Cercomela dubia*.
Photo: János Oláh (birdquest-tours.com).

Sillem's Mountain-finch *Leucosticte sillemi*.
Photo: Yann Musika.

DD **White-throated White-eye** *Zosterops meeki*

▼ POPULATION: Unknown | THREATS: Unknown

Distribution: Tagula Island, Louisiade Archipelago, Papua New Guinea (Australasia).
Notes: Very little known and not recorded during a visit in 1992; but probably a species of lowland forest and forest edge to 300 m.

DD **Emerald Starling** *Coccycolius iris*

? POPULATION: Unknown | THREATS: HUN?

20

Distribution: W & SE Guinea; Sierra Leone and W-C Côte d'Ivoire.
Notes: Appears to be a species of open country or forest edge. Large numbers may still be captured for the bird trade but effects on the wild population have not been assessed.

DD **Sombre Chat** *Cercomela dubia*

? POPULATION: Unknown | THREATS: Unknown

Distribution: E-C Ethiopia; Somalia (Africa).
Notes: Rare and little known; only one old record from Somalia. Seems to favour arid rocky areas and lava flows at 750–1,800 m.

DD **Tessmann's Flycatcher** *Muscicapa tessmanni*

? POPULATION: Unknown | THREATS: AGR?, LOG?

Distribution: Sierra Leone; Liberia; Côte d'Ivoire; Ghana; Cameroon; NE Democratic Republic of Congo; mainland Equatorial Guinea; Nigeria (not recently) (Africa). **Notes:** Usually a primary forest species; wide-ranging but only locally common. Similar to Dusky-blue Flycatcher *M. comitata*.

DD **Lake Lufira Weaver** *Ploceus ruweti*

? POPULATION: Unknown | THREATS: Unknown

Distribution: S Democratic Republic of Congo (Africa).
Notes: Occurs only in swamps bordering Lake Lufira; observed in good numbers in recent years.

DD **Black-lored Waxbill** *Estrilda nigriloris*

= POPULATION: Unknown | THREATS: Unknown

Distribution: S Democratic Republic of Congo (Africa).
Notes: Rare and little known: not seen since 1950, when recorded from grassy plains.

DD **Grimwood's Longclaw** *Macronyx grimwoodi*

= POPULATION: Unknown | THREATS: Unknown

Distribution: SW Democratic Republic of Congo; C & E Angola; NW Zambia (Africa).
Notes: Little known, locally common in grassland at 800–1,500 m.

DD **Sillem's Mountain-finch** *Leucosticte sillemi*

= POPULATION: Unknown | THREATS: Unknown

Distribution: Xinjiang and Qinghai, W China (Asia). **Notes:** Known from only two specimens collected on a barren plateau at 5,125 m in Xinjiang in 1929 until rediscovered 1,500 km to the east in Qinghai in 2012.

Acknowledgements

The production of this book would not have been possible without the generous support of so many people. An astonishing 877 photographs are featured, covering 515 of the 590 species that are currently categorized as Critically Endangered, Endangered or Extinct in the Wild and 21 of the Data Deficient species. This collection of images represents the cumulative work of 321 photographers, all of whom kindly donated their images to the project. The contribution of every photographer is gratefully acknowledged and their name appears next to each of their images wherever they appear in the book. All the photographers whose work is featured are also listed in alphabetical order by surname below, together with details of their website where this has been requested:

Omar Fadhil Abdulrahman
 (natureiraq.org/site/en)
Roger Ahlman (pbase.com/ahlman)
Al Wabra Wildlife Preservation, Qatar
Ciro Albano (nebrazilbirding.com)
Des Allen
Jose Alvarez Alonso
Ambrosini
Bjorn Anderson
Rich Andrews (cvlbirding.co.uk)
Rafael V. Arvelo C. (rafaelarvelo.com)
Asociación Civil Armonía
Nick Athanas (tropicalbirding.com)
Juan Carlos Atienza
Raffael Ayé
Ignacio Azocar (chileaves.com)
Csaba Barkóczi
Glenn Bartley (glennbartley.com)
Dolora Batchelor
Mikael Bauer
Kurt W. Baumgartner
Bill Beckon
Soner Bekir
Phil Bender
Daniel Bengtsson
Gavin Bieber (wings.com)
K. David Bishop
Jeff Blincow
Anders Blomdahl
Alejandro Boneta (aboneta.com)
Johana Andrea Borras
Nik Borrow (birdquest-tours.com)
Philippe Bourgeat
 (flickr.com/photos/avidaelinda)
Chris Bowden/RSPB
David Boyle
Dayne Braine (batisbirdingsafaris.com)
James H. Breeden Jr.
Tom Brereton
Nick Brickle
Dušan M. Brinkhuizen (sapayoa.com)
Sávio Freire Bruno (uff.br/biodiversidade)
Michael Buckham
Marie-Hélène Burle
Thomas M. Butynski & Yvonne A. de Jong
Eduardo Lugo Cabrera
 (wildlifeconnection.com)
Pablo Caceres
 (flickr.com/photos/pablocaceres)
Sarah Caceres & Jean-Noël Jasmin

Peter Candido (aviphile.smugmug.com)
Juan Manuel Cardona
 (pbase.com/caranpaima/nature)
Apolinario B. Cariño
Juan Chalco
Graeme Chapman (graemechapman.com.au)
Roger & Liz Charlwood
 (WorldWildlifeImages.com)
Danielle Chelewiak
Stefan Cherrug (cherrug.se)
Chaiwat Chinuparawat
Peter Coe
Callan Cohen & Deirdre Vrancken
 (birdingafrica.com)
Chris Collins
Murray Cooper (murraycooperphoto.com)
John Corder
Alexander Cortes
Lílian Mariana Costa
Bill Coster (billcoster.com)
Sandro Cardoso da Luz (ecophoto.com.br)
Tony Crittenden (tcphotos.net)
Anselmo d'Affonseca
Mike Danzenbaker (avesphoto.com)
Mark Darlaston
Reg Daves
Greg & Yvonne Dean
 (WorldWildlifeImages.com)
Matthias Dehling
Bram Demeulemeester
 (birdguidingphilippines.com)
Jim Denny
Paul F. Donald
Tomasz Doroń
Michael Dryden
Joseph Duff (operationmigration.org)
Guy Dutson
Michael Dvorak
Jonathan C. Eames
Kevin Easley (costaricagateway.com)
James Eaton (birdtourasia.com)
Tim Edelsten
Knut Eisermann (cayaya-birding.com)
Whaldener Endo
Edson Endrigo (avesfoto.com.br)
Gunnar Engblom (Kolibri Expeditions)
Jens & Hanne Eriksen
David Erterius
Mandy Etpison (necomarine.com)
Trevor Feltham
 (surfbirds.com/blog/albums/tf1044)

Darío Fernández
 (rovingbiologist.blogspot.com)
Diego Punta Fernández
Fletcher & Baylis (wildsidephotography.ca)
Michael & Patricia Fogden (
fogdenphotos.com)
Simon Fordham (naturepix.co.nz)
Joe Fuhrman
Fundación ProAves (proaves.org)
Devesh Gadhvi
Nicolas Gaidet & Thomas Gerdil
Julio C. Gallardo
Victor Garcia / Asociación Civil Armonía
Steve Garvie
Chris Gomersall
Gouni A/Thétys Editions/SOP Manu
Bruno Granados
Manuel Grosselet (tierradeaves.com)
Gregory Guida (gguida.com)
Roberto Güller
Phil Gunson
Marc Guyt (agami.nl)
Roy de Haas (agami.nl)
Paul Hackett
Don Hadden (donhadden.com)
Martin Hale (martinhalewildlifephoto.com)
Markus Handschuh (accb-cambodia.org)
Simon Harrap (birdquest-tours.com)
Johan Heggen (bird-picture.eu)
Peter Hodum (oikonos.org)
John & Jemi Holmes (johnjemi.hk)
Jon Hornbuckle
Steve N. G. Howell
Hu Jinglin (birdnet.cn)
Huajin Sun (birdnet.cn)
Hung Le Manh
Rob Hutchinson (birdtourasia.com)
Robert E. Hyman
Jack Jeffrey (JackJeffreyphoto.com)
Gary Jenkins
Anthony Jeremiah
Erling Jirle
Mark Sheridan Johnson
Leif Jonasson
Paul Jones
Dr Jayesh K. Joshi
Jonathan Kearvell
Aidan G. Kelly
Mohanram R. Kemparaju (kemparaju.com)
Kanit Khanikul

Robby Kohley
Maxim Koshkin
Navendu Laad
Tim Laman (timlaman.com)
Myles Lamont / Hancock Wildlife
  Research Center
Jonas Langbråten (langbraten.com)
Thiago Orsi Laranjeiras
Javier Lascurain
Greg Lasley (greglasley.net)
Peter LaTourrette (birdphotography.com)
Marcus Lawson
Ch'ien C. Lee (wildborneo.com.my)
Vincent Legendre
Valérie Lehouck
Miguel Lentino
A. P. Leventis
Patrick L'Hoir (bird-picture.eu)
Markus Lilje (rockjumperbirding.com)
Rich Lindie
Peiqi Liu (birdnet.cn)
Ken Logan
Maxime Loubon
Roy W. Lowe
James C. Lowen (pbase.com/james_lowen)
Luu Thi Thanh Lan / Vietnam Birding
Mark Alexander MacDonald
Jean-Florent Mandelbaum
Miguel Ángel Sicilia Manzo
Luiz Cláudio Marigo
Charlie Marsh
Clement Francis Martin (clementfrancis.com)
David & Nancy Massie
Luís Mazariegos
Ian R. McHenry
Shane McInnes
Craig McKenzie
  (flickr.com/photos/craigmckenzie)
H. E. Mclure
Manfred Meiners (manfredmeiners.com)
Martim Melo
Ian Merrill
Tom Middleton (reflectingthewild.com)
Michael Mills (birdingafrica.com)
John C. Mittermeier
  (flickr.com/photos/jmittermeier)
David Monticelli
  (pbase.com/david_monticelli)
Bill and Jack Moorhead
  (wildiaries.com/users/73)
Jonathan M. Morel
Michael J. Morel
Denzil Morgan
Pete Morris (birdquest-tours.com)
Rob Morris
Yann Musika
Tiwonge Mzumara
Craig Nash
Michael Neal (nealstudios.net)
Greg Neise (inplainsight.net)
Chris Newbold

Jonathan Newman
Luyen Nguyen
Paul Noakes
Ken Norris
Claudien Nsabagasani
Christian Nunes
Kurazo Okada
János Oláh (birdquest-tours.com)
Eric Olivier & Catherine Chavaillon
  (atacreation mail.pf)
Fábio Olmos
Juan Pablo López Ordóñez
Ronald Orenstein
Luís Ortiz-Catedral
Tony Palliser
Papua Expeditions/cv.Ekonexion
Jerry A. Payne / USDA Agricultural Research
  Service
David Peters (dpphotoimages.com)
Johannes Pfleiderer (zootierliste.de)
Mridu Paban Phukan
Patrick Pikacha
Pavel Pinchuk (aqua-wader.blogspot.com)
Otto Plantema (pbase.com/otto1)
René Pop
Richard Porter
H. L. Prakash
Raul Benjamin Puentespina
German Pugnali
Quan Min Li (birdnet.cn)
Alonso Quevedo / Fundación ProAves
  (proaves.org)
Houssein A. Rayaleh
Dr Paul R. Reillo (rarespecies.org)
Ernesto Reyes
Carlos Ribeiro (flickr.com/photos/cazeribeiro1)
Adam Riley (rockjumperbirding.com)
Jon Riley
Dieter Rinke / BirdLife
Craig Robson
Rafy Rodriguez
Gary Rosenberg
Daniel Rosengren (scutisorex.se)
Jonathan Rossouw
Francesco Rovero
  (mtsn.tn.it/tropical_biodiversity)
Roberto Pedraza Ruiz
  (sierragorda.net/galeria/Beto)
Tim Rumble (flickr.com/photos/timrumble)
Peter Ryan (fitzpatrick.uct.ac.za)
Mudhafar A. Salim
Daina Samba
Niranjan Sant
Ivan Sarenas
Tony Sawbridge
Fabrice Schmitt (albatross-birding.com)
Jérôme Scuiller
Dubi Shapiro (pbase.com/dubisha)
Hadoram Shirihai (The Tubenoses Project and
  the forthcoming Photographic Handbook
  of the Birds of the World, Jornvall & Shirihai;
  Bloomsbury Publishing Plc.)

H. E. Shu-hui (52pp.com)
Luís Fábio Silveira (ib.usp.br/~lfsilveira)
David Slater
Oliver Smart (smartimages.co.uk)
Martin V. Sneary (mvsneary.photoshelter.com)
David J. Southall (tropicalbirdphotos.com)
Ramki Sreenivasan (wildventures.com)
John Sterling (sterlingbirds.com)
Dr Liz Still
Rebecca Stirnemann (samoanbirds.com)
David Stowe (pbase.com/davidstowe)
Werner Suter
Andy & Gill Swash (WorldWildlifeImages.com)
Melanie Tankard
Warwick Tarboton
Vikash Tatayah
Alan Tate (aabirdpix.com)
Imam Taufiqurrahman
  (peburungamatir.wordpress.com)
Myron Tay (flickr.com/photos/28786551@N04)
Arnel B. Telesforo
Glen Tepke (pbase.com/gtepke)
Marc Thibault
Wouter Thijs
August Thomasson
Mike Thorsen (southernphotoguides.com)
David Tipling
Vivek Tiwari (flickr.com/photos/spiderhunters)
Robert Tizard (ocellata.com)
Joe Tobias
Todor Todorov
Andrew "Jack" Tordoff
Fabrice Tortey
Adams Toussaint
Tun Pin Ong (flickr.com/photos/tunpin)
Chris Tzaros
Luís Eduardo Urueña
Josef C. Uyeda
René Valdés (birdpicsandmore.com)
Glen Valentine
Eric VanderWerf (pacificrimconservation.com)
Filip Verbelen
Alexander Viduetsky
Nigel Voaden
Ross Wanless
Dave Watts (davewattsphoto.com)
Ueli Weber
Merlijn van Weerd
Emilio White
Liz Whitwell
Gehan de Silva Wijeyeratne
Edwin Winkel
Michelle & Peter Wong
Wong Chi Yin
YaBaLeX (faune-reunion.com)
Lainie Zarones
Zhang Zhengwang
Zheng Jianping

Fifteen photographers have ten or more of their images included in the book. Between them, they contributed 260 (or 30%) of the photos and particular thanks are extended to the following for their very significant involvement in the project: Ciro Albano (nebrazilbirding.com); Pete Morris (birdquest-tours.com); Andy & Gill Swash (WorldWildlifeImages. com); Adam Riley (rockjumperbirding.com); Eric VanderWerf (pacificrimconservation.com); Dubi Shapiro (pbase.com/ dubisha); David Boyle; Jon Hornbuckle; Greg & Yvonne Dean (WorldWildlifeImages.com); Denzil Morgan; Hadoram Shirihai; Nik Borrow (birdquest-tours.com); James Eaton (birdtourasia.com); Jack Jeffrey (JackJeffreyphoto.com) and Dušan M. Brinkhuizen (sapayoa.com).

Thanks are also due to Hadoram Shirihai, a friend for over 30 years, for his recognition of the importance of promoting globally threatened bird species, and for kindly contributing images of some of the rarest bird species in the world from the World Collection, some of them photographed for the first time ever. Many of these photos were obtained during photographic expeditions made specifically to obtain images for the forthcoming *Photographic Handbook of the Birds of the World*, Jornvall & Shirihai, Bloomsbury Publishing Plc. and *Albatrosses, petrels and shearwaters of the world: a handbook to their taxonomy, identification, ecology and conservation*, Shirihai & Bretagnolle, Bloomsbury Publishing Plc., and grateful thanks are extended to Hadoram for allowing their use in this book.

Unfortunately, it was not possible to feature images from all the photographers who kindly submitted their work, so high was both the number and the quality of the images provided by the 467 photographers who contributed to the project. These images did, however, prove invaluable as reference material and sincere thanks are therefore also due to the following 149 photographers:

Liz Aitken (lizaiken.com); Juan Jose Alava; Shachar Alterman; Ute Broedel Ampudia; Lily Arison Rene de Roland (peregrinefund.org); Jonathan Beilby; Boris Belchev (alcedowildlife.com); Carl Billingham; Andrew Peter Butler; Tom Butynski; John Caddick; Jeremy Calvo (jeremycalvo.com); Braulio A. Carlos (pantanalbirdclub.org); Ricardo Ceia; Chris Charles; Neil Cheshire; J. William S. Clark; Jan Axel Cubilla (janbirdingblog.blogspot.com); Francesca Cunninghame; Dave Currie; Robert A. Davis (robdavis.com.au); Matt Denton (Birdquest-tours.com); Nicola Destefano (nicoladestefano. it); Nikhil Devasar; Sudeshna Dey; Israel Didham; Bruce Doran (flickr.com/photos/30826649@N03); Yeshey Dorji; Carl Downing (birding-colombia.com); Adrian Drummond-Hill; Shahril Dzulkifli; Trevor Ellery; Monica Engstrand; Damien Farine; Dominique Filippi (stormpetrel.com); David Fisher; Alexandra Fonseca; Luís Alberto Franke; Carlos Funes (birding-elsalvador.blogspot.com); Juan Pablo Galvan; Julie Gane; Dilia E. García; Lucy Garrett; John & Judy Geeson; Richard Gibbons (ickr.com/photos/rgibbo3/); Mat & Cathy Gilfedder; Dag Gjerde; Jose Gonzalez; Chris Gooddie; Martin Goodey (martingoodeywildlifephotography.com); Carlos Otávio Gussoni; Héctor Gutiérrez Guzmán (flickr.com/photos/ hectorgutierrez); Samuel Hansson (heliangelus.se); Timo Havimo; Paquita Hoeck; Gert Huijzers; Karen & Greg Hunt; Russell Jenkins (russelljenkinsstoop.blogspot.com); Stephen John Jones; Adrian Jordi; Connie Kassner; Todd Katzner; Adam Scott Kennedy (rawnaturephoto.com); Ketil Knudsen; Ady Kristanto; Markus Lagerqvist; Kulojyoti Lahkar; Lean Yen Loong; Vincent Legrand (vincentlegrand.com); Robert M. Loudon; Barry Luckman; Tomas Lundquist (pbase.com/ zoothera); Kevin D. Mack; Petter Zahl Marki; Juan Martinez; Melanie Massaro; Menxiu Tong; Lenore McCullagh; Barry Miller; Jennifer Mortensen; Joaquim Muchaxo (flickr.com/photos/jmuchaxo); Wallace P. Murdoch Jr.; Nicholas Murray; Steve Nanz (stevenanz.com); Craig Nash; Jeffrey Newell; Anja Nusse (agami.nl); Scott Olmstead (flickr.com/sparverius); Atle Ivar Olsen; Gabor Orban; Kay Parkin; Tim Pascoe; Juan Pereira; Jean Paul Perret; Alan L. Pohl; Rob Pople; William Price (pbase.com/tereksandpiper/galleries); Mikko Pyhälä; Joao Quental; Dr. Ramakrishna (zsi.gov.in); Mark Rauzon; Matthias Reinschmidt (Loro Parque Fundacion); M. Rezzouk; Dave Rimmer; Dave Rimmer; Rob Robinson / BTO; Matthew Rodgers; Gonçalo M. Rosa; Otto Samwald; Jonny Schoenjahn; Rainer Seifert; David Simpson; Daniel L. Smith (flickr.com/photos/ yambarudan/sets/); Per Smitterberg; Kjetil Aadne Solbakken; Monika Sood; Jorge Martin Spinuzza (avespampa.com. ar); Ab Steenvoorden; Gunnar Steinholtz; Dicky T. Sutanto; Kristian Svensson; Kensuke Tanaka; Tom Tarrant; James Taylor; Larry H. Thompson; Michael Todd (wildlifing.smugmug.com); Colin Trainor; Markus Unsoeld; Arturo Valledor de Lozoya; Wim van der Schot; Inger Vandyke; Rours Vann / WCS; Nitya Vittal; Paul Walbridge; Mats Wallin (pbase.com/matswallin); David Walsh; Larry Wan (wanconservancy.org); Carleton Ward (Bahamas National Trust); Jim Watt; Alex Wegmann; Bruce Winslade; Lance Woolaver; Xie Xiao-fang; Holly Yocum; Yong Wah Sim; Cathy Zell; and Zhihua Wu (birdnet.cn).

A number of friends and colleagues provided invaluable help and support in many ways, whether suggesting or indeed making contact themselves with photographers whom they believed may be able to help by contributing images to the project, by making constructive comments during the production of this book, or helping to manage the WorldsRarestBirds.com website. In these respects, particular thanks go to: Ciro Albano; Mikael Bauer; Mike Carter; Pierre-André Crochet; Richard Craik; Sergey Dereliev; Phil Head; Sebastian K. Herzog and colleagues at Asociación Civil Armonía; Kate Jeffries; Arne Jensen; Krys Kazmierczak; Andy King; Charlie Moores; Denzil Morgan; János Oláh; Fábio Olmos; Hugo Rainey; Robin Restall; Debby Reynolds; Jennifer Rousseau; Nate A. Skinner and colleagues at Fundación ProAves; Mrs Like Wijaya; Matt Wildman and Glyn Young.

One of the incentives for photographers to offer their images to the project was the generous sponsorship provided by the quality optics company Minox, the publishers Lynx Edicions, BirdLife International and the World Migratory Bird Day.

This support was key to the success of this project and the significant contribution of these companies or organizations is gratefully acknowledged. Thanks are also due to the judges of the photo competitions – David Tipling, Andy Harmer and Steve Holmes – for their impartial and well-considered assessment of so many wonderful images.

The financial support of County Ornithological Services of Maidenhead, Berkshire, UK, is also gratefully acknowledged, as this has enabled complimentary copies of the book to be sent to BirdLife Partners around the world, to be presented to key decision-makers in the many nations that host our most threatened species of birds.

It is fair to say that the production of this book has been a labour of love. Hundreds of hours have been spent liaising with friends, colleagues, researchers, ornithologists and birdwatchers across the world. Thousands of emails have been sent and received, and as a result the species account texts have been continually updated over the past two years as new information came to light. Thanks are therefore due to the many dedicated ornithologists whose studies have provided the information that is presented. The task of condensing the often considerable amount of information available for each species proved to be a particular challenge. For this, sincere and grateful thanks are extended to Brian Clews and Gill Swash for volunteering to help in honing the text, and for doing such an exceptional job.

The job of preparing the introductory chapter on *The threats birds face*, outlining the conservation issues within each of the regions, and preparing the extended captions for the images was undertaken very ably and professionally by Nick Langley. Nick's contribution was invaluable, and he is owed a great debt of gratitude for his patience and skill.

Friends and colleagues at BirdLife have been tremendously supportive in helping to bring this book to fruition. Stu Butchart's wealth of knowledge was drawn upon frequently, and special thanks are due to him for drafting the introductory chapter on *The world's rarest birds*. Martin Fowlie provided unstinting help and support throughout the project in coordinating BirdLife's response to innumerable requests. Andy Symes was always willing to help with queries regarding changes to The IUCN Red List and threat categories. Mark Balman was immensely helpful in preparing the summary maps that appear throughout the book, and in making available the data that were used to prepare the individual species distribution maps. In addition, Tris Allinson, Nigel Collar, Mike Crosby, Ade Long, Gina Pfaff and Chris Sharpe all provided help, support, advice and constructive comments on the structure and layout of the book at various stages. Sincere thanks are due to all.

Last, but certainly not least, special thanks go to Tomasz Cofta for the 77 beautiful artworks he prepared specifically for this book. Painting birds that are well known is difficult enough, but illustrating the least-known species to show how they are likely to appear if they were ever to be seen in the wild is certainly a tall order. Tomasz's commitment to producing these amazing works of art involved detailed studies of museum specimens and hours of painstaking work. For this he cannot be thanked enough.

Critically Endangered **Ivory-billed Woodpecker** *Campephilus principalis*. Illustration: Tomasz Cofta.

335

Appendix 1: Extinct species

A species is only declared Extinct once there is no reasonable doubt that there are no individuals still in existence. The **Dodo** *Raphus cucullatus* is perhaps the best-known species of bird to have become Extinct, but since 1500, 130 species are known to have been lost, 85% of which were from islands.

All these species are listed here, with details of the date they were last recorded (approximate dates being shown in italics).

	Region	EX	Island species	
			Number	%
1	Oceanic Islands	82	82	100%
2	Australasia	25	15	60%
3	The Caribbean, North and Central America	18	12	67%
5	Asia	2	2	100%
5	Africa	2	–	0%
6	South America	1	–	0%
7	Europe and the Middle East	1	–	0%
	ALL SPECIES	**130**	**111**	**85%**

English Name	Scientific Name	Country / Area	Region	Last record
Kauai Oo	*Moho braccatus*	Hawaii, USA	Oceanic Islands	1987
Alaotra Grebe	*Tachybaptus rufolavatus*	Madagascar	Africa	1985
Kamao	*Myadestes myadestinus*	Hawaii, USA	Oceanic Islands	1985
Atitlán Grebe	*Podilymbus gigas*	Guatemala	Central America	1983
Aldabra Warbler	*Nesillas aldabrana*	Ile Malabar, Aldabra, Seychelles	Oceanic Islands	1983
Guam Flycatcher	*Myiagra freycineti*	Guam	Oceanic Islands	1983
Bishop's Oo	*Moho bishopi*	Hawaii, USA	Oceanic Islands	1981
Eiao Monarch	*Pomarea fluxa*	Marquesas Islands, French Polynesia	Oceanic Islands	1977
Colombian Grebe	*Podiceps andinus*	Colombia	South America	1977
Bar-winged Rail	*Nesoclopeus poecilopterus*	Fiji	Oceanic Islands	*1973*
Bush Wren	*Xenicus longipes*	New Zealand	Australasia	1972
Greater Akialoa	*Hemignathus ellisianus*	Hawaii, USA	Oceanic Islands	1969
Kakawahie	*Paroreomyza flammea*	Hawaii, USA	Oceanic Islands	1963
Wake Island Rail	*Gallirallus wakensis*	Wake Island	Oceanic Islands	1945
Laysan Rail	*Porzana palmeri*	Hawaii, USA	Oceanic Islands	1944
Lesser Akialoa	*Hemignathus obscurus*	Hawaii, USA	Oceanic Islands	1940
Grand Cayman Thrush	*Turdus ravidus*	Grand Cayman, Cayman Islands	Caribbean	1938
Ryukyu Pigeon	*Columba jouyi*	Nansei Shoto Islands, Japan	Asia	1936
Hawaii Oo	*Moho nobilis*	Hawaii, USA	Oceanic Islands	1934
Nuku Hiva Monarch	*Pomarea nukuhivae*	Marquesas Islands, French Polynesia	Oceanic Islands	1930s
Lord Howe Gerygone	*Gerygone insularis*	Lord Howe Island, Australia	Australasia	*ca.* 1930s
Tahiti Rail	*Gallirallus pacificus*	Tahiti, French Polynesia	Oceanic Islands	1930s
Paradise Parrot	*Psephotus pulcherrimus*	Australia	Australasia	1928
Thick-billed Ground-dove	*Gallicolumba salamonis*	Solomon Islands	Oceanic Islands	*ca.* 1927
Norfolk Island Starling	*Aplonis fusca*	Norfolk and Lord Howe Islands	Australasia	1923
Red-moustached Fruit-dove	*Ptilinopus mercierii*	Marquesas, French Polynesia	Oceanic Islands	1922
Lanai Hookbill	*Dysmorodrepanis munroi*	Hawaii, USA	Oceanic Islands	1918
Laughing Owl	*Sceloglaux albifacies*	New Zealand	Australasia	1914
Slender-billed Grackle	*Quiscalus palustris*	Mexico	North America	*ca.* 1910
Carolina Parakeet	*Conuropsis carolinensis*	USA	North America	1910
Robust White-eye	*Zosterops strenuus*	Lord Howe Island, Australia	Australasia	1908
Huia	*Heteralocha acutirostris*	New Zealand	Australasia	1907
Black Mamo	*Drepanis funerea*	Hawaii, USA	Oceanic Islands	*1907*
Chatham Bellbird	*Anthornis melanocephala*	Chatham Islands, New Zealand	Australasia	1906
South Island Piopio	*Turnagra capensis*	New Zealand	Australasia	*1905*
Choiseul Pigeon	*Microgoura meeki*	Solomon Islands	Oceanic Islands	*1904*

English Name	Scientific Name	Country / Area	Region	Last record
Guadalupe Caracara	*Caracara lutosa*	Isla Guadalupe, Mexico	North America	1903
North Island Piopio	*Turnagra tanagra*	New Zealand	Australasia	1902
Auckland Islands Merganser	*Mergus australis*	Auckland Islands, New Zealand	Australasia	1902
Greater Amakihi	*Hemignathus sagittirostris*	Hawaii, USA	Oceanic Islands	*1901*
Canary Islands Oystercatcher	*Haematopus meadewaldoi*	Canary Islands, Spain	Oceanic Islands	Early 1900s
Black-backed Bittern	*Ixobrychus novaezelandiae*	New Zealand	Australasia	*Before 1900*
Passenger Pigeon	*Ectopistes migratorius*	North America	North America	*1900*
Hawaii Mamo	*Drepanis pacifica*	Hawaii, USA	Oceanic Islands	*1898*
Greater Koa-finch	*Rhodacanthis palmeri*	Hawaii, USA	Oceanic Islands	1896
Stephens Island Wren	*Traversia lyalli*	Stephens Island, New Zealand	Australasia	1895
Hawkins's Rail	*Diaphorapteryx hawkinsi*	Chatham Islands, New Zealand	Australasia	1895
North Island Takahe	*Porphyrio mantelli*	New Zealand	Australasia	*1894*
Kona Grosbeak	*Chloridops kona*	Hawaii, USA	Oceanic Islands	1894
Lesser Koa-finch	*Rhodacanthis flaviceps*	Hawaii, USA	Oceanic Islands	1893
Seychelles Parakeet	*Psittacula wardi*	Seychelles	Oceanic Islands	1893
Ula-ai-hawane	*Ciridops anna*	Hawaii, USA	Oceanic Islands	1892
Bonin Grosbeak	*Chaunoproctus ferreorostris*	Ogasawara Islands, Japan	Oceanic Islands	*ca.* 1890s
Bonin Wood-pigeon	*Columba versicolor*	Ogasawara Islands, Japan	Oceanic Islands	1889
Cuban Macaw	*Ara tricolor*	Cuba	Caribbean	1885
Hawaiian Rail	*Porzana sandwichensis*	Hawaii, USA	Oceanic Islands	1884
Brace's Emerald	*Chlorostilbon bracei*	New Providence, Bahamas	Caribbean	*1877*
Newton's Parakeet	*Psittacula exsul*	Rodrigues, Mauritius	Oceanic Islands	1875
New Zealand Quail	*Coturnix novaezelandiae*	New Zealand	Australasia	1875
Labrador Duck	*Camptorhynchus labradorius*	Canada & USA	North America	1875
Gould's Emerald	*Chlorostilbon elegans*	Jamaica or the north Bahamas	Caribbean	1860
Kioea	*Chaetoptila angustipluma*	Hawaii, USA	Oceanic Islands	1859
Great Auk	*Pinguinus impennis*	North America & Europe	North America & Europe	1852
Norfolk Island Kaka	*Nestor productus*	Norfolk Island, Australia	Australasia	1851
Pallas's Cormorant	*Phalacrocorax perspicillatus*	Komandorski Islands, Russia	Asia	1850s
Réunion Starling	*Fregilupus varius*	Réunion	Oceanic Islands	1850s
Black-fronted Parakeet	*Cyanoramphus zealandicus*	Tahiti, French Polynesia	Oceanic Islands	1844
Oahu Oo	*Moho apicalis*	Hawaii, USA	Oceanic Islands	1837
Mauritius Owl	*Mascarenotus sauzieri*	Mauritius	Oceanic Islands	1837
Snail-eating Coua	*Coua delalandei*	Madagascar	Africa	1834
Mauritius Blue-pigeon	*Alectroenas nitidissima*	Mauritius	Oceanic Islands	*ca.* 1830s
Kosrae Starling	*Aplonis corvina*	Kosrae Island, Micronesia	Oceanic Islands	1828
Amaui	*Myadestes woahensis*	Hawaii, USA	Oceanic Islands	1825
Mysterious Starling	*Aplonis mavornata*	Mauke, Cook Islands	Oceanic Islands	1825?
Maupiti Monarch	*Pomarea pomarea*	Society Islands, French Polynesia	Oceanic Islands	1823
Kosrae Crake	*Porzana monasa*	Kosrae, Caroline Islands, Micronesia	Oceanic Islands	Late 1800s
Dieffenbach's Rail	*Gallirallus dieffenbachii*	Chatham, Mangere and Pitt Islands, New Zealand	Australasia	Late 1800s
Chatham Rail	*Cabalus modestus*	Chatham, Mangere and Pitt Islands, New Zealand	Australasia	Late 1800s
Chatham Fernbird	*Bowdleria rufescens*	Pitt and Mangere Islands in the Chatham Islands, New Zealand	Australasia	Late 1800s
New Caledonia Gallinule	*Porphyrio kukwiedei*	New Caledonia	Australasia	Early 1800s
White Gallinule	*Porphyrio albus*	Lord Howe Island, Australia	Australasia	Early 1800s
Ascension Crake	*Mundia elpenor*	Ascension Island	Oceanic Islands	Early 1800s
Kangaroo Island Emu	*Dromaius baudinianus*	Kangaroo Island, Australia	Australasia	Early 1800s

English Name	Scientific Name	Country / Area	Region	Last record
King Island Emu	*Dromaius ater*	King Island, Australia	Australasia	Early 1800s
Jamaican Green-and-yellow Macaw	*Ara erythrocephala*	Jamaica	Caribbean	Early 1800s
Bonin Thrush	*Zoothera terrestris*	Ogasawara Islands, Japan	Oceanic Islands	1800s
St Helena Cuckoo	*Nannococcyx psix*	St Helena	Oceanic Islands	1800s
Dominican Green-and-yellow Macaw	*Ara atwoodi*	Dominica	Caribbean	*ca.* Early 1800s
Martinique Amazon	*Amazona martinicana*	Martinique	Caribbean	Before 1800
Amsterdam Duck	*Anas marecula*	Amsterdam Island, French Southern Territories	Oceanic Islands	1793
Norfolk Island Ground-dove	*Gallicolumba norfolciensis*	Norfolk Island, Australia	Australasia	*ca.* 1790
Liverpool Pigeon	*Caloenas maculata*	Tahiti, French Polynesia?	Oceanic Islands	1783–1823
Guadeloupe Amazon	*Amazona violacea*	Guadeloupe	Caribbean	1779
Tahitian Sandpiper	*Prosobonia leucoptera*	Tahiti, French Polynesia	Oceanic Islands	1777
White-winged Sandpiper	*Prosobonia ellisi*	Moorea, Society Islands, French Polynesia,	Oceanic Islands	1777
Mascarene Parrot	*Mascarinus mascarinus*	Réunion	Oceanic Islands	1775
Tanna Ground-dove	*Gallicolumba ferruginea*	Tanna Island, Vanuatu	Oceanic Islands	*ca.* 1774
Mauritius Grey Parrot	*Lophopsittacus bensoni*	Mauritius	Oceanic Islands	1764
Réunion Ibis	*Threskiornis solitarius*	Rodrigues & Réunion, Mauritius	Oceanic Islands	*ca.* 1761
Lesser Antillean Macaw	*Ara guadeloupensis*	Guadeloupe & Martinique	Caribbean	1760
Rodrigues Blue-pigeon	*Alectroenas rodericana*	Rodrigues, Mauritius	Oceanic Islands	Before 1750
Réunion Gallinule	*Porphyrio coerulescens*	Réunion	Oceanic Islands	*ca.* 1730
Rodrigues Night-heron	*Nycticorax megacephalus*	Rodrigues, Mauritius	Oceanic Islands	1726
Rodrigues Starling	*Necropsar rodericanus*	Rodrigues, Mauritius	Oceanic Islands	1726
Rodrigues Owl	*Mascarenotus murivorus*	Rodrigues, Mauritius	Oceanic Islands	1726
Rodrigues Rail	*Aphanapteryx leguati*	Rodrigues, Mauritius	Oceanic Islands	1726
Miller's Rail	*Porzana nigra*	Tahiti, French Polynesia	Oceanic Islands	Late 1700s
Rodrigues Solitaire	*Pezophaps solitaria*	Rodrigues, Mauritius	Oceanic Islands	Late 1700s
Rodrigues Parrot	*Necropsittacus rodericanus*	Rodrigues, Mauritius	Oceanic Islands	Late 1700s
Raiatea Parakeet	*Cyanoramphus ulietanus*	Raiatea, French Polynesia	Oceanic Islands	Late 1700s
Guadeloupe Parakeet	*Aratinga labati*	Guadeloupe	Caribbean	Late 1700s
Jamaican Red Macaw	*Ara gossei*	Jamaica	Caribbean	Late 1700s
Réunion Pigeon	*Columba duboisi*	Réunion	Oceanic Islands	Early 1700s
Mauritius Duck	*Anas theodori*	Mauritius	Oceanic Islands	1696
Mauritius Night-heron	*Nycticorax mauritianus*	Mauritius	Oceanic Islands	1693
Mascarene Coot	*Fulica newtoni*	Réunion & Mauritius	Oceanic Islands	1693
Mauritius Shelduck	*Alopochen mauritianus*	Mauritius	Oceanic Islands	1693
Réunion Night-heron	*Nycticorax duboisi*	Réunion	Oceanic Islands	1674
Dodo	*Raphus cucullatus*	Mauritius	Oceanic Islands	1662
Broad-billed Parrot	*Lophopsittacus mauritianus*	Mauritius	Oceanic Islands	Late 1600s
Réunion Kestrel	*Falco duboisi*	Réunion	Oceanic Islands	Late 1600s
Red Rail	*Aphanapteryx bonasia*	Mauritius	Oceanic Islands	Late 1600s
Réunion Shelduck	*Alopochen kervazoi*	Réunion	Oceanic Islands	Late 1600s
Réunion Owl	*Mascarenotus grucheti*	Réunion	Oceanic Islands	1600s
St Helena Hoopoe	*Upupa antaios*	St Helena	Oceanic Islands	Early 1500s
Large St Helena Petrel	*Pterodroma rupinarum*	St Helena	Oceanic Islands	Early 1500s
St Helena Rail	*Porzana astrictocarpus*	St Helena	Oceanic Islands	Early 1500s
Small St Helena Petrel	*Bulweria bifax*	St Helena	Oceanic Islands	Early 1500s
St Helena Crake	*Atlantisia podarces*	St Helena	Oceanic Islands	Early 1500s
St Helena Dove	*Dysmoropelia dekarchiskos*	St Helena	Oceanic Islands	1500s

Appendix 2: Globally threatened bird families

This table provides a taxomonic list of the 127 bird famlies that have at least one globally threatened species. The number of species in each threat category is shown and the species that are **EN** Endangered, **CR** Critically Endangered, **PE** Possibly Extinct or **EW** Extinct in the Wild are listed, cross-referenced to the **region** and **page number(s)** on which the main species account(s) can be found. The number of **VU** Vulnerable spp. is also shown.

The **regional** codes used are: **E/M** (Europe & the Middle East); **AF** (Africa & Madagascar); **AS** (Asia); **AU** (Australasia); **OC** (Oceanic Islands); **CA** (Caribbean and North & Central America); and **SA** (South America).

	Tinamous:	Tinamidae
47 species **VU: 7** 15%		

	Cassowaries:	Casuariidae
3 species **VU: 2** 67%		

	Kiwis:	Apterygidae
4 species **EN: 1** **VU: 2** 75%		
EN	Northern Brown Kiwi *Apteryx mantelli*	**AU 164**

	Megapodes:	Megapodiidae
21 species **EN: 4** **VU: 6** 48%		
EN	Bruijn's Brush-turkey *Aepypodius bruijnii*	**AS 119**
EN	Maleo *Macrocephalon maleo*	**AS 119**
EN	Micronesian Megapode *Megapodius laperouse*	**OC 206**
EN	Polynesian Megapode *Megapodius pritchardii*	**OC 206**

	Guans and curassows:	Cracidae
51 species **EW: 1** **CR: 3** **EN: 8** **VU: 9** 39%		
EN	Baudó Guan *Penelope ortoni*	**SA 281**
EN	Cauca Guan *Penelope perspicax*	**SA 282**
CR	White-winged Guan *Penelope albipennis*	**SA 282**
CR	Trinidad Piping-guan *Pipile pipile*	**CA 249**
EN	Black-fronted Piping-guan *Pipile jacutinga*	**SA 282**
EN	Horned Guan *Oreophasis derbianus*	**CA 249**
CR	Blue-billed Curassow *Crax alberti*	**SA 283**
EN	Wattled Curassow *Crax globulosa*	**SA 283**
EN	Red-billed Curassow *Crax blumenbachii*	**SA 284**
EW	Alagoas Curassow *Mitu mitu*	**SA 282**
EN	Helmeted Curassow *Pauxi pauxi*	**SA 283**
EN	Horned Curassow *Pauxi unicornis*	**SA 283**

	Guineafowl:	Numididae
6 species **VU: 1** 17%		

	New World quails:	Odontophoridae
31 species **EN: 1** **VU: 5** 19%		
EN	Gorgeted Wood-quail *Odontophorus strophium*	**SA 284**

	Grouse, pheasants and partridges:	Phasianidae
179 species **CR: 3** **EN: 10** **VU: 25** 21%		
EN	Gunnison Sage-grouse *Centrocercus minimus*	**CA 249**
EN	Nahan's Francolin *Francolinus nahani*	**AF 81**
CR	Djibouti Francolin *Francolinus ochropectus*	**AF 81**
EN	Mount Cameroon Francolin *Francolinus camerunensis*	**AF 81**
EN	Swierstra's Francolin *Francolinus swierstrai*	**AF 80**
CR	Himalayan Quail *Ophrysia superciliosa*	**AS 119**
EN	Udzungwa Forest-partridge *Xenoperdix udzungwensis*	**AF 81**
EN	Sichuan Partridge *Arborophila rufipectus*	**AS 119**
CR	Edwards's Pheasant *Lophura edwardsi*	**AS 120**
EN	Vietnamese Pheasant *Lophura hatinhensis*	**AS 120**
EN	Hainan Peacock-pheasant *Polyplectron katsumatae*	**AS 120**
EN	Bornean Peacock-pheasant *Polyplectron schleiermacheri*	**AS 120**
EN	Green Peafowl *Pavo muticus*	**AS 121**

	Ducks, geese and swans:	Anatidae
162 species **CR: 6** **EN: 11** **VU: 15** 19%		
EN	Red-breasted Goose *Branta ruficollis*	**E/M 64, AS 121**
EN	Blue Duck *Hymenolaimus malacorhynchos*	**AU 164**
CR	Crested Shelduck *Tadorna cristata*	**AS 121**
EN	White-winged Duck *Cairina scutulata*	**AS 121**
EN	Hawaiian Duck *Anas wyvilliana*	**OC 207**
CR	Laysan Duck *Anas laysanensis*	**OC 207**
EN	Meller's Duck *Anas melleri*	**AF 82**
EN	Madagascar Teal *Anas bernieri*	**AF 82**
EN	Brown Teal *Anas chlorotis*	**AU 165**
EN	Campbell Islands Teal *Anas nesiotis*	**AU 165**
CR	Pink-headed Duck *Rhodonessa caryophyllacea*	**AS 122**
CR	Madagascar Pochard *Aythya innotata*	**AF 82**
CR	Baer's Pochard *Aythya baeri*	**AS 122**
EN	Velvet Scoter *Melanitta fusca*	**E/M 65, AS 122**
CR	Brazilian Merganser *Mergus octosetaceus*	**SA 284**
EN	Scaly-sided Merganser *Mergus squamatus*	**AS 122**
EN	White-headed Duck *Oxyura leucocephala*	**E/M 65, AF 82, AS 123**

	Penguins:	Spheniscidae
18 species **EN: 5** **VU: 6** 61%		
EN	Northern Rockhopper Penguin *Eudyptes moseleyi*	**OC 207**
EN	Erect-crested Penguin *Eudyptes sclateri*	**AU 165**
EN	Yellow-eyed Penguin *Megadyptes antipodes*	**AU 165**
EN	African Penguin *Spheniscus demersus*	**AF 84**
EN	Galápagos Penguin *Spheniscus mendiculus*	**OC 207**

	Albatrosses:	Diomedeidae
22 species **CR: 3** **EN: 5** **VU: 9** 77%		
CR	Waved Albatross *Phoebastria irrorata*	**OC 208**
CR	Amsterdam Albatross *Diomedea amsterdamensis*	**OC 208**
CR	Tristan Albatross *Diomedea dabbenena*	**OC 208**
EN	Northern Royal Albatross *Diomedea sanfordi*	**AU 166**
EN	Sooty Albatross *Phoebetria fusca*	**OC 208**
EN	Black-browed Albatross *Thalassarche melanophrys*	**AU 166, OC 209, SA 284**
EN	Atlantic Yellow-nosed Albatross *Thalassarche chlororhynchos*	**OC 209**
EN	Indian Yellow-nosed Albatross *Thalassarche carteri*	**OC 209**

	Petrels and shearwaters:	Procellariidae
80 species **PE: 1** **CR: 7** **EN: 10** **VU: 19** 46%		
EN	Barau's Petrel *Pterodroma baraui*	**OC 210**
CR	Galápagos Petrel *Pterodroma phaeopygia*	**OC 210**
EN	Henderson Petrel *Pterodroma atrata*	**OC 209**
EN	Phoenix Petrel *Pterodroma alba*	**OC 211**
EN	Zino's Petrel *Pterodroma madeira*	**OC 210**
EN	Bermuda Petrel *Pterodroma cahow*	**OC 210**
EN	Black-capped Petrel *Pterodroma hasitata*	**CA 250**
PE	Jamaica Petrel *Pterodroma caribbaea*	**CA 250**
EN	Atlantic Petrel *Pterodroma incerta*	**OC 211**
CR	Magenta Petrel *Pterodroma magentae*	**AU 166**
EN	Chatham Petrel *Pterodroma axillaris*	**AU 166**
CR	Fiji Petrel *Pseudobulweria macgillivrayi*	**OC 211**
CR	Beck's Petrel *Pseudobulweria becki*	**AU 167**
CR	Mascarene Petrel *Pseudobulweria aterrima*	**OC 211**
CR	Balearic Shearwater *Puffinus mauretanicus*	**E/M 65**

CR	Townsend's Shearwater *Puffinus auricularis*	**OC 212**
EN	Newell's Shearwater *Puffinus newelli*	**OC 212**
EN	Hutton's Shearwater *Puffinus huttoni*	**AU 167**

Storm-petrels: Hydrobatidae

23 species PE: 1 CR: 1 EN: 2 VU: 1 22%

CR	New Zealand Storm-petrel *Oceanites maorianus*	**AU 167**
EN	White-throated Storm-petrel *Nesofregetta fuliginosa*	**AU 167, OC 212**
PE	Guadalupe Storm-petrel *Oceanodroma macrodactyla*	**OC 212**
EN	Ashy Storm-petrel *Oceanodroma homochroa*	**CA 249**

Diving-petrels: Pelecanoididae

4 species EN: 1 25%

EN	Peruvian Diving-petrel *Pelecanoides garnotii*	**SA 285**

Grebes: Podicipedidae

19 species CR: 2 EN: 1 VU: 2 26%

EN	Titicaca Grebe *Rollandia microptera*	**SA 285**
CR	Junín Grebe *Podiceps taczanowskii*	**SA 285**
CR	Hooded Grebe *Podiceps gallardoi*	**SA 285**

Flamingos: Phoenicopteridae

6 species VU: 1 17%

Storks: Ciconiidae

19 species EN: 3 VU: 2 26%

EN	Storm's Stork *Ciconia stormi*	**AS 123**
EN	Oriental Stork *Ciconia boyciana*	**AS 123**
EN	Greater Adjutant *Leptoptilos dubius*	**AS 123**

Ibises and spoonbills: Threskiornithidae

34 species CR: 4 EN: 3 VU: 1 24%

EN	Madagascar Sacred Ibis *Threskiornis bernieri*	**AF 83, OC 213**
CR	White-shouldered Ibis *Pseudibis davisoni*	**AS 124**
CR	Giant Ibis *Thaumatibis gigantea*	**AS 124**
CR	Northern Bald Ibis *Geronticus eremita*	**E/M 65, AF 83**
EN	Asian Crested Ibis *Nipponia nippon*	**AS 124**
CR	Dwarf Olive Ibis *Bostrychia bocagei*	**OC 213**
EN	Black-faced Spoonbill *Platalea minor*	**AS 124**

Herons and egrets: Ardeidae

62 species CR: 1 EN: 5 VU: 3 15%

EN	Australasian Bittern *Botaurus poiciloptilus*	**AU 168**
EN	White-eared Night-heron *Gorsachius magnificus*	**AS 125**
EN	Japanese Night-heron *Gorsachius goisagi*	**AS 125**
EN	Madagascar Pond-heron *Ardeola idae*	**AF 83, OC 213**
EN	Madagascar Heron *Ardea humbloti*	**AF 83**
CR	White-bellied Heron *Ardea insignis*	**AS 125**

Frigatebirds: Fregatidae

5 species CR: 1 VU: 1 40%

CR	Christmas Island Frigatebird *Fregata andrewsi*	**OC 213**

Shoebill: Balaenicipitidae

1 species VU: 1 100%

Pelicans: Pelecanidae

8 species VU: 1 13%

Gannets and boobies: Sulidae

10 species EN: 1 VU: 1 20%

EN	Abbott's Booby *Papasula abbotti*	**OC 214**

Cormorants: Phalacrocoracidae

33 species CR: 1 EN: 2 VU: 7 30%

EN	Bank Cormorant *Phalacrocorax neglectus*	**AF 84**
CR	Chatham Islands Shag *Phalacrocorax onslowi*	**AU 168**
EN	Pitt Island Shag *Phalacrocorax featherstoni*	**AU 168**

New World vultures: Cathartidae

7 species CR: 1 14%

CR	California Condor *Gymnogyps californianus*	**CA 250**

Falcons and caracaras: Falconidae

64 species EN: 1 VU: 4 8%

EN	Saker Falcon *Falco cherrug*	**E/M 66, AF 86, AS 125**

Osprey, kites, hawks and eagles: Accipitridae

239 species CR: 10 EN: 10 VU: 28 20%

CR	White-collared Kite *Leptodon forbesi*	**SA 286**
CR	Cuban Kite *Chondrohierax wilsonii*	**CA 250**
CR	Madagascar Fish-eagle *Haliaeetus vociferoides*	**AF 84**
EN	Egyptian Vulture *Neophron percnopterus*	**E/M 66, AF 84, AS 126**
EN	Hooded Vulture *Necrosyrtes monachus*	**AF 85**
EN	White-backed Vulture *Gyps africanus*	**AF 85**
CR	White-rumped Vulture *Gyps bengalensis*	**E/M 66, AS 126**
CR	Indian Vulture *Gyps indicus*	**AS 126**
CR	Slender-billed Vulture *Gyps tenuirostris*	**AS 126**
EN	Rueppell's Vulture *Gyps rueppellii*	**E/M 66, AF 85**
CR	Red-headed Vulture *Sarcogyps calvus*	**AS 127**
EN	Madagascar Serpent-eagle *Eutriorchis astur*	**AF 85**
EN	Réunion Harrier *Circus maillardi*	**OC 214**
EN	Gundlach's Hawk *Accipiter gundlachi*	**CA 251**
EN	Grey-backed Hawk *Leucopternis occidentalis*	**SA 286**
EN	Crowned Eagle *Harpyhaliaetus coronatus*	**SA 286**
CR	Ridgway's Hawk *Buteo ridgwayi*	**CA 251**
CR	Philippine Eagle *Pithecophaga jefferyi*	**AS 127**
CR	Flores Hawk-eagle *Nisaetus floris*	**AS 127**
EN	Javan Hawk-eagle *Nisaetus bartelsi*	**AS 127**

Bustards: Otididae

25 species CR: 2 EN: 2 VU: 2 24%

CR	Great Indian Bustard *Ardeotis nigriceps*	**AS 128**
EN	Ludwig's Bustard *Neotis ludwigii*	**AF 86**
CR	Bengal Florican *Houbaropsis bengalensis*	**AS 128**
EN	Lesser Florican *Sypheotides indicus*	**AS 128**

Mesites: Mesitornithidae

3 species VU: 3 100%

Kagu: Rhynochetidae

1 species EN: 1 100%

EN	Kagu *Rhynochetos jubatus*	**AU 169**

Rails, crakes and allies: Rallidae

136 species EW: 1 CR: 4 EN: 11 VU: 18 24%

EN	White-winged Flufftail *Sarothrura ayresi*	**AF 86**
EN	Slender-billed Flufftail *Sarothrura watersi*	**AF 86**
EN	Rusty-flanked Crake *Laterallus levraudi*	**SA 286**
EN	Junín Rail *Laterallus tuerosi*	**SA 287**
CR	New Caledonian Rail *Gallirallus lafresnayanus*	**AU 168**
EN	Lord Howe Woodhen *Gallirallus sylvestris*	**AU 169**
EN	Okinawa Rail *Gallirallus okinawae*	**AS 129**
EW	Guam Rail *Gallirallus owstoni*	**OC 214**
EN	Plain-flanked Rail *Rallus wetmorei*	**SA 287**
EN	Bogotá Rail *Rallus semiplumbeus*	**SA 287**
EN	Talaud Rail *Gymnocrex talaudensis*	**AS 129**
EN	Sakalava Rail *Amaurornis olivieri*	**AF 87**
CR	Zapata Rail *Cyanolimnas cerverai*	**CA 251**
EN	Takahe *Porphyrio hochstetteri*	**AU 169**
CR	Samoan Moorhen *Gallinula pacifica*	**OC 214**
CR	Makira Moorhen *Gallinula silvestris*	**AU 169**

Finfoots: Heliornithidae

3 species EN: 1 33%

EN	Masked Finfoot *Heliopais personatus*	AS 128

Trumpeters: Psophiidae

3 species EN: 1 33%

EN	Dark-winged Trumpeter *Psophia viridis*	SA 287

Cranes: Gruidae

15 species CR: 1 EN: 3 VU: 7 73%

EN	Grey Crowned-crane *Balearica regulorum*	AF 87
CR	Siberian Crane *Leucogeranus leucogeranus*	E/M 67, AS 129
EN	Whooping Crane *Grus americana*	CA 251
EN	Red-crowned Crane *Grus japonensis*	AS 129

Buttonquails: Turnicidae

16 species EN: 1 VU: 1 13%

EN	Buff-breasted Buttonquail *Turnix olivii*	AU 170

Oystercatchers: Haematopodidae

11 species EN: 1 9%

EN	Chatham Oystercatcher *Haematopus chathamensis*	AU 170

Stilts and avocets: Recurvirostridae

9 species CR: 1 11%

CR	Black Stilt *Himantopus novaezelandiae*	AU 170

Plovers: Charadriidae

66 species CR: 3 EN: 2 VU: 3 12%

CR	Javan Lapwing *Vanellus macropterus*	AS 130
CR	Sociable Lapwing *Vanellus gregarius*	E/M 67, AF 87, AS 130
EN	New Zealand Dotterel *Charadrius obscurus*	AU 170
CR	St Helena Plover *Charadrius sanctaehelenae*	OC 215
EN	Shore Plover *Thinornis novaeseelandiae*	AU 171

Painted-snipes: Rostratulidae

3 species EN: 1 33%

EN	Australian Painted Snipe *Rostratula australis*	AU 171

Plains-wanderer: Pedionomidae

1 species EN: 1 100%

EN	Plains-wanderer *Pedionomus torquatus*	AU 171

Sandpipers and allies: Scolopacidae

89 species PE: 1 CR: 2 EN: 3 VU: 7 15%

EN	Moluccan Woodcock *Scolopax rochussenii*	AS 130
PE	Eskimo Curlew *Numenius borealis*	CA 252, SA 288
CR	Slender-billed Curlew *Numenius tenuirostris*	E/M 67, AF 87, AS 130
EN	Spotted Greenshank *Tringa guttifer*	AS 131
EN	Tuamotu Sandpiper *Prosobonia cancellata*	OC 215
CR	Spoon-billed Sandpiper *Eurynorhynchus pygmeus*	AS 131

Coursers and pratincoles: Glareolidae

18 species CR: 1 VU: 1 11%

CR	Jerdon's Courser *Rhinoptilus bitorquatus*	AS 131

Gulls and terns: Laridae

98 species CR: 1 EN: 4 VU: 7 12%

EN	Black-billed Gull *Larus bulleri*	AU 171
CR	Chinese Crested Tern *Sterna bernsteini*	AS 132
EN	Peruvian Tern *Sterna lorata*	SA 288
EN	Black-bellied Tern *Sterna acuticauda*	AS 132
EN	Black-fronted Tern *Sterna albostriata*	AU 172

Auks: Alcidae

23 species CR: 1 EN: 1 VU: 3 22%

EN	Marbled Murrelet *Brachyramphus marmoratus*	CA 252
CR	Kittlitz's Murrelet *Brachyramphus brevirostris*	AS 131, CA 252

Doves and pigeons: Columbidae

305 species EW: 1 CR: 9 EN: 15 VU: 37 20%

EN	Maroon Pigeon *Columba thomensis*	OC 215
CR	Silvery Wood-pigeon *Columba argentina*	AS 132
EN	Pink Pigeon *Nesoenas mayeri*	OC 215
EW	Socorro Dove *Zenaida graysoni*	OC 216
CR	Blue-eyed Ground-dove *Columbina cyanopis*	SA 288
CR	Purple-winged Ground-dove *Claravis geoffroyi*	SA 288
CR	Grenada Dove *Leptotila wellsi*	CA 252
EN	Tolima Dove *Leptotila conoveri*	SA 289
EN	Tuxtla Quail-dove *Geotrygon carrikeri*	CA 253
EN	Blue-headed Quail-dove *Starnoenas cyanocephala*	CA 253
CR	Mindoro Bleeding-heart *Gallicolumba platenae*	AS 133
CR	Negros Bleeding-heart *Gallicolumba keayi*	AS 133
CR	Sulu Bleeding-heart *Gallicolumba menagei*	AS 133
CR	Polynesian Ground-dove *Gallicolumba erythroptera*	OC 216
EN	Santa Cruz Ground-dove *Gallicolumba sanctaecrucis*	AU 172
EN	Wetar Ground-dove *Gallicolumba hoedtii*	AS 133
EN	Tooth-billed Pigeon *Didunculus strigirostris*	OC 216
EN	Tawitawi Brown-dove *Phapitreron cinereiceps*	AS 132
EN	Timor Green-pigeon *Treron psittaceus*	AS 134
EN	Mariana Fruit-dove *Ptilinopus roseicapilla*	OC 216
CR	Negros Fruit-dove *Ptilinopus arcanus*	AS 134
EN	Mindoro Imperial-pigeon *Ducula mindorensis*	AS 134
EN	Polynesian Imperial-pigeon *Ducula aurorae*	OC 217
EN	Marquesan Imperial-pigeon *Ducula galeata*	OC 217
EN	Timor Imperial-pigeon *Ducula cineracea*	AS 134

Parrots: Psittacidae

356 species PE: 1 CR: 15 EN: 34 VU: 55 29%

EN	Kaka *Nestor meridionalis*	AU 172
CR	Kakapo *Strigops habroptila*	AU 172
EN	Flores Hanging-parrot *Loriculus flosculus*	AS 135
EN	Baudin's Black-Cockatoo *Calyptorhynchus baudinii*	AU 173
EN	Carnaby's Black-Cockatoo *Calyptorhynchus latirostris*	AU 173
CR	Yellow-crested Cockatoo *Cacatua sulphurea*	AS 135
CR	Philippine Cockatoo *Cacatua haematuropygia*	AS 135
EN	Red-and-blue Lory *Eos histrio*	AS 136
EN	Purple-naped Lory *Lorius domicella*	AS 136
EN	Rimatara Lorikeet *Vini kuhlii*	OC 218
EN	Ultramarine Lorikeet *Vini ultramarina*	OC 218
CR	Blue-fronted Lorikeet *Charmosyna toxopei*	AS 136
CR	New Caledonian Lorikeet *Charmosyna diadema*	AU 173
CR	Red-throated Lorikeet *Charmosyna amabilis*	OC 218
EN	Uvea Parakeet *Eunymphicus uvaeensis*	AU 173
CR	Norfolk Island Parakeet *Cyanoramphus cookii*	AU 174
EN	Chatham Parakeet *Cyanoramphus forbesi*	AU 174
CR	Malherbe's Parakeet *Cyanoramphus malherbi*	AU 174
EN	Golden-shouldered Parrot *Psephotus chrysopterygius*	AU 174
CR	Orange-bellied Parrot *Neophema chrysogaster*	AU 175
EN	Swift Parrot *Lathamus discolor*	AU 175
EN	Night Parrot *Pezoporus occidentalis*	AU 175
CR	Blue-winged Racquet-tail *Prioniturus verticalis*	AS 135
EN	Mauritius Parakeet *Psittacula eques*	OC 217
EN	Hyacinth Macaw *Anodorhynchus hyacinthinus*	SA 289
EN	Lear's Macaw *Anodorhynchus leari*	SA 289
CR	Glaucous Macaw *Anodorhynchus glaucus*	SA 289
PE†	Spix's Macaw *Cyanopsitta spixii*	SA 290
CR	Blue-throated Macaw *Ara glaucogularis*	SA 290
EN	Great Green Macaw *Ara ambiguus*	CA 255, SA 290
EN	Red-fronted Macaw *Ara rubrogenys*	SA 290
EN	Thick-billed Parrot *Rhynchopsitta pachyrhyncha*	CA 253

EN	Maroon-fronted Parrot *Rhynchopsitta terrisi*	CA 253
EN	Yellow-eared Parrot *Ognorhynchus icterotis*	SA 292
EN	Golden Parakeet *Guaruba guarouba*	SA 291
EN	Socorro Parakeet *Aratinga brevipes*	OC 217
EN	Sun Parakeet *Aratinga solstitialis*	SA 291
CR	Grey-breasted Parakeet *Pyrrhura griseipectus*	SA 291
EN	Pfrimer's Parakeet *Pyrrhura pfrimeri*	SA 291
EN	Santa Marta Parakeet *Pyrrhura viridicata*	SA 292
EN	El Oro Parakeet *Pyrrhura orcesi*	SA 292
EN	Grey-cheeked Parakeet *Brotogeris pyrrhoptera*	SA 292
EN	Brown-backed Parrotlet *Touit melanonotus*	SA 293
CR	Indigo-winged Parrot *Hapalopsittaca fuertesi*	SA 293
CR	Puerto Rican Amazon *Amazona vittata*	CA 254
EN	Red-crowned Amazon *Amazona viridigenalis*	CA 254
EN	Red-browed Amazon *Amazona rhodocorytha*	SA 293
EN	Yellow-headed Amazon *Amazona oratrix*	CA 254
EN	Vinaceous-breasted Amazon *Amazona vinacea*	SA 293
EN	Imperial Amazon *Amazona imperialis*	CA 254

Turacos: Musophagidae

23 species EN: 1 VU: 1 9%

| EN | Bannerman's Turaco *Tauraco bannermani* | AF 88 |

Cuckoos: Cuculidae

141 species CR: 2 EN: 2 VU: 6 7%

EN	Bay-breasted Cuckoo *Coccyzus rufigularis*	CA 255
CR	Sumatran Ground-cuckoo *Carpococcyx viridis*	AS 136
CR	Black-hooded Coucal *Centropus steerii*	AS 137
EN	Banded Ground-cuckoo *Neomorphus radiolosus*	SA 294

Barn Owls: Tytonidae

15 species EN: 2 VU: 4 40%

| EN | Taliabu Masked-owl *Tyto nigrobrunnea* | AS 137 |
| EN | Congo Bay-owl *Phodilus prigoginei* | AF 88 |

Owls: Strigidae

182 species CR: 6 EN: 7 VU: 15 15%

EN	Sokoke Scops-owl *Otus ireneae*	AF 88
EN	Serendib Scops-owl *Otus thilohoffmanni*	AS 138
EN	Flores Scops-owl *Otus alfredi*	AS 138
CR	Siau Scops-owl *Otus siaoensis*	AS 138
EN	Seychelles Scops-owl *Otus insularis*	OC 218
EN	Biak Scops-owl *Otus beccarii*	AS 138
CR	Anjouan Scops-owl *Otus capnodes*	OC 219
CR	Mohéli Scops-owl *Otus moheliensis*	OC 219
CR	Grand Comoro Scops-owl *Otus pauliani*	OC 219
EN	Blakiston's Fish-owl *Ketupa blakistoni*	AS 137
CR	Pernambuco Pygmy-owl *Glaucidium mooreorum*	SA 294
EN	Long-whiskered Owlet *Xenoglaux loweryi*	SA 294
CR	Forest Owlet *Heteroglaux blewitti*	AS 137

Nightjars: Caprimulgidae

93 species PE: 1 EN: 3 VU: 3 8%

PE	Jamaican Pauraque *Siphonorhis americana*	CA 255
EN	Puerto Rican Nightjar *Caprimulgus noctitherus*	CA 255
EN	Itombwe Nightjar *Caprimulgus prigoginei*	AF 88
EN	White-winged Nightjar *Eleothreptus candicans*	SA 294

Owlet-nightjars: Aegothelidae

9 species CR: 1 11%

| CR | New Caledonian Owlet-nightjar *Aegotheles savesi* | AU 175 |

Swifts: Apodidae

101 species EN: 1 VU: 5 6%

| EN | Guam Swiftlet *Collocalia bartschi* | OC 219 |

Hummingbirds: Trochilidae

336 species PE: 1 CR: 7 EN: 17 VU: 9 10%

EN	Hook-billed Hermit *Glaucis dohrnii*	SA 295
EN	Santa Marta Sabrewing *Campylopterus phainopeplus*	SA 295
CR	Short-crested Coquette *Lophornis brachylophus*	CA 256
EN	Blue-capped Hummingbird *Eupherusa cyanophrys*	CA 256
CR	Sapphire-bellied Hummingbird *Lepidopyga lilliae*	SA 295
EN	Honduran Emerald *Amazilia luciae*	CA 256
EN	Mangrove Hummingbird *Amazilia boucardi*	CA 256
EN	Chestnut-bellied Hummingbird *Amazilia castaneiventris*	SA 295
EN	Scissor-tailed Hummingbird *Hylonympha macrocerca*	SA 296
EN	Purple-backed Sunbeam *Aglaeactis aliciae*	SA 296
CR	Dusky Starfrontlet *Coeligena orina*	SA 296
CR	Juan Fernández Firecrown *Sephanoides fernandensis*	OC 220
EN	Royal Sunangel *Heliangelus regalis*	SA 296
CR	Black-breasted Puffleg *Eriocnemis nigrivestis*	SA 297
CR	Gorgeted Puffleg *Eriocnemis isabellae*	SA 297
PE	Turquoise-throated Puffleg *Eriocnemis godini*	SA 297
CR	Colourful Puffleg *Eriocnemis mirabilis*	SA 297
EN	Black-backed Thornbill *Ramphomicron dorsale*	SA 298
EN	Violet-throated Metaltail *Metallura baroni*	SA 298
EN	Perijá Metaltail *Metallura iracunda*	SA 298
EN	Grey-bellied Comet *Taphrolesbia griseiventris*	SA 298
EN	Venezuelan Sylph *Aglaiocercus berlepschi*	SA 299
EN	Marvellous Spatuletail *Loddigesia mirabilis*	SA 299
EN	Chilean Woodstar *Eulidia yarrellii*	SA 299
EN	Esmeraldas Woodstar *Chaetocercus berlepschi*	SA 299

Trogons: Trogonidae

44 species EN: 1 2%

| EN | Javan Trogon *Apalharpactes reinwardtii* | AS 139 |

Ground-rollers: Brachypteraciidae

5 species VU: 3 60%

Kingfishers: Alcedinidae

93 species CR: 2 EN: 1 VU: 9 13%

EN	Kofiau Paradise-kingfisher *Tanysiptera ellioti*	AS 139
CR	Marquesan Kingfisher *Todiramphus godeffroyi*	OC 220
CR	Tuamotu Kingfisher *Todiramphus gambieri*	OC 220

Motmots: Momotidae

9 species VU: 1 11%

Hornbills: Bucerotidae

55 species CR: 2 EN: 3 VU: 8 24%

CR	Sulu Hornbill *Anthracoceros montani*	AS 140
EN	Mindoro Hornbill *Penelopides mindorensis*	AS 140
EN	Visayan Hornbill *Penelopides panini*	AS 140
CR	Rufous-headed Hornbill *Aceros waldeni*	AS 140
EN	Narcondam Hornbill *Aceros narcondami*	OC 220

Ground-hornbills: Bucorvidae

2 species VU: 1 50%

Toucans and barbets: Ramphastidae

122 species EN: 1 VU: 6 6%

| EN | Yellow-browed Toucanet *Aulacorhynchus huallagae* | SA 300 |

Woodpeckers: Picidae

219 species PE: 1 CR: 2 EN: 3 VU: 7 6%

EN	Speckle-chested Piculet *Picumnus steindachneri*	SA 300
EN	Várzea Piculet *Picumnus varzeae*	SA 300
CR	Okinawa Woodpecker *Dendrocopos noguchii*	AS 139
EN	Kaempfer's Woodpecker *Celeus obrieni*	SA 300
PE	Imperial Woodpecker *Campephilus imperialis*	CA 257
CR	Ivory-billed Woodpecker *Campephilus principalis*	CA 257

Jacamars — Galbulidae
18 species VU: 2 11%

New Zealand wrens — Acanthisittidae
2 species VU: 1 50%

Broadbills — Eurylaimidae
15 species VU: 3 20%

Asities — Philepittidae
4 species VU: 1 25%

Pittas — Pittidae
34 species EN: 1 VU: 8 26%

EN	Gurney's Pitta *Pitta gurneyi*	AS 139

Manakins — Pipridae
54 species CR: 1 VU: 4 9%

CR	Araripe Manakin *Antilophia bokermanni*	SA 301

Cotingas — Cotingidae
97 species CR: 1 EN: 8 VU: 10 20%

EN	Slaty Becard *Pachyramphus spodiurus*	SA 301
EN	Palkachupa Cotinga *Phibalura boliviana*	SA 301
EN	Peruvian Plantcutter *Phytotoma raimondii*	SA 301
EN	Banded Cotinga *Cotinga maculata*	SA 302
EN	Chestnut-capped Piha *Lipaugus weberi*	SA 302
EN	White-winged Cotinga *Xipholena atropurpurea*	SA 302
EN	Yellow-billed Cotinga *Carpodectes antoniae*	CA 257
EN	Bare-necked Umbrellabird *Cephalopterus glabricollis*	CA 257
CR	Kinglet Calyptura *Calyptura cristata*	SA 302

Tyrant-flycatchers: — Tyrannidae
415 species EN: 11 VU: 23 8%

EN	Urich's Tyrannulet *Phyllomyias urichi*	SA 303
EN	Ash-breasted Tit-tyrant *Anairetes alpinus*	SA 303
EN	Antioquia Bristle-tyrant *Phylloscartes lanyoni*	SA 303
EN	Minas Gerais Tyrannulet *Phylloscartes roquettei*	SA 303
EN	Alagoas Tyrannulet *Phylloscartes ceciliae*	SA 304
EN	Bahia Tyrannulet *Phylloscartes beckeri*	SA 304
EN	Kaempfer's Tody-tyrant *Hemitriccus kaempferi*	SA 304
EN	Lulu's Tody-flycatcher *Poecilotriccus luluae*	SA 304
EN	Santa Marta Bush-tyrant *Myiotheretes pernix*	SA 305
EN	Giant Kingbird *Tyrannus cubensis*	CA 258
EN	Rufous Flycatcher *Myiarchus semirufus*	SA 305

Antbirds: — Thamnophilidae
222 species CR: 3 EN: 10 VU: 19 14%

EN	Recurve-billed Bushbird *Clytoctantes alixii*	SA 305
CR	Rio de Janeiro Antwren *Myrmotherula fluminensis*	SA 305
CR	Alagoas Antwren *Myrmotherula snowi*	SA 306
EN	Ash-throated Antwren *Herpsilochmus parkeri*	SA 306
EN	Restinga Antwren *Formicivora littoralis*	SA 306
EN	Black-hooded Antwren *Formicivora erythronotos*	SA 306
EN	Paraná Antwren *Stymphalornis acutirostris*	SA 307
EN	Orange-bellied Antwren *Terenura sicki*	SA 307
EN	Yellow-rumped Antwren *Terenura sharpei*	SA 307
CR	Rio Branco Antbird *Cercomacra carbonaria*	SA 307
EN	Fringe-backed Fire-eye *Pyriglena atra*	SA 308
EN	Slender Antbird *Rhopornis ardesiacus*	SA 308
EN	Scalloped Antbird *Myrmeciza ruficauda*	SA 308

Tapaculos: — Rhinocryptidae
59 species CR: 2 EN: 4 VU: 1 12%

CR	Stresemann's Bristlefront *Merulaxis stresemanni*	SA 308
EN	Marsh Tapaculo *Scytalopus iraiensis*	SA 309
EN	Upper Magdalena Tapaculo *Scytalopus rodriguezi*	SA 309
EN	Ecuadorian Tapaculo *Scytalopus robbinsi*	SA 309
CR	Bahia Tapaculo *Eleoscytalopus psychopompus*	SA 310
EN	Paramillo Tapaculo *Scytalopus canus*	SA 309

Antthrushes and antpittas: — Formicariidae
64 species CR: 2 EN: 3 VU: 10 23%

CR	Táchira Antpitta *Grallaria chthonia*	SA 310
EN	Cundinamarca Antpitta *Grallaria kaestneri*	SA 310
EN	Jocotoco Antpitta *Grallaria ridgelyi*	SA 310
CR	Antioquia Antpitta *Grallaria fenwickorum*	SA 311
EN	Ochre-fronted Antpitta *Grallaricula ochraceifrons*	SA 311

Ovenbirds: — Furnariidae
243 species CR: 6 EN: 7 VU: 16 12%

CR	Royal Cinclodes *Cinclodes aricomae*	SA 311
CR	White-bellied Cinclodes *Cinclodes palliatus*	SA 311
CR	Masafuera Rayadito *Aphrastura masafuerae*	OC 221
EN	White-browed Tit-spinetail *Leptasthenura xenothorax*	SA 312
EN	Perijá Thistletail *Asthenes perijana*	SA 312
EN	Pinto's Spinetail *Synallaxis infuscata*	SA 312
EN	Blackish-headed Spinetail *Synallaxis tithys*	SA 312
CR	Marañón Spinetail *Synallaxis maranonica*	SA 313
EN	Russet-bellied Spinetail *Synallaxis zimmeri*	SA 313
CR	Hoary-throated Spinetail *Synallaxis kollari*	SA 313
EN	Bolivian Spinetail *Cranioleuca henricae*	SA 313
EN	Scaled Spinetail *Cranioleuca muelleri*	SA 314
CR	Alagoas Foliage-gleaner *Philydor novaesi*	SA 314

Woodcreepers: — Dendrocolaptidae
52 species VU: 4 8%

Scrub-birds: — Atrichornithidae
2 species EN: 2 100%

EN	Rufous Scrub-bird *Atrichornis rufescens*	AU 176
EN	Noisy Scrub-bird *Atrichornis clamosus*	AU 176

Australasian wrens: — Maluridae
27 species EN: 1 VU: 1 7%

EN	Mallee Emuwren *Stipiturus mallee*	AU 176

Honeyeaters: — Meliphagidae
176 species CR: 2 EN: 2 VU: 6 6%

EN	Mao *Gymnomyza samoensis*	OC 221
CR	Crow Honeyeater *Gymnomyza aubryana*	AU 176
EN	Black-eared Miner *Manorina melanotis*	AU 177
CR	Regent Honeyeater *Xanthomyza phrygia*	AU 177

Bristlebirds: — Dasyornithidae
3 species EN: 2 67%

EN	Western Bristlebird *Dasyornis longirostris*	AU 177
EN	Eastern Bristlebird *Dasyornis brachypterus*	AU 177

Pardalotes: — Pardalotidae
4 species EN: 1 25%

EN	Forty-spotted Pardalote *Pardalotus quadragintus*	AU 178

Thornbills and gerygones: — Acanthizidae
64 species EN: 1 2%

EN	Yellowhead *Mohoua ochrocephala*	AU 178

Wattled Crows: — Callaeatidae
2 species EN: 1 50%

EN	Kokako *Callaeas cinereus*	AU 178

Shrike-flycatchers, wattle-eyes and batises: — Platysteiridae
32 species EN: 1 3%

EN	Banded Wattle-eye *Platysteira laticincta*	AF 89

Helmet-shrikes, bush-shrikes and puffbacks:	Malaconotidae
53 species CR: 1 EN: 4 VU: 2 13%	
EN Gabela Helmet-shrike *Prionops gabela*	AF 89
EN Mount Kupe Bush-shrike *Telophorus kupeensis*	AF 89
CR Uluguru Bush-shrike *Malaconotus alius*	AF 89
EN Orange-breasted Bush-shrike *Laniarius brauni*	AF 90
EN Gabela Bush-shrike *Laniarius amboimensis*	AF 90

Vangas:	Vangidae
22 species EN: 1 VU: 4 23%	
EN Van Dam's Vanga *Xenopirostris damii*	AF 90

Cuckooshrikes:	Campephagidae
84 species CR: 1 VU: 4 6%	
CR Réunion Cuckooshrike *Coracina newtoni*	OC 221

Whistlers:	Pachycephalidae
38 species VU: 1 3%	

Shrikes:	Laniidae
30 species CR: 1 3%	
CR São Tomé Fiscal *Lanius newtoni*	OC 221

Vireos and allies:	Vireonidae
52 species EN: 1 VU: 2 6%	
EN Chocó Vireo *Vireo masteri*	SA 314

Orioles and figbirds:	Oriolidae
30 species CR: 1 VU: 2 10%	
CR Isabela Oriole *Oriolus isabellae*	AS 141

Shrike-thrushes and allies:	Colluricinclidae
13 species CR: 1 EN: 1 15%	
CR Sangihe Shrike-thrush *Colluricincla sanghirensis*	AS 141

Drongos:	Dicruridae
24 species EN: 2 VU: 1 13%	
EN Grand Comoro Drongo *Dicrurus fuscipennis*	OC 222
EN Tablas Drongo *Dicrurus menagei*	AS 141

Fantails:	Rhipiduridae
42 species VU: 2 5%	

Monarchs:	Monarchidae
99 species PE: 1 CR: 5 EN: 7 VU: 9 22%	
CR Cerulean Paradise-flycatcher *Eutrichomyias rowleyi*	AS 141
CR Seychelles Paradise-flycatcher *Terpsiphone corvina*	OC 222
EN Oahu Elepaio *Chasiempis ibidis*	OC 223
CR Tahiti Monarch *Pomarea nigra*	OC 222
EN Marquesan Monarch *Pomarea mendozae*	OC 222
PE Ua Pou Monarch *Pomarea mira*	OC 223
CR Fatuhiva Monarch *Pomarea whitneyi*	OC 223
EN Santa Cruz Shrikebill *Clytorhynchus sanctaecrucis*	AU 178
EN Chuuk Monarch *Metabolus rugensis*	OC 223
EN Flores Monarch *Monarcha sacerdotum*	AS 142
EN White-tipped Monarch *Monarcha everetti*	AS 142
CR Black-chinned Monarch *Monarcha boanensis*	AS 142
EN Biak Monarch *Monarcha brehmii*	AS 142

Crows and jays:	Corvidae
119 species EW: 1 CR: 3 EN: 2 VU: 9 12%	
CR Javan Green Magpie *Cissa thalassina*	AS 143
EN Ethiopian Bush-crow *Zavattariornis stresemanni*	AF 90
CR Banggai Crow *Corvus unicolor*	AS 143
EN Flores Crow *Corvus florensis*	AS 143
CR Mariana Crow *Corvus kubaryi*	OC 224
EW Hawaiian Crow *Corvus hawaiiensis*	OC 224

Birds of paradise:	Paradisaeidae
40 species VU: 3 8%	

Australasian Robins:	Petroicidae
44 species EN: 1 2%	
EN Black Robin *Petroica traversi*	AU 179

Rockfowl:	Picathartidae
2 species VU: 2 100%	

Tits and chickadees:	Paridae
51 species VU: 1 2%	

Swallows and martins:	Hirundinidae
82 species CR: 1 EN: 2 VU: 5 10%	
CR White-eyed River-martin *Eurochelidon sirintarae*	AS 143
EN Bahama Swallow *Tachycineta cyaneoviridis*	CA 258
EN Galápagos Martin *Progne modesta*	OC 224

Larks:	Alaudidae
91 species CR: 3 EN: 2 VU: 2 8%	
EN Ash's Lark *Mirafra ashi*	AF 91
CR Archer's Lark *Heteromirafra archeri*	AF 91
CR Liben Lark *Heteromirafra sidamoensis*	AF 91
EN Botha's Lark *Spizocorys fringillaris*	AF 91
CR Raso Lark *Alauda razae*	OC 224

Cisticolas and allies:	Cisticolidae
113 species CR: 1 EN: 2 VU: 4 6%	
EN Aberdare Cisticola *Cisticola aberdare*	AF 92
CR Taita Apalis *Apalis fuscigularis*	AF 92
EN Yellow-throated Apalis *Apalis flavigularis*	AF 92

Bulbuls:	Pycnonotidae
125 species CR: 1 EN: 2 VU: 6 7%	
EN Prigogine's Greenbul *Chlorocichla prigoginei*	AF 92
CR Liberian Greenbul *Phyllastrephus leucolepis*	AF 93
EN Streak-breasted Bulbul *Ixos siquijorensis*	AS 144

Old World warblers:	Sylviidae
291 species CR: 3 EN: 11 VU: 22 12%	
CR Long-billed Tailorbird *Artisornis moreaui*	AF 93
EN Long-legged Thicketbird *Trichocichla rufa*	OC 225
EN Grauer's Swamp-warbler *Bradypterus graueri*	AF 93
EN Basra Reed-warbler *Acrocephalus griseldis*	E/M 67, AF 93
CR Nightingale Reed-warbler *Acrocephalus luscinius*	OC 225
CR Millerbird *Acrocephalus familiaris*	OC 225
EN Kiritimati Reed-warbler *Acrocephalus aequinoctialis*	OC 225
EN Tahiti Reed-warbler *Acrocephalus caffer*	OC 226
EN Pitcairn Reed-warbler *Acrocephalus vaughani*	OC 226
EN Cape Verde Warbler *Acrocephalus brevipennis*	OC 226
EN Rodrigues Warbler *Acrocephalus rodericanus*	OC 226
EN Pulitzer's Longbill *Macrosphenus pulitzeri*	AF 94
EN Usambara Hyliota *Hyliota usambara*	AF 94
EN Turner's Eremomela *Eremomela turneri*	AF 94

Babblers and parrotbills:	Timaliidae
326 species CR: 1 EN: 7 VU: 26 10%	
EN White-throated Wren-babbler *Rimator pasquieri*	AS 144
EN Negros Striped-babbler *Stachyris nigrorum*	AS 144
EN Flame-templed Babbler *Dasycrotapha speciosa*	AS 144
CR Blue-crowned Laughingthrush *Garrulax courtoisi*	AS 145
EN Black-chinned Laughingthrush *Strophocincla cachinnans*	AS 145
EN Collared Laughingthrush *Garrulax yersini*	AS 145
EN White-throated Mountain-babbler *Kupeornis gilberti*	AF 94
EN Grey-crowned Crocias *Crocias langbianis*	AS 145

White-eyes:		Zosteropidae

99 species `CR: 5` `EN: 5` `VU: 8` **18%**

`CR`	Mauritius Olive White-eye *Zosterops chloronothus*	**OC 227**
`EN`	Seychelles White-eye *Zosterops modestus*	**OC 227**
`EN`	Bridled White-eye *Zosterops conspicillatus*	**OC 227**
`CR`	Rota Bridled White-eye *Zosterops rotensis*	**OC 227**
`CR`	Sangihe White-eye *Zosterops nehrkorni*	**AS 146**
`EN`	Splendid White-eye *Zosterops luteirostris*	**AU 179**
`CR`	White-chested White-eye *Zosterops albogularis*	**AU 179**
`EN`	Faichuk White-eye *Rukia ruki*	**OC 228**
`CR`	Golden White-eye *Cleptornis marchei*	**OC 228**
`EN`	Rufous-throated White-eye *Madanga ruficollis*	**AS 146**

Wrens:		Troglodytidae

79 species `CR: 3` `EN: 2` `VU: 3` **10%**

`EN`	Apolinar's Wren *Cistothorus apolinari*	**SA 314**
`EN`	Zapata Wren *Ferminia cerverai*	**CA 258**
`CR`	Niceforo's Wren *Thryothorus nicefori*	**SA 315**
`CR`	Santa Marta Wren *Troglodytes monticola*	**SA 315**
`CR`	Munchique Wood-wren *Henicorhina negreti*	**SA 315**

Gnatcatchers:		Polioptilidae

15 species `CR: 1` **7%**

`CR`	Iquitos Gnatcatcher *Polioptila clementsi*	**SA 315**

Nuthatches and Wallcreeper:		Sittidae

25 species `EN: 2` `VU: 3` **20%**

`EN`	White-browed Nuthatch *Sitta victoriae*	**AS 146**
`EN`	Algerian Nuthatch *Sitta ledanti*	**AF 95**

Mockingbirds and thrashers:		Mimidae

34 species `CR: 3` `EN: 2` `VU: 2` **21%**

`CR`	Floreana Mockingbird *Mimus trifasciatus*	**OC 228**
`EN`	San Cristóbal Mockingbird *Mimus melanotis*	**OC 228**
`CR`	Socorro Mockingbird *Mimus graysoni*	**OC 229**
`CR`	Cozumel Thrasher *Toxostoma guttatum*	**CA 258**
`EN`	White-breasted Thrasher *Ramphocinclus brachyurus*	**CA 259**

Starlings:		Sturnidae

109 species `CR: 3` `EN: 1` `VU: 4` **7%**

`CR`	Pohnpei Starling *Aplonis pelzelni*	**OC 229**
`EN`	White-eyed Starling *Aplonis brunneicapillus*	**AU 179**
`CR`	Bali Starling *Leucopsar rothschildi*	**AS 147**
`CR`	Black-winged Starling *Sturnus melanopterus*	**AS 147**

Thrushes:		Turdidae

170 species `PE: 1` `CR: 3` `EN: 4` `VU: 11` **11%**

`EN`	Sri Lanka Whistling-thrush *Myophonus blighi*	**AS 146**
`EN`	Spotted Ground-thrush *Zoothera guttata*	**AF 95**
`PE`	Olomao *Myadestes lanaiensis*	**OC 229**
`CR`	Puaiohi *Myadestes palmeri*	**OC 229**
`CR`	Príncipe Thrush *Turdus xanthorhynchus*	**OC 230**
`CR`	Taita Thrush *Turdus helleri*	**AF 95**
`EN`	La Selle Thrush *Turdus swalesi*	**CA 259**
`EN`	Thyolo Alethe *Alethe choloensis*	**AF 95**

Chats and Old World flycatchers:		Muscicapidae

287 species `CR: 1` `EN: 12` `VU: 18` **11%**

`EN`	Nilgiri Blue Robin *Myiomela major*	**AS 147**
`EN`	White-bellied Blue Robin *Myiomela albiventris*	**AS 147**
`EN`	Gabela Akalat *Sheppardia gabela*	**AF 96**
`EN`	Usambara Akalat *Sheppardia montana*	**AF 96**
`EN`	Rubeho Akalat *Sheppardia aurantiithorax*	**AF 96**
`EN`	Seychelles Magpie-robin *Copsychus sechellarum*	**OC 230**
`EN`	Black Shama *Copsychus cebuensis*	**AS 148**

`EN`	Amber Mountain Rock-thrush *Monticola erythronotus*	**AF 96**
`EN`	White-throated Jungle-flycatcher *Rhinomyias albigularis*	**AS 148**
`EN`	Grand Comoro Flycatcher *Humblotia flavirostris*	**OC 230**
`EN`	Lompobatang Flycatcher *Ficedula bonthaina*	**AS 148**
`EN`	Matinan Flycatcher *Cyornis sanfordi*	**AS 148**
`CR`	Rueck's Blue-flycatcher *Cyornis ruckii*	**AS 149**

Dippers:		Cinclidae

5 species `VU: 1` **20%**

Leafbirds:		Chloropseidae

11 species `VU: 1` **9%**

Flowerpeckers:		Dicaeidae

45 species `CR: 1` `VU: 2` **7%**

`CR`	Cebu Flowerpecker *Dicaeum quadricolor*	**AS 149**

Sunbirds:		Nectariniidae

124 species `EN: 3` `VU: 4` **6%**

`EN`	Amani Sunbird *Anthreptes pallidigaster*	**AF 97**
`EN`	Loveridge's Sunbird *Nectarinia loveridgei*	**AF 97**
`EN`	Elegant Sunbird *Aethopyga duyvenbodei*	**AS 149**

Sparrows, snowfinches and allies:		Passeridae

50 species `VU: 1` **2%**

Weavers and allies:		Ploceidae

106 species `EN: 7` `VU: 6` **12%**

`EN`	Bates's Weaver *Ploceus batesi*	**AF 97**
`EN`	Clarke's Weaver *Ploceus golandi*	**AF 97**
`EN`	Golden-naped Weaver *Ploceus aureonucha*	**AF 98**
`EN`	Usambara Weaver *Ploceus nicolli*	**AF 98**
`EN`	Gola Malimbe *Malimbus ballmanni*	**AF 98**
`EN`	Ibadan Malimbe *Malimbus ibadanensis*	**AF 98**
`EN`	Mauritius Fody *Foudia rubra*	**OC 230**

Waxbills, grass-finches, munias and allies:		Estrildidae

136 species `VU: 8` **6%**

Wagtails & pipits:		Motacillidae

61 species `EN: 2` `VU: 4` **10%**

`EN`	Sharpe's Longclaw *Macronyx sharpei*	**AF 99**
`EN`	Sokoke Pipit *Anthus sokokensis*	**AF 99**

Finches and Hawaiian honeycreepers:		Fringillidae

165 species `PE: 4` `CR: 7` `EN: 9` `VU: 10` **18%**

`EN`	Yellow-throated Seedeater *Serinus flavigula*	**AF 99**
`CR`	São Tomé Grosbeak *Neospiza concolor*	**OC 231**
`EN`	Red Siskin *Carduelis cucullata*	**SA 316**
`EN`	Warsangli Linnet *Carduelis johannis*	**AF 99**
`EN`	Hispaniolan Crossbill *Loxia megaplaga*	**CA 259**
`EN`	Azores Bullfinch *Pyrrhula murina*	**OC 231**
`CR`	Nihoa Finch *Telespiza ultima*	**OC 231**
`PE`	Ou *Psittirostra psittacea*	**OC 232**
`CR`	Palila *Loxioides bailleui*	**OC 232**
`CR`	Maui Parrotbill *Pseudonestor xanthophrys*	**OC 231**
`PE`	Nukupuu *Hemignathus lucidus*	**OC 232**
`EN`	Akiapolaau *Hemignathus munroi*	**OC 232**
`CR`	Akikiki *Oreomystis bairdi*	**OC 233**
`EN`	Hawaii Creeper *Oreomystis mana*	**OC 233**
`EN`	Maui Alauahio *Paroreomyza montana*	**OC 233**
`PE`	Oahu Alauahio *Paroreomyza maculata*	**OC 233**
`CR`	Akekee *Loxops caeruleirostris*	**OC 234**
`EN`	Akepa *Loxops coccineus*	**OC 234**
`CR`	Akohekohe *Palmeria dolei*	**OC 234**
`PE`	Poo-uli *Melamprosops phaeosoma*	**OC 234**

New World warblers:		Parulidae

115 species `PE: 1` `CR: 1` `EN: 6` `VU: 7` **13%**

`PE`	Bachman's Warbler *Vermivora bachmanii*	**CA 259**
`EN`	Golden-cheeked Warbler *Dendroica chrysoparia*	**CA 260**
`EN`	Whistling Warbler *Catharopeza bishopi*	**CA 260**
`EN`	Belding's Yellowthroat *Geothlypis beldingi*	**CA 260**
`EN`	Black-polled Yellowthroat: *Geothlypis speciosa*	**CA 260**
`CR`	Semper's Warbler *Leucopeza semperi*	**CA 261**
`EN`	Paria Redstart *Myioborus pariae*	**SA 316**
`EN`	Grey-headed Warbler *Basileuterus griseiceps*	**SA 316**

New World blackbirds:		Icteridae

103 species `CR: 2` `EN: 7` `VU: 5` **14%**

`EN`	Baudó Oropendola *Psarocolius cassini*	**SA 316**
`EN`	Selva Cacique *Cacicus koepckeae*	**SA 317**
`CR`	Bahama Oriole *Icterus northropi*	**CA 261**
`CR`	Montserrat Oriole *Icterus oberi*	**CA 261**
`EN`	Jamaican Blackbird *Nesopsar nigerrimus*	**CA 261**
`EN`	Mountain Grackle *Macroagelaius subalaris*	**SA 317**
`EN`	Forbes's Blackbird *Curaeus forbesi*	**SA 317**
`EN`	Tricoloured Blackbird *Agelaius tricolor*	**CA 262**
`EN`	Yellow-shouldered Blackbird *Agelaius xanthomus*	**CA 262**

Buntings, American sparrows and allies:		Emberizidae

308 species `PE: 1` `CR: 4` `EN: 13` `VU: 16` **11%**

`EN`	Rufous-backed Bunting *Emberiza jankowskii*	**AS 149**
`EN`	Sierra Madre Sparrow *Xenospiza baileyi*	**CA 262**
`EN`	Worthen's Sparrow *Spizella wortheni*	**CA 262**
`EN`	Cuban Sparrow *Torreornis inexpectata*	**CA 263**
`CR`	Gough Bunting *Rowettia goughensis*	**OC 235**
`EN`	Wilkins's Bunting *Nesospiza wilkinsi*	**OC 235**
`EN`	Plain-tailed Warbling-finch *Poospiza alticola*	**SA 318**
`EN`	Rufous-breasted Warbling-finch *Poospiza rubecula*	**SA 318**
`PE`	Hooded Seedeater *Sporophila melanops*	**SA 318**
`EN`	Marsh Seedeater *Sporophila palustris*	**SA 318**
`EN`	St Lucia Black Finch *Melanospiza richardsoni*	**CA 263**
`CR`	Medium Tree-finch *Camarhynchus pauper*	**OC 235**
`CR`	Mangrove Finch *Camarhynchus heliobates*	**OC 235**
`CR`	Antioquia Brush-finch *Atlapetes blancae*	**SA 319**
`EN`	Yellow-headed Brush-finch *Atlapetes flaviceps*	**SA 319**
`EN`	Pale-headed Brush-finch *Atlapetes pallidiceps*	**SA 319**
`EN`	Black-spectacled Brush-finch *Atlapetes melanopsis*	**SA 319**
`EN`	Yellow Cardinal *Gubernatrix cristata*	**SA 317**

Tanagers:		Thraupidae

262 species `CR: 2` `EN: 6` `VU: 18` **10%**

`EN`	Cochabamba Mountain-finch *Compsospiza garleppi*	**SA 321**
`CR`	Cone-billed Tanager *Conothraupis mesoleuca*	**SA 320**
`CR`	Cherry-throated Tanager *Nemosia rourei*	**SA 320**
`EN`	Gold-ringed Tanager *Bangsia aureocincta*	**SA 320**
`EN`	Golden-backed Mountain-tanager *Buthraupis aureodorsalis*	**SA 320**
`EN`	Azure-rumped Tanager *Tangara cabanisi*	**CA 263**
`EN`	Venezuelan Flowerpiercer *Diglossa venezuelensis*	**SA 321**
`EN`	Chestnut-bellied Flowerpiercer *Diglossa gloriosissima*	**SA 321**

Grosbeaks, saltators and allies:		Cardinalidae

58 species `CR: 1` `EN: 1` **3%**

`EN`	Black-cheeked Ant-tanager *Habia atrimaxillaris*	**CA 263**
`CR`	Carrizal Seedeater *Amaurospiza carrizalensis*	**SA 321**

Endangered **Red-crowned Crane** *Grus japonensis*. Photo: Tim Laman (timlaman.com).

Index

This index includes the English and *scientific* names of all the bird species mentioned in this book. The names of species that are Critically Endangered, Endangered, Extinct in the Wild or Data Deficient are shown in **Bold text**.

Bold figures refer to the page(s) where a species account can be found.

Blue italicised figures indicate the location of other photographs.

Bold sepia figures are the main page references for Data Deficient species.

Normal black figures refer to pages where other information on the threatened species covered in this book may be found, or to other species that are not covered in detail.

Orange figures are the page references for Extinct species.

Critically Endangered **Forest Owlet** *Heteroglaux blewitti.* Photo: Dr Jayesh K. Joshi.

359

BirdLife International

BirdLife International is a partnership of people working to protect birds and the environment. As a worldwide community, it is the leading authority on the status of birds and their habitats. Over 10 million people support the BirdLife Partnership of national non-governmental conservation organizations and local networks. Partners, operating in more than 110 territories, work together on shared priorities, programmes and policies, learning from each other to achieve real conservation results. The BirdLife Partnership promotes sustainable living as a means of conserving birds and all other forms of biodiversity.

The BirdLife Preventing Extinctions Programme was launched in 2008 in an attempt to counteract an increasingly diverse array of threats to birds by delivering conservation actions – underpinned by science – where they are most needed. The programme is implemented globally by the BirdLife Partnership, with Partners taking on different roles. The development of two new communities plays a central part in the programme: BirdLife Species Guardians – experts who will take the lead in conserving threatened species in their country; and BirdLife Species Champions – organizations or individuals who will raise awareness of and fund the vital conservation that is so urgently required. Find out more at **www.birdlife.org/extinction**.

Andorra	Argentina	Armenia	Australia	Austria	Azerbaijan	Bahamas
Bahrain	Belarus	Belgium	Belize	Bolivia	Botswana	
Brazil	Bulgaria	Burkina Faso	Burundi	Cameroon	Canada	Canada
Chile	Cook Islands	Cote d'Ivoire	Cuba	Cyprus	Czech Republic	
Denmark	Djibouti	Dominican Republic	Ecuador	Egypt	El Salvador	Estonia
Ethiopia	Falkland Islands (Malvinas)	Faroe Islands	Finland	France	French Polynesia	
Georgia	Germany	Ghana	Gibraltar	Greece	Hong Kong	Hungary
Iceland	India	Indonesia	Iraq	Ireland	Israel	
Italy	Japan	Jordan	Kazakstan	Kenya	Kuwait	Kyrgyzstan
Latvia	Lebanon	Liberia	Liechtenstein	Lithuania	Luxembourg	
FYR Macedonia	Madagascar	Malawi	Malaysia	Malta	Mexico	Myanmar
Nepal	Netherlands	New Caledonia	New Zealand	Nigeria	Norway	
Palau	Palestine	Panama	Paraguay	Philippines	Poland	Portugal
Puerto Rico	Qatar	Romania	Rwanda	Samoa	Saudi Arabia	
Seychelles	Sierra Leone	Singapore	Slovakia	Slovenia	South Africa	Spain
Sri Lanka	Suriname	Sweden	Switzerland	Syria	Taiwan	
Tanzania	Thailand	Tunisia	Turkey	Uganda	Ukraine	United Kingdom
Uruguay	USA	Uzbekistan	Yemen	Zambia	Zimbabwe	